A RECONCILIATION WITHOUT RE

An Investigation of the Foundations of Aboriginal Law in Canada

The current framework for reconciliation between Indigenous peoples and the Canadian state is based on the Supreme Court of Canada's acceptance of the Crown's assertion of sovereignty, legislative power, and underlying title. The basis of this assertion is a long-standing interpretation of section 91(24) of Canada's Constitution as a plenary grant of power over Indigenous communities and their lands, leading the courts to simply bypass the question of the inherent right of self-government.

In *A Reconciliation without Recollection?*, Joshua Ben David Nichols argues that if we are to find a meaningful path towards reconciliation, we will need to address the history of sovereignty without assuming its foundations. Exposing the limitations of the current model, Nichols carefully examines the lines of descent and association that underlie the legal conceptualization of the Aboriginal right to govern.

Blending legal analysis with insights drawn from political theory and philosophy, *A Reconciliation without Recollection?* is an ambitious and timely intervention into one of the most pressing concerns in Canada.

JOSHUA BEN DAVID NICHOLS is an assistant professor in the Faculty of Law at the University of Alberta.

A Reconciliation without Recollection?

An Investigation of the Foundations of Aboriginal Law in Canada

JOSHUA BEN DAVID NICHOLS

With forewords by John Borrows and James Tully

UNIVERSITY OF TORONTO PRESS
Toronto Buffalo London

Toronto Buffalo London
utorontopress.com
Printed in Canada

ISBN 978-1-4875-0225-6 (cloth) ISBN 978-1-4875-1498-3 (ePUB)
ISBN 978-1-4875-2187-5 (paper) ISBN 978-1-4875-1497-6 (PDF)

Library and Archives Canada Cataloguing in Publication

Title: A reconciliation without recollection? : an investigation of the foundations of Aboriginal law in Canada / Joshua Ben David Nichols.
Names: Nichols, Joshua, 1978–, author.
Description: Includes bibliographical references and index.
Identifiers: Canadiana 20190181761 | ISBN 9781487521875 (paper) | ISBN 9781487502256 (cloth)
Subjects: LCSH: Indians of North America – Legal status, laws, etc. – Canada. | LCSH: Indians of North America – Canada – Government relations. | LCSH: Indians of North America – Canada – Politics and government.
Classification: LCC KE7709 .N53 2020 | LCC KF8205 .N53 2020 kfmod | DDC 342.7108/72 – dc23

University of Toronto Press acknowledges the financial assistance of the International Law Research Program (ILRP) of the Centre for International Governance Innovation in the publication of this book. The ILRP gratefully acknowledges the funding contribution of the Province of Ontario.

Centre for International Governance Innovation

The Centre for International Governance Innovation is an independent, non-partisan think tank with an objective and uniquely global perspective. Our research, opinions, and public voice make a difference in today's world by bringing clarity and innovative thinking to global policy making. By working across disciplines and in partnership with the best peers and experts, we are the benchmark for influential research and trusted analysis.

University of Toronto Press acknowledges the financial assistance to its publishing program of the Canada Council for the Arts and the Ontario Arts Council, an agency of the Government of Ontario.

Canada Council for the Arts Conseil des Arts du Canada

ONTARIO ARTS COUNCIL
CONSEIL DES ARTS DE L'ONTARIO
an Ontario government agency
un organisme du gouvernement de l'Ontario

Funded by the Government of Canada Financé par le gouvernement du Canada
Canada

MIX
Paper from responsible sources
FSC® C016245

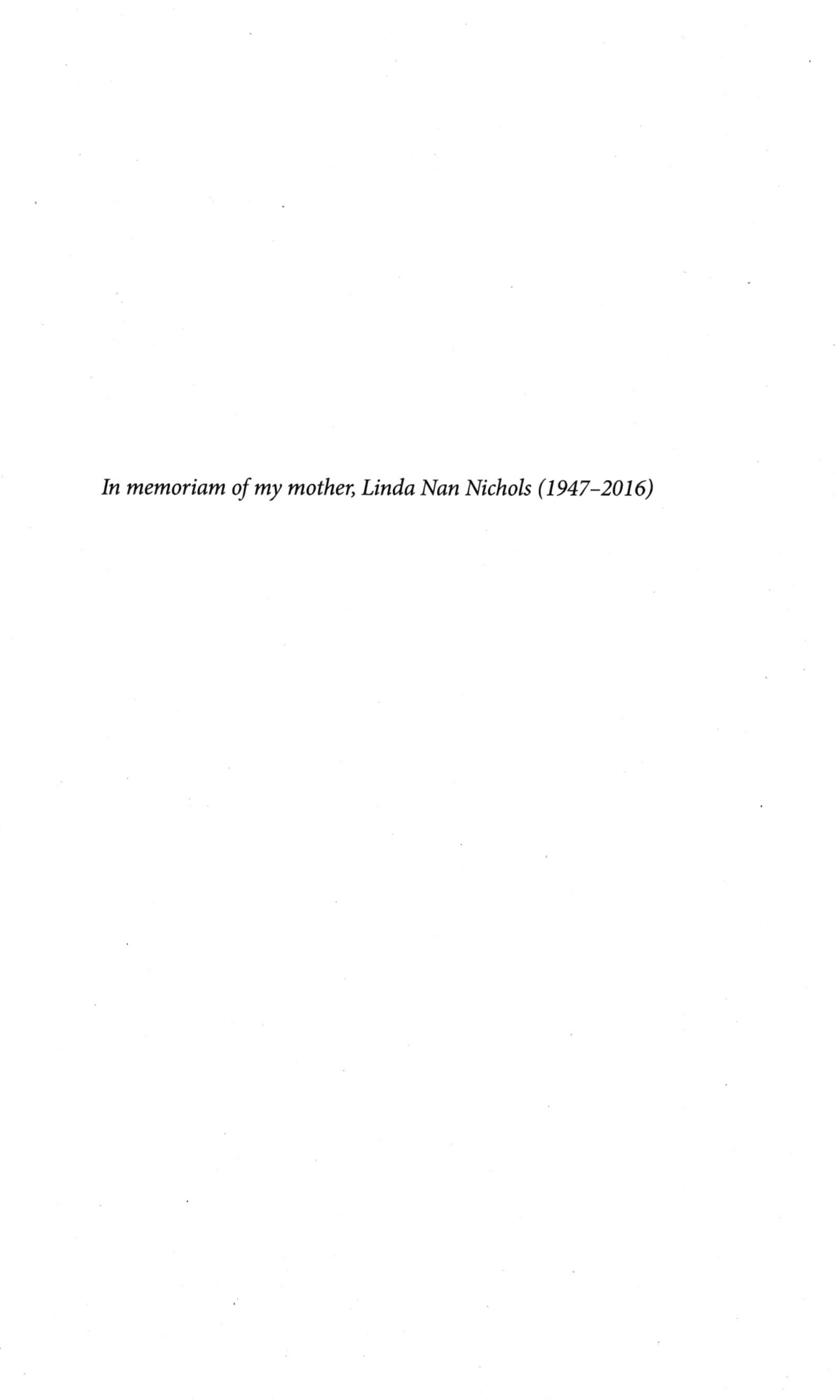

In memoriam of my mother, Linda Nan Nichols (1947–2016)

A Reconciliation without Recollection?

An Investigation of the Foundations of Aboriginal Law in Canada

JOSHUA BEN DAVID NICHOLS

With forewords by John Borrows and James Tully

UNIVERSITY OF TORONTO PRESS
Toronto Buffalo London

Toronto Buffalo London
utorontopress.com
Printed in Canada

ISBN 978-1-4875-0225-6 (cloth)
ISBN 978-1-4875-2187-5 (paper)
ISBN 978-1-4875-1498-3 (ePUB)
ISBN 978-1-4875-1497-6 (PDF)

Library and Archives Canada Cataloguing in Publication

Title: A reconciliation without recollection? : an investigation of the foundations of Aboriginal law in Canada / Joshua Ben David Nichols.
Names: Nichols, Joshua, 1978–, author.
Description: Includes bibliographical references and index.
Identifiers: Canadiana 20190181761 | ISBN 9781487521875 (paper) | ISBN 9781487502256 (cloth)
Subjects: LCSH: Indians of North America – Legal status, laws, etc. – Canada. | LCSH: Indians of North America – Canada – Government relations. | LCSH: Indians of North America – Canada – Politics and government.
Classification: LCC KE7709 .N53 2020 | LCC KF8205 .N53 2020 kfmod | DDC 342.7108/72 – dc23

University of Toronto Press acknowledges the financial assistance of the International Law Research Program (ILRP) of the Centre for International Governance Innovation in the publication of this book. The ILRP gratefully acknowledges the funding contribution of the Province of Ontario.

Centre for International Governance Innovation

The Centre for International Governance Innovation is an independent, non-partisan think tank with an objective and uniquely global perspective. Our research, opinions, and public voice make a difference in today's world by bringing clarity and innovative thinking to global policy making. By working across disciplines and in partnership with the best peers and experts, we are the benchmark for influential research and trusted analysis.

University of Toronto Press acknowledges the financial assistance to its publishing program of the Canada Council for the Arts and the Ontario Arts Council, an agency of the Government of Ontario.

Canada Council for the Arts
Conseil des Arts du Canada

ONTARIO ARTS COUNCIL
CONSEIL DES ARTS DE L'ONTARIO
an Ontario government agency
un organisme du gouvernement de l'Ontario

Funded by the Government of Canada
Financé par le gouvernement du Canada

MIX
Paper from responsible sources
FSC® C016245

Contents

Foreword

JOHN BORROWS

A Reconciliation without Recollection? highlights the challenges underlying the Crown's position relative to Indigenous peoples in Canada. This book explains how Canadian law's contingencies masquerade as necessities when dealing with Indigenous peoples. In examining these problems, Professor Nichols helps us see how untested assumptions within Canada's legal system obscure choices that diminish the potential for creating healthier relationships across the land. Mischaracterizing choice as necessity diminishes the freedom of both Indigenous peoples and the Crown and simultaneously undermines the legitimacy of Canada's legal system.

The leading Aboriginal rights case in Canada, *R. v. Sparrow*, held that "there was from the outset never any doubt that sovereignty and legislative power, and indeed the underlying title, to such lands vested in the Crown." The *Sparrow* case attempted to manufacture certainty when there was doubt: Indigenous peoples have questioned the Crown's assertions "from the outset." Crown land claims are unproven. As Professor Nichols demonstrates throughout this text, the Crown claims land through assertion in ways that the Courts do not sufficiently question and have not adequately justified. In fact, the Crown's claims are inferior when measured by the same test the courts apply to Indigenous peoples, as set out in the 2014 *Tsilhqot'in* Aboriginal title action. These deficiencies include the fact that: (1) the Crown did not legally occupy land in North America prior to their assertions of British sovereignty; (2) there have been notable breaks in the physical continuity of the Crown's occupation in places across the country since sovereignty's assertion; and (3) the exclusivity of the Crown's occupancy from the assertion of sovereignty until today is undermined by continued Indigenous governance and possession of Crown-claimed lands.

Despite these problems, the courts identify reconciliation as the purpose of Aboriginal and treaty rights in the jurisprudence. These high-sounding words do not match the lower status generally accorded to Indigenous peoples in their relationship with the Crown. In addressing this disjuncture, Professor Nichols asks us to consider whether reconciliation is possible when the law assumes that the Crown can unilaterally determine the position of Indigenous peoples within Canada's constitutional order. As his analysis unfolds, he helps us see that reconciliation with colonialism is not a goal that Indigenous peoples can support or approve.

Professor Nichols helps us see that there can be no reconciliation when we fail to recollect the colonial foundation of the existing s. 35 framework. He shows us that the law's abstraction in favour of the Crown causes Canadians to lose track of the *contingency* of that bias and thereby threatens our ability to choose other, less-oppressive alternatives. When courts or legislatures act on assumptions that the Crown is necessarily vested with power-over Indigenous peoples, reconciliation becomes an impossibility.

In making his case, Professor Nichols reminds us that the work of reconciliation cannot be done within the confines of any one tradition. This book reminds us of the importance of detailed doctrinal, philosophical, historical, and policy-oriented research when examining Aboriginal and treaty rights in Canada. He has done a superb job of highlighting challenges ahead in working towards reconciliation from these varied viewpoints. The work of reconciliation requires that we see our hidden biases, and *A Reconciliation without Recollection?* is among the best tools we have for opening our eyes to the choices that lie before us.

John Borrows
Canada Research Chair in Indigenous Law

Foreword

JAMES TULLY

A Reconciliation without Recollection? is the most thorough and scholarly study of the project of reconciliation in Canadian jurisprudence and beyond. Nichols argues that the project as currently conceived cannot reconcile the relations between Indigenous peoples and the Canadian government (Crown) because it rests on a colonial presupposition that cannot be brought into the space of questions from within the framework of reconciliation the courts set out in section 35 of the Charter. This presupposition is that section 91(24) of the Constitution gives the federal government sovereign power over Indigenous peoples and their lands. Yet the plain meaning of "reconciliation," in contrast to "resignation," is that reconciliation examines and transforms the problematic relationship between the contestants. In cases of illegitimate master–subject relationships, reconciliation consists of transforming the relationship into democratic ones in which the contestants recognize each other as equal partners, neither masters nor subjects, and learn how to exercise power-with each other. As Abraham Lincoln famously put it, "As I would not be a slave, so I would not be a master. This expresses my idea of democracy."

The courts have abandoned the legal fictions used to legitimate this power-over interpretation of 91(24) and have accepted that Crown sovereignty is only de facto. However, the procedures of litigation and negotiation initiated under section 35 since 1990 to render it de jure continue to take place on the basis of this unquestionable foundation, and thus prevent the participants from transforming the unjust relationship they bear as masters and subjects. Nichols is not the first to point this out. However, his detailed and exhaustive analysis and synopsis of the jurisprudence since 1867, the theories and legal fictions that legitimate the master–subject relationship in its various forms, the machinery of the *Indian Act* that enforces the relationship, and the secondary literature that has come before him is unparalleled.

In addition, unlike many critical scholars, Nichols does not stop there. His most important contribution, in my opinion, is to show how the background, power-over interpretation of 91(24) can be called into question and shown to be contingent and changeable. He goes on to present a de-colonial interpretation of 91(24) as the power of the federal government to relate to and with, not over, Indigenous peoples as equals, and to enter into nation-with-nation negotiations and relationships. If both parties were to interact in this way, they would bring into being a multinational, democratic federation. There is no way to reconciliation. Reconciliation is the way.

Nichols's modest proposal is neither a grand theory that solves everything in a revolution "to come" nor an inward turn of the unhappy consciousness. It is akin to the slow but sure, experimental way of his Indigenous ancestors; of finding a good path forward through attending to the dense, entangled, and interdependent ecology of the here-and-now and its history. He shows that "power-with" accords better with both the actual wording of 91(24) and the concept of just reconciliation itself. More importantly, he grounds it in a careful "recollection" of the 255-year-old history of nation-with-nation treaty-making and Indigenous peoples' demands to honour it. Furthermore, he argues that it accords with the recommendation of the Royal Commission on Aboriginal Peoples, the Truth and Reconciliation Commission, the *United Nations Declaration of the Rights of Indigenous Peoples*, as well as recent statements by the federal government. Finally, he turns to justices and common lawyers and suggests that this proposal accords with the way the Supreme Court has said it should relate to a people or peoples with the right of self-determination in the *Quebec Reference* case.

If I am not mistaken, this sort of proposal is what many Indigenous and non-Indigenous people of goodwill have been looking for: a step-by-step and potentially transformative way forward that grows out of each other's best traditions and practices and requires what he calls the "mutual labour" of all affected. The question mark in the title asks us to consider it and respond from our diverse positions and perspectives within the world we share.

James Tully
University of Victoria

He had bought a large map representing the sea,
    Without the least vestige of land:
And the crew were much pleased when they found it to be
    A map they could all understand.

"What's the good of Mercator's North Poles and Equators,
    Tropics, Zones, and Meridian Lines?"
So the Bellman would cry: and the crew would reply
    "They are merely conventional signs!

"Other maps are such shapes, with their islands and capes!
    But we've got our brave Captain to thank
(So the crew would protest) "that he's bought us the best –
    A perfect and absolute blank!"

This was charming, no doubt; but they shortly found out
    That the Captain they trusted so well
Had only one notion for crossing the ocean,
    And that was to tingle his bell.

He was thoughtful and grave – but the orders he gave
    Were enough to bewilder a crew.
When he cried "Steer to starboard, but keep her head larboard!"
    What on earth was the helmsman to do?

Then the bowsprit got mixed with the rudder sometimes:
    A thing, as the Bellman remarked,
That frequently happens in tropical climes,
    When a vessel is, so to speak, "snarked."

Lewis Carroll, *The Hunting of the Snark* (1876)

Preface

This book is first and foremost an *investigation*.[1] By this I mean that it proceeds by carefully following or tracking something of interest.[2] This requires us to focus our attention on the little concrete traces, marks, or footprints (the *vestiges*) that can so easily be overlooked. The key here is that when one sets out to follow footprints, the path is not one that can be determined. This does not mean that every investigator will follow a given trace or clue in exactly the same way. Like any other human endeavour, investigation is a practice that is subject to interpretation. It is a skill, or to borrow Aristotle's term *phronesis*, and so all investigators must start from where they are and the time that they are there. This means that they can only make use of the toolbox of ideas and concepts that are available to them in their localized and situated perspective. All that they will be able to do is make critical use of their experience and thereby refine and improve their inherited tools by applying them to a given task.

The significance of this limitation can be seen when we consider what investigators *cannot do*. The most obvious limitation is that they cannot determine in advance the path of what they are investigating by constructing a complete theory. The footprints have already been made (even if faded and difficult to decipher), and the point of the exercise is to follow them. Nor can investigators step outside of their context and systematically determine the course of all possible paths in order to provide the rigidly fixed coordinates of absolute

1 My sense of this term and the methods related to it flow from Ludwig Wittgenstein's ordinary language philosophy. In particular from his *Philosophical Investigations*. My own approach to Wittgenstein's work is heavily indebted to a number of scholars, including Stanley Cavell, Gordon Baker, James C. Edwards, Hannah Pitkin, S. Stephen Hilmy, Rupert Read, and Oskari Kuusela, but none of these debts are as significant as the one that I owe to James Tully.

2 I am referring here to the etymology of *investigation*, which comes from the past participle of the Latin *investigare* (from which we get the term *investigate*, meaning "to track or investigate") and *vestigium* (from which we get the noun *vestige*, meaning "a trace, footprint or track").

certainty. This would mean abandoning any one investigation in favour of building a comprehensive theoretical structure or model. While individual and limited theoretical models can help us find our way in difficult cases, as soon as they become *the* only approach or method, they will inevitably limit our field of view. When this happens, our model becomes like a pair of glasses that we've forgotten are there and through which we see whatever we look at.[3] Put another way, by opting for a theoretical model that holds the promise of necessity, we may confuse the theory with the object of investigation. This would leave us caught in an illusion in which "we predicate of the thing what lies in the method of representing it."[4] This kind of confusion does not necessarily result from a single decision; rather, it can occur gradually through accretion or sedimentation. As Ludwig Wittgenstein puts it, "The fundamental fact here is that we lay down rules, a technique, for a game, and that then when we follow the rules, things do not turn out as we had assumed. That we are therefore entangled in our own rules."[5] This entanglement leaves us feeling as if we were lost in a labyrinth. We look from our rules to the territory and say, "But this isn't how it is! Yet this is how it has to be!"[6] When this happens, there is no one solution that will untangle us, much like there is no single key that will open all doors. We need a more perspicuous representation of precisely where we are, so that we can see what we are missing. In other words, we need to rearrange things so that we can notice what has been hiding in plain sight.

As Stephen Toulmin helpfully points out, this dream of absolute certainty (i.e., of *the* method or key) is exposed as a dream when we remember that

> No formalism can interpret itself;
> No system can validate itself;
> No theory can exemplify itself;
> No representation can map itself;
> No language can predetermine its own meanings.[7]

The common point in all of these maxims is that each requires the practical reasoning of human actors and so cannot escape the uncertainty, ambiguity,

---

3 Ludwig Wittgenstein, *Philosophical Investigations*, 3rd ed. (Oxford: Blackwell, 2001) at §103.

4 Ibid. at §104.

5 Ibid. at §125. As I see it, entanglement is not a necessary consequence of having rules. Nor do I feel it is strictly limited to cases in which the wrong set of rules is being used. Rather, my own feeling is that the historical accumulation of rules has a tendency towards entanglement (much in the same way in which a city begins to resemble a labyrinth over time), and I further suspect that this tendency is most pronounced in heavily contested areas.

6 Ibid. at §112.

7 Stephen Toulmin, *Return to Reason* (Cambridge, MA: Harvard University Press, 2001) at 80.

and pluralism that accompanies our human condition. What this means is that the methods that I have adopted in this book were chosen because I have found them best suited to this investigation. They are by no means *the only methods* that one could choose. Rather, they are part of my set of skills and limitations as an individual investigator. They are the tools that I had on hand, and I have applied them, honed them, and shaped them to this particular task. They are, and must be clearly seen as, contingent *objects of comparison*.[8]

Another way to think of this is to consider the practice of investigation as one that makes extensive use of abductive reasoning. In contrast to the more familiar pairing of inductive and deductive, abductive reasoning is a kind of synthetic inference that allows us react to situations in which there is no clear and direct path by trying out "tentative and hazardous" suppositions.[9] It provides us with a way forward when our maps and projections fail us. This kind of guesswork, with its collection of trial balloons and ad hoc instruments, is a skill set that any investigator would be lost without. There is also an intersubjective aspect to this, as these abductive attempts are open to revision through testing it in practice, correcting for errors, saving what is relatively truthful in it, recording it in a story to share and compare with other group stories (viz. over time this becomes the set of tools, skills, and know-how that is commonly referred to as "traditional knowledge").[10] This form of reasoning is especially important when the "object" of investigation is not a specimen in a lab, but animate and out in the field or a contested concept.[11] If there is no clear path forward, the resources of abductive reasoning can be employed to find a tentative way forward by making one up in situ with what is at hand.[12] While these

---

8 Wittgenstein provides a clear summary of this: "For we can avoid ineptness or emptiness of our assertions only by presenting the model as what it is, as an object of comparison – as, so to speak, a measuring-rod; not as a preconceived idea to which reality *must* correspond." Wittgenstein, *Philosophical Investigations* at §131.

9 I encountered the concept of abductive reasoning while making my way through Alfred Gell's fascinating *Art and Agency: An Anthropological Theory* (Oxford: Oxford University Press, 1998) at 14. The phrase "tentative and hazardous" is used by Umberto Eco (who is cited by Gell) to describe abductive reasoning in *Semiotics and the Philosophy of Language* (London: Macmillan, 1984) at 40.

10 I'd like to thank James Tully for bringing this intersubjective aspect to my attention.

11 Here I have in mind Gallie's helpful notion of an "essentially contested concept." See W.B. Gallie, *Philosophy and the Historical Understanding* (London: Chatto & Windus, 1964) at 190.

12 I believe that there is a useful distinction to be made between what we could refer to as disciplined and undisciplined ways of making up an approach (i.e., of putting abductive reasoning to use). While a more thorough development of this distinction is outside the bounds of this investigation, I see this difference as closely aligned to Aristotle's use of *phronesis*, because experience and know-how often provide a helpful distinction between merely making it up as we go along and experimental approaches that succeed. I would like to thank Kerry Wilkins for drawing this distinction to my attention.

tools and techniques are invaluable, we also must be cautious about their application. As soon as we lose track of their *contingency* and treat them as *necessary*, we forgo our investigation and set off in search of snarks and jabberwocks with little more than a blank page as our guide.

This means that the map that I have managed to produce with these tools (viz. this book) *is not the territory*, nor are the tools that I made use of *the only tools possible for the job*. This book is a map of sorts, but it is not final or complete. It does not survey a field in order to master it, and the book cannot simply be catalogued into a collection of maps as a partial view that could eventually be complete. It is better thought of as a series of sketches of landscape. For the book to be of use, you need to walk the territory and see how these sketches could open up other approaches to the field. I do not mean to suggest that it is simply as good as any other map or set of tools, but rather that the *criterion* that is relevant for determining its value is how it helps you find your way through a particular territory. The book does not, nor indeed can it, spare you the trouble of *using it*. You will need to look around, think, and make your way through the thickets and brambles, but it can help you see a way out that you might not have otherwise noticed. In other words, the value of this – or indeed any – map is its ability to clear away the misunderstandings that leave us unable to make our way about.

The Question of Methodological Sources

Before I get to the subject matter of the book, I would like to address methodologies and sources. My approach to reconciliation has been to work within the Western legal, political, and philosophical tradition. Some readers may wonder why I have selected these materials and not opted to use the resources of Indigenous traditions. As I see it, this line of reasoning poses the following type of question: "If our aim is to find a way to move beyond the confines of the current system, is it not better to look for other resources than those that were used to build it?" My initial response to this concern depends on how we understand it. If the gist is that we should be seeking a diversity of resources and not opting for Wittgenstein's "one-sided diet," I agree with this concern; we should use a diversity of approaches and perspectives.[13] This means that we need to work with the tools that we have and within the confines of the problem and context that we exist within. There is more than one way to skin a cat. But if it is read as a call to reject any approach that would use the resources of the Western tradition because they may be contaminated, then I reject it. I do so because there is, as I see it, a kind of metaphysical demand

13 Wittgenstein, *Philosophical Investigations* at §593.

lurking in this reading (viz. a demand for the kind of uncontaminated or "pure" tools that would be needed to build utopia), which, if adopted, would leave us stuck in a crippling form of scepticism that would enable us only to determine that any movement fails to meet the standard we have chosen.[14] The single comfort that such a view from nowhere can offer is a hollow claim to moral superiority.[15] As Hegel forcefully points out, "It is just as foolish to imagine that any philosophy can transcend its contemporary world as that an individual can overleap his time or leap over Rhodes."[16] This point is driven home by Quentin Skinner when he maintains that "all revolutionaries are … obliged to march backwards into battle."[17] The gist is that in order to effect political change, one must work from within one's historical context.[18] This means grappling with the political, legal, and philosophical texts that are woven into its structure. The urge to simply burn these texts and begin anew is as empty as the claim that we can jump over our own shadow. These texts do not sit discreetly on library shelves. They are carried with us in our actions

---

14 While we may speak at times of "perfect tools," I am inclined to see this in a narrow sense. That is, the criterion for determining whether or not a given tool is "perfect" is the use to which it is put. This does not require that the tool have no other uses, and so the fact that it can be used to either undo a task or perform a multitude of others does not render it imperfect. This is distinct in kind from the metaphysically inflated demand for a set of tools that have no history and no other possible uses (i.e., they are not double-edged and so cannot be used differently). In my opinion this demand for new and perfect tools draws from the deeper eschatological and millennial undercurrents of eighteenth- and nineteenth-century revolutionary political ideologies; it is a kind of yearning for the end of history. Wittgenstein gets at something that I see as related to this desire when he refers to the "craving for generality" and "the contemptuous attitude towards the particular case." See Ludwig Wittgenstein, *The Blue and Brown Books*, 2nd ed. (New York: Harper & Row, 1964) at 18.

15 Here I have in mind Hegel's critique of the beautiful soul and his forceful rejection of romantic idealism in the preface to the *Philosophy of Right*. See G.W.F Hegel, *Elements of the Philosophy of Right*, ed. Allen W. Wood, trans. H.B. Nisbet (Cambridge: Cambridge University Press, 2004) at 9–23.

16 Ibid. at 21–2.

17 Quintin Skinner, *Visions of Politics*, vol. 1, *Regarding Method* (Cambridge: Cambridge University Press, 2002) at 149–50.

18 Jennifer Pitts articulates a similar point when she summarizes the intent that animates her excellent *Boundaries of the International: Law and Empire* (Harvard University Press: Cambridge, 2018) at 27: "It is my hope that an investigation of the shifting boundaries of the international, and their justifications, may help to illuminate continuing uses of ideas of international law and human rights to obscure dynamics of domination by the Global North over the Global South. There may be no untainted well from which we can draw, but recovering the perspective of ecumenical strands of the distinctive and unusual period of the late eighteenth century, as well as their occasional heirs in the nineteenth, may provide the resources for the critical scrutiny of such dynamics."

and in our words, and so to abandon them entirely is to condemn ourselves to unconsciously repeating them.[19]

I find that Audre Lorde's evocative claim that "the master's tools will never dismantle the master's house" is helpful for thinking through this problem.[20] We can imagine that the resources of the Western tradition (or any tradition) are analogous to a set of tools that have been used to construct a system of domination (viz. the master's house). If we can stretch this analogy a little, we can add in a set of actors within the system and imagine them using the tools to work on the house. What happens past this point depends entirely on *how they use the tools*. There is, undoubtedly, a way of using the tools that will result in the maintenance of the existing house or even the construction of another house that would be practically identical to the first. We could even imagine that, for experienced builders, this way of using these tools could become rather automatic (e.g., a hammer is used to drive in and extract a nail, etc.). It could even become

19 I am paraphrasing George Santayana's famous aphorism, which maintains that "those who cannot remember the past are condemned to repeat it." Santayana uses "savages" as an example of those who are condemned to repeat themselves, but my own position is that this unfortunate condition afflicts all and was by and large far more prevalent among the self-proclaimed "civilized." See George Santayana, *The Life of Reason: Reason in Common Sense*, critical ed., co-ed. Marianne S. Wokeck and Martin A. Coleman, vol. 7, bk 1 of *The Works of George Santayana* (Cambridge, MA: MIT Press, 2011) at 172.

20 Audre Lorde, "The Master's Tools Will Never Dismantle the Master's House," in *The Audre Lorde Compendium: Essays, Speeches and Journals* (London: Pandora-Harper Collins, 1996) at 160. It is interesting to note that Marx made a *very* similar observation when he was analysing the Paris Commune of 1871: "The working class cannot simply lay hold on the ready-made state machinery and wield it for their own purpose. The political instrument of their enslavement cannot serve as the political instrument of their emancipation." See Karl Marx and Friedrich Engels, *Writings on the Paris Commune*, ed. H. Draper (New York: Monthly Review, 1971) at 196. What this phrasing brings to mind for me is Marcel Duchamp's "readymades," which serve as a very helpful reminder that there are always other ways of relating to the objects (and I would argue the same applies to institutions and laws) that make up our everyday reality (viz. what is in one context a urinal is, in another, a fountain – Duchamp was a master of *making* new and surprising ways of relating to the everyday). Philip Corrigan and Derek Sayer forcefully draw out the consequences of this and show how Marx's note of caution is not to be taken as a flat rejection of "state machinery": "Revolutionary transformation, that history graphically demonstrates, is not just about changing deeds of ownership or capturing 'power,' but *making* new ways of relating, new social identities – a new moral order, a new kind of civilization, a different socialization." Philip Corrigan and Derek Sayer, *The Great Arch: English State Formation as Cultural Revolution* (Oxford: Basil Blackwell, 1985) at 207. Corrigan and Sayer also helpfully note that "history underlines … the need to start with existing resources; the only ones there are" (ibid.). As they note, Marx made much the same observation in his text on the Paris Commune. They distill his point to crystalline clarity: "There are no utopias to be introduced *par décret du people*; the starting-point for building the new world lies in the struggles of the old" (ibid.).

so automatic that they would find it difficult to conceive of any other way to use the tools and so would immediately object if another builder attempted to use a tool in a way that they did not recognize. In this case, the master's instructions on how to use tools to build a house have been internalized by the builders and they are thus captured by a picture. But, as Wittgenstein reminds us, no game is entirely circumscribed by rules.[21] Or, to rephrase this point in a way that fits with the analogy we are working with, there is no particular use that inheres within the tools themselves. They arrive to us, much like words, with a history of usage that needs to be taken into account, but this does not strictly determine the boundaries of how actors put them to use. Nor is this history solid and consistent all the way down; rather, it is analogous to a series of sedimentary layers whose regularity is occasionally subject to sudden and violent eruptions that cause the once discreet layers to criss-cross, overlap, and interpenetrate one another.[22] As Wittgenstein helpfully points out, "The aspects of things that are most important for us are hidden because of their simplicity and familiarity. (One is unable to notice something – because it is always before one's eyes.). The real foundations of his enquiry do not strike a man at all. Unless that fact has at some time struck him. – And this means: we fail to be struck by what, once seen, is most striking and most powerful."[23]

This is precisely why redescription has such an explosive potential: it can draw our attention to something that is hiding in plain sight. The master's house that once seemed to be so solid and impenetrable (consistent with itself through and through) can come to seem like nothing more than a house of cards. Once this is openly surveyable, the builders are free to explore the new uses that the tools could have. This is something that history can easily show us if we turn our eyes from generalizations and focus on particular cases. After all, in slave rebellions the master's tools were often used to destroy both the master's house and the master himself. We should remember that a hammer does not determine its use, one can use it to build, destroy, or even, as Nietzsche shows us, philosophize.[24]

21 Wittgenstein, *Philosophical Investigations* at §68.

22 I have in mind here Wittgenstein's famous image of rope from *The Brown Book*. See Wittgenstein, *Blue and Brown Books* at 87.

23 Ibid. at §127.

24 Here I have in mind Nietzsche's *Twilight of the Idols, or, How to Philosophize with a Hammer*. Another example that helps point to this feature of tools is Heidegger's use of the hammer as an example to illustrate "the worldhood of the world" in *Being and Time*. Heidegger notes that it is when tools are damaged, or the material turns out to be unusable that "we discover its unusability … not by looking at it and establishing its properties, but rather by the circumspection of the dealings in which we use it. When its unusability is thus discovered, equipment becomes conspicuous." See Martin Heidegger, *Being and Time*, trans. John Macquarrie and Edward Robinson (New York: Harper and Row, 1962) at 102. For my

I also see the approach that I have adopted as stemming from my own standpoint. I have always found myself resistant to any attempt to draw out the bright lines that are required to separate culture into strict either/or categories. My own preference is to explore the wider ranges of the neither/nor, which present themselves both at the margins of the systems of the metropole (viz. in the diverse and strange world of the borderlands, the open vistas of the hinterlands, the sublime expanse of the wastelands and the wilds) and concealed within the blind alleys, buried foundations, and hidden rooms of the metropolitan capital itself. As such, my standpoint does not come with the force of some deep reservoir of privileged cultural authority; rather, it draws me to search for the points at which connections can be made and new possibilities can be explored. This is the spirit in which I have attempted to approach the history of the Six Nations of the Haudenosaunee with Canada (and before that the British Crown). I believe that Deskaheh's appeal for justice still has many possibilities that have yet to be explored, and my aim is to use the tools and resources that I have ready at hand to carry that work forward to investigate the foundations of the current international political and legal order. As I see it, one of the greatest compliments a reader could give to the book would be to enter into a dialogue with it from the perspective of Indigenous tradition. The work of reconciliation cannot be done from the confines of any one tradition; it is a mutual labour. In this respect it draws its resources from the rich history of intercultural dialogue that we see in the networks of treaty relations that have been honoured in the breach for far too long now.

Now that we have determined that the book is an investigation (and have a rough-and-ready sense of what I mean by that), we are left with the question of *what is being investigated*. The first half of the title establishes my subject, but it does not do so directly. In order to unpack precisely what I mean by the phrase "a reconciliation without recollection" – and further, why I am using it as a question – we will need to begin with a brief contextual analysis of the word *reconciliation*. As I will be going into the finer details of this in part 1, the following should be taken as a provisional outline.

The image on the cover of the book and the epigraph also serve as (somewhat indirect) indications of my subject matter. They are taken from Lewis Carroll's nonsense poem "The Hunting of the Snark: An Agony in Eight Fits," which was written from 1874 to 1876.[25] The plot of Carroll's poem follows the voyage of a

---

purposes here, the simple point being that we can easily confuse the hammer with its most common use (i.e., a hammer is for hammering nails), but when it is broken this identification of tool and use is disrupted. In this disruption we see that it is not identical with this use and can be used otherwise. I'd like to thank Kerry Wilkins for reminding me of Heidegger's use of hammers.

25 Lewis Carroll, *The Annotated Hunting of the Snark*, ed. Martin Gardner (New York: Norton, 2006).

motley crew of ten characters who have set off to hunt the snark. The snark is their quarry. This much is certain, but what exactly is a snark? The answer to this question draws us further into the thickets. Its identity is, much like Carroll's jabberwocky, infamously enigmatic. He does not provide the reader with a definition. Instead we are given a curious bundle of improbable qualities coupled with a warning: "If your Snark be a Boojum! … You will softly and suddenly vanish away, and never be met with again!"[26] This gives us the tragically absurd stakes of the hunt: the crew is both driven by their desire for snarks and haunted by the (apparently) ever-present possibility that they have mistaken the snark for the boojum (i.e., that the quarry is in fact the hunter). But, in my view, the true character of the hunt can be seen in the description of the method for capturing snarks. The method is first set out in the third fit ("The Baker's Tale").

"You may seek it with thimbles – and seek it with care;
  You may hunt it with forks and hope;
You may threaten its life with a railway-share;
  You may charm it with smiles and soap – "[27]

This method is repeated in each subsequent fit of the poem. It serves as a kind of leitmotif for the hunt itself. The Bellman repeats it in the fourth fit ("The Hunting") and closes his speech to the crew with the following lines:

"For the Snark's a peculiar creature, that won't
  Be caught in a commonplace way.
Do all that you know, and try all that you don't:
  Not a chance must be wasted to-day!

"For England expects – I forbear to proceed:
  'Tis a maxim tremendous, but trite:
And you'd best be unpacking the things that you need
  To rig yourselves out for the fight."[28]

---

26 The qualities of the snark are scattered throughout the poem, but in the second fit ("The Bellman's Speech") we are given a bundle of "five unmistakable marks" that serve to identify genuine snarks. The qualities in the list bring to mind Edward Said's notion of "contrapuntal ensembles" as they seem to be little more than disconnected fragments of the subject that seeks the snark (viz. some of the qualities are typically associated with objects – such as flammable and edible – whereas others are those of subjects – such as laziness, a lack of humour, a fondness of bathing-machines, and ambition). The qualities that are described do not serve to cohere and give us a picture of the snark; rather, they refract and distort like a collection of funhouse mirrors, leaving only a trace of those that hunt it. See Edward Said, *Culture and Imperialism* (New York: Vintage Books, 1993) at 60.

27 Carroll, *Snark* at 38.

28 Ibid. at 42.

From the reference to Horatio Nelson's flag signal to the fleet at the battle of Trafalgar in 1805,[29] to the use of railway shares as death threats,[30] the connection with the rise of the Second Empire is difficult to miss. Also, the year of publication is a significant one for my purposes. In 1876 the federal government of the newly formed Dominion of Canada consolidated the *Gradual Civilization Act* (1857) and the *Gradual Enfranchisement Act* (1868) into the *Indian Act*. It seems to me that the description of a hunt for a quarry whose identity is fundamentally uncertain, that is guided by a blank map, and is sailing in a ship that is going backwards in a circle is a fitting indictment of both the wider British Imperial ambitions and the more localized civilizing project of the newly formed dominion.[31]

Whether or not Carroll intended "The Hunting of the Snark" to serve as such an indictment is an interesting question, but it is not my concern here. My use of the poem and its absurd imagery is linked to James Tully's use of Bill Reid's *The Spirit of Haida Gwaii* on the cover of his *Strange Multiplicity*. In the preface of that book he states that the theme (viz. "constitutionalism in circumstances of cultural diversity") is discussed "in the light of a single work of art, *The Spirit of Haida Gwaii*."[32] He continues, "In these dark and discordant times, I do not expect the lectures to move more than a few readers. Nevertheless, the only way to lessen the darkness and discord is to take up the responsibility to speak in the dialogue initiated by *The Spirit of Haida Gwaii*. This is my response."[33]

I have used the "The Hunting of the Snark" to point to the imperial darkness and colonial discord that has accompanied the Canadian ship of state for the last 150 years. I have used it as an indictment against the last 150 years of colonial constitutionalism, from the "forks and hope" of assimilation to the "smiles and soap" of reconciliation. But my intent is not to simply present

29 Ibid. at 42–3. The flag signal was "England expects every man to do his duty."

30 This could be a reference to the railway mania of the 1840s and the connections between companies, speculative investment, and empire. But the mention of railway shares is particularly suggestive in the 1870s in British North America. The first major political scandal in the Dominion of Canada after Confederation concerned the contract to build the transcontinental Canadian Pacific Railway. For more on this history and its impact on the common law, see R.W. Kostal, *Law and English Railway Capitalism 1825–1875* (Oxford: Oxford University Press, 1998). This may well be entirely coincidental for Carroll's poem, but the presence of a beaver in the crew (an animal whose emblematic relationship to Canada is long-standing) leads me to see this connection as at least a possible reading.

31 The Bellman's order in the second fit is to "Steer to starboard, but keep her head larboard!" Larboard is another name for port, and so the order seems contradictory. But it is possible to steer to starboard and keep the ship's head to port, providing that the ship is going backwards in a circle. See Carroll, *Snark* at 29–30.

32 James Tully, *Strange Multiplicity: Constitutionalism in an Age of Diversity* (Cambridge: Cambridge University Press, 1995) at xi.

33 Ibid.

an indictment and rest my case, so to speak. This would, as I see it, leave us confined to the blank map and backwards circles of the hunt. I begin with an indictment of the dark and discordant legacies of the Second Empire. I begin with this precisely because the Canadian ship of state retained far more from the nineteenth century than the "water-tight compartments" of ss. 91 and 92 of the *British North America Act, 1867*. It also retained the peculiar madness of "civilizing" and "enfranchising" Indigenous peoples. This also forms "part of her original structure" (to repurpose Lord Atkin's words), but I do not believe that it is an "essential part."[34] Rather, like Tully, I see *The Spirit of Haida Gwaii* as a representation of practices of constitutionalism whose roots extend back over 250 years and offer us another way to find our way through our current darkness to a constitution that can be "both the foundation of democracy and, at the same time, subject to democratic discussion and change in practice."[35]

34 *Canada (AG) v. Ontario (AG)*, [1937] UKPC 6, [1937] AC 326.
35 Tully, *Strange Multiplicity*, at 29.

Acknowledgments

I would like to acknowledge the tireless efforts of Michael Asch, John Borrows, and James Tully. This book would not be what it is without the many long conversations that I had with them, both in person and virtually. They have been, and continue to be, integral to my thinking. I would like to extend my thanks and sincerest gratitude to Kerry Wilkins for reading over the entire manuscript and offering inerrably detailed and insightful comments and suggestions throughout. He generously engaged with the manuscript on its own terms and suggested numerous ways of making it into the book that its author was actually attempting to write. I would also like to thank Ryan Beaton and Robert Hamilton who have, as both my friends and colleagues, read (numerous) drafts and provided me with their thoughtful comments and suggestions on my own work, while also helping me to better see the problems and possibilities in this area of law through their own work.

I would also like to acknowledge the ongoing support that I have received from the Centre for International Governance Innovation. They have provided me with the support and materials necessary to expand my work and open up lines of dialogue with other scholars and the larger policy community both within Canada and beyond its borders.

The foundations of this book are by no means separate and discreet from the projects and conversations that preceded them. While it is in some sense true that it has a single architect, I cannot say that it began on drafting paper carte blanche. I am here, as always, patching things together and (pace Descartes) "using old walls that had been built for other purposes." What I am trying to say here is simply that the foundations of this book are *not completely my own*. The components that have been salvaged and repurposed here have been taken from the flotsam and jetsam of innumerable conversations with previous supervisors, colleagues, and friends. While it can be hard (if not impossible) to trace back every component to its point of origin, I can say that many of them bear the distinctive marks of Derek Sayer and Yoke-Sum Wong. I cut my methodological teeth in their classes, and their particular approach to trouble-making in the social sciences continues to inspire me. My time in philosophy at the University of Toronto also marks the construction of this book, and so I would be remiss not to mention the influence of Rebecca Comay, Robert Gibbs, and Mark Kingwell. Then there have been the innumerable conversations and collaborations with Amy Swiffen, which provide me with the kind of open-textured space where real innovative social theory can occur. Any good qualities that this book has are, in my mind, the product of these numerous criss-crossing and overlapping lines of dialogue. Needless to say, any faults that it may have are entirely my own.

A RECONCILIATION WITHOUT RECOLLECTION?

An Investigation of the Foundations of Aboriginal Law in Canada

Introduction

Reconciliation has been a part of the everyday vocabulary of Indigenous-settler relations in Canada for some time now. It can be found in almost every area of public discourse, from political speeches, to statements of public policy, legal cases, newspapers, academic journals, commissions of inquiry, and ordinary, everyday conversation. The currency that it has is in many ways understandable. After all, the ordinary sense of the word means "to restore friendly relations" and so carries with it the notion of mutual agreement and consent. This is, as I see it, what grants the term *reconciliation* the aura of legitimacy in everyday speech, but we must remember that it is also a "term of art" in Canadian law.[1] This more specialized use of the word is important, as it determines its significance for law and policy within the Canadian constitutional structure.

If we turn our attention to how the Supreme Court uses this term, we find that reconciliation is the "grand purpose" and "governing ethos" of s. 35 of the *Constitution Act, 1982*.[2] But once you actually sit down and try to make your way through the case law to sort out precisely what this means, you quickly find yourself lost in a labyrinth of legal doctrines, tests, and fictions. For example, in *Van der Peet* we are told that s. 35 provides the constitutional framework for the "reconciliation of the pre-existence of distinctive aboriginal societies occupying the land with Crown sovereignty."[3] This seems to provide us with a

---

1 I want to note here that the term *reconciliation* has given rise to a diverse and extensive body of literature in a number of academic disciplines. I will not attempt to survey this vast literature here. Rather, I will simply state that my focus is strictly limited to the Supreme Court of Canada's use of the term.

2 *Tsilhqot'in Nation v. British Columbia*, [2014] SCC 44 at para. 17; *Beckman v. Little Salmon/Carmacks First Nation*, [2010] 3 SCR 103 at para. 10.

3 *R v. Van der Peet*, [1996] 2 SCR 507 at para. 42. There is a modification of this formulation in *Gladstone* when the Court states that what is being reconciled is "aboriginal societies with the larger Canadian society of which they are a part." See *R v. Gladstone*, [1996] 2 SCR 723 at para. 74. We should pay close attention to the shift in focus from the formula for reconciliation

framework or a process of sorts. That is, it has a kind of logical form in which we are "reconciling" *x* with *y*, but it does not provide us with a clear view of the terms or a criterion to determine whether or not the process is successful. In order to understand what the Court means by "reconciling" in this case we have to have, at the very least, a clear view of the legal difference between *occupancy* and *sovereignty*, an explanation of why these terms fit the parties that they are applied to, what the operation of "reconciling" actually entails, and an account of what grants the Court the jurisdiction to decide the matter. So even after a brief glance we can see that reconciliation is tightly bound to the concepts of sovereignty, jurisdiction, and legitimacy. And so, by pulling what initially seemed like one strand, we quickly find ourselves entangled in a web of concepts that seem to go off in all directions.

One way to get our bearings in the case law is to refer to the decision where the term was first used. This brings us to back to the Court's decision in *Sparrow* in 1990. In this case the Court was tasked with establishing the interpretive framework for s. 35(1) of the *Constitution Act, 1982*. This provision informs us that "the existing aboriginal and treaty rights of the aboriginal peoples of Canada are hereby recognized and affirmed."[4] The language used is broad, to the point of vagueness. It has the open-textured ring of preambular language, as any meaningful legal application of the term will need to have a clear sense of what "existing" and "recognized

in *Van der Peet* to *Gladstone*. Both serve to obfuscate the primary point of contention between Indigenous peoples and the Crown (i.e., was sovereignty acquired and, if so, what constitutional relationship did it establish?). The *Van der Peet* formulation loads the dice by using the terms *aboriginal societies* (avoiding the term *nations* and its legal connotations in European international law) and *occupying* (which suggests that Indigenous peoples may have had occupancy rights (*dominium*) over their territories, but they did not have sovereignty (*imperium*)). Nonetheless this formulation requires a historical and legal investigation. The *Gladstone* formula is focused on the present state of things. It is reconciling *aboriginal societies* with the "larger Canadian society of which they are a part." The nature of the relationship is presumed at the outside: Indigenous peoples are a minority within the Canadian state. This formulation of reconciliation simply leaps over the thorny constitutional and historical questions of how Indigenous peoples became a "part" of Canada and where they sit within the actual division of powers. The Court has treated these formulations as functionally interchangeable. In *Gladstone* itself the *Van der Peet* test is cited and affirmed (at para. 72) right before it is modified (in paras. 73–4). In *Delgamuukw v. British Columbia*, [1997] 3 SCR 1010 at para. 161 Lamer CJ cites the *Gladstone* formulation for the test for the justification of infringement. It is also cited in *Tsilhqot'in Nation v. British Columbia*, [2014] 2 SCR 257 at para. 16. In *Beckman v. Little Salmon/Carmacks First Nation*, [2010] 3 SCR 103 at para. 10 the Court speaks of reconciling "Aboriginal and non-Aboriginal Canadians," and while it does not cite *Gladstone*, the same presentist set of assumptions are in place. The obfuscation that is evident in both formulations is precisely what I am pointing to with the title of this book; the courts are engaged in reconciliation that is premised on forgetting the actual point of contention between the parties. They skip both the question of how the Crown became sovereign and the subsequent question of the actual nature of the sovereignty they acquired.

4 *Constitution Act, 1982.*

and affirmed" means. Without these the courts are left in a position where they do not know either the substantive content or the legal effect of these rights. This lack of clarity is not necessarily surprising. In many cases legislative drafters leave the courts with the task of drawing meaning out of their provisions by leaving them with blurred edges, so to speak (and over time even the hardest lines in a constitutional order do shift and flex). In this case the Court's task was made even more challenging by the position or context of s. 35 within the *Constitution Act, 1982*. It is not a part of the *Charter* – which extends from ss. 1 through to 34 – and so it is not subject to the limitations of ss. 1 and 33.[5] The Court recognizes the problem that this poses explicitly when they state, "There is no explicit language in the provision that authorizes this Court or any court to assess the legitimacy of any government legislation that restricts aboriginal rights."[6]

If their interpretation had simply stopped here, Aboriginal and treaty rights would not be subject to unilateral Crown infringement.[7] Rather, the provision would have offered bright jurisdictional lines more analogous to those found in

---

5 The text of s. 1 states, "The Canadian Charter of Rights and Freedoms guarantees the rights and freedoms set out in it subject only to such reasonable limits prescribed by law as can be demonstrably justified in a free and democratic society." This means that the rights set out in the *Charter* (which extends from ss. 1 to 34 and so does not include s. 35) are not absolute, but subject to unilateral Crown infringement via a judicially mediated reasonableness test. The test itself is set out by the Court in *R v. Oakes*, [1986] 1 SCR 103. Section 33 is commonly referred to as the "notwithstanding clause" or "override power." It allows for Parliament or the provincial legislatures to pass laws that temporarily override ss. 2 or 7–15 of the *Charter* and thereby nullifies any judicial review of those laws during that period of time.

6 *R v. Sparrow*, [1990] 1 SCR 1075 at 1109.

7 Kerry Wilkins helpfully reminded me that while there would be no textual grounding for the case-by-case review of instances of infringement, this does not necessarily mean that the courts would restrict unilateral infringements by the Crown. It would still be possible to interpret s. 35 as subject to *unrestricted* uniliteral Crown infringement via doctrines such as paramountcy or the residual legislative authority of Parliament. While this is certainly within the realm of theoretical possibility, it is by no means a move that cannot be countered. If anything, this would mean that the courts would be attempting to draw a bright line between law and politics and place Indigenous/Crown relations on the latter side. This would effectively render s. 35 to be a hollow provision and so directly contradict Lord Denning's words in *R v. Secretary of State for Foreign and Commonwealth Affairs, Ex parte Indian Association of Alberta*, [1982] QB 892 (CA). As he put it in that case,

> There is nothing, so far as I can see, to warrant any distrust by the Indians of the Government of Canada. But, in case there should be, the discussion in this case will strengthen their hand so as to enable them to withstand any onslaught. They will be able to say that their rights and freedoms have been guaranteed to them by the Crown, originally by the Crown in respect of the United Kingdom, now by the Crown in respect of Canada, but, in any case, by the Crown. No Parliament shall do anything to lessen the worth of these guarantees. They should be honoured by the Crown in respect of Canada "as long as the sun rises and the river flows." The promise must never be broken.

the division of powers in the *Constitution Act, 1867* than the individual rights of the *Charter*. But it would provide *only* those bright jurisdictional lines, as there are, as we have noted above, no definitions that set out the content of the "existing aboriginal and treaty rights." On its own, it is simply a container or box, but it is not a box of *rights* (at least not in the *Charter* sense of the term, which would presuppose the possibility of unilateral infringement via ss. 1 or 33). Rather, this box is made of sturdier stuff – it is *jurisdictional*. The Court was concerned that if it recognized bright jurisdictional lines around s. 35 (i.e., similar to those between the provinces and the federal government) without knowing their constitutional content, their decision could result in the creation of a legal vacuum, but this is by no means necessary.[8] Rather, as I will argue more fully later on, if the Court had recognized these lines and carved out a sphere of constitutionally protected jurisdiction for Indigenous peoples, it would require a constitutional process of mutual design that would draw content from the legal and political traditions of Indigenous peoples, the history of intercultural practices of treaty making, and the guidance of its own previous reports and commissions.[9] This was, after all, precisely what the *Penner Report* had recommended to Parliament in 1983. If the *Sparrow* Court had decided to take this route, then its jurisdiction would be limited in much the same way it was in the *Secession Reference* where their task was to "clarify the legal framework within which political decisions are to be taken 'under the Constitution,' not to usurp the prerogatives of the political forces that operate within that framework."[10] But they do not stop their analysis here. They opt to take a more well-worn path with Indigenous peoples.

> Yet, we find that the words "recognition and affirmation" incorporate the fiduciary relationship referred to earlier and so import some restraint on the exercise of sovereign power. Rights that are recognized and affirmed are not absolute. Federal legislative powers continue, including, of course, the right to legislate with respect to Indians pursuant to s. 91(24) of the *Constitution Act, 1867*. These powers must, however, now be read together with s. 35(1). In other words, *federal power must be reconciled with federal duty* and the best way to achieve that reconciliation is

8 The Court recently articulated this precise concern in the context of the finding of Aboriginal title in *Tsilhqot'in Nation v. British Columbia,* [2014] 2 SCR 257, 2014 SCC 44 at para. 147, and John Borrows has clearly pointed out that by raising the concern of legal vacuums "the Supreme Court's reasoning seems to imply that 'lawlessness' would result if provincial laws of general application did not apply to regulate Aboriginal title lands. This approach utterly fails to recognize that Indigenous peoples have (and could further create) their own laws and procedures for dealing with these issues." See John Borrows, "The Durability of Terra Nullius: Tsilhqot'in Nation v British Columbia," *UBC Law Review* 48, no. 3 (2015): 740.

9 The particular examples I have in mind here are the *Penner Report* and the *Royal Commission on Aboriginal Peoples* (*RCAP*). I will examine both further later on.

10 *Reference re Secession of Quebec*, [1998] 2 SCR 217 at para. 153.

to demand the justification of any government regulation that infringes upon or denies aboriginal rights.[11]

This is the first occurrence of the term *reconciled* in the case law. The approach that the Court establishes with it is fundamentally imbalanced. Its interpretation of s. 35(1) is based on s. 91(24), but the Court does not go on to question the meaning of that provision.[12] The text of s. 91(24) simply states that the exclusive legislative authority of the Parliament of Canada extends to all matters *in relation to* "Indians, and Lands reserved for the Indians." There is similarly no "explicit language" in s. 91(24) that would grant the Crown undoubted sovereignty, legislative power, and underlying title. And yet, since Lord Watson's decision in *St Catherine's Milling* in 1888 the courts have consistently read s. 91(24) as an unlimited grant of legislative power over Indians and their lands (vesting the provinces with the underlying proprietary interests).[13] In doing so they have treated the meaning of s. 91(24) as being somehow self-evident, but even from the limited positivistic terms of constitutional interpretation in the late nineteenth century this is clearly an *interpretation*.[14] As Toulmin would undoubtedly put it, *no law can interpret itself*. While this could well be glossed over as a truism, it is important to keep it in mind, as it means that this law can

---

11 *Sparrow* at 1109 (emphasis added).

12 What I mean here is that s. 91(24) is presented as the basis for the "federal power" to legislate with respect to Indians and so serves as the interpretive hinge that allows the Court to treat s. 35 as if it is subject to the justified infringement procedures of the *Charter*. It is worth noting that the legislative measure at issue in *Sparrow* was grounded in s. 91(12). They could have used constitutional doctrines like paramountcy to infringe s. 35 rights in this particular case, but it seems to me that they used s. 91(24), as it could serve as a kind of all-purpose hinge for this interpretive move. I would like to thank Kerry Wilkins for drawing my attention to this point.

13 *St Catherine's Milling and Lumber Company v. R* (1888), 14 App. Cas. 46.

14 It is useful to cite the specific language of s. 91:

> It shall be lawful for the Queen, by and with the Advice and Consent of the Senate and House of Commons, to make Laws for the Peace, Order, and good Government of Canada, *in relation to* all Matters not coming within the Classes of Subjects by this Act assigned exclusively to the Legislatures of the Provinces; and for greater Certainty, but not so as to restrict the Generality of the foregoing Terms of this Section, it is hereby declared that (notwithstanding anything in this Act) the exclusive Legislative Authority of the Parliament of Canada *extends to* all Matters coming within the Classes of Subjects next hereinafter enumerated; that is to say, it is patently clear that the phrases "in relation to" and "extends to" in combination with "Indians, and Lands reserved for the Indians" cannot simply be read as an unequivocal grant of unilateral *power over* Indians and their lands. (emphasis added)

See *The Constitution Act, 1867*, 30 & 31 Vict., c. 3; *St Catherine's Milling*.

be read otherwise. This should, at the very least, stop us from simply taking the Court's interpretation of s. 91(24) as self-evident.

After all, this provision has its own history as part of the *British North America Act, 1867*. Since 1982 we refer to this document as the *Constitution Act, 1867*, but it does not precisely fit the everyday assumptions that are associated with the constitutions of nation states. It is not the result of some internal process of "we *the* people," which then establishes the mechanisms and institutions that couple the nation and the state. Rather, it was passed by the imperial Parliament without any participation of Indigenous peoples, and it created a dominion that was populated by British subjects (this was not replaced by the status of Canadian citizenship until 1947).[15] Any attempt to fit this complicated history of overlapping and criss-crossing legal and political relationships into the rigid conceptual requirements of the Westphalian nation state (viz. a territorial unit with a single sovereign that derives its legitimacy from *the* people) is a Procrustean exercise where much will be left on the cutting room floor. Part of what is left out is whether or not Indigenous peoples could simply be subsumed as part of the body politic.[16] In other words, how was the imperial Parliament able to give the Parliament of its newly formed dominion *unlimited sovereignty* over Indians and their lands? It seems clear that it is impossible to give what one does not have, so there must be some accounting for its legal foundations.[17] But this account

---

15 The status of Canadian citizen was first created by the *Immigration Act*, SC 1910, c. 27, but this did not become separate from the status of British subject until *The Canadian Citizenship Act*, SC 1946, c. 15 came into effect on 1 January 1947.

16 There is some ambiguity here about what kind of subsumption takes place here. There are at least two possibilities: (1) that Indigenous peoples were made subject to the sovereign authority of the Crown, and (2) that Indigenous peoples could be assimilated into Canadian society. These possibilities were both played out historically. The imperial Crown established a somewhat ambiguous and shifting form of sovereign authority (the ambiguity hinging on the legal status of Indigenous peoples as being either nations in a federal relationship to the Crown or subjects of the Crown), and once the Napoleonic wars concluded and the imperial Crown began to grant local settler governments legislative power, which resulted in the creation of a system of administration that used assimilation to acquire lands. Andrew Fitzmaurice offers an invaluable account of this process in chapter 6 of *Sovereignty, Property and Empire, 1500–2000* (Cambridge: Cambridge University Press, 2014).

17 There is, of course, the question of what exactly the imperial Crown held when it created the dominion in 1867. What I would like to say in response is that there is a difference between what one says one has and what one legitimately has (the distinction between theft and lawful possession). But this question requires more than that response offers. There are a couple of different ways to get at the question of what the imperial Crown had to give to its newly formed dominion. First would be to take the blinkered positivistic approach of inquiring into positive sources of imperial law. I call this blinkered because it treats the question of the legal orders of the Indigenous peoples as a kind of externality. This simply moves past the messy question of who counts as an international legal actor (a question that involved the ever-shifting criteria of the term *civilization*) by rigidly maintaining that all that counts are

does not enter the case law. The meaning of s. 91(24) is simply taken as self-evident. As the Court put it, "There was from the outset never any doubt that sovereignty and legislative power, and indeed the underlying title, to such lands vested in the Crown."[18] This lack of doubt may seem to offer the kind of stability

---

the positive laws made by sovereign states. As Jennifer Pitts rightly argues, those international jurists who adhered to this position "were not just recording state practices but selecting the practices they considered worthy sources of international law, and doing so on the basis of a set of poorly defined cultural and normative assumptions." See Pitts, *Boundaries* at 26. The second would be to adopt the pluralistic approach of maintaining that the only way to obtain legitimate possession of land (or sovereignty) is through mutual recognition and consent. As Andrew Fitzmaurice notes, Kant did argue that consent is the only available standard to take lands in the possession of others: "Settlement may not take place by force but only by contract, and indeed by a contract that does not take advantage of the ignorance of those inhabitance with regards to ceding their lands." See Immanuel Kant, *The Metaphysics of Morals*, trans. Mary Gregor (Cambridge: Cambridge University Press, 1996) at 122; Fitzmaurice, *Sovereignty, Property and Empire* at 146–7. But we need to remember that Kant also held that uncivilized or savage peoples lacked legal personality (i.e., they existed in a state of nature and so were lawless). This line of argument can also be seen in the *Metaphysics of Morals*, as he maintains that prior to the establishment of the "civil condition" there is a "rightful *capacity* of the will to bind everyone to recognize the act of taking possession and of appropriate as valid, even though it is only unilateral," and that while this is a "provisional acquisition" it retains the "favor of law" so long as those subject to this taking resist entering into the "civil condition" (Kant, *Metaphysics of Morals* at 54). One of Kant's reviewers calls this might-makes-right doctrine into question, and Kant responds by reaffirming his basic premise that de facto control is the basis and precondition of de jure sovereignty, which he sets out in s. 49. He further states that it is the "actual deed (taking control)" that serves as the "condition and basis for a right" and that "the mere idea of sovereignty over a people constrains me, as belonging to the people, to obey without investigating the right that is claimed" (Kant, *Metaphysics of Morals* at 137). He reinforces this view in *Perpetual Peace*. See Immanuel Kant, *Political Writings*, ed. Hans Reiss, trans H.B. Nisbet (New York: Cambridge University Press, 1991) at 98. So Kant's model of consent begins by denying Indigenous peoples claim to sovereignty and leaves them with a kind of residual usufructuary right to lands, which they can choose to cede to colonial powers and become subject to their laws or to vacate their lands entirely. This is all part and parcel of Kant's metaphysical belief that "the good comes about unintentionally, in the long run, and providentially, by evil means," which we can see articulated in chapter 3 of *Reason within the Boundaries of Mere Reason* (James Tully, personal correspondence, 5 April 2018). I would like to thank James Tully for pointing this out to me.

18 *Sparrow* at 1103. Kerry Wilkins suggested to me that this lack of doubt is the basis for the Court's interpretation of s. 91(24) and s. 109 (i.e., the interpretations of the provisions are the consequences of the initial postulate). This makes good sense to me. The problem, as I see it, is that the Court has a tendency to treat s. 91(24) as if it were a self-interpreting provision and thereby obfuscates the actual postulate that is in play. This move functions as a kind of misdirection that enables the Court to point to a particular provision of the *Constitution Act, 1867* and thereby continue its game of procedural infringement. This allows it to avoid the legal stalemate that results from explicitly relying on the act of state doctrine (i.e., the courts simply state that they cannot inquire into the legitimacy of the state). My aim is to attempt to

required to exclude the question of the legitimacy of the nation state and thereby secure the boundary of law's empire, but this is not the case. The conceptual rigidity of this undoubtable reading of s. 91(24) is similar to that offered by the pre-Copernican model of the universe. It can serve to relate concepts to reality (or facts and values), but only at the cost of having to continually construct and reconstruct a picture of the world that becomes so absurdly complicated that it ends up simply collapsing under the weight of its own arcane explanations.[19] The similarity that I am pointing to is that, like the geocentric model of the universe,

---

point out this obfuscation and so open up the possibility of moving away from the unilateral presumption of Crown sovereignty (which bundles it with legislative power and underlying title) and towards a shared version of this sovereignty. This move is useful because it allows for a readjustment of the division of powers that moves Canada from the current model of symmetrical provincial federalism to an asymmetrical model of treaty federalism. I see this as possible in part because courts have increasingly shied away from endorsing the act of state doctrine, and for good reason. If they were to use this doctrine it would change the venue of the conflict from the courts to the political realm. There are two related worries that typically motivate courts to avoid this particular move. First, there is a long-standing concern within the Western legal tradition regarding the balance between sovereignty and the form of liberty that the rule of law permits. The worry here is that if courts allow the sovereign to operate without judicial restraint in one area it could result in a floodgates problem that would compromise the liberty of all. This position was, as Andrew Fitzmaurice points out, frequently taken by jurists in the late eighteenth and nineteenth century who were critical of European empire. See Fitzmaurice, *Sovereignty, Property and Empire* at 272. Second, there is a concern with keeping up the appearances of judicial legitimacy of Canada on the international stage. If Canadian courts explicitly resorted to the act of state doctrine to justify the unilateral infringement of Indigenous rights it would undoubtedly be seen by many as a judicial endorsement of Canada's colonial foundations.

19 The problem here bears some resemblance to Richard Lipsey and Kelvin Lancaster's theory of the second best in economics. See R.G. Lipsey and Kevin Lancaster, "The General Theory of Second Best," *Review of Economic Studies* 24, no. 1 (1956): 11–32. The gist of their argument was that in a system where there has been an uncorrectable failure in one sector, the actions taken to correct failures in other related sectors may have the unintended result of lowering the overall efficiency of the system. In other words, structural problems cannot be resolved or even held in check by patching smaller problems on an ad hoc basis, or incremental improvements in a system do not necessarily translate into a global improvement, but can in fact result in increased instability. The pre-Copernican model of the universe illustrates this point well, as the continual adaptation and modification did not maintain the structural integrity of the model, but rather undermined it by adding layer upon layer to the original problem. Lipsey and Lancaster argue that this should tell us that when we encounter a problem in a system we should hold off from immediately responding to it, as that can lead us to jump to conclusions based on the theory we are using. Instead we could carefully consider the details of the specific case we are dealing with and consider courses of action that we would have otherwise missed. In this respect the theory of the second-best also resonates with Wittgenstein's work rules, entanglement, and perspicuous representations. I would like to thank Ahmad Galal for bringing the relevance of Lipsey and Lancaster's theory to my attention.

the undoubtable assumption of Crown sovereignty requires a constant description and redescription in order to retain any plausible claim to legitimacy. This leads to an ever-growing accumulation of principles, tests, and doctrines that are calibrated to resolve one troublesome legal knot, but only progressively entangle the courts in their own rules.

Making the New Rules of the Game

Nonetheless this lack of doubt is the foundation for the entire framework of reconciliation in Canada. I do not want to suggest that the Court is unaware of the problems stemming from its interpretation. It explicitly cites an essay by Noel Lyon that indicates that it is, at least somewhat, aware of the problem posed by its interpretation of federal power. The part of Lyon's essay it cites states that "the context of 1982 is surely enough to tell us that this is not just a codification of the case law on aboriginal rights that had accumulated by 1982. Section 35 calls for a just settlement for aboriginal peoples. It renounces the old rules of the game under which the Crown established courts of law and denied those courts the authority to question sovereign claims made by the Crown."[20] The change of the "rules of the game" that is being referred to here is the shift of Aboriginal rights being a common law doctrine to being explicitly set into the *Constitution Act, 1982*. This distinction between the old and new rules is helpful, but it can also mislead one into thinking that the "old rules" were somehow solid all the way through, or that the "new rules" are actually significantly different. Neither is necessarily the case.

The basic premise of these "old rules" was that Indigenous peoples could not own the lands that they occupied (i.e., as the result of racist legal fictions that reduced their legal capacity to own their lands and govern themselves such as the so-called doctrines of discovery and *terra nullius*[21]), and so any agreements

---

20 Noel Lyon, "An Essay on Constitutional Interpretation," *Osgoode Hall Law Journal* 26 (1988): 100, cited in *Sparrow* at 1106.

21 I would like to note here that the European colonial legal fictions of discovery and *terra nullius* do not have consistent and transhistorical definitions. There is a tendency in legal reasoning to look for concepts that are discreetly and strictly defined so that they can fit into a judgment like a kind of finely machined part of an engine. These concepts are particularly important as they serve to justify the occupation of land by the European colonial empires, and so they reside at the very foundations of the settler states. The problem is that these concepts cannot serve this function; they are not load bearing. There is no solid analytic ground that they can be refined down to, no legal essence. If one attempts to follow the genealogical lines of *terra nullius* back to its foundation in hopes of securing it in place by grounding it within Roman law (in *res nullius* or *ferae bestiae*), it will be discovered instead that it is a crisscrossing and overlapping pattern of similarities and differences. For a detailed account of this, see Fitzmaurice, *Sovereignty, Property and Empire* at 51–8; and Christopher

made with them were simply surrenders of the residual "personal and usufructuary" rights that remained.[22] In these agreements, the federal Crown simply removes the "mere burden" (which it could always unilaterally remove via legislation) of these residual rights and thereby converts its title to a *plenum dominium* for its provincial counterparts.[23] Until such time as the Crown elected to do this, the courts would continue to maintain some (fairly elastic, if not simply contradictory) notion of a trust-like relationship between the Crown and Indigenous peoples.[24] But this relationship was only ever trust-*like*, as the rights in question existed only under the shadow of unexercised s. 91(24) power. This picture of the "old rules" (which is from *St Catherine's Milling*) has definitely been the dominant interpretation of the relationship between Indigenous peoples and the Crown for the last 150 years, but it is by no means uncontested.

Tomlins, *Freedom Bound: Law, Labor, and Civic Identity in Colonizing English America 1580–1865* (Cambridge: Cambridge University Press, 2010) at 116–20. There is no heraldry or hagiography to be found in the historical record; these are constructed as facades to cover over the all-too-human reality of ad hoc adaptation and use that accompanied the practices of European imperial occupation. In other words, these concepts are historical products that are born out of the need to find a way to justify the taking of lands from non-European others. What the legal fictions of discovery and *terra nullius* (add to this list the standard of civilization, the agricultural thesis, and the divine right of kings) have in common is that they are part of a set of what Kant aptly refers to as "specious reasons to justify the use of force." See Kant, *Metaphysics of Morals* at 122. Despite this fact I believe we should resist the temptation to see these "specious reasons" as merely the superficial overlay that serves to hide the truth of law and politics (i.e., that it is force that remains unmoved mover of human action). As Andrew Fitzmaurice rightly notes, "Power may well come from the barrel of a gun, but force cannot be successfully sustained, even in the more Machiavellian understandings of politics, as an everyday means of establishing political compliance (as Machiavelli himself stressed)." See Fitzmaurice, *Sovereignty, Property and Empire* at 7. What this means is that when these legal fictions are placed within their historical contexts, their hagiographic aura vanishes, leaving only a shabby set of props to mask theft as lawful possession. This does not expose a final truth (the so-called right of the strongest), but rather opens up the board for new moves in the game of justification and legitimacy.

22 *St Catherine's Milling* at 54–5. Generally speaking, in cases where the treaties did not specifically cede lands (such as the early nineteenth-century Peace and Friendship Treaties), the Crown tends to shift back to its armoury of legal fictions to maintain the legitimacy of its claims to *dominium* and *imperium*.

23 Ibid.

24 It is interesting to note that the courts have found that there are some cases in which fiduciary obligations continue post-surrender. See *Guerin v. R*, [1984] 2 SCR 335, 1984 CanLII 25 (SCC); and *Blueberry River Indian Band v. Canada (Department of Indian Affairs and Northern Development)*, [1995] 4 SCR 344. For a thorough and nuanced examination of the Supreme Court's use of fiduciary law in relation to Indigenous peoples, see Ryan Beaton, "The Crown Fiduciary Duty at the Supreme Court of Canada: Reaching across Nations, or Held within the Grip of the Crown?" in *Reflections on Canada's Past, Present and Future in International Law*, ed. Oonagh E. Fitzgerald, Valerie Hughes, and Mark Jewett, 161–79 (Waterloo, ON: CIGI, 2018).

There is a 250-year-old tradition of treaty relationships stretching back to the *Peace and Friendship Treaties* beginning in 1725, the *Royal Proclamation of 1763*, and *Treaty of Niagara* in 1764. These treaty relationships are not characterized by the singular and absolute rules of the Crown, but are rather the pluralistic and contingent product of mutual creation. I will develop this point much more extensively later on, but for now I want to highlight the fact that there is more than one set of "old rules" in play prior to 1982.

This 150-year-old picture of the "old rules" underwent a sea change in *Calder* when a majority of the Court found that the rights of Indigenous peoples were not derived solely from the Crown, but were inherent in the fact that "when the settlers came, the Indians were there, organized in societies and occupying the land as their forefathers had done for centuries."[25] This necessarily complicates the Crown's claim to sovereignty. If Aboriginal rights are inherent, how can the Crown unilaterally revoke them?[26] The "clear and plain" intent standard for extinguishment is, as we have seen, maintained by Hall J in *Calder*, but its actual legal justification is not provided.[27] What this means is that by 1973 it

25 *Calder et al. v. AG British Columbia*, [1973] SCR 313 at 328.

26 What I mean when I state that the pre-existence of Indigenous peoples "organized in societies and occupying the land" complicates the Crown's claim to sovereignty is not that the Crown is unable to respond to this challenge. After all, prior to 1982 the Crown could rely on legislative supremacy to unilaterally extinguish Aboriginal rights. The problem I am pointing out is not that the Crown did not have the requisite legal principles and doctrines at its disposal, but rather that the changing social and political context of the twentieth century had rendered the explicit use of these principles and doctrines politically unpalatable. The problem with any legal principles of doctrine that the Crown makes use of is that they all go back to the legal fictions of discovery and *terra nullius*, and this is so because it needs a way to respond to the problem of legitimacy. It had done this by using fictions that operated to negate the legal capacity of Indigenous peoples and thereby step over the need to obtain their free, prior, and informed consent. This had introduced a conceptual fissure at the foundation of the constitutional orders of the European imperial states, as they needed a system of legal justification that could maintain two distinct political-legal orders: the first based on the equal liberty of persons, and the second on administrative despotism of the civilized over the uncivilized. By the end of the Second World War this legal and political system of justification had collapsed. The legal fictions that once had been confidently proclaimed by the courts and readily accepted by the public had lost the ring of truth. The combined effects of the post–Second World War shift in the language of political and legal justification towards universal claims of human rights had combined with the movements for international decolonization and civil rights in the United States in the 1960s. This effectively rendered the continued reliance on the specious standard of civilization and the associated set of legal fictions as an embarrassing anachronism.

27 Judson J favoured a standard for extinguishment that was much more favourable to the Crown. He cites *United States v. Santa Fe Pacific R. Co.* (1941), 314 US 339 at 347 for the proposition that "extinguishment of Indian title based on aboriginal possession is of course a different matter. The power of Congress in that regard is supreme. The manner, method and time of such extinguishment raise political, not justiciable, issues." This simply leaves the question of Aboriginal title as entirely subject to unfettered parliamentary supremacy. See

was clear that the "old rules" were both incomplete and unstable. In other words, in *Calder* there is a sense that the constitutional structure of the relationship between Indigenous peoples and the Crown is exposed as being founded on little more than thin air.

The *Sparrow* Court does not signal any awareness of this foundational problem with the "old rules." Rather, following the Lyon citation, the Court states that it will "sketch the framework for an interpretation of 'recognized and affirmed' that, in our opinion, gives appropriate weight to the constitutional nature of these words."[28] The Court is thus clearly attempting to develop a new set of rules. The problem is that it does so by retaining the hinge proposition of the "old rules." It treats the *St Catherine's Milling* interpretation of s. 91(24) as a given and bases its "new rules" on it. And so the "new rules" that it wants set in place move around this seemingly magical hinge (John Borrows helpfully refers to this as "sovereignty's alchemy").[29] What we must remember here is that, like all magical artefacts, this hinge has a catch (i.e., like a sword without a hilt, it can certainly be used, but only at a substantial cost). It can serve its function as a hinge only if you *do not question it*. This is because it is fabricated out of little more than unilateral proclamations and assertions (i.e., the legal fictions of discovery, *terra nullius*, the civilization thesis, etc.) whose claim to legal authority is ultimately grounded on little more than question begging. The question that must be avoided if the hinge is to continue to serve its function in the "new rules" is, *what is the legal nature and factual basis of the relationship between Indigenous peoples and the Crown?* It must avoid this question, because if the answer is the same as the picture that is presented in *St Catherine's Milling* (i.e., that Indigenous peoples are bound in a sovereign–subjects relationship to the Crown by virtue of a *unilateral assertion*) then the magic of the hinge is broken. In other words, when it works it gives the Crown the unilateral power and authority of the great and powerful Wizard of Oz, but it can do so only as long as the curtain remains securely in place. Once the curtain drops and we can see things as they are, the magic is dispelled. Without this magic the foundation of the constitutional order, which once seemed so solid, suddenly crumbles and gives way beneath our feet.

As we can see from even this brief analysis, the Court's "new rules" are the substantive content of "reconciliation." We could say that they are the rules for

---

Calder et al. v. AG of British Columbia at 334. In *Sparrow* at 1099 Dickson CJ and La Forest J endorse the approach taken by Hall J.

28 *Sparrow* at 1106.

29 To illustrate my point here I can simply indicate how the assumption of Crown sovereignty persuades the Court in *Sparrow* to interpret s. 35 via a s. 1 style *Oakes* analysis, despite them explicitly acknowledging that s. 1 does not apply to s. 35. For Borrows's use of the term *sovereignty's alchemy* see John Borrows, "Sovereignty's Alchemy: An Analysis of Delgamuukw v. British Columbia," *Osgoode Hall Law Journal* 37 (1999): 537.

the *game of reconciliation*. This game is structured to avoid the foundational question (i.e., the legal nature and factual basis of the Indigenous–Crown relationship). It does so by operating as a kind of procedural deferral or "work in progress" that effectively brackets the question, but this can work only so long as it seems that the question is actually being worked on. The problem is that the game is structured so that there can be *no response* to this question, but there also must be a *response*. This has led the Court to gradually construct a vast and intricate case law whose labyrinthine corridors can leave even the most diligent lawyers and judges feeling bewildered. This is by no means surprising. The labyrinth of Aboriginal law has been constructed on an ad hoc basis.[30] Its walls and corridors do not remain firmly in place. Rather, they seem to move and shift behind you, so that as soon as you feel that you have adequately charted your path, you turn around and find yourself disoriented yet again.

The Court has utilized all of the considerable resources of the common law to attempt to resolve the disputes that continue to appear before it. It has drawn principles and tests from areas as diverse as property, contracts, constitutional, trusts, and administrative law. This does not require us to present it as some species of Cartesian demon who is intentionally building this labyrinth in an effort to deceive us (to my mind, the accusation of intentional deception does little more than close off avenues for dialogue). Rather the explanation that best fits this situation is the all-too-human failure of missing something that is hidden because of its simplicity and familiarity. As Wittgenstein puts it, "We fail to be struck by what, once seen, is the most striking and most powerful."[31] In this case what it is not seeing is that its undoubted and unquestioned reading of s. 91(24) – the magical hinge that enables them to set the resources of the common law in motion and decide the case before them – has tethered it in place.[32]

---

30 By *ad hoc* I mean something a little different from the normal case-by-case progression of the common law. The *difference* in this area of the common law is the question of degree. The variance within the case-by-case progression is such that attempting to follow the development of this area of the common law is, at best, disorienting. My point is that development of the case law is not easily surveyable, but labyrinthine. Kerry Wilkins helpfully suggested that this ad hoc character results from the jurisprudence in this area being resolutely result oriented.

31 Wittgenstein, *Philosophical Investigations at* §129.

32 Kerry Wilkins insightfully suggested to me that there are two ways to think of the hinge proposition here: (1) we can see the actual hinge as being the Court's unquestioned assumption of Crown sovereignty and that their interpretation of s. 91(24) is a by-product of that, and (2) the Court has treated s. 91(24) a self-interpreting expression of Crown sovereignty over Indigenous peoples, and so it becomes a magical hinge (magical because they forget that it is animated by their reading). As I see it, these two readings are not at odds, but perspectival. I believe that the first version is correct, but I feel that in order to persuade the Court that this is in fact the case we must begin by disentangling s. 91(24) from the bundled assumption of sovereignty, legislative power, and underlying title. What I mean

Its process of reconciliation can only move in circles, and this fact is concealed by the complex and shifting nature of the path. This labyrinth has been built upon an interpretation of federal "power" that the courts *cannot account for*, and without this magical "power" all of the complicated doctrines and intricate tests that it has constructed must be pulled up and put away like so many carnival booths and sideshows.

In summary, what I mean by this is that the structure of the s. 35 framework that was first put in place in *Sparrow*, and continues to be treated as *the* framework for reconciliation, is predicated on a unilateral model of federal power that the current interpretation of s. 91(24) puts into play, but its only foundation is the unquestioned assumption of the very thing that is in contention. In other words, this framework presupposes the *very sovereignty* that it is supposed to be reconciling. As long as s. 91(24) is interpreted in this manner, the Court's field of vision is fixed at the conceptual level and so can only ever result in a circular process. The game of reconciliation is fixed.

Reimagining Reconciliation and the Challenge of Constitutional Pluralism

This is what I mean when I say that what the Court is offering is a *reconciliation without recollection*. There is no memory or recollection of the colonial foundation of the existing s. 35 framework, because it is abstract.[33] There is only its

---

here is that we must start by fleshing out the distinction between *seeing that* and *seeing as*. The Court treats s. 91(24) as a self-interpreting fact that binds its reasoning, but this is only because it seems to have forgotten that this appears to be the case only because of seeing s. 91(24) as having this meaning. In other words, I am attempting to remind the Court that it is its *interpretation* of s. 91(24) that makes this provision act as the positive legal expression of "federal power" and not the reverse.

33 By this I do not mean records of the constitutional discussions that led to the *Constitution Act, 1982*. Rather, by specifying the "colonial foundation" I am referring to the continued effects of a set of nineteenth-century presumptions regarding the legal status and capacity of Indigenous peoples. This set (i.e., the standard of civilization, the stadial theory of historical development, the agricultural thesis, the doctrines of discovery and *terra nullius*, etc.) both has positioned and continues to position Indigenous peoples in a sui generis subjects-to-sovereign framework with the Crown. Whether this is as wards of the state who are incapable of managing their own affairs and thus require civilizing (let's call this the "citizen minus" approach, as it begins from a deficit and sets citizen as its aim or telos) or, to borrow the helpful phrase used by Alain Carins and the other authors of the 1966 Hawthorn Report, as "citizens plus." According to the authors of the report, Indigenous peoples would have the full benefits of Canadian citizenship, but this would be supplemented with some additional rights: "By 'plus' we referred to ongoing entitlements, some of which flowed from existing treaties while others were to be worked out in the political processes of the future, which would identify the Indian peoples as deserving possessors of an additional category of rights based on historical priority." See H.B. Hawthorn, ed., *A Survey of the Contemporary Indians*

absence of doubt in the standard that it is applying and the conceptual requirements that flow from it. There are two related problems that I am pointing to when I use this phrase:

1 The existing framework for reconciliation is founded on a model of Crown sovereignty that does not fit with any fair and balanced description of the historical relationship between Indigenous peoples and the Crown. This means that its only claims to legitimacy are the self-sealing legal fictions of discovery, and *terra nullius*.[34]

---

of Canada (Ottawa: Queen's Printer, 1967) at 12. The problem with this is that it obviates the process through which Indigenous peoples became citizens (i.e., the unilateral proclamation of the sovereignty of the imperial British Crown, which was then vested in the dominion). In my mind any move towards a federal resolution (and I should note that Carins himself favours a federal resolution – see his *Citizens Plus: Aboriginal Peoples and the Canadian State* [Vancouver: UBC Press, 2000]) to sharing sovereignty must begin with addressing this foundational problem.

34 By the term *self-sealing* I mean that there is no evidence that can be used to ultimately ground these legal fictions. They may seem to require a given set of facts or conditions to apply, but these conditions are ultimately set by a unilateral normative assertion that cannot be questioned. For example, discovery and *terra nullius* may appear to be based on evidence, as they require a certain set of conditions to apply. Their main requirement is that the party they apply to must be *savages or barbarians*, but if we attempted to determine the actual definition of these terms we find ourselves back to unilateral assertions. As Sir Edward Coke put it in 1608 in *Calvin's Case*, barbarians and infidels are "perpetual enemies" of Christians, and so "if a Christian King should conquer a kingdom of an infidel, and bring them under his subjection, there ipso facto the laws of the infidel are abrogated, for that they are not only against Christianity, but against the law of God and of nature." See Calvin's Case 7 Coke Report 1a, 77 English Reports 377 (1608) at 397–8. Once you walk through the steps and conditions, all of these fictions boil down to the vacuous justification of "I can do this because I said so." As should be obvious, this unilateralism cannot hope to serve as the foundation for a lasting and stable form of political association. Rather, it simply draws and redraws the line between the citizens who dwell in the empire of law and the enemies who roam in the state of war. The fact that the line must be redrawn points to the fact that it does not merely serve to divide one from the other, but also connects them (viz. the line between them is blurred and prey to the constant threat of conspiracy and treason, so the citizen can suddenly become the enemy). In case the danger of this way of doing politics is not immediately evident, consider Edmund Burke's prescient argument concerning the risks of excluding entire groups (in this case, Irish Catholics) "as if they were not only separate nations, but separate species." See Edmund Burke, *The Writings and Speeches of Edmund Burke*, vol. 9, *I: The Revolutionary War, 1794–1797; II: Ireland*, ed. R.B. McDowell and William B. Todd (Oxford: Oxford University Press, 2014) at 629. As he rightly states, "Our constitution is not made for great, general, and proscriptive exclusions; sooner or later, it will destroy them, or they will destroy the constitution. In our constitution there has always been a difference made between *a franchise* and *an office*, and between the capacity for the one and for the other" (601). It is also helpful to remember that the English courts did not themselves retain Coke CJ's exception regarding infidels, but rather qualified and then ultimately rejected it, in *Blankard v. Galdy* (1693) Holt

2 This legal sense of reconciliation conflicts with the everyday sense of the word and results in confusion. This is a problem because it frames how the general public views the conflict between Indigenous peoples and the Crown. It can make it seem that when Indigenous peoples contest the legal model of reconciliation that they are refusing reconciliation in the everyday sense of the word. This serves to present them as malcontents who are refusing to compromise and plays into the presumption that Indigenous peoples are simply a part of *the* people, the nation state. This confusing and conflated use of reconciliation reinforces the unitary social imaginary of Canada as a nation state with parts that need to conform (viz. French Canadians and Indigenous peoples). This constitutes a roadblock to the practical work of remembering history and *reimagining* Canada as the product of mutual negotiations and agreements between *peoples*.

This brings me to the significance of the question mark in the title. Its function is key, as it both indicates that the current framework of reconciliation is *questionable* and reminds us that this framework can be *reimagined*. This work of reimagining does not require us to engage in a Cartesian operation of tearing the constitutional order down to the ground and setting out to build an ideal one. While our constitutional machinery is certainly "composed of many pieces and made by the hands of various craftsmen," this is not a design flaw (pace Descartes and Bentham).[35] Rather, the somewhat ramshackle construction of our constitutional machinery allows us to borrow, swap, and substitute parts from the vast scrapheap of the common law.[36] There is no one way for it

---

341; 90 ER 1089 (KB); and *Campbell v. Hall* (1774) 1 Cowp 204; 98 ER 1045 (KB) respectively. What this helps to show us is that, as Jennifer Pitts eloquently reminds us,

> This history of international law, a history of universalism and hierarchy intertwined, represents an important space for the work of conceptualizing, and gaining critical purchase on, hierarchy in the international sphere. This is perhaps primarily because of the long-standing and ongoing role that law has played in structuring and justifying hierarchy and domination, and ... in occluding them ... Yet it is also because international law contains resources for critique and frameworks for envisioning greater justice and equality ... If international law is a moral and political language we can hardly avoid, we can also try to better deploy it, in part by understand its fraught past. (Pitts, *Boundaries* at 191)

35 René Descartes, *Discourse on Method and Meditations on First Philosophy*, trans. Donald A. Cress (Indianapolis: Hackett, 1998) at 7. This would set us with the impossible task of clearing the ground entirely so as to build on a foundation that is completely our own. This kind of foundational endeavour is doomed from the start, as it has jumped over the fact that constitutions are not discrete, and bounded objects but are rather *lived practices*.

36 Otto Neurath's use of the Ship of Theseus metaphor is an apt image for what I am pointing to: "We are like sailors who on the open sea must reconstruct their ship but are never able

to operate, as each configuration holds the possibility of reconfiguration. The very idea that there is a configuration or set of parts that cannot be investigated and moved is (to borrow and repurpose Bentham's evocative phrase) "nonsense on stilts."[37] Reconfiguring our constitutional machinery *does not* require us to rewrite history or evaluate the past on the basis of our current standards or needs. Rather, it requires a clear view of how the values of the past continue to animate our constitutional machinery and thereby inform our shared legal and political reality. These "values of the past" are carried with us and can easily be overlooked on account of their simplicity and familiarity. They hide in plain sight.

One of these values – and it is the one that we will find ourselves continually returning to – is the rigid conceptual requirements of the Westphalian nation state. As Tierney reminds us, "Mistaken assumptions about the unitary nature of 'the people' can generate constitutional models which fail to accommodate the specific needs of different *peoples* within the state."[38] These "mistaken assumptions" bring with them significant challenges when they are superimposed over a plurinational reality. He continues, "The challenge in terms of constitutional praxis, therefore, is for the further recognition of this reality in the narrations of constitutionalism by way of imaginative explanatory and interpretational devices. This is not to contend that law is subsumed by politics, but it does suggest that dominant interpretations of law can miss the fact that they are *merely interpretations*."[39] This helpfully articulates precisely what the question mark indicates in the title of this investigation. It is not to simply demolish the current framework and rebuild it from the ground up or even to simply walk away. My aim is to try to clearly show that the current framework is not *the only possible* interpretation of the constitution and to offer another interpretation that can accommodate the plurinational reality of Canada. So the question mark in the title invites us to wonder about our shared constitutional order again.

---

to start afresh from the bottom. Where a beam is taken away a new one must at once be put there, and for this the rest of the ship is used as support. In this way, by using the old beams and driftwood the ship can be shaped entirely anew, but only by gradual reconstruction." See Otto Neurath, "Spengler's Description of the World," in *Otto Neurath: Philosophy between Science and Politics*, ed. Nancy Cartwright, Jordi Cat, Lola Fleck and Thomas E. Uebel (Cambridge: Cambridge University Press, 2008) at 191. I would like to thank Kerry Wilkins for suggesting this connection.

37 This was Jeremy Bentham's famous dismissal of the early-modern natural law tradition. As he puts it, "*Natural rights* is simple non-sense: natural and imprescriptible rights, rhetorical nonsense, – nonsense upon stilts." See John Bowring, ed., *The Works of Jeremy Bentham* (Edinburgh: William Tait, 1838–43) at 2:501.

38 Stephen Tierney, *Constitutional Law and National Pluralism* (Oxford: Oxford University Press, 2004) at 13.

39 Ibid. at 14 (emphasis added).

What we need to recognize is that the Court has set itself the task of determining the measure of the rights of Indigenous peoples by using a standard that *cannot be legally explained.* There is, in other words, a ghost in the constitutional machine. This point requires some unpacking, so we can rearticulate it in another way. The federal power that is conferred by the unquestioned presumption of Crown sovereignty has led us to the absolute interpretation of s. 91(24). This version of s. 91(24) serves as the magical hinge of the entire s. 35 framework, but it can do so only as long as the courts *refuse to question it.* And we must remember that this strategy of avoidance *cannot hold.* That is, it cannot offer a stable constitutional order; rather, it leads to the progressive erosion of constitutional legitimacy. Each case that appears before the Court that requires some account of the foundation of Crown authority will require a repetition of this non-response. This leads to the construction of a body of law whose labyrinthine complexity mirrors Ptolemy's geocentric model of the universe. In other words, there is a cumulative effect to this repetition. At first it may seem as if the Court's lack of doubt offers a secure foundation for Crown sovereignty, but each repetition isolates the Court by making its statements more and more opaque. In the end it is left standing on a foundation that is so narrow that it can accommodate only itself. What I mean by this is that by adopting a strategy of non-response the Court sacrifices its legitimacy. Legitimacy is not simply a political question; as the Court rightly states in the *Reference re Secession of Quebec,* "In our constitutional tradition, legality and legitimacy are linked."[40]

40 *Reference re Secession of Quebec* at para. 33. The significance of this linkage between legality and legitimacy can be seen clearly if we contrast the *Secession Reference* with the *Sparrow* framework. The latter starts from the presumption of a *thick* concept of Crown sovereignty that bundles it with legislative power and underlying title. This unquestioned presumption is treated as non-justiciable and supplies the all-encompassing notion of federal "power" under s. 91(24), which, in turn, is used by the court to justify their application of a s. 1 reasonable limitation analysis to a provision that is not within the *Charter*. In the *Sparrow* framework Aboriginal peoples are positioned as cultural minorities with *Charter-like* rights that are subject to reasonable limitation via judicial mediation, whereas in the *Secession Reference* the court is focused on the constitutional obligations between equal partners in confederation. The *Secession Reference* addresses the people of Quebec as a self-determining people within the Canadian division of powers; they are "participants in the federation" (para. 150). They do not require them to prove that they have the right to self-government, nor do they maintain that such a right is subject to justifiable infringements. Rather, they note that each participant in the federation has a right to initiate constitutional change and that "this right implies a reciprocal duty on the other participants to engage in discussions to address any legitimate initiative to change the constitutional order" (para. 150). If this right is frustrated in such a way that the people of Quebec cannot achieve internal self-determination, their constitutional obligations cannot be used to foreclose the possibility of secession. The distinction here is categorical: the former presumes a sovereign-to-subject relationship; the latter presumes a nation-to-nation federal relationship. The link between legality and legitimacy implies a kind of mutual interdependence. The substance of this interdependence

While this legitimacy may not fracture in a single case, the cumulative effect of cases will erode its legitimacy piece by piece and with it the consent that provides much of the binding effect of its decisions.

If the Court were to attempt to explain this power it would be confronted with two options:

1 It could simply bar any and all inquiry into the foundations of sovereignty (i.e., the act of state doctrine). This option is a well-worn approach that was, to my mind, best articulated by Marshall CJ in *Johnson v. M'Intosh.* It also has some rather obvious benefits for the court, as the sovereignty of the state is constitutively connected to its jurisdiction and so it seems that by claiming that it lacks the jurisdiction needed to investigate the former, it shores up and preserves the latter.[41]
2 Alternatively, it could investigate the legitimacy of state sovereignty and work to provide a clear and perspicacious view of the problem. In this case it cannot decide the case (as this would require the presumption of the sovereignty it has put into question), but it can provide a clear view of it to the parties and offer them a procedure for resolving it. What I have in

---

can be seen when we consider what the court means when it says, "The Constitution is not a straitjacket" (para. 150). First, this proposition holds that the constitutional obligations of Quebec cannot be used to strictly limit or contain their democratic rights. Second, it balances this by simultaneously rejecting the notion that a people can use their democratic rights to unilaterally dissolve these obligations. This link between legality and legitimacy thus binds the parties by forming an obligation to negotiate (paras. 88–92). The distinction between the *Sparrow* framework and the *Secession Reference* is clearest at this point: the presumption of *thick* Crown sovereignty in the former serves to diminish the legal standing of Aboriginal peoples in such a way that the constitutional order is already set, whereas in the *Secession Reference* constitutional negotiations are conducted in the open without the presupposition that one party is already in unquestionable possession of sovereignty, legislative power, and underlying title. By adopting a *thick* version of Crown sovereignty, the courts have acted as if the non-justiciability of Crown sovereignty locks Aboriginal peoples into a fixed constitutional order. In doing so they have exercised their discretion in a manner that compromises their "proper role within the constitutional framework." *Reference re Canada Assistance Plan (BC)*, [1991] 2 SCR 525 at 545, cited in the *Secession Reference* at para. 99. They have read Aboriginal peoples into the constitutional order as a cultural minority, but there is no account for how this came to be. The position of Aboriginal peoples within the picture of the constitutional order is fixed by the presumption of *thick* Crown sovereignty. As a result of this presumption the courts have effectively generated a constitutional frame that *actually undermines the obligation to negotiate and renders it hollow* (to repurpose the words of the court at para. 91).

41 In 1979 the High Court of Australia adopted the former approach in *Coe v. Commonwealth of Australia* when it held that a challenge to a nation's sovereignty is "not cognizable in a court exercising jurisdiction under that sovereignty which is sought to be challenged." See *Coe v. Commonwealth of Australia*, [1979] HCA 68 at 3.

> mind here is the kind of qualified sovereignty that the Court makes use of in the *Secession Reference* when it addresses the problem of internal self-determination in a multinational society.[42] This is not a well-worn approach, but it is also not without precedent. Here again the reasoning of Marshall CJ can be of service. In *Worcester v. Georgia* he changed tack and found that the existing basis for state sovereignty (i.e., the doctrine of discovery) was an "extravagant and absurd idea" that has no place in legal reasoning. This does not necessarily leave the courts completely outside of the conversation between two (or more) separate political entities, but rather utilizes a minimal shared sovereignty to provide both a clear view of the relations of governance that exist between them and the processes and procedures for discussing and altering these relations over time.[43]

The former is certainly the most frequently adopted course of action, and this is by no means surprising. It seems to stave off the possibility of a constitutional crisis and preserve the jurisdiction of the courts by shifting the question out of the courts into the halls of parliamentary debate. It becomes a decision that "*the* people" must make in the fray of representative democracy. But, here again, these benefits come at a high cost. The problem does indeed change hands, but all this means is that a legal stalemate becomes a political stalemate. The actual problem remains untouched. In other words, all that happens here is that the court robs Peter to pay Paul. The nation state is still stuck in a crisis of legitimacy as the other *peoples* that comprise it actively contest its claim to represent "*the* people."

As James Tully reminds us,

> *Unilateral* defence of the status quo, unilateral constitutional change and unilateral secession are ALL unjust in the sense that they violate with respect to other members the very principle that is invoked to justify the act. Moreover, such unilateral acts are unstable, for the disregarded members are seldom silenced for long. All the force of the existing society or of the secessionist state cannot stabilize effectively the unjust situation or gain the recognition they need from others, as we have seen in many tragic cases.[44]

If the question cannot be opened by legal means then it can quickly lead from the relative calm of the ballot box to the chaos of riots and barricades. In

---

42 *Reference re Secession of Quebec*. See James Tully's instructive analysis of this case in chapter 6 of his *Public Philosophy in a New Key*, vol. 1, *Democracy and Civic Freedom* (Cambridge: Cambridge University Press, 2008).

43 Tully, *Public Philosophy in a New Key*, 1:191–7.

44 Ibid. at 1:201.

this case the work of governing quickly slides into a blind alley, where it seems that the only way to avoid a complete collapse of the constitutional order is to begin the grim work of closing off or delimiting "*the* people" and separating them from their enemies. In the end, this strategy is about as productive as bailing water on a sinking ship with a teaspoon.

The latter option is better, but it is by no means a simple one. It requires a step off the beaten path of the nation state. Its fiction of a single and absolute source of authority (viz. *the* sovereign that – as the representative of "*the* people" – possess both *dominium* and *imperium*) has, as Stephen Tierney rightly maintains, "been a central ideological device in legitimizing the dominant, monistic vision with which the plurinational state has masqueraded as *the* nation of the state. This vision has allowed dominant societies to renege upon the union commitments made at the time of the state's formation. The dominant society has been able to crystalize political power at the centre of the state, presenting it in the guise of legal legitimacy, and hence entrenching political hegemony in purportedly objective constitutional form."[45]

The way off this well-beaten path is to disaggregate the notions of "nation" and "state" so that we can begin to come to grips with the pluri-national reality of the Canadian state.[46] Practically speaking, this means that s. 91(24) must be interpreted in a manner that is consistent with the fact that Indigenous peoples are and have always been *peoples*.

The Canadian courts have taken a different route by willingly inquiring into the legitimacy of the nation state while, at the very same time, making full use of its power.[47] If their aim is to actually change the sovereign-to-subjects

---

45 Tierney, *Constitutional Law and National Pluralism* at 16.

46 Ibid. at 5. A complementary line of argumentation is taken up by Will Kymlicka in his excellent "Multicultural Citizenship within Multinational States," *Ethnicities* 11, no. 3 (2011): 281–302.

47 The willingness that I am pointing to here can be seen in a couple of different ways. The *longue durée* view presents us with the wavering and uncertain dialogue within the common law on the appropriate balance between the concepts of sovereignty and the rule of law. On this we could refer to classical examples such as Sir Edward Coke's arguments for the rule of law against King James I in *Fuller's Case*. For a recent study of this, see David Chan Smith, *Sir Edward Coke and the Reformation of the Laws: Religion, Politics and Jurisprudence, 1578–1616* (Cambridge: Cambridge University Press, 2014). We could also refer to the critical approaches that several key European political thinkers such as Immanuel Kant, Edmund Burke, Denis Diderot, Adam Smith, and Johann Gottfied Herder (among others) took to imperialism in the late eighteenth and early nineteenth century. As Andrew Fitzmaurice puts it, the liberal scepticism of empire was not necessarily "motivated by humanitarian sentiment, but by the self-interested concern about the endurance of the European revolutions." See Fitzmaurice, *Sovereignty, Property and Empire* at 299. In other words, their fear was more often focused on "the possibility that legal abuses in the colonies could be repatriated to Europe" (at 293). The fear was that if the courts utilized the act of state doctrine to essentially give the sovereign

relationship that has been unilaterally imposed on Indigenous peoples by the Crown for the last 150 years, then the framework that they are currently using is ill-suited to their purposes. They have acknowledged that the source of Indigenous rights resides outside the bounds of the constitutional order, and qualified Crown sovereignty as being de facto or predicated on an "assertion." And so, seeing that there is a problem here, they have set down the rules for a process of reconciliation that will remove this qualification once and for all. The game of reconciliation is meant to convert the de facto power of the Crown into *de jure* sovereignty, but it cannot hope to do so. The rules of the game are built on the presumption of the very power that is in question. A judge cannot hope to resolve a dispute between two parties by grounding their authority on the power of one party and then designing the procedures in their favour. This confuses and conflates the roles of judge and advocate and so runs the distinct risk of bringing the administration of justice into disrepute, which brings us back to the erosive effect of this strategy.

One could respond by contending that these arguments about the legitimacy of state sovereignty are by no means new and that no matter how the rules seem to change, the core will always remain the same. In other words, the Court is not willing, or perhaps even able, to compromise on the question of absolute Crown sovereignty. The problem with this contention (which we could call the *realist position*) is that it does not provide any criteria for determining whether or not there has been change over time. Or, perhaps better, the criteria that it makes use of are too crude. It presents us with a simple on/off notion of sovereignty, and

---

free reign in the colonies, they would lose the conceptual tools necessary to retain the hard-won advances of the rule of law in the metropoles. The grounds for this concern were ultimately validated in the Second World War as the legal and conceptual tools that were used to legitimize the law of occupation in the colonies were put to use in the occupation of Europe during the war. Fitzmaurice briefly touches on this crucial point and helpfully points towards the work of Raphaël Lemkin and Hannah Arendt (at 298). Finally, there is also the example we can see in the shifting articulation of the balance between sovereignty and the rule of law in the *Marshall Trilogy* as Marshall CJ moves from the strong articulation of the act of state doctrine in conjunction with the doctrine of discovery in *Johnson v. M'Intosh* to the ultimate rejection of the doctrine of discovery as a foundation for sovereignty in favour of a form of federal sovereignty that must be balanced with the inherent sovereignty of Indigenous peoples. See chapter 7 of Robert A. Williams Jr, *The American Indian in Western Legal Thought: The Discourses of Conquest* (New York: Cambridge University Press, 1990). The more recent example can be seen in how this conceptual tension is being played out in the Canadian jurisprudence on Aboriginal law since *Calder*. The trend that I will be trying to develop through the course of the book is that the courts have been reticent to fully embrace a bright line version of the act of state doctrine and have instead attempted to restrain and qualify sovereignty via the rule of law. While this strategy has its own double edges and blind alleys – as the *Sparrow* framework has clearly demonstrated – it does open up the possibility of a reconceptualization of the constitutional identity of Canada as a whole.

this makes it insensitive to gradational changes. This is like attempting to determine the stability of a volcano by merely asking if it has erupted yet, and then, if it has not, concluding that it is merely a mountain. The fact is that changes in constitutional interpretation are not always smooth and continuous. They can move at an almost glacial pace from one perspective, but underneath, the ground can give way. While it may at first appear that there is a single rigid line of Crown sovereignty that connects together the landmark Aboriginal law cases over the last 150 years (e.g., from *St Catherine's Milling*, to *Calder*, *Sparrow*, and *Tsilhqot'in Nation*), there are significant changes in how this sovereignty is being expressed, and *these changes matter*. In order to get our bearings in these cases and make sense of these changes, we need investigative tools that are honed and shaped to the requirements of the particular case. In other words, as the theory of the second-best highlights, the process of continually patching errors on an as-needed basis does not necessarily preserve the status quo. This patchwork approach to resolving deep constitutional problems erodes the stability of the constitutional order. In order to investigate these changes we need investigative tools and techniques that help us carefully consider the details of the specific case we are dealing with and thereby open up courses of action that we would have otherwise missed. These other courses of action also occur case-by-case, but they are categorically distinct from the patchwork maintenance of the status quo. Whereas the patchwork progression constrains the courts' consideration of possible interpretations and remedies (due to the assumption that that status quo is somehow fixed), an open and surveyable consideration of possible approaches will necessarily include approaches that would reorder the status quo.[48]

A number of recent policy changes in Canada seem to indicate that the sovereign-to-subject framework is not as solid as it once appeared to be. In 2015 the Truth and Reconciliation Commission delivered their Final Report and Calls to Action.[49] They recommended that Canada move beyond the old sovereign-to-subjects framework and adopt the current international norms expressed in *United Nations Declaration of the Rights of Indigenous Peoples* (*UNDRIP*). The commission forcefully reminds us, "The Doctrine of Discovery and the related concept of *terra nullius* underpin the requirement for

48 One could argue that the possibility of such a deep reordering of the law cuts against the grain of the common law virtues of consistency and continuity, but I would actually argue that it balances the demands of these virtues with those of certainty and predictability. The status quo jurisprudence in the area manifestly lacks these last two qualities, as it moves hither and thither, solving one problem only to make the next three worse, producing nothing more than a dependable area of employment for lawyers.

49 Truth and Reconciliation Canada, *Honouring the Truth, Reconciling for the Future: Summary of the Final Report of the Truth and Reconciliation Commission of Canada* (Winnipeg: Truth and Reconciliation Commission of Canada, 2015).

Aboriginal peoples to prove their pre-existing occupation of the land in court cases in order to avoid having their land and resource rights extinguished in contemporary Treaty and land claims processes. Such a requirement does not conform to international law or contribute to reconciliation. Such concepts are a current manifestation of historical wrongs and should be formally repudiated by all levels of Canadian government."[50] This is a clear and direct rejection of the absolute interpretation of s. 91(24) and the framework of reconciliation that has been built upon it. It is a rejection of the racist fictions of international law that continue to inform the interpretation of Canada's constitutional order.

They continue, "We are not suggesting that the repudiation of the Doctrine of Discovery necessarily gives rise to the invalidation of Crown sovereignty. The Commission accepts that there are other means to establish the validity of Crown sovereignty without undermining the important principle established in the Royal Proclamation of 1763, which is that the sovereignty of the Crown requires that it recognize and deal with Aboriginal title in order to become perfected. It must not be forgotten that the terms of the Royal Proclamation were explained to, and accepted by, Indigenous leaders during the negotiation of the Treaty of Niagara of 1764."[51]

This constitutes a repositioning of the basis for the validity of Crown sovereignty from the racist fictions of discovery and *terra nullius* to the processes of mutual agreement and consent that are found in the histories of treaty making.[52]

---

50 Ibid. at 6:32–3.

51 Ibid.

52 I am not suggesting that the treaties can be understood as recognitions of Crown sovereignty *over* them. Taking such a position rests on a number of deeply problematic assumptions, including the following: (1) that we know what the Indigenous signatories understood themselves to be acknowledging; (2) that the Indigenous signatories understood that this acknowledgment was permanent (this seems to be based on a deeper assumption that a legally binding relationship could be created that would be closed to the possibility of reinterpretation and renegotiation, which is an absurdly self-serving fiction); and (3) that the Indigenous signatories had the legal and political standing within their own systems to bind their descendants in perpetuity. I do not hold any of these assumptions. Rather, I take the view that the treaties establish a nation-to-nation federal-like relationship of *shared sovereignty* between the Crown and Indigenous peoples. This set of practices can also be used to treat with the Indigenous peoples in Canada who have not treated with the Crown yet. As Tully and Borrows helpfully remind us, "This relationship is based on consent and open to renegotiation or 'repolishing' over time if the partners deem it necessary." See James Tully, "Consent, Hegemony, and Dissent in Treaty Negotiations," in *Between Consenting Peoples: Political Community and the Meaning of Consent*, ed. Jeremy Webber and Colin M. Macleod (Vancouver: UBC Press, 2010) at 237; and John Borrows, "Wampum at Niagara: The Royal Proclamation, Canadian Legal History, and Self-Government," in *Aboriginal and Treaty Rights in Canada*, ed. Michael Asch (Vancouver: UBC Press, 2000) at 155–71. For more on the concept of treaty-federalism, refer to Russel Lawrence Barsh and James Youngblood Henderson, *The Road: Indian Tribes and Political Liberty* (Berkeley: University of California Press, 1980); Michael Asch, *On Being Here to Stay: Treaties and Aboriginal Rights in Canada* (Toronto: University of Toronto Press, 2014);

This also necessarily shifts Indigenous peoples from being wards who are subject to nearly unlimited sovereign power to being *peoples* in a *nation-to-nation* relationship with the Crown.[53] We can think of this as being a change from conceiving of Canada as a unitary nation state with a rigid unilateral version of sovereignty to being a plural union state whose concept of sovereignty is, and has always been (even if honoured only in the breach), *flexible and shared.*

---

and for the question of perspectives in the treaty-making process, see Aimée Craft, *Breathing Life into the Stone Fort Treaty: An Anishinabe Understanding of Treaty One* (Saskatoon, SK: Purich, 2013). I think it is also helpful to remember that "the aim of entering into negotiations is precisely to change unequal circumstances" (Tully, *Consent, Hegemony, and Dissent* at 247). It is a practice that can be used to restructure and decolonize the constitutional relationship between Indigenous peoples and the Crown. But, as Tully rightly argues, "The assumption that this ideal state of affairs must obtain prior to negotiations is illusionary. Equality and respect for difference are the aim, not the starting point. To reject negotiations because of unequal initial conditions is to be taken in by the false normative ideal of negotiation among free and equal partners that serves to obscure the real world negotiations among differently free and unequal partners. Conversely, some experts even argue that it is better in the long run to be the courageous underdog, David rather than Goliath, at the beginning, rather than the complacent and overconfident superior" (ibid.).

53 I say "nearly" unlimited sovereignty here because the limits of this sovereignty in the courts have been difficult to find. My points of reference here is the vast history of the statute known as the *Indian Act* and, prior to 1982, Parliament's ability to unilaterally extinguish Aboriginal rights. It is difficult to take the measure of legislative power that would be needed to do either of these and still be seen as existing within the rule of law. It is, to my mind, even difficult to classify the *Indian Act* as a single statute within the Canadian constitutional order. It is perhaps better thought of as a parallel constitutional order that is under a permanent state of unfettered administrative power (i.e., a state of emergency). David Dyzenhaus offers us another helpful way to conceptualize this situation with his notion of "grey holes" of legality. He uses this term to refer to situations where there are some legal limits on administrative action, but these limits "are so insubstantial that they pretty well permit government to do as it pleases." See David Dyzenhaus, *The Constitution of Law: Legality in a Time of Emergency* (Cambridge: Cambridge University Press, 2006) at 42. In other words, "grey holes" are not "true black holes" because they are not pure voids, and *some* law does apply. But this fact does not make these "grey holes" less dangerous to the rule of law. Rather, as Dyzenhaus rightly cautions, "Grey holes allow the government to have its cake and eat it too, to seem to be governing not only by law but in accordance with the rule of law, they and their endorsement by judges and academics might be even more dangerous from the perspective of the substantive conception of the rule of law than true black holes" (ibid.). The sting here is in how the "grey holes" present the appearance of the rule of law, while serving to erode its actual substance. In this the problem is similar to that presented by the strategy of indirect rule. In my view, indirect rule is a family resemblance concept that can apply to a number of related models and strategies. I review some of these models in detail in chapter 5. The similarity between Dyzenhaus's notion of "grey holes" and indirect rule lies in the relationship between appearance and substance. Indirect rule is similar to a devolved or dependent form of government, but this dependency is concealed from those who are subject to it. This concealment is its defining feature. For an excellent account of the British Empire's ideological shift towards indirect rule, see Karuna Matena, *Alibis of Empire: Henry Maine and the End of Liberal Imperialism* (Princeton, NJ: Princeton University Press, 2010).

In order to accomplish this, the commission recommended a framework for reconciliation predicated on the principles, norms, and standards of *UNDRIP*. This informs the entirety of their calls to action, but it is helpful here to cite calls 43 and 44:

43 We call upon federal, provincial, territorial, and municipal governments to fully adopt and implement the *United Nations Declaration on the Rights of Indigenous Peoples* as the framework for reconciliation.
44 We call upon the Government of Canada to develop a national action plan, strategies, and other concrete measures to achieve the goals of the *United Nations Declaration on the Rights of Indigenous Peoples*.[54]

These recommendations have begun to shape policy. In 2016 the federal government endorsed *UNDRIP* without reservation and moved towards implementation. In 2017 the federal government announced a new set of *Principles Respecting the Government of Canada's Relationship with Indigenous Peoples*, which directly recognizes that "all relations with Indigenous peoples need to be based on the recognition and implementation of their right to self-determination, including the inherent right of self-government" and that Indigenous self-government is "part of Canada's evolving system of cooperative federalism and distinct orders of government."[55] This was soon followed by the announcement that Indigenous and Northern Affairs Canada (INAC) will be dissolved and replaced with two new departments: Crown-Indigenous Relations, which will focus its attention on nation-to-nation relationships and Indigenous self-determination; and Indigenous Services, which will administer the essential services that INAC once presided over. The federal government framed this decision as a move beyond "existing colonial structures" that was based on the recommendations of the Royal Commission on Aboriginal Peoples and as a step towards "ending the *Indian Act*."[56]

On 21 September 2017 Prime Minister Justin Trudeau addressed the United Nations General Assembly and reiterated this commitment. He took this opportunity to point to the many legacies of colonialism in Canada. As he put it, "The good news is that Canadians get it. They see the inequities and they're fed up with the excuses and that impatience gives us a rare and precious opportunity

54 *Summary of the Final Report of the Truth and Reconciliation Commission* at 229.

55 See Principles 1 and 4 in Department of Justice, *Principles Respecting the Government of Canada's Relationship with Indigenous Peoples*, http://www.justice.gc.ca/eng/csj-sjc/principles-principes.html, last modified 14 February 2018.

56 Prime Minister's Office, "New Ministers to Support the Renewed Relationship with Indigenous Peoples," 28 August 2017, http://pm.gc.ca/eng/news/2017/08/28/new-ministers-support-renewed-relationship-indigenous-peoples.

to act. We now have before us an opportunity to deliver true meaningful and lasting reconciliation."[57] While we could dismiss this statement on its own as a continuation of the game of reconciliation, this is, to my mind, not an adequate reflection of his words. The prime minister maintained that the guide that Canada will be using in this process of reconciliation will be the basic norms of *UNDRIP* and stated that these are not "aspirations" but "a way forward."[58] This affirmation supports a distinct move away from the sovereign-to-subject model of the relationship (and the fictions of discovery and *terra nullius* that ultimately ground it) and towards a *nation-to-nation* model that draws on the history of treaty making between Indigenous nations and the Crown. As the prime minister noted in his speech, "We are in uncharted territory. No one has paved the way for us, but we cannot wait. The time has come for us to pave the way together. The time has come to get off the beaten path, to move away from old outdated colonial structures and to establish new structures which will respect the inherent right of indigenous people to govern themselves and to determine their future."[59]

This should clearly signal that the language of law and policy relating to reconciliation in Canada is entering a period of sudden and dramatic change. It seems that the ground of unilateral Crown sovereignty is starting to give way.

This brings me back to the purpose of *Reconciliation without Recollection?* Here I attempt to provide a perspicuous view of this problem by rearranging the familiar so as to make the problem open and available (viz. the "values of

---

57 Trudeau speech, UN General Assembly, New York, 1 September 2017.

58 Ibid.

59 Ibid. It is interesting to note that some important legislative developments followed, but they have recently proven unsuccessful. Bill C-262, entitled *The United Nations Declaration on the Rights of Indigenous Peoples Act: An Act to Ensure that the Laws of Canada Are in Harmony with the United Nations Declaration on the Rights of Indigenous Peoples*, was introduced by Romeo Saganash (who is a Cree NDP MP for the Quebec riding of Abitibi–Baie-James–Nunavik–Eeyou) as a private member's bill, which received its first reading in the House of Commons on 21 May 2016. The bill worked its way through the long and winding legislative process: it received its second reading in the House on 7 February 2018 and was then referred to committee. The House Committee delivered its report on 29 May, and the bill then quickly passed its third reading in the House on 30 May 2018. From that point it moved to the Senate, passing its first reading on 31 May 2018, and its second reading on 16 May 2019. The bill was then sent to the Standing Senate Committee on Aboriginal Peoples, which delivered its report without amendment on 11 June 2019. This left only the third reading in the Senate. Bill C-262 was ultimately scuttled by a group of Conservative senators who managed to use procedural mechanisms to delay the third reading until the Senate adjourned for the summer. The federal government is moving into an election this fall and so Bill C-262 is now a dead letter. Bill C-262 was killed on 21 June 2019 and the date is a significant one; the National Energy Board announced that it has issued the certificate for the deeply contentious Trans Mountain pipeline expansion and, in what can only be seen as a deep and bitter instance of irony, it is also National Indigenous Peoples Day in Canada.

the past" that persist, hidden in plain sight, within our laws and institutions). Once we can survey these problems clearly, it becomes possible to solve them. By this I mean the solution that I offer shows the Court, and the legal community more generally, how it can move to a *nation-to-nation* model within the confines of the Constitution by drawing on precedents in its own common law tradition, international law, federalism, and Indigenous traditions of understanding treaties. The current framework for reconciliation is based on the Court's unquestioning acceptance of the Crown's assertion of sovereignty, legislative power, and underlying title. This is what structures its interpretation of s. 91(24) and enables it to simply accept it as a plenary grant of power over Indians and their lands. This necessarily assumes that the Crown acquired sovereignty through assertion and so the imperial Parliament had plenary power to grant to the dominion.[60] This has led it to simply bypass the question of the inherent right of self-government and to generate a constitutional framework that amounts to little more than a proportionality check on the exercise of Crown sovereignty. If we are to find a meaningful reconciliation – and not simply one that is assigned by the logic of force that resides behind the unquestioned assumption of sovereignty – then we will need to address the history of sovereignty without assuming its foundations.

A Reconciliation without Recollection? sets out to expose the limitations of the current model by following the lines of descent and association that underlie the legal conceptualization of Aboriginal sovereignty. In order to follow these processes, I will employ the two methodological steps that are outlined by Tully in *Public Philosophy in a New Key*:

1 Contemporary surveys of both the language games and the practices of governance in which struggles occur that serve to expose what can be said and done within them and;
2 Historical surveys that can serve to loosen the bounds of these games by allowing participants "to see them as one *form* of practice and one *form* of

60 While it is true that conquests and/or cessions would have provided traditional grounds for the sovereignty of the imperial Crown in common and civil law, the Supreme Court has clearly stated that the Indigenous peoples in Canada have never been conquered and that *terra nullius* never applied. See *Haida Nation v. British Columbia (Minister of Forests)*, [2004] 3 SCR 511, 2004 SCC 73 at para. 25; and *Tsilhqot'in Nation v. British Columbia*, [2014] 2 SCR 257 at para. 69. We should also remember that even if these grounds applied, they do not necessarily provide a clear picture of the relationship between the Crown and Indigenous peoples, as establishing *imperium* was not necessarily understood to settle the question of *dominium*, and so the scope of Indigenous land rights (as well as the continued existence of their legal and political systems) would remain open. For more on the European understanding of the relationship between sovereignty and occupancy see Fitzmaurice, *Sovereignty, Property and Empire*.

problematization that can be compared critically with others" and so allow them to "consider the possibilities of thinking and acting differently."[61]

These more specific methodological steps reflect my more general remarks regarding investigation at the beginning of this introduction. I highlight this point here to remind the reader that I take this as a set of methods that are useful in the particular case that we are dealing with and not *the only possible set of methods*. This means that I will forgo any attempt to conduct a complete survey of all possible methods in order to justify my selection. Rather, the utility of the methods chosen should be gauged by their ability to help clarify the problem that they are being used to address.[62] I cannot guarantee this to you in advance but only hope that what I develop here can be of use in finding your own way through this problem.

The book itself is, in many ways, like Wittgenstein's sketches of landscape. What I mean by this is that the parts of the book do not fit together in a sequential path from points A to B. Rather, I have subdivided it into parts that cover the related territories of law, history, and political thought from a number of different angles and under the light of diverse methodological tools. In this

61 Tully, *Public Philosophy* at 1:31 (emphasis in original).

62 This does not mean simply accepting the methods that work and then blindly accepting the picture that results. Such an approach risks either simply cooking the books to reach the outcome desired or falling into the narrow ad hoc legal tinkering that solves one problem in one case, only to create ten more. I find that Wittgenstein's remarks on the purpose of philosophy are helpful in countering this risk. Consider his remark from the *Philosophical Investigations*: "Philosophy may in no way interfere with the actual use of language; it can in the end only describe it. For it cannot give it any foundation either. It leaves everything as it is" (§103). This may be somewhat obscure at first glance (at least in isolation), but there is, as I see it, a kind of quasi-regulative ideal (for lack of a better term) at work here. In a sense we can say that Wittgenstein moves the traditional philosophical target from a priori truth to justice. In his own words, "Our only task is to be just. That is, we must only point out and resolve the injustices of philosophy, and not posit new parties – and creeds" (§181). Oskari Kuusela makes this point in his excellent book *The Struggle against Dogmatism: Wittgenstein and the Concept of Philosophy* (Cambridge, MA: Harvard University Press, 2008) at 286. That is, his concern is, as Wittgenstein puts it in §89, "to *understand* something that is already in plain view. For *this* is what we seem in some sense not to understand." What this brings us to is that the selection of methods should be guided by a combination of the problem one is trying to describe, the demands of ordinary language (i.e., they should be used openly and plainly), and in full acknowledgment that the methods are limited and partial. This also means that the resulting redescription cannot be somehow guaranteed or certified in advance by the author alone. In a sense, it is like describing how a magic trick works. Nothing is added or taken away by the description, nor is there only one way of showing someone the distinction between "seeing that" and "seeing as," which the magic trick covers over. You only know that you're done with the work when the audience clearly has the mechanism of the trick in view and can go on.

respect it is, like the *Philosophical Investigations*, somewhat more of an album than a book in the conventional sense. Figuratively speaking, it has been my intent to cover the all-too-familiar landmarks of law, history, and politics from unfamiliar perspectives in order to open up new ways of traversing the landscape. In this endeavour I have also drawn on Walter Benjamin, who conceived of *The Arcades Project* as "an experiment in the technique of awakening" whose purpose was to transform "not-yet-conscious knowledge of what has been" into "something that just now first happened to us, first struck us."[63] In order to accomplish this, Benjamin carried "over the principle of montage into history."[64] This historical method proceeded by assembling "large scale constructions out of the smallest and most precisely cut components. Indeed, to discover in the analysis of the small individual moment the crystal of the total event."[65] Or again, from another angle, he sets out to "merely show. I shall purloin no valuables, appropriate no ingenious formulations. But the rags, the refuse – these I will not inventory but allow, in the only way possible, to come into their own: by making use of them."[66] The multiple resonances with Wittgenstein's ordinary language philosophy (and Tully's use of it) are immediately evident and deserve a far more detailed engagement than I can offer here. My point is simply that the organization of this book adopts Benjamin's notion of montage and Wittgenstein's album of sketches. It is not a simple and progressive sequence, but a set of related investigations that are assembled as a *reminder of* (or in Benjamin's terms, an *awakening to*) what is hiding in plain sight.

The book is set out in five parts, which are then internally subdivided into sections so as to help orient the reader. The parts can be read on their own, but this approach will necessarily compromise the contextual surveyability of the problem of reconciliation. Should readers find themselves somewhat disoriented in any part or subsection of the book, I recommend that they consult the roadmaps that I have provided in the table of contents and this introduction. Robert Merton offers me another illuminating way of explaining how the construction of this book came about. In the 1985 preface to *On the Shoulders of Giants* he states, "As I now reconstruct [the book's] origins, I adopted the non-linear, advancing-by-doubling-back Shandean Method of composition at the same time I was reflecting that *this open form resembles the course taken*

63 Walter Benjamin, *The Arcades Project*, ed. Roy Tiedemann, trans. Howard Eiland and Kevin McLaughlin (Cambridge, MA: Harvard University Press, 1999) at 389–90. The selection I cite here appears in Derek Sayer's masterful *Prague, Capital of the Twentieth Century: A Surrealist History* (Princeton, NJ: Princeton University Press, 2013) at 3. My own approach to Benjamin's work and methodology generally owes much to Sayer's influence.

64 Benjamin, *Arcades Project* at 461; Sayer, *Prague* at 6.

65 Benjamin, *Arcades Project* at 461; Sayer, *Prague* at 6.

66 Benjamin, *Arcades Project* at 460; Sayer, *Prague* at 6.

by history in general, by the history of ideas in particular, and, in a way, by the course taken in scientific inquiry as well. For a lifelong addict of [Thomas Sterne's] *The Life and Opinions of Tristram Shandy, Gentleman*, this complex hypothesis inexorably brought to mind the graphic depiction, in Book VI, Chapter XL, of the eccentric trajectory followed by the first four of its path-making volumes along these exact lines:[67]

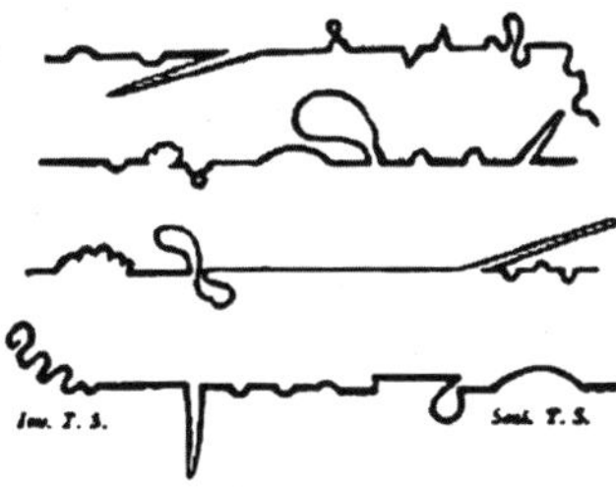

With that in mind I will outline the itinerary of this investigation:

1 We will cover the territory of reconciliation in Canadian jurisprudence. I have provided a short initial survey in this introduction, but this part of the book will delve into this line in far greater detail. By charting a course through the use of the term in the case law, I point to two conceptual themes that organize or, perhaps better, undergird the Court's discourse of reconciliation (viz. historicism and the ship of state). As I see it, these conceptual themes operate as "irrational elements" (to repurpose Max Weber's term), which structure the rule of the game of reconciliation. By investigating them we can move into the problems of history, law, and legitimacy that are at stake in the game (even if this is concealed by the obscure technical language and ad hoc developments of the common law). This leads me to a draw out the connection between the game of reconciliation that is currently being played and the problem of foundations via an in situ discussion of my methods. This connects this part of the book to the others as a kind of initial site or nexus for a number of radial paths that both lead away and return.

2 We will examine the discursive foundations of the *Indian Act* by considering the philosophical projects that grounded the legitimacy of British imperial practice in the mid-nineteenth century. The three strains of discourse that we will consider are J.S. Mill's civilizing liberal-imperialism, the extinction thesis, and Henry Maine's new culturalism. They provide

67 Robert K. Merton, *On the Shoulders of Giants: A Shandean Postscript* (Chicago: University of Chicago Press, 1993) at xix, as cited in Derek Sayer's *Making Trouble: Surrealism and the Human Sciences* (Chicago: Prickly Paradigm, 2017) at 5–6.

the discursive foundations for Indian legislation, policy, and administrative practices over the last 150 years (viz. for what I refer to as the "Crown machinery"), but they do so in different ways. My aim in this part is twofold: first, I will explore how these foundations operate in relationship to one another and how the question of legitimacy destabilizes these discourses; and second, I will explore how this foundational instability relates to the continual and haphazard legal and political renovation that has characterized the life of the Crown machinery, from the project of enfranchisement to its transformation into the project of reconciliation.

3 We will situate the *Indian Act*, s. 91(24), its associated institutions, and practices of governance in the context of these imperial foundations in the nineteenth century and follow the general line of their development to the White Paper in 1969. Part 3 follows up on the investigation of the European discursive foundations from part 2 by engaging with what the colonial institutions and authorities in Canada were doing during the same period. There is thus a shift in focus from the broader philosophical discourses to the legislative and administrative system that was being constructed and (continually) recalibrated in relation to Aboriginal resistance. The aim here will be to see both the continuities and discontinuities between the broader discursive trends and the administrative practices within Canada.

4 We will review how the courts have interpreted the *Indian Act* over time and relate their interpretations to both the active resistance of Aboriginal peoples and the foundational problems addressed in the previous parts. Part 4 focuses on three particular aspects of the case law in this area: (a) the legal nature of the authority granted in s. 91(24); (b) the definition of "Indians" and the structure and authority of "bands"; and (c) the Court's recent rejection of the doctrine of interjurisdictional immunity in relation to s. 35 in *Tsilhqot'in Nation.* When this change is seen in this light of the history of how the Court has interpreted s. 91(24), the definitions of Indians and the structure and authority of bands, we can see that the framework of reconciliation is an extension of the 150-year history of unilaterally excluding Aboriginal peoples from the division of powers that govern their lands. It highlights the fact that the s. 35 framework and the current interpretation of s. 91(24) share a common foundation. Both rely on *terra nullius,* discovery, and the civilization thesis to diminish Aboriginal peoples to such a degree that the Crown was able to acquire sovereignty and radical or underlying title to their lands by assertion alone.

5 Finally, we will consider how s. 91(24), the *Indian Act* and the practices of governance that they set in place fit into the current legal-political architecture of Canada and the ongoing struggles that continue to shape it. This is admittedly a broad field to cover, so I have divided this part

into two sections. First, I focus on the change in policy from *Calder* to the *Indian Act, 1985*. In this section I follow the three lines of policy change that stretch between these two key points. This includes the legislative changes that were considered at the federal level, the beginning of the modern land claims process with the *James Bay and Northern Quebec Agreement* in 1975, and the constitutional consultations leading up to 1982. I then move to a reconsideration of the *Penner Report* and *Bill C-52*. Despite the fact that the former was largely disregarded and the latter was never enacted, they set out to tackle the problem of self-government on a constitutional level and, by my reading, the positions taken continue to shape policy. As such, a comparative analysis of them offers us an invaluable snapshot of policy formulation in the wake of the *Constitution Act, 1982*. Second, I conclude by reconsidering what the implementation of the *United Nations Declaration of the Rights of Indigenous People* could mean for the future of reconciliation.[68] My aim in this section will be to explore what implementation could mean if the government and the courts were to reject the current interpretation of s. 91(24) and the colonial version of federalism that it entails. This will be a mapping out of an imaginary space, but it is not utopian. That is, it does not come from nowhere (despite the meaning of the name, utopias always reflect a context). Rather, it draws on the resources of the 250-year-old tradition of constitutional law that is reflected in the treaties, the *Royal Proclamation, 1763*, s. 25 of the *Constitution Act, 1982*, and the everyday practices of resistance of Aboriginal peoples. It will offer a rough-and-ready account of both what I have termed *reconciliation-with-recollection*, and what that could mean in practice.

68 An earlier version of Part 5(2)(B) was published as "'We have never been domestic': State Legitimacy and the Indigenous Question," in *UNDRIP Implementation: Braiding International, Domestic and Indigenous Laws*, by the Centre for International Governance Innovation, 2017. It is republished here with permission.

Part 1

Reconciliation without Recollection

Three degrees of latitude overthrow jurisprudence. A meridian determines the truth ... It is an odd kind of justice to have a river for its boundary. Truth lies on this side of the Pyrenees, error on the other.

Blaise Pascal, *Pensées* (23)

A "picture" held us captive. And we could not get outside it, for it lay in our language and language seemed to repeat it to us inexorably.

Ludwig Wittgenstein, *Philosophical Investigations* (§115)

What is the meaning of *reconciliation*? If we refer to the *Oxford English Dictionary* for our answer, we will find that it can refer to both an action and a state.[1] There is the transitive act of reconciling and the state of being reconciled. In the former sense it can refer to the process of restoring unity or peace between parties that have been estranged or even hostile. In this sense it can be interpreted as an essential component of settling disputes through mutual understanding and agreement. But it can also have a more unilateral sense. There is the reconciliation of bookkeepers and accountants. Here one settles discrepancies between accounts by making them compatible and consistent with one another. There is also the reconciliation of fate. One can reconcile oneself to events that are beyond one's control (whether this is death or the will of God).[2] This form of reconcilia-

1 *Oxford Dictionary & Thesaurus* (1997), s.v. "reconcile."

2 For a critical examination of the stakes of this kind of imposed reconciliation for the rule of law, see Mark D. Walters, "The Morality of Aboriginal Law," *Queen's Law Journal* 31 (2006): 472; Walters, "The Jurisprudence of Reconciliation: Aboriginal Rights in Canada," in *The Politics of Reconciliation in Multicultural Societies*, ed. Will Kymlicka and Bashir Bashir, 165–91 (Oxford: Oxford University Press, 2008); Dawnis Minawaanigogizhigok Kennedy, "Reconciliation without Respect? Section 35 and Indigenous Legal Orders," in Law Commission of Canada, *Indigenous Legal Traditions*, 77–113 (Vancouver: University of British Columbia Press, 2008); and Felix Hoehn, *Reconciling Sovereignties: Aboriginal Nations and Canada* (Saskatoon, SK: Native Law Centre, 2012).

tion may bring with it a sense of acceptance and peace or simply resignation, but can one force others to accept something as a fact that they must reconcile themselves to? Coercive force may well appear to be as irresistible as fate, but it cannot offer the same guarantees. H.L.A. Hart has this very problem in mind when he addresses the problem of authority, law, and coercive force.[3] A legal system may indeed be used to maintain a group in a position of permanent inferiority, but this comes at a price. One can simply never be sure that this forced reconciliation is real, because one can never be sure whether the other party has accepted their situation as fate or if they are simply biding their time. Quite simply, there is no way to be absolutely certain that one can tell the difference between "voluntary acceptance" and "mere obedience," and as a result, this type of legal system suffers from a kind of constitutive instability.[4] Such a system produces a vicious circle in which those who benefit from the system ground their claim to legitimacy in the phrase *salus populi suprema lex* (let the welfare of the people be the supreme law), and those who are excluded take up the revolutionary response of *fiat justitia ruat caelum* (let justice be done though the heavens fall).[5] Here the distinction between the rule of law and the rule by law is lost in the adversarial call and response of two solitudes.[6] Given its ambivalence, what can *reconciliation* mean in the context of Canadian Aboriginal law?

---

3 H.L.A. Hart, *The Concept of Law*, 2nd ed. (Oxford: Oxford University Press, 1994) at 200–3.

4 Ibid. at 201–2.

5 Robert Cover, *Justice Accused: Antislavery and the Judicial Process* (New Haven, CT: Yale University Press, 1975) at 107.

6 In other words, the consequence of conceiving of reconciliation as "reconciliation to," rather than "reconciliation with," is that one loses perspective and falls prey to seeing what one wants to see. This is where Wittgenstein's notion of being captured by a picture is quite helpful; it highlights the effect of adopting a stance that excludes the contrasting and contesting perspectives of others and mistakes what it sees (which is necessarily a product of interpretation or "seeing as") with what is actually there. It seems possible to force others to reconcile themselves to a given state of affairs only if one manages to blind oneself to the distinction between "voluntary acceptance" and "mere obedience," but, if history is any indication, even this wilful blindness is prone to a nagging suspicion that the subjects are plotting against the king. This is, in short, the path towards a politics that is grounded in fear and suspicion, which is expressed in a lineage that extends through Thrasymachus and Callicles in the Platonic dialogues to Machiavelli, Hobbes, Hegel, and Schmitt. It is not that this strain of political thought has *nothing* to show us (it is undeniable that human politics can and often does correspond to their accounts), but that their account of the role of law and legitimacy in stabilizing power (a point they all concede to) is simply unconvincingly thin. They seem to present a picture where the only possible form of legitimacy is achieved through stagecraft and illusion; legitimacy in their view is accomplished by a forced "reconciliation to" that is maintained by appearances and self-interest. This excludes the very possibility of "reconciliation with" as being anything other than a kind of mistaken perception, and with it the promise of the rule of law becomes a puppet show that distracts us from the frightening reality of our political nature (viz. Hobbes's *bellum omnium contra omnes*). My own suspicion is that political philosophers who favour this view do so from a far too comfortable chair. They achieve their grand, all-knowing perspective by writing off humanity as essentially morally

1.1 Reconciliation in Canadian Jurisprudence

The concept enters the case law in *Sparrow* when Dickson CJ and La Forest J use it to interpret the relationship between s. 35(1) of the *Constitution Act, 1982* and s. 91(24) of the *Constitution Act, 1867*.[7] What is being reconciled is, as the Court puts it, "federal power" and "federal duty" via a justificatory test.[8] This naturally has a connection with the kind of wider historical reconciliation we will see

---

bankrupt and they do so without accounting for their own position (i.e., a position that Hegel aptly characterizes as the "beautiful soul" who achieves salvation by making the world into the contrasting position of evil). It allows them to calmly accept and swallow the madness of the European colonial empires as being simply another exposure of the truth of politics as power and violence. W.E.B. Du Bois pointed to the hidden madness in this position in 1917 when looking at the wreckage of a Europe:

> As we see the dead dimly through rifts of battle smoke and hear faintly the cursing and accusations of blood brothers, we darker men say: This is not Europe gone mad; this is not an aberration nor insanity; this *is* Europe; this seeming terrible is the real soul of white culture ... Is then this war the end of war? Can it be the end so long as its prime cause, the despising and robbery of darker peoples sits enthroned even in the souls of those who cry peace? So if Europe hugs this delusion then this is not the end of war – it is the beginning. (W.E.B. Du Bois, "Of the Culture of White Folk," *Journal of Race Development* 7, no. 4 (April 1917): 437; emphasis in original)

This is not an expression of Hobbesian pessimism; the cause that Du Bois is pointing to is not *essential and unchangeable* human nature. Rather, it is the consequence of the madness of treating the non-European world as mere savages, a consequence of constructing legal and political systems on the notion that coercion yields "reconciliation to," which will hold their empires together and bring redemption through progress. Simply put, the madness is not *a priori*, but *historical*. It is the consequence of hugging the delusion that the freedom of some can be permanently secured by the enslavement of others.

7 *Sparrow* at 1109.

8 While the Court positions s. 91(24) as the hinge of "federal power," it is not the source, and so other provisions could well be put to use in this way. The actual source of this mysterious and magical power is the Court's unquestioned presumption of Crown sovereignty, legislative power, and underlying title. But in order to walk their reasoning back to this position, I feel that we must first undo the hinge that they fix in place. By this I mean the first move is a critique of the *Sparrow* framework, to clearly expose the connection between the Court's unquestioned presumption of Crown sovereignty and their reading of s. 91(24). This serves to remind them that they are given this "federal power" by virtue of their interpretation, which is not the *only* possible interpretation. Rather, it is one interpretation and one that, to my view, aligns the court so closely with the will of the sovereign that it loses track of the requirements of natural justice and with it the rule of law. Sir Edward Coke's use of the Latin phrase *nemo iudex in sua causa* brings with it the requirement that Lord Hewart CJ so neatly summarized in *R v. Sussex Justices, ex parte McCarthy*, [1924] 1 KB 256, [1923] All ER 233: "Not only must justice be done, it must also be seen to be done." It is difficult to see how the court can accomplish this in the dispute between Indigenous peoples and the Crown when it hews so closely to the act of state doctrine. Once a court embraces Marshall CJ's statement in *Johnson v. M'Intosh*, 21 US 543 (1823) at 588–9 and maintains that "conquest gives a title

later on in *Mikisew Cree*, but it is not entirely the same. The judico-historical gulf between s. 35(1) and s. 91(24) is difficult to overstate.[9] In effect, Aboriginal peoples move from being the object of a constitutional head of power to having their "existing" rights "recognized and affirmed." The interpretive complications do not end with the vague language of the provisions themselves. The Court in *Sparrow* seems to simply assume that s. 91(24) grants the federal Parliament *power over* Indians and their lands. While this is consistent with previous case law, it is one interpretation of the provision and not an unquestionable fact.[10]

---

which the courts of the conqueror cannot deny," then it has simply taken the position of the sovereign and renounced the promise of the rule of law. It seems to forget that while it may be outside of the jurisdiction of the courts to deny the sovereign's title, it seems equally absurd that they would be able to legally affirm it without losing any and all claims to impartiality. It is patently obvious that courts that find themselves in this position *are free* to take the position that the title so claimed cannot be either *affirmed or denied* in law. This marks the limits of the jurisdiction in such a way that the title in question is left as a de facto claim whose entry into *de jure* status requires a negotiated legal agreement that is based on mutual recognition and consent, and has processes by which renegotiation can take place.

9 Brian Slattery refers to this as a "sea change" in common law rules. He argues that it has given rise to two related forms of Aboriginal rights, which he terms "historical" and "generative." Historical rights are the form of Aboriginal title that existed at common law in the period following the Crown's de facto assertion of sovereignty. They are expressed in the *Royal Proclamation* and form what he refers to as the "*common law of Aboriginal rights*." They are governed by the common law *Principles of Recognition* (and he argues are the meaning of "recognized" in s. 35(1) of the *Constitution Act, 1982*). This "historical title" forms "the point of departure for any modern inquiry and a benchmark for assessing the actions of colonial governments and the scope of dispossession." This colonial dispossession has led to the transformation of the historical forms of Aboriginal right into "generative right." These are governed by the *Principle of Reconciliation* (and provide the meaning of "affirmed" in s. 35(1)). The purpose of this generative form is the successful settlement of Aboriginal claims, and as Slattery rightly maintains, this must involve "*the full and unstinting recognition of the historical reality of Aboriginal title, the true scope and effects of Indigenous dispossession, and the continuing links between an Indigenous people and its traditional lands*." Brian Slattery, "The Metamorphosis of Aboriginal Title," *Canadian Bar Review* 85 (2006): 282 (emphasis in original).

10 The history of the Supreme Court's interpretation of s. 91(24) will be addressed in detail in part 3. It is interesting to note that the Court in *Sparrow* chooses to interpret s. 91(24) as being effectively "federal power" without limit, and it is this *interpretive choice* that leads them to reconcile it with the "federal duty" that is taken on in s. 35(1). This interpretation of s. 91(24) is simply assumed (see *Sparrow* at 1103). There is no inquiry into its nature or basis, no restriction on its form or scope. This interpretive choice fits into a 150-year-old interpretive paradigm that has read s. 91(24) as an unlimited grant of power *over* Indigenous peoples. This has never been the only interpretive possibility for s. 91(24). As John Borrows argues, the basis cannot simply be the wording of the provision itself, as "the technical wording of powers granted by section 91 is '*in relation to*' matters not assigned exclusively to provincial legislatures. In particular, the exclusive federal legislative authority in section 91(24) only '*extends to*' Indians and lands reserved for Indians. There should be a vast difference between legislation *extending to* or *in*

There is also the question of the meaning of s. 35(1) within the context of the *Constitution Act, 1982* itself.[11] It is not within the *Charter* (which extends from

---

relation to a subject matter and exercising legislative power over a particular group of people." See John Borrows, "Unextinguished: Rights and the Indian Act" (unpublished) at 11. While it may be possible to attempt to shore up the Court's approach by appealing to the notion of parliamentary supremacy – which was inherited from the British constitutional tradition – this does not provide a clear-cut resolution. First, because the actual technical requirements of the common law place a very significant challenge to providing legal grounds for the claim that the absolute or "power over" reading of s. 91(24) maps onto the history of British Imperial practices pre-Confederation. For a recent account of the history from this period and beyond, see Peter H. Russell, *Canada's Odyssey: A Country Based on Incomplete Conquests* (Toronto: University of Toronto Press, 2017); for a detailed legal account of how this problem plays out in relation to the question of Aboriginal title claims in the Maritime provinces, see Robert Hamilton, "After Tsilhqot'in Nation: The Aboriginal Title Question in Canada's Maritime Provinces," *University of New Brunswick Law Journal* 67 (2016): 58108; and for an excellent examination of the common law doctrine of continuity, see Mark D. Walters, "The 'Golden Thread' of Continuity: Aboriginal Customs at Common Law and under the Constitution Act, 1982," *McGill Law Journal* 44 (1999): 711–52. Second, there is a normative conceptual problem relating to the constitutional traditions of the common law and how these translate (or fail to do so) when they move to the colonial context. In other words, appealing to parliamentary sovereignty over the claims of Indigenous peoples jumps over the question of how sovereignty was acquired. If the courts accept the claims of the sovereign at face value (as sovereign fiat alone without any account of the legal rights of Indigenous peoples), they swallow a poison pill that threatens the delicate balance between sovereignty and the rule of law within the common law (i.e., this is the contagion problem that so many European critics of imperialism were concerned with in the eighteenth and nineteenth centuries). This leads us to the question that the courts are struggling with: what are the *legal consequences* that flow from the Crown's claim to sovereignty? This is a very wide field, as it can range so far as differences in degree become differences in kind (i.e., a full "power over" account of Crown sovereignty results in a system of arbitrary power, whereas a limited "power-with" account results in a nation-to-nation federal-like relationship of shared sovereignty). This question shows us that there are other interpretive possibilities to explore. Section 91(24) can been read in light of the 250-year-old tradition that stretches back to the *Royal Proclamation of 1763*. Such an interpretation necessarily determines the form of the power (i.e., it would be a *power-with* Aboriginal peoples on a *nation-to-nation* basis within a more complicated model of treaty federalism) and limits its possible scope to accord with this form. If the Court in *Sparrow* had interpreted s. 91(24) in this light, instead of simply assuming that it grants unlimited or plenary power, there would be *no conflict* between the provisions for them to reconcile. See also Larry Chartrand, "The Failure of the Daniels Case: Blindly Entrenching a Colonial Legacy," *Alberta Law Review* 50, no. 1 (2013): 182; and for more on the meaning of the term *power-with*, see James Tully, "Violent Power-Over and Nonviolent Power-With: Hannah Arendt on Violence and Nonviolence" (paper delivered at Goethe University, 7 June 2011); James Tully, "Richard Gregg and the Power of Nonviolence: The Power of Nonviolence as the Unifying Animacy of Life," (J. Glenn and Ursula Gray Memorial Lecture, Colorado College, 1 March 2016). For more on the concept of treaty federalism, refer to Russel Lawrence Barsh and James Youngblood Henderson, *The Road: Indian Tribes and Political Liberty* (Berkeley: University of California Press, 1980); and, more recently, Asch, *On Being Here to Stay*.

11 Peter Hogg points out that s. 35 was a late addition to the *Constitution Act, 1982*. It was not included in the October 1980 version, and then it appears in the April 1981 version without the word *existing*, only to vanish entirely in the 5 November 1981 version. The omission

s. 1 to s. 34) and thus it is not subject to either s. 1 or s. 33. In *Sparrow* the Court was tasked with finding a way to read a limit into s. 35(1) without depriving it of meaning entirely. Its solution was to introduce a kind of s. 1 *Oakes* analysis via s. 91(24) and then, to avoid the colonial connotations of this provision, characterize it as the expression of a "fiduciary relationship." This constitutional form of reconciliation has been expanded through the subsequent case law.

Through *Gladstone*, *Van der Peet*, and *Delgamuukw*, reconciliation becomes both a constitutional principle and a substantive goal. The judicial process of reconciling the constitutional conflict between s. 91(24) and s. 35(1) is still in place, but it is interpreted as being a part of a larger substantive goal. That goal is the reconciliation of the pre-existence of Aboriginal peoples with the Crown's assertion of sovereignty over Canadian territory.[12] Reconciliation is thus a remedial principle that generates a judicial process. This process must reflect the fact that Aboriginal rights (including title) are not derived from the Crown. According to Lamer CJC, this means that the court must take "into account the aboriginal perspective while at the same time taking into account the perspective of the common law. True reconciliation will, equally, place weight on each."[13] The cases all seem to maintain that reconciliation, if it is to have any meaning, must be mutual, but, as we have seen, they part company on how this mutuality is to be achieved. Nowhere is the Court's hesitancy more evident than in the title cases. The Court has consistently maintained that negotiation has more to offer than litigation on the question of title.[14] This is, at least to some degree, understandable. After all, the question of title cuts to the very heart of the dispute between the Crown and Aboriginal peoples. In this question the court senses the limits of its municipal jurisdiction and so it has avoided setting a clear and determinative precedent by tripping itself over procedural technicalities (the previous cases on title have exhibited a number of methods of judicial non-decision such as, split decision (*Calder*) or *obiter dicta* (*Delgamuukw*), and when there was an actual decision it simply increased the

---

drew intense criticism and, as a result, it was added later in November with the addition of the word *existing*. The history of the provision alone demonstrates that it was the product of contention and compromise. This is also evident in the vague drafting and placement. What does *recognized and affirmed* mean? Does *existing* open the door for extinguishment? See Peter Hogg, "The Constitutional Basis of Aboriginal Rights," in *Aboriginal Law since Delgamuukw*, ed. Maria Morellato (Aurora, ON: Canada Law Book, 2009) at 5–7; and Brian Slattery, "The Constitutional Guarantee of Aboriginal Treaty Rights," *Queen's Law Journal* 8 (1982): 232–73.

12 *Delgamuuku* at 81; *Haida Nation v. British Columbia (Minister of Forests)*, [2004] 3 SCR 511 at para. 25; *Taku River Tlingit First Nation v. British Columbia (Project Assessment Director)*, [2004] 3 SCR 550 at para. 24; *Manitoba Metis Federation Inc. v. Canada (AG)*, [2013] 1 SCR 623 at paras. 71 and 73 [hereinafter *MMF*]; *Tsilhqot'in Nation v. British Columbia*, [2014] 2 SCR 257 at paras. 17–18 and 118; Hamilton, "After Tsilhqot'in Nation."

13 *R v. Van der Peet* at para. 50.

14 *Delgamuukw* at para.186.

degree of uncertainty (*Marshall; Bernard*)).[15] In this it has attempted to set the terms of negotiation, and yet the question of title keeps coming back before the Court. Indeed, if reconciliation is to have any substantive meaning, the question of title needs to be answered.[16]

With *Tsilhqot'in Nation*, McLachlin CJ (writing for a unanimous Court) provides us with an answer to this question: title now exists, but it is a title that is subject to reconciliation. Reconciliation is presented as a "project," a "process," and a "governing ethos."[17] But, again, what kind of reconciliation is this? The framework that the Court envisions for this process is the test for the justification of infringement. McLachlin states, "This framework permits a principled reconciliation of Aboriginal rights with the interests of all Canadians."[18] The problem here is that reconciliation is operating on the basis of the Crown's unilateral right of justified infringement.[19] This retains the same basic assumption that Dickson CJC maintained in *Sparrow*: "There was from the outset never any doubt that *sovereignty and legislative power*, and indeed the underlying

---

15 Two brief comments here: (1) In *Calder* the ratio of the case was the absence of a fiat and so, strictly speaking, everything in the case, aside from the holding, about the fiat is *obiter* (I would like to thank Kerry Wilkins for drawing my attention to this). (2) What I mean by "uncertainty" in *Marshall; Bernard* is that while there was a clear rejection of the title claim, this was done in such a way that the actual test for title became legally uncertain. Kent McNeil provides a detailed walk through the Court's convoluted reasoning in "Aboriginal Title and the Supreme Court: What's Happening?" *Saskatchewan Law Review* 69 (2006): 281–308. McNeil helpfully highlights the fact that although the decision in *Marshall; Bernard* was unanimous in its result, LeBel J and Fish J "expressed views on the source and proof of Aboriginal title that differed substantially from those of McLachlin CJ. LeBel J was particularly concerned that the chief justice's approach was 'too narrowly focused on common law concepts relating to property interests' and might preclude proof of Aboriginal title by nomadic or semi-nomadic peoples" (ibid. at 302). We can see this uncertainty work its way through the courts in the versions of the test for title that are articulated by Vickers J in *Tsilhqot'in Nation v. British Columbia*, 2007 BCSC 1700, Groberman J in the appeal in *William v. British Columbia*, 2012 BCCA 285, and finally in *Tsilhqot'in Nation* the uncertainty is undone while the new knot regarding interjurisdictional immunity is added.

16 See Douglas Lambert, "Where to from Here: Reconciling Aboriginal Title with Crown Sovereignty," in *Aboriginal Law since Delgamuukw*, ed. Maria Morellato, 31–54 (Aurora, ON: Canada Law Book, 2009).

17 *Tsilhqot'in Nation* at [2014] SCC 44 at paras. 17, 23, and 87; Hamilton, "After Tsilhqot'in Nation."

18 *Tsilhqot'in Nation* at para. 125.

19 The actual test for justification in *Tsilhqot'in Nation* is quite rigorous. For example, the Court states that the fiduciary duty of the Crown in a justification context requires that "incursions on Aboriginal title cannot be justified if they would substantially deprive future generations of the benefit of the land" (at para. 86). But the test for determining whether or not an infringement has *actually occurred* is unhelpfully vague. The question in this process is what constitutes a "meaningful diminution" of an Aboriginal right, and the Court cites *Sparrow* as the source of this process:

title, to such lands *vested in the Crown*."[20] But this response does little more than beg the question. If the basis of the Crown's right to unilaterally infringe on Aboriginal rights is Crown sovereignty then, one must ask, how did the Crown become sovereign? Or, to press the question a little further, did the Crown acquire sovereignty at all? This question touches on the actual heart of the Indigenous-Crown problem in Canada. And on this point, there is, paradoxically, both a lot and really not very much to say. There is a lot to say in the sense that the process of colonization of the territory now known as Canada has a long and complicated history of *incomplete conquests* (to borrow Peter Russell's apt phrase).[21] But also the Court is bound by the limits of the constitutional order that it exists within. The question of Crown sovereignty places the courts in a very difficult position, as their jurisdiction is constitutively tied to the sovereignty of the Crown, and so they are limited to determining what legal consequences flow from the Crown's claim.[22] The full scope of this question has, thus far, been largely avoided. Borrows points to this when he notes that "the Court has not articulated how (and by what legal right) assertions of Crown sovereignty grant underlying title to the Crown or displace Aboriginal governance."[23] The *Sparrow* Court bundled together Crown sovereignty with *legislative supremacy* and *underlying title*, but these do not necessarily legally

---

> The following factors will be relevant in determining whether a law of general application results in a meaningful diminution of an Aboriginal right, giving rise to breach: (1) whether the limitation imposed by the legislation is unreasonable; (2) whether the legislation imposes undue hardship; and (3) whether the legislation denies the holders of the right their preferred means of exercising the right ... All three factors must be considered; for example, even if laws of general application are found to be reasonable or not to cause undue hardship, this does not mean that there can be no infringement of Aboriginal title. (Ibid. at para. 104)

Reliance on terms like *unreasonable* and *undue hardship* provides little guidance for the exercise of judicial discretion, and it is quite possible that the theoretical utility of the more stringent justification test remains just that, theoretical.

20 *Sparrow* at 1103 (emphasis added).

21 Russell, *Canada's Odyssey*.

22 This means that the question of whether or not the Crown is in possession of sovereignty at all is beyond the purview of the Canadian courts and thus becomes a political question. For a detailed account of this limitation, see Kent McNeil, *Common Law Aboriginal Title* (Oxford: Clarendon, 1989). This question is a significant one, as the legal consequences of Crown sovereignty can range from a full "power over" account of Crown sovereignty (which results in a system of arbitrary power that cannot be conceptually explained in modern terms – i.e., it is dependent on the racist colonial legal fictions of discovery, *terra nullius*, civilization, and so on) to a limited "power-with" account (which results in a nation-to-nation federal-like relationship of shared sovereignty).

23 John Borrows, "Sovereignty's Alchemy: An Analysis of Delgamuukw v. British Columbia," *Osgoode Hall Law Journal* 37 (1999): 582.

flow together.[24] Even in cases of conquest (which does not apply in Canada, as the Court has stated that Indigenous peoples were never conquered) the doctrine of continuity would require that Indigenous legal and political order (barring only external sovereignty) and land rights would remain until extinguished by legislation.[25] Simply put, accepting the fact of Crown sovereignty does not provide a legal foundation for its claims to having either *power-over* Indigenous legal and political orders (i.e., legislative supremacy) or underlying title. The Court has silently presumed that the legally unquestionable fact of Crown sovereignty fixes Indigenous peoples in a sovereign-to-subject relationship with the Crown, but this has never been the case. By doing so it has fitted Indigenous peoples with the very constitutional straitjacket that they conscientiously avoided in the *Secession Reference*.[26] The Court's unquestioning acceptance of the legal consequences of Crown sovereignty has served to maintain the arbitrary *power-over* relationship between Indigenous peoples and the Crown,

---

24 For an interesting and insightful analysis of the implications of this version of Crown sovereignty in the cases following *Sparrow*, see *Beaver v. Hill*, 2017 ONSC 7245. I will refer to this version of Crown sovereignty as being *bundled* or *thick* (other descriptive terms such as *inflated* or *all-encompassing* could also be used). What I am pointing to with these descriptive terms is the same problem: by bundling Crown sovereignty with legislative power and underlying title, the court falls into two related errors. First, it extends the non-justiciable status of Crown sovereignty to legislative power and underlying title. Second, this inflated version of Crown sovereignty fills the constitutional framework in such a manner that the only remaining position for Aboriginal peoples is as subjects. The way out of this problem is to adopt an *unbundled, thin, deflated*, or *limited* notion of Crown sovereignty. This version of sovereignty restricts the non-justiciable shield to minimal settings (e.g., external legal personality, territorial integrity, etc.) and thus places legislative power and underlying title within the arena of constitutional law and negotiation. This is by no means a novel move. It is one that is contemplated in the *Marshall Trilogy* in the United States as the chief justice moves from a thick version of sovereignty in *Johnson v. M'Intosh* to a thinner one in *Worcester v. Georgia.* It is also by no means beyond the limits of cognizability within the common law; the United Kingdom is a pluri-national federal state (i.e., its constitutive members are *nations*), and so the issues of legislative supremacy and underlying title are necessarily subject to legal and political contestation.

25 Lord Mansfield CJ clearly sets this out in *Campbell v. Hall* (1774) 1 Cowp. 204, 98 ER 1045. For an excellent doctrinal examination of how this works in the Maritime Provinces, see Hamilton, "After Tsilhqot'in Nation" at 58. Also the arc in the legal reasoning of Marshall CJ from *Johnson v. M'Intosh*; to *Cherokee Nation v. Georgia*, 30 US 1, 8 L. Ed. 25 (1831); and finally to *Worcester v. Georgia*, 31 US 515, 8 L. Ed. 483 (1832) can be seen as working through the question of the legal implications of the claim of sovereignty in order to find a balance between arbitrary sovereign power and the rule of law. For a helpful reading of the Marshall cases on this point, see Philip P. Frickey, "Marshalling Past and Present: Colonialism, Constitutionalism, and Interpretation in Federal Indian Law," *Harvard Law Review* 107 (1993): 381–440.

26 *Reference re Secession of Quebec* at para. 150.

which was established in the mid-nineteenth century.[27] There is no legal basis for this constitutional order, aside from offering up the colonial legal fictions of the doctrine of discovery and *terra nullius*, which set out to exclude the very need for a justification for colonization by permanently stripping one party of any and all legal rights. This silent and unquestioned acceptance exposes the impossibility of the current project of reconciliation. The current version of the project begins with the assumption of Crown sovereignty, legislative power, and underlying title and then sets out to reconcile this with "Aboriginal interests."[28] In effect, the process of reconciliation thus defined begins by allowing the Crown to unilaterally determine the position of Indigenous peoples within the constitutional order. This unquestioned asymmetrical constitutional relationship cannot achieve reconciliation, no matter what extravagant constructive techniques of legal interpretation are marshalled, because it requires Indigenous peoples to reconcile themselves to a version of the constitutional order that they have consistently resisted for over 150 years. Real reconciliation

---

27 The basis of the Crown's claim being an assertion or de facto has appeared in the case law. In *Haida Nation* McLachlin CJ states that the "process of reconciliation flows from the Crown's duty of honourable dealing toward Aboriginal peoples, which arises in turn from the Crown's assertion of sovereignty over an Aboriginal people and *de facto* control of land and resources that were formerly in the control of that people." *Haida Nation* at para. 32. This opens up the possibility that the Crown's assertion of sovereignty is predicated on a de facto control of land that has yet to be made *de jure* via the formation of treaties that reconcile "pre-existing Aboriginal sovereignty with assumed Crown sovereignty" (para. 20). This is supported by *Taku River Tlingit* when McLachlin CJ states, "The purpose of s. 35(1) of the *Constitution Act, 1982* is to facilitate the ultimate reconciliation of prior Aboriginal occupation with *de facto* Crown sovereignty" (para. 42). This characterization of Crown sovereignty is also cited with approval in the Court's recent decision in *Manitoba Metis Federation Inc. v. Canada (AG)*, 2013 SCC 14 at para. 66. On a liberal reading these statements open up a number of possible arguments around the constitutional status of treaties and the nature of Crown sovereignty. Also see Walters, "Morality of Aboriginal Law" at 515; and Hoehn, *Reconciling Sovereignties*. While this may be a promising line of reasoning, it has not significantly altered the jurisprudence as, despite the questionable basis of its claim to radical title, the Crown still retains the right of unilateral infringement. I should also note that when I refer to Crown sovereignty throughout the book I am including underlying or radical title. This is important, as in *Tsilhqot'in Nation* the Court maintains that it is underlying title that gives rise to "the fiduciary duty owed and the right to encroach subject to justification" (*Tsilhqot'in Nation* at para. 112). Sovereignty remains essentially connected, as it is the assertion of sovereignty that (magically) allows the Crown to acquire "radical or underlying title" (para. 12). But one could imagine a version or theory of reconciliation that would be willing to compromise on sovereignty (e.g., to see the de facto and assertion-type qualifications the Court has been making and the final agreements or Aboriginal title as a move towards the "domestic dependent nations" model from the United States), but retain the unilateral right of infringement via underlying title. This is not a theory of reconciliation; it is little more than a shell game that conceals the problem under a different guise.

28 *Tsilhqot'in Nation* at para. 118.

can begin only when the legal consequences of Crown sovereignty are fully and directly open to question. This begins by questioning the legal basis for the assumption that Indigenous peoples are *subjects* of the Crown and not *nations* within the federation.[29] And so the current project of reconciliation is doomed to run aground before it actually sets out on its journey. Perhaps this offers us an explanation to Binnie J's cryptic metaphor in *Beckman v. Little Salmon/ Carmacks First Nation*: "The future is more important than the past. A canoeist who hopes to make progress faces forwards, not backwards."[30] Perhaps the canoeist should not look back because were he to do so he would suddenly discover that he never actually left the shore.

1.2 Reconciliation as Picture Thinking

What assumptions bind the Court to the project of reconciliation – and all of its determinations as "project," "process," "governing ethos," and "grand purpose of s. 35" – and yet keep it from moving forward in any meaningful sense?[31] It is as if the Court is held captive by a picture of reconciliation that is repeating itself in the language of each decision. On the one hand, it recognizes that if reconciliation is to have any meaning beyond a juridico-colonial procedure, it must be concerned with the mutual settlement of grievances both past and present. As Lamer CJC maintains in *Van der Peet*, true reconciliation requires that the court must place equal weight on the common law and the aboriginal perspective;[32] "we" are, after all, "all here to stay."[33] But where is "here" and who is "we"? The problem that remains constant in all cases is that there is no real justification for treating Aboriginal nations as subjects of the Crown. As Lamer J states in *Sioui*, at "the time with which we are concerned relations with Indian tribes fell somewhere between the kind of relations conducted between sovereign states and the relations that such states had with their own citizens."[34]

---

29 For a detailed version of this argument in Robert N. Clinton, "There Is No Federal Supremacy Clause for Indian Tribes," *Arizona State Law Journal* 34 (2002): 113–260; Philip P. Frickey, "A Common Law for Our Age of Colonialism: The Judicial Divestiture of Indian Tribal Authority over Nonmembers, *Yale Law Journal* 109, no. 1 (1999): 1–86; and David H. Getches, "Conquering the Cultural Frontier: The New Subjectivism of the Supreme Court in Indian Law," *California Law Review* 84, no. 6 (December 1996): 1573–1656, see Philip P. Frickey, "Adjudication and Its Discontents: Coherence and Conciliation in Federal Indian Law," *Harvard Law Review* 110 (1997): 1754–84.

30 *Beckman v. Little Salmon/Carmacks First Nation* at para. 10.

31 For the first three terms, see *Tsilhqot'in Nation* at paras. 17, 23, and 87; and for the fourth see *Little Salmon/Carmacks* at para. 10.

32 *Van der Peet* at para. 50.

33 *Delgamuukw* at para. 186.

34 *R v. Sioui*, [1990] 1 SCR 1025 at 1038.

How can one be both less than a sovereign state and not a citizen? This sui generis logic pervades the jurisprudence in this area: Aboriginal claims to land as being based in a right of "occupancy" and a "diminished" right of self-government, not pre-existing sovereignty.[35] According to this line of reasoning, there is no right to sovereignty, as this requires a level of sociocultural sophistication that is beyond the reach of "a handful of Indians."[36] The Court has avoided dealing directly with the question of Aboriginal sovereignty, because legal reasoning could not explain the basis for the superior nature of Crown sovereignty: it is simply there as an unquestionable assertion. Where does this leave us? How do we initiate an investigation into this picture of reconciliation? The metaphor of the canoeist from *Beckman v. Little Salmon/Carmacks First Nation* is, to my mind, a useful place to start, as it relies on two related assumptions that tacitly underlie the logic of the jurisprudence of reconciliation and need to be addressed before any investigation can begin.

A. Historicism

The first assumption concerns the model of history that is being offered in this picture of reconciliation. The metaphor of the canoeist collapses time and space so as to offer us, as readers, a picture in which the past is behind us and the future in front of us. The past is identified as a location of "misunderstandings" and "ancient grievances," whereas the future lies open before us.[37] So if our aim is to make progress towards reconciliation we must, like the canoeist, face the future and not the past. This simplistic model assumes that history is a single uniform continuum that all parties must agree on. Accordingly, the past is simply a set of value-free facts that need only to be summarized and ordered into sequence. Their status as historical "facts" is outside the bounds of contestation. While this may well be *a model* of history, it cannot lay claim to being objective (the degree of bias is, in my opinion, inversely proportional to its claim to being value-free). It is the colonial administrator's preferred image of history: the past

---

35 The claim concerning the "diminished" nature of the Aboriginal right to self-government is based in Marshall CJ's decisions in *Johnson v M'Intosh*; *Cherokee Nation v. Georgia*; and *Worcester v. Georgia*. For more on this, see Joshua Nichols, "A Reconciliation without Recollection? *Chief Mountain* and the Sources of Sovereignty," *UBC Law Review* 48, no. 2 (2015): 515–40; and Christopher D. Jenkins, "Marshall's Aboriginal Rights Theory and Its Treatment in Canadian Jurisprudence," *UBC Law Review* 1 (2001): 1–42. For an excellent account of how this flawed reasoning has played out in the United States, see Philip P. Frickey, "Domesticating Federal Indian Law," *Minnesota Law Review* 81 (1996): 31–95; and Frickey, "Marshalling Past and Present."

36 *R v. Syliboy* (1929), 1 DLR 307 (NS Co. Ct.) at 313. Dickson CJ strongly repudiates *Syliboy* on this point in *Simon v. R*, [1985] 2 SCR 387 at para. 21.

37 *Little Salmon/Carmacks* at para. 10.

is a set of facts that require nothing more than an occasional inventory, and then they can return to the silent shelves of the national archive. Accordingly, there is no separate view of history for the colonizer and the colonized. There is simply *the* history of *the* nation.

This model of history also determines the relationship between the past and the present by presenting itself as a factual account and concealing the limited, biased, and simply all-too-human interpretative acts that are necessarily involved in the construction of any historical narrative. This model attempts to jump over the rather obvious problem that flows from the question of perspective: if one party is able to unilaterally determine what constitutes a part of *the* past, then that same party can also determine the present reality of the conflict. The distance between the "ancient grievances" and the present can deprive the other party of grounds via a combination of laches and adverse possession (the imputed distance makes disputes concerning the content of the past out to be little more than petty grudges and self-indulgent malingering, while the present becomes simply a fact that must be accepted).[38] What the past cannot be to this mindset is open to the contestation of a plurality of parties in an ongoing conflict. It cannot be open to the possibility of the kind of radical interpretation that would derail the narrative of historical progress and its claim to an objective historical continuum, leaving us with a fractured and undetermined set of contingent histories.[39]

B. The Ship of State

The second assumption pertains to the image of the canoe – as well as to the "here" and "we" in Lamer CJ's phrase in *Delgamuukw* and Binnie J's reading of the Two Row Wampum in *Mitchell*[40] – as it suggests that the parties to the

---

38 For a detailed account of how originalism (a specific legal form of historicism) has been deployed within Aboriginal law, despite the Canadian "living tree" approach to constitutional interpretation, see John Borrows, "(Ab)Originalism and Canada's Constitution" (2012) SCLR 58:2d.

39 I share Quentin Skinner's suspicion concerning those who claim to have a "general theory about the mechanisms of social transformation" and follow his suggestion that our normative concepts are not simply statements about the world, but the "tools and weapons of ideological debate." See Quintin Skinner, *Visions of Politics* (Cambridge: Cambridge University Press, 2002) at 1:177–80. Also, for a recent and very helpful account of the question of long durations of time in historical methods, see Jo Guldi and David Armitage, *The History Manifesto* (Cambridge: Cambridge University Press, 2014).

40 *Mitchell v. MNR*, [2001] 1 SCR 911 at para. 130. This form of reasoning is also present in *Gladstone*, at para. 73, where Lamer CJC states,

> *Distinctive aboriginal societies exist within, and are a part of, a broader social, political and economic community, over which the Crown is sovereign, there are circumstances in which, in order to pursue objectives of compelling and substantial importance to that*

dispute occupy common ground and so can move forward together.[41] In effect, it assumes that "we" are all present and accounted for within the ship of state. Here again we have the false image of unity covering over the complicated legal and historical realities of settler colonialism in Canada. What does the canoe – as the "here" that contains "us" – represent? If it is the state, then how did the parties come to constitute a single vessel?[42] The "merged" sovereignty that is presented in Binnie J's concurrent decision in *Mitchell* through the metaphor of the ship of state takes the process of merging as one of historical fact, which, if accepted, would be to legitimate a form of "constructive conquest."[43]

Even if one were to ignore the problem of how the ship came to be and accept its appearance at face value, how could it be a single ship? That is, how can the parts – according to Binnie J, the ship is "composed of the historic elements of wood, iron and canvas"[44] – be considered to form a coherent whole, given the socio-economic realities of their current situation? In terms of substantive equality, it is clear that the Indigenous peoples and the rest of Canada live in separate worlds (as any cursory review of the literature on the socio-economic conditions of Indigenous peoples in Canada will demonstrate). Even under the narrow gaze of formal equality, there is the thorny problem of the distinction

---

> *community as a whole (taking into account the fact that aboriginal societies are a part of that community), some limitation of those rights will be justifiable.* Aboriginal rights are a necessary part of the reconciliation of aboriginal societies with the broader political community of which they are part; limits placed on those rights are, where the objectives furthered by those limits are of sufficient importance to the broader community as a whole, equally a necessary part of that reconciliation. (emphasis added)

The chief justice cites this paragraph with approval in relation to the first part of the test to infringements of Aboriginal title in *Delgamuukw* at para. 161. The question of how the distance between the "fact" that Aboriginal societies exist within a broader community (an obvious factual statement relating to the physical realities of settler colonialism) to the sovereignty of the Crown (a legal concept) over unceded Aboriginal territory is not answered. Much like how the Court in *Sparrow* silently bundles the legal fact of Crown sovereignty together with legislative supremacy and underlying title (both of which are questions of law and fact that cannot be simply assumed). This leads to the current incoherence of the Court's approach to s. 35, which can only address cases on an ad hoc basis and produces jurisprudence that is thin-principled and fact-bound, and frequently resorts to mysticism. I am borrowing this characterization from Philip P. Frickey's analysis of the United States Supreme Court jurisprudence in his "(Native) American Exceptionalism in Federal Public Law," *Harvard Law Review* 119 (2005): 431–90.

41 *Delgamuukw* at para. 186.

42 Gordon Christie asks precisely this question in "The Court's Exercise of Plenary Power: Rewriting the Two-Row Wampum," (2002) SCLR 16 (2d) 292–4.

43 Ibid. at 297.

44 *Mitchell* at 130.

between "citizen" (or, prior to 1949, "British subject") and "Indian." After all, the Supreme Court has held that s. 91(24) is unlike most of the other heads of power in the *Constitution Act, 1867* – which have relatively bright lines between federal and provincial jurisdiction – in that it authorizes Parliament to legislate over a racially determined group of people in an all-encompassing manner.[45] It is difficult to imagine how Indians and citizens can be simply placed into the same ship. Rather, it seems to me that Lord Atkin's famous "water-tight compartments" metaphor is a far more apt description of the relationship.[46] In order to accept the ship of state with its "merged" sovereignty offered by Binnie J in his concurrence in *Mitchell*, we would have to mistake the dream of enfranchisement as the reality of the present. Only then could "we" form a fully determinable set of peoples – the "ship of state" or "body politic" – that could move into the future under the direction of a common legal-political order.

The general problem that this assumption attempts to cover over is the plurality of communities, which also entails a plurality of legal orders. Just as there is no singular history in a settler colonial context, there is also no *singular community*, no *the* people for the sovereign to ground its claims to national interest. The implication is that there is no single sovereign that can authorize a common positive legal structure (as Austin requires), nor is there the single community that could provide the agreement necessary for a "rule of recognition" (as Hart requires). As Roger Brubaker reminds us, "'Nation' is a category of 'practice,' not (in the first instance) a category of analysis. To understand nationalism, we have to understand the practical uses of the category 'nation,' the ways it can come to structure perception, to inform thought and experience, to organize discourse and political action."[47] This provides us with a perspicacious view of the deep legal and political problems that the mythical account of the ship of state attempts to cover over. As Stanley Cavell rightly observes, the myth of the ship of state is "not merely false, but mythically false. Not just untrue but destructive of truth."[48]

These two assumptions – which I will refer to as historicism and the ship of state – lie at the foundation of modern Aboriginal law in Canada. They are the assumptions that have captured the Court and inexorably repeat themselves

45 *AG of Canada v. Canard*, [1976] 1 SCR 170, 52 DLR (3d) 548 at para. 207.

46 In *AG for Canada v. AG for Ontario*, [1937] AC 326 (PC) at para. 354, Lord Atkin wrote of Canadian federalism, "While the ship of state now sails on larger ventures and into foreign waters she still retains the watertight compartments which are an essential part of her original structure."

47 Roger Brubaker, *Nationalism Reframed: Nationhood and the National Question in the New Europe* (Cambridge: Cambridge University Press, 1996) at 10.

48 Stanley Cavell, *The Claim of Reason: Wittgenstein, Skepticism, Morality and Tragedy* (New York: Oxford University Press, 1999) at 365.

under the term *reconciliation*. They can be heard in the mysterious and magical assertions of our Supreme Court, from Dickson CJC's "there was from the outset never any doubt that *sovereignty and legislative power*, and indeed the underlying title, to such lands *vested in the Crown*,"[49] and the strange coupling of terms like *de facto* and *assertion* to characterize Crown sovereignty while maintaining the right of unilateral infringement of Aboriginal rights and title.[50] Any investigation into the meaning of reconciliation that does not address these assumptions has committed itself to the magic circle of Crown sovereignty. The termination point of such an investigation would be mistaking a refusal to re-examine the past for progress. Contrary to Binnie J's assertion, the future is not more important than the past.[51] Rather, it is a product of how we choose to imagine (and reimagine) the past.

1.3 History, Law, and Legitimacy

What is the importance of history to our understanding of the relationship between law and legitimacy? Any attempt to answer this question – with such questions there are only ever attempts – would have to begin by asking what we understand by the term *history*. If we take an everyday understanding of history – taken as a progressive series of events, names, and dates – then it seems we simply have to select a starting point and begin articulating the series associated with it. Our starting point could be any particular polity. Such an answer would naturally move from past to present, constructing a line of progression. From this we gain an orientation, a point within the present from which the open horizon of the future is, to a greater or lesser degree, constrained by the "It was" of historical time.[52]

An answer of this type is at once banal and frustrating. Confronted with the past as a *neutral* collection of events that-which-we-cannot-change, we begin to see the historian's library as little more than a graveyard where we keep an

---

49 *Sparrow* at 1103 (emphasis added).

50 *Haida Nation* at para. 32.

51 In my view, Binnie J's claim in *Little Salmon/Carmacks*, at para. 10 presumes that the importance of the future can be used to limit the scope of the Court's inquiry into what he characterizes as "ancient grievances." This approach effectively obscures the continued legal and political consequences of those presumably "ancient grievances" and encourages courts to push madly forward with its current absent-minded, ad hoc construction of thin-principled and fact-bound jurisprudence. It seems as if the position he would like the courts to adopt here is to take a page from the New Testament and tell Indigenous claimants to "let the dead bury their dead and follow the Crown."

52 See Friedrich Nietzsche, *Thus Spoke Zarathustra*, trans. Graham Parkes (Oxford: Oxford University Press, 2005) at 121–2; Hannah Arendt, *The Human Condition*, 2nd ed. (Chicago: University of Chicago Press, 1958) at 236–43.

endless series of long-unread books. Each volume accounts for the moments that preceded, and indeed led to, "us" but without the tensions and risks that gave them meaning. They present the great wars and revolutions of the past to us as if they were little more than a series of exhibits in a museum. Each would offer us a beginning, a foundation, and extend a series from that point until it reaches – and indeed explains and defines – "us," but we would inevitably find this version of ourselves strange. This historical "us" seems to anticipate who we are. It offers a sense of community and purpose, but, oddly, it is a version of ourselves that arrives before we do. It claims to anticipate who we are. But the closer we look, the more the resemblance fades. We begin to see the gaps and spaces in its history, those moments left unaccounted for when nothing seemingly happens, and we are left feeling somehow outside of this version of "us." We can't seem to fit our own experiences into this historical outline and so, for the most part, we continue on by not looking back. Once this "us" is accepted as our foundation, time is ordered according to a set mode of historical reason whose axioms are causality, continuity, and progress. These axioms set the *how* of historical time, its *modus openendi*, but its orientation is set by the fictions of beginning and end. By accepting this image of history, we trade in our historical imagination, with all of its questions, possibilities, and risks, for a sense of comfort and security that is, when we actually begin to stop and look at it, empty.

This is, of course, a misconception of what history has to offer us; it is the stuff of historicism, but it is nonetheless a common misconception. How could we begin to challenge this image of history? We could begin by refusing the necessity of the progression itself. The axioms of causality, continuity, and progress are actually dependent on the fictional co-ordinates of beginning and end. The series is, after all, not what *had* to occur. Nor are the connections between events *necessarily* causal.[53] While these are neither novel nor controversial

53 The kind of *contingency* I have in mind here is not strictly blind per se (i.e., I am not making an a priori truth claim about reality). This would, to my mind, run too far down the road of the *via negativa* and offer the kind of impossible picture that Hegel rightly ridiculed as being "the night in which all cows are black." G.W.F. Hegel, *Phenomenology of Spirit*, trans. A.V. Miller (Oxford: Oxford University Press, 1997) at 9. My own view on historical interpretation hews closely to §6.41 of Wittgenstein's *Tractatus*. As he puts it, "The sense of the world must lie outside the world. *In* the world everything is as it is and happens as it does happen. In it there is no value – and if there were, it would be of no value. If there is a value which is of value, it must lie outside all happening and being-so. For all happening and being-so is accidental. What makes it non-accidental cannot lie *in* the world, for otherwise this would again be accidental." Ludwig Wittgenstein, *Tractatus Logico-Philosophicus*, trans. C.K. Ogden (London: Routledge, 1981) at §6.41. Walter Benjamin's use of "constellations" explores a similar line of thought: "Ideas are to objects as constellations are to stars. This means, in the first place, that they are neither their concepts nor their laws. They do not contribute to the knowledge of phenomena, and in no way can the latter be criteria with which to judge the existence of ideas." Walter Benjamin, *The Origin of German Tragic Drama*, trans. John

propositions, as soon as we begin to apply them to the foundations of law we find ourselves confronted with the sternest of warnings.

In the *Metaphysics of Morals* Kant argues that questioning the historical origins of authority is, oddly, both pointless and a punishable offence akin to treason.[54] He argues that it is pointless because there is nothing to find. After all, he reminds us, "savages draw up no record of their submission to law."[55]

Osborne (New York: Verso, 1998) at 34. Benjamin draws out the consequences of this in *Arcades Project*, which he conceived of as "an experiment in the technique of awakening," or again, "an attempt to become aware of the dialectical – the Copernican – turn of remembrance." He goes on to define this "Copernican revolution in historical perception" by contrasting the former approach to history, which "thought that a fixed point had been found in 'what had been,' and one saw the present engaged in tentatively concentrating the forces of knowledge on this ground," with his notion of awakening and remembrance, which overturns the former model as "the facts become something that just now first happened to us, first struck us; to establish them is the affair of memory. Indeed, awakening is the great exemplar of memory; the occasion on which it is given to us to remember what is closest, tritest, most obvious ... There is a not-yet-conscious knowledge of what has been: its advancement has the structure of awakening." Benjamin, *Arcades Project* at 388–9. There is a family resemblance between Benjamin's "technique of awakening" and the way that Wittgenstein drives home the force of the disjunction between sense/object that he notes in the *Tractatus* in the *Philosophical Investigations* in remarks like §131 when he states that we can only avoid "ineptness or emptiness in our assertions ... by presenting the model as what it is, as an object of comparison – as, so to speak, a measuring-rod; not as a preconceived idea to which reality *must* correspond." Wittgenstein, *Philosophical Investigations* at §131. This is why he states that it may seem as if his form of investigation destroys everything interesting, but this is not the case, for what is being destroyed "is nothing but houses of cards and we are clearing up the ground on which they stood" (§118). What is difficult in this investigation is not some specialized or technical form of knowledge, but "the contrast between the understanding of the subject and what most people want to see. Because of this the very things that are most obvious can become the most difficult to understand. What has to be overcome is not a difficulty of the intellect, but of the will." Ludwig Wittgenstein, *Philosophical Occasions, 1912–1951*, ed. J. Klagge and A. Nordmann (Indianapolis: Hackett, 1993) at 161. For an excellent account of the ethical implications of Wittgenstein's approach, see Oskari Kuusela, *The Struggle against Dogmatism: Wittgenstein and the Concept of Philosophy* (Cambridge, MA: Harvard University Press, 2008).

54 Kant, *Metaphysics of Morals* at 111–12 and 136.

55 Ibid. at 112. It is interesting to note that Kant's statement here is in direct tension with his own account of the settlement of "newly discovered lands" (at 121). Here he maintains "settlement may not take place by force but only by contract" and furthermore that the contract cannot "take advantage of the ignorance of those inhabitants with respect to ceding their lands" (at 122). This is then followed by a very curious remark where Kant acknowledges that it is possible to argue that this standard for legitimate settlement of lands could be taken to mean that "the whole earth would still be in a lawless condition," but he rejects this claim by stating, "This consideration can no more annul that condition of right than can the pretext of revolutionaries within a state" (at 122). This connection between the legitimate settlement of lands and the legitimate means of changing a constitutional order places Indigenous peoples whose lands have been taken by force and fraud in a rather curious position: are

Pascal also characterizes such an inquiry as pointless; the law is simply law, there is nothing more to see: "It is self-contained, it is the law and nothing more. Whoever wanted to examine the reason for this would find it so feeble and lightweight that, if he were unaccustomed to contemplating the feats of human imagination, he would marvel that in a century it had accumulated so much pomp and reverence."[56]

But this "feeble and lightweight" answer is not without effect. It is, at least potentially, revolutionary. In this sense it has much in common with the child's observation in "The Emperor's New Clothes": "But he isn't wearing anything at all!" On the one hand it is a simple and obvious fact – the emperor is naked – but whatever comical effect this has is quite soon eclipsed by the troubling, terrorizing fact that everyone knew this and continued on "as if" they did not.

Here, I would argue, we begin to uncover the importance of history for our understanding of the relationship between law and legitimacy. History spans the gap between the empty truth and the "as if." It can serve as a kind of magical, and indeed invaluable, tool for grounding the relationship between law and

---

they forbidden from inquiring into the foundation of the settler state? This would not make sense, as it would mean that Kant's requirement for legitimate settlement is little more than a theoretical requirement that can be jumped over if the colonizing power establishes de facto control. James Tully suggested to me that the source of this muddle is the limited frame within which Kant places Indigenous peoples (his comments about Tahitians in his *Reviews of Herder's Ideas on the Philosophy of the History of Mankind* come to mind; see Kant, *Political Writings* at 219–20). As Tully puts it, "Indigenous people have 'sociality' but not 'legality.' They are by definition 'lawless'" (personal communication, 4 April 2018). This is clearly evident in a footnote from *Perpetual Peace* where he maintains that

> man (or an individual people) in a mere state of nature robs me of any such security and injures me by virtue of this very state in which he coexists with me. He may not have injured me actively, but he does injure me by the very lawlessness of his state, for he is a permanent threat to me, and I can require him either to enter into a common lawful state along with me or to move away from my vicinity. Thus the postulate on which all the following articles are based is that all men who can at all influence one another must adhere to some kind of civil constitution. (Kant, *Political Writings* at 98; emphasis added)

This means that what Kant has in mind here is that Indigenous peoples can either consent to cede their lands and accept subjection to colonial or imperial law or remove themselves from the territory being colonized. This leaves them with the same kind of *false choice* that the robber's dilemma presents to us. This point is clearly set out in Kant's response to his reviewer in the *Metaphysics of Morals* when he states that it is the "actual deed (taking control)" that serves as the "condition and basis for a right," and that "the mere idea of sovereignty over a people constrains me, as belonging to the people, to obey without investigating the right that is claimed" (at 137).

56 Blaise Pascal, *Pensées and Other Writings*, ed. Anthony Levi and trans. Honor Levi (New York: Oxford University Press, 1995) at 24.

authority. In this role its job is to make effects appear "as if" they were causes.[57] In doing so it provides the lawgiver with authority, but, as Rousseau notes, it is not the authority of reason. It is of a different order altogether, as it can "compel without violence and persuade without convincing."[58] Its power is as miraculous as it is fragile. The lawgiver mixes wisdom with sleight-of-hand and so blurs the boundary between legislator and charlatan.[59] No matter how beautiful its descriptions or astounding its logical acrobatics, the legislator's account remains, like that of the charlatan, a work of fiction. It is always grounded elsewhere. It requires access to the "there" and "then" as they never were – a state of nature, utopia, a social contract – but we are asked to not examine the details of the account too closely. This fiction is, after all, the very basis of the legislator's claim to the law; it forms the foundation of law. If the legislator is to retain the legitimacy of the legal order, its fictional foundation must be maintained; it provides the appearance of necessity. It is this "as if" that holds the progressive or, to be somewhat more specific, teleological line of historical narrative together. This leaves it vulnerable to the question of the "here" and "now" (or, to use Benjamin's phrase, to the "technique of awakening").[60] And, as Skinner's work has so clearly demonstrated, to the "contingencies of our local history and social structure."[61]

This is precisely what "The Emperor's New Clothes" so clearly illustrates. The empty truth of the relationship between law and legitimacy is open for all to see. What does this mean? Are Kant, Pascal, Rousseau, and the host of others who repeat this warning correct? Is this empty truth simply too dangerous? Is it something that only fools, demagogues, and would-be tyrants pursue? Do we need to treat the fiction of foundation as if it were a genuine and eternal truth? By doing so, do we not lose the distinction between rule *by* law and the rule *of* law? The force of this distinction can be seen in how the line between arbitrary and legitimate authority is articulated, as the modern notion of the state takes shape.[62]

In thinkers like Hobbes, Grotius, Pufendorf, Locke, Rousseau, Mill, Hume, and Kant (to name a few) we find a shifting constellation of political concepts (e.g., the social contract, natural law, popular sovereignty, the right of rebellion,

57 Jean-Jacques Rousseau, *The Basic Political Writings*, trans. Donald A. Cress (Indianapolis: Hackett Publishing, 1987) at 164.

58 Ibid.

59 Geoffrey Bennington, *Legislations* (New York: Verso, 1994) at 222; Bonnie Honig, *Emergency Politics: Paradox, Law, Democracy* (Princeton, NJ: Princeton University Press, 2009) at 21–6.

60 Benjamin, *Arcades Project* at 388. Also for an exemplary use of Benjamin's notion of history, see Sayer, *Prague, Capital of the Twentieth Century*.

61 Skinner, *Visions of Politics* at 89.

62 My view of this history is greatly indebted to Quentin Skinner's work in his magisterial *Foundations of Modern Political Thought*.

the rule of law, etc.) that are deployed in an attempt to define the connection between law and the legitimating conditions of its authority. But this line was not consistently maintained – to what was often curiously circumscribed to the *civilized* world. Beyond this uncertain and shifting border, sovereign power was – according to many of the same political thinkers – free of the problem of legitimizing its authority. An ad hoc assortment of legal fictions and philosophical arguments were marshalled to explain how the conditions of legitimacy within the European world and those outside it could be categorically distinct. Whether it was the divine right that (supposedly) flowed through the Bulls of Donation to divide the New World between the Kingdoms of Spain and Portugal[63]; the cobbled-together modifications to the law of occupation (i.e., conquest, cession by contract, *res nullius*, and its nineteenth-century cousin *terra nullius*[64]); the agricultural thesis that Locke infamously refined to justify the taking of "vacant" or "waste" in America[65]; and the "standard of civilization," which J.S. Mill and the vast majority of his contemporaries accepted as a secure analytic foundation for the rapid expansion of the colonial enterprises of the European imperial powers during the long nineteenth century.[66]

This is just a small sample of the elaborate conceptual acrobatics that European political and legal thinkers performed in order to respond to the challenge of legitimacy. Skinner helpfully draws out the nature of this challenge: "What it is possible to do in politics is generally limited by what it is possible to legitimise. What you can hope to legitimise, however, depends on what courses of action you can plausibly range under existing normative principles. But this implies that, even if your professed principles never operate as your motives, but only as rationalisations of your behaviour, they will nevertheless help shape and limit what lines of action you can successfully pursue."[67]

What this so clearly points out is that "words are also deeds."[68] With this in mind, what would it mean if we were to follow the advice of Kant and company and turn a blind eye to the historical foundations of authority? Can we count on the promise that what "was introduced once without reason" will become

63 See Anthony Pagden, *Lords of All the World: Ideologies of Empire in Spain, Brittan and France c. 1500–c. 1800* (New Haven, CT: Yale University Press, 1995).

64 See Andrew Fitzmaurice's detailed account of the use of both *res nullius* and *terra nullius* in his excellent *Sovereignty, Property and Empire*.

65 For two detailed accounts of Locke's arguments about property, see James Tully, *A Discourse on Property: John Locke and His Adversaries* (Cambridge: Cambridge University Press, 1982); and Barbara Arneil, *John Locke and America: The Defense of English Colonialism* (Oxford: Clarendon, 1996).

66 See Jennifer Pitts, *A Turn to Empire: The Rise of Imperial Liberalism in Britain and France* (Princeton, NJ: Princeton University Press, 2005); and Pitts, *Boundaries*.

67 Quintin Skinner, *Liberty before Liberalism* (Cambridge: Cambridge University Press, 1998) at 105.

68 Wittgenstein, *Philosophical Investigations* at §546.

reasonable or, as the well-worn common law metaphor holds, that the law will "work itself pure" on a case-by-case basis?[69] In order to do so it seems that we must make use of a kind of *wilful blindness* to the relationship between law and legitimacy and commit ourselves to making history serve and maintain the idols of "foundation" and "progress."

If we fail at this, then it seems to me that we have to find some way of coming to terms with foundations that amount to little more than a hodgepodge of racist legal fictions and self-serving standards of measure. We could attempt to find shelter in Hume's pessimistic claim that all foundations are effectively the same, as "the few cases where consent may seem to have taken place, it was commonly so irregular, so confined, or so much intermixed either with fraud or violence that it cannot have any great authority."[70] This may seem to offer an escape, but it provides us only with an explanation of the de facto foundations of authority. It says nothing about the normative or *de jure* foundations. The argument relies on the reader inferring that the normative question of legitimacy is somehow resolved via a description of historical facts (i.e., Hume fails to follow the requirements of one of his most famous arguments, that you cannot derive *ought* from *is*).[71] Does this mean that wilful blindness (and the bad faith that necessarily accompanies it) is the only available approach? Is there a way to understand law not from the fixed and unquestionable foundations of "there" and "then" provided by historical fiction? I suggest there is another approach to the question of legitimacy and the historical foundations of authority.[72] One that refuses the insistent claim that inquiry "into the *historical warrant* of the mechanism of government" is, at one and the same time, pointless and treasonous and takes seriously the possibility opened up by the child's exclamation, "But he isn't wearing any clothes."[73]

---

69 Pascal, *Pensées* at 24.

70 David Hume, *A Treatise of Human Nature*, ed. David Fate Norton and Mary J. Norton (Oxford: Oxford University Press, 2000) at 354.

71 James Tully sets out this argument in "Consent, Hegemony, and Dissent in Treaty Negotiations," in *Between Consenting Peoples: Political Community and the Meaning of Consent*, ed. Jeremy Webber and Colin Macleod (Vancouver: UBC Press, 2010) at 241.

72 Like Skinner, I find the answer to this question of our approach to the past in Michel Foucault's contention that "the history which bears and determines us has the form of a war." Skinner, *Visions of Politics* at 177. This is what, to my mind, connects what I have been referring to as the "empty truth" of the here and now to the study of the past: the locally contested and contingent reality that they both share.

73 Kant, *Metaphysics of Morals* at 111. I suggest that the substance of the child's charge can be interpreted as calling attention to the fact that while there is a sovereign (in the de facto sense), his claims to legitimate or *de jure* authority (i.e., clothing) are not absolute. The magical suit that the sovereign desires is this kind of uncontestable claim to *de jure* authority, which actually serves as an exposure of limitations and so an opportunity for contestation. This reading also provides a helpful way to view the role of the courts, as while they cannot use their jurisdiction to void the de facto claims of the sovereign, they can use it to interpret what legal consequences flow from that claim.

I believe that we can begin to see another angle of approach to this problem in Tully's defence of the practices of consent *contra* Hume: "Just because a particular practice of consent, such as a treaty with non-European authority, is surrounded by force and fraud, it does not follow that the practice of treaty making loses its authority.... If anything, the very fact that one can distinguish between a consensual treaty and force and fraud strengthens, rather than weakens, the practice of treaty making."[74]

This retrieval of practices of consent helps us to see that we are not painted into a corner by the force and fraud of colonialism. The Supreme Court also relies on practices of consent to legitimate authority in the *Secession Reference*. "The Constitution is not a straitjacket. Even a brief review of our constitutional history demonstrates periods of momentous and dramatic change. Our democratic institutions necessarily accommodate a continuous process of discussion and evolution, which is reflected in the constitutional right of each participant in the federation to initiate constitutional change. This right implies a reciprocal duty on the other participants to engage in discussions to address any legitimate initiative to change the constitutional order."[75]

This helps to remind us that that constitutional structures are not and cannot be absolute (in the sense of being unquestionable). It clears the ground to make our way through the "overlapping and interdependent terrain of constitutionalism" via negotiation, mutual recognition, and consent.[76] It also shows us that openly investigating the historical foundation of authority does not spell the end of sovereignty and, by extension, legal order (pace Kant and Hume). Rather, it is a move away from the unquestionable or absolute form of sovereignty (whose history is intimately bound up with the development of European imperial colonialism) and towards what Tully refers to as sovereignty in the "non-absolute sense," which is based on "the authority of a culturally diverse people or association of peoples to govern themselves by their own laws and ways free from external subordination."[77]

1.4 Problem of Reconciliation as Problem of Foundations

The problem of reconciliation is a difficult one. If we approach it via the jurisprudence, our path simply leads us in circles around the concept of sovereignty.[78] There is a labyrinthine quality to it. This is because sovereignty acts as a hidden

74 Tully, *Consent, Hegemony, and Dissent* at 238.

75 *Reference re Secession of Quebec* at para. 150.

76 Tully, *Strange Multiplicity at* 195.

77 Ibid.

78 Sovereignty resides in the jurisprudence, much like gravity: it can be seen only indirectly via its effects on a constellation of related concepts (title, jurisdiction, extinguishment,

premise that does not allow us to inquire further.[79] This limitation in the jurisprudence is reminiscent of Kant's argument that any inquiry into the historical origins of the authority of the sovereign should be a punishable offence.[80] He goes so far as to state that such an inquiry is pointless, because "we can already gather from the nature of uncivilized men that they were originally subjected to it by force."[81] This response assumes a narrow conception of the investigative possibilities that the historical question opens up. It is not simply a matter of whether the foundational act was accomplished by contractual consent or brute force (*contra* Hume/Kant), but what *de jure* consequences flow from the *de facto* sovereignty. Simply dismissing the problem of foundation or legally forbidding the investigation into the historical warrant of authority does not resolve the matter. It is about as effective as the police telling curious bystanders that "there is nothing to see here," when everyone can tell that there clearly is. As this technique fails, various *innovating ideologists* (to borrow Skinner's helpful term) – who are busily attempting to shore up the legitimacy of the colonial projects of the European imperial powers – attempt to fill the gap by making use of the civilized/uncivilized distinction, which allows an act of force to appear to be necessary. The effectiveness of this move trades on the distinction

---

infringement, and the "diminished" right of self-government). See Borrows, "Soveignty's Alchemy" at 562, 569.

79 There is a kind of logic that is reminiscent of the folktale of Bluebeard at play here: a castle is opened up for us as the reader, and we are welcome to explore each and every room with the exception of one. This excluded room is an open secret. We are simply told not to use our key to go inside. Once we violate this prohibition and enter the room, we see its simple truth: it conceals violence without measure or proportion. We also see that the violence and death that it hides (which is in a certain way, flat, or banal, as there is no real magic to be seen here) is, at least to my mind, the actual foundation of the castle and the explanation of the bizarre colour that marks the owner of the castle. The name of the door within the castle is, for the purposes of my analogy, "Sovereignty." This *Bluebeard logic* can be found in any number of political thinkers who propose to offer a system of thought that explains away the foundations of law by marking off a "state of nature" (or other open secret) in which the rules are paradoxically presented as both entirely a part of and entirely separate from the rest of the system. This Bluebeard logic can be found in any number of political thinkers (see Kant, below, for instance).

80 Kant, *Metaphysics of Morals* at 111–12, 136. Legal positivism has implicitly taken Kant's imperative as its foundation. This conceptual commitment provides it with its provincial and imperial determination. It also makes it effectively useless when attempting to understand legal systems in settler-colonial contexts. It assumes sovereignty via the assumption of a singular community, and if that community cannot be said to exist in any meaningful way, then it remains as a conceptual utopia projected into the future. In either case, it offers us a vision of law built upon the kind of justice that would have a river as its boundary. Simply put, it becomes little more than the preferred view of the colonizer.

81 Ibid. at 112.

being analytic (and so beyond the possibility of contestation). If it is accepted as such, it effectively blocks our view of the problem altogether.

In order to get past this barrier and address the source of this distinction, we have to change tactics and find a way to question the rules that have formed the game. We need what Wittgenstein refers to as a "perspicuous representation" in order to find our way about: "A main source of our failure to understand is that we do not *command a clear view* of the use of our words. – Our grammar is lacking in just this sort of perspicuity. A perspicuous representation produces just that understanding which consists in 'seeing connexions.'"[82] This entails a departure from the standard form of legal scholarship that would chart its course in and through the positive sources of the law alone. While this scholarship is necessary in order to engage in the language game of reconciliation (a game that requires all participants to position themselves within the "authority" of the law of one party while confining the other's law to the rules of evidence[83]), it constrains the scope of possible inquiry.[84]

The form of investigation that I am proposing rests more on a standpoint than on any particular thesis. Foucault summarizes this standpoint in a lecture he delivered at the College de France:

> It is an attitude that consists, first, in thinking that no power goes without saying, that no power, of whatever kind, is obvious or inevitable, and that consequently no power warrants being taken for granted. Power has no intrinsic legitimacy. On the

---

82 Wittgenstein, *Philosophical Investigations* at §122 (emphasis in original). For more on the concept of perspicuous representation (*übersichtliche Darstellung*), which can also be translated as "a surveyable representation," see G.P. Baker and P.M.S. Hacker, "Surveyability and Surveyable Representations," in *Wittgenstein: Understanding and Meaning*, vol. 1, *An Analytical Commentary on the Philosophical Investigations. Part I: Essays*, 2nd ed. (Oxford: Blackwell, 2009).

83 I am merely pointing to how in the current game of reconciliation, one jumps over the question of the legal status of Indigenous peoples (i.e., are they subjects of the Crown or nations in a federal-like relationship?), assumes that they are a sui generis set of subjects, and proceeds to accept the Crown's de facto claim to sovereignty add to it the *de jure* attributes of legislative authority and underlying title. They then make a space for the Indigenous perspective, but this subjects their legal orders to the rules of evidence and judicial discretion. This way of setting the board (to return to the analogy of a game) clearly handicaps Indigenous peoples and skews results in favour of the Crown. This fixing of the constitutional rules compromises the role of the courts, as it hews so closely to the arbitrary claims of the sovereign that it becomes difficult to tell them apart. As Lord Hewart CJ so clearly put it in *R v. Sussex Justices, ex parte McCarthy*, [1924] 1 KB 256, [1923] All ER 233, natural justice requires that "justice must not only be done, but must be seen to be done."

84 In *Mitchell* the Court, quoting from *Delgamuukw*, found it "imperative that the laws of evidence operate to ensure that the aboriginal perspective is 'given due weight by the courts'" (*Mitchell* at para. 37).

> basis of this position, the approach consists in wondering, that being the case, what of the subject and relations of knowledge do we dispense with when we consider no power to be founded either by right or necessity, that all power only ever rests on the contingency and fragility of history, that the social contract is a bluff and civil society a children's story, [and] that there is no universal, immediate, and obvious right that can everywhere and always support any kind of relation of power. Let us say that if the great philosophical approach consists in establishing a methodical doubt that suspends every certainty, the small lateral approach on the opposite track that I am proposing consists in trying to bring into play in a systematic way, not the suspension of every certainty, but the non-necessity of all power of whatever kind.[85]

Historicism attempts to provide power with a narrative that can convert the contingency of its descent into necessity and colour over the violence of its actions with the aura of progress. This standpoint, or "small lateral approach," is the first step of this investigation precisely because it is a refusal to see the past as a closed and predetermined set of facts that form the basis of power and authority; it is a rejection of the heraldry of historicism. It is a search for the descent of power, its genealogy without recourse to the fiction of divine origins. As Foucault writes, "The search for descent is not the erecting of foundations: on the contrary, it disturbs what was previously thought immobile; it fragments what was thought unified; it shows the heterogeneity of what was imagined consistent with itself."[86]

This search, or as I have chosen to call it, "investigation," does not simply uncover the way in which the rules of the language game of reconciliation came to be or how they are internally inconsistent. If this was the limit, then all that would be required would be to show that the form of reconciliation offered by the courts takes place in and through the "active forgetting" of the problem of sovereignty and that this can be seen in its use of historicism and the metaphor of the ship of state. If we stopped at this point, it could well be seen as "erecting a foundation" or perhaps simply uncovering the Crown machinery for the reader to marvel at.[87] As Wittgenstein put it, "All testing, all confirmation and

---

85 Michele Foucault, *On the Government of the Living (Lectures at the Collège de France, 1979–1980)*, trans. Graham Burchell (New York: Palgrave Macmillan, 2014) at 77–8.

86 Michele Foucault, "Nietzsche, Genealogy, History," in *The Foucault Reader*, ed. Paul Rabinow (New York: Pantheon, 1991) at 81.

87 I am grateful to James Tully for his suggestion that I refer to the combination of reconciliation, the forgetting of sovereignty through historicism and the ship of state, and the concurrent colonial governance practised under the *Indian Act* as the "Crown machinery." I will use the term (as well as the more singular variation "Crown machine") throughout the book to refer to a series of related practices and legal-philosophical arguments that are used to justify and legitimate the actions of the Crown in relation to Aboriginal peoples. This set of practices and arguments is subject to an ad hoc process of amendment that helps it recalibrate in relation to the continuous resistance of Aboriginal peoples. As a result, it

disconfirmation of a hypothesis takes place already within a system. And this system is not a more or less arbitrary and doubtful point of departure for all our arguments: no it belongs to the essence of what we call an argument. The system is not so much the point of departure, as the elements in which arguments have their life."[88]

If the investigation were to present the Crown machinery as the point of departure (viz. as an unquestionable and fixed point), it would present it as the rules of all possible games and not simply one of a multitude. Wittgenstein captures the difficulty here when he says, "It is so difficult to find the beginning. Or, better: it is difficult to begin at the beginning. And not try to go further back."[89] By this I understand him to mean that there is a temptation to continue on towards an absolute beginning, as it would then provide an absolute foundation, which would be outside of all possible language games (this is the kind of

---

has more than one aspect. Like Jastrow's picture of the duck-rabbit in the *Philosophical Investigations*, it offers a picture that has two categorically different aspects (see Wittgenstein, *Philosophical Investigations* at 165–6). What changes is not the *object* of perception or its organization, but the *way* we see it (i.e., it is not a seeing *that* but a seeing *as*). Thus, from one perspective the "Crown machine" appears to be logically organized, efficient, continuous, and impersonal (the image that the Crown wants to project – the ideal sovereign governing machine). The *Bluebeard logic* I referred to earlier is deployed to stabilize this aspect and present it as the only possible one: it is a kind of warning (i.e., do not enter, nothing to see, etc.) that is also a paradoxical concession of the very contingency of what it claims is necessary. It functions like the curtain in the Wizard of Oz (i.e., it preserves the magical illusion of sovereign power by concealing the ordinary conman on the other side). Whereas from another it is a higgledy-piggledy assortment of components that have been slapped together with very little rhyme or reason and is prone to unexpected transformations. From this aspect it is not a *machine*, but an *assemblage* – or to use Wittgenstein's register, a "language game" (i.e., a *contingent social practice* that can by altered by "acting otherwise"). Foucault's use of the term *dispositif* – which is variously translated as "device," "apparatus," "construction," "machinery," and "deployment" – draws out what I am getting at with "Crown machinery" and "Crown machine." As he articulates in an interview from 1977, "What I'm trying to pick out with this term is, firstly, a thoroughly heterogeneous ensemble consisting of discourses, institutions, architectural forms, regulatory decisions, laws, administrative measures, scientific statements, philosophical, moral and philanthropic propositions – in short, the said as much as the unsaid. Such are the elements of the apparatus. The apparatus itself is the system of relations that can be established between these elements." See Michel Foucault, *Power/Knowledge: Selected Interviews and Other Writings, 1972–1977*, ed. Colin Gordon (New York: Pantheon, 1980) at 194. This aspect is not *discovered* by the philosopher alone but is seen in and through the practices of freedom where civic actors are agonistically engaged. For an instructive account of this approach, see the chapter entitled "Public Philosophy as a Critical Activity," in *Public Philosophy in a New Key*, vol. 1, *Democracy and Civic Freedom*, ed. James Tully (Cambridge: Cambridge University Press, 2008).

88 Ludwig Wittgenstein, *On Certainty*, ed. G.E.M. Anscombe and G.H. von Wright (Oxford: Blackwell, 1974) at §105.

89 Ibid.

philosophical problem that Wittgenstein claims to arise when "language goes on holiday").[90] After all, historicism can accept the bloodiest of foundations for the state and allow it to "work itself pure" over the course of time.[91] My investigation does not stop at simply uncovering the historical contingency of the Crown machinery or the illegitimacy of the power that it produces. Rather, the point is that fragmentation and heterogeneity expose both the possibility of new moves in the language game of reconciliation and the "acting otherwise" that was always already taking place. As I see it, these new moves continually stem from the ground that resides both outside and hidden within the language game of reconciliation. The courts have termed this ground the "Aboriginal perspective," but it is much more than simply one side of the game of reconciliation. Rather, it extends beyond the confines of the game of reconciliation to the discourses and practices of law and governance (we could term these Indigenous legal and political orders) that are otherwise than the machinery of the Crown. It is not a single perspective, but a plurality of perspectives. And these perspectives offer another way of seeing the image of the ship of state and its claims to universal history. In place of the uniformity and unity – those qualities that are so firmly fixed in the language of modern constitutionalism – of Binnie J's forward-facing canoe, there is the strange multiplicity of Bill Reid's The *Spirit of Haida Gwaii.*[92] In this image the focus is no longer on the composition of the canoe itself (i.e., on how the "historic elements of wood, iron and canvas" form a singular whole[93]), but on the irreducible diversity of its passengers. Nor is the focus on moving forward, toward the future, and refusing to look back towards the past. Reid's epigram offers another perspective to counter this restless and harried movement away from the past: "The boat that goes on forever anchored in the same place."[94] It accepts that we are all here to stay, but this does not mean that we all share the same perspective. In this anchored position there is no magic circle of foundation. No Bluebeard logic forbidding others from questioning the historical warrant of sovereign authority.[95] No picture of universal history with its stages of civilization that can crown the violence of

90 Cavell, *Claim of Reason* at 226; Wittgenstein, *Philosophical Investigations* at §38.

91 Hegel's account of history – which has many similarities with Kant's – holds that the history of the world is not the "theater of happiness," but a "slaughter bench," which then serves to justify the unlimited violence of heroic vengeance. G.W.F. Hegel, *Philosophy of History*, trans. J. Sibree (New York: Prometheus Books, 1991) at 21, 26–7; Hegel, *Elements of the Philosophy of Right* at §93 and §350; and Hegel, *Lectures on the Philosophy of World History*, trans. H.B. Nisbet (Cambridge: Cambridge University Press, 1980) at 68–93.

92 See Tully, *Strange Multiplicity* at 17–29.

93 A perspective that is characteristic of modern constitutionalism and captured by the motto of the United States, *E Pluribus Unum* (Out of many, one). See *Mitchell* at 130.

94 Tully, *Strange Multiplicity* at 202.

95 I define my use of the term *Bluebeard logic* above, in note 79.

colonization as fate. As Tully puts it, "The answer given by the black canoe is that, although the passengers vie and negotiate for recognition and power, they always do so in accord with the three conventions [viz. mutual recognition, consent and continuity]."[96]

From this it follows that "we must listen to the description of each member of the crew, and indeed enter into conversation ourselves, in order to find the redescriptions acceptable to all which mediate the differences we wish each other to recognize."[97]

Their strength comes from the plurality of their perspectives, the overlapping histories that they draw on, and not from a single, unquestionable – and so uncontestable – foundation.

If we are to find a meaningful reconciliation – and not simply one that is assigned by the logic of force that resides behind the unquestioned assumption of sovereignty – then we will need to address the history of sovereignty without assuming its foundation. The problem of reconciliation and the question of sovereignty are constitutively related. As the authors of the *Royal Commission on Aboriginal Peoples* state, "The major and underlying paradox, and the key to unraveling the others, lies in the unique way Indian sovereignty has been conceptualized in Canadian legal and constitutional thinking."[98]

This paradox is, in my view, the problem of reconciliation. The work to undo it begins with following the lines of descent and association that underlie the legal conceptualization of Indigenous sovereignty. A major part of this lineage finds legislative expression in the *Indian Act*. In particular, in how the Act and its associated institutions operate to control the basic elements of self-government, such as membership, political structure, and jurisdiction.

1.5 A Genealogy of the *Indian Act*

The history of this legislation is carried in its name: "Indian," this puzzling proper noun that collects together a set of peoples whose only commonality is the fact that the names they chose for themselves were buried under the weight of a name that they were assigned through legislation. The purpose of the *Indian Act* is itself puzzling. If it succeeded on its own terms (by "civilizing" or "enfranchising"), there would be no more "Indians" within the jurisdictional

96 Ibid. at 212.

97 Ibid. at 111.

98 *Report of the Royal Commission on Aboriginal Peoples*, vol. 1, *Looking Forward Looking Back*, part 2, "False Assumptions and a Failed Relationship" (Ottawa: Canada Communication Group, 1996) at 239.

boundaries of Canada, only citizens.[99] The *Indian Act* was designed as a temporary measure. It was designed to cancel out its object. But what of its constitutional basis? While it is clear that s. 91(24) of the *Constitution Act, 1867* grants the federal government exclusive jurisdiction over *Indians, and Lands Reserved for Indians*, where does the authority to name an entire group of people as a constitutional head of power come from?[100] Here we must enter the magic circle of legal fictions.[101] It is the so-called doctrine of discovery – with its associated

---

99 *Canada* is another puzzling proper noun, as it comes from the Iroquoian word for "village" or "settlement." What can it mean to adopt a name from another people for a state in which they cannot name themselves? There is a kind of paradoxical inversion of hospitality here.

100 The formal legal response to this is the legislative supremacy of the imperial Parliament, but there is also a normative sense that I am drawing on. We could think of the normative sense as asking if it is possible to legitimate this kind of use of sovereign power. There are a number of possible responses that can be assembled by fishing around in the European colonial armoury of principles, doctrines, concepts, standards, and fictions, but, as I have argued, this higgledy-piggledy assortment can really provide only a temporary diversion. My primary point here is that the Canadian legal imagination has, to my view, become far too accustomed to reading s. 91(24) as a normal feature of our constitutional order. If we pause for a moment and really consider the normative stakes of this provision, I believe that we see something that should deeply trouble us. We can begin with the question of what kind of legal and political consequences flow into the constitutional order by accepting this kind of unilateral claim of near absolute sovereignty over multiple nations of people and their lands into the constitutional order.

101 It is necessary to point out that the Crown has consistently (and unilaterally) interpreted the meaning of s. 91(24) in its favour. A clear example can be seen when we look at how the Crown exercised power over those whom they did not explicitly recognize as being "Indian" (i.e., the Métis and Inuit). Although excluded from the *Indian Act*, this formal exclusion did not mean that the Métis and Inuit were free from unilateral Crown interference. Rather, the basic pattern has been to act either as if s. 91(24) licensed power over these peoples, or that no licence was needed because they were uncivilized, but it was a power without clear lines of responsibility. This meant that when it suited their purposes, the Crown would claim that these peoples were not Indians for the purpose of s. 91(24) (an argument that failed in *Reference whether "Indians" includes "Eskimo,"* [1939] SCR 104, and again in *Daniels v. Canada (Indian Affairs and Northern Development)*, [2016] 1 SCR 99) and/or the *Indian Act* (which formally excludes the Inuit in s. 4(1)). The history of these exclusions parallels the one that I am working through in this book, in that these divisions are tightly bound up with the colonial legal project that set out to legally define who Indians were, so as to limit (and ultimately extinguish) their rights to their lands. The removal of this layer of unilateral settler law is long overdue. Its removal does not mean that there will not be distinctions between the nations that have continued to exist under this system; rather, it will shift the existing lines imposed by the settler-state system of legal recognition and open up further points of connection and overlap that can be negotiated by the nations themselves. My point here is that while s. 91(24) and the *Indian Act* creates a complicated set of inclusions and exclusions, they have affected all of the Aboriginal peoples of Canada (i.e., Indian, Inuit, and Métis). For more on legal fictions, see Borrows, *Alchemy*. There is an extensive body of literature on the legal doctrine of discovery and *terra nullius*: see Andrew Fitzmaurice, "The

fictions of *terra nullius,* discovery, and sovereignty – that grants the Crown this arbitrary power over "Indians." This fictional foundation is the only support for the relationship between the Crown and its "Indians."[102] The *Indian Act* is

---

Genealogy of Terra Nullius," *Australian Historical Studies* 38, no. 129 (2007): 1–15; Patrick Macklem, "What Is International Human Rights Law? Three Applications of a Distributive Account," *McGill Law Journal* 52 (2007): 575 at para. 36; Patrick Macklem, "First Nations Self-Government and the Borders of the Canadian Legal Imagination," *McGill Law Journal* 36 (1991): 399–406; and Tracey Lindberg, "The Doctrine of Discovery in Canada" and "Contemporary Canadian Resonance of an Imperial Doctrine," in *Discovering Indigenous Lands: The Doctrine of Discovery in the English Colonies,* ed. Robert J. Miller, Larissa Behrendt, and Tracey Lindberg (Oxford: Oxford University Press, 2010), 89–125, 126–70.

102 There is a relationship between the Crown and the Aboriginal peoples of Canada that is a nation-to-nation relationship, which is predicated on protecting them from the threats posed by colonists. This relationship is expressed in a number of documents, from the *Royal Proclamation,* 1763, to the Rupert's Land Order and the numbered treaties. See Kent McNeil, "Fiduciary Obligations and Federal Responsibility for the Aboriginal Peoples," in *Emerging Justice? Essays on Indigenous Rights in Canada and Australia,* 309–55 (Saskatoon, SK: University of Saskatchewan Native Law Centre, 2001). There are a number of ways in which this nation-to-nation relationship can be characterized, and it has been touched on in US jurisprudence in the Marshall Trilogy (in particular in *Worcester v. Georgia*) and a few Canadian cases – *Campbell et al v. AG BC/AG Cda & Nisga'a Nation et al,* 2000 BCSC 1123; and *R v. Sioui,* [1990] 1 SCR 1025, 1990 CanLII 103 (SCC). The key problem is that even in the post-*Constitution Act, 1982,* era, the presumption of Crown sovereignty has been assumed to further entail *legislative supremacy and underlying title.* As Dickson CJ states in *Sparrow,* "There was from the outset never any doubt that sovereignty and legislative power, and indeed the underlying title, to such lands vested in the Crown." *Sparrow* at para. 1103. There has been a shift away from this presumption since *Haida Nation* – as McLachlin CJ characterizes Crown sovereignty as a combination of an "assertion" and the "*de facto* control of land and resources" (para. 32) – but the actual consequences of this shift for Aboriginal self-government and Crown jurisdiction has yet to play out. As it stands, the Crown can still infringe on Aboriginal rights and title, and the *Indian Act* enables the Crown to set the terms of engagement in its favour, but these powers are subject to justification in the courts via s. 35. The presumption of Crown sovereignty may be showing signs of wear, but it is a fiction that still shapes the day-to-day reality of Aboriginal peoples. This is the straitjacket within the Canadian constitutional order; while the courts cannot use their jurisdiction to render the Crown's de facto claim to sovereignty null and void, they can use it to determine which legal consequences flow from it. As I have argued, Marshall CJ's reasoning from *Johnson v. M'Intosh,* to *Cherokee Nation v. Georgia,* and finally to *Worcester v. Georgia* can be seen as progressively working through the legal implications of the claim of sovereignty in order to find a balance between arbitrary sovereign power and the rule of law. Generally speaking, within the Canadian context this judicial process of working through or over (and over), the balance between sovereignty and law has moved from unilaterally assigning Indigenous peoples the incapacitated legal status of wards to the current position of sui generis minority with a set of constitutionally protected rights that are subject to unilateral infringement via judicially mediated procedures of justification. The problem is that the current position shares the same colonial foundations as the previous one. The step that the Canadian courts have yet to take is to interpret the Crown's claim to sovereignty in the

the legislative expression of this relationship: it is a type of emergency legislation without chronological limitations.[103] I specify that it is a "type" because it bears the basic hallmarks of emergency legislation (i.e., a high degree of administrative discretion coupled with a suspension of the rights and freedoms that characterize the "normal" constitutional order), but it is also dissimilar to emergency legislation. The object of the legislation is not an emergency. Its object is "Indians." As John Borrows states, "The *Indian Act* makes it easier to control us: where we live, how we choose leaders, how we live under those leaders, how we learn, how we trade, and what happens to our possessions and relations when we die."[104]

This control is not the stuff of "ancient grievances," but rather it is part of the present field of our experience. It forms an unavoidable but all too often overlooked part of the history of our present – a history that can be traced back to the (seemingly) "watertight" categorical separation between the legal and political standards applicable to the civilized and the uncivilized. An investigation into the problem of reconciliation must begin here – from the lived reality of this control – and proceed to trace out the contingent processes that have brought it into being.

"non-absolute sense" (i.e., that does not automatically entitle the Crown to legislative power and/or underlying title) and thereby clear the way for a form of sovereignty that is based on "the authority of a culturally diverse people or association of peoples to govern themselves by their own laws and ways free from external subordination." Tully, *Strange Multiplicity* at 195.

103 This is an intentionally provocative statement. Naturally, to fully substantiate my point would require an extensive treatment of the literature on emergency powers. My main point here is that the *Indian Act* is not normal law (as law is understood in a common law context). It does not base its legitimacy in the consent of those whom it governs. It establishes an administrative regime with unchecked discretionary powers over a set of individuals whom it recognizes only as wards or dependents. While there are a series of fiduciary obligations that the Crown has to Aboriginal peoples (that stem back to the *Royal Proclamation*, 1763), these obligations were subject to unilateral extinguishment by the imperial Crown, and following 1867 this power was vested in the federal Crown. Since the enactment of s. 35(1) of the *Constitution Act, 1982*, this authority has been restrained by the jurisprudence of the Court. The *Indian Act* is still active in this new context – and the vast discretion vested in the Crown remains in play – but the Crown has retreated, leaving a legal vacuum in place of vital self-governing bodies.

104 John Borrows, "Seven Generations, Seven Teachings," research paper for the National Centre for First Nations Governance (2008) at 5.

Part 2

A Genealogy of Reconciliation: Civilizing, Extinction, and Culturalism as the Discursive Foundations of the *Indian Act*

The multitude of poor, and yet strong people still increasing, they are to be transplanted into Countries not sufficiently inhabited: where neverthelesse, they are not to exterminate those they find there; but constrain them to inhabit closer together, and not range a great deal of ground, to snatch what they find; but to court each little Plot with art and labour, to give them their sustenance in due season. And when the world is overcharged with Inhabitants, then the last remedy is Warre; which provideth for every man, by Victory, or Death.

Thomas Hobbes, *Leviathan* (239)

Despotism is a legitimate mode of government in dealing with barbarians, provided the end be their improvement, and the means justified by actually effecting that end. Liberty, as a principle, has no application to any state of things anterior to the time when mankind have become capable of being improved by free and equal discussion.

J.S. Mill, *On Liberty* (9)

The history of conquest as well as of commercial companies and especially that of missions afford a melancholy and in some respects a laughable picture.... We shudder with abhorrence when we read the accounts of many European nations, who, sunk in the most dissolute voluptuousness and insensible pride have degenerated both in body and mind and no longer possess any capacity for enjoyment or compassion. They are full-blown bladders in human shape, lost to every noble and active pleasure, and in whose veins lurks avenging death.

J.G. Herder, *Outline of a Philosophy of the History of Man* (185)

My purpose in this chapter is to investigate the nineteenth-century discursive foundations of the *Indian Act*. I say "foundations" because, as with all colonial law, and indeed law itself, the origin is far from being simple or uniform. There is no one thing or moment that I can point to and say, "there is the foundation."

They are always plural, always pieced together from a number of different sources. This plurality is evidenced in a number of practices and processes ranging from the nature of law making, to the resistance of Indigenous peoples and the changing aims of the colonizer. By using the phrase "discursive foundations" what I am pointing to is a limited selection or sample of the work that nineteenth-century "innovating ideologists" like J.S. Mill and H.S. Maine (and others) put into play.[1] I am not attempting to argue that the work of the authors examined in this chapter were the sole (or even primary) source that the legislators who wrote the *Indian Act* relied on. Rather, I am making the more limited claim that these authors had such a wide-ranging resonance that they helped to inform the "social imaginary" of the British Empire in the nineteenth century and into the twentieth.[2] The arguments and principles that they furnished for the imperial project are not cut from whole cloth; they are versions, adaptations, and modifications of a criss-crossing and overlapping patchwork of recovered materials. This is not to minimize the impact of the "innovating ideologists" I have selected, but to show that they need to be situated within the historical context with "the prevailing moral language of the society in which they are acting."[3] What they do provide us with is some of the strongest versions of the kinds of arguments and principles that were marshalled to legitimize the *Indian Act* and the actions of the vast administrative structure that it empowers. These foundations are important; as Skinner reminds us, "Any principle that helps legitimise a course of action will … be among the enabling conditions of its occurrence."[4] Their importance is not simply that when they are set out before us in the present we are able to see the contradictions inherent in their design. After all, how can one do anything but marvel at the kind of political alchemy that J.S. Mill has in mind when he blithely states that the best way to lead others to liberty is through despotism? Uncovering these contradictions is doubtlessly a necessary part of our investigation, but it cannot stop there. If we were to stop there, it may seem that the problems are confined to the covers of the texts that we are examining, and thus the solution is as easy as placing a text back on the shelf. They cannot simply be reshelved, because they were "among the enabling

1 Skinner, *Visions of Politics* at 148.

2 I am deeply indebted to Charles Taylor's work on this point and numerous others. As he puts it, "Our social imaginary at any given time is complex. It incorporates a sense of the normal expectations we have of each other, the kind of common understanding that enables us to carry out the collective practices that make up our social life." Charles Taylor, *Modern Social Imaginaries* (Durham, NC: Duke University Press, 2004) at 24.

3 Skinner, *Visions I* at 174. This point is, to my mind, driven home by Wittgenstein's remark in §18 of the *Philosophical Investigations* "to imagine a language means to imagine a form of life." Wittgenstein, *Philosophical Investigations* at 11.

4 Skinner, *Visions I* at 156.

conditions" of the innumerable "courses of action" that the *Indian Act* (and the prior legislative acts that were folded into it) set into motion.

The approach I am taking focuses on how the conceptual instability of these foundations (which is so clearly exemplified in J.S. Mill's attempt at setting the limits of liberty with the bright line of "civilization") relates to the constant legal and political renovation on the so-called Indian Question (i.e., the question of how to legally secure and normatively legitimate the taking of Indigenous lands and the assimilation of Indigenous peoples).[5] I am interested in how the seemingly endless string of experiments, unintended consequences, and failures generated by these projects were rationalized and legitimated – and further, how these rationalizations gradually change these projects. This process of change is key. It is how the conceptual foundations that we can no longer accept return to us dressed in new clothes and yet bearing a striking family resemblance to those that preceded them. What else can begin to account for how the answer to the Indian Question in Canada has shifted from the term *enfranchisement* to *reconciliation*? Despite all claims to the contrary, there is a genealogical connection between these terms. Their shared heritage is plainly exhibited in their unquestioning acceptance of Crown sovereignty. I am not saying that the differences between these terms are a mere surface phenomenon that conceals their true identity. Rather, I am saying that, aside from the unquestioning acceptance of Crown sovereignty, these terms (and the discourses, practices, and policies associated with them) have no one thing in common, no single defining characteristic or essence, but there is "a complicated network of similarities overlapping and criss-crossing: sometimes overall similarities, sometimes similarities of detail."[6] Simply put, they are genealogically related, and it is the specific details of their relation that concerns us in this chapter.

In order to begin our investigation into this genealogical relationship, we will need to focus on three strains of political thought in imperial Britain that were utilized during the mid-nineteenth century shift to devolve more powers to the settler colonies. This shift (which begins after the War of 1812, is signalled by the *Durham Report* in 1839 and formalized with the passage of the *1867*

5 The kind of "conceptual" I have in mind here has much in common with how Jeanne Morefield explains the limits that are entailed in legitimating the project of *liberal imperialism* (an oxymoron akin to *unfree freedom, led them to liberty*). As she explains, "Liberal imperialist storytellers are at all times both producers of meaning and prisoners of their own conceptual worlds, often pushed into very tight discursive corners by the difficult juggling act at the heart of their political project. There is a reason, then, that their arguments are often so profoundly tautological: the more closed-in the rhetorical walls, the tighter circles that they are forced to pace." See Jeanne Morefield, *Empires without Imperialism: Anglo-American Decline and the Politics of Deflections* (Oxford: Oxford University Press, 2014) at 25.

6 Wittgenstein, *Philosophical Investigations*, at §66.

British North America Act and, ultimately, the first version of the *Indian Act* in 1876) leads to the complete refiguring of the Indian-to-Crown relationship. The imperial federation of military alliances that was formalized with the *Royal Proclamation of 1763* and the *Treaty of Niagara* in 1764 was suddenly shifted to municipal jurisdiction under s. 91(24), effectively refiguring Indigenous nations into wards of the state. The three strains of discourse that led in this transformation are the civilizing liberal imperialism articulated by James and J.S. Mill, the new culturalism put forward in the work of Henry Maine, which informed imperial Britain's post-1857 shift towards the theory and practice of indirect rule, and the extinction thesis, which developed in the 1860s and was associated with Charles Darwin, Herbert Spencer, and T.H. Huxley (prefigured in the pessimism of Malthus and Hobbes).

Generally speaking, these strains are active in a distinct of events. Following the War of 1812, the rebellions in Upper and Lower Canada 1837 and 1838, the intense colonial rebellions of the 1850s and 1860s (Ireland in 1848, India in 1857, and Jamaica in 1865), and the end of the American Civil War, the imperial Crown generally adopts the indirect rule model advanced by Henry Maine to minimize administrative costs and maximize the extraction of revenue (this change was possible as they did not require direct control over land).[7] For the settler colonies this translated into the devolution of powers that left them

7 There is a repetition of this transition from civilizing to indirect rule on the international stage in the middle of the twentieth century as the mandate system gives way to the informal world of international relations that characterizes *Pax Americana*. For a detailed account of this transformation, see Antony Anghie, *Imperialism, Sovereignty and the Making of International Law* (Cambridge: Cambridge University Press, 2005); and Marti Koskenniemi, *The Gentle Civilizer of Nations: The Rise and Fall of International Law 1870–1960* (Cambridge: Cambridge University Press, 2001). Also, for an excellent account of the British Empire's ideological shift away from the liberal-imperial model to Maine's culturalism and indirect rule, see Matena, *Alibis of Empire*. For a response that maintains the importance of the civilizing vision of empire in British imperial ideology, see Duncan Bell, *Reordering the World: Essays on Liberalism and Empire* (Princeton, NJ: Princeton University Press, 2016). In regards to the definition of indirect rule, my own position is that it constitutes a kind of family resemblance concept for a number of related models and strategies. My own view on the traits that these different versions or strains share is set out in some detail at 311–13. The gist is that indirect rule is similar to a devolved or dependent form of government, but this dependency is concealed from those who are subject to it. The sheer diversity of the modes or forms of concealment give rise to the criss-crossing and overlapping pattern of similarities and differences between the version offered by Maine and the forms of neocolonial or neo-imperial models that take shape in the mid-twentieth century. On the origins of the concept of neocolonialism, see Jean-Paul Sartre, *Colonialism and Neocolonialism*, trans. Azzedine Haddour, Steve Brewer, and Terry McWilliams (New York: Routledge, 2006); and Noam Chomsky and Edward S. Herman, *The Washington Connection and Third World Fascism* (Montreal: Black Rose Books, 1979).

responsible for administering the relationship between the Crown and Indigenous nations.[8] As Mill noted,

> It is now a fixed principle of the policy of Great Britain, professed in theory and faithfully adhered to in practice, that her Colonies of European race, equally with the parent country, possess the fullest measure of internal self-government.... How liberal a construction has been given to the distinction between imperial and colonial questions is shown by the fact that the whole of the unappropriated lands in the regions behind our American and Australian Colonies have been given up to the uncontrolled disposal of the colonial communities; though they might, without injustice, have been kept in the hands of the Imperial Government, to be administered for the greatest advantage of future emigrants from all parts of the empire.[9]

These "unappropriated lands" were by no means vacant, and, following the transfer from the imperial government to the settler colonies, there is a sudden shift of focus on how these lands were to be administered.

The devolution of self-governing powers and the "giving up" of these "unappropriated lands" draws the settler colonies to focus their attention on the so-called Indian Question.[10] While Mill does not address this issue in the settler colonies in particular (his model of governing a dependency is British India

8 The imperial Parliament retained sole responsibility for maintaining relations with the Indian nations and tribes. This responsibility was, at least in theory, maintained by the imperial Parliament until 1860, but the de facto reality of this administrative system was subject to erosion after the end of the War of 1812. Throughout the 1820s the Imperial Colonial Office questioned the necessity of the Indian Department. This concern over the costs of the Indian Department led to a series of commissions and reports (e.g., the Darling Report of 1828, the Bagot Commission of 1844, the Pennefather Commission in 1858), which were accompanied by legislative encroachment from the colonial legislatures. In effect, the imperial government simply withdrew and the colonial legislatures assumed their responsibilities. Then the *Indian Lands Act* of 1860 (which was largely a response to the recommendations of the Pennefather Commission) transferred authority over Indians and Indian lands to the colonial legislature, bringing to an end "the three-way Imperial federal system so purposefully constructed in 1763 and so strictly maintained by Imperial administrators thereafter." John S. Milloy, *A Historical Overview of Indian-Government Relations 1755–1940* (Ottawa: Department of Indian Affairs and Northern Development, 1992) at 59. The text of the *Indian Lands Act* itself states, "From and after the 1st day of July next, the Commissioner of Crown Lands, for the time being, shall be Chief Superintendent of Indian Affairs" (23 Vict. (1860), c. 151, s. 1).

9 J.S. Mill, *On Liberty and Considerations on Representative Government*, ed. R.B. McCallum (Oxford: Basil Blackwell, 1948) at 309.

10 I am not suggesting that there was no Indian Question for the imperial Crown – as I have previously noted the question of the financial costs of Indian administration arises shortly after the War of 1812. Rather, the devolution of powers to the settler colonies shifted the focus of the Indian Question from the more removed questions of imperial military and

under his employer, the East India Company), his liberal-imperial model bears a striking resemblance to the one that was put into practice in Canada. It is well suited to the purposes of the settler colonies, as it simply requires that the colonizer make the determination that the colonized are "savages" (as Mill readily admits, this is a "truth" whose recognition is "for the most part" empirical[11]), and the issue of consent becomes irrelevant, as the appropriate mode of government is one of force. The criteria that Mill uses to determine who is and is not "savage" is important. As Mill writes, "A savage tribe consists of as handful of individuals, wandering or thinly scattered over a vast tract of country."[12] The influence of this characterization of savagery on Canadian case law is unmistakable. It is this type of reasoning (and even phrasing) that has been used to deny Indigenous nations a claim to anything beyond a conditional right to occupy land. In *R v. Syliboy* the Mikmaq are referred to as "a handful of Indians," and the language of "vast tracts" and the concerns about the claims of "nomadic" or "semi-nomadic" peoples is found throughout the case law on title from *St Catherine's Milling* to *Tsilhqot'in Nation.*[13]

According to Mill, the legitimacy of this despotic mode of government over the uncivilized hinges on the colonizer facilitating the transition of the colonized into a higher stage of civilization.[14] Without this promise of progress, the line that divides the civilized from the uncivilized becomes permanent. This conceptual shift serves to narrow the practical options to containment and/or extirpation, and this unvarnished form of imperial coercion could provide no normative shelter to distinguish between legitimate and illegitimate imperial projects (viz. the British could no longer claim moral superiority over Spain and later Germany).[15] Mill's commitment to the universal perfectibility of human-

---

economic concerns to the localized questions of the newly formed dominion and its interests in western expansion, securing unburdened title to land and normalizing the body politic.

11 Mill, *On Liberty* at 130.

12 J.S. Mill, "Civilization," in *Collected Works of John Stuart Mill*, ed. J.M. Robson (Toronto: University of Toronto Press, 1977) at 18:119.

13 *Syliboy* at 313; *Tsilhqot'in Nation v. British Columbia*, [2014] 2 SCR 257; *St Catherine's Milling and Lumber Company.*

14 Mill, *On Liberty* at 9, 313.

15 I am not suggesting that there are not models of imperial governance which adopt this permanent line between the civilized and uncivilized. It is, after all, a feature of several models that purport to provide legitimacy. For example Hegel's account of world history has large blank areas where it seems that history simply does not occur. The highly influential 1918 pamphlet by Jan Smuts (who was strongly influenced by the late nineteenth-century British idealists) "The League of Nations: A Practical Suggestion" sets out a hierarchy of peoples according to their level of civilization, and the lowest tier was not educable (a somewhat unsurprising position, given he was also a founder of apartheid in South Africa). This pamphlet served to shape both the League of Nations mandate system and the United Nations Trust Territories. Interestingly this permanently uncivilized or uneducable tier was

ity and to the moral and intellectual education of the colonized alleviates this problem and widens the scope of practical policy options. It is also directly connected to the question of land and private property (a connection that can be seen in the work of a constellation of thinkers from Hobbes, Locke, and Kant to Mill). The desired result was simple: once the colonized were successfully civilized they would focus their labour on private plots of land as individual citizens and the Crown would possess radical title to all lands. This explains why "enfranchisement" (the assimilation of Indigenous peoples into the body politic, and with them, their lands) was the single consistent guiding aim of Indian policy from the 1830s through to the White Paper in 1969 (and one could argue it is still present in the logic of Bill C-31 in 1985 and the 6(1)–6(2) status system).[16]

The continual resistance of Indigenous peoples to the assimilative policies of enfranchisement led colonial administrators towards the extinction thesis as an explanatory framework (their resistance to the process of civilizing being little more than a symptom of their inevitable extinction). It is manifest from the very beginning of the transformation we are concerned with here, as Sir Francis Bond Head's Manitoulin Island experiment in the 1830s demonstrates. While this kind of cultural palliative care model provided a useful moral explanation for the process of colonization (the innate inferiority of Indigenous peoples means that their demise was as inevitable as fate, leaving colonists free from moral responsibility beyond providing palliative care), it offered few practical policies that allow for the control of land beyond relocation and containment (which tended to produce immediate resistance and require more repressive force).[17] As a result of this limitation, the extinction strain plays a constant but

---

not adopted into these systems. Rather, they maintained a commitment to the universal perfectibility of humanity coupled with a kind of Lockean notion of tabula rasa. Their adherence to this seems to me to have two benefits from the imperial perspective: (1) within the metropoles it can serve to respond to rule-of-law criticisms by rendering the despotic use of force temporary, and (2) it offers some limited means of responding to the resistance of the colonized by claiming that it is for their own benefit and splitting allegiance via education and co-opting. While these later tactics are admittedly weak ones at best, they are superior to the permanent walling off and/or extirpating of peoples, as that leaves no room for anything other than a Hobbesian war of all against all. See Morefield, *Empires without Imperialism* at 192–3.

16 Robert G. Moore, *The Historical Development of the Indian Act*, ed. J. Leslie and R. Maguire, 2nd ed. (Ottawa: Treaties and Historical Research Centre, Indian and Northern Affairs, 1978) at 191.

17 As Sir Francis Bond Head writes in a letter from 1836:

> So long as we were obtaining possession of their country by open violence, the fatal result of the unequal contest was but too easily understood; but now that we have succeeded in exterminating their Race from vast regions of land, where nothing in

lesser role in the history of Indian Question in Canada. As for the final strain, the real emergence of a type of culturalism within the domestic sphere does not come until after the White Paper in 1969, and it is mainly via the development of Aboriginal law in the Courts from *Calder* to *Tsilhqot'in Nation* (the recognition of innate rights of Aboriginal peoples and the requirement that the Court take some account of the "aboriginal perspective").[18] It exists as one possible view on what s. 35 and reconciliation means, namely, an internal form of indirect rule where self-government is strictly confined to the bounds set by the de facto power of the Crown.

This brief overview serves to explain why our inquiry will begin by focusing on the relationship (or, to be more specific, family resemblance) between Mill's model of liberal-imperialism and the project of enfranchisement. In order to explore this relationship, it will be necessary to map out the conceptual requirements and lines of tension that are endemic to this model of governance. The main line of tension centres on Mill's use of universal historical-developmental stages in order to justify the use of coercive force to govern those peoples who are deemed to be uncivilized. The only requirement to legitimate this despotic mode of governance is that it has the improvement of the uncivilized as its end. Mill's ideal form of government for the uncivilized is presented as temporary. As he states, "It has been the destiny of the government of the East India Company to suggest the true theory of the government of a semi-barbarous dependency by a civilized country, and after having done this, to perish."[19] This model of a temporary despotism that is justified by its end (the complete unification

the present dam remains of the poor Indian but the unnoticed bones of his ancestors, it seems inexplicable how it should happen, that even where the race barely lingers in existence, it should still continue to wither, droop, and vanish before us like Grass in the Progress of the Forest in flames. "The Red Men," lately exclaimed a celebrated Miami Cacique, "are melting like Snow before the Sun!" The mysterious inevitability of this extermination led him to the three following conclusions: "1) That an attempt to make farmers of the Red Men has been, generally speaking, a complete failure; 2) That congregating them for the purpose of civilization has implanted many more vices than it has eradicated; and, consequently, 3) That the greatest kindness we can perform towards these intelligent, simple-minded people, is to remove and fortify them as much as possible from all communication with the Whites." (Bond Head to Glenelg, no. 32, 20 November 1836, *British Parliamentary Papers* (Shannon, Ireland: Irish University Press, 1969) at 12:353)

18 For an instructive analysis of this shift and the Court's development of Aboriginal rights, see James Tully, *Public Philosophy in a New Key* (Cambridge: Cambridge University Press, 2008) at 1:268–73; and Michael Asch, "From 'Calder' to 'Van der Peet': Aboriginal Rights in Canadian Law, 1973–1996," in *Indigenous Peoples' Rights in Australia, Canada and New Zealand*, ed. Paul Havemann, 428–45 (Oxford: Oxford University Press, 1999).

19 Mill, *On Liberty* at 324.

of the body politic) meets its analogue with Marx's articulation of the dictatorship of the proletariat (that grim spectre that continues to haunt the history of communist political struggles).

In 1852 Marx wrote, "Long before me, bourgeois historians had described the historical development of this struggle between the classes, as had bourgeois economists their economic anatomy. My own contribution was (1) to show that the existence of classes is merely bound up with certain historical phases in the development of production; (2) that the class struggle necessarily leads to the dictatorship of the proletariat; [and] (3) that this dictatorship, itself, constitutes no more than a transition to the abolition of all classes and to a classless society."[20] The parallel with Mill is even more striking in "The British Rule in India" (1853) when Marx applies this model of history to a colonial context, "England, it is true, in causing a social revolution in Hindostan, was actuated only by the vilest interests, and was stupid in her manner of enforcing them. But that is not the question. The question is: can mankind fulfil its destiny without a fundamental revolution in the social state of Asia? If not, whatever may have been the crimes of England she was the unconscious tool of history in bringing about that revolution."[21]

Mill's liberal-imperial despotism shares the fate of Marx's dictatorship of the proletariat: the temporary government of force becomes permanent, as the end goal moves constantly further and further into the future. The mode of government this logic establishes, despite all claims to the contrary, has no real limitations on its use of coercive force.

With this in mind, let us consider the course of our investigation for this chapter. I will begin by following four related lines of inquiry through Mill's texts:

1 How is the distinction between the civilized and uncivilized determined?
2 What type of governmental body is best suited to this mode of government?
3 What legitimates the government of the uncivilized by the civilized?
4 How can one determine when the end (its goal is, after all, its termination) of this government is reached?

By following these lines of inquiry we will be able to relate the implicit commitments and paradoxes within his text to points of tension and struggle that relate to both the persistence of the project of enfranchisement and its eventual

20 Karl Marx and Frederick Engels, *Collected Works* (New York: International Publishers, 1983) at 39:62–5.

21 Karl Marx, "The British Rule in India," *New York Daily Tribune*, 25 June 1853.

transformation. From that basis, we will then move on to consider the extinction strain, which serves as a constitutive companion to the project of enfranchisement. It also has a role in shaping the response to the Indian Question in Canada during the nineteenth century and into the twentieth, but it tends to be entwined with the project of enfranchisement and its logic of civilizing the colonized. It provides a rhetorical evasion of responsibility when the colonized resist and/or there is no sign of the continual progress that the enfranchisement project requires for its own legitimacy. The final section of this chapter will focus on how the ultimate failure of the project of enfranchisement leads (via a curious repetition of the course of imperial British policy in the nineteenth century and of international law following the collapse of the mandate system in the middle of the twentieth century) to a culturalism and domestic model of indirect rule known as the project of reconciliation.[22] My aim is not to simply provide the reader with a historical summary of the relevant sections of each author's work. Rather, I am interested in how the conceptual instability of these discursive foundations relates to the constant process of legal and political renovation on the Indian Question from the project of enfranchisement and its transformation into the project of reconciliation.

2.1 Liberty and Legitimate Despotism: The Liberal-Imperialism of J.S. Mill

It is difficult to read Mill's political philosophy without experiencing a sense of disorientation. On the one hand there is his careful analysis of the dangers of majoritarian rule within liberal democratic states and the need for finding a way to protect minorities. In this respect Mill's text opens up before us like a familiar street with the commonplace signs and slogans of liberal democracy, which have been a part of our political reality since the eighteenth century. With its language of rights, constitutions, and individualism, a text like *On Liberty* can easily draw readers into seeing an account of their own political struggles. For example, "The 'people' who exercise the power are not always the same people with those over whom it is exercised; and the 'self-government' spoken of is not the self-government of each by himself, but of each by all the rest. The will of the people, moreover, practically means the will of the most numerous or the most active part of the people; the majority, or those who succeed in making themselves accepted as the majority; the people, consequently may desire to

22 I follow Tully's argument on this point: "The present application of the right of internal self-determination within the prevailing constitutional order constitutes a form of indirect colonial rule." Tully, *Philosophy in a New Key* at 1:286.

oppress a part of their number; and precautions are as much needed against this as against any other abuse of power."[23]

This observation on the dangers that majoritarian politics belongs as much to our present as to 1859.[24] At certain points Mill's defence of the liberty of the individual could almost be mistaken for some of the more revolutionary political thinkers of the Enlightenment. Consider the following selection on free speech: "If all mankind minus one, were of one opinion, and only one person were of contrary opinion, mankind would be no more justified in silencing that one person, than he, if he had the power, would be justified in silencing mankind."[25]

Or his articulation of the "harm principle" as the only standard for the restriction of individual liberty: "That the only purpose for which power can be rightfully exercised over any member of a civilised community, against his will, is to prevent harm to others. His own good, either physical or moral, is not a sufficient warrant.... The only part of the conduct of any one, for which he is amenable to society, is that which concerns others. In the part which merely concerns himself, his independence is, of right, absolute. Over himself, over his own body and mind, the individual is sovereign."[26]

But it is here, at the very heart of his defence of individual liberty, that the comforting familiarity of our surroundings begins to fade away. The detail that triggers this shift can easily be missed; it is, after all, a single word, but this single word is the single qualification on the rightful use of power and so should stand out. That word is *civilized.* With this single word another aspect comes into view, and the everyday street of familiar normative language suddenly becomes strange, unfamiliar, a collection of scaffolding and facades. Mill is clear on this point: "Despotism is a legitimate mode of government in dealing with barbarians, provided the end be their improvement, and the means justified by actually effecting that end. Liberty, as a principle, has no application to any state of things anterior to the time when mankind have become capable of being improved by free and equal discussion."[27]

Here we encounter the aspect that shifts our perception from the familiar street to the scaffolds and facades of the movie set (or perhaps simply to the scaffold itself). This is not to suggest that the language and associated practices

---

23 Mill, *On Liberty* at 3–4.

24 This was a danger that was painfully clear to Mill, as by 1859 the 1848 revolutions and "spring time of the people" had long since collapsed, leaving Europe under the rule of reactionary conservative movements. For more on this, refer to Eric Hobsbawm, *The Age of Capital, 1848–1875* (New York: Vintage Books, 1996) at 9–28.

25 Mill, *On Liberty* at 14.

26 Ibid. at 8–9.

27 Ibid.

of liberal-imperialism are relics of the nineteenth century that we have since left behind. Rather, following the end of the mandate system in the middle of the twentieth century, we have grown accustomed to seeing despotism as a symptom of the absence of political liberty (or the product of cultural difference) and not as a prescription for attaining it.[28] Seeing a political philosophy focused on the principle of liberty prescribing despotism is, to my mind, akin to seeing Jastrow's picture of the duck-rabbit in Wittgenstein's *Philosophical Investigations*: we encounter a single picture that has two categorically different aspects. What changes is not the object of perception or its organization, but the *way* we see it.[29] The key part of this analogy for my purposes is that these are two aspects of a single picture. In other words, Mill's defence of liberty for the individual in the civilized community and prescription of despotism for the uncivilized are not modular elements or compartments that can simply be removed or replaced (as the shallower defences of Mill via his historical context would have us believe). They are, rather, two aspects of a single political philosophy.[30] The contrast between these two aspects is so stark that it seems as if night and day are divided by a line that can be crossed in a single step. This stark contrast brings us to our first question: how does Mill determine this line?

28 While the emphasis that President George W. Bush placed on democratic regime change did signal a return to a more Millian approach to American imperialism, it is distinguished by its emphasis on "shock and awe" military interventions that remove a regime and allow for the spontaneous development of liberal democracy. In contrast, Mill's liberal-imperialism prescribes a mode of government (modelled on the East India Company) to facilitate a gradual transition, and this process is by no means certain (he maintains that civilization can go backwards on his universal developmental scale). For a text that does an exemplary job of tracking the shift in the techniques of legitimating imperial practices from the late nineteenth century to today, see Morefield, *Empires without Imperialism*.

29 Wittgenstein, *Philosophical Investigations* at 165–6.

30 Kerry Wilkins asked a helpful question on this particular point: do these two aspects of Mill's political philosophy require one another in such a way that neither can defensibly stand without the other? A satisfying answer to this question goes beyond what I can offer here, so I will confine my response to a tentative placeholder. I think the only reasonable attempt at salvaging Mill would be to try to excise the civilized/uncivilized distinction from his account of liberty. There are certainly salvageable components to be had here, but I am also reticent about his kind of operation. I think that this civilized/uncivilized distinction is dug in quite deeply and that its removal is no simple task. It metastasizes in Mill's texts, distributing itself widely and deeply into its conceptual structure. This does not mean that we need to necessarily make some kind of final pronouncement along the lines of "Mill is dead" or "Mill lives"; rather, we need to exercise great caution when making use of his work so we do not unwittingly adopt our own version of this distinction and the "waiting room of history" (as Dipesh Chakrabarty evocatively put it) that it constructs. See Dipesh Chakrabarty, *Provincializing Europe: Postcolonial Thought and Historical Difference* (Princeton, NJ: Princeton University Press, 2000) at 9.

2.2 The Science of Savage Character: The Uncivilized and Mill's Philosophy of History

The distinction between the civilized and the uncivilized is put forward as a line with four stages: savagery, slavery, barbarism, and civilization.[31] The line that connects these stages is progressive: history moves from savagery to civilization, or rather, the only history that exists is precisely the movement along the line. This movement is neither certain nor is it unidirectional: civilization can move backwards or stop progressing altogether.[32] As Mill states in the third chapter (entitled "Of Individuality, as one of the elements of well-being") of *On Liberty*, "The progressive principle, however, in either shape, whether as the love of liberty or of improvement, is antagonistic to the sway of Custom, involving at least emancipation from that yoke; and the contest between the two constitutes the chief interest of the history of mankind. The greater part of the world, has, properly speaking, no history, because the despotism of Custom is complete."[33]

There is no history at the beginning of the line of civilization. The same sentiment is found in Hegel's lectures on the philosophy of history given at the University of Berlin between 1822 and 1830 (it is also found in Kant's "Idea for a Universal History with a Cosmopolitan Purpose" (1784).[34] Mill's own philosophy of history is strikingly similar on this count (this similarity – which also connects his work to Kant's – is not confined to the idea of there being periods without history, but relates to the role of coercion as a means of progress, as I

---

31 This taxonomy (a ladder whose rungs seem clearer when seen at a distance) is set out in his 1836 essay "Civilization."

32 As Mill states,

> If civilization has got the better of barbarism when barbarism had the world to itself, it is too much to profess to be afraid lest barbarism, after having been fairly got under, should revive and conquer civilization. A civilization that can thus succumb to its vanquished enemy, must first have become so degenerate, that neither its appointed priests and teachers, nor anybody else, has the capacity, or will take the trouble, to stand up for it. If this be so the sooner such a civilization receives notice to quit, the better. It can only go on from bad to worse until destroyed and regenerated (like the Western Empire) by energetic barbarians. (Mill, *On Liberty* at 83)

33 Ibid. at 63.

34 As the lecture notes state, "The History of the World is not the theater of happiness. Periods of happiness are blank pages in it, for they are periods of harmony – periods when the antithesis is in abeyance." G.W.F. Hegel, *Philosophy of History*, trans. J. Sibree (New York: Prometheus Books, 1991) at 26–7.

will draw out further on).[35] According to Mill, the "blank pages" of the history of mankind are a result of the "despotism of Custom." This is a period in which "custom is there, in all things, the final appeal; justice and right mean conformity to custom; the argument of custom no one, unless some tyrant intoxicated with power, thinks of resisting."[36]

But it should also not be mistaken for being stationary. There can be movement, "provided all move together."[37] What this period lacks – and the reason it lacks history – is individuality. This is the key for Mill's philosophy of history, but it is also qualified, as savagery is a condition that is characterized by individuality. As Mill writes in "Civilization" (1836), "A savage tribe consists of a handful of individuals, wandering or thinly scattered over a vast tract of country."[38] He

---

35 Mill would undoubtedly be displeased by this connection, as his attitude towards German philosophy (Hegel in particular) was far from complimentary. Consider this excerpt from his letter to Alexander Bain in 1867:

> I found by actual experience of Hegel that conversancy with him tends to deprave one's intellect. The attempt to unwind an apparently infinite series of self contradictions not disguised but openly faced & coined into [illegible word] science by being stamped with a set of big abstract terms, really if persisted in impairs the acquired delicacy of perception of false reasoning & false thinking which has been gained by years of careful mental discipline with terms of real meaning. For some time after I had finished the book [Stirling's *Secret of Hegel*] all such words as reflexion, development, evolution, &c., gave me a sort of sickening feeling which I have not yet entirely got rid of. (John Stuart Mill, *The Collected Works of John Stuart Mill*, vol. 16, *The Later Letters of John Stuart Mill 1849–1873 Part III*, ed. Francis E. Mineka and Dwight N. Lindley (Toronto: University of Toronto Press, 1972) at 1324)

36 Mill, *On Liberty* at 63. Mill mentions Hegel (usually in conjunction with Schelling) a number of times throughout his works, but the engagements are limited. Hegel is set up to play the role of the metaphysician of the a priori who refuses the law of contradiction and holds that Being and Nothing are the same (at best, Mill's rendition presents Hegel as a kind of straw man for mysticism who is meant to show the superiority of the English empiricist tradition). This can be seen in the following selection from John Stuart Mill: "'What kind of an Absolute Being is that,' asked Hegel, 'which does not contain in itself all that is actual, even evil included?' Undoubtedly: and it is therefore necessary to admit, either that there is no Absolute Being, or that the law, that contradictory propositions cannot both be true, does not apply to the Absolute. Hegel chose the latter side of the alternative; and by this, among other things, has fairly earned the honour which will probably be awarded to him by posterity, of having logically extinguished transcendental metaphysics by a series of *reductiones ad absurdissimum*." *The Collected Works of John Stuart Mill*, vol. 9, *An Examination of William Hamilton's Philosophy and of the Principal Philosophical Questions Discussed in His Writings*, ed. John M. Robson and intro. Alan Ryan (Toronto: University of Toronto Press, 1979) at 47.

37 Mill, *On Liberty* at 63.

38 Mill, "Civilization" at 119. The influence of this characterization of savagery on Canadian case law is, as I have noted, unmistakable. This form of reasoning (and others related to it – in particular I have in mind Locke's notion of property and "empty" or "waste" lands)

expands on this point just a few pages later: "Consider the savage: he has bodily strength, he has courage, enterprise, and is often not without intelligence: what makes all savage communities poor and feeble? The same cause which prevented the lions and tigers from long ago extirpating the race of men – the incapacity of co-operation. It is only civilized beings that combine. All combination is compromise: it is the sacrifice of some portion of individual will, for a common purpose. The savage cannot bear to sacrifice, for any purpose, the satisfaction of his individual will. His social cannot even temporarily prevail over his selfish feelings, nor his impulses bend to his calculations."[39]

And so we see that the savage has no history because he is, at one and the same time, far too individualistic and far too communitarian. He is both animal and child.[40] He both follows his own will and blindly accepts the authority of his superiors. Whereas the slave lacks history because he is "habituated to control, but not to self-control," and barbarism – for which, unlike savagery and slavery, Mill does not provide a clear and consistent definition – seems to function at times as a catch-all term to refer to the uncivilized generally as being too passive.[41] In this they all have the wrong kind of individuality and the wrong kind of sociality to facilitate progress. In order for history to begin – and for it not to be simply movement or duration – there must be progress towards

---

has been used to deny Indigenous nations a claim to anything beyond a conditional right to occupy land. In *Syliboy* at 313 the Mikmaq are referred to as "a handful of Indians," and the language of "vast tracts" is found throughout the case law on title from *St Catherine's Milling* to *Tsilhqot'in Nation*. The co-constitutive relationship between the land use and the level of development is also found in Mill, as he states, "There are two elements of importance and influence among mankind: the one is, property: the other, powers and acquirements of mind" (ibid. at 121).

39 Mill, "Civilization" at 122.

40 Mill explicitly connects savages and children often. The connection is that both require what he refers to as "an education of restraint" in order "to fit them for future admission to the privileges of freedom" (Mill, "Civilization" at 91).

41 Mill provides us with his characterization of the slave right after the one on the savage, and so it is worth considering at length:

> Look again at the slave: he is used indeed to make his will give way: but to the commands of a master, not to a superior purpose of his own. He is wanting in intelligence to form such a purpose: above all, he cannot frame to himself the conception of a fixed rule: nor if he could, has he the capacity to adhere to it: he is habituated to control, but not to self-control: when a driver is not standing over him with a "whip," he is found more incapable of withstanding any temptation, or "restraining" any inclination, than the savage himself. (Mill, "Civilization" at 122)

For a consideration of his use to the term *barbarism*, see Michael Levin, *Mill on Civilization and Barbarism* (New York: Routledge, 2004) at 31–2.

a certain form of individuality. After all, we are told that it is in "the natural growth of civilization [that] power passes from individuals to the masses."[42] There is a strange repetition of terms at work here, as we are informed that history begins and ends with individuals and is both halted (despite moving) and driven by despotism.[43] This brings us to the following question: what is the role of the individual in the progress of history?

Mill informs us that a people "may be progressive for a certain length of time, and then stop; when does it stop? When it ceases to possess individuality."[44] The connection between historical progression and individuality is explicit, so what is "individuality" for Mill? The answer to this question can be found in the third and, to a lesser degree, the fourth chapter of *On Liberty*. He does not provide us with a definition: at least in the more common sense that would follow the formula "*x* is *y*" – that is, in the sense that would provide us with a categorical distinction between the "individuality" of savages and that form of genius that propels the motor of history. Rather, he provides us with a definition through contrasts and roles:

> No government by a democracy or a numerous aristocracy, either in its political acts or in the opinions, qualities, and tone of mind which it fosters, ever did or could rise above mediocrity, except in so far as the sovereign Many have let themselves be guided (which in their best times they always have done) by the counsels and influence of a more highly gifted and instructed One or Few. The initiation of all wise or noble things, comes and must come from individuals; generally at first from some one individual. The honour and glory of the average man is that he is capable of following that initiative: that he can respond internally to wise and noble things, and be led to them with his eyes open. I am not countenancing the sort of "hero-worship" which applauds the strong man of genius for forcibly seizing on the government of the world and making it do his bidding in spite of itself. All he can claim is, freedom to point out the way. The power of compelling others into it is not only inconsistent with the freedom and development of all the rest, but corrupting to the strong man himself.[45]

---

42 Ibid. at 126.

43 In this there is another interesting parallel with Hegel, as the *Phenomenology* begins with "sense certainty" and ends with "absolute knowledge," and yet his descriptions of the state of "absolute knowledge" echo his descriptions of "sense-certainty." One could argue that the only difference between the beginning and the end (or the individuality of the savage and the civilized genius) is one of emphasis. See G.W.F. Hegel, *Phenomenology of Spirit*, trans. A.V. Miller (Oxford: Oxford University Press, 1997).

44 Mill, *On Liberty* at 63.

45 Ibid. at 59.

This constellation of the one and the many is a familiar one within the Western political thought (from Plato's philosopher king to Hegel's "right of heroes"). The relationship as presented here requires some parsing.

First the many: they are the mass who remain inert in their "collective mediocrity."[46] They are resistant to change and without history. Their mode of government (if left to themselves) is the "despotism of custom." Why is it characterized as "despotism"? For the same reason there can be (paradoxically) movement but no history (and so that Mill – and those in his philosophical family – can justify using despotism as a means to counter and correct it). The many move together as a (seemingly) formless mass and resist the guidance of the one or few and in this they are guilty of a transgression against history (indeed against nature itself). The only way that they can have history is by producing what one does not know how to make: the individual. "It is through the cultivation of these [who have the strongest natural feeling] that society both does its duty and protects its interests: not by rejecting the stuff of which heroes are made, because it knows not how to make them."[47]

The language of "duty" and "interests" here is key, as they are indicative of a leap over the distinction of "is" and "ought." The many cannot produce the one (they do not know how) and so it can only be the deus ex machina of necessity, fate, or providence. Mill finds this in nature:[48] "Human nature is not a machine

---

46 Ibid. at 58.

47 Ibid. at 53.

48 There is, it seems to me, a vitalism at work in Mill's use of "inward forces." While he explicitly rejects essentialism (in *A System of Logic Part 1*, §3 is entitled "Individuals have no essences"), he holds that "the real essence of an object has, in the progress of physics, come to be conceived as nearly equivalent, in the case of bodies, to their corpuscular structure." John Stuart Mill, *The Collected Works of John Stuart Mill*, vol. 7, *A System of Logic Ratiocinative and Inductive, Being a Connected View of the Principles of Evidence and the Methods of Scientific Investigation (Books I–III)*, ed. John M. Robson and intro. R.F. McRae (Toronto: University of Toronto Press, 1974) at 115. By taking his account of "inward forces" as the *real essence* of the humanity, Mill begs the question. We are left with a strange ostensive definition of the individual taken from a particular set of examples. He points the way to a definition by saying "this here" or "this is a genius." By doing this he is able to gain access to a concept that has the philosophical force of the a priori (it can be used to determine the nature of man and map out an entire philosophy of history and political order) by claiming to have discovered it in nature via induction. His proposal for a science of the formation of character (which he referred to as "ethology") sought to determine the empirical laws that govern human nature. These were to be collected "*à posteriori* from observation of life" through inductive reasoning. As Mill put it,

> Ethology is the science which corresponds to the art of education; in the widest sense of the term, including the formation of national or collective character as well as individual. It would indeed be vain to expect (however completely the laws of the formation of character might be ascertained) that we could know so accurately the

to be built after a model, and set to do exactly the work prescribed for it, but a tree, which requires to grow and develop itself on all sides, according to the tendency of the inward forces which make it a living thing."[49]

The contrast between mechanics and organic nature is often repeated as he compares those who do not have their own "desires and impulses" (they are externally determined by the many) as having as much character as a "steam-engine."[50] Automation is presented as the condition of the many under their "blind and mechanical adhesion" to custom.[51] The individual is possessed of a set of "inward forces." This "force of nature" argument is clearly laid out in Mill's account of the genius:

> Persons of genius, it is true, are, and are always likely to be, a small minority: but in order to have them, it is necessary to preserve the soil in which they grow. Genius can only breathe freely in an *atmosphere* of freedom. Persons of genius are, *ex vi termini*, more individual than any other people – less capable, consequently, of fitting themselves, without hurtful compression, into any of the small number of moulds which society provides in order to save its members the trouble of forming their own character. If from timidity they consent to be forced into one of these moulds, and to let all that part of themselves which cannot expand under the

---

circumstances of any given case as to be able positively to predict the character that would be produced in that case. But we must remember that a degree of knowledge far short of the power of actual prediction, is often of much practical value. There may be great power of influencing phenomena, with a very imperfect knowledge of the causes by which they are in any given instance determined. It is enough that we know that certain means have a tendency to produce a given effect, and that others have a tendency to frustrate it. When the circumstances of an individual or of a nation are in any considerable degree under our control, we may, by our knowledge of tendencies, be enabled to shape those circumstances in a manner much more favourable to the ends we desire, than the shape which they would of themselves assume. This is the limit of our power; but within this limit the power is a most important one. (John Stuart Mill, *The Collected Works of John Stuart Mill*, vol. 8, *A System of Logic Ratiocinative and Inductive, Being a Connected View of the Principles of Evidence and the Methods of Scientific Investigation (Books IV–VI and Appendices)*, ed. John M. Robson, and intro. R.F. McRae (Toronto: University of Toronto Press, 1974) at 861–70)

If he is asked why it is legitimate that the one uses force to subjugate the many, his only answer is "because of the strength of their inward forces." This is, to my mind, akin to offering us a kind of ostensive definition where the speaker points to the object and says "this is that" and thereby neglects the fact that a subjective judgment is being offered. In this he is like the magician finding a coin behind a spectator's ear and joining in everyone's astonishment as he forgot that he placed it there by sleight of hand.

49 Mill, *On Liberty* at 52.

50 Ibid. at 53.

51 Ibid. at 52.

> pressure remain unexpanded, society will be little the better for their genius. If they are of a strong character, and break their fetters, they become a mark for the society which has not succeeded in reducing them to commonplace, to point at with solemn warning as "wild," "erratic," and the like: much as if one should complain of the Niagara river for not flowing smoothly between its banks like a Dutch canal.[52]

There is a conditional that we should pay close attention to here: the key characteristic for geniuses to possess (the one that will mark their society) is strength of character. If they have it then they are able to "break their fetters" (the "moulds" that the masses impose) and mark their society. The "moulds" thus serve as a kind of sorting mechanism or test of strength. This plays directly into Mill's account of historical development and his justification for the subjugation of the uncivilized by civilized foreign governments. As Mill states,

> From the general weaknesses of the people or of the state of civilization, the One and his counsellors, or the Few, are not likely to be habitually exempt; except in the case of their being foreigners, belonging to a superior people or a more advanced state of society. Then, indeed, the rulers may be, to almost any extent, superior in civilization to those over whom they rule; and subjection to a foreign government of this description, notwithstanding its inevitable evils, is often of the greatest advantage to a people, carrying them rapidly through several stages of progress, and clearing away obstacles to improvement which might have lasted indefinitely if the subject population had been left unassisted to its native tendencies and chances. In a country not under the dominion of foreigners, the only cause adequate to producing similar benefits is the rare accident of a monarch of extraordinary genius. There have been in history a few of these who, happily for humanity, have reigned long enough to render some of their improvements permanent, by leaving them under the guardianship of a generation which had grown up under their influence.[53]

The course of historical development is a difficult one (because in reality it is little more than legerdemain). It requires the arrival of an individual who will bring the many to submission by acting as a "prophet supposed to be inspired from above, or conjurer regarded as possessing miraculous power."[54] For this account, this is the only possible course of history (Mill informs us that he is "not aware that history furnishes any [other] examples"): the only way for the mass of "political atoms or corpuscles" to coalesce into a "body" and learn to "feel themselves one people" is through the "previous subjection to a central authority common to all."[55] The civilized foreign government

52 Ibid. at 57–8.
53 Ibid. at 157–8.
54 Ibid. at 154.
55 Ibid. at 156.

thus serves as surety for the "rare accident" that is the local or autochthonous monarch, and as a colonizer the civilized provide the uncivilized with the governmental "focus at which all its scattered rays are collected, that the broken coloured lights which exist elsewhere may find what is necessary to complete and purify them."[56]

The arrival of the individual on the stage of history is necessary (to combat the despotism of the many), and its means are justified before he arrives because his ends are not his own.[57] Mill's presumption of purpose in nature echoes the very first proposition in Kant's *Idea for a Universal History with a Cosmopolitan Purpose*: "All the natural capacities of a creature are destined sooner or later to be developed completely and in conformity with their end."[58] It is this presumption that acts as the motor or history (Mill's genius or "uncontented character,"[59] Kant's "unsocial sociability," and Hegel's "right of heroes"), and without it there is nothing but the passage of time without history under the tyranny of custom.[60] The problem (and perhaps also the benefit, as it offers colonial administrators near-unlimited discretion) with this argument is that *it cannot be wrong*. In fact, it can even learn to profit from its mistakes through experimentation. As Mill maintains in his *System of Logic*, "It is enough that we know that certain means have a tendency to produce a given effect, and that others have a tendency to frustrate it. When the circumstances of an individual or of a nation are in any considerable degree under our control, we may, by our knowledge of tendencies, be enabled to shape those circumstances in a manner much more favourable to the ends we desire, than the shape which they would

56 Mill uses this analogy to argue for centralized as opposed to local representative bodies, but the logic he uses is the same as he applies to colonial contexts (ibid. at 289).

57 The sudden and unexplained development of a hero who uses coercion to counter the coercion of custom parallels Hegel's account of the hero. There are two references to the "right of heroes" in the *Philosophy of Right*. The first occurs in §93 in section 3 ("Coercion and Crime") of part 1 ("Abstract Right"). The second appears in §350 in the third subsection ("World History") of section 3 ("The State") in part 3 ("Ethical Life").

Hegel provides a more detailed account of the hero and its role in history in 1830 in the second draft of his *Lectures on the Philosophy of World History*, trans. H.B. Nisbet (New York: New York University Press, 1975) at 68–93. This account draws heavily from a set of borrowed, but unstated set of concepts from Christian theology like predestination, which, outside of their context, strike me as little more than legerdemain and chicanery.

58 Kant, *Political Writings* at 42. This point is also connected to Kant's work on natural or organic teleology in the second half of the third *Critique*.

59 Mill, *On Liberty* at 145. He goes on to refer to the "function of Antagonism" (at para. 200).

60 Consider Kant's comments on a world without this "unsocial sociability": "Man would live an Arcadian, pastoral existence of perfect concord, self-sufficiency and mutual love. But all human talents would remain hidden forever in a dormant state, and men, as good-natured as the sheep they tended, would scarcely render their existence more valuable than that of their animals" (ibid. at 45).

of themselves assume. This is the limit of our power; but within this limit the power is a most important one."[61]

The initial determination is simple: the question of who is uncivilized is as unmistakable as what is good. The subject simply knows it and points, saying, "I desire this," or "That is a savage." Once the term is applied, then there is no need to bother attempting to gain their consent. As Mill puts it in *A Few Words on Non-Intervention* in 1859, "Barbarians have no rights as a *nation*, except a right to such treatment as may, at the earliest possible period, fit them for becoming one."[62] In fact, he recognizes that the rules of what he calls "ordinary international morality" imply reciprocity, but claims that "barbarians will not reciprocate," as their minds are incapable of it.[63] If one wished to justify the suppression of any group, then all that would be required would be to characterize them as "savage" (or any other mode of the uncivilized), and there would be no limit to the force that could be used to ensure that they were "taught obedience" and to "submit to the restraints of a regular and civilized government."[64] After all, Mill informs us that "human beings are only secure from evil at the hands of others" if they are both "self-*protecting*" and "self-*dependent*."[65]

The line that divides the uncivilized and the civilized – or, for that matter, the savage and the genius – is presented as an obvious and uncontroversial fact for those who are civilized. In this it bears the mark of G.E. Moore's naturalistic fallacy: it is possible to perform philosophical alchemy by concealing your subjective judgment in nature and then receiving its fruit as the product of historical necessity.[66] The key interpretive means to distinguish between the savage and the genius is the magic of the philosopher (who, oddly, also happens to be a genius). As Wittgenstein states in *On Certainty*, "I want to say: We use judgments as principles of judgment."[67] To answer our first question: the distinction between the civilized and the uncivilized (the savage and the hero) is a judgment dressed up as a principle. But, aside from its subjective

---

61 Mill, *Collected Works* 8:870.

62 John Stuart Mill, *The Collected Works of John Stuart Mill*, vol. 21, *Essays on Equality, Law, and Education*, ed. John M. Robson and intro. Stefan Collini (Toronto: University of Toronto Press, 1984) at 119.

63 Ibid.

64 Mill, *On Liberty* at 111 and 133.

65 Ibid. at 142.

66 As Moore states, "Mill has made as naïve and artless a use of the naturalistic fallacy as anybody could desire. 'Good,' he tells us, means 'desirable,' and you can only find out what is desirable by seeking to find out what is actually desired … The fact is that 'desirable' does not mean 'able to be desired' as 'visible' means 'able to be seen.' The desirable means simply what ought to be desired or deserves to be desired; just as the detestable means not what can be but what ought to be detested." G.E. Moore, *Principia Ethica* (Amherst: Prometheus Books, 1988) at 66–7.

67 Wittgenstein, *On Certainty* at §124.

basis (which deprives it of its claim to necessity and thereby the historical justification of destiny), it presents us with a set of properties that determine how to govern – the main one being that power should be exerted on the "inner force" of the individual. It should be used to shape and grow them like a tree. As Mill states,

> Among the works of man, which human life is rightly employed in perfecting and beautifying, the first in importance surely is man himself. Supposing it were possible to get houses built, corn grown, battles fought, causes tried, and even churches erected and prayers said, by machinery – by automatons in human form – it would be a considerable loss to exchange for these automatons even the men and women who at present inhabit the more civilized parts of the world, and who assuredly are but starved specimens of what nature can and will produce. Human nature is not a machine to be built after a model, and set to do exactly the work prescribed for it, but a tree, which requires to grow and develop itself on all sides, according to the tendency of the inward forces which make it a living thing.[68]

This exchange would be a "considerable loss," as we would fail to cultivate man. This cultivation is not done through the imposition of external force on him (as it would be with an automaton), but on his "inward forces." This is a model of power that requires the freedom of those it governs. This brings us to our next question: what type of governmental body is best suited to this mode of government?

A. Governing the Uncivilized: The Role of the Intermediate Body

Mill believed that a key distinguishing feature of his political philosophy was that it recognized that the form that government takes must be adapted to the stage of advancement of those whom it governs. His articulation of this aspect of his work in *Considerations on Representative Government* is particularly explicit on this point and should be considered at length: "It is otherwise with that portion of the interests of the community which relate to the better or worse training of the people themselves. Considered as instrumental to this, institutions need to be radically different, according to the stage of advancement already reached. *The recognition of this truth, though for the most part empirically rather than philosophically, may be regarded as the main point of superiority in the political theories of the present above those of the last age*; in which it was customary to claim representative democracy for England or France by arguments which would equally have proved it the only fit form of government for Bedouins or Malays."[69]

---

68 Mill, *On Liberty* at 52.

69 Ibid. at 130–1 (emphasis added).

He contrasts this method with his understanding of Bentham's utilitarianism, which he viewed as being too abstract.[70] The "truth" that Bentham failed to appreciate was his failure to appreciate the effect of character on political form. Mill believes that this "truth" (which, as I have argued above, is clearly exhibited in his account of individuality and human nature in *On Liberty*) is recognized more through empirical observation than philosophical speculation alone.[71] This required, as Pitts notes, the combination of a "rough dichotomy between savage and civilized" with a philosophy of history (adapted from the conjectural historiography of the Scottish Enlightenment) and utilitarianism to justify "despotic, but civilizing, imperial rule."[72] Returning to the citation above, Mill goes on to say,

> The state of different communities, in point of culture and development, ranges downwards to a condition very little above the highest of the beasts. The upward range, too, is considerable, and the future possible extension vastly greater. A community can only be developed out of one of these states into a higher, by a concourse of influences, among the principal of which is the government to which they are subject. In all states of human improvement ever yet attained, the nature and degree of authority exercised over individuals, the distribution of power, and the conditions of command and obedience, are the most powerful of the influences, except their religious belief, which make them what they are, and enable them to become what they can be. They may be stopped short at any point in their progress, by defective adaptation of their government to that particular stage of advancement. And the one indispensable merit of a government, in favour of which it may be forgiven almost any amount of other demerit compatible with progress, is that its operation on the people is favourable, or not unfavourable, to the next step which it is necessary for them to take, in order to raise themselves to a higher level.[73]

This is the basis for Mill's account of what the term *good government* means (chapter 2 of *Considerations on Representative Government* is entitled "The Criterion of a Good Form of Government"). There is no one form of "good government" that could be applicable to all. It must be adapted to the stage that the people it is going to govern are at and this process of adaptation will shift the "nature and degree of authority," "distribution of power," and "conditions of command and obedience." There is thus a range of possible configurations

70 For more on the relationship between Mill and Bentham, see Pitts, *Turn to Empire* at 133–8.

71 I find this to be a curious qualification for a philosopher who never left the confines of Western Europe. How can one argue for such a subtle grasp of the particularity of human character and yet have never encountered the nations that you determine to be savages or barbarians?

72 Mill, *On Liberty* at 133.

73 Ibid. at 130–1.

of government in response to the stage of civilization, ranging from savages (as Mill notes, a stage that is "very little above the highest of the beasts" who have to learn how to "obey"[74]), slaves (who need to learn how to act for themselves and so need a government of "leading-strings"[75]), barbarians (who form a passive mass and so need to be taught the discipline of individuality), and the civilized (who require representative government so as to preserve the best *soil* and *atmospheric* conditions for the cultivation of the individual genius that prevents it from stagnating or moving backwards[76]). These may occur in hybrid forms (Mill will sometimes use the term *semi-barbarous*) but, as he notes, "to attempt to investigate what kind of government is suited to every known state of society, would be to compose a treatise, not on representative government, but on political science at large."[77] He thus confines himself to providing only its "general principles."

Now that we understand that the aim of government (of "good government") is to further the orderly progress of those it governs from one stage to the next, we can narrow the focus of our inquiry to the form of government best suited for this purpose. While Mill insists that the form that government must take varies in accordance with the level of civilization of those it governs, his model has two general categories: the uncivilized and the civilized. The civilized are to be governed by representative democracy. On the other hand, the uncivilized are governed without their consent, and so the general form of government that applies is non-representative. There is a high degree of variability within this general category. After all, the language that Mill adopts to describe governance is borrowed from agriculture and animal husbandry (i.e., he speaks of cultivation, soil, atmosphere, trees, ripening, taming, softening, and hardening[78]). This means that within the general form of non-representative government the actual practices of governing (the nature and degree of authority, distribution of power, and conditions of command and obedience[79]) vary in accordance with the unique qualities of the population being governed. This process

74 Ibid. at 132.

75 Ibid. at 132–3.

76 Ibid. at 57–8 and 83.

77 Ibid. at 133.

78 Consider this selection from his "Remarks on Bentham" in 1833: "For a tribe of North American Indians, improvement means, taming down their proud and solitary self-dependence; for a body of emancipated negroes, it means accustoming them to be self-dependent, instead of being merely obedient to orders: for our semi-barbarous ancestors it would have meant, softening them; for a race of enervated Asiatics it would mean hardening them." John Stuart Mill, *The Collected Works of John Stuart Mill*, vol. 10, *Essays on Ethics, Religion, and Society*, ed. John M. Robson and intro. F.E.L. Priestley (Toronto: University of Toronto Press, 1985) at 16.

79 Mill, *On Liberty* at 130–1.

is both deductive and experimental: it is a knowledge of "tendencies."[80] In the final chapter of *Considerations on Representative Government* (entitled "Of the Government of Dependencies by a Free State") he clearly states that the best form of government for the uncivilized is what he refers to as a delegated or intermediary body:

> It is of no avail to say that such a delegated body cannot have all the requisites of good government; above all, cannot have that complete and ever-operative identity of interest with the governed, which it is so difficult to obtain even where the people to be ruled are in some degree qualified to look after their own affairs. Real good government is not compatible with the conditions of the case. There is but a choice of imperfections. The problem is, so to construct the governing body that, under the difficulties of the position, it shall have as much interest as possible in good government, and as little in bad. Now these conditions are best found in an intermediate body. A delegated administration has always this advantage over a direct one, that it has, at all events, no duties to perform except to the governed. It has no interests to consider except theirs. Its own power of deriving profit from misgovernment may be reduced – in the latest constitution of the East India Company it was reduced – to a singularly small amount: and it can be kept entirely clear of bias from the individual or class interests of any one else.[81]

He recognizes that this cannot be the fullest expression of "good government" (as the result of its obvious lack of consent or representation of their interests), but this fault is due to the fault within the people it is set to govern. They are incapable of the practice of liberty: they are either too individualistic (savage), selfless (slaves), or simply caught up in the passivity of the masses that necessarily accompanies the despotism of custom (barbarians). They need a delegated body that has no other interest than in their cultivation (aside from the inevitable motivations of self-interest and profit that can be reduced legislatively). This form is superior to allowing Parliament to govern dependencies, as it is "swayed by those partial influences in the exercise of the power reserved to them."[82] In contrast, "the intermediate body is the certain advocate and champion of the dependency before the imperial tribunal."[83] It is a body composed of specialists. Returning to Mill,

> The intermediate body, moreover, is, in the natural course of things, chiefly composed of persons who have acquired professional knowledge of this part of their country's concerns; who have been trained to it in the place itself, and have

80 Mill, *Collected Works* 8:870.
81 Mill, *On Liberty* at 320.
82 Ibid.
83 Ibid.

> made its administration the main occupation of their lives. Furnished with these qualifications, and not being liable to lose their office from the accidents of home politics, they identify their character and consideration with their special trust, and have a much more permanent interest in the success of their administration, and in the prosperity of the country which they administer, than a member of a Cabinet under a representative constitution can possibly have in the good government of any country except the one which he serves.[84]

In summary, the intermediate body is, according to Mill, the best possible model for the governing of the uncivilized, because it is designed with one sole purpose in mind: it is a system that is calculated to form the population that it governs.[85] Once it accomplishes this transformation and converts the uncivilized into the civilized, it completes its destiny and perishes.[86] Its problem (the problem that pervades it from start to finish) is that there is no way to determine when this process is complete. Without a way to verify (via a "view from nowhere") that it has reached its destination, the intermediate body ceases to be temporary, the experiments of civilizing cease to have an orientation or goal, and it becomes next to impossible to distinguish between the pedagogical purposes of its coercive practices. What is left resembles Kafka's penal colony: it is an intricately customized system of domination held together by a mixture of self-serving faith and the blind inertia of custom.[87] It is a place without orientation (as the truth that it promised remains always on the horizon) and with the passage of time without progress, without hope. Its last vestige of purpose is reactive. It exists (much like Carl Schmitt's *katechon*) in a continual state of siege, waiting only for its own fall, as the teeming masses of the uncivilized threaten to drag it back into the "blank pages" of time without history.

B. *Peace, Order, and Good Government: Mill and the Indian Question*

The phrase "peace, order and good government" appears in a number of the imperial Acts of Parliament in the nineteenth and twentieth centuries. Examples of its use include the constitutions of Canada (*British North America Act 1867*), Australia (*Commonwealth of Australia Constitution Act 1900*), and, formerly, New Zealand (*New Zealand Constitution Act 1852*) and South Africa (*South Africa Act 1909*). It stands in contrast to a number of other prominent tripartite mottoes from the late eighteenth and nineteenth centuries, such as

84 Ibid. at 320.

85 Ibid. at 321.

86 Ibid. at 324.

87 Franz Kafka, "In the Penal Colony," in *The Complete Short Stories*, ed. Nahum N. Glatzer and trans. Willa and Edwin Muir, 140–67 (New York: Schocken Books, 1971).

the motto of the French Republic (*Liberté, égalité, fraternité*[88]) and the rendition of John Locke's "Life, Liberty, and Property" in the *United States Declaration of Independence* (Life, liberty and the pursuit of happiness). Even at first glance the values expressed in these three mottoes are very distinct: where "*Liberté, égalité, fraternité*" has the ring of a rallying cry to be shouted from the barricades, and "Life, liberty and the pursuit of happiness" the promise of a bucolic agrarian utopia, "Peace, order and good government" reflects its distinctly imperial origins. While "peace" and "order" are undoubtedly necessary qualities for both a government and those it governs, they provide only the most minimal conditions for government of any kind (even the most restrictive dictatorship would see their inherent value). This leaves significant weight on the meaning of "good government." Naturally, because the meaning of the word *good* is "open-textured" (to borrow H.L.A. Hart's expression) there will be a host of possible variations. Within Canadian constitutional law the phrase (which occurs in the opening paragraph of s. 91 of what is now referred to as the *Constitution Act, 1867*) has been interpreted as a wide-ranging grant of residual legislative authority in Parliament. This residual power has been limited by the jurisprudence to include three branches (matters that are purely residual, national concern, and emergency powers), which are all subject to specific limitations via legal tests.[89] The implicit meaning of "good government" in this sense would be, at the very least, respect for the constitutional limitations of federal legislative power. But Mill provides us with a definition of the term that, to my mind, has significant explanatory value within the Canadian context. As we noted above, he maintains that the "good" of government is necessarily connected with the cultivation of humanity within a series of set stages of civilization. What is "good" for those in one stage is not so for those in others. The term does not simply vary in degree, but also in kind. The uncivilized are governed by force. They are, at best, wards. The force exerted on them

88 The history of the inclusion of *fraternité* in the motto is a complicated one. Unlike *liberté* and *égalité*, its roots are decidedly Christian. While the association between *liberté* and *égalité* is seen as being essential – one ensuring the other, as in isolation there can be "liberty for some" and/or "equality in servitude" – the inclusion of *fraternité* is much less direct. Among the host of mottoes that the revolutionary period produced, *fraternité* was by no means always included. There were terms that were both less specifically Christian terms (i.e., *Amitié*) and Christian terms that were not gender exclusive (i.e., *Charité*), but it is ultimately *fraternité* that remains. For a more detailed examination, refer to Mona Ozouf's article on fraternity in *A Critical Dictionary of the French Revolution*, ed. Francois Furet and Mona Ozou, trans. Arthur Goldhammer, 694–703 (Cambridge, MA: Belknap, 1989); Jacques Derrida, "In Human Language, Fraternity …" in *Politics of Friendship*, trans. George Collins, 000–000 (New York: Verso, 2000); and in the chapter on Nancy and Derrida in my book *The End(s) of Community* (Waterloo, ON: Wilfrid Laurier University Press, 2013).

89 The leading case on this doctrine is *R v. Crown Zellerbach Canada Ltd.*, [1988] 1 SCR 401.

is, from the perspective of those who govern them, "for their own good" (as long as one can maintain the universal validity of the mould they are being forced into), but it is also behind their backs. This means that there could be a state that simultaneously maintained two distinct kinds of government within its bounds: this state is Canada. The way in which the powers granted to the federal government under s. 91(24) of the *British North America Act 1867* were realized in legislation (and anticipated in the Indian legislation that preceded it from the 1830s onwards) formed two distinct orders of "good government" in Canada. In one order this claim to the "good" is founded on the representation of citizens; in the other, it is an order of force (akin to that of emergency powers, but lacking a clear limit) used to make those whom it governs "to submit to the restraints of a regular and civilized government."[90]

The significance of Mill's work extends beyond constitutional structure. His version of liberal-imperialism provided the Crown machine with a justification that it could draw upon to immunize it to contestation by the colonized. Once the determination is made that a population on a territory is uncivilized, there is no need to secure their full and informed consent (this process can now be seen as simply one instrument that can be used to reduce conflict, as it is divorced from the question of legal legitimacy). Nor is there any need to investigate how sovereignty was acquired. The entire concept of reciprocity is inapplicable to them because they lack capacity.[91] They have no right to be considered a nation, as their only social existence is either as a handful of individuals or a passive mass. The only requirement that the colonizer must meet in order to justify its actions (to those others who are also civilized) is that the coercion exercised on them is oriented towards civilizing them (it must be pedagogical coercion). As Deputy Superintendent-General Duncan Campbell Scott explained to a special committee of the House of Commons in 1920, "Our object is to continue until there is not a single Indian in Canada that has not been absorbed into the body politic and there is no Indian question, and no Indian department."[92] This is the line of reasoning that connects the unswerving acceptance of Crown sovereignty (whether *de jure* or de facto) to McEachern J's "tin ear,"[93] and the idea that the only rights that they can lay claim to exist are a "mere burden" that is "dependent upon the good will of the sovereign" and

90 Mill, *On Liberty* at 111.

91 Mill, *A Few Words on Non-Intervention* at 119.

92 Moore, *Historical Development* at 114.

93 At the trial level of *Delgammuukw* a Gitxsan elder wanted to sing her *limx'oy* (songs that are part of the *adaawk*), and the judge responded by saying, "I can't hear your Indian song Mrs Johnson because I have a tin ear." *Delgammuukw v. British Columbia* (8 March 1991), Smithers No. 0843 (BCSC).

so can be revoked unilaterally.[94] It is based on a position or perspective that refuses the principle of reciprocity and so refuses the most basic principles of natural justice (*audi alteram partem* and *nemo judex in sua causa*). Its ability to determine the rights and capacities of the other party enables it to frame them as uncivilized, justify the use of force to acquire sovereignty, and present any resistance as a product of false consciousness (the influence of the "despotism of custom") comes at a cost, as its legitimacy is tied to an impossible undertaking (i.e., civilizing them).[95]

The basic logic of Mill's liberal-imperialism enables the colonizer to separate the colonized from the settler-citizens and treat them as wards of the Crown. It does this by employing a pessimistic view of human nature (a tradition that connects Hobbes and Malthus as well as Kant and Hegel).[96] While many variations fit this general description, there are some important common points:

1 The state of nature (viz. the lawless condition of the uncivilized) begins in a way that is contrary to *the truth* of human nature.[97] Whether humanity

---

94 This line of reasoning extends from *St Catherine's Milling* in 1888 to *Calder* in 1973. The words are Lord Watson's from *St Catherine's Milling & Lumber Company v. R* (1888), 14 App. Cas. 46 (PC) at 54–8.

95 Mill would doubtlessly see this as difficult and perhaps even uncertain, but without an actual objective measure there is no way to measure progress, and so its claim to pedagogical value vanishes, leaving only coercion. Also, regarding the use of force to acquire sovereignty, the Court has been clear that "Aboriginal peoples were here first, and they were never conquered." See *Haida Nation* at para. 25, and cited with approval in *MMF* at para. 67. This bars the acquisition of *de jure* sovereignty via force, but it leaves the unanswered question of what its de facto use of force has left it with. This is clearly the legal and normative gulf that the Court's project of reconciliation is being tasked to bridge, but if its terms are set by the undoubted sovereignty of one party, does it not simply attempt to work backwards from the result that the Crown favours? If so, then what is the distinction between *de jure* and de facto sovereignty? It seems to me that this amounts to little more than some judicial legerdemain or, as Borrows refers to it, *sovereign alchemy*.

96 In 1823 Mill was arrested for distributing neo-Malthusian pamphlets to women in working-class areas. Nicholas Capaldi, *John Stuart Mill: A Biography* (Cambridge: Cambridge University Press, 2004) at 41.

97 Mill favoured using the uncivilized distinction, as opposed to the state of nature, which he saw as a useful fiction. As he put it in *Use and Abuse of Political Terms* in 1832, "The question is not whether [the state of nature] ever existed, but whether there is any advantage in supposing it hypothetically; as we assume in argument all kinds of cases which never occur, in order to illustrate those which do. All discussions respecting a state of nature are inquiries into what morality would be if there were no law." And he agreed with Locke that "all independent governments, in relation to one another, are actually in a state of nature, subject to moral duties but obeying no common superior." See John Stuart Mill, *The Collected Works of John Stuart Mill*, vol. 18, *Essays on Politics and Society Part I*, ed. John M. Robson (Toronto: University of Toronto Press, 1977) at 10–11.

is presented as being primarily predatory (the familiar theme captured by the phrase *Homo homini lupus est*[98]) or passive (like Kant's reference to the pointless life of Tahitians[99]), the point remains the same: the state of nature is one of *original sin.*

2 This leads to the concept of pedagogical coercion. The fact that the state of nature begins in a position that is contrary to *the* human nature means that coercion directed against it is justified as a response (i.e., it is a form of self-defence) and, further, this coercion is a form of correction or teaching.[100]

---

98 A Latin proverb (meaning "man is a wolf to man") that stretches from Plautus's *Asinaria* to Francisco de Vitoria and Thomas Hobbes (among several others). Derrida addresses the relationship between various iterations of this proverb and the concept of sovereignty in Jacques Derrida, *The Beast and the Sovereign*, vol. 1, trans. Geoffrey Bennington (Chicago: University of Chicago Press, 2009).

99 In *Reviews of Herder's Ideas on the Philosophy of the History of Mankind* (1785) Kant poses the following question to Herder: "Does the author really mean that, if the happy inhabitants of Tahiti, never visited by more civilized nations, were destined to live in their peaceful indolence for thousands of centuries, it would be possible to give a satisfactory answer to the question of why they should exist at all, and of whether it would not have been just as good if this island had been occupied by happy sheep and cattle as by happy human beings who merely enjoy themselves?" Kant, *Political Writings* at 219–20. This is a curious argument, as the existence of a peaceful people contradicts the fourth proposition in Kant's *Idea for a Universal History*, which holds that antagonism (or "unsocial sociability") is primary (ibid. at 44–5). So it seems that Kant can see the pacific nature of the Tahitians only as an indication of their pointlessness or possibly self-exterminating nature. Herder's response to Kant's antagonistic thesis (or, as Herder refers to it, Kant's "evil doctrine") can be seen in his *Ideas for a Philosophy of History*: "Men of all quarters of the globe, who have perished over the ages, you have not lived solely to manure the earth with your ashes, so that at the end of time your posterity should be made happy by European culture. The very thought of a superior European culture is a blatant insult to the majesty of Nature." J.G. Herder, *Herder on Social and Political Culture*, ed. and trans. F.M. Barnard (Cambridge: Cambridge University Press, 1969) at 311.

100 Hegel draws the logic of this argument out very clearly in the *Philosophy of Right*:

> Pedagogical coercion, or coercion directed against savagery and barbarism [*Wildheit und Rohheit*], admittedly looks like a primary coercion rather than one which comes after a primary coercion which has already occurred. But the merely natural will is in itself a force directed against the idea of freedom as that which has being in itself, which must be protected against this uncivilized [*ungebildeten*] will and given recognition within it. Either an ethical existence [*Dasein*] has already been posited in the family or state, in which case the natural condition referred to above is an act of violence against it, or there is nothing other than a state of nature, a state governed entirely by force, in which case the Idea sets up a right of heroes against it. (Hegel, *Philosophy of Right* at 120–1)

This logic can be seen in Mill, as his extension of the licence to use coercive force on the uncivilized is based upon his concept of the "despotism of custom." We are told that savagery, slavery, and barbarism are contrary to the destiny of human nature and that only movements towards this destiny can be considered to be historical (all others, we can assume, are simply the passing of time – which again aligns with the account of universal history in Kant and Hegel). The problem that this logic is inevitably confronted with is its inability to come to an end: it cannot determine when it has produced the civilized subject and so is caught in what we could refer to as a paradox of a permanently temporary form of government. This is a problem that goes to the very root of the system of justification that this logic establishes. If the coercion that was used to secure sovereignty over the colonized is to retain its status as a response (as self-defence), then the colonizer must be able to civilize them. If the difference between the uncivilized and the civilized is persistent, then either the colonizer must question its foundational claims concerning human nature (and thereby expose its use of coercive force as unprovoked and wrongful) or it must shift the onus to the colonized yet again.

The latter possibility provides the connection between Mill's liberal-imperialism, the extinction thesis, and culturalism. The extinction thesis provides one possible solution to the problem of difference by framing it as a product of biological constitution (a solution Mill consistently rejected, as he maintained that difference was environmentally determined).[101] The answer is attractive as it retains the foundational status of the colonizer's definition of human nature and with it the legitimacy of the colonizer's sovereignty. There is no need to examine the past, as conquest was inevitable. But it offers few practical policy options as, at best; it can justify a palliative version of the *cordon sanitaire* (the Manitoulin Island experiment being the obvious example; another was the *Removal Act* of 1830 in the United States) or the active extermination of the population (the so-called Black War in Tasmania during the early nineteenth century).[102] Culturalism provides the next response by attributing the problem of difference to the thickness of the culture of the colonized. The general line of this type of argument holds that cultural difference is irresolvable, and so the colonizer (whose sovereignty remains unquestioned) should proceed by abandoning the civilizing project and start to practise governance via *indirect rule*. The key point to remember here is that all of these approaches to colonization are related – their commonality

101 Bell, *Reordering the World* at 224–5.

102 For more on the Black War and the *Removal Act of 1830*, see Patrick Brantlinger, *Dark Vanishings: Discourse on the Extinction of Primitive Races, 1800–1930* (Ithaca, NY: Cornell University Press, 2003) at 124–30 and 56–7.

being that that they all are responses to the problem of difference (which each addresses unilaterally) and that each accepts and attempts to legitimate the use of coercive force to obtain sovereignty over the colonized. The following section will further explore the relation between the liberal-imperial civilizing project and the extinction thesis.

2.3 Reading the Right of History: Universal History and the Extinction Thesis

The project of civilizing the colonized is both conceptually and historically related to the extinction strain. An example of this conceptual connection can be seen within Marx's "The British Rule in India" (1853) as he concludes by quoting a poem by Goethe:

> whatever bitterness the spectacle of the crumbling of an ancient world may have for our personal feelings, we have the right, in point of history, to exclaim with Goethe:
>
> "Sollte diese Qual uns quälen
> Da sie unsre Lust vermehrt,
> Hat nicht myriaden Seelen
> Timur's Herrschaft aufgezehrt?"
>
> [Should this torture then torment us
> Since it brings us greater pleasure?
> Were not through the rule of Timur
> Souls devoured without measure?]
>
> Goethe, "An Suleika," Westöstlicher Diwan[103]

It is easy to overlook the reasoning here. But we should pause and ask ourselves what kind of "right" history can provide. There is an admission of tension here over the spectacle of human suffering. The tension is split between two perspectives: first, the personal, which can see only torment (which, we can assume, troubles its conscience), and second, a collective historical perspective that provides a "right" to take pleasure in this spectacle, as "we" can see the arc of historical necessity in it. Hegel provides a detailed account of this tension between perspectives:

> We endure in beholding it a mental torture, allowing no defense or escape but the consideration that what has happened could not be otherwise; that it is a fatality

103 Marx, "British Rule in India."

> which no intervention could alter. And at last we draw back from the intolerable disgust with which these sorrowful reflections threaten us, into the more agreeable environment of our individual life – the Present formed by our private aims and interests. In short we retreat into the selfishness that stands on the quiet shore, and thence enjoy in safety the distant spectacle of "wrecks confusedly hurled." But even regarding History as the slaughter-bench at which the happiness of peoples, the wisdom of States, and the virtue of individuals have been victimized – the question involuntarily arises – to what principle, to what final aim these enormous sacrifices have been offered. From this point the investigation usually proceeds to that which we have made the general commencement of our enquiry. Starting from this we pointed out those phenomena which made up a picture so suggestive of gloomy emotions and thoughtful reflections – as the very field which we, for our part, regard as exhibiting only the means for realizing what we assert to be the essential destiny – the absolute aim, or – which comes to the same thing – the true result of the World's History.[104]

Here again one's "moral reflections" (the "mental torture") are presented as being the product of a picture that shapes one's perspective (one cannot experience anything more than "a gloomy satisfaction in the empty and fruitless sublimities"). The truth of the slaughter-bench (the "true result" or "absolute aim" that gives redemption by accepting slaughter as sacrifice) can be seen only from the perspective of universal history. This revaluation of the spectacle of suffering and death via a universal historical perspective (or "view from nowhere") can be found in Kant, Hegel, and Mill, but it is by no means confined to them. Whether it is Hobbes's *bellum omnium contra omnes*, Smith's claim that savages are self-terminating as a result of their inefficient customs,[105] or Malthus's expansion of this logic in his *Essay on Populations,* they all see progress as the outcome of disaster.[106] They belong to a constellation of thinkers who combine a "struggle for existence" model of human nature with a universal and progressive model of history. The result is a kind of dark theodicy that held that evil means ("pathological" in the Kantian sense) are *necessary* to reach moral ends (J.G. Herder referred to this as Kant's "evil doctrine").[107] Following this logic, the problem we are confronted with when we consider the wreckage of violence and suffering that fills the course of history is not the question of responsibility

104 Hegel, *Philosophy of History* at 21.

105 Adam Smith, *The Wealth of Nations*, ed. Edwin Cannan (Chicago: University of Chicago Press, 1976) at 1:2.

106 For a through account of the development of the extinction thesis, see Brantlinger, *Dark Vanishings* at 85.

107 I would like to thank James Tully for drawing my attention to Herder's critique of Kant on this point. He explores Herder's critique of Kant's concept of culture in his *Public Philosophy in a New Key*, vol. 2, *Imperialism and Civic Freedom* (Cambridge: Cambridge University Press, 2008) at 27–30.

(the "slaughter-bench" is animated by *necessity*), but rather it is a matter of finding the right seat to view it from. The philosophy of history and morality becomes the practice of *anamorphosis.*[108]

The logic is effectively repeated in their accounts of the use of capital punishment (an institution that each supported). Each sees the death of the condemned as having positive significance: Kant sees a natural equality between murder and the death penalty (viz. that the act of murder *necessitates* capital punishment), which allows execution to establish the authority of the lawgiver; Hegel expands on Kant and places it as the very beginning of the state, as the execution of the murderer enables those who witness it to internalize the law and become moral subjects;[109] and Mill (whose views are articulated in a speech he gave to Parliament in 1868) holds that it is an invaluable deterrent as a result of the strong impression that it makes on the innocent.[110] The death of the condemned is, for each, a necessary object lesson in the law. This is its connection to the historical perspective exemplified by Marx above: in each there is a claim to a perspective from which we would be able to read (and to be able to teach others how to read) the true meaning of the suffering of others. This perspective would enable the individual to see purpose and necessity in "the panorama of sin and suffering that history unfolds."[111] It is also why the project of civilizing has always been related to the extinction strain. Whether the uncivilized live under the rule of the colonized or simply die, the same "right" is exercised and the same lesson is learned; all that changes is who survives to learn it. In both versions, colonizers are potentially able to see their rule as being "crowned by fate."[112] The only difficulty that remains is teaching others how to overcome

---

108 Anamorphosis is a technique of perspective in which a distorted image can be reconstituted when the viewer either uses a special object or occupies a specific vantage point.

109 Immanuel Kant, *The Metaphysics of Morals*, ed. and trans. Mary Gregor (New York: New York University Press, 2006) at 17 and 106–7; Hegel, *Philosophy of Right* at 130–2. What this means for Hegel is that the state has to wait for a murder in order to get underway. I have written on this issue in both Kant and Hegel in my book *The End(s) of Community: History, Sovereignty and the Question of Law* (Waterloo, ON: Wilfrid Laurier University Press, 2013).

110 John Stuart Mill, *The Collected Works of John Stuart Mill*, vol. 28, *Public and Parliamentary Speeches Part I November 1850–November 1868*, ed. John M. Robson and Bruce L. Kinzer (Toronto: University of Toronto Press, 1988) at 266–72.

111 Hegel, *Philosophy of History* at 21.

112 The phrase I cite here is taken from Benjamin's "Critique of Violence": "An attack on capital punishment assails, not legal measure, not laws, but law itself in its origin. For if violence, violence crowned by fate, is the origin of law, then it may be readily supposed that where the highest violence, that over life and death, occurs in the legal system, the origins of law jut manifestly and fearsomely into existence." The same association is at work here: the right of the colonizer is presented as being the product of fate (historical necessity) and not the contingent (and thus contestable) actions of human actors. This claim to historical necessity does not simply respond to the question of "right" but jumps over it entirely (viz. the claim

their personal feelings and see the course of reason through history: this is the role of Mill's individual (hero and genius). The problem – both of governing and of history – is that while their appearance is the product of necessity, their cultivation is, at best, an uncertain undertaking.

The capacity to adopt the universal historical perspective is a limited one: solving the anamorphosis of reason in history requires that rare touch of philosophical genius. One's endurance is always being tested, as the tension between one's own limited perspective and the universal perspective remains constant. Much like Mill's account of the progress of civilization, there is always the risk of losing the narrative and backsliding into "moral reflections" that can see the course of history only as "wrecks confusedly hurled." Few are able to find the right seat in the theatre of history. It is this problem that leads Mill towards what Duncan Bell refers to as "melancholic resignation" in the later years of his life.[113] In a letter to A.M. Francis in 1869 Mill writes, "The common English abroad – I do not know if in this they are worse than other people – are intensely contemptuous of what they consider inferior races, & seldom willingly practise any other mode of attaining their ends with them than bullying & blows."[114] His resignation here is not due to the use of coercive force per se, but the inability or unwillingness of the "common English" to use it *correctly* (i.e., they use it for "pathological" and not rational ends of civilizing). It is not that Mill doubts the validity of his own perspective: on this point he never wavers. Rather, as the colonial violence spread during the middle of the nineteenth century, he assigned the failure to the settlers, the colonial administrators, and the uncivilized themselves. There were simply not enough of the "highly gifted and instructed" individuals to guide the many though the process of civilizing the world.[115] This line of reasoning allows a further layer of insulation to the universal historical perspective. If there are failures in the project of

---

of fate effectively brackets and neutralizes the very question of "right"). The claim that "we have the right, in point of history" – which is, as we have seen, by no means confined to Marx – is an indicator that there is, as Benjamin notes concerning the death penalty, "something rotten in the law." Walter Benjamin, "Critique of Violence," in *Reflections: Essays, Aphorisms, Autobiographical Writings*, ed. Peter Demetz and trans. Edmund Jephcott, 277–300 (New York: Schocken Books, 1986) at 286.

113 Bell, *Reordering the World* at 12. Also, for an excellent account of the varieties of historicism and their relation to empire in Victorian Britain, refer to chapter 5 of Bell's aforementioned book.

114 Bell also cites this letter as an example of Mill's melancholic resignation at 232. For the original, see John Stuart Mill, *The Collected Works of John Stuart Mill*, vol. 17, *The Later Letters of John Stuart Mill 1849–1873 Part IV*, ed. Francis E. Mineka and Dwight N. Lindley (Toronto: University of Toronto Press, 1972) at 1599.

115 Mill, *On Liberty* at 59.

civilizing, they can be attributed to the one, the few, or the many, but not the perspective itself.

The universal historical perspective is necessary to the project of civilizing (it provides, in Marx's words, the "*right in point of history*"), as it immunizes the colonizer from the contestation of the colonized. In this it follows a kind of kettle logic that allows the colonizer to respond to the colonized accusation:

1 The coercive force that we used did not harm you, it benefited you.
2 You were already destroying yourselves when we found you.
3 You would have died in any case.

The three statements are inconsistent: the first denies that the wrong was actually harmful, the second attributes the wrong to the colonized themselves, and the third denies any involvement in the wrong whatsoever.[116] All three are active forms of justification in the project of civilizing put forward by thinkers such as Mill, Smith, and Malthus. The extinction thesis is simply one member of a family of arguments. Its utility is that when the civilizing project shows signs of failing it allows the colonizer to attribute that failure to the biological constitution and/or the thick cultural organization of the colonized.[117] Like the civilizing project of liberal-imperialism, its strength is due to its basis in a "view from nowhere": it treats the colonized as objects of knowledge. This, in turn, provides both a justification for the process of colonization and an explanation that can soothe the conscience of the colonizer. In practical terms the argument offers very little: the colonized can be isolated, scientifically studied, or simply exterminated.[118] The Darwinian revolution in the mid-nineteenth century

---

116 The term "kettle logic" derives from a story that Sigmund Freud relates in both *The Interpretation of Dreams* and *Jokes and Their Relation to the Unconscious* in which a man is accused by his neighbour of returning a kettle in a damaged condition, and he responds with three inconsistent arguments: (1) that he had returned the kettle undamaged, (2) that it was already damaged when he borrowed it, and (3) that he never borrowed it in the first place. See *The Interpretation of Dreams*, ed. and trans. James Strachey (New York: Basic Books, 2010) at 143–5; *Jokes and Their Relation to the Unconscious*, ed. and trans. James Strachey (New York: W.W. Norton, 1989) at 72 and 254–5.

117 For more on the theme of the auto-extinction of Aboriginal peoples, see Brantlinger, *Dark Vanishings* at 1–3.

118 It is important to note that the isolation of the Aboriginal peoples of Canada from the settler population was not driven by the extermination thesis. Rather, it was based on the imperial policy of non-interference or non-molestation that finds expression in the *Royal Proclamation, 1763*. While it was possible to use the extermination thesis to repurpose or reimagine this division (as was done in the Manitoulin Island experiment), its basis lies in the nation-to-nation relationship that pre-existed the process of internal colonization, which

did little to change this pre-existing discursive structure. Rather, as Brantlinger notes, it strengthened it.[119]

The common feature that relates the extinction thesis to the civilizing project of liberal-imperialism is that both foreclose the possibility that the practice of colonization (the use of coercive force to take lands and to civilize others) constitutes a wrong. This is foreclosed at a conceptual level because if it is put into question it would also entail that the universal historical perspective (which is, in Wittgenstein's terms, the "world-picture" or *Weltbild* that provides the unmentioned "matter-of-course foundation" for both[120]) is *not universal.* Fichte's response to Kant's argument for the rational necessity of the death penalty for murderers draws out the implicit connection between an *absolute* right to use coercive force (a feature that is present in Mill's liberal-imperialism) and *absolute* sovereign authority. Fichte responds to Kant by conceding that his argument would be correct *if* we lived "in a moral-world, governed by an omniscient judge in accordance with moral laws."[121] But, he asks, "from where does a mortal get the right of this moral world-order, the right to render the criminal his just deserts?"[122] He advances his argument further and argues that anyone who could maintain this argument within this world would also be committed "to say that the sovereign's rightful title to it is unexaminable; to derive the sovereign's authority from God; and to regard the sovereign as God's visible representative and every government as a theocracy."[123]

This same argument applies to the project of colonization and all of its justifications. If it was possible to secure a "view from nowhere" and see the rationality of history, then it would also be possible to ignore the demands of the colonized and act as the judge of our own actions (the principles of *audi alteram partem* and *nemo judex in sua causa* do not apply to God). Without these (impossible) conditions, how does a mortal individual living within the confines of this world get the right to determine who is civilized and who is not? Is this not simply a variation to the theological question of who is among the saved and the damned or the living and the dead?[124] This is the problem with the civilizing arguments. They are immune to

---

began in the mid-nineteenth century. For a thorough explanation of the process of "internal colonization," see Tully, *Philosophy in a New Key* at 1:259–61.

119 Brantlinger, *Dark Vanishings* at 164.

120 Wittgenstein, *On Certainty* at 24.

121 J.G. Fichte, *Foundations of Natural Right*, ed. Frederick Neuhouser and trans. Michael Baur (New York: New York University Press, 2000) at 246. I explore Fichte's arguments against Kant on this point in more detail in *The End(s) of Community*.

122 Ibid.

123 Ibid.

124 A question whose absurdity Christ points to in John 8:7 when he states, "He that is without sin among you, let him cast the first stone."

contestation, but as a result they are caught in their own snare. There is no possibility of progress towards the end goal: all that is left is melancholic resignation as the laboratories of civilizing become nothing more than Kafkaesque penal colonies.

2.4 From Enfranchisement to Reconciliation: Culturalism and Indirect Rule

The liberal-imperial civilizing project had grounded itself on the assumption that culture was thin. This was the practical point of contact for its entire grand historical narrative: once the "scattered rays" and "broken coloured lights" of the world had been collected, catalogued, and sorted, all that was left to do was "to complete and purify them."[125] This meant that the "despotism of custom" (whose existence justified colonial despotism as a kind of universal historico-civilizational act of self-defence) had to be broken up in order to free the creative energy of the individual. For this assumption to hold true, the resistance of the colonized (which, from the confines of this framework, could be seen only as a kind of misguided atavism) would need to gradually dissipate. As it became clear that the colonial rebellions of the first half of the nineteenth century were intensifying, the promises of the liberal-imperial civilizing project soon began to fade, and a crisis of legitimacy set in. Culture had proven to be far too thick. This led to a turning point in British imperial ideology as it moved from universalism to culturalism and *indirect rule*.[126] This approach started from the assumption that culture was thick. This meant that the invasive array of political institutions and experimental civilizing technologies would need to be removed, as they were destabilizing native societies and thereby threatening imperial order.[127] For this order to be stabilized, governing powers would need to be devolved to the colonies themselves. And this, in turn, brought about a distinct shift in the justification of imperial legitimacy as it moved from being the universal historical destiny of civilization to being a necessary rehabilitative framework.[128] The continuity that maintains the relation between the civilizing project and culturalism is that, despite all of their differences, both serve as modes of imperial legitimation.[129] They are also bound together in a dialectical

125 Mill, *On Liberty* at 289.

126 For a detailed review of this transition, see Mantena, *Alibis of Empire*.

127 Ibid. at 171.

128 Mantena refers to this mode of legitimation as the "alibi" of empire (ibid. at 12).

129 In the chapter entitled "The Negotiation of Reconciliation" Tully states that what has remained constant through the phases of colonial domination that have occurred since the establishment of the *Indian Act* is that "Aboriginal peoples are subordinate and subject to the

relation as the wreckage of the former provides the need for the rehabilitative framework of the latter.

The problematic that I am attempting to address follows this mid-nineteenth-century transition from a different perspective. As imperial Britain devolved powers to the settler colonies, internal colonization began.[130] Within Canada this process was informed and structured by the liberal-imperial project of civilizing that operated under the term *enfranchisement*. The project followed the liberal-imperial formula that Mill set out: Indigenous forms of government were systematically broken up and replaced with *bands*; individual members of the previously self-determining peoples were catalogued and registered as a population of *Indians*; their children were forcefully removed and placed in residential schools; their lands were divided up into a system of reserves; and everything occurs under the all-encompassing non-representative power of the Department of Indian Affairs. The legal-political order established under the authority of s. 91(24) and enacted through the *Indian Act* existed as a parallel system within Canada whose closest family member is the state of emergency. There is the system of responsible representative government for the settler-citizen (the form of "good government" Mill saw as appropriate for the civilized), and then there is the non-representative and authoritarian system that was designed for the colonized.[131]

The aim of this parallel system was the complete unification of the body politic: *Indians* were seen as a temporary impediment. This aim remains in place from the 1830s through to the White Paper in 1969. Its mandate was ultimately derived from a "view from nowhere," which enabled it to legitimize its existence as "good government" for the uncivilized subjects of the Crown.

Canadian Government, rather than equal, self-governing nations subject to the agreements reached though the treaty system." Tully, *Philosophy in a New Key* at 1:226–7.

130 Duncan Bell argues – contra Uday Singh Meta and the historical work on empire that has followed his lead by focusing on the colonial experience of India from Pitts to Mantena – that "many British liberals regarded settler colonialism as a preferable model of empire to the conquest and alien rule associated with India." Bell, *Reordering the World* at 9 and 366. This is a crucial point to keep in mind, because "most of the so-called 'anti-imperialists' from the eighteenth century to the late nineteenth, from Bentham through Spencer to Hobson and Hobhouse, promoted settler colonialism of one kind or another" (at 369).

131 While the band governance model first set in place through the *Gradual Enfranchisement Act* in 1869 – this was later incorporated into the *Indian Act* in 1873 and forms the basis of the current system – does establish a system of "responsible government" on the municipal model, it is difficult to characterize it as "representative." The system of band councils was imposed as part of the civilizing process, and so to characterize it as "representative" raises the question of what it *represents* (viz. the nineteenth-century project of unifying the Canadian nation state by taking Indigenous lands and civilizing Indigenous peoples). See the *Act for the gradual enfranchisement of Indians, the better management of Indian affairs, and to extend the provisions of the Act 31st Victoria, Chapter 42*, SC 1869, c. 6.

There are, as I have argued, limits to this approach. As Quinten Skinner notes in *Liberty before Liberalism*, "What it is possible to do in politics is generally limited by what it is possible to legitimize. What you can hope to legitimize, however, depends on what courses of action you can plausibly range under existing normative principles. But this implies that, even if your professed principles never operate as your motives, but only as rationalizations for your behavior, they will nevertheless help to shape and limit what lines of action you can successfully pursue."[132]

By the late 1960s it was no longer possible to legitimize the project of enfranchisement, because there had been a shift of the normative principles. The constant and increasing resistance of the Indigenous peoples in Canada, combined with the growing resistance to colonial authority on a global scale (e.g., the American Indian Movement in the United States and the growing resistance of peoples in the "Third World" for decolonization), had brought about a political sea change. It was no longer acceptable to unilaterally determine the limits of the principle of liberty. In short, the "*right in point of history*" that Marx claimed for Europeans in 1853 had expired.

Within Canada, the White Paper was the last explicit attempt to use the Crown machine to unilaterally answer the Indian Question. Its ultimate failure was extended by the *Calder* decision in 1973 when a majority of the Supreme Court of Canada found that the rights of Indigenous peoples were not derived solely from the Crown, but were inherent in the fact that they were here before the Europeans arrived. This entailed a complete reorganization of the Crown's response to the Indian Question. The project of enfranchisement becomes the project of reconciliation.[133] This is not to say that a complete legal and political project simply takes shape overnight. Rather, the change in normative principles (from the unilateral "*right in point of history*" or "view from nowhere" to consent) changed the plausible range of actions that could be used to legitimize the authority of the Crown.

---

132 Skinner, *Liberty before Liberalism* at 105.

133 This is somewhat of an oversimplification as the project of enfranchisement was a statutory arrangement under the legislative authority of Parliament, whereas the project of reconciliation is an invention of the courts. Despite this changing of hands (sleight-of-hand is a more apt phrase as the lines of power remain unilateral, but they are recessed behind the curtains of jurisprudence) from one branch of government to another, much of the nineteenth-century administrative apparatus that was designed to assimilate Indigenous peoples remains in place. This nineteenth-century apparatus has been gradually repurposed and reframed as the settler colonies in the Americas, Australia, and New Zealand "gained independence from their empires by revolution or devolution and developed the institutions of modern civil citizenship in ways similar to Europe. After the Second World War, they developed modern minority rights in domestic and international law as a tactic of 'internal colonization.'" See Tully, *Public Philosophy* at 2:259.

The most basic outlines of this transformation echo the change in imperial British policy in the mid-nineteenth century: culture is thick, and the previous policies have brought little more than resistance and rebellion, and so the basis of Crown authority needed to be shifted in order to prevent further collapse. This shift to "indirect governance" in nineteenth-century imperial British policy bears a family resemblance to the shift to reconciliation in Canada; both are rehabilitative tactics for stabilizing the existing power structure by concealing its strings. But there are also differences between the nineteenth-century model of "indirect governance" and reconciliation. In particular, the context of internal colonization shifts the importance of lands.[134] While the imperial Crown could withdraw and continue to pursue its interests via informal mechanisms of economics and trade from the security of the metropole, the domestic Crown could not. The apparatus of the previous project remains in place but is gradually repurposed in an ad hoc manner. There has been an informal devolution of powers, but the basic structure of the *Indian Act* remains in place. This gives the Crown a number of powers that cannot be accounted for in principle, as they are remnants from the previous normative *world picture*, which rely on the "view from nowhere."[135] The most obvious of these are the unilateral powers of infringement and recognition (Parliament's ability to use s. 91(24) and the *Indian Act* to determine who and who is not an *Indian* or a *band* is both extended and buffered by the Court's unquestioned assumption of Crown sovereignty).[136] By continuing to grant these powers legal force, we fall prey to what John Borrows has referred to as the alchemy of sovereignty.[137] This is a difficult trap to escape from. As Quintin Skinner states, "It is remarkably difficult to avoid falling under the spell of our own intellectual heritage. As we analyse and reflect on our normative concepts, it is easy to become bewitched into believing that the ways of thinking about them bequeathed to us by the

134 Interestingly in Canada this is more than merely an alibi for the power of the federal Crown, as the Indian Association of Alberta (under the leadership of Harold Cardinal) responded to the White Paper with *Citizens Plus* (it takes its title from a term used in the Hawthorn Report and it is also known as the Red Paper), which argued for the retention of the *Indian Act* as a means of protecting their lands. See Indian Association of Alberta, *Citizens Plus* (Edmonton: Indian Association of Alberta, 1970).

135 This includes the legal doctrines that are based in this world picture such as *terra nullius* and discovery.

136 The Court determines standing by determining whether or not claimants are "bands" within the meaning of the *Indian Act*. The collective nature of Aboriginal rights (which has been assigned through colonial law and not by the actual political-legal practices and structures of Indigenous peoples) was recently upheld by the Court in *Behn v. Moulton Contracting Ltd.*, [2013] 2 SCR 227.

137 Borrows, "Sovereignty's Alchemy," 537. Also see the recent continuation of this in Borrows, "Durability of Terra Nullius."

mainstream of our intellectual tradition must be *the* ways of thinking about them."[138] Freeing ourselves from this spell (or to use Wittgenstein's terminology "picture") requires that we expose the provisional "system of judgments" that holds it in place and makes it seem as if it is beyond question and contestation.[139]

We will pause here a moment and reconsider our course thus far from a broader vantage point. The purpose of this chapter was to explore how the discursive foundations of nineteenth-century British imperialism addressed (or failed to address) the question of legitimacy. Mill's liberal-imperialism offers legitimacy for despotic modes of governance, but the legitimacy hinges on civilizing the colonized population (i.e., the legitimacy was contingent upon the despotism being temporary and for the improvement of the colonized). Since there are no possible objective, a priori criteria to determine who is or is not civilized, the legitimacy that is promised is always tied to a future that is yet to come (viz. the best that can be offered is philosophical legerdemain to buffer claims by deferral and distraction). In practice this means that the system of governance becomes unable to account for resistance over time, and the promise of legitimacy fades. It can turn to the extinction thesis, which fixes the blame on the colonized themselves, but this too is tied to the promise of a future event (i.e., it is legitimate only if the colonized become extinct). Maine's culturalism rejects the civilizing thesis and argues that culture is "thick," and so colonized peoples are best left to govern their internal affairs. This offers a set of pragmatic instructions for maintaining an indirect system of colonial rule, but it does not offer legitimacy for it. Rather, it simply accepts domination as part of the status quo and moves to stabilize it by ignoring the question of legitimacy altogether. Its claim to stability rests on the colonized either not noticing or simply accepting this arrangement of governance. All of these discourses work to *finesse* rather than *face* the question of legitimacy. They are designed to provide a foundation for relationships of domination, but their solutions are, as we have seen, constitutively flawed. The Crown machinery has used all three of these discursive strains; they have overlapped and criss-crossed through its 150-year historical development from the project of enfranchisement to the project of reconciliation. The upshot is that the question of legitimacy *remains open*. My aim in the chapters that follow will be both to show how the Crown machinery has dealt with this question, and to help open up the possibility of facing it directly so as to offer the possibility of a *reconciliation with* Indigenous peoples.

138 Skinner, *Liberty before Liberalism* at 116.
139 Wittgenstein, *On Certainty* at §105. Also see Tully, *Philosophy in a New Key* at 1:32–3.

Part 3

A Despotism for Dealing with Barbarians: A Survey of the Foundations of Indian Policy in Canada

To seek it with thimbles, to seek it with care;
  To pursue it with forks and hope;
To threaten its life with a railway-share;
  To charm it with smiles and soap!

For the Snark's a peculiar creature, that won't
  Be caught in a commonplace way.
Do all that you know, and try all that you don't:
  Not a chance must be wasted to-day!

For England expects – I forbear to proceed:
  'Tis a maxim tremendous, but trite:
And you'd best be unpacking the things that you need
  To rig yourselves out for the fight.

Lewis Carroll, *The Hunting of the Snark* (42)

In this chapter I will situate the *Indian Act*, s. 91(24), its associated institutions and practices of governance – viz. the machinery of the Crown[1] – in the context

1 As in previous chapters, I will employ this term to refer to a system of legal-philosophical arguments that are used to justify and legitimate the actions of the Crown in relation to Aboriginal peoples (viz. the series of arguments that are deployed to justify the unilateral taking of lands and the despotic governance of Aboriginal peoples – e.g., Lockean conceptions of property and agriculture, Mill's model of culture and universal history, the concept of the struggle for existence that connects Hobbes, Malthus, and Darwin, etc.). I use the term to convey a number of key characteristics: (1) The arguments make subjective judgments appear to be objective statements (i.e., they appear to be impersonal, objective, or mechanical – e.g., nomads are incapable of owning land – and are therefore presented as being immunized against contestation). (2) The arguments do not form a single coherent and constant system,

of its imperial foundations in the nineteenth century and follow the general line of their development to the White Paper in 1969.[2] This chapter follows up on the investigation of the European discursive foundations from the previous chapter by engaging with what the colonial institutions and authorities in Canada were doing during the same period. There is thus a shift in focus from the broader philosophical discourses, to the legislative and administrative system that was being constructed and (continually) recalibrated in relation to Aboriginal resistance. The aim here will be to see both the continuities and discontinuities between the broader discursive trends and the administrative practices within the dominion. I have selected this specific period, as it covers the transition from British imperial rule through to the devolution of powers to the dominion in 1867, and the development of the "vast administrative dictatorship" of the *Indian Act*.[3]

These changes and the practices of resistance that responded to them shaped the Crown's administrative aims and practices. This construction was by no means smooth or continual (i.e., the Crown machinery did not move from the draughtsman's sketchbook to the reality of the colony in one continuous move). Rather, the machinery of the Crown takes shape in and through the concurrent interaction of related and conflicting processes that stretch from philosophical propositions, legislative drafting, administrative interpretation, enforcement, institutional design, scientific discourse, and the continually adapting

but rather an ad hoc assemblage that can be reordered and recalibrated in accordance with resistance (e.g., there is much to distinguish the relationship between the Crown and Aboriginal peoples in the position taken by the Privy Council in *St Catherine's Milling* and the most recent articulation in *Tsilhqot'in Nation*, but they both maintain unilateral Crown sovereignty. Just as there is much to distinguish J.S. Mill's model of imperial liberalism – with its civilized/uncivilized distinction and universal history – from Henry Maine's culturalism and indirect rule, their political consequences bear a striking resemblance, as both maintain the legitimacy of imperialism). (3) The constant element is the intransigent character (i.e., metaphysical) of the arguments (e.g., the Court in *Sparrow* stating that Crown sovereignty was never doubted. Another example would be Kant's claim that questioning the historical warrant of the mechanism of government is futile or even criminal, or Mill's paradoxical claim that a "good despotism" is impossible *except as a means to a temporary purpose*). I have attempted to capture this last characteristic with the term *Bluebeard logic* (i.e., an open contradiction within a system of propositions and arguments that cannot be accounted for and so is supported only by the use or threat of physical violence – see note 79 of part 1). Wittgenstein captures this characteristic in §112 of the *Philosophical Investigations*: "A simile that has been absorbed into the forms of our language produces a false appearance, and this disquiets us. 'But *this* isn't how it is!' – we say. 'Yet *this* is how it has to *be*!'"

2 See the "Statement of the Government of Canada on Indian Policy 1969," presented to the first session of the twenty-eighth Parliament by Jean Chrétien, minister of Indian affairs and northern development, 25 June 1969.

3 Tully, *Strange Multiplicity* at 90–1.

and innovating practices of resistance of Aboriginal peoples.[4] Its formation is more analogous to sedimentation interacting with the sudden eruption of volcanic activity or, to follow the mechanistic line of comparison, it is like the ad hoc construction and maintenance of an engine from a scrapyard, where the haphazard selection of parts never quite fit the task at hand, which necessarily entails that the engine never runs smoothly – it continually resides on the very edge of collapse. Any attempt to provide an exhaustive – or even general – survey of this vast and complicated territory would require a far more extensive treatment than I can offer here. My aim is not to provide an exhaustive map of this period so that I could somehow settle what was going on once and for all. Such a complete map is an impossibility, akin to the map in Lewis Carroll's *Sylvie and Bruno Concluded* that had "the scale of a mile to the mile."[5] Accordingly, the criterion of success here will not be to somehow discover that the general administrative program from 1867 to 1969 was *identical* to the civilizing imperialism set out by J.S. Mill. Rather, my aim here is to provide a few brief surveys of the historical landscape as seen from different scales and assemble them as a kind of sketchbook of reminders. As a survey (in line with Wittgenstein's concept of "perspicuous representation"), I am looking to provide a few landmarks or points of reference that will enable us to find our way about. The aim is not to provide the definitive map at this – or indeed any other – scale, but to provide a different *point of view*. The map is *not* the territory, but this does not render maps useless.[6] The landmarks and points of reference offer us a way of seeing

4 Refer to Foucault's comments on his use of the term *dispositif* in Foucault, *Power/Knowledge at* 194.

5 Lewis Carroll, *Sylvie and Bruno Concluded* (London: Macmillan, 1893) at 169. J.L. Borges draws out the absurdity of such a metaphysical desideratum in his short story "Del rigor en la ciencia" (On rigour in science), where he presents (through the device of literary forgery as it is presented as a citation from Suárez Miranda, *Travels of Prudent Men*, bk 4, ch. 45, Lérida, 1658), an empire where the science of cartography has become so exact that only a 1:1 scale will suffice:

> In that Empire, the Art of Cartography attained such Perfection that the map of a single Province occupied the entirety of a City, and the map of the Empire, the entirety of a Province. In time, those Unconscionable Maps no longer satisfied, and the Cartographers Guilds struck a Map of the Empire whose size was that of the Empire, and which coincided point for point with it. The following Generations, who were not so fond of the Study of Cartography as their Forebears had been, saw that that vast map was Useless, and not without some Pitilessness was it, that they delivered it up to the Inclemencies of Sun and Winters. In the Deserts of the West, still today, there are Tattered Ruins of that Map, inhabited by Animals and Beggars; in all the Land there is no other Relic of the Disciplines of Geography. (J.L. Borges, *Collected Fictions*, trans. Andrew Hurley (New York: Penguin, 1998) at 325)

6 I am making use of Gordon Baker's distinction between what he refers to as the "Bird's eye View Model" approach to Wittgenstein (viz. that he – much like Gilbert Ryle – is mapping

things again, from a different angle, under a different light, so that we can see what once seemed immutable and constant to be conventional and accidental, thereby opening up the possibility of other paths.

With this in mind, I have limited the scope of this investigation to two particular lines or aspects: membership and political form. The structure of the chapter will be divided up as follows:

1 I will begin by setting out a sketch of the pre-Confederation changes in Indian administration from 1812 to 1867. This will provide the reader with a sense of the transition from treaty federalism under imperial rule to administrative despotism within the confines of the dominion. The scale of focus here is broad and meant to place the series of transitions that are occurring in British North America within their imperial context (viz. the mid-nineteenth-century transition to a model of indirect rule). My aim is to provide a picture of the pre-Confederation landscape that can serve as an object of comparison (in Wittgenstein's sense of the term), so that we can see the transformations in Indian policy that have followed.
2 I will shift the scale of my focus down slightly and concentrate on the importance of the Indian Question from the perspective of the dominion from 1867 to the 1920s. I will move from providing a general survey of western expansion and the numbered treaties and then focus my attention

out *the* grammatical geography and policing its limits) and his more open-ended approach to "perspicuous representation." See Gordon Baker, *Wittgenstein's Method: Neglected Aspects*, ed. Katherine Morris (Oxford: Blackwell, 2004) at 28–46. I would also add the caveat that I do not adhere to the therapeutic reading of Wittgenstein as, by my understanding, the pictures do not simply make *individual philosophers* – or, for that matter, philosophers as a *particular group* – suffer disquiet. While there are undoubtedly pictures whose enchanting effects are confined to the cloistered ranks of professional philosophers, they can have a far wider social reach, one that I believe Charles Taylor captures with his use of the term *social imaginary*. As he puts it, "What I'm calling the social imaginary extends beyond the immediate background which makes sense of our particular practices. This is not an arbitrary extension of the concept, because just as the practice without the understanding wouldn't make sense for us, and thus wouldn't be possible, so this understanding supposes, if it is to make sense, a wider grasp of our whole predicament, how we stand to each other, how we got to where we are, how we relate to other groups, etc." See Taylor's magisterial book *A Secular Age* (Cambridge, MA: Belknap, 2007) at 172–3. If we take Wittgenstein's pictures in this wider sense, we can begin to get a sense of the stakes involved, as they provide the normative *justification for* and *legitimization of* violence. This latter aspect is what I feel gets lost in all of the therapeutic approaches. It is not merely a balm to the troubled mind (which would make it much more related to the ethical project of the *Tractatus* and a certain reading of Heidegger's concern with authenticity), but a work that is *for others* and focused on the intersubjective aspects of justice. For this I draw more on the political readings of Wittgenstein (in particular, James Tully). For a recent and thorough account of this reading, see Michael Temelini, *Wittgenstein and the Study of Politics* (Toronto: University of Toronto Press, 2015).

on how these processes and policies led to the first phase of wide-scale confrontation (e.g., the rise of pan-Indian political resistance and the increasing use of cultural and political suppression via legislative amendments to the *Indian Act* and more informal enforcement mechanisms). This section will – like the previous section – be restricted to a picture of the landscape of Indian policy during this period. My focus will be on the legislation and policy that is dominant in this period, as this connects it to current government practices. I note this specifically because there is still, even at this point, a counter-narrative within the various governments of the Crown that advises a different course of action. This can be found in a number of speeches by key political actors or even in parliamentary debates, and while it is valuable for enriching our sense of the debates leading up to legislation, it is not our focus here. The main purpose of this section is to allow us to see the shift from one mode of Indian administration to another (viz. imperial to the dominion). This will also provide some background for the more detailed case study that follows it.

3 The following section forms the heart of the chapter. Here I will narrow the focus to a particular event: the Six Nations' appeal for justice at the League of Nations in 1923. I believe that this event offers us a useful point of reference or landmark for determining the overall form of Indian policy during this period (i.e., from its first full articulation in the *Indian Act* of 1876 through to its crisis of legitimacy in the 1950s and partial collapse with the White Paper in 1969). It is ideally suited to this function for a number of reasons. First, it involves a direct political confrontation between an Aboriginal nation and the dominion over the question of legitimacy and self-government and so constitutes "a direct challenge to the very foundations of federal policy."[7] Second, this confrontation reaches the international stage, and Canada is forced to justify its Indian policies to other states during the first period of decolonization (the delegates of Estonia, Ireland, Panama, and Persia – nations all very familiar with the vicissitudes of imperial realpolitik – supported the Six Nations' cause[8]). Third, Canada's response is written by Duncan Campbell Scott, who served as deputy superintendent of the Department of Indian Affairs from 1913 to 1932, and one of the events leads to one of the most aggressive periods of assimilation policy in Canadian history (e.g., in response, a permanent police presence was established at Grand River, the hereditary council was replaced, a network of informers was employed to break local resistance,

7 E. Brian Titley, *A Narrow Vision: Duncan Campbell Scott and the Administration of Indian Affairs in Canada* (Vancouver: University of British Columbia Press, 1986) at 134.

8 Ibid. at 123.

and in 1927 s. 141 of the *Indian Act* was adopted, which effectively barred Indians from accessing legal representation until its repeal in 1951[9]).

4 In the final section I will zoom out again to provide a brief overview of the transformations in Indian policy that followed the Second World War. I will address the 1951 amendments to the *Indian Act*, which followed Canada's commitment to the United Nations *Universal Declaration of Human Rights*. My aim here will be to place the changes going on within Canada in the international context of this wave of decolonization. This leads to the ultimate crisis of legitimacy for the policy of assimilation, which took shape with the White Paper in 1969. The detail in this section will be general, as its purpose is to provide a bridge to the following chapters on what

---

9 Ibid. at 59, 134, and 157. I should note two points here. First, this was not the first time that the colonial government barred access to legal representation. *An Act to make better provision for the Administration of Justice in the unorganized tracts of Country in Upper Canada, 1853* prohibited "any person" from "inciting Indians or half-breeds." The terms "incitement" and "disturbance of the public peace" are flexible, as they depend on who comprises the "public" and what its "peace" requires. Their effect in this context was to place a blanket ban on any form of resistance to the unilateral imposition of justice in "unorganized tracts" (i.e., Indigenous territories). This was extended to all persons, so it precluded anyone from acting as legal counsel for Indians on land issues and was passed as a direct result of Aboriginal "intransigence" regarding the Robinson-Huron treaty. I'd like to thank Robert Hamilton for drawing my attention to this early predecessor to s. 141. See Janet E. Chute, "Singwaukonse: A Nineteenth-Century Innovative Ojibwa Leader," *Ethnohistory* 45 (1998): 86. Second, s. 141 was not introduced *solely* to deal with the Six Nations status case. The land claims issue in British Columbia was another source of legal resistance to DIA policy (cf. Titley, *Narrow Vision* at 135–61). The hearings of the 1920 Special Committee of the House of Commons examining the *Indian Act* amendments are instructive here. Counsel for the Six Nations (arguing for independence) and the Nisga'a (arguing for recognition of their title) appeared before the committee and were met with considerable annoyance from the MPs on the committee – especially the committee chair (my thanks to Kerry Wilkins for pointing this out to me). In addition, decisions of the Judicial Committee of the Privy Council from the 1918 decision in *Re Southern Rhodesia Land* and the 1921 decision in *Amodu Tijani v. Secretary, Southern Nigeria* had held that Aboriginal title pre-existed British authority and remained in place unless explicitly extinguished. This was a distinct reversal from the position that Lord Watson had taken in *St Catherine's Milling and Lumber Company v. R* (1888), 14 App. Cas. 46, which held that Aboriginal title was created by the British Crown and could be removed at its pleasure. As Paul Tennant points out, it is reasonable to presume that this played a major role in Parliament's move to ban claims-related activities in 1927. He also notes that the removal of this policy in the 1951 revisions to the *Indian Act* could be due to the fact that after 1949 the Supreme Court of Canada becomes the final court of appeal, and this means that the cases of the Judicial Committee of the Privy Council would henceforth only serve as precedents. See Paul Tennant, *Aboriginal Peoples and Politics: The Indian Land Question in British Columbia, 1849–1989* (Vancouver: University of British Columbia Press, 1992) at 214–15. Peter H. Russell also provides a compelling account of events in the early years of the dominion (and beyond) in his excellent new book *Canada's Odyssey: A Country Based on Incomplete Conquests* (Toronto: University of Toronto Press, 2017).

I am referring to as the era of reconciliation and indirect rule, which will cover from 1969 to Canada's endorsement of the *United Nations Declaration on the Rights of Indigenous Peoples* in 2016.

3.1 Pre-Confederation to the *Indian Act* of 1876

In keeping with the analogy of sedimentation, we can say that, generally speaking, three layers of Indian policy exist prior to Confederation under the *British North America Act, 1867*. For the sake of clarity, I will refer to the three layers as imperial federalism, imperial civilizing, and assimilation/indirect rule. These layers are by no means entirely distinct. There is interaction across and between the layers. Some principles are retained but repurposed to suit new goals, whereas others seem to be suddenly discarded but are then followed by variations that resemble them operating under new names. These three layers are merely a rough-and-ready guide to help the reader get a sense of the gradual administrative transitions and volcanic changes that the nineteenth century brings to Indian policy.

A. Imperial Federalism

This could also be referred to as *suzerainty*, or *treaty-federalism*.[10] The origins of this layer stretch back to the period prior to the *Royal Proclamation of 1763*. During this period the official policy was to leave relations with Indian nations to the governors of colonial governments. By the end of the seventeenth century it had become abundantly clear to the British imperial authorities that this policy was, at best, impractical. The problem was that the local settler populations were continually expanding into Aboriginal lands and displacing them. At its basis this stems from a distinction between imperial and colonial interests regarding land-acquisition (i.e., the difference in their respective scales of governance translated into conflicting interests in land). This had led to escalating conflicts that threatened "trade, travel, and diplomacy and could even lead to

---

10 John Milloy uses the term *Imperial federalism* in *Historical Overview*. For the term *suzerainty*, refer to Brian Slattery, "Making Sense of Aboriginal Treaty Rights," *Canadian Bar Review* 79 (2000): 198, 201, and 209–10. It appears in the case law in Lamer J's (as he was then) decision in *R v. Sioui*, [1990] 1 SCR 1025 and again in Binnie J's concurring decision in *Mitchell* at 142, where he cites Slattery's article while attempting to square the Crown's circular reasoning on the issue of sovereignty by providing an account of "merged sovereignty" (for more, see my engagement with this case in the Introduction to this book). For more on the concept of treaty federalism, refer to Barsh and Henderson, *Road: Indian Tribes and Political Liberty*; and, more recently, Asch, *On Being Here to Stay*.

war when settlers were unrestrained."[11] Simply put, the local settler population was focused on continual expansion, whereas the imperial Crown was more interested in overall stability and control (an expression of this can be seen in the colonial grievances that precipitated the American Revolutionary War in 1775 and in the subsequent use of the concept of *manifest destiny* in the nineteenth century).[12] This problem continued and was clearly restated in the

---

11 John Borrows, *Freedom and Indigenous Constitutionalism* (Toronto: University of Toronto Press, 2016) at 66.

12 The concept of "manifest destiny" was, in most respects, a uniquely American expression of settler expansionism. It is one that I would argue is connected to how the American Revolution combined the two reigning notions of legitimacy in the late eighteenth century (viz. the "ancient constitution" with its backwards-looking claims to a foundation in time immemorial, and the explosive force of popular sovereignty that is expressed in "We, the people"). For an invaluable comparative account of the development of the sovereign people in the United States and France, see Taylor, *Secular Age* at 196–207. What holds between the concept of "manifest destiny" and the relationship between settler populations and Indigenous peoples generally is an adversarial relationship focused on the control and ownership of lands. As the court in *United States v. Kagama*, 118 US 375, 6 S. Ct. 1109 (1886) put it, for Indigenous communities, "the people of the States where they are found are often their deadliest enemies" at 383. This is not to suggest that the imperial Crown was *uninterested* in land; rather, they sought to maximize their sovereign control by making these new lands a part of the royal demesne (and so outside the jurisdiction of Parliament and the common law) while avoiding the Spanish contagion that had been associated with the doctrine of conquest (i.e., the legitimacy of Spanish conquest was linked to the "divine" grants from papal authority, and without the glimmer of divinity they appeared to be little more than unjust wars that the Indigenous peoples could contest). This problem with the doctrine of conquest was further complicated for the English, as the continuity theory from the Norman conquest provided that the pre-existing legal and political structures survived conquest. The colonists' interest in land was different, as they wanted to secure as much independence from the Crown as possible (i.e., they did not want to recognize conquest as their basis, as this would leave them as vassals of the sovereign, and this led them to argue for Aboriginal sovereign rights, as then they could acquire title by purchase – the notion of sovereignty applied was thin and flexible so that it could be used to validate a contract of sale and then simply discarded). This difference in priorities between the empire and its colonists translated into constant tension and competing discourses on the question of the legal status of Indian lands. Robert Williams Jr summarizes the competing discourses during the later eighteenth century prior to the American War of Independence:

> The British Crown's discourse of empire asserted a Norman-derived royal prerogative right to control the disposition of Indian lands on the frontier in the Proclamation of 1763. Virginia and the other landed colonies asserted their controlling rights to the West on the basis of their Crown charters and the purer legal discourse of the natural-law-based Saxon Constitution realized by their colonies' governments. And finally, a large group of frontier speculators who cared for neither the Crown's nor the landed colonies' pretensions claimed that under natural law and natural right, the Indians

Report of the Parliamentary Select Committee on Aboriginal Tribes in 1837: "The protection of Aborigines should be considered as a duty peculiarly belonging and appropriate to the executive government, as administered either in this country or by the governors of the respective colonies. This is not a trust which could conveniently be confided to the local legislatures.... [T]he settlers in almost every colony, having either disputes to adjust with the native tribes, or claims to urge against them, the representative body is virtually a party, and therefore ought not to be the judge in such controversies."[13]

The imperial Crown responded to this problem with the *Royal Proclamation of 1763* and a subsequent series of treaties that were designed to protect

---

> themselves as sovereign princes of the soil they occupied could sell land to whomever they wished. (Williams Jr, *American Indian in Western Legal Thought* at 287)

Williams's summary does not cover the Lockean arguments for taking land, which can be seen in the *United States Declaration of Independence 1775* (i.e., Indians are characterized as "inhabitants of our frontiers" and "Savages whose known rule is warfare"). This offers a fourth line of argumentation whereby colonists can acquire rights in the land though their Anglo-Saxon allodial rights (viz. Lockean labour-derived rights), which were not extinguished by the Norman Conquest and the coming of royal prerogative. Marshall CJ rejects these arguments in *Worcester v. Georgia*, 6 Pet. 515 (US 1832), but it could well be argued that they are followed by President Jackson's Indian removal policies. I'd like to thank James Tully for drawing my attention to this important point. For an excellent summary of this conflict between the Crown and the settlers over the legal basis for land acquisition in North America, see Anthony Pagden, "Conquest, Settlement, Purchase, and Concession: Justifying the English Occupation of the Americas," in *The Burdens of Empire 1539 to the Present*, 120–52 (Cambridge: Cambridge University Press, 2015). Also see Tomlins, *Freedom Bound*; and Fitzmaurice, *Sovereignty, Property and Empire*.

13 See United Kingdom, *Report of the Parliamentary Select Committee on Aboriginal Tribes (British Settlements)* (London: William Ball, Aldine Chambers, Paternoster Row, 1837) at 117. This report is a reaction against the larger trend – which begins after the War of 1812 – of devolving administrative responsibilities to local settler governments in order to reduce the costs associated with maintaining a network of military alliances that were no longer necessary. For a more extensive treatment of this trend, see John Giokas, "The Indian Act: Evolution, Overview and Options for Amendment and Transition," research paper prepared for the Royal Commission on Aboriginal Peoples, 1995. It is interesting that the normative force of this statement draws on a principle of natural justice (viz. *Nemo judex in causa sua*). I say "interesting," as this principle is mobilized despite the fact that Aboriginal peoples are clearly being judged by the laws of an occupying force in both cases (except, of course, where a treaty concedes some jurisdiction, but even here there is the question of degree that leads to the problem of a conflict of laws). Neither the imperial nor the colonial governments could lay claim to neutrality in relation to Aboriginal peoples. This points to a long-standing picture of Aboriginal sovereignty as being *lesser-than* or diminished in relation to European states. For more on this, refer to Williams Jr, *American Indian;* Pagden, *Burdens;* Tomlins, *Freedom Bound;* Fitzmaurice, *Sovereignty, Property and Empire;* and for the relationship with international law, see Anghie, *Imperialism*.

Indigenous peoples from the European settlers.[14] This translated into an administrative apparatus (the Indian Department, which was established in 1755 as an operational arm of the military) that was focused on supervision and separation.[15] Superintendents were appointed by the imperial Crown to maintain military and trading alliances (by distributing gifts as symbols of alliance between the imperial Crown and allied Aboriginal Nations[16]) and ensure that settlers were not encroaching on Aboriginal lands.

B. *Imperial Civilizing*

Following the British victory in the War of 1812, the military importance of their alliances with Aboriginal nations began to decline. This led the Colonial Office to begin to look for ways to reduce its costs by eliminating the system of gifts and annuities associated with the treaty system (a trend that has been referred to as "imperial financial retrenchment"[17]). This, in turn, led to a general

14 This policy was by no means uniformly applied in North America. The imperial authorities adopted a regional approach. As such, the Maritime Indian population never received the same protections as those in Upper and Lower Canada. For a more detailed analysis of what was occurring within the Maritimes, see Robert Hamilton, "'They Promised to Leave Us Some of Our Land': Aboriginal Title in Canada's Maritime Provinces" (LLM thesis, York University Osgoode Hall Law School, 2015); and Leslie F.S. Upton, *Micmacs and Colonists: Indian-White Relations in the Maritimes, 1713–1867* (Vancouver: University of British Columbia Press, 1979).

15 Giokas, "Indian Act" at 16–19; Darlene Johnson, "The Quest of the Six Nations Confederacy for Self-Determination," *University of Toronto Faculty Law Review* 44, no. 1 (1986): 15.

16 Cary Miller provides some instructive insight into the significance of gifts among the Anishinaabeg in the early nineteenth century in "Gifts as Treaties: The Political Use of Received Gifts in Anishinaabeg Communities, 1820–1832," *American Indian Quarterly* 26, no. 2 (2002): 221–45.

17 John Leslie, *Commissions of Inquiry into Indian Affairs in the Canadas, 1828–1858: Evolving a Corporate Memory for the Indian Department* (Ottawa: Treaties and Historical Research Centre, DIAND, 1985) at 10. Part of the rationale for this financial retrenchment was the drastic decline of the Indigenous population between 1780 and 1880. Smallpox was responsible for killing 80–90 per cent of the Indigenous population during this period. This decline became a major factor in the policy shift as the once-powerful and populous nations whose alliances had helped secure British dominance in the area were now drastically weakened. Meanwhile, the British policy shifted towards the kind of unilateralism that characterizes the civilizing and palliative models (here I am thinking of Bond Head's Manitoulin Island experiment). This decline was exacerbated by the British withholding the vaccine that was readily available to the settlers in this period, an action that we would refer to today as genocide. This connection between the laws of occupation, the practices of colonization, and the European wars of the twentieth century has been pointed to by others. Andrew Fitzmaurice provides a helpful and insightful overview of how late nineteenth-century jurists reacted to the Berlin Conference (viz. Charles Salomon and Gaston Jéze). As he puts it, these critical jurists foresaw that "the practices that had been

shift in policy away from a more lateral *nation-to-nation* relationship (a key characteristic of imperial federalism), which supported the self-governing autonomy of Aboriginal nations, towards the concept of civilizing. This concept was appealing from an economic perspective precisely because it promised to unify the body politic – by taking the settlers as the model of normality – and thereby place the responsibility for all citizens (and wards) under the local colonial governments. This shift was further supported by the popularity of new "progressive" ideas (viz. Millian liberal-imperialism that was in vogue in imperial policy circles in the first half of the nineteenth century) amongst the new bureaucrats within the Indian Department itself as well as missionary and humanitarian societies. By the 1820s the Imperial Colonial Office had begun to question the continued existence of the Indian Department. They initiated inquiries to explore their policy options. The first was the Darling Report of 1828, which recommended a policy of effectively segregating the Aboriginal population on reserves that would be focused on converting them to Christianity and transforming them into farmers.[18] This was by no means a new idea, as similar types of reserves were a part of Indian policy in Quebec from the mid-seventeenth century.[19] This policy was approved in 1830 on the condition that

---

employed in empire were being repatriated to the occupation of Europe during the wars. This critique was later taken up in the twentieth century by figures such as Raphaël Lemkin and Hannah Arendt." See Fitzmaurice, *Sovereignty, Property and Empire* at 298. For more on the nineteenth-century practices of genocide, refer to James Daschuk, *Clearing the Plains: Disease, Politics of Starvation, and the Loss of Aboriginal Life* (Regina: University of Regina Press, 2014); Shelley A.M. Gavigan, *Hunger, Horses, and Government Men: Criminal Law on the Aboriginal Plains, 1870–1905* (Vancouver: UBC Press, 2013); Robert Boyd, *The Coming of the Spirit of Pestilence: Introduced Infectious Diseases and Population Decline among the North-West Coast Indians* (Vancouver: UBC Press, 1999); and for sources that deal with the broader context of smallpox, see Gareth Williams, *Angel of Death: The Story of Smallpox* (London: Palgrave Macmillan, 2010); Donald R. Hopkins, *The Greatest Killer: Smallpox in History* (Chicago: University of Chicago Press, 2002); Elizabeth Fenn, *Pox Americana: The Great Smallpox Epidemic 1775–1782* (New York: Hill and Wang, 2001); Jonathan B. Tucker, *Scourge: The Once and Future Threat of Smallpox* (New York: Grove, 2001); Jared Diamond, *Guns, Germs and Steel: The Fates of Human Societies* (New York: Norton, 1999); and David E. Stannard, *American Holocaust: The Conquest of the New World* (New York: Oxford University Press, 1994).

18 This report was prepared by Major General H.C. Darling, who was the military secretary to the governor general and later the chief superintendent of Indian affairs for Upper Canada. For more a more detailed review of the report, see chapter 2 of John Leslie's *Commissions of Inquiry*. The report itself can be found in Library and Archives Canada, RG10, Records Relating to Indian and Inuit Affairs Program, vol. 5.

19 The first of these was created at Sillery in 1637 so that "Indians could be taught the Catholic catechism, farming techniques and other useful trades …" See Giokas, "Indian Act" at 20. For more on this, see G.F.G. Stanley, "The First Indian 'Reserves' in Canada," *Revue d'histoire de l'Amérique française* 4, no. 2 (September 1950): 168–85.

it would not increase costs. In about this period the Indian Department was divided into two separate offices (one in each of the Canadas – only the office in Lower Canada remained under military supervision).[20] This led to two separate policy initiatives being pursued at the same time – Darling's civilizing reserves in Lower Canada and Bond Head's Manitoulin Island experiment (which, as we have previously noted, was driven by the extinction thesis and took the form of a kind of palliative care) in Upper Canada. By the late 1830s both of these approaches had failed to produce anything but increased resistance. But the bulk of the criticism was focused on the approach taken by Bond Head. The general civilizing approach of the Darling Report was continued,[21] as can be seen in the passing of the *Crown Lands Protection Act* in Upper Canada in 1839.[22] This Act classified all lands that were "appropriated for the residence of certain Indian Tribes" as Crown lands.[23] This move positioned the Crown as the formal guardian of Indian lands (a move that effectively expropriated the Indigenous interest in their lands), which, in turn, furthered the ends of civilizing policy by maintaining the necessary degree of separation and supervision.

The slow progress of the civilizing project – which was due primarily to Aboriginal resistance to policies that were destroying their entire form of life – led to a number of inquiries. By far the most influential of these during this period was the Bagot Commission of 1844. The commission conducted a systemic review of the cost effectiveness and efficiency of Indian policy. In its final report it made far-reaching recommendations that prefigure the colonial policies that followed it – some of which are still in operation today (e.g., the centralization and eventual phasing out of the Indian Department; the transition from Indian title towards freehold title in order to encourage assimilation;[24]

---

20 The Maritime colonies remained under a comparatively less administratively structured system of Indian commissioners. For a detailed view of the history of colonial practices in the Maritimes and their current legal implications, see Hamilton, "'They Promised to Leave Us Some of Our Land.'"

21 This policy is clearly outlined in a communication from the colonial secretary (Lord Glenelg) to the governor general and lieutenant governor of Upper Canada: "Wandering Indians were to be settled on land: those who were settled had to become farmers. Indians were to be given a sense of permanency on their improved lands, with the title to their reserve locations assured under the great Seal of the province. As well, reserve land would be protected from creditors and would be alienable only with the consent of the Governor General, principal Chief and resident missionary. Since Indian education was also a basic aspect of Indian civilization every encouragement was to be given to missionaries and instructors were to be issued to Indian department officials to cooperate with them." See Giokas, "Indian Act" at 21.

22 *An Act for the Protection of Lands of the Crown in this Province from Trespass and Injury* RSUC 1792–1840 (1839, c. 15).

23 Ibid.

24 This was a precursor to how the federal Crown would respond to the Métis peoples in the *Manitoba Act*. See *An Act to amend and continue the Act 32–33 Victoria, chapter 3; and*

and the establishment of a register of Indians – via a complete census – that could be used to establish band lists that could be used to restrict the costs of annuities and gifts[25]). This recommendation was taken up – at least in part – by the colonial legislatures in the *Indian Land Acts* of 1850, which were designed to *protect* reserve lands by restricting who could access them.[26] They did this by – for the first time in Canadian law – legally defining the term *Indian* for the purpose of determining eligibility to reside on reserve lands. Thus two of the most basic elements of the Crown machinery (viz. the *unilateral* determination of membership and land use) were set in place by the colonial legislatures seventeen years before Confederation.

C. *Assimilation and Indirect Rule*

The civilizing policies that were directed by the Colonial Office in London (as well as the India and Foreign Offices) led to a series of intense colonial rebellions of the 1830s and 1860s (rebellions in Upper and Lower Canada 1837 and 1838, Ireland in 1848, India in 1857, and Jamaica in 1865). This – as I have previously detailed in part 2 – led the imperial Crown to move away from the more centralized structure of the civilizing model and towards the devolved structure of the indirect rule model advanced by Henry Maine, which promised to minimize administrative costs and maximize the extraction of revenue. In the case of British North America this trend can be seen in the growing concern with the costs of maintaining the Indian Department. In

---

to establish and provide for the Government of the Province of Manitoba (assented to 12 May 1870). As a side note, it is clear that the origins of Métis land rights are distinct from Aboriginal title by *design*, and thus treating individual freehold title as some sort of essential feature of Métis land interests is deeply problematic. In my mind the Court's treatment of this issue in *MMF* at paras. 51–9 highlight this problem. The presumption is that Métis land interests are individual and not communal, but this stems from the civilizing policies of the imperial Crown and the dominion. The argument thus simply shifts to "historic use and occupation," which is part of a general pattern of originalism in the case law that, as John Borrows has argued, "should be diminished in Aboriginal rights cases. This is because Aboriginal agency is severely restricted when the Court interprets rights through the prism of unilateral Crown actions." See Borrows, *Indigenous Constitutionalism* at 144.

25 This last recommendation was by far the most prescient, as it contains the seeds of both the status and the band council system. It also recommended that the following classes of persons be ineligible to be listed as Indians: Indian women who married white men, mixed children, and Indian children educated in industrial schools.

26 *An Act for the better protection of the Lands and Property of the Indians of Lower Canada*. S. Prov. C. 1850, c. 42; *An Act for the protection of the Indians in Upper Canada from the imposition, and the Property occupied or enjoyed by them from trespass and injury*, S. Prov. C. 1850, c. 74.

1856 the Pennefather Commission was established and instructed to report on two points:

1 The best means of securing the future progress and civilization of the Indian tribes in Canada.
2 The best mode of managing the Indian property to secure its full benefit to the Indians, without impeding the settlement of the country.[27]

In 1858 they offered their opinion on the general state of the imperial government's Indian policy:

> The position in which the Imperial Government stands with regard to the Indians of Canada, has changed very materially within the last fifteen years. The alteration, however, is rather the working out of a system of policy previously determined on, than any adoption of new views on the part of the English Cabinet.
>
> As the object of this system was gradually to wean the Indians from perpetual dependence upon the Crown, successive years show an increasing loosening of the ties to which the Aborigines clung. Many of the officers appointed to watch over their interests were removed, vacancies were not filled up, the annual presents were first commuted, and subsequently withdrawn and the Indian Department is being gradually left to its own resources.[28]

The commissioners noted that while the Manitoulin Island experiment was "practically a failure," they remained optimistic about the overall project of civilizing and assimilating the Indians.[29] They blamed the slow progress of the project on the "apathy" and "unsettled habits" of the Indians, but overall they maintained that there was "no inherent defect in the organization of the Indians, which disqualifies them from being reclaimed from their savage state."[30] The final recommendations of the commission were directed to the complete assimilation of Indians (foreshadowing the termination policies that were later pursued by both the United States and Canada). Their recommendations included moving from communal reserves to allotting lands to individuals (also a recommendation of the Bagot Commission in 1844); combining the smaller reserves into larger units; consolidating Indian legislation; dismantling the tribal governance structures and, once the civilizing process was complete,

27 Moore, *Historical Development of the Indian Act* at 28.
28 Ibid.
29 Ibid.
30 Leslie, *Commissions* at 138; Moore, *Historical Development* at 29.

abolishing the Indian Department itself.[31] From the imperial standpoint, the primary benefit of assimilation was that it promised to eliminate the costs associated with the imperial federal model by producing a uniform body politic of British subjects (with a single land code) within the colony. But, contrary to the position taken in the Pennefather Commission, assimilation was not the *only* way to achieve these ends. Indirect rule – which, in the context of settler colonies, means transferring jurisdiction to the colonial governments, thereby creating dominions – also offered the imperial Crown a way to step away from its legal and economic obligations to Aboriginal nations.

The recommendations of the Pennefather Commission were quickly translated into imperial Indian policy. The practice of distributing treaty presents (symbols of the *nation-to-nation* relationship between the imperial Crown and Aboriginal nations) ended in 1858. The *Indian Lands Act* of 1860 formally ended the era of imperial federalism, as it transferred authority for Indians and Indian lands to the colonial legislature.[32] This Act fundamentally reconfigured the relationship between the Crown and Aboriginal nations. This transfer of jurisdiction is where the *indirect rule* model fits into the policy landscape of the mid-nineteenth century. The imperial Crown *unilaterally* transferred its responsibilities for Aboriginal nations to the colonial legislature – thereby stepping out of the tripartite imperial federal system that was set in place by the *Royal Proclamation of 1763.* From this point forward, the administration of Indian policy cannot be described as either disinterested or neutral – assimilation will continue, but it will be carried out by the emerging dominion.[33]

---

31 Giokas, "Indian Act" at 27.

32 *An Act respecting the Management of Indian Lands and Property*, SC 1860, c. 151, s. 4.

33 Milloy, *Historical Overview* at 59. Kerry Wilkins pointed out that it is interesting that it was the dominion, and not the constituent provinces, that assumed these responsibilities. After all, the default position, after 1860, would have been to leave this with the provinces, to which, as colonies, the 1860 legislation had assigned it. In my view the explanation for distribution of responsibilities and powers is connected to a series of criss-crossing and overlapping changes in the social imaginary of the second empire in the mid-nineteenth century. Part of this division seems to hail back to the position of the imperial Crown following the *Royal Proclamation 1763* (viz. in the hierarchically stratified view of the Crown, the logic that makes sense is to move the responsibility one level down and thereby preserve the protective oversight of local settler populations), but I believe that another part of this story can be found when we look into how the settler colonies were being positioned and repositioned by innovating ideologists who were intent on legitimating the Second British Empire by distinguishing it from its European rivals (which, by the late nineteenth century, was clearly Germany, whose imperial ambitions were painted in colours that bear a striking resemblance to those used on the Spanish Empire in the sixteenth and seventeenth centuries). The move towards conceiving of the second empire as a federal union of self-governing Anglo-Saxon states that would oversee the development of their non-European colonial dependencies was articulated by federationists such as Sir John Seeley in *The Expansion of*

The colonial legislature was more than ready to assume these responsibilities. In fact, it had further advanced its encroachment on Indian policy before the Pennefather Commission even issued its report in 1858. With the passage of the *Gradual Civilization Act* in 1857 it signalled that it would continue to follow the line of civilizing policy – the line that connects the Darling Report to the Bagot and Pennefather Commissions – towards total assimilation of Indians and the absorption of their lands. While it did continue the overall trajectory of imperial civilizing policies, it also exhibited a number of innovations in key policy areas.

1 *Lands*: In a stark departure from the procedures set up in the *Royal Proclamation of 1763*, the Act allowed for the *unilateral* reduction of reserve lands without a formal public surrender or compensation.[34]
2 *Political form*: Whereas previous civilizing policies had largely attempted to respect Aboriginal political autonomy (or at least not directly oppose it), the process of civilizing that the Acts put forward is, again, *unilateral*. The strategy of "enfranchisement" bypasses the need for the consent of tribal councils (first by making it a voluntary option for individuals – thus breaking up political cohesion – and later as a mandatory condition imposed via shifting administrative mechanisms), which had been increasingly resistant to civilizing policies. Aboriginal nations were keenly aware of this shift and immediately called for the repeal of the *Gradual Civilization Act*. The colonial legislature refused and instead passed the *Gradual Enfranchisement Act* in 1868, which marked the first attempt to uproot the traditional political systems of Aboriginal nations and replace them with "simple municipal

England (1883) and later taken up and adapted by those working on the "imperial problem" in the early twentieth century (e.g., the members of the Round Table and Jan Smuts – who was known as the empire's handyman). It is part of a more complicated story where the notions of Greater Britain as a peaceful and free global federation built on cosmopolitanism, free trade, and self-determination (often painted up as a modern Achaean League) gets folded into the modern institutions of international law (i.e., the League of Nations, and later the United Nations), along with the darker side of colonial domination and its Millian tones of pedagogical coercion (from the mandate system to the trustee system, and now operative under the vague confines of informal empire as "development"). There are a number of instructive texts on the history of the late second empire and its process of restructuring; see Bell, *Reordering the World*; Morefield, *Empires without Imperialism*; and, for a Canadian-centred account, Carl Berger, *The Sense of Power: Studies in the Ideas of Canadian Imperialism 1867–1914* (Toronto: University of Toronto Press, 1970).

34 This served as a precedent for provisions in later versions of the *Indian Act* that allowed for the expropriation and leasing of reserve lands without band consent. Giokas, "Indian Act" at 29.

institutions" that would prepare them for "responsible government."[35] As Giokas rightly notes, "These measures were clearly seen by the government as a way of bringing recalcitrant traditional Indian governments to heel by seeing to their elimination or control."[36] The resulting conflict set an adversarial tone that characterizes Crown-Aboriginal relations to this day.[37]

3 *Membership*: This legislation extended the power of the colonial legislatures – which originated in Lower Canada's *Indian Land Act* of 1850 – to determine who was to be considered an "Indian."[38] It imposed Victorian norms of family structure, sex, and gender (a practice that is built upon in subsequent legislation and whose implications are still playing out), as it made it so that the enfranchisement of a man automatically entailed the enfranchisement of his wife and children.

These innovations indicate the distinction between the interests of the imperial Crown and those of the local settler governments. They are all extensions of pre-existing imperial policies – which stem from the cost-cutting imperatives that followed the War of 1812 – but they also all move beyond the confines of their predecessors by making these policies *unilateral*. Some vestiges of the more lateral *nation-to-nation* relationship remained in play beyond the mid-nineteenth century (e.g., the continuation of the treaty-making process, the centralization of the responsibility for Indian affairs with the federal Crown, the unique communal quality of Aboriginal title, etc.). These vestiges were ultimately connected to a legitimating principle of popular sovereignty, with its connections to concepts of equality and consent. These vestiges, or perhaps better, vestigial practices, were carried out haphazardly and unevenly, so most often ended up directly contradicting this principle. There was, as we have noted, a hodgepodge of bad faith colonial gambits from excessive qualifications, narrow and formalistic legal interpretation, racist legal fictions, and blatant breech, but the legitimating principle was nevertheless still there ("more honoured in the breach than the observance," so to speak). These vestiges and the various colonial actors and factions that supported them were ultimately overshadowed by the growing influence of those who adopted a different legitimating principle

35 *Annual Report of the Indian Branch of the Department of the Secretary of State for the Provinces*, Canada, *Sessional Papers*, no. 23 (1871) at 4. Cited in Giokas, "Indian Act" at 33; *Act for the gradual enfranchisement of Indians, the better management of Indian affairs, and to extend the provisions of the Act 31st Victoria, Chapter 42*, SC 1869, c. 6 [hereinafter the *Gradual Enfranchisement Act*].

36 Giokas, "Indian Act" at 33.

37 Ibid. at 30.

38 *An Act for the better protection of the Lands and Property of the Indians in Lower Canada*. *Statutes of Canada* 1850, c. 42 (13 and 14 Vict.).

altogether – one taken from what Taylor aptly characterizes as the "dark side of our Western social imaginary": civilizational superiority.[39] The perspective offered by this dangerously false principle can be seen clearly in Lord Watson's decision in *St Catherine's Milling* as the Crown is presented as having unquestioned sovereignty, underlying title, and legislative power, while Aboriginal nations appear as a "mere burden."[40]

D. Striation or Continuity?

There are commonalities between the Indian policy of the imperial Crown and the colonial governments. Generally speaking, the principles of protection, supervision, and separation extend throughout the strata of Indian policy in the nineteenth century (and persist today), but they are directed towards new ends. One way of thinking of this shift is to return to the machine/assemblage analogy and think of these principles as engine components that can be retooled and placed in a different configuration in order to achieve different outcomes. For example, the protective component of Indian policy extends from its basis in the eighteenth century to today. It has been deployed to support the often pernicious "trust-like" relationship that presented the Crown as the guardian of Indian wards. While this relationship was not always practised in bad faith – there were dangers that threatened Indigenous nations and required something like alliance or suzerainty, such as the incursions of local colonists, ravages of disease, and imperial wars – it could be used as a gambit to avoid the issue of consent by making use of a paternalistic conception of best interests (viz. shifting it from a relationship of mutual defence in treaty federalism to the paternalism of the guardian–ward relationship). There is no distinguishing mark that allows us to strictly determine the difference between imperial Indian policy and the policies put forward by colonial governments. Rather, there is a series of distinctions, shifts in emphasis, and changes of degree that, when taken together, transform the overall shape of policy. The system that begins to take shape from the *Indian Land Acts* of the 1850s through the *Gradual Civilization Act* in 1857 is given form by the *British North America Act, 1867* – in particular through the ambiguity of s. 91(24) and its grant of power *in relation to* Indians and their lands. This system continues to expand with the *Gradual Enfranchisement Act* of 1869 and the first *Indian Act* in 1876, but we must remember that it is distinct from what preceded it.[41] This accumula-

39 Charles Taylor, *Modern Social Imaginaries* (Durham, NC: Duke University Press, 2004) at 182–3.

40 These are Lord Watson's words in *St Catherine's Milling* at 58.

41 For more on the significance of s. 91 being a set of powers that are "*in relation to*" – i.e., there is no textual basis to assume that s. 91(24) confers plenary *power-over* Indians and

tion of similarities and differences follows a general shift away from a political relation that held *power-with* Aboriginal nations (a relation that – no matter its selfish motivations or how racketeering-like its tactics – *relied* on their consent) towards the despotic *power-over* system that eventually gives shape to the *Indian Act.* Put somewhat differently, during this nineteenth-century process of *ad hoc* legal adaptation and local colonial retooling of imperial administrative systems, there is a shift in the dominant legitimating principle of the Crown–Indigenous relationship from popular sovereignty to civilizational supremacy.

In my opinion these differences stem (at least in part) from the difference of scale in the respective viewpoints of the British Empire and its colonies. That is, imperial policies are driven by a concern with minimizing the costs of governing several colonies. This scale of focus leads imperial administrators to view resistance and conflict somewhat differently. Imperial federalism can be seen as an expression of this difference. Even following the War of 1812 – as it is dismantling imperial federalism and transferring its responsibilities to the local colonial governments – the imperial Crown is focused on lowering costs by minimizing conflict. The colonial governments, on the other hand, have a direct and pressing concern with the *acquisition of land.* This is precisely why the court in the *United States v. Kagama* held that "the people of the States where they are found are often their deadliest enemies."[42] This focus on land acquisition necessarily gives rise to an increase in resistance from Aboriginal nations and so – as it is no longer possible to gain their consent – the favoured model of governance becomes *unilateral.* The parallels between this and J.S. Mill's liberal imperialism are strong. Both are based on the false legitimating principle of civilizational superiority. The unilateral *power-over* relationship that takes shape with the *Indian Act* in 1876 is explained and justified by the civilized/uncivilized distinction. Mill's philosophy of history seems to offer a viewpoint (or rather an exemplary articulation or version of a viewpoint) that is perfectly

---

their lands – matters not assigned exclusively to provincial legislatures, see Borrows, "Unextinguished" at 11. This is by no means a knock-down argument, as it is doubtlessly possible to read "in relation to" as "legislative authority over," but the ambiguity in the phasing leaves open a space to move past the limits of "narrow and technical construction," past the unspoken assumption of civilizational superiority, and allow the "living tree" to grow and expand past its colonial limits (*Edwards v. AG for Canada*, [1930] AC 124 (PC) at 136). As Borrows argues, "History should always be calibrated to non-discriminatory standards for judgement when used as a source of constitutional authority; it should rarely be determinative. Contemporary constitutional standards should not replicate the views held by past generations of Canadian leaders who regarded Aboriginal peoples as inferior and denied their governance and land rights. Constitutional doctrines that transmit these and other historically discriminatory beliefs should have no place in Canada's highest law." See Borrows, *Freedom and Indigenous Constitutionalism* at 145.

42 *Kagama* at 383.

suited to the ends of colonial governments.[43] He offers a ladder that allows the settlers to survey the vast expanses of time and geography that exist under the name of British North America and see nothing more than a "handful of individuals, wandering or thinly scattered over a vast tract of country."[44] This philosophical viewpoint provides a key part of the explanatory background, or more precisely the "social imaginary," for the administrative despotism that characterizes Indian policy from the mid-nineteenth century on.[45] The problem is that once this ladder is climbed, it disappears.[46] It provides an exception from the normal conditions of morality, and it connects the actions it justifies to a future state. The legitimacy of this "temporary despotism" is tied to the progressive civilization of those who are deemed to be savages. But it leads to a paradox. As John Tobias notes concerning the *Gradual Civilization Act*, "The paradox that was to become and remain a characteristic of Canada's Indian policy was given a firm foundation in this act.... Thus, the legislation to remove all legal distinctions between Indians and Euro-Canadians actually established them. In fact, it set standards for acceptance that many, if not most, white colonials could not meet, for few of them were literate, free of debt, and of high moral character. The 'civilized' Indian would have to be more 'civilized' than the Euro-Canadian."[47]

The policies that are designed to remove all distinctions between the civilized and uncivilized actually establish and maintain them – precisely because they are all based in a view from nowhere. Mill's universal history is predicated on the idea that the civilized/uncivilized distinction is an objective, value-neutral fact, but there is no secure anchoring point for it. As soon as we sit down to make a practical, real-world determination with this distinction, we find only a loose bundle of qualities without a determinative criterion. There is no litmus test in this colonial field kit, no means of measuring civilization. Rather, there is just a kind of hollow "know it when you see it" guarantee that can be buffered

---

43 This viewpoint is, as I noted above, part of the "dark side of our Western social imaginary." See Taylor, *Social Imaginaries* at 182–3.

44 Mill, "Civilization" at 119.

45 I am using Charles Taylor's concept as it is articulated in *Social Imaginaries* and *Secular Age*.

46 I am borrowing and altering the metaphor of the ladder from Wittgenstein's *Tractatus Logico-Philosophicus* at §6.54, my alteration being that this ladder does not allow those who use it to get to a vantage point where they see the world rightly. Quite the opposite, it leaves those who climb it trapped by a picture of things that is dangerously false. A picture that can be retained only if we fall into a kind of false consciousness or "cover-up, averting our gaze from various excluded and disempowered groups or imagining that their exclusion is their own doing." See Taylor, *Social Imaginaries* at 183.

47 John L. Tobias, "Protections, Civilization, Assimilation: An Outline History of Canada's Indian Policy," in *Sweet Promises: A Reader on Indian-White Relations in Canada*, ed. J.R. Miller (Toronto: University of Toronto Press, 1991) at 130.

by (over) only inflating the degree of training and expertise necessary to do so. Put another way, Mill's universal history is unable to distinguish between the map and the territory; any policy framework that bases itself on it is left tilting windmills and hunting snarks. Without this madness, what once seemed to be historical necessity is seen for what it always was, *an arbitrary assertion of sovereign power over others*. In other words, once the floor falls out of civilizational supremacy the legal status of Indigenous peoples becomes a live problem. The set of settler colonial political and legal practices that had been available under the (dangerously false) principle of civilizational supremacy could not be salvaged by retrospectively reinterpreting them with the legitimating principle of popular sovereignty. This leaves a large repertory of social, legal, and political practices normatively unmoored (viz. it initiates a legitimation crisis within the Western social imaginary). Nevertheless, we must remember that the components of the Crown machine retain the possibility of being reconfigured for different ends. Even during its initial phase of construction, nothing was necessary; its design was haphazard, open to constant change, and layered with possibilities for reconfiguration.[48]

3.2 The Indian Question and the Dominion

The dominion is formed with the *British North America Act, 1867*, and the Indian Question is a primary component of its policy agenda. This prioritization was due, in large part, to the rapid territorial expansion of Canada. It acquired Rupert's Land and the North-Western Territory from the Hudson's Bay Company in 1870 – a process that also led to the creation of the province of Manitoba. This acquisition led to Métis resistance (led by Louis Riel in the Red River colony) and the unhappy history of the *Manitoba Act* and

---

48 One of these possibilities stems from the protective component of the Crown machine. As John Borrows puts it, "The law in North America developed to ensure that local governments had substantial obstacles placed in their path in dealing with First Nations. The *Royal Proclamation* and 250 years of Canadian law, as affirmed in subsection 91(24) of the *Constitution Act, 1867*, interposed a more distant imperial or federal power between First Nations and colonial/state/local/provincial governments." See Borrows, "Durability of Terra Nullius" at 736. Borrows contrasts this 250-year-old constitutional principle – which he, following Brian Slattery, refers to as *The Aboriginal Constitution* – with the more recent 150-year-old principle of unilateral Crown dominance, which he refers to as Canada's Colonial Constitution. See John Borrows, "Canada's Colonial Constitution" (paper delivered at the Faculty of Law, University of British Columbia, 19 January 2016); and Brian Slattery, "The Aboriginal Constitution" (2014) 67 SCLR (2d) 319. See also Pagden, *Burdens* at 144–7, as he contextualizes the protective component of the proclamation in relation to the colonists' desires to distance themselves from the reach of the sovereign authority of the Crown (i.e., the question of the nature of Aboriginal rights becomes entangled in this struggle between the British Crown and the colonists).

Métis scrip lands.[49] The creation of a province by federal legislation gave rise to constitutional concerns in the newly formed dominion. This led the imperial Parliament to pass the *British North America Act, 1871*, which clearly granted Parliament the powers necessary to create, alter the boundaries (with provincial consent), and legislate for non-provincial territories.[50] Less than a month after its passing, British Columbia entered Confederation. These acquisitions led to a concern with governing – and preventing possible US encroachment on – the sparsely settled and vast geographic expanse of its new western frontiers.[51] The solution was a national policy that focused on the construction of a transcontinental railway and the promotion of western settlement.[52] This project necessitated securing of vast tracts of lands from a diverse set of Aboriginal nations, and the experience of the Red River Resistance had made the high stakes of this problem clear. The importance of the Indian Question can be clearly seen in the legislation from this period.

In 1868 Parliament passed an Act that gave the secretary of state the role of superintendent-general of Indian affairs and control over the management of Indian lands, property, and all of their funds, as well as all Crown lands across the dominion.[53] This was the first national legislation that addressed the Indian Question. It effectively consolidated much of the previous legislation concerning Indian lands that had been passed by the colonial legislatures in the decade preceding Confederation – continuing the "guardianship policy" – and extended it throughout the dominion. It also entrenched the definition of the term *Indian* on a patrilineal model (i.e., it excluded non-Indian men who lawfully married Indian women, but included non-Indian women who lawfully married Indian men). This was quickly followed by the passage of the *Gradual Enfranchisement Act* in 1869, which marked the formal implementation of assimilation as a guiding principle of Indian policy in Canada. The general purpose of this legislation is clearly summarized in an official government report issued in 1871:

> The Acts framed in the years 1868 and 1869, relating to Indian affairs, were designed to lead the Indian people by degrees to mingle with the white race in

49 *Manitoba Act.*

50 *British North America Act, 1871*, 34–5 Vict., c. 28 (UK).

51 This sense of urgency was further exacerbated by the gradual withdrawal of the British from their commitments in the North American colonies: see Berger, *Sense of Power* at 60–6.

52 Eden and Molot refer to this era of national policy – which, in their opinion, is the first of three discernible policies and extends from Confederation in 1867 to 1940 – as "defensive expansionism." The third component of this policy is the protectionist tariffs introduced by the Macdonald government in 1878. See Lorraine Eden and Maureen Appel Molot, "Canada's National Policies: Reflections on 125 Years," *Canadian Public Policy* 19, no. 3 (1993): 232–51.

53 *An Act providing for the organisation of the Department of the Secretary of State of Canada, and for the management of and Ordnance Lands* (31 Vict., c. 42), 22 May 1868.

> the ordinary avocations of life. It was intended to afford facilities for electing, for a limited period, members of bands to manage as a Council, local matters – that intelligent and educated men, recognized as chiefs, should carry out the wishes of the male members of mature years in each band, who should be fairly represented in the conduct of their internal affairs.... Thus establishing a responsible, for an irresponsible system, this provision, by law was designed to pave the way to the establishment of simple municipal institutions.[54]

The use of the phrase "pave the way" (with its connotations of covering over and flattening out) is particularly revealing. It had become clear that the failure of pre-Confederation attempts at assimilation was due, in large part, to the resistance of traditional Indigenous governments. These legislative measures provided the means to remove that resistance by redefining the traditional governments as "irresponsible systems." It is from this point forward that federal control of on-reserve governmental systems becomes, as John Milloy aptly phrases it, "the essence of Canadian-Indian constitutional relations."[55]

The difficulty, to my mind, is in determining exactly where this "essence" is derived from – viz. what is the basis of authority and legitimacy for this extraordinary *power-over* Aboriginal nations. This is by no means a simple task. Nor is

---

54 *Annual Report of the Indian Branch*, at 4. Cited in Giokas, "Indian Act" at 33. The use of "responsible government" as a premise for legitimating the unilateral displacement of the traditional systems of government used by Aboriginal nations is a particularly interesting use of rhetoric in this context. For the first half of the nineteenth century the colonists had been locked in a struggle between their elected assemblies and the unelected executives. As Jeremy Webber puts it, the struggle was a Canadian variation of "the long contest between king and parliament." Responsible government was (understandably) the primary objective of the colonists. Their aim was to ensure that the government of each colony was answerable to the citizens who elected it and not the imperial Crown. The shift to applying this argumentative framework to Aboriginal nations is fundamentally at odds with the principles of this aim. Within this frame the traditional governments are being presented as "irresponsible" in the same manner that the British monarch is. This supplies the premise for their removal, but the impetus does not come from those who live under this "irresponsible system." Rather, it comes from the colonists. This is the addition that contradicts the fundamental premise of the call for responsible government (with its connotations of democratic equality). For this to make sense it must be the case that the Aboriginal people are not able to make their own decisions at this point – they must lack the requisite degree of reason for responsible self-government. The civilized/uncivilized and ward/guardian argument sits here as a hidden premise. Without it, this is simply a repetition of the same imperialistic system of governance that the colonists had rallied against. Only this time the Indian agent would assume the role of the imperial executive, and both the conditions of membership and system of governance would be arbitrarily imposed. See Jeremy Webber, *The Constitution of Canada: A Contextual Analysis* (Portland, OR: Hart Publishing, 2015) at 14–20.

55 John S. Milloy, "The Early Indian Acts: Developmental Strategy and Constitutional Change," in *Sweet Promises: A Reader on Indian-White Relations in Canada*, ed. J.R. Miller (Toronto: University of Toronto Press, 1991) at 145.

it one that starts from the premise that this essence is hidden from us (i.e., that it is, as Wittgenstein puts it, "something that lies *beneath* the surface").[56] Rather, the difficulty is that what we are trying to understand is "already in plain view."[57] What obscures it is a particular picture of federalism and the constitutional order of Canada. In this picture Aboriginal nations are presented as being paradoxically *entirely within* and yet somehow *outside of* the normal constitutional order (i.e., lacking the rights of British subjects).[58] This plenary or *power-over*

---

56 Wittgenstein, *Philosophical Investigations* at §92.

57 Ibid. at §89.

58 Kerry Wilkins drew my attention to Estey J's comments on s. 91(24) and s. 15 of the *Charter*, in his concurring reasons in *Reference re Bill 30, An Act to Amend the Education Act (Ont.)*, [1987] 1 SCR 1148. He attempts to use s. 91(24) as an example of how s. 93 of the *Constitution Act, 1982*, fits with the division of powers that was established with the *Constitution Act, 1867*. As he puts it,

> Once section 93 is examined as a grant of power to the province, similar to the heads of power found in s. 92, it is apparent that the purpose of this grant of power is to provide the province with the jurisdiction to legislate in a prima facie selective and distinguishing manner with respect to education whether or not some segments of the community might consider the result to be discriminatory. In this sense, s. 93 is a provincial counterpart of s. 91(24) (Indians, and lands reserved for Indians) which authorizes the Parliament of Canada to legislate for the benefit of the Indian population in a preferential, discriminatory, or distinctive fashion vis-à-vis others. (*Reference re Bill 30* at para. 79)

The gist of this argument seems to be that s. 93 and s. 91(24) are buffered against s. 15 of the *Charter* because they are discriminatory by design, and, as Esty J reminds us at para. 80, s. 15 "cannot be interpreted as rendering unconstitutional distinctions that are expressly permitted by the *Constitution Act, 1867*." This kind of originalist approach raises the question by acting as if the constitutional provisions have a hard-coded interpretation (viz. originalism) and thereby jumps over the fact that Canada's constitutional order is "a living tree capable of growth and expansion within its natural limits" (*Edwards v. AG for Canada* at 136). While Esty J does not cite any authority for this interpretation of the purpose of s. 91(24), his reasoning is virtually identical with that of Pigeon J's dissent in *R v. Drybones*, [1970] SCR 282 at 303, and then by Ritchie J's in *AG of Canada v. Lavell*, [1974] SCR 1349 at 1358–9. The positions taken in all these cases rely on an appeal to the hierarchy of laws coupled with a narrow originalist interpretation of the meaning of s. 91(24) to preserve a colonial system of domination against the challenge posed by the concept of equality. What the Court ends up offering here is little more than the all-too-familiar logic of the "separate but equal" doctrine in the United States or apartheid in South Africa. Laskin J provides a strong and clear counterargument to this pale juristic legerdemain in his dissent in *Lavell*. He simply reminds the Court that while it is true that s. 91(24) does give Parliament exclusive legislative power in relation to Indians and their lands, "Discriminatory treatment on the basis of race or colour or sex does not inhere in that grant of legislative power" (at 1389). The gist of this counterargument is to remind the Court that it cannot act as if s. 91(24) interprets itself so as to shield it from all possible challenges. What is lurking unsaid in this exchange is the balance between sovereign prerogative powers and the rule of law. After all, if s. 91(24) is immune to the effects of instruments like the *Bill or Rights* or the *Charter* because it is discriminatory by

interpretation of s. 91(24) has left Aboriginal nations subject to the power of Parliament to an entirely undetermined degree – so much so that the courts are left with the unenviable (if not entirely impossible) task of determining exactly how this plenary *power-over* Indians and their lands fits within the division of powers in ss. 91 and 92.[59] In order for this picture to make sense, Aboriginal nations are redefined by the dominion as "Indians," who, *by their very nature*, lack the capacity to either own land (they can merely *occupy* it, as the Crown is simply presumed to hold the underlying title – hence Lord Watson's definition of Indian title as "personal and usufructuary right, dependent upon the good will of the Sovereign"[60]) or to govern themselves.[61] The foundation of all of this

---

design, then it seems that the Court has argued itself out of its own jurisdiction and (at least in theory) left the sovereign a non-legal space of unlimited administrative discretion. I will analyse these arguments in more detail in part 4.

59 It may be tempting to argue that there is a similarity between s. 91(24) and s. 91(25) (i.e., "Naturalization and Aliens"). This could be because on the surface it seems that the legal extension of the terms *Indians* and *Aliens* are similarly constructed by broad legislative discretion. But there are distinctions that cause this apparent analogy to break down rapidly on closer inspection. First, the category of individuals captured under s. 91(25) has entered the territorial jurisdiction of Canada from elsewhere, and this freedom of movement (for lack of a better term) allows for a limited presumption of consent to the authority exercised under s. 91(25) (i.e., the basic assumption that they elected to enter Canadian jurisdiction). In the case of s. 91(24) the term *Indians* is applied to a limited set of Indigenous peoples whose presence within Canadian territorial jurisdiction is categorically distinct from those covered under s. 91(25). Second, s. 91(24) specifically targets "lands reserved for Indians." This ties back to the complicated legal status of Indians noted in the first distinction. In other words, the connection between Indians and their lands necessarily raises the attendant problems of sorting out the questions of the Crown's claims to *dominium* and *imperium*. None of these concerns with land and territorial sovereignty are in play with s. 91(25). Laskin J made a similar argument against the analogy between these provisions in his dissent in *Cardinal v. Alberta (AG)*, [1974] SCR 695 at 728.

60 *St Catherine's Milling* at 54–5.

61 The problem here is twofold: first, the picture of land ownership the settlers brought with them is tenurial, under which all estates in land derive ultimately from Crown grants; and second, this common law tenurial picture is projected over the pre-existing Indigenous systems of land ownership and governance. This makes for deep confusion, as under the presumption of the Crown holding underlying title, Indigenous peoples can have only the capacity to own lands within the rules of that system. The question of how the Crown obtained the *dominium* required to legitimate this picture of land ownership (even on its own Western legal and normative terms) is simply jumped over. When pressed for an explanation for how the Crown acquired sovereignty, underlying title, and legislative power, we find ourselves supplied with a hodgepodge of nineteenth-century legal fictions that restrict (or even eliminate) the legal capacity of Indigenous peoples. This singular focus on the observation, evaluation, and measurement of the supposedly indicative qualities of Indigenous peoples is grounded in the conclusion that the Crown (or those who support it) desires. This one-sided search for evidence to support the Crown's claims to *dominium* and *imperium* makes all of those who adopt it blind to any facts that contradict it. This blindness

is, like any other despotism, built upon a magical circle of legal fictions (e.g., discovery, *terra nullius*, etc.), which is vulnerable to the simplest question of legitimacy, or, to borrow Kant's phrasing, *historical warrant*: viz. "what gives you the right"? The only available response to this question, aside from the obscure non-responses supplied by legal fiction, or absurdly one-sided constructions of treaties, is *the right of the strongest*. It was as if the "right of the strongest" was all that is great and important in the constitutional history of Canada, but, as soon as we rearrange the picture and see it from another angle, we see "nothing but a house of cards."[62]

In 1874 federal legislation extended the Indian legislation (and broadened the laws on alcohol) to the western frontier.[63] This was quickly followed in 1876 by the consolidation of all laws relating to Indians into the first *Indian Act*. This firmly established the direction of Indian policy of the newly formed dominion. As Moore notes, it "created a framework of Indian legislation that remains fundamentally intact today."[64] This framework expanded on the basic formula of the *Gradual Enfranchisement Act* by extending parliamentary control over political structures, membership, and lands.[65] Like the *Gradual Enfranchisement Act* that preceded it, the *Indian Act* was, as Milloy notes, designed to ensure "that Indians would lose control of every aspect of their corporate existence."[66]

---

brings with it a vulnerability; if the direction of the inquiry is shifted from the status of the Indigenous party to the Crown, then it has little to show, other than its desire for a decision in its favour and a one-dimensional patchwork collection of facts that serve only to point back to the biased manner in which they were selected. This vulnerability can be avoided only if the Crown is able to maintain a one-sided legal game where the judiciary maintains the reality of their desired conclusion by refusing to question it.

62 Wittgenstein, *Philosophical Investigations* at §118. Some could disagree with my claim that the right of the strongest cannot form a legitimate basis for the state. They would likely respond by invoking the spirit of Hobbes (or indeed the tradition that stretches from Thrasymachus, Machiavelli, Bodin, Schmitt, etc.) and maintain that the right of the strongest is the only possible foundation for political association. I do not agree with this position – as should be rather obvious by this point – but I also do not take it lightly. The members of this tradition require sustained critical engagement and have much to teach us. In lieu of my own response to the Hobbesian viewpoint, I would refer any reader drawn to this position – or curious about it – to Quentin Skinner's exemplary scholarship. In particular, *Hobbes and Republican Liberty* (Cambridge; Cambridge University Press, 2008); and *Liberty before Liberalism*.

63 *An Act to amend certain Laws respecting Indians, and to extend certain Laws relating to matters connected with Indians to the Provinces of Manitoba and British Columbia*, SC 1874, c. 21. This law made it a punishable offence for an Indian to be found "in a state of intoxication" and refusing to name the supplier.

64 Moore, *Historical Development* at 60.

65 Moore maintains that the three principal areas of concern in the *Indian Act* are "lands, membership, and local government." See *Historical Development* at 51.

66 Milloy, *Historical Overview* at 99.

The founding principle of this policy was clearly articulated in the 1876 *Annual Report to the Department of the Interior*:

> Our Indian legislation generally rests on the principle, that the aborigines are to be kept in a condition of tutelage and treated as wards or children of the State. The soundness of this principle I cannot admit. On the contrary, I am firmly persuaded that the true interests of the aborigines and of the State alike require that every effort should be made to aid the red man in lifting himself out of this condition of tutelage and dependence, and that it is clearly our wisdom and our duty, through education and other means, to prepare him for a higher civilization by encouraging him to assume the privileges and responsibilities of full citizenship.[67]

The legal basis of this entire framework is the *power-over* interpretation of s. 91(24). This is where the *Indian Act* derives its authority and its claim to legitimacy. It is this unlimited *power-over* Indians and their lands that enabled Parliament to fashion the machinery to complete the unfinished policies of civilization that it had inherited from its colonial predecessors. The structural tension in this machinery is clear; the general principle of Indian legislation, its very foundation, is *unsound*. This is, to my mind, the key characteristic of this legislation and settler-colonialism in general. Once the foundation is admitted to be *unsound*, the machinery can continue forward; the Crown machine was designed as a "temporary despotism."[68] Without this temporal bracketing the reassuring developmental analogy of children and pedagogy would dissolve and leave only the static position of the slave and the *idée fixe* of divine right.[69]

---

67 *Annual Report to the Department of the Interior*, cited in Giokas, "Indian Act" at 36–7.

68 Consider Mill's account of the destiny of the East Indian Company in Mill, *On Liberty* at 324. It is as if by admitting that the principle of inequality is unsound that it is suddenly immunized to the moral force of the contestations of those who are subjected to it. It reverses the onus of the question of legitimacy (viz. "what gives you the right?") by admitting that what is being done is normally wrong but is necessary due to the nature of the subject (i.e., savages, criminals, children, women, terrorists, etc.). This move is successful only as long as those who employ it remain committed to a view from nowhere – as only this can provide the absolute universal developmental hierarchy that enables them to determine the "true" position of the subject and assign the appropriate treatment.

69 When I refer to the master–slave relationship as "static" I am simply referring to its design (i.e., ideally the relationship would be a permanent and stable asymmetry between the parties). Naturally, the practical realities of this relationship are – as Hegel and Marx famously illustrated – dialectical, or, to remove the heavy presumptions that accompany that term, agonistic. My point here is limited: the guardian–ward relation is *different* from the master–slave relation and I am employing it as an object of comparison so that we can see the guardian–ward relationship from a different angle (i.e., more clearly than the shallow historical moralism of good but misguided intentions). The difference is that the relationship is designed to be impermanent; it is just a transitional phase towards an ultimate state of equality. This provides those who assume the

Thus, in order to retain a claim to universal legitimacy, this principle can serve only as an interim measure to the ultimate goal of unifying the body politic (much like the concept of the state of emergency, which suspends the operation of the normal constitutional order in order to "save" it).

The *Indian Act* was not uniformly applied across the dominion.[70] Rather, it was applied on a more regional basis in relation to how "developed" or "advanced" the Indians were determined to be. It specifically excluded the western bands from many provisions, including those relating to enfranchisement and the election system for band councils.[71] The excluded bands were by no means free of the administrative controls of the dominion. The Act included any "tribe, band or body of Indians," whether or not they had entered into treaty relations with the Crown.[72] Indian agents supervised elections and could either appoint the council (as was often the case on the prairies) or allow the customary process to occur (a practice more common in British Columbia).[73] In either case, the three-year term limit was often enforced, irrespective of whether it legally applied to the band in question. The so-called advanced tribes of central Canada – those who were supposed to be the beneficiaries of the enfranchisement and elective system – rejected it.[74] As Tobias notes, "They knew that the superintendent general would have not only

mantle of guardianship with a kind of self-sealing moral position. They have a ready-made and self-issued response to the question of legitimacy; the moral obligation they assume magically pays all debts in advance via promissory notes (i.e., what Rudyard Kipling referred to in 1899 as the White Man's Burden). As soon as they are challenged for their unilateral and arbitrary assertion of *power-over* those they deem to be wards, they acknowledge that the system is despotic and so normally illegitimate, but it is excepted from this standard because it is merely the temporary means to the greater good. This entire game is predicated on the ability and entitlement to make the determination of who is civilized and who is uncivilized (as well as on the very significance of these categories). Its claim to legitimacy rests on a model of universal history that – like the Last Judgment – requires the absolute certainly that only a view from nowhere can provide. When this relationship collapses, its great and important institutions suddenly fall like houses of cards or "buildings, leaving behind only bits of stone and rubble," because the ground on which they stood was not the divine ordination but human language. Wittgenstein, *Philosophical Investigations* at §118.

70 As Prime Minister Alexander Mackenzie put it in 1876, the "wild nomad of the North-West" could not be judged by the same standards as "the Indian of Ontario." See Moore, *Historical Development* at 81.

71 *Indian Act*, SC 1876, c. 18, s. 94. Parliament has subjected western bands to special rules as recently as 2014: see *Indian Act*, RSC 1985, c. I-5, ss. 32–3.

72 Ibid. at §1–2. Those who had not entered into treaty relations and did not have reserve lands were defined as "irregular bands." This is a clear indication of the nature of the presumption of Crown sovereignty that was in play; consent was simply not a requirement.

73 Giokas, "Indian Act" at 39.

74 Only one band is known to have adopted the system during this period. See Giokas, "Indian Act" at 39.

supervisory and veto power over band decisions, but also, according to the provisions of the act, he could force the band council to concern itself with issues with which it did not wish to deal."[75] The band councils themselves were, by design, little more than nominal governments (or puppets) under the effective control of the dominion. This is clearly demonstrated by the sheer number of discretionary powers that the Act originally conferred on the superintendent general.[76] For a more specific example, we can simply refer to the limited measure of jurisdiction the band councils had on reserve lands. Initially band councils were granted the power to make by-laws, but they were given no means to enforce them.[77] In 1879 they were granted the power to enforce their by-laws, by imposing a fine of thirty dollars or a jail term (thirty days) for violations, but the provision for a hearing was not added until 1880.[78] These provisions established a procedure that required a justice of the peace, which meant that proceedings for on-reserve by-law violations had to be held in the settler towns. This oversight was amended in 1881 when officers of the Indian Department were granted the power to act as ex officio justices of the peace on reserve lands.[79] This did not increase the jurisdiction of the band council. Rather, it simply added a jurisdictional buffer to the wide-ranging administrative powers of the Department of Indian Affairs and its Indian agents to enforce their own civilizing regulations (a vague and continually shifting set of regulations targeting moral character). It allowed a single administrative apparatus (indeed, in many cases the very same individual) to act as both the police and the judiciary. This clearly violated the basic principles of criminal law and procedural fairness, but nevertheless the amendments that followed reinforced this structural arrangement.[80] In 1882 Indian agents were granted

---

75 Tobias, *Protections, Civilization, Assimilation* at 133.

76 The term *superintendent-general* occurs eighty-six times over the 100 provisions that make up the first *Indian Act.*

77 *Indian Act 1876* at s. 63.

78 *Indian Act*, SC 1879, c. 34, s. 4; *Indian Act*, SC 1880, c. 28, s. 74. Incidentally, the 1880 amendments also included new provisions (viz. §70–2) that significantly reduced the autonomy of band councils by giving the governor in council sole discretionary powers as the trustee for the proceeds from the sale of Indian lands and resources (a power that has remained in place ever since).

79 *Indian Act*, SC 1881, c. 17, s. 12.

80 I am referring to the related principles of judicial independence and *Nemo judex in causa sua*, which have a distinctive twist in this context, given that Aboriginal peoples were formally excluded from the legislative process. This fact was not lost on those who were operating within this system at the time. In fact, the North-West Mounted Police (a police force created in 1873 – and modelled on the paramilitary Royal Irish Constabulary – to respond to fears of US expansion and Aboriginal resistance) repeatedly expressed concerns about the legality of the pass system and the restrictions on ceremonial dances. The gist of the concern was that if these practices were challenged in court and found to be illegal, it would bring the

the same enforcement powers accorded to the police (i.e., to charge and arrest), which, when combined with their adjudicative powers, offered them the rare opportunity to act as judge, jury, and executioner. In 1884 an amendment reinforced this all-in-one model of administrative power by granting Indian agents authority over any and all matters "affecting Indians" as well as the discretion to conduct their trials wherever they deemed conditions to be "conducive to the ends of justice."[81] This remarkably wide-ranging grant of jurisdiction was – at least formally – limited to the bounds of the *Indian Act* by the introduction of the *Criminal Code* in 1886. But the potential limitations of a uniform *Criminal Code* were practically negated by the continued expansion of the civilizing regulations within the *Indian Act* via an ad hoc series of amendments.[82] These regulations covered practically every facet of daily life, both on and off the reserves, and included the infamous legislative prohibitions on ceremonial practices and the informal administrative structure of the pass system.[83]

This continual administrative encroachment was by no means uncontested. Rather, its expansion is correlated directly with Aboriginal practices of resistance and the general context of the dominion during this period. The initial

---

administration of justice into disrepute. See Titley, *Narrow Vision* at 165–8; F. Laurie Barron, "The Indian Pass System in the Canadian West, 1882–1935," *Prairie Forum* 13, no. 1 (1988): 25–42.

81 *Indian Act*, SC 1882, c. 30, s. 3; *Indian Act*, SC 1884, c. 27, ss. 22–3.

82 *Criminal Code*, RSC 1886, c. 43, s. 117.

83 For example, amendments in 1884 banned the potlach and the tamanawas dance. See *Indian Act*, SC 1884, c. 28, s. 3. This use of legislation to authorize the administrative control over Indigenous sociocultural practices was extended to the Blackfoot Sun Dance and the Cree and Saulteaux Thirst Dance in the *Indian Act*, SC 1895, c. 35, s. 6. In 1914 an amendment was passed prohibiting all western Indians from participating in any off-reserve "dance, show, exhibition, stampede or pageant" in "aboriginal costume" without official permission. See *Indian Act*, SC 1914, c. 35, s. 8. Interestingly this particular restriction proved to be very unpopular with the settler population, as the Indigenous performances in local stampedes were in high demand. Additionally, these provisions proved to be very difficult to actually enforce, and these factors eventually led to the deletion of the prohibition on the use of "aboriginal costume" in the *Indian Act*, SC 1933, c. 42, s. 10. For a review of this period of anti-ceremonial administrative policy, see J.R. Miller, "Own Glendower, Hotspur, and Canadian Indian Policy," in *Sweet Promises: A Reader on Indian-White Relations in Canada*, ed. J.R. Miller, 323–52 (Toronto: University of Toronto Press, 1991). As for the pass system, it was instituted without legislative sanction in the prairies to restrict mobility off or between reserves. Apparently the system was developed informally by government officials in the early 1880s as a response to fears that the Cree in Saskatchewan would organize a resistance similar to the Red River resistance. The pass system fell into disuse by the 1890s (while occasionally used in some areas into the twentieth century). This was due in part to the fact that the RCMP disliked enforcing the pass system, because they believed that the courts would find it illegal and so it would bring their law-enforcement practices into disrepute. For more on the pass system, see note 80.

stages of the dominion's territorial and administrative expansion were fraught with anxieties. The British had been redefining their model of imperial administration following from the War of 1812 (as we have previously detailed in part 2); by the time of the *British North America Act, 1867* the measured distance of indirect rule was in place. This brought with it a fear of imperial abandonment within the pre-Confederation colonies, and later, the newly formed dominion. The English-speaking population – which had previously been concentrated in Upper Canada, the Maritime colonies, and a scattering of Hudson Bay Company outposts – were keenly aware of the growing power and instability of their southern neighbour.[84] The fear of annexation (and the resulting territorial loss) formed a primary motivation for the western expansion of the dominion. In addition, the question of western expansion added to the long-standing conflict between the English and French colonists. In this context Aboriginal resistance was seen as a distinct and pressing threat. The Red River resistance – and indeed, the North-West War later on in 1885 – was seen through a lens coloured by both the external loyalist/republican distinction and the internal English/French divisions.[85] This can be seen in both the militaristic responses

84 See "Critique of the Republic," in Berger's *Sense of Power*.

85 The usual reference to these events is to term them "rebellions," but this presumes the very authority that was being contested here. I would like to thank Larry Chartrand for highlighting this point. Further, this lens is clearly evidenced by the anti-francophone legislation passed in Manitoba in 1890, viz. the *Public Schools Act*, SM 1890, c. 38; and *An Act to Provide that the English Language shall be the Official Language of the Province of Manitoba*, SM 1890, c. 14. This trend was by no means confined to the provincial boundaries of Manitoba, as the Northwest Territories also removed French as an official language in 1892 (this trend continued as Alberta and Saskatchewan followed suit in 1905). This, combined with the execution of Riel in 1885, strengthened the developing sense of French nationalism in Quebec during the late nineteenth century. There is a family resemblance between the repressive techniques that the dominant English-speaking settlers used to supress Indigenous peoples and those used on the French-speaking settler populations. While a full exploration of this resemblance extends far beyond the confines of this book, I would like to point to the criss-crossing and overlapping pattern of similarities and differences that connects the course of events from the *Royal Proclamation of 1763* – and the Indigenous adhesion in the *Treaty of Niagara* in 1764 – with the widespread resistance of the *Canadiens* in Lower Canada and the subsequent creation of the *Quebec Act of 1774*. It is interesting to see how the fourfold relationship between the imperial Crown, French-speaking colonists, and Indigenous peoples shifts back and forth from models of federalism that support self-determination (to greater or lesser degrees) to models of assimilation that aim at dissolving their diverse socio-political identities altogether. For example, the proclamation was used to recognize and protect Indigenous nations, while at the same time attempting to break up and assimilate the *Canadiens*. The *Quebec Act of 1774* marks a shift away from assimilation and towards federal self-determination, which bore some resemblance to treaty-federalism. But once the War of 1812 was concluded, the relationships begin to shift again. Indigenous nations are no longer needed as military allies, and so the imperial Crown begins to search for cost-effective alternatives through commissions of inquiry and special reports. The system of

during the war and the overall changes that take place in Indian administrative policy during this period. The pass system – an informal administrative policy to control the movement of Indians – was introduced during the North-West Resistance in 1885.[86] This was accompanied by the legal suppression of ceremonial practices (e.g., the Sun Dance of the Blackfoot, Thirst Dance of the Cree, and a vast array of other dances and gift-giving practices), which were seen as a potential threat.[87] These repressive techniques or mechanisms were not extraordinary measures within Indian policy; they were a natural extension of it.

The main structural lines of Indian policy were set by the first *Indian Act* in 1876. The administrative apparatus that it generated was focused from the

---

treaty-federalism (at once formal and informal) is gradually disassembled and repurposed as the imperial Crown (informally) devolves the administrative responsibilities to local colonial governments who predominantly favour assimilation, as it allows for the unilateral taking of lands. As this imperial reorganization continues, the *British North America Act, 1867,* creates a federal dominion that unilaterally excludes Indigenous peoples but includes Lower Canada as the province of Quebec. The *Canadiens* do not simply achieve internal self-determination at Confederation, but there is a clearly defined position for the province of Quebec within the machinery of government that the 1867 division of powers sets out. This remains absent for Indigenous peoples. My sense is that there is largely unexplored common ground between the federalists in Quebec who have been attempting to reimagine the structure of Canadian federalism through terms such as sovereignty-association and Indigenous nations who have been drawing on the history of treaty-federalism to redraw the colonial bounds that exclude them from the division of powers. Both are long-standing political and legal projects that are practically contesting the internal mechanisms of the Canadian constitution that have been used to impose a singular model of Canadian national identity onto them. The challenge (and indeed the opportunity) presented by these diverse sub-state nationalists extends beyond substantive constitutional reform. As Stephen Tierney rightly argues, it is a challenge that "seeks a new constitutional culture within deeply diverse liberal democracies; it challenges these states to pluralise their conception of both of the demos and hence, through a recognition of the historical foundations of the constitution, of the sources of supreme legal authority which underpins the origins and continuing legitimacy of the state." See Tierney, *Constitutional Law and National Pluralism* at 16.

86 The pass system (cf. notes 80 and 83) was studied by a commission from South Africa in 1902. See Giokas, "Indian Act" at 46. At this time South Africa was adapting and expanding its own system of pass laws. This coincided with the transition of the colony to a self-governing dominion in 1910. The newly formed dominion passed, and a series of legislations (e.g., the *Native Land Act* in 1913, which was renamed the *Bantu Land Act*, 1913, and *Black Land Act*, 1913) regulated the acquisition of land and controlled the movement of the Black population by instituting a system of "reserves," which were the precursors of the infamous apartheid system that was in place from 1948 to 1994. For more on the pass laws in South Africa and their role in development of apartheid, see Leonard Monteath Thompson, *A History of South Africa*, 3rd ed. (New Haven, CT: Yale University Press, 2001); and Deborah Posel, *The Making of Apartheid 1948–1961: Conflict and Compromise* (Oxford: Oxford University Press, 1991).

87 See note 83 and Titley, *Narrow Vision* at 164–5.

outset on the unilateral control of lands, membership, and local government.[88] It based this power in its own interpretation of the authority it was granted in s. 91(24) of the *British North America Act, 1867* (this power-over interpretation is based on the assumption that the Crown holds sovereignty, underlying title, and legislative power).[89] This interpretation necessarily implies a picture of federalism that *unilaterally* excludes Aboriginal nations. For those who adopted this picture, the only constitutional question that s. 91(24) gave rise to was how this unlimited *power-over* Indians and their lands affected the division of powers between Parliament and the provincial Legislatures. This question led to litigation soon after Confederation with the *St Catherine's Milling* case. The decision of the Privy Council supported this picture of federalism by presenting Aboriginal rights and title as a "mere burden" that exists at the pleasure of the sovereign and holding that once this "burden" is released, the provinces' underlying interest in the lands becomes plenary and unencumbered.[90] The fact that this case is decided without an Aboriginal party is a clear indication of just how captivating this picture of federalism was. The dominion used this picture to move forward with its project of western expansion and national unification.[91] The *Indian Advancement Act* of 1884 set out to accelerate this

88 Moore, *Historical Development* at 51.

89 An interpretation, which, as we have already detailed, reads "in relation to" as being plenary *power-over*. See note 41.

90 *St Catherine's Milling* at 58. By legally determining the meaning of s. 91(24) and sorting out which parts of the Crown machine are responsible for administering the "mere burden" and those who receive the underlying lands, this case resolves a vexing problem with the picture of federalism that was developing in the dominion (i.e., sorting out the finer details of the unilateral exclusion of Indigenous peoples from the division of powers). This centralization of legislative authority over Indian affairs was a repetition of the older imperial administrative model; Parliament now took the place of the imperial Crown and the provincial legislatures that of the colonies. Despite the basic structural similarity, the reality for Aboriginal peoples within the dominion was radically different. The relative internal autonomy that they had experienced under imperial rule had vanished; what was left was a Crown machine that was intent on transforming them into British subjects and thereby unburdening title to all lands within the bounds of the dominion.

91 The post-Confederation continuation of the treaty process (i.e., the eleven "numbered treaties," which date from 1871 to 1921) also fits within this unilateral model as the *Indian Act* extended to *all* Indian bands, regardless of whether or not they had entered into treaty relations (see *Indian Act 1876* at ss. 1–2). The vast administrative despotism of the *Indian Act* did not rely on the treaty process for its legitimacy (its principle of legitimacy was civilizational supremacy). Rather, the treaty process is a practical remnant of the imperial system of treaty-federalism, which was tied to the legitimating principle of popular sovereignty. Even if the practical realizations were done in bad faith or even outright fraud, they were accountable (i.e., defended, attacked, and judged) via the conceptual registers of popular sovereignty. Within the context of the (dangerously false) principle of civilizational superiority, the treaties cannot count as legitimating the sovereignty of the Crown (as Indigenous peoples are either legally diminished to the status of wards or excluded entirely irredeemable savages); rather, the treaties can be only a gambit or ploy to avoid open conflict.

process by moving the more "advanced" eastern bands to a one-year elective band council system and extending the power of the superintendent-general (locally represented by the Indian agents) to direct every aspect of the political affairs of the "advanced" bands.[92] Sir John A. Macdonald clearly articulated the guiding aim of Indian policy in the House of Commons in 1887 when he stated that the "great aim of our legislation has been to do away with the tribal system and assimilate the Indian people in all respects with the inhabitants of the Dominion."[93] Subsequent amendments to the *Indian Act* continually enhanced the powers of the superintendent-general. For example, an amendment in 1887 granted the superintendent-general the ability "to determine who is or is not a member of any band of Indians."[94] Further amendments in 1894 extended the effect of this power by granting the superintendent-general sole authority to determine whether non-Indians could reside on reserve lands.[95] While the

---

The conflict between these two principles of legitimacy can be seen in the process of treaty making and their judicial interpretation (i.e., in their shifting and inconsistent status as somehow both political tools of colonial settlement without legal significance and legitimacy-granting instruments of cession). Their connection to treaty-federalism and the legitimating principle of popular sovereignty remains a crucial site for contesting the legitimacy of the administrative despotism of the *Indian Act* and the colonial picture of federalism that has confined Indigenous peoples in the constitutional order as wards. They can be utilized as critical resources and unstruck from this colonial picture by refusing to read them as merely sui generis surrender documents and seeing them as products of inter-societal law. As Brian Slattery states, the treaties are (along with the *Royal Proclamation, 1763*) a part of "a diffuse body of customary law and practice that was neither wholly Indigenous nor European but a form of inter-societal law that bridged the gulf between Aboriginal and English legal systems." See Slattery, "Aboriginal Constitution" at 323 and note 9.

92 *An Act for conferring certain privileges on the more advanced Bands of the Indians of Canada, with the view of training them for the exercise of municipal powers*, SC 1884, s. 28. Section 10 of the Act grants council the power to make certain by-laws, rules, and regulations (subject to approval of the superintendent-general), which are set out specifically in fourteen subsections. These subsections are a puzzlingly amalgam, as they vary from being almost hopefully broad (e.g., s. 10(1) the care of the public health) to being concerned with decorum at meetings, the repression of moral offences (i.e., s. 10(4) targets intemperance and profligacy), the care and maintenance of buildings and bridges, trespass, and raising taxes. While this could be read as an expansion of the powers and responsibilities of the council, this is strictly an apparent increase, as it is eclipsed by the enlarged powers of the superintendent-general, which included the ability to direct every aspect of elections and band council meetings. See Giokas, "Indian Act" at 44–5. Parliament also attempted to increase the speed of assimilation by passing a *Franchise Act* in 1885 that gave all Indian males the vote, but objections from the settler society (centring on differences regarding property ownership, taxes, and rational capacities) led to its repeal in 1898. See Moore, *Historical Development* at 51; Titley, *Narrow Vision* at 113.

93 "Return to an Order of the House of Commons, May 2." Canada, *Sessional Papers*, no. 20b (1887) at 37. Cited in Giokas, "Indian Act" at 47.

94 *Indian Act*, SC 1887, c. 33, s. 1.

95 *Indian Act*, SC 1894, c. 32, s. 2.

Indian Act was subject to an almost endless series of amendments, they were primarily changes in degree. The Crown machinery was constantly recalibrated and adjusted, but its structural lines (i.e., its focus on the *unilateral* control of lands, membership, and local government) remained as fixed as the steel rails that stretched across and bound together the new dominion. It was these structural lines – which were designed as a one-way street to assimilation – that, not surprisingly, drew the remaining traditional Indigenous governments into escalating confrontations with the dominion. In order to get a better sense of how Indigenous peoples responded to these lines, we will need to shift to a more ground-level perspective. That is, we will need to focus our attention on an example of such a confrontation.

3.3 The Six Nations Status Case

The conflict between the Six Nations and the dominion was the first to be taken to an international legal body: the League of Nations. In 1923 Chief Deskaheh (also known as Hi-wyi-iss and Levi General) issued "The Redman's Appeal for Justice."[96] The appeal was addressed to the secretary-general of the League of Nations and outlined the Six Nations' case against the dominion. The dominion quickly found itself the object of international criticism (as a number of former colonies – Persia, Estonia, Ireland, and Panama – supported a more official hearing of the case): it responded by defending its Indian policy in an official letter to the secretary-general. The letter – written by the deputy superintendent of the Department of Indian Affairs, Duncan Campbell Scott – is, to my knowledge, the only articulation of the dominion's Indian policy that is addressed to other nations during this period.[97] This episode provides us with an excellent example of how the Crown machinery responded to Indigenous resistance, and vice versa.[98]

---

96 Deskaheh, "The Redman's Appeal for Justice," in *Strange Visitors: Documents in Indigenous-Settler Relations in Canada from 1876*, ed. Keith D. Smith (Toronto: University of Toronto Press, 2014) at 143–8.

97 The letter itself was signed by Joseph Pope (the under-secretary of state for external affairs) and printed in the official journal of the League of Nations in 1924. See Government of Canada, "Appeal of the 'Six Nations' to the League," *League of Nations Official Journal* 5, no. 6 (1924): 829. Many Indigenous nations (including the Six Nations) had taken their petitions to the British Crown. This was a clear demonstration of their view of the *nation-to-nation* relationship between them and the British Crown. That relationship preceded the dominion, and they did not consent to end it. The practice of the British Crown was to simply relay these petitions back to the dominion, as these matters were seen to be within the exclusive jurisdiction of the dominion. For an account of an instance of this practice, see Titley, *Narrow Vision* at 117.

98 The Six Nations Confederacy is the English term for the *Haudenosaunee* (People of the Longhouse). The French refer to them as the Iroquois. The confederacy consists of six Indigenous nations: Mohawk, Oneida, Onondaga, Seneca, Cayuga, and Tuscarora.

I do not mean that this particular conflict can stand for all others in a strict sense. This would simply repeat the very same nonsense that resides within the collective noun *Indian* (i.e., it would not reveal any particular quality that is shared by all members of the group aside from the name and the unilateral process of naming). The grievances, methods of resistance, and desired ends of each Indigenous nation are all highly variable. The conflict between the Six Nations and the dominion is not interchangeable with the Dene, Nuu-chah-nulth, Tsilhqot'in, Mi'kmaq, or any other Indigenous nation. Each of these conflicts has a history of its own. But there is a constant. The constant is what I have been referring to as the picture of federalism – the picture that *unilaterally* excludes Indigenous nations by positioning them as "Indians" – and the Crown machinery that operationalizes it. It is this constant that this case exemplifies. Naturally, the Six Nations status case showed us some of the more precise details of how the Crown machinery was geared or calibrated and how it pursued assimilation. This much is true of any point in the history of Indian policy, but the particular historical context makes this case particularly useful for my purposes. This is because this part of the conflict between the Six Nations and the dominion takes place during volcanic change in the international legal order. This period marks the initial stages of the project of dismantling the European empires that had dominated the nineteenth century with their vast networks of colonial dependencies.[99] The positivist legal arguments that had once unilaterally justified (or, more accurately, been buried outside the boundaries of universal history) the conquest and exploitation of non-European peoples were no longer seen as incontestable.[100] The former colonies

---

Also I note that this is an "episode" because it is part of a conflict that extends from pre-Confederation to today, cf. Johnson, "Quest of the Six Nations."

99 For an excellent history of the League of Nations and the development of the modern international order, see Susan Pedersen, *The Guardians: The League of Nations and the Crisis of Empire* (Oxford: Oxford University Press, 2015); and for an intellectual history of the relationship between imperialism and idealist liberalism during the period, see Jeanne Morefield, *Covenants without Swords: Idealist Liberalism and the Spirit of Empire* (Princeton, NJ: Princeton University Press, 2005).

100 The philosophical discourses that provided the foundations of the colonial world were obsessed with mapping out the geographical dimensions of universal history and pointing out its limits. Hegel's *Lectures on the Philosophy of History* is probably the most detailed example, but, as we saw in part 2, Kant, Mill, and Marx also make contributions. Those peoples and places that are deemed to be outside of history could be shown the light of civilization via the slavers bonds; this was, after all, the compromise that Charles V reached following the Valladolid debate in 1551. For an instructive account of this history and its various legacies, refer to Anthony Pagden, *The Fall of Natural Man: The American Indian and the Origins of Comparative Ethnology* (Cambridge: Cambridge University Press, 1986); and Pagden, *Lords of All the World*. The absurdity of this cartography is aptly parodied by Lewis Carroll in *The Hunting of the Snark*, as the crew (whose number includes a beaver

were pressing for self-government and inclusion in the international system as sovereign, independent nation states.[101] These changes forced the dominion to justify its Indian policy within a new international legal context. It also made clear that the assimilationist policies were not producing "docile bodies" that could be grafted into the body politic as British subjects.[102] Rather, they

---

whose emblematic association with Canada stretches back to its use in the coat of arms of the Hudson's Bay Company in 1678) is guided by a map of the ocean that is nothing more than a blank sheet of paper. It is this same absurd absence of reason (or carte blanche assertion, so perfectly exemplified by the *Requerimiento* of 1513) that Pascal puts his finger on in his remark about boundaries of justice (see the epigraph for part 1) in his *Pensées and Other Writings* at 23.

101 Anghie, *Imperialism* at 115–19.

102 Foucault uses this term in *Surveiller et punir: Naissance de la prison* (translated as Discipline and punish: The birth of the prison). He uses the term to illustrate how the disciplinary technologies of the late eighteenth century related to the body, a relation that he contrasted with slavery, which was based on the appropriation of bodies as object or chattel. In contrast to the owned body of the slave, a docile body "may be subjected, used, transformed and improved." What was new in this was not that the body was the object or site of power, but that the techniques, the "scale of control," had changed. As he puts it, "It was a question not of treating the body, *en masse*, 'wholesale,' as if it were an indissociable unity, but of working it 'retail,' individually; of exercising upon it a subtle coercion, of obtaining holds upon it at the level of the mechanism itself – movements, gestures, attitudes, rapidity: an infinitesimal power over the active body." See Michel Foucault, *Discipline and Punish: The Birth of the Prison,* trans. Alan Sheridan (New York: Vintage Books, 1995) at 136–7. My aim in using this term is simply to highlight the fact that there are many points of connection between Foucault's account of the rise of disciplinary technology and those developed and applied in those lonely laboratories of civilization where the Crown machinery continually carried out its work. I cannot begin to explore these points of connection here. It opens a landscape that is so unfathomably vast and dark that it is utterly bewildering to me. The precise details of the operation of the "vast administrative despotism" – i.e., the residential schools, experimental farms, moral education, policing of moral character, supervisory and penal roles of the Indian agents, etc. – constitutes a missing chapter in the history of discipline. All I can really say with any certainty is that the Crown machinery was geared to produce something that, to my mind, strongly resembles Foucault's account of docile bodies, but it starts from a different set of presumptions and employs a very different procedural model. Its task was to transform Indians into British subjects; figuratively speaking, to transform a kind of foreign tissue into one that could be seamlessly grafted into the body politic. This, to me, constitutes a difference from Foucault's account of the development of discipline in France. The British system (as it is expressed in Indian policy) does not begin with the presumption of complete docility and move towards systematicity; rather, it begins with resistance and adopts a haphazard, experimental approach to achieve its ends. The complex interaction of legislation, policy, administration, enforcement, and resistance brings with it an endless series of unexpected turns and detours (no matter the overall configuration, whether it is set to civilize or to indirect rule). From the French perspective (which is informed by and, to my mind, reflects the civil law tradition with its more vertically structured system of codification), this haphazardness would constitute a failure. In the British case, it is not a failure at all; rather, it is its modus operandi. It reflects, in many ways,

were (much like the British civilizing policies of the first half of the nineteenth century) increasing resistance. The nature of the dominion's response to this increased resistance, which can be seen in the effective ban on the right to seek legal counsel via s. 141 to the *Indian Act* in 1927, pushed the Crown machinery towards the crisis of legitimacy that began to take hold in the 1950s.[103] This is why I believe that this particular moment can serve as a landmark to help us find our way about Indian policy in the early twentieth century and begin to trace out the paths that will eventually lead to the White Paper in 1969.

In order to appreciate the significance of positions that these documents articulate, we will need to get a better sense of both the history of the conflict between the parties and the context of the intended audience. Without this the documents could well seem to simply hang in the air as an abstract exchange of legal propositions. In my opinion, it is just this sort of ahistorical abstraction that grounds the position of the dominion with its refrain of sovereignty (i.e., they are British subjects by birth, by location, by once using the salutation "Our Sovereign Lord" in a legal document, etc.). Without a sense of the actual history of the relationship, it may well appear that the position of the Six Nations lacks the "foundation for any real grievance" or is even "fanatical."[104]

In order to avoid this appearance I will begin by providing the reader with a brief overview of the history of the relationship between the Six Nations and the British. My aim will be to give the reader a sense of the deep historical roots of the conflict (e.g., the military alliance between the Six Nations and the British, the Two Row Wampum of 1613, the Haldimand Proclamation of 1784, etc.). My main focus will be on how the administrative transition that begins

---

how the common law functions. As Pagden states, "The English common law, unlike the law in Spain and France during the sixteenth century, was uncodified. The absence of any accepted body of legislation made the resulting conflict between the Parliament, the Crown, and the various colonies and overseas dependencies hard to resolve." Pagden, *Burdens* at 121. The common laws structure lent itself to a more open and experimental modus operandi; in it, series of policy initiatives are deployed and then adjusted, recalibrated or substituted in and through the case law. Its movements are haphazard and muddled, but they are *movements* (i.e., it does have a general trajectory). There is a set of boundary principles, which exhibit what I have been referring to as *Bluebeard logic* (i.e., they cannot be challenged or contested directly, but they are not hidden). The nature of Crown sovereignty and its corresponding picture of federalism (which excludes or diminishes the rights of Aboriginal nations *ab initio*) are like this. Within these boundaries, the Crown machinery is an open system that can be recalibrated and reconfigured. If these boundaries are put directly into question, the engine seizes; what remains is the bare assertion of force as law (here again, we encounter Bluebeard, as this is what happens after the prohibition on the room is transgressed; see note 79 of part 1).

103 See *supra* note 8.

104 These are the words of Duncan Campbell Scott in a letter to the minister of the interior, Charles Stewart, 13 September 1922. Cited in Titley, *Narrow Vision* at 118.

after the War of 1812 (i.e., shifting the responsibility for Indian administration from the imperial Crown to the colonial governments) led to a conflict, which escalated from Confederation on to this episode in the early 1920s. Next, I will provide a similarly brief account of the international changes following the end of the First World War. My focus here will be on the formation of the League of Nations and the position of the settler colonies in the dismantling of the colonial empires via the mandate system. From that basis I will then turn my attention to the documents themselves and examine the positions that they take. Finally, I will end this section with a short summary of how the Crown machinery was set in motion to respond to the Six Nations in the fallout from the exchange at the League of Nations.

A. *The Six Nations of the Grand River*

The historical roots of the relationship between the Six Nations Confederacy and the British run deep.[105] When the British and the French arrived in the northeastern reaches of North America, the confederacy (which was composed of five nations up until the addition of the Tuscarora – who were fleeing from colonial encroachment on their territory – in 1714 and whose territories longitudinally extended from present-day New York to Illinois and latitudinally from southern Québec to Kentucky)[106] was the predominant regional force. The Europeans soon recognized that they were key to tipping the balance of power in their struggle for control of the continent. As Felix Cohen observes, "The friendship of these Indians was a highly important, if not decisive, factor in the struggle of France and England for the continent. The history of this struggle, as enacted in America, is largely the history of these Indians, who in defending their own lands, played an international role which brought them recognition in treaties between France and England. It is no wonder that the Iroquois were

105 I am indebted to Darlene Johnson's excellent article on the history of the Six Nations struggle in Canada; see Johnson, "Quest of the Six Nations."

106 The Six Nations confederacy is characterized by an elaborate and long-standing legal system and democratic structure, which features three governing bodies that roughly resemble the division of powers between the legislative, executive, and judicial branches of the parliamentary system. The Covenant Circle Wampum represents this structure. As Johnson explains, "The intertwining strands that form the circle represent the fifty chiefs of the confederacy. Their hands are bound symbolically together so firmly and so strongly that, if a tree should fall upon the circle, it could not shake or break it. Inside the circle, the clans, laws, ceremonies, ways, and traditions of the confederacy are protected. The people and their future generations remain in security, peace, and happiness. People are free to leave the circle – that is, to submit to the law of a foreign nation – by passing underneath the arms of the chiefs. But, to stand on the outside of the circle is to stand without a language, without a culture." Johnson, "Quest of the Six Nations" at 9.

'courted and conciliated' by England and that their national character was scrupulously observed and recognized."[107]

The Six Nations formed an alliance with the British in the Treaty of Fort Albany in 1664. They expressed the significance of this relationship (and, indeed, its formal structure) by presenting the British with the Two Row Wampum Belt (or *Kaswentha*). As Taiaiake Alfred explains, "The metaphor for this relationship – two vessels, each possessing its own integrity, travelling the river of time together – was conveyed visually on a wampum belt of two parallel purple lines (representing power) on a background of white beads (representing peace). In this respectful (co-equal) friendship and alliance, any interference with the other partner's autonomy, freedom, or powers was expressly forbidden."[108]

The alliance proved to be invaluable to the British, as the Six Nations assisted them in securing their victory over the French in the Seven Years' War. Following this victory, the British formally acknowledged their obligations to Indigenous peoples with the *Royal Proclamation of 1763*.[109] Many of the Six Nations continued to maintain the alliance during the American War of Independence; this conflict led to their relocation to Grand River.[110] The British had made no provisions for their allies in the Treaty of Paris in 1783. This meant that they were seemingly left with neither lands nor rights in the newly formed United States. The Six Nations, through their leader Joseph Brant, protested this to the governor of Quebec (Sir Frederick Haldimand) by reminding him of the long-standing alliance. In response, the governor offered them territory under British protection. Brant chose the Grand River valley, a region west of Lake Ontario, and in 1784 the governor purchased this territory from the Mississauga. The land was transferred to the Six Nations that same year under the Haldimand Proclamation.[111] The Six Nations regarded (and indeed still regard) this proclamation as full recognition of their status as an independent nation.[112]

---

107 Felix Cohen, *Handbook of Federal Indian Law* (New York: LexisNexis, 2012) at 417.

108 Taiaiake Alfred, *Peace, Power, Righteousness: An Indigenous Manifesto*, 2nd ed. (Oxford: Oxford University Press, 2009) at 76.

109 The preamble makes the military and political significance of these alliances clear: "And whereas it is just and reasonable, and essential to our interest and the Security of the Colonies, that the several Nations or Tribes of Indians with whom We are connected ... should not be molested or disturbed." George R, Proclamation, 7 October 1763 (3 Geo III), rept. in RSC 1985, App II, No 1 [*Royal Proclamation of 1763*]. See also Pagden, *Burdens* at 144.

110 The civil nature of the conflict led to some internal confusion and division, but the British promised compensation, and so Joseph Brant (an influential Mohawk war chief) rallied a large portion of the Six Nations to the British side. See Johnson, "Quest of the Six Nations" at 12.

111 Ibid. at 13.

112 This interpretation was actually affirmed by Lieutenant Governor John Graves Simcoe (Haldimand's successor) at a council with the Six Nations in which he presented a series of past and present agreements between the British and the confederacy and stated,

Following the War of 1812 the military importance of the confederacy to the British declined. This was, as we have seen, the beginning of a transition in Indian policy and administration. The guiding star of policy had shifted from maintaining important military alliances (via a system of treaties, gifts, protection, and separation) to the reduction of administrative costs. This ushered in a series of commissions and reports (e.g., Darling, Bagot, and Pennefather), which recommended that the Indians be civilized. This was seen as the surest means to the end of reducing costs and ensuring the continued settlement of the colony. The administrative machinery was gradually repurposed to effect these new ends. The Indians were slated to become British subjects; the only question that remained was how to effect this transformation. By 1830 the Indian Department – which had been established in 1755 as part of the military – had become a branch of the public service, and in 1860 control was transferred from the imperial Crown to the province of Canada.[113] This devolution continued with the formal creation of the dominion in 1867, which in turn brought more legislative machinery to task. With the *Gradual Enfranchisement Act*, *Indian Lands Act*, and finally the *Indian Act*, the main structural lines of Indian policy were set; the federal Crown would now have *unilateral* control over lands, membership, and local government. These were seen as the main levers or points of control that were required to civilize the Indians and enfranchise them into the body politic.

Now let's take a step back from this series of legislative shifts and administrative changes for a moment and try to imagine the policy aim that was guiding them, that is, let's try to express it as a picture. It is a picture of a single ship of state (or body politic, depending on the preferred political metaphor). The ship is structured upon a series of principles (federalism, democracy, constitutionalism, etc.), but it is a single ship. The current version of it has a separate compartment that operates on different principles – viz. administrative despotism – but it is presented as only temporary or transitional state to the single, unified ship.[114] The contrast with this picture and the one we find in the Two Row Wampum is stark. It contemplates two ships. They are travelling together, but they remain separated at a respectful distance, each managing its own affairs. The conflict between these pictures is obvious. So how do we explain how one

---

"These authentic papers prove that no King of Great Britain ever claimed absolute power or sovereignty over any of your lands that were not fairly purchased or bestowed by your Ancestors at Public Treaties, they likewise prove that your natural independency has been preserved." Cited in Johnson, "Quest of the Six Nations" at 14.

113 The *Indian Lands Act* of 1860 ended the era of imperial federalism by transferring authority for Indians and Indian lands to the colonial legislature. See *An Act respecting the Management of Indian Lands and Property*, SC 1860, c. 151, s. 4.

114 This is, to my mind, the picture that informs Binnie J's reinterpretation of the Two-Row Wampum in *Mitchell*. I deal with this at length in part 1.

is given the *force of law*, or, to make the question a bit more precise, what is the legal foundation for the dominion's picture?

The letter we will examine will provide responses to this question. Its author will marshal the evidence and lay out the case, but at its basis it is an assertion. It is the same assertion at the basis of the unlimited *power-over* interpretation of s. 91(24). And it is, in turn, reliant on a view of history that adds a series of caveats and qualifications on the human species. J.S. Mill clearly illustrates the upshot of this view point when he states, "Despotism is a legitimate mode of government in dealing with barbarians."[115] This view is, to borrow an analogy from Wittgenstein, like the case of the eye and the visual field. It looks out and says, "This is my world," or "Those are barbarians." But it does not see itself. Nothing in the visual field allows it to infer that it is seen by an eye, and so the limits of perspective are forgotten. The limits its perspective are simply taken as the limit of *the world*.[116] This forgetting of the limits perspective, or "view from nowhere," helps to insulate one viewpoint by disqualifying (with the *force of law*) the view of others who contest its claims to truth by reminding those who adopt it that their chosen view is simply *one way of seeing* things. And so Wittgenstein's example of eye and the visual field shows us how it is possible to mistake one perspective for the a priori order of things. The order that it sees seems as though "it is *prior* to all experience, must run through all experience; no empirical cloudiness or uncertainty can be allowed to affect it – It must rather be of the purest crystal. But this crystal does not appear as an abstraction; but as something concrete, indeed, as the most concrete, as it were the *hardest* thing there is."[117]

It is, as Wittgenstein puts it, held captive by a picture.[118] But, despite appearances, the eye is not suspended in a void; rather, the strange and diverse passengers of the black canoe in Bill Reid's sculpture *The Spirit of Haida Gwaii* have continually struggled to assemble reminders of what already lies open to view (viz. that true legitimacy can be based only on mutual recognition, consent, and continuity).[119]

115 Mill, *On Liberty* at 9.

116 Wittgenstein, *Tractatus* at §5.63–5.634.

117 Wittgenstein, *Philosophical Investigations* at §97. The use of the term *crystal* is particularly evocative in this context. It leads us to the role of "crystallization" in the case law from *Guerin*, to *Van der Peet*, and *Delgamuukw*. How is it that mere assertion of sovereignty can "crystallize" (to absolutely fix) the rights of the other party? This is, to my mind, where we begin to enter the magical circle of legal fictions (*terra nullius*, discovery, the civilization thesis, etc.). For a recent and instructive critique of this, refer to John Borrows's "(Ab) originalism and Canada's Constitution," in *Freedom and Indigenous Constitutionalism*.

118 Wittgenstein, *Philosophical Investigations* at §115.

119 Tully, *Strange Multiplicity* at 212.

The Six Nations continually resisted the administrative encroachment of the dominion into their affairs. In 1839 (following the transfer of the Indian Department from military to civilian control in 1830) they demanded to be governed by their own laws, but the government of Upper Canada refused. In 1890 they responded to the growing bureaucratic control of the Crown machinery by delivering a petition to Ottawa demanding recognition of their autonomy and exemption from the *Indian Act*. The government responded in a predictable fashion by stating, "The Superintendent-General of Indian Affairs is unable to concur in the view put forward in this petition, and he is of the opinion that there is no ground on which the same can be supported."[120]

During this period internal divisions began to form within the confederacy. A group of reformers sought to replace the hereditary council with an elective one. The reformers (who were known by a series of names, from Dehorners, the Warriors Association, and the Six Nations' Rights Association, to the Indian Rights Association) included members from each of the nations within the confederacy. The only discernible line that separated the supporters of the hereditary council from the reformers was religion; the majority of the former adhered to the longhouse religion, whereas the latter were largely Christian.[121] The reformers delivered a petition to Ottawa in 1907 requesting that the traditional council be removed, but it represented only a small portion of the electorate, so Ottawa refused.[122] After this refusal, the movement faded, but the traditional council feared that its authority was going to be undermined. This led to a shift in the leadership of the council away from the members who supported the status quo to a group who favoured total sovereignty. The latter group (led by Chief Deskaheh) established a special committee to plan a campaign for sovereignty in 1919. They sought legal advice and hired a lawyer to compile evidence to support their claims.

In 1920, under Duncan Campbell Scott's leadership, an amendment to the *Indian Act* was proposed that included mandatory residential school attendance and granted the government the unilateral power to enfranchise Indians who were over the age of twenty-one.[123] The amendment proved to be highly controversial among both the Indian and settler communities.[124] The Six Nations sent their lawyer to Ottawa to appear before the committee considering the amendment. He put forward the sovereignty argument; the committee's response was that they intended to replace the traditional government as soon as a majority

120 Cited in Titley, *Narrow Vision* at 112.

121 Ibid. at 110–13.

122 The petition only had 300 signatures, which was one quarter of the adult male population (ibid. at 113).

123 Moore, *Historical Development* at 115; Titley, *Narrow Vision* at 114.

124 For an account of the response, see Moore, *Historical Development* at 116–17.

of the adult male electorate approved.[125] The amendment became law later that year, and this prompted the Six Nations to press their case forward. They sent a petition outlining their position to the governor general in 1920. This led Scott to recommend that the petition be considered by the Supreme Court and that the compulsory enfranchisement provisions would not apply to them until a decision had been reached.[126] This apparent success was, in fact, simply part of Scott's plan to remove the traditional council from power, as he was convinced that the Court would provide the kind of final and full response that would (in his view) restore proper administrative order. The deputy minister of justice reviewed the Six Nations' petition and informed Scott that it was "a hopeless case," and on 27 November 1920 the Privy Council handed down an Order in Council rejecting the Six Nations' demand for judicial review.[127] Scott then informed the Six Nations that enfranchisement provisions would be applied to them. This, combined with concerns raised by the *Soldier Settlement Act*,[128] prompted them to issue a second petition, which was referred back to Scott. In his response he cited a statement made by John B. Robinson, the attorney general for Upper Canada, in 1824: "To Talk of treaties with the Mohawk Indians residing in the heart of one of the most populous Districts of Upper Canada upon lands purchased for them and given to them by the British Government is much the same in my humble opinion as to talk of making treaty alliances with the Jews in Duke Street or with the French Emigrants who have settled in England."[129]

Scott then went on to state, "With reference to enfranchisement I may say that the policy of the Government is to carefully protect and educate the Indians and to thus contribute towards their civilization in order that they may eventually be merged into the general body of citizenship. If this in any way conflicts with the aspirations of Indians whose faces are set against ultimate destiny, it can only be regretted."[130]

---

125 Titley, *Narrow Vision* at 114.

126 Ibid. at 115.

127 Ibid.

128 The concern was that the Act (which was assented to in 1919) would empower the government to unilaterally surrender reserve lands for soldiers. See *Soldier Settlement Act*, RSC 1927, c. 188, s. 10.

129 Cited in Titley, *Narrow Vision* at 115–16. The position taken here exhibits a curious mix of practical difficulty (or to a term from the register of international law, the principle of territorial integrity) and comparisons that distort the relationship between the British and the Six Nations by comparing them to minority groups living in uncontested sovereign territory. The position implicitly relies on the assumption that British sovereignty to the lands of Upper Canada is equivalent to that which Britain possesses over England.

130 Cited in Titley, *Narrow Vision* at 116. It is clear here that the picture was indeed crystallized, as it is presented as the "ultimate fate" of Indians.

The Six Nations sought legal advice and responded by taking their case to the king of England in 1921. Chief Deskaheh personally delivered the petition, which was forwarded to Winston Churchill (then the secretary of state for the colonies). Churchill simply forwarded it to the governor general in Canada, as it was, in his opinion, a matter that was within the exclusive jurisdiction of the dominion.[131] Chief Deskaheh's visit to England had generated considerable attention and sympathy from the media. Scott, who was also in London at the time, was approached by the editor of *Canada* (a weekly magazine published in London) for an official reaction, but he refused. This increased the media attention, which increased Scott's frustration.

The Mackenzie King government was elected in 1921; it adopted a somewhat more conciliatory approach to the Indian Question. It repealed the compulsory enfranchisement provisions (against Scott's protests) and moved to set up a Royal Commission to settle the dispute with the Six Nations. Any progress made was soon lost when an incident occurred at the Grand River reserve involving police officers (who were investigating reports of liquor manufacturing) and a group of armed Indians. The presence of an armed force on their lands convinced the traditional council that the negotiations were not sincere.[132] This led them to take their case to the newly formed League of Nations.

B. The League of Nations and the Mandate System

The League of Nations was established in the wake of the First World War at the Paris Peace Conference in 1919. Its principal mission was to maintain world peace by forming a community of nations that would settle their disputes through negotiation and arbitration. While the idea itself was far from new (Kant's *Perpetual Peace* was written in 1795), the institutionalization of it brought about a seismic shift in international law. The world view of the positivist tradition, which had served as the legal basis for the European empires throughout the nineteenth century, was now fundamentally contested. This world view had maintained (contra the natural law tradition) that the sovereign was the only source of law. Once that was accepted, the study of law itself became an autonomous field of scientific inquiry (a field that was, from the outset, focused on defining the concept of sovereignty by determining which entities were in fact "sovereign").[133] The international legal order that it gave rise to was ruled by a kind of mechanistic formalism, which divided the world into sovereign states and uncivilized tribes.[134] As Antony Anghie points out,

131 Ibid. at 117.
132 Ibid. at 119.
133 Anghie, *Imperialism* at 56.
134 Ibid. at 56–65.

the league challenged this world view in at least two different respects: "First, it challenged the positivist idea that international law is the law governing states and that states are the only actors in international law. Second, and more importantly, the existence of the League suggested new ways of approaching the problem of sovereignty, and led inter-war lawyers to question conceptions of sovereignty that been fundamental to the positivist international law of the nineteenth century."[135]

In effect, the First World War had highlighted a deep fissure in the positivists' world view: viz. the community of civilized nations had collapsed, leaving a straight line from unilateral nature of state sovereignty to the normalization of war. This left the interwar jurists the task of constructing a system that limited sovereignty while recognizing the centrality of the sovereign state. This new approach was embodied in the mandate system, which was designed to deal with the former German colonial territories in Africa and the Pacific as well as a number of non-Turkish provinces of the Ottoman Empire.

The basic principles of the mandate system are set out in Article 22 of the League Covenant,

> To those colonies and territories which as a consequence of the late war have ceased to be under the sovereignty of the States which formerly governed them and which are inhabited by peoples not yet able to stand by themselves under the strenuous conditions of the modern world, there should be applied the principle that the well-being and development of such peoples form a sacred trust of civilization and that securities for the performance of this trust should be embodied in this Covenant.... The best method of giving practical effect to this principle is that the tutelage of such peoples should be entrusted to advanced nations who by reason of their resources, their experience or their geographical position can best undertake this responsibility, and who are willing to accept it, and that this tutelage should be exercised by them as Mandatories on behalf of the League.... The character of the mandate must differ according to the stage of the development of the people, the geographical situation of the territory, its economic conditions and other similar circumstances.[136]

This was a departure from the stark boundaries that characterized the positivists' world view in the nineteenth century. The uncivilized peoples of the colonial territories were slated to become part of the international community of sovereign states.[137] The principles of "well-being and development" (which formed the "sacred trust of civilizations") were directly connected to that of

135 Ibid. at 125.

136 *League of Nations Covenant*, Article 22, paras. 1–3.

137 This is by no means a full and complete departure from the earlier paradigms of sovereignty and legitimacy that were used by the European colonial empires. James Tully provides us

self-determination.[138] This entailed a shift from the positivist focus on the autonomous sphere of law to a pragmatic jurisprudence based on rules, procedures, policies, and administration.[139] The uncivilized world was no longer simply outside of law and history, it was the site of their administrative realization.

This system of international "tutelage," with its linear continuum of stages of development, was by no means entirely new. As Anghie clearly details, league lawyers returned to the work of Francisco de Vitoria, whose characterization of the natives as "infants" supported the guardianship model.[140] But it also bears some resemblance to the civilizing machinery that the British had developed in the first half of the nineteenth century (and the Crown machinery that the dominion of Canada was busily attempting to perfect since its formation in 1867). If we consider the general outline of the mandate system itself, this similarity is, to my mind, striking. Generally speaking, the mandate system drew

---

with a perspicuous overview of how these apparent changes continue a system of imperial relationships by rendering them informal and thus less easy to clearly see:

> The nominally sovereign and independent non-European states recognized by international law are in fact the former colonies, whose legal and political structures were constructed by the European powers to serve their interests over two periods of colonial imperialism: 1500–1776 and the second period of hyper-colonization, 1800–1905, when 85 per cent of the non-European world was under formal and informal imperial rule. Under the "standard of civilization" of the nineteenth-century international law, these "uncivilized" colonies were opened to free trade and structured accordingly by the imperial powers under the Mandate System of the League of Nations and the Trustee System of the United Nations. During the period of decolonization, state building, and the Cold War competition between the United States and the Soviet Union, the Indigenous, westernized elites wrested formal political power from their former masters, but this involved a "transfer of power" and the "continuation" of existing "informal" imperial relationships. (Tully, *Public Philosophy* at 2:139)

138 This connection was clearly set out by President Woodrow Wilson to a joint session of Congress on 8 January 1918. In this address he laid down what he saw as a "programme of the world's peace, … the only possible programme" in a set of fourteen numbered points (now known as the Fourteen Points speech). The issue of the colonies was addressed in point five, which required "a free, open-minded, and absolutely impartial adjustment of all colonial claims, based upon a strict observance of the principle that in determining all such questions of sovereignty the interests of the populations concerned must have equal weight with the equitable government whose title is to be determined." See John Milton Cooper, *Breaking the Heart of the World: Woodrow Wilson and the Fight for the League of Nations* (Cambridge: Cambridge University Press, 2001) at 24; and Erez Manela, *The Wilsonian Moment: Self-Determination and the International Origins of Anticolonial Nationalism* (Oxford: Oxford University Press, 2007) at 40.

139 Anghie, *Imperialism* at 188.

140 As he aptly puts it, "The circle was complete: in seeking to end colonialism, international law returned to the origins of the colonial encounter" (ibid. at 145).

on the social sciences to develop a new set of technologies and methods of control (i.e., the creation of international institutions allowed for a fusion of practical administrative technologies and law).[141] These enabled it to access the structural and functional components that make up states (i.e., what we could figuratively refer to as the organelles of states). This made it possible to move past the simplistic binary of civilized/uncivilized. The presence of sovereignty and the capacity for self-government was now measured on a gradational scale that went from backward to advanced.[142] Naturally, the very possibility of a scale (whether binary or gradational) was based on the presumptions supplied by universal history. This provided an abstract model of the ideal (and therefore sovereign) state. This singular model provided the mandate system with what Anghie refers to as the "fantastic universalizing apparatus."[143] With this in hand, it was possible to measure differences and set to work straightening the "crooked timber of humanity."[144] The mandate system sought to selectively eliminate those customs and traditions that were seen as barriers to creating efficient communities of rational individuals.[145] Native governments and legal structures were slated to be replaced with the modern political intuitions of responsible government.[146] This program is undoubted by now. All basic components of Canadian Indian policy from the mid-nineteenth century on are repeated here. We may not see the familiar legislative terms of the *Gradual Civilization Act*, *Gradual Enfranchisement Act*, *Indian Act*, or the *Indian Advancement Act*, but their substantive content and operational procedures are all here. It also led to the very same paradoxical dead end. The system that was set up to liberate the mandate peoples from the "strenuous conditions of the modern world" actually maintains those conditions.[147] This is, to my mind,

141 This kind of amalgamated judico-administrative system was already very familiar within the settler colonies. In the Canadian context it is an assemblage of Indian legislation, policy, and administrative practices that I have been referring to as the Crown machinery. It should come as no surprise that this system was internationalized in the early twentieth-century institutions of the League of Nations and the United Nations, as their architects were very familiar with these British settler colonial models.

142 Ibid. at 155.

143 Ibid. at 149.

144 These measurements were by no means immune to political pressures. The determination that the former German colonies in Africa and Asia were at the lowest scale was made to placate the desire of the dominions (viz. Australia, New Zealand, and South Africa) to annex them entirely. They were unwilling to accept any determination that would suggest that these territories would ever become independent. See Anghie, *Imperialism* at 121. The phrase "the crooked timber of humanity" is Isaiah Berlin's; see *The Crooked Timber of Humanity: Chapters in the History of Ideas* (Princeton, NJ: Princeton University Press, 2013).

145 Anghie, *Imperialism* at 162.

146 Ibid. at 168–9.

147 Ibid. at 178. As Anghie points out, "The peculiar cycle thus creates a situation whereby international institutions present themselves as a solution to a problem of which they are an

the same paradox that Tobias notes concerning the *Gradual Civilization Act.* As he puts it, "The legislation to remove all distinctions between Indians and Euro-Canadians actually establishes them."[148] Simply put, the mandate system internationalized the Anglo-American model of the Indian reservation.[149]

Returning now to the historical context of the appeal of the Six Nations to the league, by the early 1920s this volcanic change to the international legal order (i.e., the transition from nineteenth-century legal positivism – bolstered by the bright lines supplied by the "standard of civilization" – to a looser, more informal, and administratively pragmatic system of development) is in full swing. The war had weakened the Imperial powers in their military capacities and their legitimacy. Their symbolic status as the pinnacle of civilization was shaken, and with it the hierarchy of metropole and colony. In response, nationalist movements were rapidly expanding and gaining strength (e.g. the Egyptian Revolution and the Turkish War of Independence in 1919, as well as rebellions throughout the colonized world).[150] This trend was bolstered by the success of the Bolshevik Revolution in Russia, which provided inspiration to those resisting imperial domination. Mahatma Gandhi's first satyagraha

---

integral part. Such a situation is very much part of contemporary international relations." My contention is that this is also the case in Canada and that the two problems are related.

148 *Tobias*, "Protections, Civilization, Assimilation" at 130.

149 By "internationalized" I do not mean to suggest that they simply adopted the model holus-bolus; rather, they took a familiar judico-administrative structure and adapted it for use on a different scale. The connection I am making is thus not strict identity but family resemblance. This resemblance should not be altogether surprising, considering that Jan Smuts (one of the two principal drafters and architects of the covenant) was a prominent South African statesman who was doubtlessly familiar with the *Native Land Act* of 1913 (renamed the *Bantu Land Act*, 1913) and *Black Land Act*, 1913. As previously stated, these acts regulated the acquisition of land and controlled the movement of the blacks by creating a system of "reserves," which were the precursors of the infamous apartheid system that took shape in 1948. Naturally, substantiating the similarity between the mandate system and Anglo-American Indian administration (beyond a rough-and-ready comparison) would require, among other things, a thorough comparative examination of the initial proposals (e.g., the Phillimore Commission, the Fourteen Points), as well as an investigation into US administrative policies relating to Indians and the colonies ceded in the Spanish-American War (with a particular focus on the Philippines from 1898 to 1919). What I am positing here is a *family resemblance* between the model of Indian administration that was developed within the dominions of the British Empire in the second half of the nineteenth century. The Crown machine that was to prepare the Indians for a higher state of civilization may not have been designed to create independent states (as the mandate version of it was), but it was designed to build their atomic components (the citizens). In both cases the same abstract system of measurement (civilization) was unilaterally imposed under the rubric of guardianship. It should not be surprising that the socio-legal technologies could be applied to both.

150 Anghie, *Imperialism* at 139.

campaigns in Champaran and Kheda take place in 1917–18. The remaining imperial powers responded with repressive measures (e.g., the French suppression of the Cochinchina uprising in 1916 and the British use of military force in the massacre at Amritsar in 1919), but this only increased resistance. This tense atmosphere of anticolonial resistance and volcanic international change forms the context for the exchange between the Six Nations and Canada.

C. The Documents

In order to properly interpret the exchange that takes place in these documents I will need to provide the reader with a little more detail regarding each of them. The first to appear was Chief Deskaheh's *The Redman's Appeal for Justice*, which was published as a pamphlet – and so it was publicly circulated in the British press – in London in August 1923.[151] It is addressed to the secretary-general of the League of Nations (Sir James Eric Drummond). On 4 September Deskaheh presented it to the president of the Assembly (Cosme de la Torriente y Peraza), who responded by informing him that for procedural reasons no action could be taken in that session.[152] Nevertheless, the Canadian delegate (George P. Graham) was concerned that future appeals may be more successful and wrote to Ottawa recommending that Canada issue a more detailed response. Scott volunteered to prepare the statement, which he completed by 17 December. "Statement Respecting the Six Nations' Appeal to the League of Nations" was reviewed and subsequently endorsed by the minister of the interior (Charles Stewart), the deputy minister of justice (E.L. Newcombe[153]), and the Canadian delegate to the league (Graham). It was then forwarded to the under-secretary of state for external affairs (Sir Joseph Pope) in January 1924 for circulation to the league and was published in its official journal.[154]

These details are important, as they highlight the fact that these documents articulate official positions on a legal conflict (a fact that is also reflected in their form, content, and tone). With this in mind, my aim now is to provide the reader with a brief analysis of each. I will focus on how each document

151 It is unclear whether Deskaheh is the sole author of the document. Given its formal structure and official purpose (by this I mean that Deskaheh is writing under the authority of his political role – a fact that is made clear in the introduction of the document – within the Six Nations), it may have been drafted with the assistance of legal counsel. The counsel for the Six Nations at this time was George T. Decker (a prominent attorney from Rochester). I mention this to highlight the fact that this is an official statement of a legal and political position and not a personal letter or pamphlet. See Titley, *Narrow Vision* at 116–17.

152 Titley, *Narrow Vision* at 122.

153 Newcombe was subsequently appointed to the Supreme Court in 1924, where he served until his death in 1931.

154 Titley, *Narrow Vision* at 123.

presents three elements of its case: (1) the relationship between the parties; (2) The nature of the present conflict, and (3) The remedies sought.

THE REDMAN'S APPEAL FOR JUSTICE

The appeal is relatively brief and to the point. It sets out the Six Nations' case in twenty numbered paragraphs. These paragraphs can be further subdivided into the elements we will be analysing: the relationship between the parties is set out in paras. 3–8; the nature of the present conflict in paras. 10–19; and, finally, the remedies in the closing paragraph. The first two paragraphs clearly establish the overall position of the Six Nations and so are best cited at length,

> Under the authority vested in the undersigned, the Speaker of the Council and the Sole Deputy by choice of the Council composed of forty-two chiefs, of the Six Nations of the Iroquois, being a state within the purview and meaning of Article 17 of the Covenant of the League of Nations, but not being at present a member of the League, I, the undersigned, pursuant to the said authority, do hereby bring to the notice of the League of Nations that a dispute and disturbance of peace has arisen between the State of the Six Nations of the Iroquois on the one hand and the British Empire and Canada, being Members of the League, on the other.... The Six Nations of the Iroquois crave therefore invitation to accept the obligations of Membership of the League for the purpose of such dispute; upon such conditions as may be prescribed.[155]

This paragraph establishes the identity of the parties (i.e., both the Six Nations and Canada are presented as states) and the purpose of the document (i.e., to gain membership in the league and initiate dispute resolution set out in Articles 12–17 of the Covenant).

The Six Nations' case for membership in the league is made on the basis of an account of their long history of interactions with European states in the colonies of North America. This history provides the Six Nations' account of their relationship to the dominion of Canada:

> Great Britain and the Six Nations of the Iroquois (hereinafter called "The Six Nations") having been in open alliance for upwards of one hundred and twenty years immediately preceding the Peace of Paris of 1783, the British Crowns in succession promised the latter to protect them against encroachments and enemies making no exception whatever, and King George the Third, falling into war with his own colonies in America, promised recompense for all losses which might be sustained by the Six Nations in consequence of their alliance in that war and they remain entitled to such protection as against the Dominion of Canada.[156]

155 Dekahh, "Redman's Appeal" at 143.
156 Ibid. at 144.

What is invoked here – and it is a position that the Six Nations have maintained from the *Two Row Wampum in 1664* on – is imperial federalism. The specifics of this position are reinforced by their explanation of the acceptance of the Grand River lands under the *Haldimand Proclamation of 1784*: "The Six Nations (excepting certain numbers of those people who elected to remain), at the invitation of the British Crown and under its express promise of protection, intended as security for their continued independence, moved across the Niagara and thereafter duly established themselves and their league in self-government upon the said Grand River lands, and they have ever since held the unceded remainder thereof as a separate and independent people, established there by sovereign right."[157] The emphasis here is on *self-government, separate,* and *independent.* Again, this position is entirely consistent with their long-standing position as being a self-governing people under the protection of the British imperial Crown. This point is driven home in paragraph 7: "The Six Nations have at all times enjoyed recognition by the Imperial Government of Great Britain of their right to independence in home-rule, and to protection therein by the British Crown – the Six Nations on their part having faithfully discharged the obligations of their alliance on all occasions of the need of Great Britain, under the ancient covenant chain of friendship between them, including the occasion of the late World War."[158] This underlines the ultimate basis of the Six Nations' appeal. That is, a relationship that they have consented to and honoured from 1664 onwards was unilaterally altered when the British devolved powers to the dominion in 1867 (a process that, as we have seen, began after the War of 1812). So while the specific case concerns a dispute with the dominion, it occurs as the result of a unilateral breach by the imperial British Crown.

From this basis Deskaheh goes on to outline the current dispute between the Six Nations and the dominion. There are five related grievances, and I will review them in order of occurrence in the appeal:

1 Enfranchisement: This is presented as an attempt to unilaterally "impose Dominion rule upon" the Six Nations and their lands (by parcelling out lands to those who were to be enfranchised).[159]
2 Penal Jurisdiction: As Deskaheh states, "The Dominion Government is now engaged in enforcing upon the people of the Six Nations certain penal laws of Canada." This is seen as a violation of the Six Nations' own jurisdiction on their territory and over their nationals, which are being held in Canadian prisons.[160]

157 Ibid.
158 Ibid. at 145.
159 Ibid. at 145–56.
160 Ibid. at 146.

3 Misappropriated Funds: This issue is briefly touched on, the gist of it being that Six Nations funds – which are held in trust by the dominion – have been and are still being "misappropriated and wasted without consent of the Six Nations."[161]

4 Inciting Rebellion: This grievance is tied to the issue of misappropriation, as Deskaheh maintains that the dominion "has been using these trust funds to incite rebellion within the Six Nations, to furnish occasion for setting up of a new Government for the Six Nations, tribal in form but devised by the Dominion Parliament and intended to rest upon Canadian authority under a Dominion Statute known as the 'Indian Act.'"[162]

5 Hostile Invasion: This refers to the incident with the RCMP that prompted the Six Nations to leave negotiations with the dominion and appeal to the league. This incident is detailed in paragraph 15, which I will cite as a whole: "To the manifest end of destroying the Six Nations Government, the Dominion Government did, without just or lawful cause, in or about December of the year 1922, commit an act of war upon the Six Nations by making an hostile invasion of the Six Nations domain, wherein the Dominion Government then established an armed force which it has since maintained therein, and the presence thereof has impeded and impedes the Six Nations Council in the carrying on of the duly constituted government of the Six Nations people, and is a menace to international peace."[163]

The legal substance of these specific grievances is that they constitute a "violation of the nationality and independence" of the Six Nations, which is contrary to the treaties that exist between them and the British Crown.[164]

Deskaheh summarizes the basis of the Six Nations' case at the close of paragraph 16: "The said acts and measures were and are in violation as well of the recognized law of Nations, the Six Nations never having yielded their right of independence in home-rule to the Dominion of Canada, and never having released the British Crown from the obligation of its said covenants and treaties with them, but they have ever held and still hold the British Crown thereto."[165]

The appeal closes with a list of the remedies sought.

1 Recognition of their independent right of home rule.

2 Appropriate indemnity for the said aggressions for the benefit of their injured nationals.

161 Ibid.
162 Ibid.
163 Ibid. at 146–7.
164 Ibid. at 147.
165 Ibid.

3 A just accounting by the imperial government of Great Britain, and by the Dominion of Canada of the Six Nations' trust funds and the interest thereon.
4 Adequate provision to cover the right of recovery of the said funds and interest by the Six Nations.
5 Freedom of transit for the Six Nations across Canadian territory to and from international waters.
6 Protection for the Six Nations hereafter under the League of Nations, if the imperial government of Great Britain shall avow its unwillingness to continue to extend adequate protection or withhold guarantees of such protection.[166]

They also seek interim relief in the form of unrestricted access to the fund held in trust and a suspension of all "aggressive practices" by the dominion.

The appeal puts its finger on the flashpoint that was tearing the colonial empires apart: viz. the *unilateral* basis of colonization – as expressed in its legal incantations of discovery, *terra nullius*, the civilization thesis, etc. – which continued on in the guise of the so-called community of nations. The treaties and promises that had secured the alliances and helped to build the British Empire could be revised at will. Their meaning was – and, to my mind, still is – lost in a sort of strange riddle: "What begins as a treaty, ends as a surrender document, but never changes a single word?"[167] This must have been what drew the attention and support of the formerly colonized states in 1923 (i.e., Estonia, Ireland, Panama, and Persia). It was a joke that they were all, in one way or another, sadly familiar with. The league was set up as a means of reconciling the empires with their colonies by levelling the ground. This was the idea of the community of nations; to open access to the principle of equality and thereby move the boundary of justice beyond the limits of Europe. The mandate system clearly demonstrates the failure of this idea. The only honest motto for this version of the community of nations is captured in George Orwell's *Animal Farm*: "All animals are equal but some animals are more equal than others."[168]

THE DOMINION'S RESPONSE

The dominion's response is much longer than the appeal. This is the result, in large part, of its format. As Scott states in the opening paragraph, "The undersigned has the honour to submit herewith a categorical statement respecting the petition to the League of Nations entitled 'The Red Man's Appeal for Justice'

166 Ibid.
167 The reasoning in *Logan v. Styres*, [1959] OWN 361, 20 DLR (2d) 416 (Ont. HC), which came much later, is an instance of this.
168 George Orwell, *Animal Farm and 1984* (New York: Houghton Mifflin Harcourt, 2003) at 80.

communicated by Levi General, otherwise Chief Deskaheh, on behalf of the Council of the Six Nations of Brantford, to the President of the Assembly on September 4th, 1923, arranged in sections numerated in correspondence with those of the petition, the verbiage of which is quoted and indented at the beginning of each."[169]

As I see it, there are two points of note here. First, the response is referred to as a "categorical statement," and it adopts the format of quotation and response. The Six Nations appeal is cited in full, and there are extensive citations from Canadian case law, Orders in Council, the *Royal Proclamation of 1763*, the *Indian Act*, and an annex that contains a copy of the *Simcoe Deed*, an example of a land surrender, a financial statement of the Six Nations trust account, as well as a copy of the *Indian Act* in full. This helps explain the length of the document and points out that the actual arguments in response to the appeal make up only a small portion of it. Second, the references to both the author of the document and the other party serve to reposition them so as to imply that the dispute is a domestic matter.[170]

The response is set out as a point-by-point refutation of the Six Nations' appeal. The gist of the dominion's position is that the league is not the appropriate venue for this dispute, because it is a domestic matter (i.e., the Six Nations are under the exclusive jurisdiction of the dominion). The counterarguments that are marshalled against the Six Nations are easily summarized, so I will begin by providing the reader with a list of them in order of occurrence:

1 The Six Nations are not a state because they are "subjects of the British Crown domiciled within the Dominion of Canada and owing a natural debt of allegiance to His Majesty's Government thereof, and are therefore not competent to apply for or receive membership in the League."[171]
2 "The Six Nations are not now, and have not been for 'many centuries' a recognized or self-governing people but are, as aforesaid, subjects of the British Crown residing within the Dominion of Canada. The statement that the Six Nations have treated with the Dominion of Canada is incorrect. The Dominion of Canada has at no time entered into any treaty with the Six Nations or recognized them as having any separate or sovereign rights."[172]

169 Canada, "Appeal" at 829.
170 Chief Deskaheh is referred to first by his English name, which seems to suggest that the appeal is personal and that his official title is of secondary importance or perhaps even illegitimate in some way. The reference to the Six Nations includes the addition of a specific location (i.e., "of Brantford"), which is a way of situating them within Canadian jurisdiction without needing to provide the legal and normative basis.
171 Canada, "Appeal" at 829.
172 Ibid. at 830.

3 In a land surrender dated 4 August 1826 "the Indian council speaks of the King as 'Our Sovereign Lord.' The same language is used in other similar documents, and thus the Six Nations, through their Council, have officially recognized their allegiance to the British Crown."[173]
4 In regard to the enfranchisement provisions of the *Indian Act*, it explains that they "provide legislative machinery whereby Indians who so desire, and who are duly qualified, may acquire full Canadian citizenship. This legislation was enacted to stimulate progress among the Indians and to afford them an opportunity for self-development and advancement." This and the Soldier Settlement provisions "exists solely for the benefit of the Indians themselves and can only be invoked of their own motion."[174]
5 The dominion has not misused the Six Nations' funds, as the Indian Department allows the council to "take part in the administration and expenditure of their capital and interest funds … [and] leaves decisions with respect to expenditure of band funds to the discretion of the Council, in so far as possible, consistent with proper economy and due regard for the interests of the Indians."[175]
6 The Six Nations are subject to Canadian criminal law because "Indians are subject to the laws of the land in the same manner as other of His Majesty's subjects. It is necessary to maintain order and punish offenders for the protection of the Indian community itself. Ever since their arrival in the country they have had the protection of the laws and access to the Courts. They have fully availed themselves of these privileges and have in no way conducted or maintained any separate courts or legal machinery of their own."[176]
7 The presence of the RCMP on the Six Nations lands has "no political significance or bearing upon the agitation of the petitioners. Such measures as have been taken are in pursuance of the regular administration of law, without which the Indians would be deprived of the benefit of police protection. No military force has been used in any way."[177]
8 As for the treaties between the Six Nations and the British, Scott explains that "there has been no treaty of any kind between His Majesty's Government in Canada and the Six Nations." The *Haldimand Proclamation of 1784* and the *Simcoe Deed of 1793* are simply grants of land "not involving any political recognition whatsoever." Additionally, the treaties that Canada does make with Indians are not "treaties" "in the meaning comprehended

173 Ibid. at 833.
174 Ibid. at 833–4.
175 Ibid. at 834.
176 Ibid.
177 Ibid. at 835.

> by international law." Rather, in the Canadian context the term "denotes the plan of negotiation adopted by the Government in dealing with the usufructuary rights which the aboriginal peoples have been recognized as possessing in the land from the inception of British rule."[178]

These arguments are supported by a litany of legislation, case law, and Orders in Council, but what is their actual substance? That is, what assumptions do they rely on in order to bear weight? I would say that the foundation for the entire set of arguments is on the two contrary meanings of the term *treaty*. Without this distinction, the remaining arguments are little more than question begging (i.e., stating that the Six Nations are British subjects tells us nothing of how they actually became so; without some evidence of consent it is simply an arbitrary assertion). So what is in the distinction that we are given? The normal sense of the term *treaty* is that found within international law. It necessarily implies mutual recognition of each party as a state. The second, or special, sense of the term withholds recognition. It is simply part of a "plan of negotiation" – or what I would refer to as the Crown machinery – and it deals with the "usufructuary rights" of Aboriginal peoples (Scott does not cite Lord Watson from the *St Catherine's Milling* decision of the Privy Council, but it is undoubtedly what he had in mind).[179] The gist of the difference is that a normal treaty starts on the recognition of equal legal standing, whereas the special treaty starts from an imbalance between the parties standing. Simply put, Aboriginal peoples can possess only "usufructuary rights." Why? The usual response centres on a set of criteria (e.g., government, population, and territory) and/or legal fictions (e.g., *terra nullius*, discovery, the civilization thesis, etc.), but, at its basis, it is simply a matter of *recognition*. These special "treaties" were used by the colonizing powers to draw Indigenous peoples into national constitutional systems – this process has since been termed "domestication."[180] It was common practice throughout Africa, Australasia, and the Americas – a fact that was surely not lost on the membership of the newly formed league. Scott seems to be alive to this particular concern. We can see this evidenced in his extensive attempts to reinforce the legitimacy of this practice by pointing to its continuity. He states, "It may be interesting to note that one of these 'treaties' was negotiated with the inhabitants of the large territory comprised in the Mackenzie River district so

178 Ibid. at 835–6.

179 *St Catherine's Milling and Lumber Company v. R (Ontario)* (1889) LR 14 App. Cas. 46, [1888] UKPC 70, 14 App. Cas. 46.

180 UNCHR (Sub-Commission), "Final Report Submitted by Miguel Alfonso Martinez, Special Rapporteur, Treaties, Agreements, and Other Constructive Agreements between States and Indigenous Populations" (22 June 1999) UN DocE/CN.4/Sub.2/1999/20, 26–38[168]–[244]. Cited in Duncan B. Hollis, ed., *The Oxford Guide to Treaties* (Oxford: Oxford University Press, 2012) at 133.

recently as the summer of 1921, and within the past few months a 'treaty' has been negotiated with tribes of Mississagua and Chippowa Indians resident in the province of Ontario."[181] Immediately after this he adds another layer of fortification: "Naturally and obviously it was not the intention in this or preceding 'treaties' to recognize or infer the existence of any independent or sovereign status of the Indians concerned. Such a principle, if admitted, would apply as much, if not more, to these other groups of Indians as to the Six Nations, and the entire Dominion would be dotted with independent, or quasi-independent Indian States 'allied with but not subject to the British Crown.' It is submitted that such a condition would be untenable and inconceivable."[182]

This argument is well-worn in international law (i.e., it is an expression of the principle of territorial integrity).[183] It acts as a kind of rearguard action. That is, if the primary argument of special "treaties" is refused, the tack shifts to practical impossibility. Its weakness is not that it is somehow factually incorrect (un-domesticating Aboriginal nations would *undoubtedly* be a very difficult process), but that it has about the same moral basis as a thief pleading that the funds have already been expended.

Scott is not content to leave the field on that note and so launches one last volley: "It may here be explained that Indian affairs are administered by a department of the Dominion Government under a special Act of the Canadian Parliament known as the Indian Act, which provides that the Minister of the Interior, or the head of any other Department appointed for that purpose by the Governor-General in Council, shall be the Superintendent-General of Indian Affairs, and shall, as such, have the control and management of the lands and property of the Indians of Canada."[184] The last point is that these "treaties" are legitimate by virtue of the manner in which they are subsequently administered. The chances that the guardianship model would help to bolster the legitimacy of these "treaties" in the eyes of those in the league who were sympathetic to the Six Nations' case are, at best, negligible.

The sheer volume and detail of Canada's response indicates how frightened it was by the Six Nations' appeal. Scott's exhaustive defence of the legitimacy of the special "treaties" is indicative of both its importance to the dominion and of its weakness.[185] You get the feeling that Scott is convinced of the legitimacy

181 Canada, "Appeal" at 836.

182 Ibid.

183 For an instructive analysis of the relationship between the principle of self-determination and territorial integrity in the context of in the Six Nations status case, see Johnson, "Quest of the Six Nations" at 27–31.

184 Canada, "Appeal" at 836.

185 The possibility for excessively strong and detailed arguments having a contraindicative and self-defeating effect is well captured by the phrase "The lady doth protest too much, methinks." The line itself is from *Hamlet*; it is Queen Gertrude's ironic response to the queen in the play-within-a-play.

of his position, but, at the same time, when the list of reasons is set out in front of him on paper they seem to be, in some way, insufficient.

I believe that Wittgenstein puts his finger on just this phenomenon in *On Certainty*: "And now if I were to say 'It is my unshakable conviction that etc.,' this means in the present case too I have not consciously arrived at the conviction by following a particular line of thought, but that it is anchored in all my *questions and answers*, so anchored that I cannot touch it."[186] There is no particular line of argument that secures the legitimacy of the dominion's position. But the lines of argument do "form a system, a structure."[187] The question is what anchors this structure. Scott cannot articulate it and so he seems to be left drowning, clutching at straws. It is not that the arguments that he offers are not related to one another; quite the reverse: the positions he articulates are all related. Rather, he is drowning because they require a shared mythology to anchor them in a way that they make sense; the ultimate anchor then is that Aboriginal peoples are *uncivilized*. This is the premise that explains why treaties made with them do not involve any form of political recognition and why they can be *unilaterally* domesticated within the dominion. We could say that this forms the riverbed of the dominion's arguments (i.e., its principle of legitimation). Unlike a foundation, a riverbed shifts, it moves with the flow of the water in such a way that "there is not a sharp division of one from the other."[188] The problem for the dominion was that in the early 1920s the riverbed had shifted so significantly that what had appeared to be hard rock was now being washed away like sand. Put more directly, the reigning notions of legitimacy in Britain and Canada were shifting. The standards of civilizational supremacy – which had been relied on as simply being part of the taken-for-granted background of the nineteenth century – were no longer being accepted as objective fact. This explains why the British government elected to intervene after these arguments were delivered. The Foreign Office contacted the governments who had expressed sympathy with the Six Nations and informed them that their attempts to reopen the case constituted an "impertinent interference" in the internal affairs of their empire by a group of "minor powers."[189] This exercise of realpolitik was effective (at least in the short term), as the "minor powers" quickly abandoned the case.[190]

---

186 Wittgenstein, *Certainty* at §103.

187 Ibid. at §102.

188 Ibid. at §97.

189 Cited in Titley, *Narrow Vision* at 123.

190 I specify "in the short term," as by abandoning the tools of persuasion and resorting to realpolitik, the British only highlight the fact that they lacked the kind of normative foundations that could secure the consent of the "minor powers." Antonio Gramsci's account of hegemony provides a useful and detailed account of the contraindicative and

AFTERMATH

The repercussions did not end there. The plan to depose the hereditary council was set in motion as soon as they had broken off negotiations with Ottawa in the early months of 1923. Because they could not agree on who would sit on the proposed royal commission, Scott selected a partisan to conduct an inquiry. Col. Andrew Thompson was appointed for the task on 1 March 1923. His report was ready by 22 November, and its principal recommendation was that the hereditary council be immediately replaced, regardless of popular support.[191] Even before the report was complete, Scott was preparing for possible resistance. In October he appointed Col. C.E. Morgan (a veteran of the Boer War who had experience working as a colonial administrator in South Africa) as the Indian superintendent at Brantford. Col. Morgan prepared his own special report on reserve conditions for Scott, which he delivered in early August of the following year. It recommended the immediate removal of the hereditary council and cautioned that this would require a strong police presence.[192] With these two reports in hand, Scott moved to secure an Order in Council that imposed an elective council on the Six Nations.

On 17 September 1924 the Order in Council was passed; it stated, "In consideration of this report and recommendation and in view of the fact that this Band is considered fit to have Part II of the *Indian Act,* entitled 'Indian Advancement' applied to it, the Minister recommends that from and after the date thereof, the said Part II of the *Indian Act* shall apply to the Six Nations Band of Indians."[193]

On 7 October 7 – little more than a month after Chief Deskaheh presented the appeal to the president of the assembly – Col. Morgan arrived at a council meeting with the RCMP, read the Order in Council that authorized the imposition of the elective council, and expelled them from the hall.[194] The election for the new council saw a low turnout (16–30 per cent of the electorate) and resulted in a twelve-member council who were primarily Christian (i.e., the faction that had petitioned Ottawa for this very action back in 1907).[195] These aggressive and unilateral tactics were yet another demonstration of just how unpersuasive the dominion's position on Indian policy was. The only way that it could deal with resistance was through more and more suppression. It relied

---

self-defeating effects that the use of political violence can have on political authority. See Antonio Gramsci, *Prison Notebooks*, 3 vols, ed. and trans. Joseph A. Buttigieg (New York: Columbia University Press, 1992).

191 Titley, *Narrow Vision* at 124–5.

192 Ibid. at 125.

193 Cited in Johnson, "Quest of the Six Nations" at 20.

194 Titley, *Narrow Vision* at 126.

195 Ibid. at 113 and 126.

on making an example of those who dared to resist. But despite the excessive measures that the Crown machine resorted to (including a permanent police presence and the use of informants), in this case it did not actually achieve its aims.[196] The support for the traditional council persisted, and the elective council has been consistently regarded by many within the Six Nations as illegitimate.[197] The Crown machine's show of strength was simply a demonstration of its inability to secure consent without coercion.

3.4 A Building Crisis of Legitimacy

The trajectory of Indian policy during the first half of the twentieth century was characterized by a continual increase in control and complexity.[198] The broad policy aims remained constant (to civilize, assimilate, and then disappear – aims that can be dated back to the pre-Confederation period), but the technical means of achieving these ends had become the focus. Special acts and detailed amendments had become the modus operandi of Indian policy in the dominion. The 1906 version of the *Indian Act* was, at 195 sections, twice the length of the original act. Simply put, the Crown machinery was expanding; new components were constantly being added. These components increased the discretionary powers of the superintendent-general and the governor-in Council.[199] For example, amendments passed in 1911 allowed

196 Ibid. at 134.

197 There have been a number of legal challenges to the legitimacy of the elected council (most often by challenging the legitimacy of the Order in Council that established it). The first case was initiated in 1957. It resulted in the decision in *Logan v. Styres*, [1959] OWN 361, 20 DLR (2d) 416 (Ont. HC), which held that the Six Nations are British subjects because they accepted the protection of the Crown. The decision relied on little historical evidence, as it based itself on two unilateral declarations by British officials (see Johnson, "Quest of the Six Nations" at 21). In 1970 supporters of the confederacy took direct action and locked the elected council out of the council house. Members of the elected council sought an injunction, which resulted in the *Isaac v. Davey*, [1973] 3 OR 677, 38 DLR (3d) 23 (Ont. HC) case. The question before the court was whether or not the Six Nations constituted a "band" within the meaning of the *Indian Act*. Osler J reviewed the official results of band elections in 1969 and concluded that the hereditary council had a better claim and dismissed the plaintiffs' request for an injunction (the issue of the Six Nations' sovereignty was not considered in this case). The elected council appealed the decision and in *Isaac v. Davey*, [1974] 51 DLR (3d) 170 Arnup JA held that because the tract of land is vested in the Crown, it fits the definition of a "reserve," and so the Six Nations fall within the definition of a "band." The hereditary council appealed, and in *Davey v. Isaac* (1977) 77 DLR (3d) 481 [1977], 2 SCR 897 the Supreme Court of Canada held that the Six Nations were a band, as they have trust funds held for them by the Crown (see Johnson, "Quest of the Six Nations" at 22).

198 For a comprehensive account of this period, see Giokas, "Indian Act" at 47–55.

199 Any concerns about treaty rights were pushed aside. In 1911 Frank Oliver (the minister of the interior) outlined the general approach of the government to treaties in the House

any authority with statutory powers of expropriation to expropriate reserve lands for public works.[200] In 1914 the superintendent-general was granted the authority to make health by-laws that would supersede any of those made by band council.[201] In 1927 the superintendent-general gained the right to require anyone soliciting funds for an Indian legal claim to obtain a licence from him (effectively removing the right to seek legal counsel).[202] In 1936 an amendment was passed that enabled the superintendent-general to apply existing provincial laws to reserves by incorporating them by reference.[203] These are just a few examples of a dizzying array of amendments that deal with every aspect of daily life on the reserves, from the regulation of ceremonial practices, to pool halls and school attendance (not to mention the more informal policies, which

---

of Commons: "For while we believe that the Indian having a certain treaty right is entitled ordinarily to stand upon that right and get the benefit of it, yet we believe that there are certain circumstances and conditions in which the Indian by standing on his treaty rights does himself an ultimate injury, as well as does an injury to the white people, whose interests are brought into immediate conjunction with the interest of the Indians." Cited in Giokas, "Indian Act" at 50. This position should be compared with Lamer CJC's use of the "public interest" framework for dealing with what he refers to as "unlimited rights" in *Gladstone* at para. 60 and its use in the infringement standards for Aboriginal title in *Tsilhqot'in Nation v. British Columbia,* [2014] 2 SCR 257. The only difference is that the unilateral power of the Crown is articulated in the register of reconciliation.

200 In addition, municipalities with over 8000 people could apply to a judge to expropriate reserve lands; the only standing being whether or not it was "expedient" to do so. See *Indian Act*, SC 1911, c. 14, ss. 1–2.

201 *Indian Act*, SC 1914, c. 35, s. 6.

202 *Indian Act*, SC 1926–7, c. 32, s. 6.

203 *Indian Act*, SC 1936, c. 20, s. 2. Kerry Wilkins informed me that a more limited version of this provision, authorizing the superintendent-general to apply the game laws of Manitoba and "the Western Territories" (what became Alberta, Saskatchewan, and the Northwest Territories) to some or all Indians in respect of some or all of the territory in those jurisdictions, had existed since 1890 (SC 1890, c. 29, s. 10). It became s. 69 of the *Indian Act*, RSC 1927: the provision that SC 1936, s. 20, s. 2 amended. This is part of a curious trend of incorporating provincial law by reference into federal law, which expands the enforceable reach of provincial standards. The effect is rather curious, as it is not, strictly speaking, an extension of the jurisdiction of the provinces over Indians and their lands. It renders valid provincial (that could otherwise be *ultra vires* by virtue of the position of s. 91(24) within the *Constitution Act, 1867*) law as federal law. But this does seem like an attempt to normalize the legislative and administrative structure of the provinces. Perhaps it is a move to set the stage for the post-assimilation legal environment where the "mere burden" (the federal responsibility for administering Indians) is removed, and the provinces are made territorially whole by having perfected their underlying title to the lands reserved for Indians. In any case, this trend continues with the addition s. 87 of the 1951 *Indian Act* (now s. 88), the recommendation for "fused federalism" in the Hawthorn Report in 1966. Cited in Giokas, "Indian Act" at 76, and can be seen as part of the overall trend in the case law towards the so-called modern approach to federalism in relation to s. 91(24). I will address this trend in detail in part 4.

included the infamous pass and the everyday disciplinary control exercised in situ by Indian agents).[204]

By the 1940s it had become clear that this approach was not generating the desired results. The Crown machinery had expanded by leaps and bounds. There seemed to be no real limits to its reach. It had reduced the powers of the band council to be little more than advisory.[205] It had effective control over all aspects of the lives of Indians and their lands. As a result, it should have constituted a "fantastic universalizing apparatus," but for all of its elaborate and detailed construction it simply did not work.[206] It provided ample resources for seizing lands, but it could not produce citizens that it had promised, and therefore it could not produce legitimacy. In effect, the system was plagued by its own foundational principle. As J.S. Mill put it, "A good despotism is an altogether false ideal, which practically (except as a means to some temporary purpose) becomes the most senseless and dangerous of chimeras."[207] The despotic powers were legitimate *only if* they could be demonstrated to be in the best interests of those who were subjected to them. Additionally, this "best interests" rationale could retain the aura of legitimacy only if the despotism was temporary; any system adopting this legitimating principle needed to provide some evidence of progress towards civilization. But the Crown machinery could show no evidence of progress on this front. It could forcibly enfranchise Indians (even entire bands), but it could not generate the kind of mass voluntary enfranchisement that would legitimize its "vast administrative despotism."[208] In order to actually supply the legitimacy that it promised it would have to completely assimilate the Indians and their lands into the body politic and then, once the transition was complete, to have them simply wither away and perish.[209] But it was actually following the opposite trajectory entirely; it was growing, its administrative structures were deepening the cultural and economic divides between its wards and the "civilized" citizens they were purportedly slated to become. Without the promise of being "temporary," it was seen as being a growing expenditure with no real purpose or sense of direction. Simply put, the promise that had given birth to the Crown machinery (i.e., the promise of financial savings and the realization of the ideal body politic via civilizing) had turned against it.

204 See notes 80–3.

205 In 1936, amendments (*Indian Act*, SC 1936, c. 20, s. 4) were passed that enabled Indian agents to cast the deciding vote in band council elections that resulted in a tie and to sit in and direct all band council meetings.

206 Anghie, *Imperialis* at 149.

207 Mill, *On Liberty* at 141.

208 Tully, *Strange Multiplicity* at 90–1.

209 As Marx says of the role of dictatorship of the proletariat or J.S. Mill says of the East India Company. See ibid. at 324, and Karl Marx and Frederick Engels, *Collected Works* (New York: International Publishers, 1983) at 39:62–5.

The Second World War was a kind of catalyst to shift the government's focus away from the narrow and haphazard technical modifications of the machinery (an approach favoured by the bureaucratic staff who serviced it) towards the broader horizons of policy.[210]

The spectacle of the Nuremburg Trials (not to mention the unspeakable realities that preceded it) stripped the last vestiges of legitimating capacity from the principle of civilizational supremacy. This made it clear that the current trajectory (or lack thereof) of Indian policy was no longer economically sustainable or politically desirable; it could no longer explain itself in intelligible terms. It had become, if anything, an embarrassing relic of nineteenth-century imperialism, which was no longer acceptable, given the rising tide of international human rights. The fracture in the relationship between the concepts of sovereignty and civilization – which the League of Nations had been designed to patch – was now complete. The atrocities of the war made it undeniably clear that Europe could no longer claim to be the model for all historical progress. This left the concept of sovereignty untethered.[211] It could serve as a basis for law within the boundaries of the state, but beyond that was simply a legal grey area in which Hobbesian leviathans drifted, like ships passing in darkness. The *Universal Declaration of Human Rights* in 1948 was designed to provide the bright lines needed for a "community of nations."[212] It universalized a set of individual rights that had once been confined to the boundaries of the metropole. As J.S. Mill had so confidently stated, "Liberty, as a principle, has no application to any state of things anterior to the time when mankind have become improved by free and equal discussion."[213] But the lines that had once separated the liberty of the civilized from the despotism that was to improve the uncivilized were now unclear.

Wittgenstein offers us a way to reimagine the construction of these boundaries: "To say 'This combination of words makes no sense' excludes it from the sphere of language and thereby the bounds of the domain of language. But when one draws a boundary it may be for various kinds of reason. If I surround an area with a fence or a line or otherwise, the purpose may be to prevent someone from getting in or out; but it may also be part of a game and the players supposed, say, to jump over the boundary; or it may be to show where the

210 Giokas, "Indian Act" at 54.

211 This position itself is by no means a new one. There is a long tradition of political thought that dismisses the possibility of international law entirely due to its lack of a *true* (sovereign) binding force (e.g., Hobbes, Hegel, Schmitt, etc.).

212 It may have been designed to provide these lines, but they have never been particularly bright. Rather, they have been, from the very outset, contested as being anything but universal in nature. The Saudi Arabian delegation voiced its opposition to the committee responsible for drafting the Declaration in 1947 by stating that the committee had "for the most part taken into consideration only the standards recognized by Western civilization." Pagden, *Burdens* at 243.

213 Mill, *On Liberty* at 9.

property of one man ends and that of another begins, and so on. So if I draw a boundary line that is not yet to say what I am drawing it for."[214]

As soon as one can no longer be certain that the distinction between civilized and uncivilized is *objective*, then the act of drawing the line becomes subjective. The line is not drawn by the hand of history. It does not contain its own rules. They are assigned. Suddenly the fixed position of liberty becomes suspect and so, open to contestation. The barbarians had been excluded from liberty; they had been, to borrow Wittgenstein's phrase, "withdrawn from circulation."[215] But now that Europe had exhibited all of the traits and qualities that they had associated with the barbarians, the gates were open. Even the barbarians could lay claim to liberty. Quite simply, the push for self-determination was redoubled. This set the stage for a shift in the confrontation within the settler states as the Millian model of the "temporary" despotism was no longer possible. This left Canada with few explanations for its Indian policy (aside from the shallow comforts offered by sovereignty).[216]

Following the war, Canada moved to establish a joint committee of the Senate and the House of Commons to examine the general structure of its Indian administration. Its focus was to look into eight topics:

1 treaty rights and obligations;
2 band membership;
3 Indian liability to pay taxes;
4 voluntary and involuntary enfranchisement;
5 Indian eligibility to vote in federal elections;
6 non-Indian encroachment on reserves;
7 the operation of Indian day and residential schools; and
8 "Any other matter or thing pertaining to the social and economic status of Indians and their advancement which ... should be incorporated into the revised Act."[217]

---

214 Wittgenstein, *Philosophical Investigations* at §299.

215 Ibid. at §300.

216 It took some time before this lack of a legitimating principle began to show in the everyday de facto Crown machinery. In the Canadian case it would not come to a head until the White Paper in 1969. A crisis of legitimacy can, in a sense, be a somewhat disappointing kind of crisis. Institutional machinery can continue its normal operations (or at least the appearance of doing so), but it is doing so on borrowed time. What is missing is the organization's capacity to account for its big-picture policy aims, to make sense of its raison d'être. Without this it can explain its operations only in relation to itself (i.e., the tautological responses of an organization whose only purpose is to continue to exist) and narrow its view to day-to-day operations. These are a small comfort to administrators whose job description includes justifying their institution's budget to governments.

217 Cited in Giokas, "Indian Act" at 55.

The limits of the Joint Committee's commitment to egalitarianism can be seen in what this list omits (e.g., self-government, the state of band funding, and the role of the provinces).[218] It established hearings with government officials and experts before meeting with Indigenous representatives. The first Indigenous person to speak before the committee was the president of the newly formed North American Indian Brotherhood (Andrew Paull), who criticized the form of the committee (it was not the independent royal commission that had been requested), its composition (there were no Indigenous representatives), and its limited scope of inquiry.[219] This seemed to have little effect; a motion to permit five Indigenous observers failed.[220] There was a wealth of testimony from Indian bands (mostly in the form of letters), and this level of consultation was a first. But we must ask, what was its effect?

A statement made by the co-chairman (D.F. Brown) after the first year of hearings clearly indicates the direction of the "new" Indian policy: "And I believe that it is a purpose of this Committee to recommend eventually some means whereby Indians have rights and obligations equal to those of all other Canadians. There should be no difference in my mind, or anybody else's mind, as to what we are, because we are all Canadians."[221] The substantive content of this position can be seen in the testimony of a key government anthropologist (Diamond Jenness). He proposed a twenty-five-year plan to "abolish, gradually, but rapidly, the separate political and social status of Indians (and Eskimos); to enfranchise them and move them into the rest of the population on an equal footing."[222]

It should be obvious at this point that there is nothing new in these statements. In fact, it is simply a statement of the primary desideratum of Indian policy stretching back to the Darling Report of 1828: to be rid of the "little colony of unwelcome foreigners" once and for all, to be free of the costs associated with maintaining them, and to, finally, unify the body politic.[223] The only question that the Joint Committee actually entertained was the question of how to achieve it.

In 1949 the government made its first substantive step in its "new" Indian policy by transferring the responsibility for the Indian Branch to the Department

218 Ibid.

219 Ibid. at 56.

220 Ibid. at 57.

221 Cited in ibid.

222 Cited in ibid. at 57–8.

223 The words are Alexis de Tocqueville's; as he described the conditions of the Indigenous peoples in the United States in the nineteenth century, "Isolated within their own country, the Indians have come to form a little colony of unwelcome foreigners in the midst of a numerous and dominating people." See *Democracy in America*, trans. George Lawrence, ed. J.P. Mayer (New York: Harper and Row, 1988) at 334.

of Citizenship and Immigration.[224] This enabled them to introduce Bill 267 of 1950 by stating that its goal was to integrate "the Indians into the general life and economy of the country," but this would require "a temporary transition period" during which "special treatment and legislation are necessary."[225] The actual content of the *Indian Act* of 1951 was largely a return to the original Act of 1876. As John Tobias notes, "The new act definitely differs from the Indian acts between 1880 and 1951, but only because it returned to the philosophy of the original act: civilization was to be encouraged but not directed or forced on the Indian people. Assimilation for all Indians was a goal that should be striven for without an abundance of tests or the compulsory aspects of the preceding acts."[226]

The Crown machine was thus effectively reset. Its accumulated bulk was reduced, its profile streamlined, but it was far from "new." The main structural lines of Indian policy (the ones that were so clearly set by the first *Indian Act* in 1876: viz. the unilateral control of lands, membership, and local government) had never changed. That being said, this "new" version was also not entirely the same. One change in particular foreshadows a significant change: the addition of s. 87 (now s. 88).[227] This provision, which we will deal with extensively in the next chapter, incorporated provincial laws of general application as federal law. It was an extension of a discretionary power that was given to the superintendent-general in 1936. But this version was automatically applied (subject to the confusing limits of treaties and federal legislation). It represents, to my mind, the first real shift in Indian policy since 1876: viz. the decentralization of federal jurisdiction over Indians and their lands in favour of an increasing role for the provinces.

The 1951 revision did not settle the issue. It merely marked the beginning of an extended crisis of legitimacy that was marked by increasing political pressures. The civil rights movement in the United States, the steady dissolution of the remaining European empires, and the so-called Quiet Revolution in Quebec, all made the "temporary transition period" increasingly uncomfortable.[228] Throughout the 1950s and 1960s there was a proliferation of internal reviews, committees, and inquiries. All culminated in what became known as the White Paper in 1969.[229]

---

224 Its home since 1936 had been in the Ministry of Mines and Resources and prior to that the Ministry of the Interior.

225 Cited in Giokas, "Indian Act" at 63.

226 Moore, *Historical Development* at 150–1.

227 The changes also include the creation of the register, which continues to unilaterally regulate Indian status.

228 In 1960 the *Canadian Bill of Rights* was passed (*Canadian Bill of Rights*, SC 1960, c. 44). In that same year citizenship was granted to all status Indians.

229 Canada, "Statement of the Government of Canada on Indian Policy" – the White Paper. The term *White Paper* refers to a kind of policy document that had, as Sally Weaver notes, "been used for purely informational purposes in announcing completed policies, or as

There is a somewhat pleasing (if not magical) circularity to the White Paper; what begins as a *unilateral* civilizing policy ends with a *unilateral* proclamation: "You are now all equal before the law!" The problem was that the audience did not erupt into applause. In fact, the simple incantation failed and the magic show fell apart. As Weaver states, "Although the policy-makers struggled to produce a 'good' policy, the White Paper was basically a self-serving policy designed to free the government from criticism, protecting it from future accusations of discrimination."[230]

It was indeed self-serving, but it was, to my mind, more than a desire to free the government from the accusation of discrimination. It was also, consciously or not, repeating the picture that had captivated policymakers of the nineteenth century: viz. the unified and uniform body politic. What could not be accomplished by social engineering was now being attempted by political fiat. The problem was that equality (which was the guiding star of the White Paper), much like self-defence, has a universal appeal, but lacks clear boundaries.[231] As Tully rightly states, "Abstract moral principles can literally mean anything the user wishes them to mean unless they are grounded and articulated in relation to the experiential self-understanding of those to whom they are applied."[232]

The Indigenous response was a complete rejection. The Alberta Indian Association published a position paper entitled "Citizens Plus" (the title explicitly referring to the term used in the Hawthorn Report) and this was, after some revisions, adopted as the National Indian Brotherhood's response to the White Paper. The Red Paper was presented before the full Cabinet of the Trudeau government by Chief Adam Soloway and Chief John Snow (both in traditional regalia) on 4 June 1970. They read the papers in the form of a dialogue:

CHIEF ADAM SOLOWAY: "The White Paper states: The legislative and constitutional basis of discrimination should be removed."

CHIEF JOHN SNOW: "The Red Paper states: The legislative and constitutional basis for Indian status and rights should be maintained until such times as Indian people are prepared and willing to renegotiate them."

---

mechanisms for enhancing consultation with the provinces, the public, and opposition members in Parliament during minority governments." See Sally M. Weaver, *Making Canadian Indian Policy: The Hidden Agenda 1968–1970* (Toronto: University of Toronto Press, 1981) at 122.

230 Ibid. at 197.

231 For a classic exploration of this lack of boundary, see Peter Westen, "The Empty Idea of Equality," *Harvard Law Review* 95, no. 3 (1982): 537–96.

232 James Tully, "Deparochializing Political Theory and Beyond: A Dialogue Approach to Comparative Political Thought," *Journal of World Philosophies* 1, no. 1 (2016): 51–74.

CHIEF ADAM SOLOWAY: "The White Paper states: There should be a positive recognition of the unique contribution of Indian culture to Canadian life."

CHIEF JOHN SNOW: "The Red Paper states: These are nice sounding words which are intended to mislead everybody. The only way to maintain our culture is for us to remain as Indians."[233]

The government quickly retracted the policy, but the landscape had fundamentally shifted.[234] The question was what the new landscape looked like.

The broad contours of this landscape can be found in the most significant and wide-ranging study of this period, the Hawthorn Report.[235] It recommended that the government address the Indian problem by adopting a number of new approaches. The two most significant ones were first, to include the provinces via a system of "fused federalism"; and second, to move away from the paternalistic administrative management of Indian bands towards a system of self-governing bands within a provincial municipal framework.[236] The proposed "new" landscape of Indian governance thus gave more power to band councils (by removing some supervision), but it simultaneously limited them by situating them as municipalities under the concurrent jurisdiction of Parliament and the provincial legislatures. The pattern here is very similar to what the British imperial government was doing near the tail end of its civilizing policy: viz. it began to decentralize its authority by devolving powers to the colonial governments. The difference was that the *British North America Act* of 1867 was a clear and structured legal framework put in place by the imperial Parliament to increase the governing powers of its colonists. The Canadian version of devolution is far more *unilateral*; the pre-existing legal and political systems of Indigenous nations are ignored, the treaties are read down into little more than surrender documents, and the power of Parliament under s. 91(24) is read as being unlimited. This result is not a change in substance from the goal of assimilation; it is a change in form. It created a picture of federalism that enabled the band to continue on as a municipality and Indians as "citizens plus." This residual difference could fit squarely within the confines of the existing constitutional structure, so there would be no need to really be concerned about the possibility of "independent, or quasi-independent Indian States."[237]

With that worry pushed aside, it was possible to leave the precise details to the courts. This did not necessarily mean that the Crown machine suddenly

233 Cited in Weaver, *Making Canadian Indian Policy* at 183.

234 Ibid. at 185–9.

235 Interestingly, in the same year that the first volume of the report was published, the government moved the Indian Branch from the Department of Citizenship and Immigration and created the Department of Indian Affairs and Northern Development. See Giokas, "Indian Act" at 73.

236 Ibid. at 79–82.

237 Canada, "Appeal" at 836.

ceased to function. It was simply modified; the spells became unspoken. Sovereignty (and underlying title) was never to be questioned or subjected to doubt. All that was required to animate the machinery was to invoke (or, more appropriately, conjure up) the unlimited *power-over* Indians and their lands that were given by the British in s. 91(24). It contained the force of all of the old spells and incantations, which now appeared to be, if spoken, little more than "nonsense on stilts."[238] The trick was that one could simply never ask how the British were able to give what they never had; this was to be evaded at all costs. If pressed, the courts have little recourse but to silently trace and retrace the lines of those inscrutable and mysterious numbers: s. 91(24). The words of Bluebeard logic warn off all those who dare to ask what lies behind the numbers: "Beyond this there is nothing to see!" Naturally, it is precisely this question that Aboriginal peoples began to put forward through the courts from *Calder* on.

At this point we will take a step back for a moment here and reconsider the ground that we covered in this chapter. I began by outlining the pre-Confederation changes in Indian administration from 1812 to 1867. This provided us with a sense of how the transition from treaty federalism to administrative despotism worked at the level of legislation, policy, and practice. From this I shifted to a consideration of the way the dominion addressed the Indian Question from 1867 to the 1920s. It highlighted how the system of administrative despotism (viz. the Crown machinery) was put in place and continually reconfigured in relation to Aboriginal resistance. In this third section I narrowed the focus to address the particular case of the Six Nations' appeal for justice at the League of Nations in 1923. This offered us a clear example of how the Crown machinery operated in this period, and it shows that the question of self-determination in international law was in play from the beginning of the twentieth century. I then closed the chapter by zooming out and providing an overview of the transformations in Indian policy that followed the Second World War. This placed the changes going on within Canada in the international context of the 1960s wave of decolonization. This provides the context for part 4, which will address key changes in the case law following *Calder*.

238 See note 37 in the Introduction.

Part 4

A Law without Measure for a Land without Citizens: The *Indian Act* in Canadian Jurisprudence

A good despotism is an altogether false ideal, which practically (except as a means to some temporary purpose) becomes the most senseless and dangerous of chimeras.

J.S. Mill, *Considerations on Representative Government* (141)

It is *futile* to inquire into the *historical warrant* of the mechanism of government, that is, one cannot reach back to the time at which civil society began (for savages draw up no record of their submission to law; besides, we can already gather from the nature of uncivilized men that they were originally subjected to it by force).

Immanuel Kant, *The Metaphysics of Morals* (§52)

The fundamental fact here is that we lay down rules, a technique, for a game, and that then when we follow the rules, things do not turn out as we had assumed. That we are therefore as it were entangled in our own rules.... This entanglement in our rules is what we want to understand (i.e. get a clear view of).

Ludwig Wittgenstein, *Philosophical Investigations* (§125)

What is the *Indian Act*?[1] The question is, at least at first glance, simple and direct. It seems that one could simply respond by quoting the Act itself and saying that it is "an act respecting Indians" (the use of the word "respecting" here verging on irony) or by reciting two basic facts: (1) the *Indian Act* is an Act of Parliament originally passed in 1876; and (2) it is a legislative expression of the exclusive jurisdiction given in s. 91(24) of the *British North America Act* passed by the imperial Parliament in 1867 (now referred to as the *Constitution Act*, 1867). This provides us with a formal definition that relates the legislation to its constitutional basis. And while it does allow us to generally situate

1 *Indian Act* (RSC, 1985, c. I-5).

this specific Act within the legal architecture of Canada by giving us its "pith and substance," it provides us with no information about the object of the Act or how it operates within the "mechanism of government" (to borrow Kant's phrasing from the epigraph).[2] So how does the set of possible responses change if we shift our focus to the object and purpose of the legislation? On this front we are presented with several possible avenues of investigation, from the "modern principle" of statutory interpretation to the legislative history of the Act and its precursors.[3] The words of the Act are of little assistance, as the terms that would indicate who the Act applies to (i.e., Indian and band) are defined by the unilateral procedures within the Act itself. This is unhelpful, as it leaves us with legislative tautologies like an Indian is a person who is or is entitled to be registered as an Indian, or a band is a body of Indians.[4] If we are to escape from this circular path, our investigation will need to consider the history of the Act.

Even a cursory historical examination (and, because the roots of the *Indian Act* are inextricably intertwined with the project of settler colonialism, it is a history that precedes both Confederation and the *Royal Proclamation, 1763*) will lead us to the legislative acts that preceded it and gave it shape. There is the *Gradual Civilization Act* (1857), the *Gradual Enfranchisement Act* (1869), and a host of commissions and reports with names such as Darling, Bond Head, Pennefather, and Bagot, among others. The titles of these two acts alone begin to give us an indication of the object and purpose of the *Indian Act*: its purpose is captured in the verbs that it sets out to address its object (*to civilize*, *to enfranchise*, etc.). If we adopt these verbs into the working response to our initial question, then we can say that the *Indian Act* sets out the powers and procedures that give form to the project of "civilizing" the "Indians," or, to put it another way, it is the legislative basis for the *mechanism of governing* "Indians." The Act is a response – or rather, given the fact that the Act has been subject to a continual ad hoc process of amendment, a series of responses – to a problem: what is to be done about the "Indians"?

The response that the Crown articulates with the *Indian Act* is, as James Tully states in *Strange Multiplicity*, "a vast administrative dictatorship which governs every detail of Aboriginal life," and this "entire regime was imposed without the consent of Aboriginal peoples."[5] Another way of expressing this is to say that it exists as a "good despotism," which Mill – as long as we ignore his

---

2 Kant, *Metaphysics of Morals* at 111–12.

3 As the Court holds in *Rizzo & Rizzo Shoes Ltd. (Re)*, [1998] 1 SCR 27 at para. 21, "The words of an Act are to be read in their entire context and in their grammatical and ordinary sense harmoniously with the scheme of the Act, the object of the Act, and the intention of Parliament."

4 *Indian Act*, definitions in s. 2(1).

5 Tully, *Strange Multiplicity* at 90–1.

exception – rightly refers to as "the most senseless and dangerous of chimeras."[6] But, it seems to me, we have lost sight of this danger and are still living in the shadow of Mill's exception. The *Indian Act* continues to unilaterally determine the identity of its subjects and govern every aspect of their lives without their consent, but this blatant despotism somehow escapes us. It is as if we have recited its words so often that their nonsense has been disguised. And so, in a kind of semantic version of prescription (or adverse possession), it has acquired the appearance of truth and legitimacy through continuous repetition. We have forgotten its strangeness and with that its danger. The "temporary purpose" of the *Indian Act* (to civilize Indians) has been abandoned, but its mechanisms of governance continue to move under the banner of reconciliation. Its presence under this banner is by no means an easy one. The Act cannot be seamlessly grafted into the reconciliation paradigm (it is cut from an altogether different cloth), but it can be and has been redescribed as a kind of necessary halfway house between a colonial past and self-government. Its only justification is that it is necessary because it provides some structure in the (perpetually extended) interim. It thus hides in plain sight as a kind of unhappy idée fixe that obscures our view of other possibilities. Wittgenstein provides, what is to my mind, an appropriate analogy for this situation: "You think that after all you must be weaving a piece of cloth: because you are sitting at a loom – even if it is empty – and going through the motions of weaving."[7]

How can we begin to move out of the shadow and see the disguised nonsense of this "good despotism"? How can we begin to understand our entanglement in these rules? One possible approach is to turn to the law to review the basis of its authority, or, to borrow Kant's phrase, its historical warrant. This method of inquiry has been made possible (contrary to Kant's claim concerning "savages" and record keeping in the epigraph) by the wealth of records that have been generated by the continuous resistance of Aboriginal peoples to Crown domination.[8] These records enable us to enquire into the historical

---

6 Mill, *On Liberty*, 141.

7 Wittgenstein, *Philosophical Investigations* at §414.

8 The particular examples I have in mind here include the Six Nations status case and the Nisga'a petitions on the land issue, as both occur at key moments in the late nineteenth and early twentieth centuries. But this resistance extends far beyond what is captured in the jurisprudence. Law's province has the unfortunate tendency to only see the resistance that it recognizes through the lens of the rules and tests that it itself generates. An example of this tendency towards solipsism is the distinction between law and custom, which was used as a kind of criterion for determining who was or was not civilized. The problem was that the concept of law affords itself no generally accepted and therefore correct or standard use. It is an essentially contested concept (this, despite W.B. Gallie's own doubts on the matter, which I believe vanish as soon as the implications of legal pluralism and history of colonialism are taken seriously). See Gallie, *Philosophy and the Historical Understanding* at 190. While

warrant of this mechanism of government with a view to challenging its legitimacy. And we must remember that legitimacy is not simply a *political question*; as the Court reminds us in the *Reference re Secession of Quebec*, "In our constitutional tradition, legality and legitimacy are linked."[9] The *Indian Act* has been imposed without the consent of those it governs and so it ignores the most fundamental constitutional convention: *quod omnes tangit ab omnibus comprobetur* (*q.o.t.*)[10] (what touches all should be agreed to by all).[11] Its only possible claim to a historical warrant is found in the unilateral logic of colonialism and some shabby, bankrupt legal fictions that would purport to convert force into law by opening up an exception in the qualifications for the fundamental equality of human beings.

Our task in this chapter will be to travel over the wide field that the 150-year history of this "vast administrative dictatorship" opens up before us. An exhaustive survey of this field is an immense undertaking, as it would need to cover the legislative, juridical, political, and administrative dimensions, in addition to the numerous contrapuntal practices of resistance practised by Aboriginal peoples.[12] Our investigation in this chapter will be confined to one aspect of

---

there can be dominant schools of thought (e.g., law as being commands laid down by a sovereign, law as a distinctive structure or set of institutions, etc.), there can be no single universally acceptable criterion to determine the boundary between law and custom. When this distinction was used to discount the complex legal systems of entire cultures as being merely custom, it cannot stand as anything more than a self-serving assertion of power. It is as absurd as weaving on an empty loom or claiming that the "self" consists mainly of "peculiar motions in the head or between the head and throat." Wittgenstein, *Philosophical Investigations* at §413. Aboriginal self-government has not been extinguished, despite the past 150 years of the Crown's administrative despotism. Rather, it inheres in the continuous and multiform practices of resistance that Aboriginal peoples live out daily. For an example, see John Borrows, "A Genealogy of Law: Inherent Sovereignty and First Nations Self Government," *Osgoode Hall Law Journal* 30, no. 2 (1992): 291–353.

9 *Reference re Secession of Quebec* at para. 33.

10 *Q.o.t.* is the abbreviation for *quod omnes tangit ab omnibus debet supportari.*

11 One could argue that this is not unusual, as legislatures do not hold referenda every time they enact legislation, but this rather banal defence is unconvincing. It operates on a set of assumptions concerning the "normal" relationship between the government and its citizens (i.e., the legitimacy supplied by some notion of a social contract, representation, etc.), but this Act was not founded on these assumptions. The fundamental presupposition of the Act was (and in many respects remains – although in a thinner, or at least less explicit form) unquestioned Crown sovereignty, legislative power, and underlying title. The Act was thus explicitly an administrative dictatorship whose legitimacy was supplied by the promise of civilizing Indians (i.e., the structure of its legitimating principles is clearly – and to my mind paradigmatically – articulated by J.S. Mill's notion of a "good" despotism). See Tully, *Strange Multiplicity* at 74.

12 For my use of the term *contrapuntal*, see the phrase *contrapuntal reading* in Said, *Culture and Imperialism* at 66–7.

this colonial landscape: the juridical interpretation of the *Indian Act*. Even this field is vast, so we will narrow our focus further to the lines of authority and resistance[13] that relate to the problem of self-government most directly:

1 *The legal nature of the authority granted in s. 91(24)*: In this section our guiding line of inquiry will be to ask how s. 91(24) can be understood to confer the authority necessary to support the *Indian Act* or to allow for concurrent provincial jurisdiction without the expressed consent of Aboriginal peoples. This line can be rephrased into a clear and direct question: where does s. 91(24) – i.e., Indians and their lands – fit within the division of powers set out in the *Constitution Act, 1867*? The answer to this question is of fundamental importance, as it will explain how Aboriginal sovereignty has been unilaterally excluded from the picture of Canadian federalism that is being put forward by the Supreme Court. This line will take us from *St Catherine's Milling* – where the Privy Council establishes the picture that excludes Aboriginal peoples – through a series of cases dealing with the doctrine of interjurisdictional immunity in relation to s. 91(24) and s. 88 of the *Indian Act*. I believe that this set of cases offers us the most detailed account of how the courts have attempted to interpret both the scope of s. 91(24) and how it fits into the broader constitutional framework. From the 1970s through to the early 1980s the majority decisions in *Cardinal*, *Natural Parents*, and *Four B* extend the reasoning of *St Catherine's Milling* to offer us a picture of federalism that places Aboriginal peoples in a labyrinth of concurrent jurisdiction that is overseen by the "vast administrative dictatorship" of the *Indian Act*. But in true common law fashion, there are a series of dissents in these cases that offer us another possibility. Laskin CJ (as he was then) put forward a theory of s. 91(24) that views Indian lands as federal enclaves that are immune to provincial jurisdiction.[14] While this possibility is by no means a complete deviation from the picture of federalism put forward in *St Catherine's Milling*, it reveals the tension within the Court on this question and the continued possibility of another way forward.
2 *The definition of Indians and the structure and authority of bands*: In this section we will consider how the definitions of Indians and bands (from

13 I refer to these cases as lines of authority and resistance in order to highlight a basic fact that is too often taken for granted. On the one hand they are lines of authority because they are decisions that stand as legal authority in terms of the common law in Canada. On the other hand they are also lines of resistance because they are the product of one form of Aboriginal resistance.

14 His first articulation of the enclaves theory was in *Cardinal v. AG of Alberta*, [1974] SCR 695, just prior to his appointment as the fourteenth chief justice of Canada on 27 December 1973.

their nineteenth-century legislative foundations) fit within the picture of federalism that the Court has formulated in and through its interpretation of s. 91(24). This is directly connected to the preceding section of the interpretation of s. 91(24), as it concerns who resides within the ambit of that authority and what kind of political structure can exist there. Simply put, if the Court's interpretation of s. 91(24) provides us with a picture of federalism, then the question of who Indians are and what form of political structure governs them determines their place within this picture. This, in turn, helps us to see what form of legal justification could possibly support such a picture. This section is divided into two main subsections:

a The definition of Indians: This section begins with a brief overview of the legislation from 1850 to the first version of the *Indian Act* in 1876 and its revision in 1880. This legislation provides a backdrop for case law that follows from it. With the overview in place we will then turn to the judicial interpretation of the definition of *Indians* from the 1939 *Eskimo Reference* through to *Lavell*, the United Nations Human Rights Committee finding in *Lovelace v. Canada* 1981, the legislative changes to registration in the 1985 revision of the *Indian Act*, *McIvor*, *Daniels*, and the recent decision in *Descheneaux*, and the (spectacularly complicated) amendments to s. 6 that it generated.
b The definition of band councils: The aim in this section is to provide a survey of how the courts have interpreted the authority of the band council. These cases develop from situations in which a band makes a move away from the normal rules of the *Indian Act* game (my discussion of the Six Nations' petition to the League of Nations in part 3 is one example of precisely this agonistic process). This is unsurprising, as the "normal rules" of the *Indian Act* are unambiguous. The source of authority and of ultimate administrative power is the Crown. But there are some moves that have been taken by bands to move away from this power *over* relationship. I have limited my focus to three specific examples of these moves:

    i. First, in *Pamajewon* we see an example of band councils asserting laws outside the bounds of the *Indian Act*. This leads to a direct confrontation with the unilateral authority of the Crown.
    ii. Second, a band council uses the mechanisms of the *Indian Act* to request to switch from the election procedures in s. 74 and form a custom election code.[15] This enables them to change rules

15 The procedures for changing elections were changes by *The First Nations Elections Act* (SC 2014, c. 5), but the cases I will be focusing on arise out of the previous *Indian Act* mechanisms.

concerning eligibility, term of office, and size of council, and to integrate hereditary leaders. But what happens when there is a dispute within the band over the results of an election? This has led to a body of cases in which the federal courts are forced to determine whether or not a custom band council fits within their jurisdiction under the *Federal Courts Act.*

iii. And finally, we will conclude this section by considering how the courts have dealt with the constitutionality of the legislative and self-government powers set out in Final Agreements (also known as modern treaties).

3 *Tsilhqot'in Nation and the Meaning of s. 91(24):* In the concluding section of this chapter we will reconsider the implications of the Court's rejection of the doctrine of interjurisdictional immunity in *Tsilhqot'in Nation* for both federalism and the future of reconciliation. When this change is seen in the light of the history of how the Court has interpreted s. 91(24), the definitions of Indians and the structure and authority of bands, we can see that the framework of reconciliation is an extension of the 150-year history of unilaterally excluding Aboriginal peoples from the division of powers that govern their lands. It highlights the fact that the s. 35 framework and the current interpretation of s. 91(24) share a common foundation. Both rely on the racist legal fictions of *terra nullius* and discovery to diminish Aboriginal peoples to such a degree that the Crown was able to acquire sovereignty and radical or underlying title to their lands by assertion alone. Both are based on little more than a stated absence of doubt. What this means is that even if Parliament were to suddenly repeal the *Indian Act,* the picture of federalism would remain the same. In effect, the era of reconciliation has changed the procedures, but it has not even begun to address the issue of the *historical warrant* of the Crown's mechanism of government. In order to address warrant (or lack thereof), we need to have a clear view of how the s. 35 framework has become entangled with s. 91(24). It is this entanglement that has left us with a picture of federalism in which Aboriginal peoples are left with little more than the simple municipal institutions and abandoned laboratories of civilization that were set in place in the nineteenth century. My hope is that by finding other ways to see this picture – a position from which we can begin to survey its course through history and see its contingency – we can also see how this is not the only possibility. Our reconciliation need not be one without recollection. *The Spirit of Haida Gwaii* shows us that life within *the boat that goes on forever anchored in the same place* can always be otherwise than it is.[16]

---

16 I am referring to James Tully's use of Bill Reid's sculpture *The Spirit of Haida Gwaii* in *Strange Multiplicity.*

4.1 The Authority of s. 91(24)

The precise nature of the legal authority conferred on the federal Parliament by s. 91(24) of the *Constitution Act, 1867* is, much like the *Indian Act*, neither simple nor direct. On a plain reading of the provision itself it seems clear: Parliament has the exclusive jurisdiction to make laws in relation to "Indians, and lands reserved for Indians." But even in venturing this far, we have complications that need to be accounted for. First, there is the fact that the provision contains two heads of power, namely "Indians" and "lands reserved for Indians." Second, there is the question of the purpose or nature of this section. Its position within the *Constitution Act, 1867* is unique, as it is a power to make laws in relation to a specific category of people who, unlike "aliens" in s. 91(25),[17] are racially defined and have proprietary claims to land that pre-exist those of the state.[18] This adds a higher than normal degree of concern regarding the limits

17 Laskin J made this point (minus the racial determination) very directly in his dissent in *Cardinal v. Alberta (AG)*, [1974] SCR 695 at 728: "It was contended by the respondent Attorney-General of Alberta that federal power in relation to 'Indians' was akin to its power in relation to aliens (s. 91(25)) and that Indians like aliens were subject to provincial laws of general application. I do not pursue the analogy because it breaks down completely when regard is had to the fact that we are dealing here not only with Indians but with 'lands reserved for the Indians.'"

18 I use the term "proprietary claim" here to indicate how the settler legal system interprets the claims of Aboriginal peoples. This claim has been characterized in different ways within the common law over time (e.g., as a "mere burden" on title that exists at the pleasure of the sovereign to a sui generis right that is derived from prior occupation), but it is always tied to the question of land. It is not simply a dispute over land. It is a dispute over sovereignty and the right of self-government. My position is that the confusing system of rights and title that has been developed is predicated on the unquestioned sovereignty of the Crown (within this system judges, much like blind men confronting an elephant, discover what they believe to be separate and distinct rights from something that is, when seen from another perspective, actually coherent only as parts of a whole). This has led to an asymmetry that the legal system cannot (or rather will not) investigate. It can and does qualify sovereignty by adding terms such as *de facto* or *assertion* or substitutions like *suzerainty*, but as long as the Crown retains the unilateral right to infringe Aboriginal right and title, the asymmetry remains firmly in place (an asymmetry whose sheer and unquestionable degree brings to mind Job's position in relation to God in the Old Testament). This unilateral right of infringement is not unlimited. Rather, the exercise of the Crown's (unquestioned) sovereignty and legislative power is subject to judicial scrutiny via a justification requirement that is analogous to the Court's s. 1 analysis in *R v. Oakes*, [1986] 1 SCR 103. The Court itself points to the analogy between its s. 1 *Oakes* analysis and the justification requirement for s. 35 in *Sparrow* at 1102. While I do not suggest that this requirement is without value, the constitutional assumptions that inform the s. 1 *Oakes* analysis (i.e., a sovereign–subjects relationship judicially mediated by a written charter of rights) are different in kind from those that have informed the interpretation of s. 91(24) (i.e., a sovereign–wards relationship with a limited form of judicial mediation via a shifting set of principles borrowed from the law of trusts, human rights, contracts, property, etc. and then cobbled together into sui generis and sometimes contradictory forms) and the Indigenous perspectives

of the legislative authority that it confers. As Peter Hogg states, "The federal Parliament has taken the broad view that it may legislate for Indians on matters which otherwise lie outside its legislative competence, and on which it could not legislate for non-Indians."[19]

What is the basis of this "broad view" and what limits does it have?[20] If we read s. 91(24) in line with British imperial policy prior to Confederation, it seems that the primary purpose would be to protect the Indians from the interests of local settlers and other European powers via the establishment of treaties. This point is reinforced by the fact that Aboriginal peoples did not consent to or participate in the enactment of the *Constitution Act, 1867*. This means that the imperial Parliament would have no legitimate basis for changing the special horizontal relationship between Aboriginal peoples and the Crown. And so, by conferring this power on the federal Parliament, the imperial Crown could ensure that there was a clear successor to its responsibilities under both the treaties and the *Royal Proclamation of 1763*.[21] This relationship between the Crown and the Aboriginal peoples is best described by the terms *suzerainty* or

---

that have consistently argued for self-determination and mutual recognition as nations (i.e., a multi- or pluri-national federal relationship). By opting to build the s. 35 analysis by analogy with s. 1 of the *Charter*, characterizing the claims of Aboriginal peoples as sui generis right of occupancy, confining the Aboriginal perspective to the rules of evidence, and establishing a complicated and costly system of adjudicating these disputes, the Court simply articulates a new doctrine of constructive conquest under the banner of reconciliation and thereby reduces the law to "the most vital and effective instrument of empire." See Williams Jr, *American Indian in Western Legal Thought* at 6.

19 Peter W. Hogg, *Constitutional Law of Canada*, 5th ed. (Toronto: Carswell, 2007) at 618.

20 As John Borrows notes, the basis cannot simply be the wording of the provision itself, as "the technical wording of powers granted by section 91 is '*in relation to*' matters not assigned exclusively to provincial legislatures. In particular, the exclusive federal legislative authority in section 91(24) only '*extends to*' Indians and lands reserved for Indians. There should be a vast difference between legislation *extending to* or *in relation* to a subject matter and exercising legislative power over a particular group of people." See Borrows, "Unextinguished" at 11.

21 This is Lord Watson's position in *St Catherine's Milling and Lumber Company v. R* (1888), 14 App. Cas. 46 at 59. The decision – which serves as the conceptual model for the relationship between the Crown and Aboriginal peoples in Canada until *Calder* – holds that Aboriginal title is "a personal and usufructuary right, dependent upon the good will of the Sovereign" (ibid. at 54). As Lord Watson states, "The Crown has all along had a present proprietary estate in the land, upon which the Indian title was a mere burden. The ceded territory was at the time of the union, land vested in the Crown" (ibid. at 58). Crown sovereignty is taken as a given. The conceptual picture of the relationship between the Crown and Aboriginal peoples is puzzling. The only source of Aboriginal title is the power of the Crown (as expressed by the proclamation), and so the "burden" is inherited (via the doctrine of continuity, which holds that pre-existing rights and legal arrangements survive the Crown's acquisition of sovereignty), but its continued existence is self-imposed, and the Crown retains the unilateral power to extinguish this "burden." The problem here is where this asymmetry derives from. Is it to be found in the terms of the treaties? What about unceded territory? And if it has no

treaty federalism.[22] This form of relationship is categorically distinct from that of sovereignty in that both parties maintain their internal autonomy (as graphically illustrated by the separation between the rows in the *Two Row Wampum Treaty Belt* in 1613).[23] This interpretation places specific limits on "the exclusive power of legislation and administration" that was vested in Parliament with s. 91(24), which affect both its legislative capacity and the place of Aboriginal peoples within the federal structure.[24]

> 1 The conflict between this interpretation of Canadian constitutional history and the *Indian Act* is obvious. The *Indian Act* unilaterally governs every aspect of the lives of those it determines to be Indians and leaves no possible space for Aboriginal self-government.[25] Simply put, the conflict between the two possible interpretations of s. 91(24) is a conflict between two categorically distinct constitutional relationships. The "broad view" version of s. 91(24) that serves as the constitutional grounding for the *Indian Act* is predicated on the (unquestioned) assumption that the Crown

---

basis in these texts and historical records, what are we left with? Can the Crown acquire title to lands by unilateral proclamation?

22 For the term *suzerainty*, refer to Slattery, "Making Sense" at 198, 201, 209–10. It appears in the case law in Lamer J's (as he was then) decision in *R v. Sioui*, [1990] 1 SCR 1025, and again in Binnie J's concurring decision in *Mitchell* at 142, where he cites Slattery's article while attempting to square the Crown's circular reasoning on the issue of sovereignty by providing an account of "merged sovereignty" (for more, see my engagement with this case in the Introduction to this book). For more on the concept of treaty federalism, refer to Barsh and Henderson, *Road* and, more recently, Asch, *On Being Here to Stay*.

23 The history of the Two-Row Wampum Treaty or Tawagonshi Treaty of 1613 between the Haudenosaunee and the Dutch has been subject to long-standing debates. For a recent and helpful analysis of the documentary record of the Haudenosaunee oral tradition regarding the two-row wampum belt (*kaswentha*), see Jon Parmenter, "The Meaning of *Kaswentha* and the Two Row Wampum Belt in Haudenosaunee (Iroquois) History: Can Indigenous Oral Tradition Be Reconciled with the Documentary Record?" *Journal of Early American History* 3 (2013): 82–109.

24 *St Catherine's Milling* at 59.

25 The conceptual disjunction between the *Royal Proclamation of 1763* and the *Indian Act, 1873* is even more evident when one takes into consideration the *Quebec Act of 1774*. The proclamation recognized and protected Indian Nations, but did not do so for the *Canadiens*. They protested, and their resistance led to the passing of the *Quebec Act*, which provided them similar protections (e.g., restoring the use of the civil law, guaranteeing the free practice of Catholicism, etc.). How is it that they were treated as legally similar in 1763 and 1774 (even though Quebec was technically conquered) yet different in kind in 1867 (when the *Quebec Act* was used to protect the rights of provinces against the central government)? In 1867 Quebec is granted a clear position in the division of powers, whereas Aboriginal peoples are placed under the exceptional jurisdiction of s. 91(24) and then in 1873 the administrative despotism of the *Indian Act*. There is a sea change that needs to be accounted for here. I would like to thank James Tully for drawing my attention to this important contrast.

has sovereignty, legislative power, and underlying title. This necessarily places Aboriginal peoples *under* the sovereign legislative power of Parliament (i.e., it presumes a *power-over* or sovereign-to-subject relationship).[26] The version of s. 91(24) that is consistent with the pre-existing relationship of suzerainty or treaty federalism necessarily *shares power* between the parties as nations (viz. Crown sovereignty is *not bundled* with either legislative power or underlying title, as those components are subject to mutually negotiated constitutional agreements). And so, if s. 91(24) is to be read in the light of the relationship between the imperial Crown and Aboriginal peoples prior to Confederation, then the vast majority of the *Indian Act* is simply and utterly *ultra vires* (the exception being those protections that are consistent with the *Proclamation*).[27]

---

26 The precise form of this power-over relationship has gradually changed. The introduction of s. 35 has subjected the *Indian Act* (and the explicitly colonial sovereign-to-wards administrative despotism it set in motion) to judicially mediated standards of justification. This has served as a kind of benchmark in the last 150 years of the constitutional relationship between the Crown and Aboriginal peoples, as the remaining vestiges of wardship have been reframed into the *Charter*-like sovereign–subjects relationship (albeit of a sui generis variety). Again, I stress that this move – despite the beneficial changes it has offered – is predicated on the *same* unquestioned presumption of Crown sovereignty (which bundles it with legislative power and underlying title) that gave rise to the *Indian Act* and its despotic sovereign-to-wards system of governance.

27 A further consequence is that the current *Sparrow* framework of s. 35 collapses as its interpretation of federal "power" under s. 91(24) requires the Crown to be in possession of sovereignty, legislative power, and underlying title. Once this presumption is questioned, this bundle of qualities unravels and with it the Courts rationale for applying a s. 1 analysis to s. 35, which, we must remember, is a constitutional provision that is not within the *Charter*. While the Court cannot question the sovereignty of the Crown, it has a constitutional responsibility to determine the sources of the legal consequences that flow from sovereignty. Legislative power and underlying title are not necessarily bound to sovereignty. If they are removed from the bundle, then the character or type of the constitutional relationship that is possible between the Crown and Aboriginal peoples changes from the *power-over* sovereign–subjects relationship to a *power-with* multinational federal relationship. This may seem to be a bridge too far for the Court, but it provides them with an opportunity to step away from the unhappy double bind that the *Sparrow* framework has placed them in (i.e., by starting from the presumption of Crown sovereignty, legislative power, and underlying title, the Court is confined to making determinations within a constitutional framework that presumes a sovereign–subjects relationship whose very existence cannot be explained without recourse to the legal fictions of discovery and *terra nullius*) and occupy the more familiar judicial position that they so clearly articulated in the *Secession Reference* (i.e., "clarify the legal framework within which political decisions are to be taken 'under the Constitution,' not to usurp the prerogatives of the political forces that operate within that framework"; see *Reference re Secession of Quebec* at para. 153). It seems to me that if the Court carries on fashioning the planks and timbers of reconciliation in accordance with a colonial constitutional framework, it has undertaken a task whose only outcome can be paradox. Is a ship whose "historic elements of wood, iron and canvas" (to borrow Binnie J's words from

2 The second limitation that this reading of s. 91(24) necessarily implies relates to the division of powers. The horizontal nation-to-nation relationship between Aboriginal peoples and the Crown gives the federal government exclusive (but not plenary) jurisdiction to pass laws dealing with "Indians and lands reserved for Indians."[28] Its purpose, as Bruce Ryder rightly states, is to guarantee "political spaces to the founding cultural groups in which they could define their own policies and preserve their institutions."[29] This adds a unique emphasis to the references to "exclusivity" throughout ss. 91 and 92 of the *Constitution Act, 1867* and places hard limits on the theory of federalism that is applicable. This means that when the courts are faced with a division-of-powers question relating to s. 91(24), the only appropriate model of federalism is the so-called classical paradigm.[30] Its use of watertight jurisdictional, compartments is consistent with the purpose of s. 91(24), which is necessarily different from any other head of power.[31] The classical paradigm provides the courts with the necessary interpretive tools to limit the scope and application of provincial laws, thereby preserving space for Aboriginal self-government. These tools include a more robust version of the doctrine of interjurisdictional

Mitchell at para. 130) have been meticulously removed and replaced at sea the same ship when it returns to port? Put differently, attempting to use the *Sparrow* framework to move beyond Canada's colonial constitutional history has led us to try to build our way out of a problem using the same plans; the reconciliation that this framework can offer is little more than a colonial Ship of Theseus.

28 Borrows, "Durability of Terra Nullius" at 734–8.

29 Bruce Ryder, "The Demise and Rise of the Classical Paradigm in Canadian Federalism: Promoting Autonomy for the Provinces and First Nations," *McGill Law Journal* 36 (1991): 362. This seminal article provides a clear and consistent "autonomist" approach to interpreting both s. 91(24) and s. 88 of the *Indian Act*. It bases this in the elements of Canadian constitutional history that I have outlined here (i.e., the special constitutional status of Aboriginal peoples as recognized in the treaty-making process and the *Royal Proclamation of 1763*, the exclusive jurisdiction that s. 91(24) grants to the federal government, and the fact that Aboriginal peoples did not consent to or participate in the enactment of the *Constitution Act, 1867*). My own approach to s. 91(24) and s. 88 takes its lead from Ryder's "autonomist approach." My contribution is to expose the necessary assumptions that ground the argument for applying the "modern approach" to this area (i.e., it depends on unquestioned and unexplained Crown sovereignty, legislative power, and underlying title).

30 For a summary of the "classical paradigm," see note 39.

31 This is directly against the long-standing (and unexplained) position that the Supreme Court has taken in regards to s. 91(24), which Abella J articulates in *NIL/TU,O Child and Family Services Society v. BC Government and Service Employees' Union*, [2010] 2 SCR 696 at para. 20: "There is no reason why, as a matter of principle, the jurisdiction of an entity's labour relations should be approached differently when s. 91(24) is at issue. The fundamental nature of the inquiry is – and should be – the same as for any other head of power."

immunity[32] that supports an "enclave" theory of jurisdiction over Indian lands; a broader "covering the field" approach to paramountcy; and the prohibition on federal inter-delegation. This is the only approach to the division of powers that respects the purpose of the imperial Parliament's division of legislative authority of the *Constitution Act, 1867* into two lists of "exclusive" spheres and its pre-existing responsibilities under the treaties and the *Royal Proclamation of 1763*. In contrast, the modern principle with its overlapping spheres of concurrent jurisdiction and more flexible double aspect and paramountcy doctrines is utterly inconsistent with the purpose of s. 91(24).[33] In order for it to it to gain the appearance of coherence within the four corners of the constitution, it endeavours to treat s. 91(24) as in no way different from any other head of power.[34] While this may appear attractive for the purposes of administrative efficiency for both levels of government to enjoy concurrent jurisdiction, it raises the question of where this jurisdiction is derived from and where the space for Aboriginal self-government went.

The only possible explanation for how s. 91(24) could be understood to confer the authority necessary to support the *Indian Act* without the expressed consent of Aboriginal peoples is absolute sovereignty (i.e., a form of sovereignty that would be immune to both *q.o.t.* and the basic principles of natural justice[35]), which itself can be based only in the legal fictions of *terra nullius* and discovery.[36] And yet, in *Tsilhqot'in Nation* the Court has informed us that

32 I agree with Robin Elliot's argument that the term *interjurisdictional immunity* is an unhappy one, as it encourages the misconception that the purpose of the doctrine is to protect the interests of particular entities rather than jurisdictional exclusivity. We should follow his suggestion and rename it the "doctrine of jurisdictional exclusivity." See Robin Elliot, "Interjurisdictional Immunity after Canadian Western Bank and Lafarge Canada Inc.: The Supreme Court Muddies the Doctrinal Waters – Again," (2008) 43 SCLR (2d) at 495.

33 Borrows, *Durability of Terra Nullius* at 734–8.

34 Hogg presents a version of this argument in *Constitutional Law* at 624. See note 76 in this chapter as well.

35 I am referring, of course, to *audi alteram partem* and *nemo judex in causa sua*.

36 An example of this reasoning can be seen in *Kruger et al. v. R*, [1978] 1 SCR 104 at 107, when Dickson J (as he was then) cites Robertson J from the BCCA decision: "The Proclamation of 1763 was entirely unilateral and was not, and cannot be described as, a treaty. Assuming (without expressing any opinion) that the Proclamation has the force of a statute, it cannot be said to be an act of the Parliament of Canada: there was no Parliament of Canada before 1867 and by no stretch of the imagination can a proclamation made by the Sovereign in 1763 be said to be an act of a legislative body which was not created until more than a hundred years later." A number of necessary assumptions undergird this interpretation. First, in order to maintain the logic that the unilateral nature of the *Proclamation of 1763* reflects unilateral

"the doctrine of terra nullius (that no one owned the land prior to European assertion of sovereignty) never applied in Canada, as confirmed by the Royal Proclamation of 1763."[37] This claim raises the question of the legal basis for Parliament's "broad view" of its own legislative powers under s. 91(24) and the Court's ability to interpret it as a double-aspect matter.[38] So we must ask, what

---

Crown sovereignty, it is necessary to ignore the treaties and imperial policy towards Aboriginal peoples prior to Confederation. Second, Aboriginal peoples would have had to consent to this unilateral sovereignty or be subjected to it via conquest without conditions. Third, this unilateral sovereignty is then passed on to the colonial Parliament with the *British North America Act, 1867,* and from that point forward it has the seemingly unlimited capacity to despotically govern Aboriginal peoples (the only qualification on their power being clear and plain legislative intent, and the division of powers). If these assumptions are accepted, then it explains why Dickson J asserts that "claims to aboriginal title are woven with history, legend, politics and moral obligations" (ibid. at 109). It is curious that this position requires the interchangeability of history and legend; how else can the Crown move from a set of horizontal nation-to-nation treaties to the kind of unilateral sovereignty that it would need to give the colonial Parliament absolute sovereignty over them in s. 91(24)? It is as if the court had taken a page from *The Surprising Adventures of Baron Munchausen,* as the Crown is seemingly able to lift itself out of the swamp of its contested historical and legal obligations by pulling its own hair. No wonder that Dickson CJC will later state in *Sparrow,* at 1103, "There was from the outset never any doubt that sovereignty and legislative power, and indeed the underlying title, to such lands vested in the Crown." The sovereignty of the Crown is a fact by virtue of having never been doubted. Its only authority is the fiction that the Crown could obtain sovereignty over Aboriginal peoples simply by virtue of legislating it. This requires the unstated premise that lies at the root of both Crown sovereignty and the process of reconciliation: *terra nullius.* Dickson CJC effectively admits this by citing CJ Marshall's *Johnson v. M'Intosh* (1823), 8 Wheaton 543 (USSC) as authority for his undoubtable concept of Crown sovereignty.

37 *Tsilhqot'in Nation v. British Columbia,* [2014] 2 SCR 257, 2014 SCC 44 at para. 69; Hamilton, "After Tsilhqot'in Nation." For an investigation into this claim, see Borrows, "Durability of Terra Nullius"; and Gordon Christie, "Who Makes Decisions over Aboriginal Lands?" *UBC Law Review* 48, no. 3 (2015): 743–92.

38 The Court has recognized the varying scope of different heads of powers. In *Reference re Employment Insurance Act (Can.), ss. 22 and 23,* [2005] 2 SCR 669 at para. 11, the Court states, "Some heads that set forth narrow powers leave little room for interpretation. Other, broader, heads result in legislation that can have several aspects." But, the "broad view" that Parliament has taken to s. 91(24) has an even more tenuous claim to authority, following the passage of s. 35(1) of the *Constitution Act, 1982.* In *Sparrow* at 1109 the Court held, "Federal legislative powers continue, including, of course, the right to legislate with respect to Indians pursuant to s. 91(24) of the *Constitution Act, 1867.* These powers must, however, now be read together with s. 35(1). In other words, federal power must be reconciled with federal duty and the best way to achieve that reconciliation is to demand the justification of any government regulation that infringes upon or denies aboriginal rights." This attempt to reconcile the juridico-historical gulf between s. 35(1) and s. 91(24) was the first sense of reconciliation within the jurisprudence. It is a task that has still barely begun. Contrary to the Court in *Sparrow,* the best way to achieve reconciliation is not through a justificatory test for infringement (a test that – unlike the *Oakes* test that it is based on – has no basis within the *Constitution Act, 1982,* as neither s. 1 nor s. 33

determines the limit of Parliament's authority over "Indians, and lands reserved for Indians"?

This question brings us to our aim in this section. We will investigate the legal nature of the authority granted in s. 91(24) by following how the courts have read this provision. Since *St Catherine's Milling*, this body of jurisprudence has been developed in and through the question of how s. 91(24) affects provincial legislative power.[39] In *Tsilhqot'in Nation* the Supreme Court has made a significant

---

applies to s. 35), but rather, it is through asking how legislation *extending to* or *in relation* to Indians and lands reserved for Indians became the kind of *power over* a particular group of people that could support the despotism of the *Indian Act*.

39 The fact that the case law on s. 91(24) develops out of a conflict over jurisdiction between two branches of the Crown and not between the Crown and Aboriginal peoples is a symptom of the implicit premise that provides the Crown with unquestionable sovereignty (*terra nullius*). A set of cases following passage of the *Canadian Bill of Rights*, SC 1960, c. 44, attempted to use its guarantee of "equality before the law" and its prohibition on "discrimination by race" against the *Indian Act*. The first such case is *R v. Drybones*, [1970] SCR 282. In this case the Court held that the use of the racial classification "Indian" in s. 95 of the Act (a provision that made it illegal to be intoxicated on a reserve) violated the equality guarantee in the *Canadian Bill of Rights*. The majority does not touch on the problem that this finding could pose to the entire *Indian Act* and s. 91(24). Pigeon J notes this issue in his dissent and provides an argument for retention of the *Indian Act* (despite its obvious conflict with the *Canadian Bill of Rights*), based on s. 91(24) and the division of powers at 303: "In the instant case, the question whether all existing legislation should be considered as in accordance with the non-discrimination principle cannot fail to come immediately to mind seeing that it arises directly out of head 24 of s. 91 of the *BNA Act* whereby Parliament has exclusive legislative authority over 'Indians, and Lands reserved for the Indians.'" As was pointed out by Riddell J in *Rex v. Martin*, this provision confers legislative authority over the Indians qua Indians and not otherwise. Its very object insofar as it relates to Indians, as opposed to lands reserved for the Indians, is to enable the Parliament of Canada to make legislation applicable only to Indians as such, and therefore not applicable to Canadian citizens generally. This legislative authority is obviously intended to be exercised over matters that are, as regards persons other than Indians, within the exclusive legislative authority of the provinces. Complete uniformity in provincial legislation is clearly not to be expected, not to mention the fact that further diversity must also result from special legislation for the territories. Equality before the law, in the sense in which it was understood in the Courts below, would require the Indians to be subject in every province to the same rules of law as all others in every particular, not merely on the question of drunkenness. Outside the territories, provincial jurisdiction over education and health facilities would make it very difficult for federal authorities to provide such facilities to Indians without "discrimination" as understood in the Courts below. This argument provides the constitutional insulation necessary to immunize the *Indian Act* against further challenges stemming from the *Canadian Bill of Rights* in *AG of Canada v. Lavell*, and *AG of Canada et al. v. Canard*, [1976] 1 SCR 170. In short, it repeats the "broad view" of s. 91(24) that we find in the division of powers cases, and it uses this to override the *Canadian Bill of Rights*. This leads to Sandra Lovelace taking her case to the United Nations Human Rights Committee in 1977; in 1981, the committee reached its decision that, inter alia, found Canada to be in breach of Article 27 of the *International Covenant on Civil and Political Rights* (*Lovelace v. Canada*, Communication no. R.6/24, UN Doc. Supp. No. 40 (A/36/40)).

change to this jurisprudence by holding that there is no longer any role for "the doctrine of interjurisdictional immunity and the idea that Aboriginal rights are at the core of the federal power *over* "Indians" under s. 91(24) of the *Constitution Act, 1867*."[40] The Court has thus followed Dickson CJ's (as he was then) view that "the history of Canadian constitutional law has been to allow for a fair amount of interplay and indeed overlap between federal and provincial powers. It is true that doctrines like interjurisdictional and Crown immunity and concepts like 'watertight compartments' qualify the extent of that interplay. But it must be recognized that these doctrines and concepts have not been the dominant tide of constitutional doctrines; rather they have been an undertow against the strong pull of pith and substance, the aspect doctrine and, in recent years, a very restrained approach to concurrency and paramountcy issues."[41]

---

40 *Tsilhqot'in Nation* at para. 140 (emphasis added).

41 *OPSEU v. Ontario (AG)*, [1987] 2 SCR 2 at para. 17. The contrast that the Court is outlining here is between two competing juridical responses to constitutional interpretation in the division of powers in s. 91 to s. 95 of the *Constitution Act, 1867*. Ryder provides us with an instructive overview of the main point of distinction between the two: "The classical and modern paradigms represent different judicial approaches to defining 'exclusivity' of federal and provincial powers, and thus of preserving provincial autonomy." Ryder, "Demise and Rise" at 312. The classical paradigm adopts a "strong" interpretation of exclusivity. It refuses the possibility of overlap between federal and provincial heads of power. It works to retain "watertight compartments" of jurisdiction by taking a strong position on paramountcy (i.e., when there is federal legislation in place it "covers the field" and prevents the effect of provincial law), interjurisdictional immunity (which, as we have seen, address the issue of valid laws passed by one body that affect the jurisdiction of another), and a prohibition on inter-delegation (the delegation of federal power to the provinces, or vice versa, which was ruled against in *Nova Scotia (AG) v. Canada (AG)*, [1951] SCR 31). In contrast, the modern paradigm allows for interplay and overlap. Once again, Ryder provides the overview: "The modern paradigm, on the other hand, is premised on a weaker understanding of exclusivity. Instead of seeking to prohibit as much overlap as possible between provincial and federal powers, the modem approach to exclusivity simply prohibits each level of government from enacting laws whose dominant characteristic ("pith and substance") is the regulation of a subject matter within the other level of government's jurisdiction. Exclusivity, on this approach, means the exclusive ability to pass laws that deal predominantly with a subject matter within the enacting government's catalogue of powers. If a law is in pith and substance within the enacting legislature's jurisdiction, it will be upheld notwithstanding that it might have spillover effects on the other level of government's jurisdiction." Ryder, "Demise and Rise" at 312. Ryder has clearly explained the function of the "pith and substance" approach, and this leaves us to briefly address the aspect or double aspect doctrine and the restrained approach to paramountcy. The aspect doctrine is an interpretive tool that is used when both levels of government have equally valid constitutional rights to legislate on an issue (i.e., each has the capacity to legislate, depending on the aspect from which the subject is approached). This approach rejects the idea of the "watertight compartments" and moves towards the overlap and interplay that characterizes the modern or flexible approach to federalism. The classic example of this doctrine at work is *Multiple Access Ltd. v. McCutcheon*, [1982] 2 SCR 161 at 181–3. Finally, the modern approach to paramountcy is to move to requiring an

My position is that in the case of s. 91(24) the "dominant tide" (i.e., the modern paradigm of federalism) and the "undertow" (i.e., the classical paradigm of federalism) necessarily entail two categorically distinct models of the relationship between the Crown and Aboriginal peoples. By following the "strong pull" of the modern approach to federalism, the Court has altered the meaning of the "exclusive authority" of s. 91(24) and thereby overlooked the distinct constitutional status and history of Aboriginal peoples.[42] But because the explicit wording in *Tsilhqot'in Nation* relates to only one head of s. 91(24) ("Indians"), this sea change in this jurisprudence is not complete.[43] The question of the application of interjurisdictional immunity to "lands reserved for Indians" (aside from Aboriginal rights and title subject to s. 35[44]) remains open. This small opening offers us the opportunity to urge the Court to reconsider what the "strong pull" of co-operative federalism necessarily implies in the context of s. 91(24).[45] We will do this by tracing its course through the jurisprudence on the relationship between s. 91(24) and valid provincial laws of general application.

"express conflict" between the federal and provincial legislation before finding the latter to be *ultra vires* or reading it down (for more on the how the courts have applied the express conflict standard, see note 55).

42 Borrows, "Durability of Terra Nullius" at 734–8.

43 Kerry Wilkins has reminded me it is by no means clear that this is the case, as the Court in *Delgamuukw* at paras. 174–6 holds that Aboriginal title lands are "Lands reserved for Indians" (unsurprisingly the authority they cite for this is the judgment of the Privy Council in *St Catherine's Milling*). But, on the off chance that indeed the specific wording in *Tsilhqot'in Nation* at para. 140 applies only to the first head of s. 91(24), then it could still hold open the possibility of most of Ryder's autonomist approach (depending, of course, on what approach it takes to questions of paramountcy regarding "Indians"). As Ryder states, "While autonomy for First Nations people would be furthered by interpreting federal jurisdiction over 'Indian lands' as creating 'constitutional reserves' immune from provincial legislation, it is not a plausible alternative to similarly interpret federal jurisdiction over the first branch of s. 91(24) ('Indians') as creating an 'enclave' around all First Nations people that would shield them from the application of provincial laws off reserves.... At the same time, subjecting First Nations people to the full operation of provincial laws off reserves in the same manner as other Canadian citizens ignores their distinct constitutional status." See Ryder, "Demise and Rise" at 368. This is by no means certain as the wording at paras. 150–1 state that the doctrine will not be applied in cases where lands are held under Aboriginal title, which seems to suggest that "lands" in s. 91(24) are being restricted to reserve and treaty lands. If this is the case the possibility of the autonomist approach has been narrowed to the point of insignificance.

44 *Tsilhqot'in Nation* at paras. 150–1.

45 Robin Elliot points out that when courts attribute wide purviews of overlapping legislative authority it does not necessarily lead to co-operation (after all, it is obvious that overlapping powers do not *necessarily* lead to co-operation; they can just as easily lead to legislative duplication and/or competition) and that clearly defined and distinct compartments of legislative authority are more likely to promote co-operation. See Robin Elliot, "Interjurisdictional Immunity after Canadian Western Bank and Lafarge Canada Inc.: The Supreme Court Muddies the Doctrinal Waters – Again," (2008) 43 SCLR (2d) at 433–98.

A. St Catherine's Milling, *s. 91(24), and the Division of Powers*

It is telling that *St Catherine's Milling* – a case where there is no Aboriginal party to plead its case before the Privy Council – forms the first chapter in both the judicial interpretation of s. 91(24) and Aboriginal title. The case establishes two connected points:

1 Lord Watson interprets the *Royal Proclamation, 1763* as showing that "the tenure of the Indians was a personal and usufructuary right, dependent upon the good will of the Sovereign."[46] He adds that "the Crown has all along had a present proprietary estate in the land, upon which the Indian title was a mere burden."[47]

2 Section 91(24) confers upon the Parliament of Canada power to make laws for "Indians, and lands reserved for the Indians." The wording of the provision is "sufficient to include all lands reserved, upon any terms or conditions, for Indian occupation."[48] But this legislative power does not carry with it a proprietary right over the subject matter. This means that Parliament has "the power of legislating for Indians, and for lands which are reserved to their use," and the provinces retain the underlying title to the land.[49]

With this interpretation the *Proclamation* is effectively reversed: it moves from the Crown formally recognizing and protecting Indian nations to a document that grants absolute sovereignty over them.[50] This is done without even

---

46 *St Catherine's Milling* at 54.

47 Ibid. at 58.

48 Ibid. at 59.

49 Ibid. The provincial claim to underlying title did not apply to the Prairie provinces until Parliament passed the three *Natural Resource Transfer Acts*, 1930. Prior to that, Parliament had exercised jurisdiction over Crown lands and natural resources in the region that it purchased from the Hudson's Bay Company in 1870. These three Acts turned that jurisdiction over to the provinces of Manitoba, Saskatchewan, and Alberta.

50 While on its face the proclamation could accommodate either interpretive approach, it is difficult to fit the *St Catherine's Milling* interpretation to the actual history of the legal and political relationships that existed between the British imperial Crown and Aboriginal nations. In order for it to be consistent we have to either square this *power-over* interpretation of the proclamation with the treaties that the Crown made with Aboriginal nations (i.e., shoring up the claim to legitimacy by constructing Aboriginal consent, which requires interpretive acrobatics that quickly veer into absurdity) or by relying on the legal fictions of discovery and *terra nullius* to attribute magical properties to the British imperial Crown (i.e., an ability to excuse itself from the legal and moral obligations that structure its own political architecture and social imaginary). Lord Watson's reading retains whatever plausibility it can (in my view, it is a thin veneer at best) by strictly avoiding any engagement with the history

a passing reference to the actual pre-Confederation relationship between the imperial Crown and Aboriginal Peoples. It is as if Lord Watson reads the *Proclamation* through the lens of the wording of s. 91(24), when he could have just as easily used the *Proclamation* to restrict the seemingly limitless grant of authority that the words of the provision itself seem to grant.[51] He could have done so by using the history of the relationship to explicitly define what the limits of legislation *extending to* or *in relation* to "Indians, and lands reserved for Indians" are. Instead we are told that Indian title is a "mere burden" under the exclusive jurisdiction of Parliament; this will remain authoritative until *Calder* in 1973.[52] From this basis the only question concerning s. 91(24) left to resolve was how this exceptionally broad or even unlimited provision fits within the division of powers.[53]

This question has led to a number of cases that have formed a general rule, which holds that provincial laws apply to both "Indians" and "lands reserved for Indians."[54] Sanders summarized this trend in the case law by stating, "'Indians'

---

and context of the proclamation. I engage with the history of the proclamation in greater detail in part 3.

51 As Kerry Wilkins rightly points out, "Section 129 of the *Constitution Act, 1867* continues pre-Confederation laws, including the Proclamation, in force until they are superseded by valid legislation enacted by the order of government having legislative authority over their subject matter. Because it was Parliament that acquired exclusive legislative authority over 'Indians, and Lands reserved for the Indians,' the relevant parts of the Proclamation continue as federal law, with priority over conflicting provincial law; only Parliament now has authority to amend or to repeal them." Kerry Wilkins, "'Still Crazy after All These Years': Section 88 of the Indian Act," *Alberta Law Review* 38, no. 2 (2000): 478; cf. Brian Slattery, "Understanding Aboriginal Rights," *Canadian Bar Review* 66 (1987): 773, 777–8. Even if we were to concede that the proclamation was susceptible to supersession by subsequent imperial legislation (a view that does conform to common law procedures and principles, but also jumps over the inter-national character of the proclamation, the effect of the treaties and thus requires a strong or absolute version of Crown sovereignty, which brings us back to the legitimation problem), the wording of s. 91(24) of the *British North America Act, 1867*, does not necessarily supersede it. It seems to me that even a minimal clear and plain intent standard would preserve the terms of the proclamation.

52 *Calder et al. v. AG of British Columbia*, [1973] SCR 313.

53 This not to say that Aboriginal peoples did not attempt to use the courts to challenge the nature of the Crown's authority (e.g., the Six Nations Status Case detailed in part 3). In fact, in 1927 Parliament made use of its seemingly unlimited legislative authority to make it illegal for Indians to hire a lawyer by adding s. 141 to the *Indian Act*. This provision made it a summary offence to receive any payment or promise of payment from an Indian for the prosecution of a claim without the written consent of the superintendent general. See *Indian Act* SC 1927, c. 32, s. 6, consolidated as s. 141 of RSC 1927, c. 98.

54 Hogg, *Constitutional Law* at 623. Examples of cases that establish this rule include *R v. Hill* (1907) 15 OLR 406 (CA); *Four B Manufacturing v. United Garment Workers*, [1980] 1 SCR 1031; *R v. Francis* [1988] 1 SCR 1025; and *Paul v. British Columbia* [2003] 2 SCR 585.

fall into a 'double aspect' area in which provincial laws will always apply in the absence of special federal legislation. No case states this proposition bluntly."[55]

The basis for treating s. 91(24) as a double aspect matter (despite its obvious uniqueness) has not been explored by the courts. Nonetheless, in the jurisprudence that has developed there are a number of exceptions. Some of these exceptions are relatively uncomplicated, as they concern cases where there is a clear violation of the division of powers (i.e., those that would be caught on a pith and substance analysis of the matter).[56] For example, provincial laws that explicitly single out Indians or lands reserved for Indians are invalid, as that power is within s. 91.[57] Likewise the doctrine of federal paramountcy holds that where there is an inconsistency between provincial and federal law, the federal law trumps it (the question being whether the Court takes the classical "covering the field" or modern "express conflict" standard).[58] The most serious complications arise when an otherwise valid provincial law of general application affects

---

55 Douglas Sanders, "The Application of Provincial Laws," in *Aboriginal Peoples and the Law: Indian, Metis and Inuit Rights in Canada*, ed. B.W. Morse (Ottawa: Carleton University Press, 1984) at 452–3. Kerry Wilkins notes that while it is true that Indians are not immune from valid provincial legislation unless it has the effect of impairing "Indianness" (or conflicts with valid federal law), this exception counts for something. The potential shielding effect of these exceptions is limited by the uncertain process of determining both the measure of "Indianness." As Wilkins points out, "One cannot always tell at a glance whether a given provincial measure applies, as such, to Indians or whether its application to them depends on s. 88 because its effect is to regulate them 'qua Indians.' Such determinations are often profoundly difficult." See Wilkins, "'Still Crazy,'" at 471. He further argues that the core of the "lands reserved" power is a more secure shield, as it is (or at least should be) broad enough to exclude most provincial land law. He deals with the (dizzying) intricacies involved in the s. 91(24) lands question and s. 88 of the *Indian Act* in the aforementioned article from 483 to 497.

56 For a recent (but ultimately unsuccessful) example of this type of division of powers argument, see *Kitkatla Band v. British Columbia (Minister of Small Business, Tourism and Culture)*, [2002] 2 SCR 146 at paras. 51–78.

57 For cases that deal with what counts as "singling out," see ibid.; *R v. Sutherland* [1980] 2 SCR 451; *Four B*; *Dick v. R*, [1985] 2 SCR 309; and *Leighton v. British Columbia* (1989) 57 DLR (4th) 657 (BCCA).

58 The language that the Court has used to determine if there is an "express conflict" that requires the neutralization of provincial legislation (paramountcy) is that there is either a "practical and functional incompatibility" between the two schemes (*Bell Canada v. Quebec (Commission de la Santé et de la Sécurité du Travail)*, [1988] 1 SCR 749 at paras. 866–7) or where the federal regulations "display a sufficient intent that [the federal government] wished to cover the field exclusively" (*Francis* at 10). Also, there is a similar limitation on provincial legislative powers in Manitoba, Saskatchewan, and Alberta as the *Natural Resource Transfer Agreements* (which have constitutional status by virtue of a constitutional amendment passed in 1930) contain a clause that provides for subsistence hunting and fishing rights for Indians. In *R v. Badger*, [1996] 1 SCR 771 the Court held that provincial infringement of those rights can be justified, in accordance with *Sparrow*.

the essential aspects of federal responsibility and there is no competing federal law in existence. In this case the courts are faced with the difficulty of deciding what *exclusive* means in the case of s. 91(24) by treating it as a double aspect matter, limiting provincial jurisdiction via the doctrine of interjurisdictional immunity or referential incorporation via s. 88 of the *Indian Act*.[59] This decision is particularly significant, as it necessarily implies very different conceptions of both federalism and the constitutional status of Aboriginal peoples.

I believe that this penumbra of cases offers us the most detailed account of how the courts have attempted to interpret both the scope of s. 91(24) and how it fits into the broader constitutional framework. We will begin by reviewing how the courts have applied the doctrine of interjurisdictional immunity in relation to s. 91(24). Here our focus will be on Laskin J's (as he was in *Cardinal*; he was the chief justice by the time of *Natural Parents*) articulation of the theory of federal "enclaves" in his dissenting judgment in *Cardinal*, his concurring decision in *Natural Parents*, and the Court's rejection of it in favour of the more flexible concept of "Indianness" in *Four B* and *Francis*.[60] From there we will review the shift in the Court's interpretation of s. 88 of the *Indian Act* from the declaratory theory put forward in *Kruger* to the theory of referential incorporation in *Dick v. R*.[61] We will then consider how the definition of *Indians* and *bands* (from its nineteenth-century legislative foundations) fits within the picture of federalism that the Court has formulated in and through its interpretation of s. 91(24). Finally, we will conclude the chapter by reconsidering the implications of the Court's rejection of the doctrine of interjurisdictional immunity in *Tsilhqot'in Nation* for both federalism and the future of reconciliation.[62]

B. Interjurisdictional Immunity and s. 91(24)

The doctrine of interjurisdictional immunity is based on the references to *exclusivity* throughout ss. 91 and 92 of the *Constitution Act, 1867*. For instance, the opening paragraph of s. 91 states that the Parliament of Canada has "exclusive"

---

59 This decision is further complicated by the referential incorporation theory of s. 88 set out by Beetz J in *Dick*. This is highlighted in *R v. Morris*, [2006] 2 SCR 915 at para. 44 where the Court states, "Section 88 reflects Parliament's intention to avoid the effects of the immunity imposed by s. 91(24) by incorporating certain provincial laws of general application into federal law." This interpretation further narrows the ambit of "exclusivity" in s. 91(24) and complicates its judicial application, as laws that go to "core Indianness" can still be unilaterally incorporated into federal law by s. 88 of the *Indian Act*. This process makes a mockery of both the history of federalism in Canada and the constitutional status of Aboriginal peoples.

60 *Cardinal v. Alberta (AG)*, [1974] SCR 695; *Four B*; *Francis*.

61 *Kruger et al. v. R*, [1978] 1 SCR 104; *Dick*.

62 *Tsilhqot'in Nation*.

legislative authority in matters coming within the listed classes of subjects. What does *exclusive* mean? If the limits are strictly formal, then it would have very little practical meaning, as creative drafting techniques would allow for concurrent (not to mention confused) jurisdiction on all matters. If, on the other hand, the limits are strictly enforced in both form and effect, then legislating becomes next to impossible. In this case, the legislative branches would be faced with the nearly impossible task of having to anticipate all possible effects that their laws may have on matters within the jurisdiction of the other branch. Between these two extremes lies the penumbra of cases in which otherwise valid, generally worded legislation enacted by one order of government intrudes on the core area of the jurisdiction of the other order.[63] When this type of case concerns s. 91(24), the courts are effectively tasked with determining the limits of core federal jurisdiction over Indians and the lands reserved for them. In these cases, the courts must answer the following question: what is the meaning of *exclusive* legislative authority in regards to s. 91(24)? Broadly speaking, this question has given rise to two approaches: the "enclaves" theory of Indian lands and the much narrower "core of Indianness" theory. The most comprehensive articulation of the "enclaves" theory of s. 91(24) comes from Laskin CJ's dissents in *Cardinal* and *Natural Parents* in the mid-1970s.[64] It remains the best defence for applying the classical approach to federalism to s. 91(24), and it offers the possibility of providing jurisdictional space for meaningful Aboriginal self-government (assuming that federal power is constrained to the limits of the shared and negotiated model of sovereignty that we see in treaty federalism and not given the "broad view" that enables the kind of unilateral and unrestrained power that we find exemplified in the *Indian Act*).[65]

---

63 This expression of the doctrine is paraphrased from Beetz J in *Bell Canada v. Quebec (Commission de la Santé et de la Sécurité du Travail)*, [1988] 1 SCR 749 at 833. The expression holds true for both the enclave and Indianness theories of jurisdiction. The difference between them is the location of the core (one holds it at the boundaries of lands; the other, on the vague boundaries of judicial discretion to determine the limits of Indianness).

64 Older cases suggest that Indian reserves should be regarded as federal enclaves: *R v. Rogers* (1923), 33 Man. R. 139, [1923] 3 DLR 414 (CA).

65 Ryder offers a useful argument for using the classical approach for s. 91(24): "If provincial autonomy is a value frequently cited in, although imperfectly promoted by, existing Canadian constitutional doctrine, autonomy for First Nations people is a hidden constitutional value whose injection into interpretive practices is long overdue." Ryder, "Demise and Rise" at 363. I agree with this sentiment and approach. My own concerns relate to how this has remained a "hidden constitutional value" for the last 150 years. It seems that thus far the courts have been willing to accept that s. 91(24) provided the jurisdiction required for both the creation of a federally administered despotism and provincial legislative interference. It has done so without providing any basis for its interpretation. It simply assumes it, and so the debates concerning s. 91(24) have been effectively carried out as a division of powers issue between Parliament and the legislatures. The real underling issue here is not

The second approach adopts the more flexible modern approach to federalism by limiting the intrusion to what Beetz J referred to as the "basic, minimum and unassailable content" of the matter in question.[66] In the case of s. 91(24) the Court developed the unhappy terms *Indianness* and *Indians qua Indians* to refer to this essential or core content.[67] The overall trend has been one of decline, as the Court has followed the "dominant tide" of the modern paradigm of federalism. In doing so they have relied strongly on the assumption that s. 91(24) is in no way different from any other head of federal power in the *Constitution Act, 1867* (or that it is different only insofar as it necessarily has a double aspect).[68] They have simply accepted a "broad view" of the Crown's legislative capacity and, as such, they have enabled the Crown's despotic governmental practices under the *Indian Act*; unilaterally subjected Aboriginal peoples to a confused system of concurrent provincial and federal jurisdiction; and continued the implicit use of the *doctrine of discovery* in Canadian law. In the following section, we will trace how the Court has defined federal jurisdiction under s. 91(24) by reviewing the theory of "enclaves" in *Cardinal* and *Natural Parents* and the rejection of it in *Four B* and *Francis*.

C. The Theory of Enclaves

In *Cardinal* the appellant, a treaty Indian, sold a piece of moose meat to a non-Indian. The transaction took place at his home on a reserve in Alberta. He was charged with unlawful trafficking in big game, in breach of s. 37 of the

---

whether s. 91(24) is strictly federal or a double aspect matter, but what these two different approaches to federalism necessarily imply about the relationship between the Crown and Aboriginal peoples. Put differently, placing Indians strictly under federal jurisdiction on the classical model *without redefining what s. 91(24) means* retains the same colonial power *over* relationship as the modern vision (i.e., the Crown is still presumed to be in possession of sovereignty, legislative power, and underlying title). This exercise of constitutional interpretation requires the assumption that Aboriginal peoples are an internal component of the constitutional order that can be unilaterally moved within the constitutional order. The question driving this is how s. 91(24) can be interpreted as fundamentally changing the treaty federalism relationship that existed between Aboriginal peoples and the imperial Crown.

66 *Bell Canada v. Quebec* at 839.

67 *Natural Parents v. Superintendent of Child Welfare et al.*, [1976] 2 SCR 751 at 760–1.

68 The Court has also argued that s. 91(24) is in fact distinguished from the other enumerated heads of federal power, but only insofar as it can support interjurisdictional immunity. This position is set out in *Canadian Western Bank v. Alberta*, [2007] 2 SCR 3. After a (shockingly) brief summary of the case law, the Court summarized the "special position" of Aboriginal peoples in the constitutional order: "In their federal aspect ('Indianness'), Indian people are governed by federal law exclusively, but in their activities as citizens of a province, they remain subject to provincial laws of general application. As it is with Indians, so it must be with chartered banks" (para. 61). There is, to my eye, a kind of gallows humour to be found in the legal equation of Indianness and bankness.

provincial *Wildlife Act*.[69] He argued that the provincial law was not applicable to him as an Indian on a reserve and was acquitted at trial on the ground that the *Wildlife Act* was *ultra vires* in its application to the appellant by virtue of s. 91(24).[70] The province appealed the case and the judgment at trial was reversed. At the Supreme Court the case resulted in a majority decision from Martland J (supported by Fauteux CJ, and Abbott, Judson, Ritchie, and Pigeon JJ) and a dissent from Laskin J (supported by Hall and Spence JJ).

The majority held that s. 12 of the *Alberta Natural Resources Agreement of 1929* made the provisions of the *Wildlife Act* applicable to all Indians, including those on reserves. This was due to the fact that, by their interpretation, s. 1 of the *British North America Act, 1930*, gave the agreement the force of law, notwithstanding anything contained in the *British North America Act, 1867* (now referred to as the *Constitution Act, 1867*), any amendment, or any federal statute.[71] This argument provided a solid constitutional basis for concurrent jurisdiction, but, due to the specific wording of the agreement,[72] it did not provide a clear answer concerning the application of provincial law on reserves. On this question Martland J stated,

> Section 91(24) of the *British North America Act, 1867*, gave exclusive legislative authority to the Canadian Parliament in respect of Indians and over lands reserved for the Indians. Section 92 gave to each Province, in such Province, exclusive legislative power over the subjects therein defined. It is well established, as illustrated in *Union Colliery Company v. Bryden*, that a Province cannot legislate in relation to a subject matter exclusively assigned to the Federal Parliament by s. 91. But it is also well established that Provincial legislation enacted under a heading of s. 92 does not necessarily become invalid because it affects something which is subject to Federal legislation. A vivid illustration of this is to be found in the Privy Council decision a few years after the *Union Colliery* case in *Cunningham*

69 RSA 1970, c. 391.

70 The Court's use of *ultra vires* here is a bit confusing. If the law is *ultra vires*, it has no force or effect at all. But that was not the argument here. What we have instead is a valid provincial law deemed (at trial) inapplicable in certain circumstances because of IJI. I would like to thank Kerry Wilkins for pointing this out to me.

71 *Cardinal* at 698–9.

72 Section 12 of the *Alberta Natural Resources Agreement of 1929* reads: "In order to secure to the Indians of the Province the continuance of the supply of game and fish for their support and subsistence, Canada agrees that the laws respecting game in force in the Province from time to time shall apply to the Indians within the boundaries thereof, provided however, that the said Indians shall have the right, which the Province hereby assures to them, of hunting trapping and fishing game and fish for food at all seasons of the year *on all unoccupied Crown lands and on any other lands to which the said Indians may have a right of access*" (emphasis added). This wording could be read as excluding reserves, as it is an open question as to whether they are included in the jurisdictional boundaries of the provinces. The appellant makes just this argument and Martland J addresses it directly at 709–10.

> *v. Tomey Homma*, which sustained Provincial legislation, pursuant to s. 92(1), which prohibited Japanese, whether naturalized or not, from voting in Provincial elections in British Columbia.[73]

It is a curious coincidence that the line of reasoning here qualifies the exclusivity of federal power under s. 91(24) on the basis of a case on s. 91(25), which upholds the right of the province to exclude a specific ethnic group from voting.[74] The reasoning of the Lord Chancellor in *Cunningham v. Tomey Homma* makes use of a pith and substance interpretive approach to hold that the mere mention of aliens is not enough to make a provincial law *ultra vires*. Rather, the court must determine the limits of the subject matter. From this Martland J goes on to hold,

> A Provincial Legislature could not enact legislation in relation to Indians, or in relation to Indian Reserves, but this is far from saying that the effect of s. 91(24) of the *British North America Act, 1867*, was to create enclaves within a Province within the boundaries of which Provincial legislation could have no application. In my opinion, the test as to the application of Provincial legislation within a Reserve is the same as with respect to its application within the Province and that is that it must be within the authority of s. 92 and must not be in relation to a subject-matter assigned exclusively to the Canadian Parliament under s. 91. Two of those subjects are Indians and Indian Reserves, but if Provincial legislation within the limits of s. 92 is not construed as being legislation in relation to those classes of subjects (or

---

73 *Cardinal* at 702–3.

74 It is worth considering the words of the Lord Chancellor in *Cunningham v. Tomey Homma*:

> Could it be suggested that the Province of British Columbia could not exclude an alien from the franchise in that Province? Yet if the mere mention of alienage in the enactment could make the law *ultra vires*, such a construction of section 91(25) would involve that absurdity. The truth is that the language of that section does not purport to deal with the consequences of either alienage or naturalization. It undoubtedly reserves these subjects for the exclusive jurisdiction of the Dominion, that is to say, it is for the Dominion to determine what shall constitute either the one or the other, but the question as to what consequences shall follow from either is not touched. The right of protection and the obligations of allegiance are necessarily involved in the nationality conferred by naturalization, *but the privileges attached to it, where these depend upon residence, are quite independent of nationality.* (*The Collector of Voter for the Electoral District of Vancouver City and the Attorney General for the Province of British Columbia v. Tomey Homma and the Attorney General for the Dominions of Canada (British Columbia)* [1902] UKPC 60 at 3–4; emphasis added)

It is difficult to understand how it could be "absurd" that s. 91(25) could cover all laws that pertain to naturalization, and yet entirely reasonable that it can be severed from the most basic of civic privileges.

> any other subject under s. 91) it is applicable anywhere in the Province, including Indian Reserves, even though Indians or Indian Reserves might be affected by it. My point is that s. 91(24) enumerates classes of subjects over which the Federal Parliament has the exclusive power to legislate, but it does not purport to define areas within a Province within which the power of a Province to enact legislation, otherwise within its powers, is to be excluded.[75]

The point that Martland J makes concerning the nature of the exclusivity in s. 91(24) is based on his own interpretive approach. Its reasoning relies on the idea that all heads of power in ss. 91 and 92 are the same, but it seems to jump past the fact that this sameness is produced by the juristic perspective he adopts. That is, by electing to determine the effect of s. 91(24) by virtue of the text of the provision alone, the meaning of s. 91(24) is determined without a consideration of its actual historical, political, and legal context of Aboriginal peoples.[76] These are taken as mere externalities: all that is left for the Court to do is to maintain the balance of federalism by interpreting the pith and substance of legislation on a case-by-case basis. In effect, by limiting itself to a *law qua law* perspective the Court is able to pronounce the magical words "*mutatis mutandis,*" and suddenly Indians are akin to railways.[77] It is this magical reasoning that is able to convert the pre-Confederation "treaty federalism" of the imperial Crown into the domestic Crown's absolute sovereignty over Aboriginal peoples (i.e., the bundled notion of Crown sovereignty that assumes legislative power

---

75 *Cardinal* at 703.

76 For another iteration of this argument, see Hogg, *Constitutional Law* at 624: "The [enclave] theory was always implausible, because it involved a distinction between the first and second branches of s. 91(24) for which there is no textual warrant, and it placed the second branch ('lands reserved for the Indians') in a privileged position enjoyed by no other federal subject matter. It is plain that there is no constitutional distinction between 'Indians' and 'lands reserved for the Indians,' and that provincial laws may apply to both subject matters." Ryder responds to this by stating, "I believe these authors are wrong to suggest that federal jurisdiction under s. 91(24) should not be treated differently than any other head of power. To suggest that it should is not simply a 'politically-based perception,' rather, it is one that brings to the fore the hidden constitutional history of First Nations people, and interprets s. 91(24) with that history in mind. If this seems to be an unusual or 'political' theory, I would suggest that it is only because the legitimate constitutional claims to autonomy of First Nations people have been neglected or ignored for so long." Ryder, "Demise and Rise" at 363. I would add to this that it is curious that Hogg notes that s. 91(24) has allowed the federal Parliament to make laws "for Indians on matters which otherwise lie outside its legislative competence, and on which it could not legislate for non-Indians," and that the validity of these laws has been determined by the courts via pith and substance but then argues that s. 91(24) cannot have a distinction between its two branches because no other head of power does. It appears that in Hogg's estimation s. 91(24) is both exceptional and ordinary. See Hogg, *Constitutional Law* at 618.

77 *Cardinal* at 706.

and underlying title). Martland J supports this logic by citing the words of Riddel J in *R v. Martin*, "In other words, no statute of the Provincial Legislature dealing with Indians or their lands as such would be valid and effective; but there is no reason why general legislation may not affect them."[78]

There is *no reason* because there is no contextual inquiry into the purpose and scope of the words of s. 91(24). Here the thinking of the Court plays a queer trick that is akin to the one Wittgenstein touches on in §352 of the *Philosophical Investigations*: "Here saying 'There is no third possibility' or 'But there can't be a third possibility!' – expresses our inability to turn our eyes away from this picture: a picture which looks as if it must already contain both the problem and its solution, while all the time we *feel* it is not so."[79]

Martland J excludes the possibility that s. 91(24) could be distinct as a result of his commitment to a picture of federalism and that places Aboriginal peoples under federal power. Whether they are positioned as wards or subjects, the constitutional division of power remains the same, as both positions start with the (unquestionable) background presumption of Crown sovereignty, legislative power, and underlying title. It is this picture that excludes the possibility of Aboriginal self-government (a picture that we have yet to fully turn away from). Instead, it sets out to determine the meaning of federal jurisdiction in s. 91(24) on a case-by-case basis under the wide ambit of judicial discretion available under the doctrine of "pith and substance." Under this approach the legal world of Aboriginal peoples in Canada is determined by judges who are concerned with a picture of federalism that does not involve these peoples as anything more than an object to be weighed and measured (perhaps with more care following s. 35 of the *Constitution Act, 1982*). It is in this way that Indians end up sharing the same uncertain measure that John Seldon saw at work in equity in the seventeenth century: "Equity is a roguish thing: for law we have a measure, know what to trust to; equity is according to the conscience of him that is Chancellor, and as that is larger or narrower, so is equity. 'Tis all one as if they should make the standard for the measure we call a foot, a Chancellor's foot; what an uncertain measure would this be? One Chancellor has a long foot, another a short foot, a third an indifferent foot: 'tis the same thing in a Chancellor's conscience."[80]

The difference here is that the "uncertain measure" of judicial discretion is being used to determine the legal boundaries for entire cultures, over their lands, without their consent. Near the end of his decision Martland J makes use of this discretion to determine the meaning of s. 12 and thereby holds that the

78 Ibid., citing *R v. Martin* (1917), 41 OLR 79 at 83.

79 Wittgenstein, *Philosophical Investigations* at §352.

80 John Selden, *Table Talk*, quoted in M.B. Evans and R.I. Jack, eds, *Sources of English Legal and Constitutional History* (Sydney: Butterworths, 1984) at 223–4.

provisions of the *Wildlife Act* apply "to all Indians, including those on Reserves, and governed their activities throughout the Province, including Reserves."[81] This argument hinges on including reserves into the phrase "any other lands to which the said Indians may have a right of access."[82] As Laskin J notes in his dissent, this argument must ignore both the fact that the accused was not hunting for food (which is the object of s. 12) and that s. 10 of the same Act deals with reserves explicitly.[83] It must also assume that s. 91(24) is in no way different from any other head of power in s. 91. As we have previously noted, this assumption grants the federal government sovereignty *over* Aboriginal peoples by reading the words of the provision alone, and thus it closes off jurisdictional spaces for self-government (not to mention that it presumes that the imperial Parliament had the curious power of being able to give what it did not have simply by virtue of legislating it).[84] The conceptual problem here arises in the first step (i.e., reading s. 91(24) as conferring legislative authority *over* Aboriginal peoples), which, as Wittgenstein notes, "is the one that altogether escapes notice ... (the decisive movement in the conjuring trick has been made, and it was the very one that we thought quite innocent.)"[85] I believe that the reasoning of Martland J (or rather what remains as the implicit premise for his reasons) provides us with an example of how s. 91(24) has remained the basis for laws without measure governing lands without citizens. So does Laskin J depart from this picture?

Laskin J starts his dissent by clearly stating the uniqueness of the issue before the Court in this case. As he puts it, "This appeal raises, for the first time in this Court, the question whether provincial game laws apply to a Treaty Indian on an Indian Reserve so as to make him liable to their penalties for engaging on the Reserve in activities prohibited by the provincial legislation."[86] By characterizing the issue in this manner he makes it clear that he is approaching the issue as a precedent-setting division-of-powers case (as

81 *Cardinal* at 710.

82 Ibid. at 698–9.

83 Ibid. at 710. Laskin J responds to this interpretation of the words of s. 12 in his dissent in the case at 723: "Even if the words in s. 12, 'any other lands to which the said Indians may have a right of access,' are taken in a broad general sense as capable, if s. 12 stood alone, of embracing Indian Reserves, they must be read to exclude such Reserves which are specially dealt with in s. 10. The canon of construction enshrined in the maxim *generalia specialibus non derogant* is particularly apt here."

84 Even the broad view of s. 91(24) and the bundled notion of Crown sovereignty that grounds it (or perhaps better, leaves it ungrounded) does not necessarily exclude the possibility of an Aboriginal right of self-government, as Williamson J demonstrates in *Campbell et al. v. AG BC/AG Cda & Nisga'a Nation et al.*, 2000 BCSC 1123.

85 Wittgenstein, *Philosophical Investigations* at §308.

86 *Cardinal* at 698–9.

opposed to the more limited and technical approach of the majority, which manages to avoid this issue).

He quickly moves to setting out a classical "watertight compartments" approach to the second branch of s. 91(24). "Apart entirely from the exclusive power vested in the Parliament of Canada to legislate in relation to Indians, its exclusive power in relation also to Indian Reserves puts such tracts of land, albeit they are physically in a Province, beyond provincial competence to regulate their use or to control resources thereon. This is not because of any title vested in the Parliament of Canada or in the Crown in right of Canada, but because regardless of ultimate title, it is only Parliament that may legislate in relation to Reserves once they have been recognized or set aside as such."[87]

The basis for this "exclusivity" is set strictly on a theory of the exclusivity of federal legislative powers in the *Constitution Act, 1867* and not a pre-existing right of Aboriginal self-government. Considering that this case is decided in the immediate wake of *Calder,* this theory of s. 91(24) is all the more curious. After all, as Judson J stated in *Calder*, "It is clear that Indian title in British Columbia cannot owe its origin to the Proclamation of 1763, the fact is that when the settlers came, the Indians were there, organized in societies and occupying the land as their forefathers had done for centuries. This is what Indian title means."[88]

How could title be placed outside the bounds of the prescriptive powers of the Crown while social organization (a concept that is necessarily connected to both politics and law) remained squarely within it? Laskin J may be anticipating this concern by stating that this legislative power exists "regardless of ultimate title."[89] But this hardly settles the matter and it is a question that remains unanswered even today.[90]

87 Ibid. at 714.

88 *Calder* at 328.

89 Ibid. at 714.

90 The only case that the Supreme Court has given us so far on the right of self-government is *R v. Pamajewon*, [1996] 2 SCR 82 at 832–4, which sidesteps the issue altogether by characterizing the right in a narrow manner. This approach is briefly mentioned in *Delgamuukw* at paras. 170–1. But the reasoning in *Pamajewon* presumes that Aboriginal peoples would have to prove that they have such via the *Van der Peet* test on a case-by-case basis. This presumption is built on the unquestioned assumption of Crown sovereignty over Aboriginal peoples in s. 91(24). See Brad Morse, "Permafrost Rights: Aboriginal Self-Government and the Supreme Court in *R v. Pamajewon*," *McGill Law Journal* 42, no. 4 (1997): 1011–44; Patrick Macklem, *Indigenous Difference and the Constitution of Canada* (Toronto: University of Toronto Press, 2001) at 173–4; P.G. McHugh, *Aboriginal Societies and the Common Law: A History of Sovereignty, Status and Self-Determination* (Oxford: Oxford University Press, 2004) at 471–4; Kent McNeil, *Emerging Justice? Essays on Indigenous Rights in Canada and Australia* (Saskatoon, SK: Native Law Centre, 2001) at 82–95.

Laskin J continues to elaborate on his theory of federal jurisdiction on reserve lands. He maintains that reserves are "enclaves" that "are withdrawn from provincial regulatory power," but they are nonetheless subject to the plenary nature of federal jurisdiction, which includes the capacity to referentially incorporate provincial legislation.[91] Laskin J is clear that in his opinion "provincial regulatory legislation cannot, *ex proprio vigore*, apply to a Reserve."[92] Additionally, he views s. 88 of the *Indian Act* as being limited to the first branch of s. 91(24) ("Indians") as a result of its own wording.[93] This preserves the boundaries of the enclave, but what kind of enclave is a reserve? "The significance of the allocation of exclusive legislative power to Parliament in relation to Indian Reserves merits emphasis in terms of the kind of enclave that a Reserve is. It is a social and economic community unit, with its own political structure as well according to the prescriptions of the *Indian Act*. The underlying title (that is, upon surrender) may well be in the Province, but during its existence as such a Reserve, in my opinion, is no more subject to provincial legislation than is federal Crown property; and it is no more subject to provincial regulatory authority than is any other enterprise falling within exclusive federal competence."

A curious tension in his argument requires further consideration here. We are told that the exclusive nature of federal jurisdiction on reserve lands is related to the fact that a reserve "is a social and economic community unit, with its own political structure."[94] But again he maintains that this political structure is set according to "prescriptions of the *Indian Act*."[95] This point echoes the dissent of Hall J in *Calder* when he states that "the right to possession claimed is not prescriptive in origin because a prescriptive right presupposes a prior right in some other person or authority."[96] This same logic equally applies

91 *Cardinal* at 716.

92 Ibid. at 727.

93 It is helpful to consider the wording of this (deeply) complicated section. I will cite the version of s. 88 that Laskin J (as he was then) cited in *Cardinal* at 727, which was s. 88 of the *Indian Act*, RSC 1970, c. I-6: "Subject to the terms of any treaty and any other Act of the Parliament of Canada, all laws of general application from time to time in force in any province are applicable to and in respect of Indians in the province, except to the extent that such laws are inconsistent with this Act or any order, rule, regulation or by-law made thereunder, and except to the extent that such laws make provision for any matter for which provision is made by or under this Act." The current version was amended in 2012 but remains largely the same, except for the explicit inclusion of the *First Nations Fiscal Management Act*, SC 2005, c. 9. Laskin CJ (as he was then) continues this approach to s. 88 in *Natural Parents* at 763. Also Kerry Wilkins believes that Laskin J was correct on the lands issue and has persuasively argued this point in his excellent essay on Section 88 (see Wilkins, "'Still Crazy'" at 488–96).

94 Ibid.

95 Ibid.

96 *Calder* at 353.

to the question of Aboriginal self-government. By maintaining that the social, economic, and political structure of Aboriginal peoples living on reserve lands accord with the prescriptions of the *Indian Act*, Laskin J (with Hall and Spence JJ) seems to suggest that it is this accordance with the Act that excludes provincial legislation. While the reasoning here could provide some jurisdictional space for Aboriginal self-government, it also presupposes the bundled or thick version of Crown sovereignty. Put differently, it maintains the "broad view" of s. 91(24) but strictly holds it to federal jurisdiction on reserve lands. As he states, "The present case concerns the regulation and administration of the resources of land comprised in a Reserve, and I can conceive of nothing more integral to that land as such. If the federal power given by s. 91(24) does not preclude the application of such provincial legislation to Indian Reserves, the power will have lost the exclusiveness which is ordained by the Constitution."[97]

Laskin J is correct when he states that jurisdictional boundaries that surround Indian lands are integral to the meaningful regulation and administration of resources.[98] In effect, the enclave theory of jurisdiction over Indian lands provides a bright line for the limits of provincial jurisdiction. But what about the first branch of s. 91(24)?

It does not seem plausible that this would create an "enclave" around Aboriginal people that would shield them from the application of provincial laws when off reserve.[99] But subjecting them to the full operation of provincial laws ignores their distinct constitutional status. This means that the boundaries of provincial jurisdiction over the first branch of s. 91(24) will be much more difficult to practically determine. In 1976, Laskin (now the chief justice) addresses this problem in the *Natural Parents* case by introducing the concept of "Indianness" to refer to the core of federal jurisdiction that provincial legislation cannot touch. In this case, he argued that a provincial adoption law could not constitutionally apply of its own force to the adoption of a child with Indian status by non-Indians: "It could only embrace them if the operation of the Act did not deal with what was integral to that head of federal legislative power, there being no express federal legislation respecting adoption of Indians. It appears to me to be unquestionable that for the provincial *Adoption Act*

97 *Cardinal* at 717–18.

98 The absence of these jurisdictional boundaries has, at least to my mind, contributed to confusion concerning internal limitations within the case law on Aboriginal rights. By refusing to acknowledge territorial limitations within provincial jurisdiction, the Crown is able to either confine rights to food, social, and ceremonial purposes (which can easily fit within existing regulatory schemes) or grant a commercial level right while altering the infringement test to include the interests of the Canadian society as a whole, as in *Gladstone*, at paras. 73–5.

99 Ryder, "Demise and Rise" at 368.

to apply to the adoption of Indian children of registered Indians, who could be compelled thereunder to surrender them to adopting non-Indian parents, would be to touch 'Indianness,' to strike at a relationship integral to a matter outside of provincial competence."[100]

But it is clear that provincial legislation that does not touch "Indianness" could apply to native people:

> Such provincial legislation is of a different class than adoption legislation which would, if applicable as provincial legislation simpliciter, constitute a serious intrusion into the Indian family relationship. It is difficult to conceive what would be left of exclusive federal power in relation to Indians if such provincial legislation was held to apply to Indians. Certainly, if it was applicable because of its so-called general application, it would be equally applicable by expressly embracing Indians. Exclusive federal authority would then be limited to a registration system and to regulation of life on a reserve. The fallacy in the position of the respondents in this case and, indeed, in that of all the intervenors, including the Attorney General of Canada, is in the attribution of some special force or special effect to a provincial law by calling it a "provincial law of general application," as if this phrase was self-fulfilling if not also self-revealing. Nothing, however, accretes to provincial legislative power by the generalization of the language of provincial legislation if it does not constitutionally belong there.[101]

By drawing attention to the use of the phrase "provincial law of general application," Laskin CJ highlights a key concern with the concept of "Indianness": it subjects Aboriginal peoples to the "uncertain measure" of judicial discretion. The uncertain measure of "Indianness" may be a practical necessity beyond the limits of Indian lands, but if it is set as the standard for both branches of s. 91(24), then Aboriginal peoples are effectively surrounded by the presumption that "provincial law[s] of general application" apply.

This theory of enclaves is, at least potentially, useful, as it provides space for Aboriginal jurisdiction on Aboriginal lands, but this is dependent on the answer to the question that it leaves unanswered: what are the origins of and the limits to federal power in s. 91(24)?[102] The courts have been consistently silent on this. As Martland J expressed it in 1976 in his concurring decision

---

100 *Natural Parents* at 760–1.

101 Ibid. at 761.

102 Kerry Wilkins drew my attention to the fact that there are two senses to this "limits" question: what are the limits on the core of exclusive federal authority, and what are the limits to the federal capacity to legislate in relation to Indians? The first is the division-of-powers question that the Courts have engaged with thus far, whereas the second question has not been directly addressed. As Peter Hogg insightfully notes, Parliament has taken the

in *Natural Parents*, "The ambit of that authority is uncertain, in that it has not been positively defined by the Courts."[103] These words remain true today. We can only infer its limits via the case law that deals with the limits of provincial jurisdiction. On this front the enclave theory is rejected, and the concept of "Indianness" is extended to both branches of s. 91(24) in *Four B* and *Francis*.

D. The Uncertain Measure of Indianness

In 1979 the Court delivered its decision in the *Four B* case. The chief justice mounts yet another defence of his enclave theory in his dissenting judgment, but this time only one other justice follows (Ritchie). The majority (delivered by Beetz J) decides the case on the basis of the functional test from the *Stevedoring Reference*.[104] The focus of our attention will be on how the majority

---

"broad view" of its legislative competence under s. 91(24) (see Hogg, *Constitutional Law* at 618). I would add that the courts have done little to determine the limits of this view.

103 *Natural Parents* at 772. In *NIL/TU,O Child and Family Services Society v. BC Government and Service Employees' Union*, [2010] 2 SCR 696 at paras. 62–73, McLachlin CJ and Fish J attempt to delineate the scope of the core of s. 91(24). They only address the limits on the core of exclusive federal authority. They do not address the limits of federal capacity to legislate in relation to Indians. But even on this technical division-of-powers aspect of s. 91(24) they provide little more than a thin survey of the Court's previous statements on Indianness. On this basis, at para. 73 they find the conclusion that they were clearly looking for at the outset: "The scope of the core of s. 91(24) is admittedly narrow. That, however, is as it should be. A narrow test for when activities fall within the core of Indianness reserved to the federal government is consistent with the dominant tenor of jurisprudence since *Four B*, as well as the restrained approach to interjurisdictional immunity adopted by this Court in recent cases." The legal reasoning that supports this conclusion is, at best, unconvincing. In my view it is a shabby and threadbare stalking horse for their actual aim, viz. advancing the "dominant tide" of (so-called) co-operative federalism (the phrase "dominant tide" is Dickson CJ's from *OPSEU v. Ontario (AG)*, [1987] 2 SCR 2 at 17).

104 *In the matter of a reference as to the validity of the Industrial Relations and Disputes Investigation Act*, [1955] SCR 529. Cited in *Four B* at 1047. This test is based on a pith-and-substance approach, which maintains that in labour relations exclusive provincial jurisdiction is the rule. The exception, as Beetz J notes, "comprises, in the main, labour relations in undertakings, services and businesses which, having regard to the functional test of the nature of their operations and their normal activities, can be characterized as federal undertakings, services or businesses" (ibid. at 1045). This approach allows him to focus on the factual details of the business in the case (he is careful to distance it from the band council and present it as a private business) and put the fact that it is physically situated on reserve lands to the side. It is interesting to note that in *NIL/TU,O* and *Native Child*, the majority, by adopting this approach, felt able to avoid the "Indianness" question entirely (see *NIL/TU,O Child and Family Services Society v. BC Government and Service Employees' Union*, [2010] 2 SCR 696; and *Communications, Energy and Paperworkers Union of Canada v. Native Child and Family Services of Toronto*, [2010] 2 SCR 737). I would like to thank Kerry Wilkins for bringing this to my attention.

responds to the appellant's argument on the nature of exclusive federal jurisdiction under s. 91(24). Beetz J summarizes their position: "What is submitted on behalf of appellant is that the matter to be regulated in the case at bar is the civil rights of Indians on a reserve; that this matter falls under the exclusive legislative authority of Parliament to make laws relating to 'Indians and Lands reserved for the Indians' pursuant to s. 91.24 of the *British North America Act, 1867*; that provincial law is inapplicable to this matter even in the absence of relevant federal law."[105]

He continues this summary later: "Counsel for appellant has also stressed that the civil rights in issue are not only the civil rights of Indians, but Indian civil rights exercised on a reserve. The import of this submission, as I understand it, is that the exclusive character of federal jurisdiction is somehow reinforced because it is derived from two related heads of federal authority instead of one, federal authority over Indians and over Lands reserved for the Indians."[106]

His response to this line of reasoning is problematic and merits closer consideration. According to his understanding, the appellant is arguing that the exclusive nature of federal jurisdiction in s. 91(24) is reinforced as a result of the presence of two heads of power. This would, according to Beetz J, lead to the possibility that "provincial laws would not apply to Indians on reserves although they might apply to others."[107] He seems to suggest that the possibility that non-Indian citizens might be subject to federal laws when on reserve lands would be an unacceptable result. We can only assume that this would be so as a result of the risk of uncertainty or even that old common law bugbear, the legal vacuum. Yet it seems to be perfectly acceptable that the law would vary in this manner for Indians. This reading produces its own absurdity. It does so by avoiding the issue at the heart of the enclave theory from *Cardinal*: that the two heads of s. 91(24) require two distinct interpretive approaches. Without these approaches it is impossible to give meaning to the exclusive nature of federal jurisdiction *and* respect the distinct constitutional status of Aboriginal peoples. The possibility of Aboriginal jurisdiction on Aboriginal lands within a co-operative federal structure is simply non-cognizable (viz. the questions of who has legislative power and underlying title is foreclosed). Put differently, the interpretive approach he adopts begins with the unstated presumptions regarding the structure of federalism and the meaning of sovereignty, and these presumptions lead him to the result. Unsurprisingly Beetz J rejects the argument as an attempt to "revive the enclave theory of the reserves in a modified version" and then goes on to offer a rationale for his own interpretive approach:[108] "Section 91.24 of the *British North America Act, 1867* assigns jurisdiction to Parliament over two distinct subject

105 *Four B* at 1046.
106 Ibid. at 1049.
107 Ibid. at 1048.
108 Ibid. at 1049.

matters, Indians *and* Lands reserved for the Indians, not Indians *on* Lands reserved for the Indians. The power of Parliament to make laws in relation to Indians is the same whether Indians are on a reserve or off a reserve. It is not reinforced because it is exercised over Indians on a reserve any more than it is weakened because it is exercised over Indians off a reserve."[109]

While it may be true that the power of Parliament under s. 91(24) is the "same whether Indians are on a reserve or off a reserve," this reasoning does not determine the reach of valid provincial laws of general application. Nor does it necessarily require that the same standard be applied to both of the "two distinct subject matters." Instead it simply suggests that the power to make laws is the same, and so either we would have to imagine that provincial laws simply do not apply to Indians (regardless of whether or not they are on reserve lands), or that they are subject to concurrent jurisdiction that can be qualified in some cases. Despite a glaring absence of justification for this position, Beetz J confines the exclusive federal jurisdiction in s. 91(24) to "Indianness" (the standard Laskin CJ applied in *Natural Parents* to the first branch alone).[110] By doing so this "uncertain measure" is used to set the jurisdictional boundaries on both a federal category of person and their lands.

This leads us to ask where exactly are the limits of exclusive federal jurisdiction over Indians and the lands reserved for them. Beetz J clearly maintains that the labour relations of a private business on reserve lands cannot be considered to fit within this exception (even if both the employers and employees were all Indians[111]), but this does not tell us what kind of things would count. He does provide a few examples to help us determine the jurisdictional boundary: "registrability, membership in a band, the right to participate in the election of Chiefs and Band Councils, reserve privileges, etc."[112] It is telling that these examples are all clearly governed by the *Indian Act*. If we are to understand that these examples set the limit, it would seem that the measure of Indianness is set by Parliament alone (viz. curiously the core of the unhappy term *Indianness* or even less happy phrase *Indian qua Indian* is legislatively defined).[113] Beetz

109 Ibid. at 1049–50.

110 I do not mean to suggest that he does so in a way that closes the possibility of future inquiry into this branch. The Court has since examined (in less than unsatisfying ways) the nature of exclusive federal authority over "Lands reserved for Indians" in *Derrickson v. Derrickson*, [1986] 1 SCR 285; and *Delgamuukw*.

111 A possibility he addresses in *Four B* at 1047–8.

112 Ibid. at 1048.

113 I say "seem" as it is not strictly necessary to assume that these examples set the limit, or at least not a final or immovable limit. After all, the Court has tended to avoid limiting parliamentary legislative authority under s. 91(24). And even if we hold that these examples *do set the limit*, it could just be that Parliament just so happened to legislate within the precise confines of their legislative authority under s. 91(24). Finally, what I see as curious

J reinforces this suggestion when he leaves open the question of Parliament's ability to pass legislation that would regulate labour relations under s. 91(24).[114] He does so again when he holds that provincial laws apply "as long as such laws do not single out Indians nor purport to regulate them *qua* Indians, and as long also as they are not superseded by valid federal law."[115] If the positive content of Indianness is determined by federal law, then this is little more than a repetition of the doctrine of paramountcy.[116] By this reading Indians are subjected to the uncertainty of concurrent jurisdiction on both their legal status as Indians and their lands. And yet this accords with the approach that the courts have taken. As Ryder states, "The courts have been willing to see the legal status of an

---

about how Indianness or "Indian qua Indian" are being defined is that Aboriginal peoples do not define their legally significant difference within the Canadian constitutional order. The colonial picture of the constitutional order – which presumes at the outset that the Crown has unquestioned (and seemingly unquestionable) sovereignty, legislative power, and underlying title – can only see or recognize Aboriginal peoples as a sui generis species of legal subject. Aboriginal peoples cannot be seen as nations within (and founding partners of) the federal constitutional order, as this would necessarily entail that legislative power and underlying title were open questions and not components that could simply be bundled with Crown sovereignty.

114 *Four B*. It is worth considering Beetz J's words on this point: "I come to the conclusion that the power to regulate the labour relations in issue does not form an integral part of primary federal jurisdiction over Indians or Lands reserved for the Indians. Whether Parliament could regulate them in the exercise of its ancillary powers is a question we do not have to resolve any more than it is desirable to determine in the abstract the ultimate reach of potential federal paramountcy."

115 Ibid.

116 This means that if we reject the idea that Parliament can unilaterally determine the content of "Indianness" (viz. if we move to a constitutional order when Aboriginal peoples can, as self-governing *peoples*, define their own legally significant difference within the Canadian constitutional order), then IJI can play a helpful role in re-mapping jurisdictional lines of federalism as it would operate even in the absence of conflicting federal law to limit the application of valid provincial laws that "regulate them qua Indians." This somewhat limited precedence for the core of Indianness being something other than a creature of statute as in *Natural Parents*, Laskin CJ included Indian family relationships within the core of Indianness, even though there was (at the time) no federal legislation dealing with them (see *Natural Parents v. Superintendent of Child Welfare et al.*, [1976] 2 SCR 751 at 760–1. As Laskin CJ put it, "It appears to me to be unquestionable that for the provincial Adoption Act to apply to the adoption of Indian children of registered Indians, who could be compelled thereunder to surrender them to adopting non-Indian parents, would be to touch 'Indianness,' to strike at a relationship integral to a matter outside of provincial competence" (ibid.). This seems to be an example of judicial discretion to take notice of an obvious fact (i.e., family relationships must be included in the core of "Indianness") without a clear statutory basis. It is, admittedly, a small step from the definition of Indians under the *Indian Act*, but a potentially significant one for the future of IJI. This was subsequently cited by Beetz J with approval in *Bell Canada v. Quebec*, as did the majority in *Canadian Western Bank v. Alberta*, [2007] 2 SCR 3 at para. 61.

Indian created by federal government legislation as being a matter at the core of federal jurisdiction, while they have not been willing to so characterize cultural and economic aspects of First Nations peoples' lives."[117]

This leaves Aboriginal peoples subject to valid provincial laws of general application and the Court's "broad view" of the undefined federal powers of s. 91(24).[118] It is by this interpretation (or lack thereof) that Indians become little more than creatures of statute whose creator may withhold, grant, or withdraw their powers and privileges as it sees fit in its sovereign will. And so we must ask, again, where are the limits of exclusive federal jurisdiction over Indians and their lands? In *Francis,* La Forest J held that where there is federal legislation, the doctrine of paramountcy can tolerate concurrent jurisdiction in the absence of an express conflict[119] (especially in cases where the court sees the matter as being somewhat removed from the "Indian way of life," which seems to be a matter that is so blatantly obvious that it can be addressed by judicial notice alone).[120] But what about cases in which a provincial law of general application does affect

117 Ryder, "Demise and Rise" at 370. Since Ryder's article, the Court has touched on some cultural and economic aspects; for example, see *Kitkatla Band v. British Columbia (Minister of Small Business, Tourism and Culture)*, [2002] 2 SCR 146.

118 Noel Lyon, "Constitutional Issues in Native Law," in *Aboriginal Peoples and the Law: Indian, Metis and Inuit Rights in Canada*, ed. B.W. Morse, 408–51 (Ottawa: Carleton University Press, 1984).

119 See note 47 for how the courts have defined this standard. Also, pace La Forest J, we should remember that paramountcy assumes that the relevant federal and provincial laws have already been found to be valid. If either is found to be invalid, the question of paramountcy does not arise. This means that paramountcy doctrine does not tell us anything useful about when (or, really, whether) federal and provincial legislative authority are concurrent. I'd like to thank Kerry Wilkins for pointing this out to me.

120 *Francis*. A point he was quite certain of as he stated at para. 4: "In *Kruger v. The Queen*, [1978] 1 SCR 104, this Court held that general provincial legislation relating to hunting applies on reserves, a matter which is obviously far more closely related to the Indian way of life than driving motor vehicles." It is interesting to note that Beetz J assumed the contrary to reach the s. 88 issue in *Dick v. R,* [1985] 2 SCR 309. In this case hunting is found to be within the scope of Indianness and so the *Wildlife Act* could not apply *ex proprio vigore*. Nevertheless, Beetz J holds that the *Wildlife Act* is a law of general application and thus saved by s. 88 of the *Indian Act* because it was not obvious that "this particular impact has been intended by the provincial legislator" (para. 35). So according to this line of reasoning the only provincial legislation that s. 91(24) actually bars is what both impairs the status or capacity of Indianness and intentionally "singles out Indians for special treatment or discriminates against them" (ibid.). Intention is a notoriously slippery concept. A court relying on it as the determinative criterion for legislative interpretation brings to mind John Selden's quip about the Chancellor's foot. If the Court in *Dick* means that the standard for singling out Indians will be something like legislation that explicitly states "this law only applies to Indians," then it seems that the real target is not intent at all but a particular form of phrasing. After all, as any legislator knows, legal effects can be achieved without explicit wording.

Indians qua Indians? Surely this is where the exclusivity of s. 91(24) serves as a shield and protects the special constitutional status of Aboriginal peoples? The simple answer is, "not necessarily." At this point the courts still have to consider the possibility that the law can be referentially incorporated by s. 88 of the *Indian Act.*

E. Section 88 and Provincial Law

The interpretive approach that the Court has adopted on s. 91(24) of the *Constitution Act, 1867* means that provincial laws apply to Indians in two ways. First, they may apply directly and of their own force (*ex propio vigore*) as long as they do not infringe on exclusive federal jurisdiction (i.e., "Indianness" or Indians "*qua* Indians"); conflict with a valid federal law (via the "restrained" or modern approach to paramountcy); or be deemed by the court to be inconsistent with the purpose animating the relevant federal law (e.g., paramountcy can be triggered by what the Court has termed "operational conflict" or "incompatibility").[121] The second way is via s. 88, which operates to incorporate into federal law those provincial laws of general application that do affect "Indianness" or derogate from the "status and capacities" of Indians.[122] This theory of the meaning of s. 88 is the one that Beetz J set in place in *Dick v. R*, which we will turn to in more detail later. Prior to this, the courts had found it very difficult to determine the meaning of s. 88: was it a declaration of the limits on the application of provincial laws to Indians (a reiteration of the shielding effect of federal exclusivity) or an incorporation of provincial laws at the federal level to ensure that they will apply?

---

121 For the modern approach to the division of powers, see note 32. Beetz J touches on the second aspect of paramountcy in *Dick v. R*, *supra* note 57 at para. 43, when he says, "It would not be open to Parliament in my view to make the Indian Act paramount over provincial laws simply because the Indian Act occupied the field. Operational conflict would be required to this end." The Court puts this point more clearly in *Canadian Western Bank v. Alberta*, [2007] 2 SCR 3 at para. 69 when it states,

> According to the doctrine of federal paramountcy, when the operational effects of provincial legislation are incompatible with federal legislation, the federal legislation must prevail and the provincial legislation is rendered inoperative to the extent of the incompatibility. The doctrine applies not only to cases in which the provincial legislature has legislated pursuant to its ancillary power to trench on an area of federal jurisdiction, but also to situations in which the provincial legislature acts within its primary powers, and Parliament pursuant to its ancillary powers. This doctrine is much better suited to contemporary Canadian federalism than is the doctrine of interjurisdictional immunity.

122 *Dick v. R*, *supra* note 57 at 33.

In 1978 Dickson J (as he was then) decided the *Kruger* case and held that the phrase "laws of general application" in s. 88 would be determined by two *indicia*: that the law apply uniformly throughout the territory of the province, and that it not be "in relation to" one class of citizens in object and purpose.[123] He followed the approach that Martland and Ritchie JJ took in *Natural Parents,* which held the section to be little more than a declaration that provincial laws of general application apply to Indians, but laws that affect them "*qua* Indians" do not.[124] This approach is fairly consistent with the classical "watertight compartments" approach to federalism (as it retains some sense of federal exclusivity), but it also introduces confusion, as it requires that the closing words of the section – "except to the extent that such laws make provision for any matter for which provision is made by or under this Act" – be read as meaning that federal and provincial powers are concurrent, not exclusive.[125]

In 1985, in *Dick v. R*, the Court united behind a single approach.[126] It strictly narrowed the test for "laws of general application" by placing the onus on Aboriginal peoples to show that "the policy of such an Act was to impair the status and capacities of Indians"[127] and entirely reversed the approach taken in *Kruger* by holding that the purpose was to referentially incorporate laws that *do* affect Indians "*qua* Indians."[128] This approach may have resolved the problem concerning the meaning of the closing words, but it introduced another set of problems. First, there is no mention of lands in s. 88, and so either it is limited to the first branch of s. 91(24), or the term *Indians* must be understood as referring to both branches. This latter possibility has perverse implications, as it would mean that the laws s. 88 referentially incorporates would apply as federal law only to those whom the *Indian Act* deems to be Indians and not to others. This flies in the face of the established principle "that statutes relating to Aboriginal peoples are to be construed generously and liberally, and any

123 *Kruger* at 110. For the text of s. 88 see note 93.

124 Martland J is cited in *Kruger* at 117: "The extent to which provincial legislation could apply to Indians was stated to be that the legislation must be within the authority of s. 92 of the *British North America Act, 1867* and that the legislation must not be enacted in relation to Indians. Such legislation, generally applicable throughout the Province, could affect Indians." Dickson J also cites Ritchie J at 116–17: "In my view, when the Parliament of Canada passed the *Indian Act* it was concerned with the preservation of the special status of Indians and with their right to Indian lands, but it was made plain by s. 88 that Indians were to be governed by the *laws of* their Province of residence except to the extent that such laws are inconsistent with the *Indian Act* or relate to any matter for which provision is made under that Act."

125 Wilkins, "'Still Crazy.'"

126 In *Four B* the majority noted the two competing views of s. 88 but did not need to try to decide between them.

127 *Dick v. R, supra* note 57 at 31.

128 Ibid. at 33.

ambiguities resolved in their favour."[129] Second, while it saves the meaning of the closing words, it deprives the phrase "laws of general application" of meaning, as it is connected with the vague and unhappy judicial concept of "Indianness." Finally, there are the administrative implications, as the laws that s. 88 pertains to apply as federal law to Indians. This means, as Wilkins details, that "such measures, when applied to Indians, are subject, as a matter of course, to federal procedures, policies, priorities, and discretion but to provincial priorities and procedures when applied to anyone else."[130] There is no clear answer to the question of who is responsible for administering this system or even paying for it, and there is "room for doubt, in circumstances such as these, whether the federal order has constitutional authority to require that provinces assume the added financial and administrative burden of applying these hybrid measures beyond the permissible range of their application as provincial legislation."[131]

---

129 This phasing can be found in *Nowegijick v. R*, [1983] 1 SCR 29 at 36, and the Court cites *Jones v. Meehan*, 175 US 1 (1899). La Forest J (writing for the majority) in *Mitchell v. Peguis Indian Band*, [1990] 2 SCR 85 at 143 alters this principle when it applies to statutes, as he finds that

> somewhat different considerations must apply in the case of statutes relating to Indians. Whereas a treaty is the product of bargaining between two contracting parties, statutes relating to Indians are an expression of the will of Parliament. Given this fact, I do not find it particularly helpful to engage in speculation as to how Indians may be taken to understand a given provision. Rather, I think the approach must be to read the Act concerned with a view to elucidating what it was that Parliament wished to effect in enacting the particular section in question. This approach is not a jettisoning of the liberal interpretative method. As already stated, it is clear that in the interpretation of any statutory enactment dealing with Indians, and particularly the *Indian Act*, it is appropriate to interpret in a broad manner provisions that are aimed at maintaining Indian rights, and to interpret narrowly provisions aimed at limiting or abrogating them. Thus if legislation bears on treaty promises, the courts will always strain against adopting an interpretation that has the effect of negating commitments undertaken by the Crown. (*United States v. Powers*, 305 US 527 (1939) at para. 533)

While this may well not be "jettisoning" the liberal interpretive method, it is certainly an approach that necessarily grounds itself on the presumption of a colonial picture of the Canadian constitutional order. Placing weight on Parliament's intent presumes that Aboriginal peoples are simply and entirely under its legislative power, and this in turn rides on the assumption that the treaties are little more than a sui generis species of surrender documents. For an insightful engagement with these issues and others, see Kent McNeil, "Aboriginal Title and Section 88 of the Indian Act," *UBC Law Review* 34 (2000): 180.

130 Wilkins, "'Still Crazy.'"

131 Ibid. at 471. This suggests that the provinces could potentially use the doctrine of interjurisdictional immunity to shield themselves from the costs and administrative complications of s. 88.

What unites the declarative and referential incorporation theory is the conviction that s. 91(24) vests Parliament with the authority to unilaterally determine which laws do and do not apply to Indians and their lands, and the absolute silence on where this power was derived from. All we are left with is the repetition of Riddel J from 1917 assuring us that, although provincial legislatures cannot pass laws dealing with Indians, "there is no reason why general legislation may not affect them."[132] This "no reason why" depends entirely on how one sees the authority of Parliament over Indians and their lands. It is part of a picture of Canadian federalism that positions Aboriginal peoples as objects of a federal head of power and not founding partners. Furthermore, it is a picture that cannot account for how it came to be, yet it is repeated ad nauseum. Wilkins clearly articulates this lack of doubt: "No one doubts Parliament's legislative authority to do what s. 88, broadly speaking, does: incorporate certain provincial laws for the purpose of applying them to Indians. No one doubts, either, that Parliament also has a constitutional mandate to apply the incorporated laws to section 91(24) lands."[133]

While this is true, to the extent that it is consistent with how the courts have interpreted s. 91(24), it says nothing about how the Crown obtained this sovereignty over Aboriginal peoples (a key point, given the Court's recent claim that *terra nullius* never applied in Canada).[134] This is the point on which the Court consistently maintains that there is no room for doubt; so consistently in fact that it makes room for what it seeks to exclude. As Dickson CJC and La Forest J state, "There was from the outset never any doubt that sovereignty and legislative power, and indeed the underlying title, to such lands vested in the Crown."[135] This stated and restated lack of doubt has about the same sense as the phrase "There is nothing to see here," in that, it is more about the authority of the speaker than the literal meaning of the words themselves. Wittgenstein provides some insight into the possible origins of this picture of federalism; its "main cause" is "a one-sided diet: one nourishes one's thinking with only one kind of example."[136] The one example that nourishes the Court in this case is the unquestioned assumption of Crown sovereignty (a diet that flies in the face of the most basic principles of natural justice, which require that we listen to the other side and do not act as a judge in our own cause). This diet has yet to be

---

132 This statement first appears in *R v. Martin*. It is cited by Martland J in *Cardinal* at 706, and by Dickson J in *Kruger* at 111.

133 Wilkins, "'Still Crazy'" at 489–90.

134 *Tsilhqot'in Nation supra* notes 40 and 62 at para. 69.

135 *Sparrow* at 1103. We can see this in Judson J's words from *Calder* (who is citing the words of Lord Watson from *St Catherine's Milling*): "There can be no question that this right was 'dependent on the goodwill of the Sovereign'" (*Calder* at 328).

136 Wittgenstein, *Philosophical Investigations* at §593.

balanced by the Aboriginal perspective, as it has been confined to the vagaries of the common law rules of evidence, which are always subject to the tin ear of the judiciary.[137] Given the foundational implications for both the meaning of federalism and the special constitutional status of Aboriginal peoples, we would imagine that the legislative process that introduced this section would assist us in determining its meaning. We turn to this now.

THE ORIGINS OF S. 88

The section was first introduced in 1950 as s. 87 of Bill 267, *An Act Respecting Indians* (the term *respecting* being confined to its unilateral sense of "referring to").[138] The bill itself gave rise to considerable opposition from the public and within Parliament. It was the first major revision of federal Indian law in seventy years, and it was done without consulting Indian leaders (a point of key importance, as Indians did not have the right to vote in Canada until 1960).[139] The government of the time responded by withdrawing the bill and revising it. It was introduced in 1951 as Bill 79, and while there were a number of changes, s. 87 remained the same.[140] The current version of the section reads, "Subject to the terms of any treaty and any other Act of Parliament, all laws of general

137 See part 2, n 92.

138 d Sess., 21st Parl., 1950. This is cited by Wilkins, "'Still Crazy'" at 459. He provides an excellent overview of the legislative history of this provision and a detailed analysis of its implications. As I noted in part 3, there is an earlier precedent for s. 88. The *Indian Act*, SC 1936, c. 20, s. 2 enabled the superintendent-general to apply existing provincial laws to reserves by incorporating them by reference.

139 The deliberations that lead up to the legislative changes in 1951 included the role that the provinces had to play in the process of assimilation. As Wilkins states, "The other clearly relevant theme that emerged from those deliberations was the growing federal conviction, identified most clearly in the 1948 report, that the provinces had a role to play in achieving the recognized long-term goal of assimilation – or, in a later idiom, 'integration' – of the Indian peoples into mainstream society." Wilkins, "'Still Crazy'" at 463. Section 88 was, at a minimum, consistent with that conviction.

140 Bill 79, *An Act Respecting Indians*, 4th Sess., 21st Parl., 1951. The section was altered in 2005 and again in 2012, but these changes were simply to add the *First Nations Fiscal and Statistical Management Act* (in 2005), which was changed to *First Nations Fiscal Management Act* in 2012 (it was passed as s. 678 in an omnibus bill entitled the *Jobs, Growth and Long-Term Prosperity Act*, SC 2012, c. 19). Curiously the 2005 amendments also substituted "Act of Parliament" for "Act of the Parliament of Canada" in the opening clause. It is also interesting to note that the United States Congress enacted a very similar law (Public Law 280) in 1953. This law enabled states to assume criminal and civil jurisdiction in matters involving Indians as litigants on reserve lands. Prior to its enactment these issues were dealt with in either tribal or federal court. For more on this and the problems it raises for the place of Aboriginal self-government in US federalism, see Kyle S. Conway "Inherently or Exclusively Federal: Constitutional Preemption and the Relationship between Public Law 280 and Federalism," *Journal of Constitutional Law* 15, no. 5 (2013): 1323–72.

application from time to time in force in any province are applicable to and in respect of Indians in the province, except to the extent that those laws are inconsistent with this Act or the *First Nations Fiscal Management Act*, or with any order, rule, regulation or law of a band made under those Acts, and except to the extent that those provincial laws make provision for any matter for which provision is made by or under those Acts."[141]

While it is possible to simply accept this as validly enacted law and move towards its interpretation by the courts, we should pause here and consider its practical implications. This is a statutory provision in a federal law that states that provincial law applies (as federal law) to a class of subjects that the constitution assigns exclusively to federal legislative authority. This alone is, or should be, shocking. Wilkins notes that, to the best of his knowledge, "s. 88 was unprecedented" and that he knows of no other statutory provision in federal law that acts in this way.[142] It seems to be little more than a technological shortcut that allows the "*unilateral federal* imposition of provincial legislative regimes on Indians."[143] But beyond that, what does it say about the meaning of s. 91(24)? It requires the "broad view" that this provision grants Parliament sovereignty *over* Indians and their lands and, as we have noted, the *historical warrant* of this authority can have no other basis than *terra nullius* and discovery. How else can a law that they were neither consulted on, nor consented to, be used to delegate authority to the provinces to infringe on Aboriginal rights?[144] It

141 *Indian Act*. Note that the wording of the section explicitly excludes treaties from the referential incorporation it sets in place and does not mention lands (i.e., the second branch of s. 91(24)). For more on the question of application to lands, see Wilkins, "'Still Crazy'" at 483–97.

142 Wilkins, "'Still Crazy'" at 460.

143 Ibid. at 464 (emphasis in original). The distinction between legislating a general rule of referential incorporation and the long-standing prohibition on inter-delegation is a so fine as to be practically undeterminable. In *McEvoy v. New Brunswick (AG)*, [1983] 1 SCR 704 at 720 the Court held that "Parliament can no more give away federal constitutional powers than a province can usurp them." (See also *Nova Scotia (AG) v. Canada (AG)* at 34, 54, and 58). It seems odd that, despite this, Parliament can make a general rule that referentially incorporates provincial laws. The only distinction between this and delegation is that provincial legislatures are restricted to passing valid laws (i.e., they cannot pass laws that single out Indians or the lands reserved for them), but this limitation can be negated by creative legislative drafting (let alone by the fact that "Indianness" is a vague concept).

144 Kerry Wilkins notes that there was a conference with selected Indigenous leaders about Bill 79 on 28 February 28 to 3 March 1951. Section 87 (as it then was) received very brief attention at the conference. This means that there was at least some semblance of consultation about the bill, or the provision. See Wilkins, "'Still Crazy.'" As I see it, this concern with the "semblance of consultation" betrays an awareness of a crisis of legitimacy in the Crown's constitutional relationship with Aboriginal peoples. It is as if the Crown (and here I mean its varied, multiform, and often conflicting collection of actors and institutions) operates under the presumption that it has sovereignty, legislative power, and underlying

seems to be designed to practically nullify the very possibility of Aboriginal self-government (or, perhaps more accurately, constructed within a picture of Canadian constitutionalism whose background assumptions conceptually excluded Aboriginal self-government). Borrows provides us with an invaluable critique of the effect of s. 88, which we will consider at length:

> Section 88 of the *Indian Act* drastically constrains jurisdictional spaces which should be filled by Indigenous sovereignty. It does so by delegating vast fields of political activity to provincial governments by referentially incorporating, as federal law, provincial laws of general application. This severely limits First Nations' political power in Canada. It also creates very few incentives for the federal government to work with First Nations and pass legislation recognizing and affirming Aboriginal and treaty rights throughout the country.... The federal government's "transfer" of legislative responsibility from itself and First Nations to provincial governments is a significant reason why Canada lags behind the United States in developing politically healthier Indigenous communities. This is a national tragedy. Section 88 does not enhance self-determination by making provincial laws applicable to "Indians." At a federal level, this allows the federal government to almost completely abandon its section 91(24) constitutional responsibility concerning "Indians and lands reserved for Indians." By "passing the buck" to the provinces the federal government does not face the consequences of its delegation of authority to the provinces. First Nations must comply with provincial laws which they have no real role in crafting or administering. In fact, if provinces were to "single out" Indians in the passage of provincial legislation such action would be *ultra vires*, or unconstitutional, because acting in relation to Indians is beyond provincial authority. Thus, section 88 of the *Indian Act* removes incentives from both the provincial and federal governments to work with Indians on the detail of laws which most effect Indian peoples' lives. The "idea" of assimilation built into the *Indian Act* and other Canadian legislative action usurps First Nations' authority. The *Indian Act* essentializes Canada's treatment of Indigenous peoples in Canada and subjects them to a false "form" of organization, subordinate to other governments in the land.[145]

This provides us with a clear and sustained view of the impact that s. 88 has on Aboriginal peoples. It is part of the Crown machinery that continues to animate the "vast administrative dictatorship which governs every detail

title, but when it moves to exercise this unilateral power-over Aboriginal peoples it attempts to buffer its actions by adding a veneer of consent. But the effect of these practices is not to buffer at all. Rather, it simply indicates an awareness of a crisis of legitimacy (the common law phrase "honour in the breach" captures what I am attempting to point to here).

145 Borrows, *Freedom and Indigenous Constitutionalism* at 167–8.

of Aboriginal life."[146] And at its basis is the spectre of the *doctrine of discovery*, which remains firmly in place with the undoubted and undetermined power of s. 91(24). The courts have doubled the effect of this power *over* Aboriginal peoples by adopting the modern approach to federalism and reading down the meaning of *exclusive* in the *Constitution Act, 1867*. This has left them and their lands subject to a confusing labyrinth of concurrent jurisdiction whose last remaining openings are closed off by allowing generally worded provincial legislation that regulates Indians qua Indians to be referentially incorporated under s.88. This interpretive approach has confined exclusive federal jurisdiction to the "uncertain measure" of "Indianness."

We have seen the confusion that this has generated via our considerations of the doctrine of interjurisdictional immunity and s. 88, but it does not stop here. This picture is further complicated by the fact that the determination of *who Indians are* has been subject to continual contestation and resistance. It is puzzling how the courts are to begin to define what Indians qua Indians means, when the definition in the *Indian Act* (which Beetz J used in *Dick v. R* as the example of the kind of "Indianness" that resides under the exclusive jurisdiction of the federal government) does not cover all of those whom the courts have included in the ambit of the authority of s. 91(24). This draws us to ask a series of related questions. Who has been placed within this ambit? How were they placed there? How does this determine how they are governed? It is this line of questioning that brings us to the next section of the chapter.

4.2 The Definition of Indians and the Authority of Bands

This section reviews how the courts have dealt with the definition of Indians and the authority of bands in s. 91(24) and the *Indian Act*. This is directly connected to the preceding discussion of the interpretation of s. 91(24), as it concerns who resides within the ambit of that authority and what kind of political structure can exist there. Simply put, if the Court's interpretation of s. 91(24) provides us with a picture of federalism, then the question of who Indians are and what form of political structure governs them determines their place within this picture. This, in turn, helps us to see what form of legal justification could possibly support such a picture. As Tully so clearly reminds us, "If the Constitution does not rest on the consent of the people or their representatives, or if there is not a procedure by which it can be so amended, then they are neither self-governing nor self-determining but are governed and determined by a structure of laws that is imposed on them. They are unfree. This is the principle

146 Tully, *Strange Multiplicity* at 90–1.

of popular sovereignty by which modern peoples and governments are said to be free and legitimate."[147]

Our investigation into the judicial interpretation of the definition of Indians and the structure and authority of bands will require a brief overview of the legislation from 1850 to the first version of the Indian Act in 1876 and its revision in 1880. This legislation provides the backdrop for case law that follows. Following the overview, I will first turn to the judicial interpretation of the definition of *Indians* from the 1939 *Eskimo Reference* through to *Lavell*, the United Nations Human Rights Committee finding in *Lovelace v. Canada* 1981, the legislative changes to registration in the 1985 revision of the *Indian Act, McIvor, Descheneaux*, and the recent *Daniels* case and then, to the authority of band councils.[148]

A. Legislative Origins

The process of unilaterally defining who Indians are via legislation began prior to Confederation. It was a part of the systemic changes that were taking place between the colonial legislatures and the imperial Parliament during the mid-nineteenth century (i.e., it is part of the devolution of powers to the dominion that would ultimately be expressed in the *British North America Act, 1867*). The imperial Parliament had retained sole responsibility for maintaining their relationship with Aboriginal peoples until 1860. This is when the legislative assembly of the province of Canada passed the *Indian Lands Act*, which vested control over Indian affairs in the province.[149] But the first specific legislation

147 Tully, *Public Philosophy in a New Key* at 1:286.

148 *Reference whether "Indians" includes "Eskimo,"* [1939] SCR 104 [hereinafter *Eskimo Reference*]; *Lovelace*; *Lavell*; *McIvor v. Canada (Registrar of Indian and Northern Affairs)*, [2009] BCCA 153; *Daniels v. Canada*, 2013 FC 6 [hereinafter *Daniels I*]; *Canada (Indian Affairs) v. Daniels*, [2014] FCA 101 [hereinafter *Daniels II*]; *Daniels v. Canada (Indian Affairs and Northern Development)*, [2016] 1 SCR 99; *Descheneaux c. Canada (Procureur Général)*, 2015 QCCS 3555.

149 Victoria (1860), c. 151, s. 1. "From and after the 1st day of July next, the Commissioner of Crown Lands, for the time being, shall be Chief Superintendent of Indian Affairs." This process of devolution was influenced by the adoption of regional approaches to Indian administration by the Colonial Office in London, which was formalized in the 1840s and 1850s. Broadly speaking, this regional approach translated into a policy of "insulating" Indians from settlers in the Maritimes, whereas in Upper and Lower Canada it was "amalgamating," and in Rupert's Land and the Northwest it was providing support for Hudson's Bay Company policy (see Giokas, "Indian Act" at 22). In the Maritime colonies the process of devolution was underway by the 1840s. This is evidenced most clearly by the New Brunswick, Nova Scotia, and Prince Edward Island *Indian Acts* of the 1840s and 1850s, but also in the earlier transfer of power over Crown lands (which was considered to include Indian reserve lands). These acts are a useful point of reference, as they highlight

aimed at defining who Indians are was passed in 1850. The Act dealt with the protection of lands and property of Indians in Lower Canada (now Quebec), and s. 5 defined the people it was intended to cover:

> Be it declared and enacted: That the following classes of persons are and shall be considered as Indians belonging to the Tribe or Body of Indians interested in such lands:
>
> First. All persons of Indian blood, reputed to belong to the particular Body or Tribe of Indians interested in such lands, and their descendants.
> Secondly. All persons intermarried with any such Indians and residing amongst them, and the descendants of all such persons.
> Thirdly. All persons residing among such Indians, whose parents on either side were or are Indians of such Body or Tribe, or entitled to be considered as such: And
> Fourthly. All persons adopted in infancy by any such Indians, and residing in the Village or upon the lands of such Tribe or Body of Indians, and their descendants.[150]

---

the colonial legislatures' perspective on the Indian Question. The preamble to the New Brunswick *Indian Act* of 1844 provides a clear indication of this perspective: "Whereas the extensive Tracts of valuable Land reserved for the Indians in various parts of this Province tend to greatly retard the settlement of the Country, while large portions of them are not, in their present neglected state, productive of any benefit to the people, for whose use they were reserved: And whereas it is desirable that these Lands should be put upon such footing as to render them not only beneficial to the Indians but conducive to the settlement of the Country" (see *An Act to regulate the management and disposal of Indian Reserves in this Province* 7 Victoria (1844), c. 47). The focus on the "valuable" tracts of underutilized lands (with its heavy Lockean overtones) followed by the protective (and paternalistic) pretext of guardianship is by no means unique, but it does provide us with a snapshot of the interests of the local settler governments. The upshot is that legislative authority over Indians was already with the colonial legislatures, and they were focused on the acquisition of reserve lands. Laws dealing with Indians required imperial approval, but this was true of all laws, and that approval was never withheld. What this seems to mean is that the colonial legislatures were being permitted to exercise the legislative authority of the imperial Parliament without any formal delegation. If correct, this would account for the curious fact that these powers were formally delegated to the dominion at Confederation with s. 91(24). I would like to thank Robert Hamilton for turning my attention to these important precursors to the *Indian Lands Act*. For a more detailed analysis of this legislation, see Hamilton, "'They Promised to Leave Us Some of Our Land'"; and Hamilton, "After Tsilhqot'in Nation."

150 and 14 Vict. (1850), c. 42; *An Act for the Better Protection of the Lands and Property of the Indians in Lower Canada*. In the same year the provincial legislature passed *An Act for the Protection of Indians in Upper Canada from Imposition, and the Property Occupied or Enjoyed by them from Trespass and Injury* (13 and 14 Vict. (1850), c. 74 (Province of

This unilateral determination is targeted directly at the connection between Indians and their lands. It places a set of restrictions on who can qualify as an Indian. The qualifications are broad, as they encompass marriage, adoption, and blood relation (a status that can be imputed to an individual). The expressed purpose of this cordon is to protect their lands and property, but it is curious that the best way of doing this is by removing their capacity to determine their own membership (beyond the narrow limits of discretion afforded by marriage and adoption, which were later removed by legislation). It seems to me that this is *the key step* in the construction of what I have termed the Crown machinery. This move to unilaterally define Aboriginal peoples and place "protective" limits on who can occupy their lands is a distinct shift from the nation-to-nation relationship that had characterized the imperial federal practices; it places them in a ward–guardian relationship to the settler-state. It has obvious practical utility from this perspective, as it provides a legal mechanism by which Aboriginal peoples can be separated from the body politic of the settler-citizens as a determinable and thus governable population (a necessary step in the deployment of the civilizing process of Mill's liberal-imperialism).[151] From this point forward an externally imposed administrative language of blood and descent will be used to set the boundaries of Indian lands.

This connection between blood and land must not be confused with the familiar logic of determining citizenship by the *jus sanguinis* or *jus soli*. As soon as Aboriginal peoples are legislatively defined by a government that they

---

Canada)). Interestingly this Act does not define who Indians are but simply states that it is for "Indians and persons intermarried with Indians."

151 I specify "practical utility" here so as to focus attention on the everyday effects of these legal mechanisms. I am avoiding venturing into the attribution of "intent," as this is where the waters are quickly muddied by the self-proclaimed moral goals of the actors involved. The question of intent draws us into the endless cacophony of explanation, justification, and excuse that permeates the history of the colonial and imperial projects of the Western European powers. While this is indeed fertile territory for investigation (viz. it exposes aspects of what Charles Taylor helpfully terms the "social imaginary" of the actors involved). But my aim here is to shed a cold light on a set of mechanisms and structures that actually did things in the world. Not to see it "objectively" but to see an aspect (or set of aspects) of these mechanisms and structures that is all too readily obscured by the (shallow) reassurance of the "good intentions" of those who fashioned them. The appeal to "good intentions" has always puzzled me. It seems to work to (magically) remove the moral blame from everyone involved in the settler-colonial system, both past and present. Those in the past were simply living their lives in accordance with a world view that positioned their actions as moral and those in the present point to the (now obvious) flaws of this world view and, in doing so, hold this observation up as evidence of moral progress. The cure-all character of this particular (pseudo-)historical explanation should be enough to raise suspicion that perhaps the wrongs of the past require investigations that go beyond "good intentions."

did not participate in or consent to, they become subjects who have been deprived of the right to determine who they are. In and through the process of legislative definition and the imposition of a register to administer status, the meaning of blood *fundamentally changes*. It is no longer a chosen sign of membership. Its significance is assigned and regulated externally. This is how Indian blood becomes the bond that, at one and the same time, connects them to their lands and divides them from the body politic of settler-citizens (as well as creating divisions within Aboriginal communities between the members who have status and those who do not). This bond between blood and soil is set in place by the settler-state so that it can be severed. By controlling the definition of the term *Indians*, the settler-state could continue to unilaterally narrow its boundaries and move towards its ultimate goal of removing the burden of Indian blood from the radical title to their lands once and for all. It is part of the legislative and administrative extirpation of the Indian (i.e., enfranchisement). In this process the settler-state takes the place of a fiduciary that can (paradoxically) infringe upon and extinguish the class of beneficiaries at will. This process of narrowing the definition starts less than a year after first definition.

In 1851 the provincial legislature passed an Act repealing the 1850 definition of Indians[152] and replaced it with the following:

> The following persons and classes of persons, and none other, shall be considered as Indians belonging to the Tribe or Body of Indians interested in any such lands or immoveable property:
>
> Firstly. All persons of Indian blood, reputed to belong to the particular Tribe or Body of Indians interested in such lands or immoveable property, and their descendants:
>
> Secondly. All persons residing among such Indians, whose parents were or are, or either of them was or is, descended on either side from Indians, or an Indian reputed to belong to the particular Tribe or Body of Indians interested in such lands or immoveable property, and the descendants of all such persons: And
>
> Thirdly. All women, now or hereafter to be lawfully married to any of the persons included in the several classes hereinbefore designated; the children issue of such marriages, and their descendants.[153]

152 Vict. (1850), c. 74. *An Act for the protection of the Indians in Upper Canada from imposition, and the property occupied or enjoyed by them from trespass and injury*. This Act does not strictly define the term *Indians* (one could assume it was taken as obvious). But there is a minimal definition of sorts, as the effects of the Act itself are directed at a class of subjects referred to by the phrase "Indians or persons inter-married with Indians."

153 and 15 Vict. (1851), c. 59.

This change in the definition removed the sole mechanism for Aboriginal peoples to determine their own membership (adoption). It also applies a patrilineal model that excludes non-Indian men who married Indian women, but includes non-Indian women who marry Indian men.

The definition is narrowed again in 1857 when the province of Canada passed the *Gradual Civilization Act*.[154] This purpose of this Act is clearly set out in its preamble: "Whereas it is desirable to encourage the progress of Civilization among the Indian Tribes in this Province, and the gradual removal of all legal distinction between them and Her Majesty's other Canadian Subjects, and to facilitate the acquisition of property and of the rights accompanying it, by such Individual Members of the said Tribes as shall be found to desire such encouragement and to have deserved it."[155]

This purpose is then applied to the target population, which is detailed in s. 1:

> Shall apply only to Indians or persons of Indian blood or intermarried with Indians, who shall be acknowledged as members of Indian Tribes or Bands residing upon lands which have never been surrendered to the Crown (or which having been so surrendered have been set apart or shall then be reserved for the use of any Tribe or Band of Indians in common) and who shall themselves reside upon such lands, and shall not have been exempted from the operation of the said section, under the provisions of this Act; and such persons and such persons only shall be deemed Indians within the meaning of any provision of the said Act or of any other Act or Law in force in any part of this Province by which any legal distinction is made between the rights and liabilities of Indians and those of Her Majesty's other Canadian subjects.[156]

The phrases "removal of all legal distinction" and "facilitate the acquisition of property" betray the true purpose of this legislation. It is part of a basic bait-and-switch tactic that holds out the promise of legal citizenship (i.e., as citizens they will now be able to purchase the lands they once only "occupied") and by choosing it the Indians disappear along with their claim to their lands.[157] The actual purpose of this Act – and indeed of all Indian law issued from the settler-state – is clearly expressed in the phrase "to facilitate the acquisition of

154 Vict. (1857), c. 26. *An Act to Encourage the Gradual Civilization of the Indian Tribes in this Province, and to Amend the Laws respecting Indians* [hereinafter the *Gradual Civilization Act*].

155 Ibid.

156 Ibid. It is interesting to note that the *Gradual Civilization Act* uses the broader definition of Indians from the 1850 legislation (i.e., "Indians or persons of Indian blood or intermarried with Indians") and not the exclusive patrilineal 1851 definition. The patrilineal 1851 definition returns in 1869 in s. 6 of the *Gradual Enfranchisement Act*.

157 It is hardly surprising that only one Indian was enfranchised between 1857 and the enactment of the first Indian Act in 1876. It should also be noted that Aboriginal peoples protested the *Gradual Civilization Act* and petitioned for its repeal. See Giokas, "Indian Act."

property." With this Act the definition of *Indians* is now set as a term within a larger system whose explicit purpose is to eliminate all legal distinctions within the body politic and thereby unburden the Crown's claim to radical title to all lands. It also makes clear that the relationship between the settler-state and Indians is strictly unilateral: not only are Indians defined by the settler-state, but those Indians who express the desire to be enfranchised must be deemed to "deserve" it (an expression of the role of morals in the process of civilizing the Indian, which is so clearly articulated in the regulation of alcohol).

In 1868 the Senate and House of Commons of Canada enacted legislation that made the definition set out by the provincial legislature in 1851 national policy.[158] This was quickly followed by the passage of the *Gradual Enfranchisement Act* in 1869. This Act marked a substantial set of changes to Indian policy.

1 It provided (for the first time) that any Indian woman who married a non-Indian man would lose Indian status and band membership (as would any children of that marriage).[159]
2 It placed a blood quantum qualification (i.e., "no person of less than one-fourth Indian blood") on the division of annuity money. This is the only time in Canadian history that blood quantum has been explicitly used.[160]
3 It established the band council system as an attempt to prepare Indians for "responsible government."

The law was designed to establish a set of "simple municipal institutions" that would be entirely subject to the discretion of the governor in council.[161] This was the first time that the settler-state extended its legislative intrusion beyond land-holding patterns to the legal and political systems of Aboriginal peoples. It was purposively designed to break the resistance of the existing Aboriginal governments by replacing them with a set of dependent band councils, which were designed to be little more than temporary placeholders in the larger process of assimilation referred to as "enfranchisement."[162] Like the introduction of Indian status, the introduction of the band council system imposes an artificial

158 *Act providing for the organisation of the Department of the Secretary of State of Canada, and for the management of Indian and Ordinance Lands*, SC 1868, c. 42, s. 15.

159 Ibid., s. 6. The Act contains a set of provisions that directly target and systematically disempower Indian women (e.g., preventing them from voting in band council elections and allowing enfranchised men to draw up wills regarding his land that favour his children, but not his wife).

160 Ibid., s. 4; Giokas, "Indian Act" at 34.

161 *Annual Report of the Indian Branch of the Department of the Secretary of State for the Provinces*. Canada, *Sessional Papers*, No. 23 (1871) at 4. Cited in Giokas, "Indian Act" at 33.

162 Giokas, "Indian Act" at 35. See also *Report of the Royal Commission on Aboriginal Peoples*, vol. 1, *Looking Forward Looking Back*, part 2, *False Assumptions and a Failed Relationship*

set of legal and political structures, which fail to recognize the "Nations and Tribes" that the *Proclamation* refers to and continue the Crown's despotic rule over Aboriginal peoples.

As we have seen, this legislative definition of Indians shifts from its introduction in 1850 to its ultimate incorporation (via the consolidation of previous Indian legislation) into the first *Indian Act* in 1876.[163] The term *Indian* is defined as:

> *First*. Any male person of Indian blood reputed to belong to a particular band;
> *Secondly*. Any child of such person;
> *Thirdly*. Any woman who is or was lawfully married to such person.[164]

This definition – which remained in place until 1951 – explicitly determines the inheritability of status by imposing a patrilineal model (introduced in 1851) and placing the legal qualification on marriage. This gives colonial officials the ability to determine what would constitute a legitimate form of marriage (i.e., to impose their own cultural norms as law) and exclude the children of unions they would not recognize as illegitimate children.[165]

According to John Milloy, the first versions of *Indian Act* in 1876 and 1880 built upon the "political formula of 1869" to effectively ensure "that Indians would lose control of every aspect of their corporate existence."[166] The annual report of the Department of the Interior in 1876 clearly expressed this formula:

> Our Indian legislation generally rests on the principle, that the aborigines are to be kept in a condition of tutelage and treated as wards or children of the State … the true interests of the aborigines and of the State alike require that every effort should be made to aid the Red man in lifting himself out of his condition of tutelage and dependence, and that is clearly our wisdom and our duty, through education and

---

(Ottawa: Canada Communication Group, 1996) at 237, 240, and 253 [hereinafter *RCAP* 1:2].

163 SC 1879, c. 34 at s. 4(3). This Act divides bands into two categories: regular and irregular. The distinction is meant to *encourage* groups that have not adopted the band council system or initiated the treaty process to do so (the encouragement being the legal disadvantages placed on irregular bands and "non-treaty Indians"). For more on this distinction in the *Indian Acts* of 1876 and 1880, see Giokas, "Indian Act" at 36–40.

164 SC 1876, c. 18 at s. 3(3).

165 Ibid. at s. 3(3)(a) to 3(3)(e). It is also interesting to note that "half-breeds" (a term that the Act leaves undefined) are formally excluded, and the s. 3(3)(b) allows for the exclusion of Indians who are residing in another country for a continuous period of five years (limiting the mobility of Aboriginal groups whose traditional territories straddle the border with the United States).

166 Milloy, "Early Indian Acts" at 151.

> every other means, to prepare him for a higher civilization by encouraging him to assume the privileges and responsibilities of full citizenship.[167]

The *Indian Act* collected together the protective features of the previous legislation and clarified them; fashioning, testing, calibrating, and recalibrating the legal components required for administering the civilizing of Indians. The 1880 Act made a number of advancements down this line. The Act replaced the Indian Branch of the Department of the Interior with the Department of Indian Affairs.[168] It centralized the control over Indian monies by removing this control from the band councils and placing it in the hands of the governor in council.[169] Another example can be found in the provisions against trespassing, which made it so that no one other than an "Indian of the band" could reside on reserve lands without obtaining a licence from the superintendent general (a provision that combined with the "marrying-out" rule so that Indian women who married either a non-Indian or an Indian from another band were effectively exiled).[170] Through its legislated control over Indian status, Indian legal and political structures, land-holding patterns, and resources, it presents us with the first fully functional version of the Crown machinery. This version of the machine remains essentially the same – despite the ad hoc process of amendment that helps recalibrate it in relation to the continuous resistance of Aboriginal peoples – until it is substantially overhauled in 1951. It is interesting to note that the net effect of the 1951 overhaul was actually to return Canadian Indian legislation to its original 1876 form.[171] It seems that when it comes to the Indian Question in Canada, the more things change, the more they remain the same. In any case, one key event leading up to this overhaul occurred in 1939 when the Supreme Court delivered its decision in the *Eskimo Reference*. This decision introduces a distinction between the definition of Indians in s. 91(24) and the *Indian Act* whose significance the courts are still struggling to come to terms with.

B. The Judicial Definition of Indians

In the *Eskimo Reference* the Court was asked to determine whether Inuit in Quebec were under federal or provincial jurisdiction. The federal government did not want to assume responsibility, and so it argued that the term *Indians* in s. 91(24) should be read in light of the *Royal Proclamation of 1763*. It argued

167 Department of the Interior, *Annual Report for the year that ended 30th June, 1876* (Parliament, *Sessional Papers*, no. 11, 1877) at xiv. Cited in *RCAP* 1:2 at 255.

168 SC 1880, c. 28 at s. 74(7).

169 Ibid. at ss. 70, 71.

170 Milloy, *Historical Overview* at 11–12.

171 *RCAP* 1:2 at 285.

that the Inuit were not covered in the *Proclamation* for two reasons: first, the terms *nation* and *tribe* are not employed in relation to them; and second, they were never "connected" to or "under the protection" of the imperial Crown.[172] The Court rejected both arguments. It adopted an originalist interpretive approach to determining the meaning of the term and found that "the *British North America Act*, in so far as it deals with the subject of Indians, must, in my opinion, be taken to contemplate the Indians of *British North America* as a whole."[173] The problem with the decision is less the finding itself than the way it arrives at it. By anchoring the meaning of the term *Indians* in its historical context, the Court reinforces the "broad view" of s. 91(24), which grants the federal government an undetermined ambit of power *over* "the Indians of *British North America* as a whole." The practical outcome was limited because Parliament has no obligation to legislate to the full limits of its authority. As a result, the Inuit became Indians for the purposes of s. 91(24), but not as defined within the *Indian Act*. This placed them under the ambit of "exclusive" federal jurisdiction. But as we have seen, the case law has restricted that ambit of legislative authority over the Indians qua Indians (a term whose meaning is unilaterally determined by the courts and most often drawn from the *Indian Act*).

The next series of challenges to the definition of *Indians* begins with the *Lavell* case in 1974.[174] This case followed on the seemingly successful use of the equality provision of the *Canadian Bill of Rights* in *Drybones* to challenge the provision in the *Indian Act* that deprived Indian women of their status when they married non-Indian men.[175] Ritchie J (writing for the plurality of Fauteux CJ, Martland, and Judson JJ) held that

> the effect of the *Bill of Rights* on the *Indian Act* can only be considered in light of the provisions of s. 91(24) of the *B.N.A. Act* whereby the subject of "Indians and lands reserved for Indians" is assigned exclusively to the legislative authority of the Parliament of Canada ... [T]he exclusive legislative authority vested in Parliament under s. 91(24) could not have been effectively exercised without enacting laws establishing the qualifications required to entitle persons to status as Indians and to the use and benefit of Crown "lands reserved for Indians." The legislation enacted to this end was, in my view, necessary for the implementation of the authority so vested in Parliament under the constitution.... To suggest that the provisions of the *Bill of Rights* have the effect of making the whole *Indian Act* inoperative as discriminatory is to assert that the Bill has rendered Parliament powerless to exercise the authority entrusted to it under the constitution of enacting legislation

172 *Eskimo Reference* at 115.
173 Ibid.
174 *Lavell*.
175 *Indian Act* RSC 1970, c. I-6, s. 12(1)(b); *Drybones*.

> which treats Indians living on Reserves differently from other Canadians in relation to their property and civil rights.[176]

This argument (first used by Pigeon J in his dissent in *Drybones*[177]) is a curious one. At first it appears that Ritchie J is simply holding that the *Canadian Bill of Rights* cannot be used to limit Parliament's capacity to define *Indian* under s. 91(24), which is unsurprising, as it is a standard hierarchy of laws argument (i.e., a statute must be considered in light of a constitutional provision). But he does not stop with this argument. He buffers this standard constitutional argument by claiming that the *Indian Act* is "necessary for the implementation of the authority so vested in Parliament under the constitution." By closing off the space between s. 91(24) and the *Indian Act*, he can make it seem as if the *Canadian Bill of Rights* cannot be used to counter the discriminatory effect of the *Indian Act* (viz. the *Indian Act*, not merely another statute – it is the necessary expression of Parliament's constitutional authority). This argument places no limits on the legislative authority vested in Parliament by s. 91(24) and holds any change to this "broad view" to the clear-and-plain intent standard.[178] In effect, the implication is that equality before the law would make it impossible for the Parliament of Canada to "discharge ... its constitutional function under s. 91(24)." This "function" is "to specify how and by whom Crown lands reserved for Indians are to be used."[179] This allows the Court to simply refer to the way in which Parliament exercised its authority under s. 91(24) to define what the term *Indian* means (i.e., the *necessary* meaning of s. 91(24) is legislatively defined by the "broad view" of Parliament).[180] This argument adopts the kind of threadbare interpretation of the concept of equality, which allows for categorical distinctions (i.e., the familiar double-dealing logic of the "separate but equal" doctrine in the United States). Laskin J responds to this in his dissent:

> In my opinion, the appellants' contentions gain no additional force because the *Indian Act*, including the challenged s. 12(1)(b) thereof, is a fruit of the exercise of Parliament's exclusive legislative power in relation to "Indians, and Lands reserved for the Indians" under s. 91(24) of the *British North America Act*. Discriminatory treatment on the basis of race or colour or sex does not inhere in that grant of legislative power. The fact that its exercise may be attended by

176 *Lavell* at 1358–9.

177 *Drybones* at 303.

178 *Lavell* at 1360.

179 Ibid. at 1372.

180 At this time the *Indian Act* SC 1951, c. 29 at s. 2(1)(g) had changed the definition: "'Indian' means a person who pursuant to this Act is registered as an Indian or is entitled to be registered as an Indian." This circular definition retains the unilateral power of the previous definition, but conceals how the determination is actually being made by the register.

> forms of discrimination prohibited by the *Canadian Bill of Rights* is no more a justification for a breach of the *Canadian Bill of Rights* than there would be in the case of the exercise of any other head of federal legislative power involving provisions offensive to the *Canadian Bill of Rights*.[181]

This draws out the problem with reasoning used by both Ritchie and Piegon JJ: it begs the question of the meaning of s. 91(24). This reasoning relies on the premise that discriminatory treatment *inheres* in the grant of legislative power under s. 91(24), but this is circular. It assumes the meaning of *Indians* in s. 91(24) and the *Indian Act* is the same (a curious conclusion, given the distinction that the *Eskimo Reference* had already made). But it actually leaves the term entirely undefined. It does not define the term *Indians*; it simply holds it open to definition by Parliament. As a result, it holds that Parliament has unlimited legislative authority over Indians and their lands. This "broad view" does not *inhere* in the wording of s. 91(24). It acquires this magical meaning only through interpretation, but the actual act of interpretation is hidden from view. This is, to borrow Wittgenstein's analogy, the decisive movement in the conjuring trick. It is the movement that escapes notice because "it was the very one that we thought quite innocent."[182]

In 1976 Laskin (now the chief justice) revisits this argument in the *Canard* case, where he holds that the argument of the majority in *Lavell*

> resides in the view that the *Indian Act* is a self-contained code which if it exhibits any dissonance with the *Canadian Bill of Rights* is justified by the very fact that Indians have been designated as a special class for which Parliament may legislate. I did not accept that view in *Lavell* and I do not accept it now, because I do not regard the mere grant of legislative power as itself authorizing Parliament to offend against its generally stated protections in the *Canadian Bill of Rights*. If Parliament deems it necessary to treat its grant of legislative power under s. 91(24) of the *British North America Act* in terms that would be offensive to the *Canadian Bill of Rights*, it is open to Parliament to do so, but s. 91(24) is not, in my opinion, an invitation to the Courts to do what Parliament has not chosen to do. It seems to me patent that no grant of federal legislative power, as a mere vehicle for legislation, should be viewed as necessarily carrying with it a built-in exclusion of the mandates of the *Canadian Bill of Rights*.[183]

This forceful repetition of his argument in *Lavell* provides a valuable additional observation concerning the role of the Courts. It reverses the force of the clear and plain intent standard. Ritchie J had held that the *Canadian Bill of Rights* did not meet this standard, so it could not be interpreted as applying to the *Indian Act* in

181 *Lavell* at 1389.

182 Wittgenstein, *Philosophical Investigations* at §308.

183 *Canard* at 184.

that case. Laskin CJ holds that this position rests on the Court overstepping its jurisdiction and assuming the meaning of s. 91(24). It is open for Parliament to shield legislation anchored in s. 91(24) from the *Canadian Bill of Rights* (as prior to 1982 Canada operated on the principle of parliamentary sovereignty), but without a clear and plain expression of this, it was not open to the Court to simply assume the meaning of s. 91(24) and thereby shield it from the effect of the *Canadian Bill of Rights*. But in *Canard,* the majority (Beetz J writing) rejects this line of reasoning:

> The *British North America Act, 1867,* under the authority of which the *Canadian Bill of Rights,* was enacted, by using the word "Indians" in s. 91(24), creates a racial classification and refers to a racial group for whom it contemplates the possibility of a special treatment. It does not define the expression "Indian." This Parliament can do within constitutional limits by using criteria suited to this purpose but among which it would not appear unreasonable to count marriage and filiation and, unavoidably, intermarriages, in the light of either Indian customs and values which, apparently were not proven in *Lavell,* or of legislative history of which the Court could and did take cognizance.[184]

This is exactly the problem with the Court's approach: s. 91(24) does not define *Indian*, nor does it express the form of constitutional relationship. It could accommodate a nation-to-nation federal relationship. But the Court reads the provision as conferring power *over* and so leaves it open for Parliament to define its meaning. Beetz J does specify that Parliament's power is confined within "constitutional limits," but these limits have not been set. Put otherwise, the Court repeats the "broad view" of s. 91(24) that we find in the division-of-powers cases and uses this to override the effect of the *Canadian Bill of Rights* on federal Indian legislation. It seems to me that the only meaningful "constitutional limits" that Beetz J can be referring to are those provided by the division of powers, but, following the decisions in *Cardinal* and *Four B*, these limits apply only to Indians qua Indians (a cipher whose positive content is most often provided by federal legislation or judicial fiat and can be bypassed via s. 88 if necessary). The upshot is that the Courts operate under the presumption that Indians are subject to overlapping jurisdiction and have no access to the *Canadian Bill of Rights* until clear and plain legislation tells them otherwise. This tactic led Sandra Lovelace to take her case to the United Nations Human Rights Committee in 1977. In 1981 the committee found Canada to be in breach of Article 27 of the *International Covenant on Civil and Political Rights.*[185]

In 1976 Canada became a signatory to the *International Covenant on Civil and Political Rights.*[186] Article 27 of the *ICCPR* provides, "In those States in

184 Ibid. at 207.

185 *Lovelace.*

186 Adopted 16 December 1966, entry into force 23 March 1976. GA Res. 2200A (XXI) accession by Canada 19 May 1976, Can. TS 1976, No. 47.

which ethnic, religious or linguistic minorities exist, persons belonging to such minorities shall not be denied the right, in community with the other members of their group, to enjoy their own culture, to process and practice their own religion, or to use their own language." The testimony of Mary Two-Axe Earley (president, Quebec Equal Rights for Indian Women) before the Standing Committee on 13 September 1982 provides a vivid picture of the discrimination that Indian women have faced in Canada:

> We are stripped naked of any legal protection and raped by those who would take advantage of the inequities afforded by the Indian Act. We are raped because we cannot be buried beside the mothers who bore us and the fathers who begot us, although dogs from neighbouring towns are buried on our reserve land: because we are subject to eviction from the domiciles of our families and expulsion from the tribal roles; because we must forfeit any inheritance or ownership of property; because we are divested of the right to vote; because we are unable to pass our Indian-ness and the Indian culture that is engendered by a woman in her children: because we live in a country acclaimed to be one of the greatest cradles for democracy on earth, offering asylum to refugees while, within its borders, its native sisters are experiencing the same suppression that has caused these people to seek refuge by the great mother known as Canada.[187]

The continuous resistance to the restrictions on Indian status, combined with the passage of both s. 15 of the *Charter* and s. 35 of the *Constitution Act, 1982*, led to the most recent revision of the *Indian Act*. In 1985 Parliament introduced *Bill C-31* and (prospectively) removed the influence of marriage on status.[188] It replaced the previous system of registration with an even more complicated one. We will touch on only a few of the most controversial features of the new system.[189] The Royal Commission on Aboriginal Peoples argues that *Bill C-31* introduced several issues:

1 The Two-Parent Rule and the Second-Generation Cut-Off: Prior to 1985 Indian status was passed through the male line (via one parent). Section 6(1)(f) changes this requirement so that s. 6(1) Indian status can now be passed on only if both parents have status. This means that if one parent

187 Cited in *McIvor v. The Registrar, Indian and Northern Affairs Canada*, 2007 BCSC 827 at para. 37 [hereinafter *McIvor BCSC*].

188 *An Act to amend the Indian Act*, SC 1985, c. 27. I specify "prospectively," as *McIvor* and *Descheneaux* demonstrate that the discriminatory effects of the previous regime persist past this point.

189 For an overview of how both the previous and the new system work to discriminate against women and usurp the right of Aboriginal peoples to determine their own identity see Mary Eberts, "McIvor: Justice Delayed – Again," *Indigenous Law Journal* 9, no. 1 (2010): 15–46.

has s. 6(1) status and the other parent does not have status, the child is eligible only for s. 6(2) status. Section 6(2) allows a person who has only one parent with status to get a "life interest" in status, but this cannot be passed on unless the other parent has status.[190] This means that in order for those who regained their status under s.6(1)(c) to pass their status on, the other parent must have status. In this sense, we can see this new system of registration as an extension of the project of assimilation that began in 1857. While the Act now presents itself in the bare and technical language of a modern statute, it maintains the system whereby the federal government is able to set the legal limits of Indian status. The courts then give this (magical) ability to set the terms of Indian status the aura of legal legitimacy, but they do so on the unquestioned assumption of Crown sovereignty, legislative power, and underlying title. Cases such as *McIvor*, *Descheneaux*, and *Daniels* show us that the precise limits of eligibility in both the *Indian Act* and s. 91(24) are open to legal contestation. This can result in changes that do have real, practical benefits for people, but the actual constitutional question of how the Crown came to have the power to legally define Indian status is left unanswered. It seems to me that the foregrounding of the limits of eligibility serves as a kind of stalking horse or screen to prevent any inquiry into the origins and structure of the constitutional relationship between Aboriginal peoples and the Crown.[191] As the *RCAP* states, this complicated system of registration works to "continue the policy of assimilation in disguised but strengthened form."[192]

2 Band membership: Section 10 of *Bill C-31* allows bands to create their own membership codes. This largely separates Indian registration from band membership.[193] This has led to two paradoxical results: First, there are now individuals who have Indian status but do not have membership within a

190 As Eberts notes, the two-parent rule should be contrasted with the reform of Canadian citizenship law which came into effect in 1977 via *An Act Respecting Citizenship*, SC 1974–75–76, c. 108. This legislation retained the one-parent rule for passing on Canadian citizenship, but simply broadened it so that it could be passed by either the mother or the father (ibid. at 23).

191 In this sense it seems to me that the current use and interpretation of s. 91(24) and the *Indian Act* bear some resemblance to the legislative practices and strategies of the Jim Crow laws of the southern United States following Reconstruction. In that case the practical legal effects of the previous system of slavery were largely retained by a combination of indirect legislative means and legal principles whose flexibility could tolerate contradictory formulations (i.e., "separate but equal"). For an exemplary treatment of the jurisprudence from this period in US history, see Cover, *Justice Accused*.

192 *RCAP* 1:2 at 279–83.

193 I specify "largely," as s. 4(1) of the *Indian Act* includes a set of purposes whereby any person named on a band list is included in the term *Indian*. My main point is that inclusion on a band list does not confer Indian status.

band. The lack of band membership has serious repercussions as a result of the collective nature of Aboriginal and treaty rights. In practical terms, this means that these status Indians can be barred from exercising those rights and lack the standing to challenge infringements of their rights in the courts.[194] Second, by restricting band funding so that they receive funds only for members with Indian status, the Crown is able to use its economic powers to indirectly control band membership. In addition, under the *Indian Act* a band's ability to hold reserve lands depends on the band having registered Indians in its membership.[195] While it is true that s. 4(1) extends some specific applications of the term *Indian* to anyone whose name is on the band list, it is unclear what would happen if no members were eligible for status. In other words, by decoupling membership and status, it becomes possible to remove Indians from their lands. This may sound like a far-fetched scenario, but when we seriously consider the potential long-term implications of rules of registration that work to reduce the number of eligible individuals, it seems clear that at some point a band without Indians becomes possible. Once this occurs it would raise a troubling question: does a band without registered Indians have a legal claim to Indian lands?

This brings us to the *McIvor, Descheneaux*, and *Daniels* cases. The *McIvor* case provides us with a vivid illustration of just how resilient the Crown machinery is. Sharon McIvor regained status after 1985, and her son was given 6(2) status. This meant that her grandchildren would not be registered unless her daughter-in-law was also an Indian. Instead of challenging s. 6(2) directly, they sought to expand s. 6(1)(a) to all of those born before 17 April 1985. They argued that *Bill-31* was failed remedial legislation and that registration is a benefit of the law within the meaning of s. 15 of the *Charter*.[196] At the trial their argument succeeded. Ross J recognized that the Crown's argument that status is

194 For more on this problem, see Bruce Miller, *Invisible Indigenes: The Politics of Nonrecognition* (Lincoln: University of Nebraska Press, 2008). This implication can be seen in the discussion of standing in *Behn v. Moulton Contracting Ltd.*, at paras. 26–36. Also see Giokas, "Indian Act" at 66.

195 For an insightful analysis of how membership controls work within the Indian Act system, see Sébastien Grammond, *Identity Captured by Law: Membership in Canada's Indigenous Peoples and Linguistic Minorities* (Montreal and Kingston: McGill-Queen's University Press, 2009).

196 The gist of the case was that the effects of the second-generation cut-off are inconsistent with the equality provision of the *Charter*. The similarity with *Lavell* is obvious, but, one would imagine, the result should be different as the equality provision is now part of the constitution itself and so not vulnerable to the principle of parliamentary supremacy. The factual components of the case are convoluted as a result of the changes in the registration system over time. See Eberts, "McIvor" at 27–46.

a personal right "would treat status as an Indian as if it were simply a statutory definition pertaining to eligibility for some program or benefit."[197] This is inappropriate (to say the least) as "having created and then imposed this identity upon First Nations peoples, with the result that it has become a central aspect of identity, the government cannot now treat it in that way, ignoring the true essence or significance of the concept."[198] In closing she found that s. 6 of the 1985 Act violates s. 15(1) of the *Charter*; she refused the Crown's request for a twenty-four-month suspension of relief.[199] At the Court of Appeal, Groberman J curtailed the scope of the remedy by changing the comparator group and thereby narrowing the definition of the discrimination and suspending the order.[200] The result was passage of *Bill C-3* in 2010, which has been heavily criticized for the lack of meaningful consultation during its drafting process and for its narrow and technical language.[201] There is more than a passing resemblance between the outcome of *McIvor* and that of *Descheneaux*. The issue in the case concerned specific situations within the post-*McIvor* system of registration where there were demonstrable sex-based inequalities.[202] The Superior Court of Quebec found that paragraphs 6(1)(a), (c), and (f) and subsection 6(2) of the *Indian Act* unjustifiably infringe s. 15 of the *Charter* and declared these provisions to be of no force of effect.[203] This declaration of invalidity was suspended for eighteen months to allow Parliament to amend the legislation accordingly. This resulted in Parliament passing *Bill S-3* in 2017.[204] The changes that this legislation makes to the *Indian Act* have only increased the complexity of the provisions governing eligibility. Both *McIvor* and *Descheneaux* demonstrate the limitations of using the *Charter* to address the inequalities imposed by the *Indian Act*. The courts can and will make use of the *Charter* to alter the precise

---

197 *McIvor BCSC* at para. 193.

198 Ibid.

199 Ibid. at paras. 343–50.

200 Eberts, "McIvor" at 35–40; *McIvor v. Canada*.

201 *An Act to promote gender equity in Indian registration by responding to the Court of Appeal for British Columbia decision in McIvor v. Canada (Registrar of Indian and Northern Affairs)* 3rd Sess., 40th Parliament, 59 Elizabeth II, 2010; Sarah E. Hamill, "McIvor v Canada and the 2010 Amendments to the Indian Act: A Half-Hearted Remedy to Historical Injustice," *Constitutional Forum constitutionnel* 19, no. 2 (2011): 75–84.

202 I have avoided a more detailed description of the specific issues (i.e., the cousins, siblings, and omitted minors issues), as their technical details do not have a direct bearing on my argument. Those interested in these details can refer to the decision *Descheneaux c. Canada (Procureur Général)*, 2015 QCCS 3555 and the legislative response to it in *An Act to amend the Indian Act in response to the Superior Court of Quebec decision in Descheneaux c. Canada (Procureur général)*, SC 2017, c. 25.

203 *Descheneaux c. Canada (Procureur Général)*, 2015 QCCS 3555 at 245–4.

204 *An Act to amend the Indian Act in response to the Superior Court of Quebec decision in Descheneaux c. Canada (Procureur général)*, SC 2017, c. 25.

terms of the *Indian Act*, but this leaves the deeper constitutional problems untouched. The unquestioned presumption of Crown sovereignty, legislative power, and underlying title remains fixed in these cases. They still occur within a picture of a constitutional order in which Aboriginal peoples are subjects, not *self-governing peoples* who are contesting the Crown's claim to legislative power and underlying title.[205] Both *McIvor* and *Descheneaux* demonstrate that the "broad view" interpretation s. 91(24) and the colonial constitutional picture that it presumes can withstand *Charter* litigation. This type of litigation may even buffer this colonial constitutional picture. It narrows the scope of the conflict over statutory provisions, which, like so many cogs and gears, can simply be removed, recalibrated, and replaced without interrupting the overall operation of the Crown machinery. This kind of litigation enables the court to see and evaluate particular components of the picture but not the actual constitutional framework thereof. In other words, it focuses the court's attention on the (many) injustices that result from the criteria of eligibility that Parliament uses to define who is or is not entitled to be registered as an Indian. But it leaves untouched the larger (and far more troubling) question of how Parliament is able to define Indians in the first place.

The *Daniels* case is the current chapter in the judicial definition of "Indians." Abella J (writing for a unanimous Court) began her decision with the following observation: "As the curtain opens wider and wider on the history of Canada's relationship with its Indigenous peoples, inequities are increasingly revealed and remedies urgently sought. Many revelations have resulted in good faith policy and legislative responses, but the list of disadvantages remains robust. This case represents another chapter in the pursuit of reconciliation and redress in that relationship."[206]

The imagery of the opening curtain is evocative. It presents us with a picture of a stage and a curtain. Though these are the only physical elements of the theatre that are mentioned, it seems clear that we (and seemingly the court) are being drawn into the seats as spectators. The curtain separates the spectators from the stage and marks off the boundaries of what can be seen. We are told that as the curtain is drawn back it reveals the "history of Canada's relationship with its Indigenous peoples." There are aspects of this picture that should give us pause: to begin with, it is unclear how this relationship could be so completely concealed by a curtain. After all, the curtain in a theatre conceals what is on the stage only so long as the audience participates by following the rules of this social game. If concern, or even mere curiosity, drew them from

205 I am not suggesting that Aboriginal peoples are not contesting Crown sovereignty. Rather, I am focusing on the questions that the courts can address.

206 *Daniels* at para. 1.

their seats, they could quickly see what lies behind the curtain. And given that the history of this relationship would be a lived reality (both in the past and the present), for many it seems that the audience members must have been drawn from a group that was somehow left in the dark. So who exactly fills the seats of this theatre? How are they so unaware of this "history"? The very use of the term *history* suggests a kind of temporal distance that not everyone can share in. What is simply "history" for some is, for others, a criss-crossing and overlapping set of experiences and memories that are inseparable from their everyday reality. Putting these questions to the side for a moment and retuning to Abella J's picture, we are told that as the curtain opens "wider and wider" we can see inequities and disadvantages. She immediately attempts to reassure us that many of the "revelations have resulted in good faith policy and legislative responses" but, she acknowledges, that much remains to be done. This appeal to the ever so slippery concept of good faith leaves the reassurance offered sounding thin, strained, and unconvincing. After all, the concept of "good faith" is ready-to-hand whenever we want to draw attention away from the actual results of our actions. It provides us with a makeshift moral shelter of sorts, one that is very difficult to challenge. Nonetheless she moves on to explain that the work of addressing these inequities and disadvantages forms another "chapter in the pursuit of reconciliation."

While I do not want to place too much interpretive stress on this relatively commonplace metaphor, it seems to me that it illustrates a problem that is central to all three decisions in *Daniels*. What seems important to me in Abella J's picture of the curtain and the stage is that the work of reconciliation is confined to what appears on this stage. In this view, whatever adjustments or alterations are required to redress the (historical) inequities and disadvantages in this relationship, they are confined to what can be seen in the foreground of the stage. What is not open to question is how the very framework of the stage itself shapes the relationship between the Crown and Indigenous peoples. Put differently, in all three levels of the *Daniels* case, the most basic constitutional character of the relationship between the Crown and Indigenous peoples is simply assumed. Each begins with the presumption that the Crown has sovereignty, legislative power, and underlying title, and so Indigenous peoples can exist only as subjects (with a judicially mediated set of sui generis rights) within a colonial picture of the Canadian constitutional order. This allows them to take the "broad view" of s. 91(24). They speak of the purposes and definitional contours of its terms but not the actual origins of the Crown's legislative power over Aboriginal peoples.

As Dawson JA rightly states in the decision of the Federal Court of Appeal, "This is a division of powers case about the interpretation of section 91(24) of the *Constitution Act, 1867*."[207] The question before the Court – much like the

207 *Daniels II* at para. 16.

Eskimo Reference – was "whether the federal government has jurisdiction over Métis and non-status Indians pursuant to section 91(24) of the *Constitution Act, 1867*."[208] The response of the courts to this question (at the trial and both appeals) was yes. There are two related problems with this case: first, it maintains the "broad view" of s. 91(24) (i.e., that it confers plenary power *over* Indians and their lands). This can clearly be seen in the list of the purposes of s. 91(24) that Phelan J adopts in the trial decision (which are cited in both appellate decisions):

- to control native people and communities where necessary to facilitate development of the Dominion.
- to honour the obligations to natives that the Dominion inherited from Britain while extinguishing interests that stood in the way of the objects of Confederation.
- eventually to civilize and assimilate native people.[209]

The purposes are obviously mutually inconsistent: how could it be possible to "honour the obligations to natives that the Dominion inherited from Britain" while controlling them, extinguishing their interests, and eventually assimilating them? Abella J elaborates on this point when she finds that

> historically, the purpose of s. 91(24) in relation to the broader goals of Confederation also indicates that since 1867, "Indians" meant all Aboriginal peoples, including Métis. The trial judge found that expanding British North America across Rupert's Land and the North-West Territories was a major goal of Confederation and that building a national railway was a key component of this plan. At the time, that land was occupied by a large and diverse Aboriginal population, including many Métis. A good relationship with all Aboriginal groups was required to realize the goal of building "the railway and other measures which the federal government would have to take." With jurisdiction over Aboriginal peoples, the new federal government could "protect the railway from attack" and ensure that they did not resist settlement or interfere with construction of the railway. Only by having authority over *all* Aboriginal peoples could the westward expansion of the Dominion be facilitated.[210]

There is no inquiry into the justifications that were used to legitimate the means to pursue these "broader goals of Confederation." Or, for that matter, what exactly gave them the new federal government "authority over *all* Aboriginal peoples"? What possible legal basis could the imperial Crown or the dominion use to legitimate policies of control, extinguishment, and assimilation? If

208 Ibid. at para. 1.

209 Ibid. at para. 5; *Daniels I* at para. 353; *Daniels II* at para. 36.

210 *Daniels* at para. 25.

there is none, how can they possibly be accepted as the purposes of this head of power today? Furthermore, how can they be accepted via a "purposive" or "living tree" approach to constitutional interpretation? As Phelan J rightly maintained in the trial decision, "I accept the Plaintiffs' submission that the purposive approach – the 'living tree' doctrine – is the appropriate approach (see *Reference re Same-Sex Marriage*, 2004 SCC 79, [2004] 3 SCR 698). History helps to understand perspectives on the purpose but does not necessarily determine the purpose for all time. This is particularly the case with a constitution power which has, at some level, racial tones and which involved people who were seen in a light which today we would find offensive. Racial stereotyping is not a proper basis for constitutional interpretation."[211]

If racial stereotyping is not a proper basis for constitutional interpretation, how can it be possible to accept the idea that the purpose of s. 91(24) is to pursue policies of control, extinguishment, and assimilation? The only basis for these policies is *racial stereotyping* (i.e., that there is a civilizational hierarchy, so there is no need to acquire consent). Dawson JA was faced with the question of whether Phelan J failed to follow the approach to constitutional analysis mandated by the Supreme Court. His response was that "there is ample evidence to support the view that Métis were considered within section 91(24) at the time of Confederation. A progressive interpretation was, therefore, unnecessary, and the Judge did not err by failing to address the social changes that would underlie such an interpretation."[212]

This is plainly correct. The conclusions that Phelan J reaches *do not* require a progressive interpretation. I would go further than Dawson JA and say that the reasons do not show that a progressive interpretation was used in the first place.[213]

This leads to the second problem with the case: it accepts a race-based view of the basis of s. 91(24).[214] Dawson JA qualifies this finding, but in doing so he simply follows the logic that Beetz J sets out in *Canard* (i.e., he holds the term *Indians* open so that it can be adapted).[215] Abella J similarly uses examples of how Parliament had exercised its legislative authority in the past to show that *Indian* is "a general term referring to all Indigenous peoples, including

211 *Daniels I* at para. 538.

212 *Daniels II* at para. 148. Abella J confirmed this same point when she found that "the purpose of s. 91(24) in relation to the broader goals of Confederation ... indicates that since 1867, 'Indians' meant all Aboriginal peoples, including Métis." See *Daniels* at para. 25.

213 The blame for this cannot be laid entirely on Phelan J, as the plaintiffs themselves conceded that s. 91(24) is a broad plenary power. See an instructive analysis in Chartrand, "Failure of the Daniels Case."

214 *Daniels I* at para. 568.

215 *Daniels II* at paras. 83–124.

mixed-ancestry communities like the Métis."[216] Allowing the discrete and multiple Indigenous identities to fit into the term *Indians* does not cure the problem of racism. It continues it. As Chartrand rightly notes, this logic "fails to appreciate that the provision is, without imposing a check on its unilateral reliance [on] federal authority, inherently racist as it offends fundamental human rights."[217]

The logic that the court is using here assumes that s. 91(24) confers absolute legislative power *over* Indians and their lands. This is dependent on the prior and unstated assumption that the Crown is sovereign and that its sovereignty is necessarily bundled with legislative power and underlying title. If this unstated assumption is simply accepted, then it seems that the "broad view" of s. 91(24) simply follows from the principle of parliamentary supremacy (i.e., s. 91(24) is the legislation of the imperial Parliament whose sovereignty the courts cannot question). But no possible basis can support this unstated assumption, other than the set of racist legal fictions that can no longer be accepted as valid law (i.e., *terra nullius*, discovery, etc.). The unquestioned assumption of Crown sovereignty, legislative power, and underlying title leads the reasoning of the courts into circles. In the trial decision Phelan J attempted to prove the purpose of s. 91(24) based on a premise that itself requires proof. Both Dawson JA and Abella J simply follow the same course. They fashion their definition of s. 91(24) out of the purposes, goals, and beliefs of the federal government. After all, as Abella J reminds us, "Only by having authority over *all* Aboriginal peoples could the westward expansion of the Dominion be facilitated."[218] In the end *Daniels* offers nothing new. It is simply the application of the finding of the Court in the *Eskimo Reference* and *Canard*.[219]

---

216 *Daniels* at para. 23.

217 Chartrand, "Failure of the Daniels Case" at 184.

218 *Daniels* at para. 25.

219 Dawson JA notes this at *Daniels II* at para. 124; *Eskimo Reference* at 118; *Canard* at 207. The recent decision of the Supreme Court in *Daniels v. Canada (Indian Affairs and Northern Development)*, 2016 SCC 12 does nothing to change the problems that are in both the previous decisions. The short unanimous decision that is written by Abella J simply passes over the history of s. 91(24) quickly and offers no analysis of the distinction between a power that "extends to" versus one that is a power *over*. As she states at para. 34, "Moreover, while it does not define the scope of s. 91(24), it is worth noting that s. 35 of the *Constitution Act, 1982* states that Indian, Inuit, and Métis peoples are Aboriginal peoples for the purposes of the Constitution." The fact that s. 35 can be read in a way that *does not* restrict the scope of s. 91(24) is an indication of their shared foundation. The "grand purpose" of reconciliation remains anchored to the *doctrine of discovery* (this is why Binnie J's canoe can never leave the shore; see *Mitchell v. MNR* at paras. 127–8). What we are left with is that Abella J states at para. 46, "A broad understanding of 'Indians' under s. 91(24) as meaning 'Aboriginal peoples,' resolves the definitional concerns raised by the parties in this case. Since s. 91(24) includes all Aboriginal peoples, including Métis and non-status Indians,

Wittgenstein provides a description of the interpretive trap that the Court is caught in when it repeats the "broad view" of s. 91(24): "It is like a pair of glasses on our nose through which we see whatever we look at. It never occurs to us to take them off," and so we "predicate of the thing what lies in the method of representing it."[220] If the Court were to actually remove these "glasses" and employ a purposive or "living tree" approach to s. 91(24), it could not possibly find that its purposes are to control, extinguish, and assimilate.

This set of historical purposes form one historical narrative that is in direct conflict with the nation-to-nation treaty relationship that related to honouring "the obligations to natives that the Dominion inherited from Britain."[221] A "living tree" approach would have to balance s. 91(24) with s. 35 and remove any purpose that does not have a basis in the free, prior, and informed consent of Aboriginal peoples. This would go beyond the approach that the Court took in *Sparrow* (i.e., "reconciling" the *unquestioned assumption* of federal "power" Indians and their lands with the self-imposed "duty" that is expressed in s. 35), as it would place the assumption of federal power under s. 91(24) directly into question.[222] In so doing, it would have to uphold the basic constitutional principle of *q.o.t.* and the requirements of natural justice (i.e. *audi alteram partem* and *nemo judex in causa sua*).

As Chartrand suggests, one possible version of such a reinterpretation of s. 91(24) would restrict it to a "treaty power" that would allow Parliament to "negotiate with nations and peoples who occupy and possess territory that Canadian authority wished to acquire."[223] A broader way to characterize this type of interpretation – and sharpen the distinction between it and the current "power-*over*" model – is to use the phrase "power-*with*."[224] This serves as an object of comparison that challenges the foundational claim of the current picture of federalism in Canada and moves towards the kind of democratic

---

there is no need to delineate which mixed-ancestry communities are Métis and which are non-status Indians. They are all 'Indians' under s. 91(24) by virtue of the fact that they are all Aboriginal peoples." Aboriginal peoples now all enter an undetermined ambit of authority that is founded on nothing but an assertion and an absence of doubt (by the party that benefits from it). It seems that this picture of life in the black canoe is predicated on seeing the figure in the centre as a king holding a sceptre (a paradigmatic symbol of European sovereign power and divine right) in place of the ambiguous tall figure of the chief (that may or may not be the Spirit of Haida Gwaii) holding a talking stick.

220 Wittgenstein, *Philosophical Investigations* at §103–4.

221 *Daniels I* at para. 353.

222 *Sparrow* at 1109.

223 Chartrand, "Failure of the Daniels Case" at 185.

224 I would like to thank James Tully for suggesting that I adopt this term. He develops this term (via the work of thinkers such as Mary Follette, Hanna Arendt, Richard Greg, and Gandhi) in two unpublished essays: "Violent Power-Over and Nonviolent Power-With"; "Richard Gregg and the Power of Nonviolence."

constitutionalism that could offer the possibility of a reconciliation based on dialogue and consent.[225] This is not a model that naively presumes to end all conflict and open the way to perpetual peace (i.e., it is not the confession of a *beautiful soul* that, as Hegel notes, remains "*dumb*, shut up within its inner life" as it cannot find a way to make the world conform to the picture it sees).[226] Rather, as Tully argues, "The treaty system is a living human practice in which, by great effort, the battle for recognition by arms has been transformed into the conflict of words. This does not end the strategies of fraud and deceit humans play under the colour of the conventions. It only stops the killing, and this is only as long as the participants continue to listen to each other."[227]

This view of the concept of constitutionalism does not adopt a singular foundation of authority (i.e., the one that the "broad view" of s. 91(24) silently presumes). It invites us to view the plurality of foundations as a source of strength rather than dissolution or lawlessness. As Wittgenstein puts it, "The strength of the thread does not reside in the fact that some one fiber runs through the whole length, but in the overlapping of many fibers."[228]

Instead, we are left with a repetition of the same baseless logic that presents s. 91(24) as plenary power *over* the undefined term *Indians*. This means that those who fit within these bounds fall through a rabbit hole in the constitutional order. They are caught in a sui generis space within the division of powers that has been fashioned by judicial interpretation. The Court is captured by a picture of federalism that grants Parliament unquestioned sovereignty *over* Indians and their lands. It has consistently refused to inquire into the basis of this presumption. Instead, it simply repeats that it is beyond doubt or qualifies sovereignty by employing the terms *assumption, assertion*, or de facto while retaining the unilateral power to infringe on Aboriginal and treaty rights.[229]

---

225 Tully, *Strange Multiplicity* at 136.

226 Hegel, *Phenomenology of Spirit* at §653.

227 Tully, *Strange Multiplicity* at 138.

228 Wittgenstein, *Philosophical Investigations* at §67.

229 *Haida Nation* at para. 32; *Taku River Tlingit*. This characterization of Crown sovereignty is also cited with approval in the Court's recent decision in *MMF*. The full expression of this confusing qualification of sovereignty can be found in *Tsilhqot'in Nation* at para. 69: "At the time of assertion of European sovereignty, the Crown acquired radical or underlying title to all the land in the province. This Crown title, however, was burdened by the pre-existing legal rights of Aboriginal people who occupied and used the land prior to European arrival. The doctrine of *terra nullius* (that no one owned the land prior to European assertion of sovereignty) never applied in Canada, as confirmed by the *Royal Proclamation* of 1763. The Aboriginal interest in land that burdens the Crown's underlying title is an independent legal interest, which gives rise to a fiduciary duty on the part of the Crown." For a detailed exploration of the problems with the concept of "Crown title" in this case, see Ryan Beaton, "Aboriginal Title in Recent Supreme Court of Canada Jurisprudence: What Remains of Radical Crown Title?" *National Journal of Constitutional Law* 33 (2014): 61–81.

This has left us in a position where there is something that is "already in plain view," but this is precisely why "we seem in some sense to not understand."[230]

Wittgenstein provides us with tools that we need to break this spell. By assembling and rearranging "reminders for a particular purpose" it is possible to begin to offer a survey of aspects that have been forgotten.[231] What has been forgotten is the Aboriginal perspective and the *historical warrant* of Crown sovereignty and its limits.[232] This is evident when we reconsider the definition of *Indians* under s. 91(24) and the *Indian Act*, which has, as we have seen, been subject to continuous resistance and ongoing litigation. The legal definition of *Indians* is part and parcel of a narrative of imperial despotism. From the introduction of the first legislative definition in 1850 through to today it remains a unilaterally imposed (or withheld) legal status. In order to maintain the constitutional legitimacy of the *Indian Act* the courts have had to assume that the powers conferred to the dominion by the imperial Parliament under s. 91(24) were a plenary or sovereign power *over* Indians and their lands. In doing so the courts have committed themselves to a circular picture of federalism. They have not been able to either hear the Aboriginal perspective or explain the *historical warrant* of this theory of s. 91(24). Instead they confine the former to the bounds of evidence (which is subject to the translation effect of judicial discretion) and simply assume the latter is in place. Without this assumption they would not be able to retain the "broad view" of s. 91(24), as they would need to explain how the imperial Parliament was able to give something that it did not have (thereby cloaking the federal government of the newly formed dominion as the bona fide purchaser for value). While this kind of legal alchemy was once possible, the required legal fictions (i.e., *terra nullius* and discovery) no longer retain even the appearance of legitimacy. This has left the courts in a position where they must either simply confess that there is no basis for the unilateral and unrestricted theory of s. 91(24) or continue to indulge in the kind of assumptions and hidden premises that have been leading them in circles since *Calder* was decided in 1973. By adopting the expression "Indians *qua* Indians"

230 Wittgenstein, *Philosophical Investigations* at §89.

231 Ibid. at §92, §127, §92.

232 While the question of Crown sovereignty may well be non-justiciable within its courts, the questions of who has legislative power and underlying title and how they came to be in lawfully possession of them certainly are. The Court cannot simply use the non-justiciability of sovereignty as a magical hat where one can place unilateral assertions and then pull out lawful powers. The Court has an obligation as the guardian of the Constitution to adjudicate conflicts over the relationship between Indigenous peoples and the Crown. This includes conflicts over who is in lawful possession of legislative power and underlying title. This should not be seen as a zero-sum historical inquiry; rather, it is a constitutional relationship that is subject to ongoing contestation and revision (viz. it is a "living tree"). The *Secession Reference* provides a clear defence of this power-with model of the Constitution.

to define the area of exclusive federal jurisdiction, they have made their choice rather clear.

But what of bands? In *Four B,* Beetz J used "membership in a band" and "the right to participate in the election of Chiefs and Band Councils" as examples of the kind of "Indianness" that resides under the exclusive jurisdiction of the federal government.[233] So how have the courts interpreted this aspect of Indians qua Indians? Does the spectre of the *Gradual Enfranchisement Act* (with its "simple municipal institutions") still determine the lived reality of self-government?

C. The Judicial Definition of Bands

The band council is, as we have seen, a colonial invention. It was first introduced in 1869 with the *Gradual Enfranchisement Act.* Its explicit purpose was to prepare Indians for "responsible government."[234] This framed all Indigenous political and legal systems as "irresponsible" and thus illegitimate. The contradictory nature of this gesture is blatantly obvious. The basic democratic principle of consent is being used as the justification for interfering with the self-government of Aboriginal peoples without their consent and despite their continual resistance.[235] It employs the basic institutional forms of representative government (e.g., elections and representatives), but the ultimate control is not in the hands of the membership. In fact, as we have seen, the membership itself is defined and/or controlled externally (i.e., a band may elect to control its membership list, but the funding is based on the number of registered Indians). The powers of the band council are strictly bound by the *Indian Act,* and it cannot be considered to be a constitution that can lay any claim on the will of the people that it governs.[236] This model was designed to maintain colonial domination during a process of assimilation. It was designed to disappear. The policy of enfranchisement saw no future for these simple municipal institutions. Their purpose was pedagogical. Once the Indians were fully absorbed into the body of citizens, they would not require a separate form of government. The authority and structure of bands fits this model from its inception in 1869 to the most recent form of the *Indian Act.* The arrangement of authority in the legislation

233 *Four B* at 1048.

234 Giokas, "Indian Act" at 34.

235 The imposition of the *Indian Act* electoral scheme on the Six Nations is a good illustration; see part 3.

236 More recently, certain other opt-in statutory schemes have been used to modify the *Indian Act* scheme. Examples of such legislation include the *First Nations Land Management Act,* SC 1999, c. 24; the *First Nations Fiscal Management Act,* SC 2005, c. 9; and the *Family Homes on Reserves and Matrimonial Interests or Rights Act,* SC 2013, c. 20.

is unequivocal. There have been periods of adjustment and recalibration over the course of the last 150 years, but the general form of administrative despotism remains constant. The ambit of discretional authority that the minister has within the *Indian Act* is difficult to exaggerate. For example, if we consult s. 3(1) of the current version of the Act, we are told that the "Act shall be administered by the Minister" and that within this role the minister is "the superintendent general of Indian affairs."[237] The language used to describe the role clearly conveys the power-*over* arrangement. We can think of the relationship between the minister and the Act as that between a machine and its operator. The machine presents a set of levers and buttons that allow the operator to set it in motion. This is by no means unique. Ministers are often placed in the seats of administrative power. But this machine was originally designed to control and assimilate Indians. This is clearly evident in the sheer number of discretionary levers and buttons that it features and how they connect to bands.[238]

Consider the language of the provisions relating to the elections of chiefs and band councils: "Whenever he deems it advisable for the good government of a

---

237 *Indian Act*, RSC, 1985, c. I-5.

238 It is interesting to note that s. 4(2) enables the Governor in Council (this is a term that refers to the governor general – the Queen's representative – who acts by and with the consent of the Queen's Privy Council for Canada) or, more colloquially, the federal Cabinet, to suspend these features with the (rather telling) exception of the sections dealing with the definition and registration of Indians and the surrender and designation of lands. These are, after all, the two main targets of assimilation and the heads of power that compose s. 91(24). Additionally, in s. 17 we are told that "the Minister may, whenever he considers it desirable" amalgamate bands (if there is a request based on a majority vote), constitute new bands, and establish band lists (on the basis of existing lists or from the register – meaning that he cannot make new Indians, as this is done at the discretion of the register in s. 5). Curiously the definition of *band* in s. 2(1) takes no account of s. 17. In any case, this discretionary power combines with the changes in registration under *Bill C-3* and the ability for bands to control their own membership. This combination leads to a situation in which there can be registered Indians who do not have a band. They cannot exercise Aboriginal rights, as these are collective and not individual rights (assuming that the band is the proper collectivity to which such rights belong); the Court has been somewhat difficult to pin down on this issue. For example, see the Court's analysis on the question of the rights holder in *Behn v. Moulton Contracting Ltd.*; and *Tsilhqot'in Nation v. British Columbia*, [2014] 2 SCR 257. They cannot be recognized as a legitimate collective without the minister. But the minister is under no obligation to remedy this situation, and so these groups fall through an exception within the law. For a long period of time they were seen as a mere "handful of Indians" (*Syliboy* at 313). This perspective has most certainly shifted. As Dickson CJ put it in *Simon*, "The language used by Patterson J, illustrated in this passage, reflects the biases and prejudices of another era in our history. Such language is no longer acceptable in Canadian law and indeed is inconsistent with a growing sensitivity to native rights in Canada" (*Simon* at para. 21). While this rejection of the language of *Syliboy* is laudable the actual substance of them (i.e., how these words express the place of Aboriginal peoples within the Canadian constitutional order) remains in place.

band, the Minister may declare by order that after a day to be named therein the council of the band, consisting of a chief and councillors, shall be selected by elections to be held in accordance with this Act."[239] This provision enables the minister to dissolve a band council and hold a new election.[240] The only restriction on this discretionary power is that the minister deems it "advisable for the good government of a band." There is no need to consult the group in question. Their powers are strictly bound within the Act. The minister is the one who determines what is and is not advisable for the "good government" of Indians, and the standard of judicial review for these determinations is most likely reasonableness.

This high level of discretionary authority is obvious when we consider the section dealing with the powers of the council: "The council of a band may make by-laws not inconsistent with this Act or with any regulation made by the Governor in Council or the Minister."[241] This is stated prior to the twenty-one subsections that detail the matters that the council can regulate. The language is not ambiguous. The governor in council and the minister maintain power over the band council. It remains a creature of statute strictly bound by the Act. If one were to condense the entire Act down to a single phrase it would simply state, "The minister or governor in council may do whatever they deem necessary for the good government of Indians." Naturally this somewhat overstates the ambit of their authority as, at an absolute minimum, their spending authority would be subject to the norms of parliamentary appropriations. Nevertheless, the asymmetrical distribution of discretionary authority within the Act is clear: the band is a part of the municipal order of government.

It does not matter whether or not this immense discretionary power is actually used. If the minister either neglects or simply chooses not to use certain levers or buttons for an extended period of time, it may seem as if the band council is a self-governing body. But the relationship of power-*over* remains firmly in place, despite the neglect. It is and remains tied to the strings of power that initially gave it form. This does not mean that its use is, as Wittgenstein puts it, "everywhere circumscribed by rules."[242] It can be used otherwise, but this remains the legal structure of its authority.

---

239 *Indian Act*, RSC, 1985, c. I-5.

240 Some limitations are relevant: first, the band must have been established in accordance with the *Indian Act*. This means that if the band was chosen via the *First Nations Elections Act* or by the custom of the band, then those procedures apply. This is all outlined in s. 2(1) of the *Indian Act*. Second, once the minister has invoked s. 74, its terms determine the frequency of band council elections and the procedures for carrying them out.

241 Ibid.

242 Wittgenstein, *Philosophical Investigations* at §68.

The Aboriginal perspective is not taken into account within the bounds of the colonial law (viz. aside from highly structured consultative processes aimed at adding the veneer of consent). It can be manifest only by acting otherwise within the *Indian Act* game. This resistance has a history that can be seen in each and every adjustment and recalibration of the crown machinery (e.g., the Six Nations status case detailed in part 3 is a prime example, but it is one of many). These cases develop from situations in which a band makes a move away from the normal rules of the *Indian Act* game. This is unsurprising, as the "normal rules" of the *Indian Act* are unambiguous. The source of authority and of ultimate administrative power is the Crown. But bands have (repeatedly) tried to move away from this power-*over* relationship.

I have limited my focus to three specific examples of these moves. First, in *Pamajewon* we see an example of band councils asserting laws outside the bounds of the *Indian Act*. This leads to a direct confrontation to the unilateral authority of the Crown. Second, a band council requests to switch from the *Indian Act* election procedures in s. 74 and form a custom election code. This enables them to change rules concerning eligibility, term of office, and size of council, and to integrate hereditary leaders. But what happens when there is a dispute within the band over the results of an election? This has led to a body of cases in which the federal courts are forced to determine whether or not a custom band council fits within their jurisdiction under the *Federal Court Act*. Finally, we will consider how the courts have dealt with the constitutionality of the legislative and self-government powers set out in Final Agreements (also known as modern treaties).

PAMAJEWON AND THE RIGHT OF SELF-GOVERNMENT

In *Pamajewon* two band councils passed laws relating to gambling on their territory. These laws were not passed pursuant to s. 81 of the *Indian Act*, and neither sought a provincial licence.[243] They consciously stepped outside of the bounds of the *Indian Act* game and asserted their right to self-government. The Crown's response was to charge a number of members from each first nation with criminal offences relating to gambling.[244] At the trial, both first nations

243 *Pamajewon* at paras. 5–10. For a detailed examination of the factual details of gambling and provincial licensing, see Bradford W. Morse, "Permafrost Rights: Aboriginal Self-Government and the Supreme Court in *R v. Pamajewon*," *McGill Law Journal* 42 (1997): 1011–44. It is particularly interesting to note that the Shawanaga First Nation Council was offered a provincial licence but refused; they believed that accepting it would compromise their position on the inherent right of self-government (1024).

244 There were two sets of appellants in the case. First, Pamajewon and Jones, who were members of the Shawanaga First Nation. They were charged and found guilty of keeping a common gaming house contrary to s. 201(1) of the *Criminal Code*, RSC, 1985, c. C-46. Second, Arnold Gardner, Jack Pitchenese, and Allan Gardner, who were all members of

pled not guilty. The members of the Shawanaga First Nation put forward three arguments at trial:

1 The Crown had failed to prove the essential elements of the offence.
2 They should not be convicted because their actions were taken pursuant to laws enacted by persons in possession of de facto sovereignty as per s. 15 of the *Criminal Code*.
3 The application of s. 201(1) of the *Criminal Code* was an unconstitutional violation of their inherent right of self-government.

Carr J rejected all three. He held that they had not demonstrated that they were acting in "obedience" to the lottery law, any right of self-government was extinguished, and that they did not have de facto sovereignty.[245] The de facto sovereignty argument was not pursued on appeal, but the Ontario Court of Appeal decision followed this line of reasoning and held that the right of self-government was extinguished.[246]

While the Supreme Court did not adopt this line of argumentation, Lamer CJC provides us with a clear and concise summary of it: "Relying on the terms of the *Royal Proclamation of 1763* and the Robinson Huron Treaty of 1850, and the granting of exclusive jurisdiction over 'Indians, and Lands reserved for the Indians' to the federal government under s. 91(24) of the *Constitution Act, 1867*, Carr Prov. Ct. held that any right of self-government which was once held by the Shawanaga First Nation had been extinguished by the clear and plain intention of the Crown, with the result that the appellants could not rely on such a right as a defence to the charges against them."[247] This argument clearly relies on the "broad view" of s. 91(24). Only the presumption of unlimited sovereign power-*over* could extinguish the right of self-government. The only legitimate *historical warrant* for this power is consent or conquest. In this case there is neither. While Lamer CJC does not adopt this particular approach to determining the question, the result is, as we will see, effectively the same.

The members of the Eagle Lake First Nation argued that they should not be convicted because s. 206 of the *Criminal Code* unjustifiably interfered with their s. 35(1) right to self-government. At trial Flaherty J held that this argument was an attempt to base the right to self-government on the economic disadvantages suffered by the First Nation. As the trial judge put it, "However one may wish to complain about one's economic disadvantage and however apparent it might

the Eagle Lake First Nation, were found guilty of conducting a scheme for the purpose of determining the winners of property, contrary to s. 206(1)(*d*) of the *Criminal Code*.

245 *R v. Jones and Pamajewon*, [1993] 3 CNLR 209 (Ont. Prov. Div.) at 211.

246 *R v. Pamajewon*, [1994] OJ No. 3028.

247 Cited in *Pamajewon* at para. 14.

be, redress needs to be found in other ways. People need to find ways of creating wealth and generating revenue that are not contrary to the Criminal law.... I am not persuaded that the economic disadvantages of the Eagle Lake First Nations people as evident as they have been established to be in these proceedings and of First Nations people generally can be addressed by activity which contravenes the Criminal law nor can I strike down a section of the *Criminal Code* which is otherwise constitutionally valid for the reasons carefully and ably submitted in this case."[248]

This characterization sidesteps the substantive issue altogether. It is analogous to interpreting a prisoner's claim to a right to liberty on the basis of innocence as arising from the discomfort of confinement and not the actual details of the offence that resulted in the imprisonment.[249] At appeal the cases were combined, the de facto sovereignty argument was dropped, but the appellants again argued that their convictions violated their respective bands' rights to self-government. They maintained that the right to self-government existed either as a necessary component of their Aboriginal title or as an inherent aboriginal right.

Osborne JA ruled that that the content of Aboriginal title is determined by the nature of the traditional Aboriginal use and occupation of that land.[250] This meant that the specific right of self-government would have to be argued on a rights basis. Furthermore, he held *Sparrow* as authority for the proposition that any broad inherent right to self-government was extinguished by the British assertion of sovereignty. Osborne JA cited Dickson CJC and La Forest J: "While British policy towards the native population was based on respect for their right to occupy their traditional lands, a proposition to which the Royal Proclamation of 1763 bears witness, there was from the outset never any doubt that sovereignty and legislative power, and indeed the underlying title, to such lands vested in the Crown."[251]

Here again the case stands on the thin air of an absence of doubt. From this basis Osborne JA narrows any possible claim to self-government to fine-grained historical and cultural details of each particular case. He states, "If the Shawanaga First Nation and Eagle Lake Band had some rights of self-government which existed in 1982 (I am prepared to assume that they did), the right of governance asserted must be viewed like other claimed aboriginal rights; it must be given an historic context. Here, there is no evidence that gambling on the reserve lands generally was ever the subject matter of aboriginal regulation.

248 Cited in *Pamajewon* at para. 16.

249 The analogy here is imperfect, as typically the prisoner–state relationship is not complicated by questions of jurisdiction and the legitimacy of sovereign authority.

250 *R v. Pamajewon*, [1994] OJ No. 3028 at 400.

251 *Sparrow* at 1103, as cited in *R v. Pamajewon*, [1994] OJ No. 3028 at 400.

Moreover, there is no evidence of an historic involvement in anything resembling the high stake gambling in issue in these cases."[252]

Lamer CJC adopts the approach set out by Osborne JA and finds that "the appellants themselves would have this Court characterize their claim as to 'a broad right to manage the use of their reserve lands.' To so characterize the appellants' claim would be to cast the Court's inquiry at a level of excessive generality. Aboriginal rights, including any asserted right to self-government, must be looked at in light of the specific circumstances of each case and, in particular, in light of the specific history and culture of the aboriginal group claiming the right."[253]

The weight of this standard effectively shuts off this approach to asserting a right of self-government. Asking a First Nation to show that self-government is "an element of a practice, custom or tradition integral" to their "distinctive culture" that can be traced back prior to contact with Europeans is an impossible task.[254] It is akin to the Court asking a First Nation to prove that their language contains meaning that could be said to be a "defining feature" of their culture.[255] The thrust of the analogy can also be expressed as a question: how can one possibly untangle a culture from its legal and political structures? The worry here is that the phrase "defining feature" operates like a filter that removes *universal features* (e.g., language or self-government). Even if this worry can be resolved by making the contours of the "defining feature" more flexible (i.e., permitting distinctive forms or types of universal features), the remark about "excessive generality" suggests that the evidentiary criterion is fine grained and strict. This worry leads us to a host of others. For instance, by what authority can the Court confine the Aboriginal perspective to questions of fact that are cognizable within the common law? Naturally there must be some consideration of *mutual cognizability*, but how can the terms of this be so strictly set by one party? And furthermore, how can the Court bind the development of their diverse cultures to the moment of contact with Europeans? This focus on historical context shifts the onus. It is not the Crown that needs to articulate how it acquired sovereign power *over* Aboriginal peoples. This maintains its

252 *R v. Pamajewon,* [1994] OJ No. 3028 at 400.

253 *Pamajewon, supra* note 75 at para. 27.

254 *Van der Peet.* See also Morse, *Pamajewon* at 1035–7. For critiques of the *Van der Peet* test, see Borrows, "Trickster"; Leonard I. Rotman, "Hunting for Answers in a Strange Kettle of Fish: Unilateralism, Paternalism and Fiduciary Rhetoric in *Badger and Van der Peet,*" *Constitutional Forum constitutionnel* 8, no. 2 (1997): 40–6; Russel Lawrence Barsh and James Youngblood Henderson, "The Supreme Court's *Van der Peet* Trilogy: Naive Imperialism and Ropes of Sand," *McGill Law Journal* 42 (1997): 993–1010; and Kent McNeil, "How Can Infringements of the Constitutional Rights of Aboriginal Peoples Be Justified?" *Constitutional Forum constitutionnel* 8, no. 2 (1997): 33–9.

255 *Van der Peet* at para. 59.

force from the simple fact that it was never doubted. It is the assumption of this foundation – a foundation that can be based only on the legal fictions of discovery, *terra nullius* and the civilization thesis – that grants the Court the jurisdiction necessary to place the onus on the Aboriginal claimant and the judicial discretion to determine the weight of the indigenous laws expressed in their oral histories. This is what determines the substantive content of the Court's repeated commitment to reconciliation.

As Lamer CJC states in *Van der Peet*, "It is possible, of course, that the Court could be said to be 'reconciling' the prior occupation of Canada by aboriginal peoples with Crown sovereignty through either a narrow or broad conception of aboriginal rights; the notion of 'reconciliation' does not, in the abstract, mandate a particular content for aboriginal rights. However, the only fair and just reconciliation is, as Walters suggests, one which takes into account the aboriginal perspective while at the same time taking into account the perspective of the common law. True reconciliation will, equally, place weight on each."[256]

The question here is how weight is to be determined and at what level. By confining the Aboriginal perspective to the facts of the case, the substantive question is avoided. The question of "reconciling" is bound up in judicial discretion. This balancing game maintains that the judiciary must take the Aboriginal perspective into account and accord it equal weight, but they must also "do so in terms which are cognizable to the non-aboriginal legal system."[257] It is hardly surprising that the Court adopts the analogy of translation in *Marshall; Bernard*.[258] This is an apt description of the game that is being played.[259]

---

256 *Van der Peet* at para. 50.

257 Ibid. at para. 49.

258 *R v. Marshall; R v. Bernard*, [2005] 2 SCR 220 at para. 48 [hereinafter *Marshall; Bernard*]. As Slattery argues, translation "artificially constrains and distorts the true character of Aboriginal title and risks compounding the historical injustices visited on Indigenous peoples. Far from reconciling Indigenous peoples with the Crown, it seems likely to exacerbate existing conflicts and grievances." Slattery, "Metamorphosis of Aboriginal Title."

259 It leads to the same well-intentioned but hollow and ineffective process that we find in the criminal law context with the *Gladue* reports and the use of sentencing provisions to address the problem of the over-representation of Aboriginal people within the Canadian prison system. Subsection 718.2(e) of the *Criminal Code*, RSC, 1985, c. C-46. is part of the process of sentencing, and it provides the judiciary with a "guiding principle," not a substantive power. This means that it cannot change the available sentencing range. It offers the accused the opportunity to bring a broader consideration of the circumstances before the judge, but it does so in a way that places the accused in the position of having to decide to simply accept "normal" sentencing or to reveal the most intimate details of their personal history as an Aboriginal. This is an optional process, but it has strong confessional overtones. In a settler-colonial context, these overtones cover over the legacy of colonization and reaffirm the jurisdiction of the Crown over Aboriginal peoples. It invites the judge to see into the life of the accused through the lens of Indian qua Indian (to borrow the language from

The real question centres directly on jurisdiction: how can the Court simply decide that the Aboriginal perspective is to be determined as a matter of fact? As Morse argues, the debate between the majority and the two dissents on the significance of the activity in question in *Van der Peet* "misses the central point, which is the existence of Aboriginal governmental jurisdiction and its relationship to the legislation of other governments. The conflict should rather be envisaged as one between competing governments, each attempting to exercise its legislative jurisdiction, akin to the lengthy history of federal provincial constitutional conflicts."[260]

As Wittgenstein states in *On Certainty*, "Knowledge is in the end based on acknowledgment."[261] This game is fixed in advance: it is not about the evidence or the facts. It is about the ability to set the rules of the game and the discretion to acknowledge or ignore the moves. This is based on the unquestioned assumption of sovereign power *over* Aboriginal peoples.

D. Custom Band Councils and the Question of Jurisdiction

The case of custom bands under the *Indian Act* is similarly limiting.[262] While it may initially appear that providing bands with the ability to choose to determine their membership and election codes was a move away from the legacy of despotism and assimilation, this appearance is, at best, misleading. Allowing bands to control their own lists provides a degree of self-determination. It is an example of the kind of limited or hedged discretionary powers that the

---

the s. 91(24) jurisprudence) and offer some small clemency on that basis. It also places an onerous fact-finding process on the accused, who must produce (through legal counsel) the report and present it to the court. As in the Aboriginal rights jurisprudence, the Aboriginal perspective is confined to a factual inquiry that is subject to judicial discretion. For commentary on these issues, see Kent Roach and Jonathan Rudin, "Gladue: The Judicial and Political Reception of a Promising Decision," *Canadian Journal of Criminalogy* 42, no. 3 (2000): 355–88; Kent Roach, "Blaming the Victim: Canadian Law, Causation, and Residential Schools," *University of Toronto Law Journal* 64, no. 4 (2014): 556–95; and for a recent comparative analysis, see Samantha Jeffries and Philip Stenning, "Sentencing Aboriginal Offenders: Law, Policy, and Practice in Three Countries," *Canadian Journal of Criminal Justice* 56, no. 4 (2014): 447–94.

260 Morse, *Pamajewon* at 1034.

261 Wittgenstein, *On Certainty* at §378.

262 I am referring to the default arrangement under the *Indian Act* (for bands for which the minister has not invoked s. 74). The default *Indian Act* arrangement has been in place since at least 1951. Bands have been able to take control of their own membership since 1985. Since 2014 the *First Nations Elections Act* has allowed participating First Nations to create their own election codes. The processes and procedures for this are somewhat different, but the larger point of where the authority flows from and where the band council fits within the larger picture of the Canadian constitutional order remains the same.

Indian Act provides to bands, but this discretion is situated within a legislative framework that forecloses on the possibility of self-government. This can be seen in a series of cases in which the Federal Courts attempt to determine their jurisdiction over custom bands. In *Lavell* Laskin J (as he was then) expressed doubt as to whether any type of band council would fit the definition in the *Federal Court Act*:

> I share the doubt of Osler J whether a Band Council, even an elected one under s. 74 of the *Indian Act* (the Act also envisages that a Band Council may exist by custom of the Band), is the type of tribunal contemplated by the definition in s. 2(g) of the *Federal Court Act* which embraces "any body or any person or persons having, exercising or purporting to exercise jurisdiction or powers conferred by or under an Act of the Parliament of Canada." A Band Council has some resemblance to the board of directors of a corporation, and if the words of s. 2(g) are taken literally, they are broad enough to embrace boards of directors in respect of powers given to them under such federal statutes as the *Bank Act*, R.S.C. 1970, c. B-1, as amended, the *Canada Corporations Act*, R.S.C. 1970, c. C-32, as amended, and the *Canadian and British Insurance Companies Act*, R.S.C. 1970, c. I-15, as amended. It is to me an open question whether private authorities (if I may so categorize boards of directors of banks and other companies) are contemplated by the *Federal Court Act* under s. 18 thereof. However, I do not find it necessary to come to a definite conclusion here on whether jurisdiction should have been ceded to the Federal Court to entertain the declaratory action brought by Mrs. Bédard against the members of the Band Council. There is another ground upon which, in this case, I would not interfere with the exercise of jurisdiction by Osler J.[263]

The problem here has to do with where the powers of band councils derive from. If their powers are conferred by Parliament, then they are a creature of statute. But this simply begs the question. It leads back to the question of the Aboriginal perspective and the inherent right of self-government. If the powers of the band council flow from the inherent (or perhaps even de facto) right of self-government, then the resemblance to "a board of directors of a corporation" is significantly reduced and with it the likelihood that the Federal Court has the necessary jurisdiction.[264] Given this, it is unsurprising that Laskin J would have doubts

---

263 *Lavell* at 1379.

264 Under s. 2(1) of the *Federal Courts Act*, RSC, 1985, c. F-7: *federal board, commission or other tribunal* means any body, person, or persons having, exercising, or purporting to exercise jurisdiction or powers conferred by or under an Act of Parliament or by or under an order made pursuant to a prerogative of the Crown, other than the Tax Court of Canada or any of its judges, any such body constituted or established by or under a law of a province or any such person or persons appointed under or in accordance with a law of a province or under section 96 of the *Constitution Act, 1867*.

concerning the jurisdiction of the Federal Courts. Despite this, the Federal Court decided the issue just four years after *Lavell* in *Gabriel*.[265] Thurlow J arrived at this conclusion by reviewing the powers the *Indian Act* confers on a band council and deciding that the scheme of the statute *resembled* a restricted form of municipal government by the council on the reserve. On the basis of this resemblance he concluded that such a council was a "federal board, commission or other tribunal" within the meaning of the *Federal Court Act* (viz. without this resemblance the question of jurisdiction was open to litigation). This argument was later affirmed by the Federal Court of Appeal without any further elaboration.[266]

A similar (but far more explicit) analogy was put forward by Cameron JA of the Saskatchewan Court of Appeal in 1982: "As municipal councils are the 'creatures' of the Legislatures of the Provinces, so Indian band councils are the 'creatures' of the Parliament of Canada."[267] He also elaborated on this point later on in the same decision:

> In summary, an Indian band council is an elected public authority, dependent on Parliament for its existence, powers and responsibilities, whose essential function it is to exercise municipal and government power – delegated to it by Parliament – in relation to the Indian reserve whose inhabitants have elected it; as such it is to act from time to time as the agent of the Minister and the representative of the band with respect to the administration and delivery of certain federal programmes for the benefit of Indians on Indian reserves, and to perform an advisory, and in some cases a decisive role in relation to the exercise by the Minister of certain of his statutory authority relative to the reserve.[268]

This characterization is simple and direct: band councils (whether custom or not) are "creatures" of the Parliament of Canada. This alone is not surprising, as the band council is a form of government that was introduced by the *Indian Act*. The problem with this reasoning is that it simply jumps over the question of the inherent right of self-government. It seems reasonable to consider the possibility that the statutory definition of the band council does not preclude the possibility that its authority is *also* derived from the inherent right of self-government. Instead the courts have favoured the view that band councils are simply "creatures" of statute and so entirely within their jurisdiction.

---

265 *Gabriel v. Canatonquin*, [1978] 1 FC 124 [*Gabriel*].

266 In *Gamblin v. Norway House Cree Nation Band Council*, 2012 FC 1536 at para. 35, Mandamin J refers to *Gabriel* as "the seminal case for the proposition that a First Nation council is a 'federal board, commission or other tribunal.'"

267 *Re Whitebear Indian Council and Carpenters Provincial Council of Saskatchewan* (1982), 135 DLR (3d) 128, 3 WWR 554, 15 Sask. R. 37 (Sask. CA) at 133.

268 Ibid. at 134.

But there have been some cases that have returned to the doubts expressed by Laskin J. For instance, in *Devil's Gap* Dawson J (as she was then) cited Dickson J's decision in *Guerin*, which held that a First Nation's interest in reserve lands is "a pre-existing legal right not created by Royal Proclamation, by s. 18(1) of the *Indian Act*, or by any other executive order or legislative provision."[269] From this basis she found that, "Given that nature of the First Nation's interest in the reserve lands, and the reservation of rights in Treaty No. 3, I am unable to conclude that the decision to refuse to proceed with a lease extension agreement is an exercise of any power conferred under the Act or any other Act of Parliament. As such, I find that the Chief and Council were not acting as a 'federal board, commission or other tribunal' when they refused to consent to an extension of the Cottagers' lease. It follows that the Court does not have jurisdiction to deal with this application for judicial review."[270]

This doubt does not necessarily disturb the jurisdiction of the Federal Court. It may simply be that in her view the power to grant or withhold consent in this instance is an implied power, not a statutory power. But even the issue of implied powers can lead to the broader issue of what kind of decision is before the court. She responds to the reasoning in both *Gabriel* and *Whitebear* by stating that the "argument that a band council obtains its existence, powers, and responsibilities from Parliament ... exemplifies the narrow conception of a band council and its powers" and that this view is inconsistent with the jurisprudence.[271] She articulates a broader view that holds that band councils have "at least all of the powers necessary to effectively carry out their responsibilities, even if not specifically provided under the Act."[272] What this has translated to in the case law is simply a qualification on the general presumption that the Federal Court retains the jurisdiction necessary to judicially review decisions of band councils (including custom councils).[273] The issue hinges on how the judge views the nexus between the nature of the council decision and the source of the authority applicable to that decision. This two-step process is set out by Nadon J in Anisman: "A two-step enquiry must be made in order to determine whether a body or person is a 'federal board, commission or other tribunal.'

269 *Guerin et al. v. R et al.*, [1984] 2 SCR 335 at 379; cited in *Devil's Gap Cottagers (1982) Ltd. v. Rat Portage Band No. 38B*, [2009] 2 FCR 276 at para. 44.

270 *Devil's Gap Cottagers* at para. 45.

271 Ibid. at paras. 58–9.

272 Ibid.

273 One such example can be found in *Wood Mountain First Nation No. 160 Council v. Canada (AG)* (2006), 55 Admin. LR (4th) 293 (FC) at para. 8, where Strayer J finds that the *Indian Act* "does not create the authority for custom elections but simply defines them for its own purposes" and so "such elections are not held under the authority of an Act of Parliament." This entails that "the Minister has no authority over such elections. Nor does INAC have any role in determining what is band custom for the purpose of governance of an election."

First, it must be determined what jurisdiction or power the body or person seeks to exercise. Second, it must be determined what is the source or the origin of the jurisdiction or power which the body or person seeks to exercise."[274]

In addition, in the *Algonquins of Barriere Lake* case Mainville J found that the common law of Aboriginal title and Aboriginal and treaty rights was part of the federal common law under the meaning of s. 101 of the *Constitution Act, 1867*.[275] And in *Gamblin* Mandamin J takes this to necessarily include the Aboriginal right of governance.[276] This means that the jurisdiction of the Federal Court over custom band councils (and if Mandamin J is correct, over all possible forms of Aboriginal self-government) hinges on a determination of the nature of the decision in relation to the source of authority. This determination is made on the basis of judicial discretion. The test for determining jurisdiction allows the court to make use of analogies between the decision of the band council and the *Indian Act* (as well as other federal statutes). This effectively circumscribes the possibility of a band council having any certainty regarding its jurisdiction. It also means that the *Indian Act* can be set as "the source or the origin of the jurisdiction or power" for all band councils (custom or not). The ambit of independent authority they have has been effectively limited to the specific section of the *Indian Act* that they have received ministerial permission to be exempted from. Beyond that, they are bound by the assumption that their powers are delegated by federal Parliament (either directly or indirectly via the *resemblance* of the decision). It seems as if even the ghost of the *Indian Act* can determine the authority of band councils.

As for what this says about the actual basis of the jurisdiction of Aboriginal governments it is difficult to say. The Federal Court is still citing *Gabriel* as authority for its jurisdiction, but its reasoning, as we have already seen, is predicated on the *resemblance* to the *Indian Act*. Even if the jurisdiction of the Aboriginal government is held to be based on a "pre-existing legal right," the courts can read this right as being part of federal common law. When this is combined with the reasoning in *Pamajewon*, the possibility of using the band council as a vehicle for moving out from the administrative despotism of the *Indian Act* seems impossible. According to the jurisprudence, the *Indian Act* can determine the jurisdiction of all bands: if not by letter, then by resemblance. When a band council passes a law on the basis of its inherent right to

274 *Anisman v. Canada (Border Services Agency)*, 2010 FCA 52 at paras. 29–30. This seems to be the full extent of the independence of custom bands (i.e., they are released from s. 74 and so they can determine the form of their council and elections, but beyond that they are bound by the assumption of delegation).

275 *Elders of Mitchikinabikok Inik v. Algonquins of Barriere Lake Customary Council*, [2010] FC 160 at para. 102.

276 *Gamblin* at para. 59.

self-government it will need to prove that such a right exists via the test in *Van der Peet*.[277] This, as we have seen, effectively closes the door to such actions. It seems that there is little difference between the current understanding of band councils and the "simple municipal institutions" envisioned over 150 years ago in the *Gradual Enfranchisement Act*. Is there a path left open within the current configuration of the Crown machinery for Aboriginal peoples to pursue self-government? In order to answer this question, we will have to turn our attention to the modern treaties.

MODERN TREATIES AND FEDERALISM

In *Beckman v. Little Salmon/Carmacks*, Binnie J articulated the purpose of the modern treaties: "The reconciliation of Aboriginal and non-Aboriginal Canadians in a mutually respectful long term relationship is the grand purpose of s. 35 of the Constitution Act, 1982. The modern treaties … attempt to further the objective of reconciliation not only by addressing grievances over the land claims but by creating the legal basis to foster a positive long-term relationship between Aboriginal and non-Aboriginal communities."[278]

In view of this grand purpose, we must ask how have the courts situated modern treaties within the current picture of federalism. The only response to this question thus far has come from the British Columbia Court of Appeal in the *Chief Mountain* decision.[279] The issue in this case was the constitutional-

277 For an example of this problem, see Sharpe JA's application of the *Van der Peet* test in *Mississaugas of Scugog Island First Nation v. National Automobile, Aerospace, Transportation and General Workers Union of Canada*, 2007 ONCA 814. The emphasis in this decision is decidedly on the notion that, whatever the inherent right of self-government is, it *must* be consistent with "Crown sovereignty or basic common law principles [and] not strain Canada's constitutional structure" (at para. 15). It is curious that in the next sentence he notes, "Treaty rights are consensual in nature and arise from agreements reached between the Crown and aboriginal peoples" (ibid.). These can be consistent only if one assumes that Crown sovereignty is (for lack of a better term) free floating. It is hard to explain how this could be the case without recourse to the racist legal fictions of *terra nullius* or discovery. If Crown sovereignty is derived from the treaties, then the constitutional structure would likely require some balancing of the common law principles with those of Indigenous legal traditions.

278 *Beckman v. Little Salmon/Carmacks First Nation*, 2010 SCC 53 at para. 10. This characterization of the purpose of modern treaties is echoed (and cited) by Karakatsanis J when she states, "As expressions of partnership between nations, modern treaties play a critical role in fostering reconciliation. Through s. 35 of the *Constitution Act, 1982*, they have assumed a vital place in our constitutional fabric. Negotiating modern treaties, and living by the mutual rights and responsibilities they set out, has the potential to forge a renewed relationship between the Crown and Indigenous peoples" *First Nation of Nacho Nyak Dun v. Yukon*, 2017 SCC 58 at para. 1 [hereinafter *Nacho Nyak Dun*].

279 *Sga'nism Sim'augit (Chief Mountain) v. Canada (AG)*, 2013 BCCA 49, 359 DLR (4th) 231, leave to appeal to SCC refused, 35301 (22 August 2013) [hereinafter *Chief Mountain*]. I have

ity of the legislative and self-government powers set out in the Nisga'a Final Agreement (NFA). The appellants (who are members of the Nisga'a Nation) argued that the NFA and the attending settlement legislation effectively created a "third order of government" via s. 35 of the *Constitution Act, 1982* that is inconsistent with the distribution of powers set out in ss. 91 and 92 of the *Constitution Act, 1867*.[280] Harris JA followed the trial judge in rejecting the appellants' reasoning and upholding the constitutionality of the NFA; the Supreme Court of Canada denied leave to appeal that decision.[281] Accordingly, *Chief Mountain* now sits as the current authority on the constitutionality of the NFA and the validity of modern treaties. Given that fact, the importance of the case is rather difficult to overstate. Simply put, this case deals with the future of reconciliation. Harris JA clearly follows the Supreme Court's view on the "grand purpose" of the modern treaties, as it informs us that they are designed to "achieve reconciliation" and "lay the foundation" for the new relationship between Aboriginal peoples and the Crown.[282] As such, we need to pay very close attention to precisely how he determines the fit between the NFA and "the wider constitutional fabric of Canada."[283]

Harris JA found that the powers given in the NFA were "valid delegations of power."[284] It is this finding that allows him to maintain that that it is "unnecessary to decide whether some or all of the self-government powers derive from an inherent Aboriginal right."[285] The reasoning here is puzzling. How can it be "unnecessary" to identify the actual source of these powers? After all, when we are considering the meaning of a legal agreement, the relationship between the parties can change the character of that agreement. This possibility is reflected on a very general level in the difference between a unilateral act of delegation and a treaty. A unilateral act of delegation is premised on an asymmetrical relationship: one party gives another something that they do not have (i.e., authority), and this transfer is a conditional one,[286] whereas a treaty is normally understood as a compact made between two or more independent nations.[287] Of course, this is not the case in the Canadian jurisprudence. As Dickson CJC states in *R v. Simon*, "An Indian treaty is unique; it is an agreement sui generis which is neither created nor terminated according to the rules of international

written on this case previously, and my reasoning here is simply an abbreviation of that more extensive examination of the case. See Nichols, "Reconciliation without Recollection?"

280 *Chief Mountain* at para. 5.

281 SCC docket 35301; leave denied 22 August 2013.

282 *Chief Mountain* at para. 49.

283 Ibid.

284 Ibid. at para. 8.

285 Ibid.

286 *Black's Law Dictionary*, 5th ed., s.v. "delegation."

287 Ibid., s.v. "treaty."

law."[288] But whichever rules do actually govern the creation of these sui generis treaties, it is clear that the relationship is not analogous to a unilateral act of delegation.[289] If it were, it would entail that either the sui generis treaties are surrender documents or that Aboriginal peoples were subject to Crown authority without consent.[290] And if these types of arguments are going to be used to explain the rules that govern the sui generis treaties, then the Court will need to provide evidence to support them; they cannot simply stand as self-evident facts and unquestioned assumptions. So how is it that in *Chief Mountain* we encounter something that is called a "treaty" and has the characteristics of a "valid act of delegation"? Is the ultimate achievement of the process of reconciliation a treaty that can be – like any act of delegation – "withdrawn or amended" by the Crown?[291] If so, it would certainly shift the connotations of Binnie J's (somewhat enigmatic) assertion that "the future is more important than the past."[292]

This was not the first time that the validity of the NFA was contested. In *Campbell* Williamson J faced the same question but adopted an entirely different approach to determining the fit between the modern treaties and "the wider constitutional fabric of Canada."[293] In response to the problem of sovereign incompatibility, he found that "the *Constitution Act, 1867* did not distribute all

---

288 *Simon* at 404.

289 See *Syliboy*; *Badger*; *R v. Marshall*, [1999] 3 SCR 456 at para. 76. In *Badger* Cory J states that treaties are "analogous to contracts," but this analogy is qualified by the fact that they are (once again) sui generis, as they are of a "very solemn and special, public nature." As such, finding that treaties are "valid delegations of power" could well – without further explanation – represent a distinct shift in the characterization of treaties within the case law. For more on the problems surrounding the sui generis status of treaties in Canadian jurisprudence, see Gordon Christie, "Justifying Principles of Treaty Interpretation," *Queen's Law Journal* 26 (2000): 143–224; Leonard Rotman, "Defining Parameters: Aboriginal Rights, Treaty Rights, and the Sparrow Justificatory Test," *Alberta Law Review* 36 (1997): 149–79; and J.Y. Henderson, "Interpreting *Sui Generis* Treaties," *Alberta Law Review* 36 (1997): 46–96; Royal Commission on Aboriginal Peoples, *Report of the Royal Commission on Aboriginal Peoples: Restructuring the Relationship*, vol. 2 (Ottawa: Minister of Supply and Services, 1996) [hereinafter *RCAP* 2]; Joshua Nichols, "A Narrowing Field of View: An Investigation into the Relationship between the Principles of Treaty Interpretation and the Conceptual Framework of Canadian Federalism," *Osgoode Hall Law Journal* 56, no. 2 (2019).

290 In "Justifying Principles," Christie argues that the Court's approach to interpreting treaties makes sense only if the treaties are thought of as surrenders. This shifts the burden directly onto the Court, as in order for this interpretation to claim legitimacy, the Court would have to determine how and why this is the case (ibid. at 161 and 198–200).

291 *Chief Mountain* at para. 48.

292 *Beckman* at para. 10.

293 The phrase "wider constitutional fabric" is Harris JA's from *Chief Mountain* at para. 48; *Campbell*.

legislative power to the Parliament and the legislatures."[294] These bodies have the powers set out in ss. 91 and 92, but this distribution is of the powers that the colonies (or the imperial Crown) had until 30 June 1867.[295] It does not distribute an absolute or final set of powers, and so it "does not end, what remains of the royal prerogative or aboriginal and treaty rights, including the diminished but not extinguished power of self-government which remained with the Nisga'a people in 1982."[296] This makes it clear that the picture of federalism that each case offers is quite distinct: one avoids a positive determination by treating it as if it were a "valid delegation of power"; the other fits the inherent right of self-government into the residual spaces between the division of powers set out in the *Constitution Act, 1867*. But the key difference between these cases is that each offers us a different method for testing the constitutional validity of the NFA. In *Chief Mountain* Harris JA presents us with the "valid delegation" model, which maintains that "the source of the treaty rights, whether they are rooted in Aboriginal rights or rights delegated from either federal or provincial governments, is not, therefore, the critical question in assessing the validity of a treaty. What matters is that the rights have been agreed to by parties with the necessary capacity and authority."[297] Whereas in *Campbell* Williamson J addresses the issue of source directly and finds the "diminished sovereignty" that is the Aboriginal right of self-government.

At first glance, the distinction between *Campbell* and *Chief Mountain* seems obvious, yet when we begin to examine the actual legal effects of this difference in terms of the legal status and vulnerability of the NFA we find that they are virtually identical. In each the NFA is found to be constitutionally valid and the *Sparrow/Badger* test for infringement is found to apply. Yet there is a difference here to be accounted for. It concerns what these approaches hold for the future of reconciliation and the picture of federalism. As Karakatsanis J reminds us, "The Final Agreements address past grievances, and yet are oriented towards the future."[298]

In *Campbell* the recognition of an Aboriginal right to self-government opens the door to a shift within the Canadian jurisprudence. While it is by no means a leap out of the "magic circle" of Crown sovereignty and the various legal fictions that have served as its foundation thus far (i.e., the doctrine of discovery,

294 *Campbell* at para. 180.
295 Ibid. at paras. 76 and 180.
296 Ibid. at para. 180.
297 *Chief Mountain* at para. 51.
298 *First Nation of Nacho Nyak Dun v. Yukon*, [2017] 2 SCR 576, 2017 SCC 58 at para. 10. While she does not cite Binnie J directly, the resemblance is worth noting; see *Beckman* at para. 10.

terra nullius, adverse possession, etc.), it does suggest a line for future development.[299] It could be bolstered by a reconsideration of the "enclaves" approach taken by Laskin CJC in *Cardinal*.[300] This could have the benefit of removing the suggestion that Aboriginal self-government fits between the spaces of ss. 91 and 92 and, instead, situate it directly in s. 91(24). Naturally, this would also require removing the "broad view" of s. 91(24) with its unquestioned assumption of unlimited power *over* Aboriginal peoples. It would require strictly confining s. 91(24) to honouring the obligations that the Crown has to Aboriginal peoples and abandoning the legacy of control, assimilation, and extinguishment.[301] Given the more recent developments on the nature of the Crown's sovereignty in relation to Aboriginal peoples in *Haida Nation* and *Taku River Tlingit*, the reasoning in *Campbell* and *Cardinal* could be revisited.[302] The Crown's sovereignty could be decoupled from legislative power and underlying title. This would open the door for constitutional legitimacy, as Aboriginal peoples are included via practices of negotiation, mutual recognition, and consent. But this shared (or treaty federalist) notion of Crown sovereignty would be unable to support either the power of unilateral extinguishment prior to 1982 or the

---

299 Borrows, "Sovereignty's Alchemy" at 562, 569. See also Kent McNeil, "Challenging Legislative Infringements of the Inherent Aboriginal Right of Self-Government," *Windsor Yearbook of Access to Justice* 22 (2003): 329–62.

300 The Court's removal of IJI in *Tsilhqot'in Nation v. British Columbia* bars this. For an excellent analysis of the effect of recent Supreme Court decisions on s. 91(24), see Kerry Wilkins, "Life among the Ruins: Section 91(24) after *Tsilhqot'in* and *Grassy Narrows*," *Alberta Law Review* 55, no. 1 (2017): 91–126.

301 This would offer some certainty: a classical approach to federalism would adopt a territorial limit to the issue of lands, which would serve to ease the fears of the Crown around the bugbear of unlimited rights (e.g. in *Gladstone; Ahousaht Indian Band and Nation v. Canada (AG)*, 2009 BCSC 1494; *Ahousaht Indian Band and Nation v. Canada (AG)*, 2011 BCCA 237). It would also limit the vague Indians qua Indians reasoning to the first head of s. 91(24).

302 In *Haida Nation* McLachlin CJ states that the "process of reconciliation flows from the Crown's duty of honourable dealing toward Aboriginal peoples, which arises in turn from the Crown's assertion of sovereignty over an Aboriginal people and *de facto* control of land and resources that were formerly in the control of that people": *Haida Nation* at para. 32. This opens up the possibility that the Crown's assertion of sovereignty is predicated on a de facto control of land that has yet to be made *de jure* via the formation of treaties that reconcile "pre-existing Aboriginal sovereignty with assumed Crown sovereignty": ibid. at para. 20. This is supported by *Taku River Tlingit*, where the Court states, "The purpose of s. 35(1) of the *Constitution Act, 1982* is to facilitate the ultimate reconciliation of prior Aboriginal occupation with *de facto* Crown sovereignty"; *Taku River Tlingit* at para. 42. This characterization of Crown sovereignty is also cited with approval in the Court's recent decision in *MMF* at para. 66. On a liberal reading, these statements open up a number of possible arguments around the constitutional status of treaties and the nature of Crown sovereignty. Also see Walters, "Morality of Aboriginal Law" at 515; Hoehn, *Reconciling Sovereignties*.

unilateral conception of federal power under s. 91(24) that makes s. 35 into a justification test for unilateral infringements (i.e., *Sparrow/Badger* test).[303] This could open the way to the possibility of revisiting the top end of the duty to consult in *Delgamuukw* and *Haida Nation* so as to require the consent of the Aboriginal nation in cases of the Crown either infringing an acknowledged treaty provision or proposing changes in a treaty (effectively barring the possibility of unilateral infringement).[304] With this change, treaties would have to cease being seen as merely documents with a measure of constitutional protection (that measure being determined by the courts) and start being viewed as constitutional documents.[305] While this is only a possible (even if unlikely) line of jurisprudential development, it is one that the reasoning in *Campbell* and *Cardinal* holds open. This offers at least the possibility of a form of federalism based on holding power *with* Aboriginal peoples. It is only by finding such a perspicuous picture of federalism that we can arrive at a reconciliation that would *not* be dependent on the support of legal fictions that can no longer be reasonably defended.

With *Chief Mountain* we find that the question of the source of authority and jurisdiction is set aside as being unnecessary to the resolution of the question of constitutional validity. As such, the NFA is reviewed "as if" it was a simple municipal charter. The legislation is deemed valid to the extent that it conforms to the ability of Parliament and the legislatures to delegate powers to subordinate bodies. The only trace of difference in the case of the NFA is its constitutional protection under s. 35, which is deemed acceptable because the *Sparrow/Badger* test applies and extends unilateral Crown authority over it on the basis of unquestioned Crown sovereignty, legislative power, and underlying title.

What kind of future does this kind of reasoning open to us? What picture of federalism does this offer us? The answer is far from certain. On the one hand, the reasoning fits with an established pattern within the jurisprudence where the courts avoid the issue of an Aboriginal right to self-government by speaking instead of rights and title. Within this line of reasoning the Crown is granted unquestionable sovereignty and underlying title, while Aboriginal nations are left with a series of residual rights that act as a burden on this claim. *Chief Mountain* fits comfortably within this pattern. The only real distinction is that it explicitly holds back from actually determining the source of authority and jurisdiction (for at least one party to the treaty). We are simply told that it is possible to determine "validity" of a treaty without determining the source of

303 Rotman, "Defining Parameters."

304 *Haida Nation* at paras. 24, 30, 48; *Delgamuukw* at para. 168.

305 Christie, "Justifying Principles" at 202. See Borrows, "Sovereignty's Alchemy"; Henderson, "Interpreting *Sui Generis* Treaties"; Walters, "Morality"; Tully, *Strange Multiplicity*.

authority.[306] Looking into the actual source of authority is as unnecessary to the result as it is to the "true nature" of the treaty.

If this is the "future of reconciliation," it seems we have to reverse Binnie J's dictum and maintain that *the past is more important than the future.*[307] After all, it is the unquestioned presumption of Crown sovereignty, legislative power, and underlying title that gives rise to the "broad view" of s. 91(24), which, in turn, gives the federal Crown the power to control, assimilate, and extinguish.[308] This unquestioned *historical warrant* is offering a picture of federalism where Aboriginal peoples remain stuck within a set of "simple municipal institutions." By following the Bluebeard logic of the Court and not inquiring into the past, we are left with a future in which the foundations of reconciliation are based on the *mere possibility* of valid delegations.[309]

But how can the Crown *validly* delegate power to Aboriginal peoples when its power *over* them is founded on the *thin air* of its own unilateral assertions? If it is possible for the Crown to *validly* give what it never legally had, then it seems the Crown can simply launder its own sovereignty, legislative power, and underlying title. As it stands, it seems that there is no way out of the "magic circle" of Crown sovereignty.[310] This is, to my mind, precisely because the *only way out* is through questioning the validity of the Crown's *historical warrant* (this is what the various practices of resisting and acting otherwise have always contested). Without doing this, the unquestioned presumption of Crown sovereignty, legislative power, and underlying title will continue to silently determine the course of the future and all paths will remain circular.

4.3 Tsilhqot'in Nation and the Meaning of s. 91(24)

We have travelled over a wide field of jurisprudence criss-crossing in every direction in search of some arrangement of perspectives or set of reminders that could begin to loosen the grip of the current picture of federalism that is holding the Supreme Court captive. The sections of this chapter offer a number of "sketches of landscapes" in which "the same or almost the same points were always being approached afresh from different directions."[311]

Now that we have come to the end of these "long and involved journeyings," how can we arrange them so as to get a more perspicuous picture of the landscape? I believe that the best vantage point is to return to *Tsilhqot'in Nation* and

306 *Chief Mountain* at para. 51.
307 *Beckman* at para. 10.
308 *Daniels* at para. 25; *Daniels I* at para. 353; *Daniels II* at para. 36.
309 I defined what I mean by the term *Bluebeard logic* in note 79 of part 1.
310 Borrows, "Sovereignty's Alchemy."
311 Wittgenstein, *Philosophical Investigations* at preface.

reconsider the *basis for* and *significance of* the removal of interjurisdictional immunity from issues characterized as involving treaty or Aboriginal rights.

In the opening paragraphs the chief justice offers a summary of the six conclusions she reaches in the case, but we will focus on one of them: "Once Aboriginal title is established, s. 35 of the *Constitution Act, 1982* permits incursions on it only with the consent of the Aboriginal group *or if they are justified by a compelling and substantial public purpose and are not inconsistent with the Crown's fiduciary duty to the Aboriginal group; for purposes of determining the validity of provincial legislative incursions on lands held under Aboriginal title,* this framework displaces the doctrine of interjurisdictional immunity."[312]

The reasoning here connects the "framework" of s. 35 to the place of s. 91(24) in the division of powers. My question is simple and direct: what is the basis of this displacement? The chief justice's response to this is split. Part of the response can be found in how the s. 35 framework is set out. The subsection on the justification of infringement is particularly relevant in this regard. The second, and more direct, part of the response is found in the closing subsection of the decision, which is on the division of powers. This subsection is part of the Court's response to the question of whether or not the *Forest Act* (as provincial legislation) is ousted by the *Constitution.*[313]

The first subsection that responds to this question provides a short outline of the s. 35 test for infringement and maintains that "this framework permits a principled reconciliation of Aboriginal rights with the interests of all Canadians."[314] This is, to my mind, the justification for the displacement of the doctrine of interjurisdictional immunity. This justification can be rephrased as follows: the framework of s. 35 permits a "principled reconciliation" that makes the limited protections offered by the "exclusive" nature of federal jurisdiction over Indians and their lands unnecessary. This means that in order to explain the basis for this displacement – and the resulting alteration of the picture of federalism – we will need to turn our attention to this "principled reconciliation."

This articulation of reconciliation poses some serious problems. First, the use of reconciliation here is *unilateral.* This is because *Aboriginal rights* do not speak for themselves. They are "recognized and affirmed" only *after* they have been subjected to the legal tests that have been designed (again unilaterally) to determine whether or not they can be said to "exist." Only those rights that can pass through the alchemical processes of crystallization (simply another term for the magical effects of discovery) and the "integral/distinctive" test can be placed in the curatorial collection of Aboriginal rights that have constitutional

312 *Tsilhqot'in Nation* (emphasis added).

313 *Forest Act,* RSBC 1996, c. 157.

314 *Tsilhqot'in Nation* at para. 125.

protection. Once they have been subjected to this process, the Court can begin reconciling them as legally defined rights. This brings us to the second problem: on the other side of this process of justification, the Court places "the interests of all Canadians." This can only ever be an amalgam of what the provincial legislatures and federal Parliament say this interest is and how the Court interprets it. Furthermore, in *Sparrow* the Court held that "the Court of Appeal below held, at p. 331, that regulations could be valid if reasonably justified as 'necessary for the proper management and conservation of the resource *or in the public interest*.' We find the 'public interest' justification to be so vague as to provide no meaningful guidance and so broad as to be unworkable as a test for the justification of a limitation on constitutional rights."[315]

Why is the Supreme Court using a justification that it previously found effectively meaningless and unworkable? In this model of reconciliation, one party is restrained by a series of deeply restrictive standards (whose only possible justification is the presumption of Crown sovereignty, legislative power, and underlying title, which, in turn, can be grounded only on the legal fictions of discovery and *terra nullius*) that determine the possible significance of their perspective, while the other party enjoys the unquestioned presumption of both sovereignty and underlying title as well as the ability to cloak its perspective in the "public interest." How can this be a part of the framework that is supposed to make reconciliation possible?

Part of the response is, I would assume, found in *Gladstone*. In this case Lamer CJC attempts to deal with a right that extends beyond the limits of "moderate livelihood"[316] and food, social, and ceremonial purposes (i.e., purposes that can be said to have the "internal limitation," as they are not "unlimited" commercial rights). As he put it, "The only circumstance contemplated by *Sparrow* was where the aboriginal right was internally limited; the judgment simply does not consider how the priority standard should be applied in circumstances where the right has no such internal limitation."[317]

From this he goes on to argue that "under *Sparrow*'s priority doctrine, where the aboriginal right to be given priority is one without internal limitation, courts should assess the government's actions not to see whether the government has

315 *Sparrow* at 1113 (emphasis added).

316 A standard from the United States Supreme Court in *State of Washington v. Washington State Commercial, Passenger, Fishing Vessel Association*, 443 US 658 (1979) (known as the *Boldt* decision) introduced into the Canadian case law by Lambert J in *R v. Van der Peet* (1993) 80 BC L. Rev. (2d) 75 at 126. The majority at the BCCA disagreed and found the standard irrelevant. At the Supreme Court Lamer CJ rejected this standard; see *R v. Van der Peet*, [1996] 2 SCR 507 at para. 279. It was later recognized in a treaty context in *R v. Marshall*, [1999] 3 SCR 456 at para. 59.

317 *Gladstone* at para. 60.

given exclusivity to that right (the least drastic means) but rather to determine whether the government has taken into account the existence and importance of such rights."[318]

What kind of standard can the Court apply to determine whether or not one party to a conflict is "taking into account the existence and importance" of the other's rights? Is this not simply bypassing the need for the other party to consent? After all, it seems that in a normal situation the determination of the "importance" of a given right is, and must be, mutually agreed upon (i.e., thus offering a secure basis for judicial determinations). If it is not, then it is not a form of reconciliation that relies on the mutual consent of the parties involved. This means that it can be only a unilateral reconciliation of *judicial concepts*. Lamer CJC clearly sets out the framework for dealing with "unlimited" rights:

> Aboriginal rights are recognized and affirmed by s. 35(1) in order to reconcile the existence of distinctive aboriginal societies prior to the arrival of Europeans in North America with the assertion of Crown sovereignty over that territory; they are the means by which the critical and integral aspects of those societies are maintained. Because, however, distinctive aboriginal societies exist within, and are a part of, a broader social, political and economic community, over which the Crown is sovereign, there are circumstances in which, in order to pursue objectives of compelling and substantial importance to that community as a whole (taking into account the fact that aboriginal societies are a part of that community), some limitation of those rights will be justifiable. Aboriginal rights are a necessary part of the reconciliation of aboriginal societies with the broader political community of which they are part; limits placed on those rights are, where the objectives furthered by those limits are of sufficient importance to the broader community as a whole, *equally* necessary part of that reconciliation.[319]

The key move here – which cloaks this version of reconciliation with the appearance of legitimacy – is the claim that "distinctive aboriginal societies exist within, and are a part of, a broader social, political and economic community, over which the Crown is sovereign." In what sense can Aboriginal peoples be said to be "a part of" the broader community? If this is simply a kind of factual statement – along the lines of his statement in *Delgamuukw* that "we are all here to stay"[320] – then the claim concerning Crown sovereignty would not necessarily flow from it. But even if we attempt to interpret this as a description of a factual situation, the prepositions do not make sense (i.e. "exist within,

318 Ibid. at para. 63.
319 Ibid. at para. 73.
320 *Delgamuukw* at para. 186.

and are a part of"). It is these unilaterally determined prepositions that make it appear as if the Crown's claim to sovereignty, legislative power and underlying title is simply a matter of fact. It does so in much the same manner as Binnie J's reinterpretation of the Two-Row Wampum in *Mitchell* or as McLachlin CJ's use of the concept of translation in *Marshall; Bernard*.[321] By this reasoning, the inherent rights of Aboriginal peoples – those rights that exist by virtue of the fact that when the colonists arrived they were "organized in societies and occupying the land as their forefathers had done for centuries"[322] – are suddenly and entirely absorbed by the Crown. Here the entire 150-year project of colonization and assimilation is realized and legitimated by judicial fiat. Lamer CJC clearly recognizes this and hedges the position slightly: "The objectives which can be said to be compelling and substantial will be those directed at either the recognition of the prior occupation of North America by aboriginal peoples or – and at the level of justification it is this purpose which may well be most relevant – at the reconciliation of aboriginal prior occupation with the assertion of the sovereignty of the Crown."[323]

The problem here, once again, is that the Court is *reconciling* the parties by and through a process that it determines in order to arrive at a resolution that it assigns. The only element of consent it can attempt to lay claim to is the fact that the Aboriginal claimant brought the dispute before the court. But submitting a claim before an adjudicative body cannot be transmuted – no matter what legal alchemy is employed – into a consent to the sovereignty of the state that grants that body jurisdiction. This reasoning would fundamentally confuse the concept of dispute with that of surrender. It is the Court – as the "guardian of the constitution"[324] – that is unilaterally determining whether the infringement that the Crown is proposing either *recognizes* "the prior occupation of North America by aboriginal peoples" or *reconciles* that occupation with the assertion of Crown sovereignty.[325] This necessarily implies that this process can take place entirely *within* the bounds of the constitution. Only those rights that the Court can *hear* and *translate* into the common law will receive protection, because only those rights can be *recognized and affirmed* as "existing." But if this is the case, then the form of reconciliation that the Court is referring to can only be the *internal process* of reconciling the *federal power* with *federal duty*.[326]

321 *Mitchell* at para. 130; *Marshall; Bernard* at para. 48.

322 *Calder* at 328.

323 *Gladstone* at para. 60; cited in *Tsilhqot'in Nation* at para. 81.

324 *Hunter v. Southam Inc.*, [1984] 2 SCR 145 at paras. 16, 44.

325 *Gladstone* at para. 60; cited in *Tsilhqot'in Nation* at para. 81.

326 This was how the Court first characterized reconciliation in *Sparrow* at 1109: "Federal legislative powers continue, including, of course, the right to legislate with respect to Indians pursuant to s. 91(24) of the *Constitution Act, 1867*. These powers must, however, now be

This was, after all, how the Court first characterized reconciliation in *Sparrow*. It is based on the "broad view" of s. 91(24) and the unquestioned assumption of the Crown's power *over* Aboriginal peoples. It is – despite the Court's explicit claims to the contrary in *Tsilhqot'in Nation*[327] – *necessarily* reliant on the doctrine of discovery and *terra nullius*. This explains how the Court can maintain that "there was from the outset never any doubt that sovereignty and legislative power, and indeed the underlying title, to such lands vested in the Crown."[328] The only possible basis for the nexus between Crown sovereignty and underlying title is *legal fiction* – this is "what is left when Aboriginal title is subtracted from it."[329] And it is this that explains how the Court can unilaterally determine that provincial laws apply to land held under Aboriginal title.[330]

The removal of the doctrine of interjurisdictional immunity from disputes involving s. 35 rights fundamentally alters the picture of federalism in Canada. It does so without addressing the history of Aboriginal peoples or listening to their perspectives. It is a unilateral assertion that has the same degree of legitimacy as the introduction of s. 88 of the *Indian Act* when it was introduced (without meaningful consultation or consent) in 1951. The effect of this change is substantial and must not be understood as a *diminution* of the Crown's powers under s. 91(24). It is certainly a reduction of the *limited protections* that "exclusive" federal jurisdiction under s. 91(24) offered to Aboriginal peoples. But it is also a fundamental expansion of the "broad view" of s. 91(24). The Court has stated that it will treat Aboriginal title as a double aspect matter.[331] Now that the limited shielding of Indians qua Indians has been removed, the ground has been cleared for the provinces to draft legislation of general application for Aboriginal title lands (the modern approach at least restricts the legislatures from singling out Indians in this legislation). A picture of federalism that has been in place – even if only in limited forms – for 250 years has been unilaterally altered.[332]

So how does the Court explain this change? The chief justice briefly summarizes the s. 35 framework: "As discussed, s. 35 of the *Constitution Act, 1982* imposes limits on how both the federal and provincial governments can deal with land under Aboriginal title. Neither level of government is permitted to legislate in a way that results in a meaningful diminution of an Aboriginal or

read together with s. 35(1). In other words, federal power must be reconciled with federal duty." After *Tsilhqot'in Nation* it seems that what is being reconciled is the double aspect of federal and provincial power in s. 91(24) with the Crown's duty under s. 35.

327 *Tsilhqot'in Nation* at para. 69.

328 *Sparrow* at 1103.

329 *Tsilhqot'in Nation* at para. 70; Borrows, "Durability of Terra Nullius" at 742.

330 *Tsilhqot'in Nation* at para. 101.

331 Ibid. at para. 129.

332 Borrows, "Durability of Terra Nullius" at 735–7.

treaty right, unless such an infringement is justified in the broader public interest and is consistent with the Crown's fiduciary duty owed to the Aboriginal group. The result is to protect Aboriginal and treaty rights while also allowing the reconciliation of Aboriginal interests with those of the broader society."[333]

The logic here is, as we have already detailed, puzzling. What constitutes a "meaningful diminution" of an Aboriginal or treaty right? It seems that this is what the Court believes it is determining by applying this framework. It allows it to distinguish between what is a "meaningful diminution" and what is simply consistent with the standard of recognition that it feels to be appropriate. How can the Court hope to possibly make this determination have any significance whatsoever when it is using the "public interest" as a unit of measure in its justification analysis? What kind of reconciliation is this? It seems to be one in which a solitary accountant balances the books. The Aboriginal perspective is reduced to a curated collection of crystalline legal objects that can be weighed and measured. Wittgenstein aptly points out the kind of disguised nonsense at work here: "I want to say: We use judgments as principles of judgment."[334] But this constellation of unilateral judgments is passed off as a "framework." This leads the Court to state, "What role then is left for the application of the doctrine of interjurisdictional immunity and the idea that Aboriginal rights are at the core of the federal power over 'Indians' under s. 91(24) of the *Constitution Act, 1867*? The answer is none.... The doctrine of interjurisdictional immunity is directed to ensuring that the two levels of government are able to operate without interference in their core areas of exclusive jurisdiction. This goal is not implicated in cases such as this. Aboriginal rights are a limit on both federal and provincial jurisdiction."[335]

It is difficult to fully appreciate the significance of this statement. It is a sea change in the jurisprudence. John Borrows clearly articulates the stakes of this change:

> The court's conclusion cuts against a two-hundred-fifty year constitutional principle first outlined in the *Royal Proclamation of 1763*, and accepted by many First Nations in central Canada in the 1764 Treaty of Niagara. These principles prevented local colonial governments from molesting or disturbing First Nations in their use and occupation of land. Governments who are the closest to First Nations have the greatest incentive to benefit from Indigenous lands. For example, British Columbia stands to gain the most from infringing Aboriginal title; any diminishment of Aboriginal title accrues to their benefit. Therefore, the law in

---

333 *Tsilhqot'in Nation* at para. 139.

334 Wittgenstein, *On Certainty* at §124.

335 *Tsilhqot'in Nation* at paras. 140–1.

> North America developed to ensure that local governments had substantial obstacles placed in their path in dealing with First Nations. The *Royal Proclamation* and 250 years of Canadian law, as affirmed in section 91(24) of the *Constitution Act, 1867*, interposed a more distant imperial or federal power between First Nations and colonial/state/local/provincial governments. The exclusion of the provinces from dealing with First Nations was one of the few checks and balances Indigenous peoples enjoyed under Canadian law throughout history. In fact, our country was partially formed on this basis. While the 13 former American Colonies rebelled against this principle in the American War of Independence, governments north of the border have largely upheld the Proclamation and Treaty of Niagara's principles – that is until June 26, 2014 when the *Tsilhqot'in* decision was released. With the *Tsilhqot'in* decision the Supreme Court of Canada has overturned First Nations' *Marta Carta*.[336]

By relying on the framework of s. 35 and ignoring the history of s. 91(24), the Court follows the unquestioned assumption of Crown sovereignty as articulated by Lord Watson in *St Catherine's Milling* and repeated by Dickson CJ in *Sparrow*. It highlights the fact that the s. 35 framework and the "broad view" s. 91(24) share a common foundation. Both rely on *terra nullius* and discovery to diminish Aboriginal peoples to such a degree that the Crown was able to acquire sovereignty, legislative power, and underlying title to their lands by assertion alone. As Borrows argues, "The assertion of radical title retroactively affirms the Crown's appropriation of Indigenous legal interests without their knowledge or consent. In most other contexts this would be called stealing."[337]

The Court concludes that "applying the doctrine of interjurisdictional immunity to exclude provincial regulation of forests on Aboriginal title lands would produce uneven, undesirable results and may lead to legislative vacuums."[338] This clearly shows the picture of federalism that the Court has adopted. It forecloses on the very idea that Aboriginal peoples – who have always had their own legal and political systems – form a part of the federal structure of Canada. Borrows drives this point home:

> A legal vacuum would not be created if the Court recognized the pre-existing and continuing nature of Indigenous jurisdiction along with Aboriginal title. Indigenous law exists in Canada. The recognition of Aboriginal title is contingent on the recognition of Aboriginal social organization and its continuity down to the present day. Thus, as noted, the very existence of Tsilhqot'in title recognizes

336 Borrows, "Durability of Terra Nullius" at 735–7.

337 Ibid. at 724.

338 *Tsilhqot'in Nation* at para. 147; Borrows, "Durability of Terra Nullius" at 738–9.

> that Aboriginal peoples effectively occupied land at the time sovereignty was asserted; it affirms that they have continuously retained such control, exclusive of other Aboriginal groups, down to the present day. The Court's own reasoning presupposes a legal presence, rather than a vacuum, when it recognizes Aboriginal title.[339]

Simply put, the legal vacuum that it fears is its own creation. Overall by declaring that the s. 91(24) allows for provincial laws of general application, the Court has fully adopted the modern approach to federalism. This, as we have already seen, relies on the idea that s. 91(24) is *in no way different* from any other head of power in the *Constitution Act, 1867*. It is an approach that ignores the special constitutional status of Aboriginal peoples as recognized in the treaty-making process, the *Royal Proclamation of 1763*, and the fact that Aboriginal peoples did not consent to or participate in the enactment of the *Constitution Act, 1867*. It assumes that the exclusive jurisdiction that s. 91(24) grants to the federal government is unlimited power *over* Indians and their lands (what I have been referring to as the "broad view") and unilaterally broadens this power in favour of the provincial Crown by interpreting it as a double aspect matter. This subjects Aboriginal peoples to a confused system of concurrent provincial and federal jurisdiction and continues the implicit use of the doctrine of discovery in Canadian law.

This decision did not have to take this form. Aboriginal title is not unlimited in the same way that Lamer CJC was so concerned about in *Gladstone*. It is by definition geographically limited. The Court could have used this opportunity to revive the "enclaves" theory of s. 91(24) and adopt the "autonomist" approach to the division of powers that Bruce Ryder mapped out in 1991.[340] This approach would offer the benefit of protecting Aboriginal title lands from provincial incursion. It would open the space required for the Tsilhqot'in Nation to govern their lands by their laws in a nation-to-nation relationship. This would clarify the purpose of and limits to s. 91(24) by reading it as a "treaty power" and finally ending the colonial "broad view" with its legacy of control, assimilation, and extinguishment.[341] This would open up a space where Aboriginal peoples could negotiate with the Crown on more even constitutional ground (one that *does not* begin with the presumption of Crown power *over* Aboriginal peoples) – a space that could be used to move towards the equal federal relationship that the Royal Commission of 1664 recommended (viz. Aboriginal nations would be equal "partners in confederation").[342] This more diverse

---

339 Borrows, "Durability of Terra Nullius" at 738–9.

340 Ryder, "Demise and Rise."

341 Chartrand, "Failure of the Daniels Case" at 185.

342 Cited in Tully, "Strange Multiplicity" at 137.

picture of federalism would have constituted a step towards actually honouring the obligations that the dominion inherited from the imperial Parliament.[343] It would also offer a clear and reasonable solution to the problem of "unlimited rights" (which remains an ongoing jurisdictional bugbear for the provinces), as territorial boundaries would provide areas in which First Nations have the authority to effectively co-manage the land base.[344] This would put the bugbear of "unlimited" rights (a curious fear, as it is precisely the nature of the right the Crown claims over Aboriginal peoples and their lands) to bed and with it this use of the "public interest" standard of justification in *Gladstone* and *Tsilhqot'in Nation*. This approach offers an opportunity to move towards a model of federalism that would meaningfully share power *with* Aboriginal peoples.

Instead, the Court has opted to continue (or, at a minimum, not question) the "extravagant and absurd idea" that the Crown acquired sovereignty, legislative power, and underlying title by unilaterally proclaiming it.[345] This can be seen, as Borrows maintains, in the Court's reasoning on the test for determining the existence of Aboriginal title, the test for infringement, the rejection of interjurisdictional immunity, and its remarks on legal vacuums.[346] It is, to my mind, also the basis of its framework of reconciliation, which it has used to continue to expand a picture of federalism that constitutively excludes Aboriginal

---

343 What I have in mind here is the obligations of the imperial Parliament under the historical treaties and the *Royal Proclamation, 1763*. What it cannot simply pass on is the unquestioned presumption that it was in possession of sovereignty, legislative power, and underlying title. Rather, the concept of sovereignty that the dominion inherited was one in which legislative power and underlying title were subject to negotiated agreements between *all* members of the federation. This means that s. 91(24) should be limited to a power to make negotiated agreements with Indians concerning jurisdiction over their lands. By taking the "broad view" of s. 91(24) and acting as if the non-justiciable nature of the Crown's claim to sovereignty extends to legislative power and underlying title, the judiciary abandons its constitutional responsibilities and compromises the integrity of the rule of law.

344 This is the main problem in both *Gladstone* and the more recent – and far reaching, as it is not limited to a single species – *Ahousaht* (see note 301) decision: the federal and provincial regulatory agencies refuse to co-manage the resource and claim that they cannot fit an "unlimited right" into their management model. They continue to argue that an "unlimited right" for Aboriginal fisheries is both unfair and unworkable (the logic that justifies the "public interest" justification for infringement). The solution is to grant Aboriginal fisheries priority within their territory and work with them to co-manage the resource within those areas. But the resistance to this approach is, I would imagine, that it would constitute Crown recognition of title and compromise its general approach of treating Aboriginal rights as extinguished until litigated.

345 John Marshall CJ stated that the doctrine of discovery was based on the "extravagant and absurd idea, that the feeble settlements made on the sea coast, or the companies under whom they were made, acquired legitimate power by them to govern the people, or occupy the lands from sea to sea." *Worcester v. Georgia*, 6 Pet. 515 (US 1832) at 544–5.

346 Borrows, "Durability of Terra Nullius."

peoples. In order to see the actual form of this framework, it must be considered from the Aboriginal perspective. Here the undefined and unchecked powers of s. 91(24) continue the work of legislatively defining Indians so that the Court can legally evacuate their lands and transform the Crown's *fictional* claims to underlying title to full and unburdened title. Bill C-31 continues to reduce the number of Indians as if status "were simply a statutory definition pertaining to eligibility for some program or benefit."[347] At the same time, the *Indian Act* defines and determines the governing powers of band councils (either directly or by judicially interpreted *resemblance*). The Courts work to close off any action that could depart from this "administrative despotism" by using its alchemy to determine the rights that the Court can *hear* and what it cannot under the guise of judicial discretion or factual inquiry. It has ushered Aboriginal peoples towards negotiation with the Crown that has resulted in little but crippling debt and modern treaties whose place within the federal order is *seemingly* much the same as the "simple municipal institutions" that were set in place over 150 years ago.[348] The process of reconciling s. 91(24) with s. 35, which began in *Sparrow,* has now assumed a discernible systemic shape. The power to unilaterally infringe on Aboriginal title, rights, and treaties all stems from the unquestioned presumption of Crown sovereignty, legislative power, and underlying title. This presumption is the real basis of the "broad view" of s. 91(24). It is a power without positive definition or justifiable basis. The era of reconciliation has changed the procedures, but it has not even begun to address the issue of the *historical warrant* of the Crown's mechanism of government. This means that in every case in which the Court uses s. 91(24) it is repeating the content of the doctrine of discovery and *terra nullius* (which, despite their differences, all maintain the ability of one party to determine the rights of the other without seeking their consent). While s. 35 does introduce a measure of judicial mediation into this picture, it is one that presumes that one party has the capacity to unilaterally infringe the rights of the other. It is subjecting Aboriginal peoples to a picture of federalism they never consented to. And it is doing it under the aegis of "reconciliation." In the words of the chief justice in *Haida Nation*: "This is not reconciliation. Nor is it honourable."[349] This is *indirect rule.*

---

347 *McIvor BCSC* at para. 193. As noted earlier, the *Indian Act* amendments enacted in response to *McIvor* and *Descheneaux* do little to address or mitigate this problem.

348 It is true that Indigenous communities operating under governance arrangements set out in modern treaties have considerably more authority than band councils operating exclusively under the *Indian Act*. But the lack of clarity concerning their actual place within the division of powers leaves them confined to the same sui generis municipal level and dependent on the same "uncertain measures" of reconciliation under s. 35.

349 *Haida Nation* at para. 33.

Before we move on, we will pause here and review the ground we have covered in this chapter. I began by investigating the way in which the courts have interpreted s. 91(24). This line took us from *St Catherine's Milling* to a series of cases dealing with the doctrine of interjurisdictional immunity in relation to s. 91(24) and s. 88 of the *Indian Act*. It showed us that the current interpretation of s. 91(24) has remained largely constant since 1888, and it unilaterally subjects Indians and their lands to an undetermined and unquestioned administrative despotism (viz. as objects of a head of power within this picture of federalism, such that the only possible form of self-government is via devolved municipal powers). It also showed that, despite this, there have been a number of dissents that held open the possibility of changing this interpretative framework and thereby altering the current model of federalism. From this, I moved on to a consideration of how the definitions of *Indians* and *bands* fit within the picture of federalism that the Court has formulated in and through its interpretation of s. 91(24). This involved two subsections. In the first, I reviewed the definition of *Indians* from the nineteenth-century legislation through to the judicial interpretation of it in cases from the *Eskimo Reference* in 1939 to more recent cases of *Lovelace*, *McIvor*, *Descheneaux*, and *Daniels*. In the second subsection, I provided a similar review of the definition of *bands*, from the earliest legislation through to the modern case law. This showed how the current set of self-government forms remain locked within the municipal confines put in place by the current interpretation of s. 91(24). I then closed the chapter by reconsidering the implications of the Court's rejection of the doctrine of interjurisdictional immunity in *Tsilhqot'in Nation* for both federalism and the future of reconciliation. My purpose was to show that the Court's s. 35 framework and the current interpretation of s. 91(24) share a common foundation. Both rely on *terra nullius*, discovery, and the civilization thesis to diminish Aboriginal peoples to such a degree that the Crown was able to acquire sovereignty and radical or underlying title to their lands by assertion alone. With this in mind we can now move forward to the final chapter.

Part 5

An Era of Reconciliation, an Era of Indirect Rule: From the White Paper to the Full Box of Rights

It was the best of times, it was the worst of times, it was the age of wisdom, it was the age of foolishness, it was the epoch of belief, it was the epoch of incredulity, it was the season of Light, it was the season of Darkness, it was the spring of hope, it was the winter of despair, we had everything before us, we had nothing before us, we were all going direct to Heaven, we were all going direct the other way – in short, the period was so far like the present period, that some of its noisiest authorities insisted on its being received, for good or for evil, in the superlative degree of comparison only.

Charles Dickens, *A Tale of Two Cities* (7)

What *we* do is to bring back words from their metaphysical to their everyday use.

Ludwig Wittgenstein, *Philosophical Investigations* (§116)

I ended the last chapter by suggesting that the project of reconciliation has been misnamed. One could dismiss this concern by arguing that the name is of less consequence than the practical substance of the project itself. My response to this line of reasoning is, following Wittgenstein, "Words are also deeds."[1] This is especially important in the context of a conflict. Quentin Skinner's work is particularly helpful on precisely this point:

> People generally possess strong motives for seeking to legitimize any conduct liable to appear questionable. One implication is that they will generally find it necessary

1 Wittgenstein, *Philosophical Investigations* at §546. This remark also shows the connection between Wittgenstein's approach to ordinary language philosophy and the work of J.L. Austin, in particular in Austin's seminal *How to Do Things with Words*, ed. J.O. Urmson and Marina Sbisá (Oxford: Oxford University Press, 1980). My own appreciation of the points of connection and distinction between Wittgenstein and Austin have been shaped by the work of James Tully, Quentin Skinner, and Stanley Cavell.

> to claim that their actions were motivated by some accepted principle. A further implication is that, even if they were not motivated by any such principle, they will find themselves committed to behaving in such a way that their actions *remain compatible* with the claim that their professed principles genuinely motivated them. To recognize these implications is to accept that the courses of action open to such agents will in part be determined by the range of existing principles they can hope to profess with some degree of plausibility.[2]

Reconciliation is a term that is used to legitimate conduct, and so, as Skinner rightly argues, when it is employed, its meaning and use restrict the range of available actions.[3] When it is applied to a conflict, in its everyday use, it suggests that two or more parties are engaged in settling a dispute by mutual understanding and agreement. But this is, as I have previously noted, not its only sense. It is also a word that belongs to the more solitary world of bookkeepers and accountants. They also reconcile, but they do so in order to make one account consistent with another. Reconciliation is how they balance their books. Its entrance into Canadian jurisprudence leaned in this latter direction.

In *Sparrow*, Dickson CJC and La Forest J use the word *reconciliation* to balance the terms of the *Constitution Act, 1982* with those of the *Constitution Act,*

2 Skinner, *Visions of Politics* at 1:155.

3 By "restrict" I do not mean to suggest that legitimating words like *reconciliation* serve only a limiting function; they do not and cannot supply bright lines, because their usage is subject to contestation and change. Reconciliation opens up a number of possible avenues of action that are bounded by blurred edges. The Crown machine has consistently used the unilateral sense of reconciliation, which I referred to as *reconciliation-to* in part 1. What I have in mind when I refer to the practice of "reconciling-to" can be seen clearly in the context of a game wherein one party attempts to define the boundaries of the game itself. It is an attempt by one party to have the other accept its picture of the rules of the game. This attempt to set the boundaries is often presented indirectly. The party asserting avoids a direct command (i.e., "these are the rules of the game"), because this naturally leads the other party to ask how anyone has the authority to define the rules. As such, the party asserting often displaces the origin of the rules from the realm of subjective judgment to that of objective fact (i.e., merely describing the conditions of the possibility of the game). Put otherwise, it attempts to cloak a subjective claim in the guise of an objective (and thus uncontestable) fact. We can see this kind of displacement, misdirection, or legerdemain at work in the Crown's attempt to present its claim to sovereignty, legislative power, and underlying title as a necessary and unquestionable fact. Once this picture is accepted as the framework or background for the game, it determines which moves are possible. This "reconciliation-to" does not exhaust the potential of the term *reconciliation*. There is still the path of mutual consent; there is still the possibility of *reconciliation-with* the older 250-year-old consent-based constitutional relationship with Aboriginal peoples. The difference here is categorical, as both parties make their respective moves and claims in the context of a set of rules whose terms are open to mutual contestation and legitimated by mutual agreement.

1867. As they put it, "Federal power must be *reconciled* with federal duty."[4] But what is the character of this federal power? They tell us that "there was from the outset never any doubt that sovereignty and legislative power, and indeed the underlying title, to such lands vested in the Crown."[5] Then they cite *Johnson v. M'Intosh*, the *Royal Proclamation*, and *Calder*.[6] It is hard to see how these can serve as authority for this lack of doubt. After all, *Johnson v. M'Intosh* is the first case in the Marshall Trilogy and lays out a version of the doctrine of discovery that the subsequent cases go on to reject.[7] In addition, the specific pages cited from *Calder* include Hall J's move from *Johnson v. M'Intosh* to *Worcester v. Georgia* and Judson J's statement that the origin of title does not come by way of European recognition, but the fact "that when the settlers came, the Indians were there, organized in societies and occupying the land as their forefathers had done for centuries."[8] The *Royal Proclamation* itself can be read as the Crown formally recognizing and protecting Indian nations (as the Haudenosaunee have argued for centuries), or as an assertion of absolute sovereignty over them (as Lord Watson held in *St Catherine's Milling*).[9] Simply put, the division between the inherent rights of Aboriginal peoples and the nature of Crown sovereignty is not settled in these materials; it is merely repeated. But none of this is reflected in how Dickson CJC and La Forest J interpret s. 91(24). It is simply the provision that grants the federal government the power to legislate

---

4 *Sparrow* at 1109 (emphasis added).

5 Ibid. at 1103.

6 *Calder*.

7 The other two being *Cherokee Nation v. Georgia*, 30 US (5 Peters) 1 (1831); and *Worcester v. Georgia*, 31 US (6 Pet.) 515 (1832). While Marshall CJ does not question the sovereignty of the United States, he *does* significantly change the legal consequences that flow from it. In brief, the version of sovereignty presented in *Johnson v. M'Intosh* is bundled with legislative power and underlying title and buffered by the doctrine of discovery. Whereas the version in *Worcester v. Georgia* is no longer buffered by that pernicious legal fiction, and this lack of a buffer changes the form of sovereignty the United States can legitimately claim in its relationship with Indigenous peoples. It is an unbundled or thin version of the concept of sovereignty wherein legislative power and underlying title are open to negotiation and contestation. There are still problems with Marshall CJ's notion of "domestic dependent nations" (i.e., the notion of dependency and its connection with guardianship), but it does clear a path towards constitutional legitimacy via practices of mutual recognition and consent in a pluri-national federal order.

8 *Calder* at 328, 383, and 402. This finding is held in tension with the fact that none of the justices doubted that the Crown had the power to extinguish Aboriginal rights. As Judson J put it at 328, "There can be no question that this right was 'dependent on the goodwill of the Sovereign.'" The question of how exactly this hierarchy of sovereignties can be accounted for in law is not answered; we are simply confronted by the plain statement that "there can be no question." This prohibition in further inquiry is yet another manifestation of what I have termed *Bluebeard logic* (see note 79 of part 1).

9 I offer an extended account of the origins of these contrasting interpretations in part 3.

with respect to Indians. We should recall Peter Hogg's understated analysis of this power: "The federal Parliament has taken the broad view that it may legislate for Indians on matters which otherwise lie outside its legislative competence, and on which it could not legislate for non-Indians."[10]

This "broad view" has, as I demonstrated in the previous chapter, never been qualified or restricted by the court. *Sparrow* does not alter that pattern; it extends it. When Dickson CJC and La Forest J turn to the text of s. 35, they state that there is "no explicit language" in s. 35 that would authorize the courts to "assess the legitimacy of any government legislation that restricts aboriginal rights." They find that the words *recognition* and *affirmation* incorporate the fiduciary relationship and so "import some restraint on the exercise of sovereign power."[11] Let us hold onto this for a moment and reflect on its content. There is no "explicit language" in s. 35 that enables the courts to question the legitimacy of the federal power contained in s. 91(24); what can this possibly mean? I do not think that there can be a definitive answer to this question because the difficulty encountered by the court here is *self-imposed*. What kind of "explicit language" would meet this threshold? It seems that the court is perfectly comfortable with assessing the legitimacy of the claims of Aboriginal peoples. While it is true that there is no list of Aboriginal and treaty rights to assist the Court, the course of action it chose to take is constitutionally unbalanced.

The basis of this unbalanced approach remains the Court's unquestioned assumption of Crown sovereignty, legislative power, and underlying title. By bundling Crown sovereignty in this manner and treating it as non-justiciable, it has adopted a picture of the constitutional order that is entangled in the very legal fictions that they so conscientiously avoid (viz. discovery, *terra nullius*, adverse possession, the civilization thesis, etc.). If the basis of the "broad view" of s. 91(24) cannot be called into question, then the courts cannot reconcile it with s. 35 by virtue of the fact that you cannot reconcile an *undetermined value*. Put somewhat differently, if the Court simply presumes that Crown has this bundled form of sovereignty, then its "power" under s. 91(24) has no internal limits.[12] This interpretation of s. 91(24) does not lead it to *reconcile* competing but equal constitutional provisions. Rather, it uses one provision of the

---

10 Hogg, *Constitutional Law of Canada* at 618.

11 *Sparrow* at 1109.

12 What I mean by the lack of "internal limit" can be thought of as a lack of specificity and/or clarity regarding how s. 91(24) fits within the broader contours of the division of powers set out in ss. 91 and 92 of the *Constitution Act, 1867*. This lack of internal limits results from the presumption of Crown sovereignty that grounds the "broad view" of s. 91(24). Once the courts adopt this view of s. 91(24), it brings with it a host of spillover problems for the division of powers between Parliament and the provincial legislatures. This is clearly evident in the s. 91(24) jurisprudence (see part 4).

constitution to enframe the other. By this I mean that it uses the "broad view" s. 91(24) to set the constitutional framework that determines the form and function of s. 35. This framework operates like a set of glasses that determines the legal identities of the parties that appear before the courts. When Aboriginal peoples bring their grievances to the courts, they are not seen as *peoples* contesting the structure of the constitutional order; they are seen as *subjects* seeking the recognition of special rights within it. Thus, the game of reconciliation in *Sparrow* operates within a framework of unquestionable federal "power" that determines the results of the game in advance. The decisive move, the move that establishes the nature of the constitutional relationship between the Crown and Aboriginal peoples, occurs outside of the game. It is part of a presumed background that the courts treat as being simply non-justiciable. If we can agree that the everyday sense of reconciliation minimally refers to a process of settling disputes by *mutual understanding and agreement*, then it seems clear that what we find in *Sparrow* is a special use of the term. Simply put, there is a conflict between the very concept of reconciliation and the "broad view" of s. 91(24).

In *Van der Peet*, Lamer CJC alters the conception of reconciliation we found in *Sparrow*. He notes the effect that the word *reconciliation* has on the judicial process that the Court develops to adjudicate disputes between the Crown and Aboriginal peoples: "It is possible, of course, that the Court could be said to be 'reconciling' the prior occupation of Canada by aboriginal peoples with Crown sovereignty through either a narrow or broad conception of aboriginal rights; the notion of 'reconciliation' does not, in the abstract, mandate a particular content for aboriginal rights. However, the only fair and just reconciliation is, as Walters suggests, one which takes into account the aboriginal perspective while at the same time taking into account the perspective of the common law. True reconciliation will, equally, place weight on each."[13]

There are two significant departures from the conception of reconciliation we found in *Sparrow*. First, the objects or terms that are being reconciled are different. In *Van der Peet* the Court is reconciling *prior occupation* with *Crown sovereignty*. This does bear a strong resemblance to the *Sparrow* Court's language of *power* and *duty*. It is, after all, the presumption of the bundled from of Crown sovereignty that shapes what the Court means by the "power" of s. 91(24). But the terms have now moved outside the confines of the two written constitutional documents and into history. Second, the conception of reconciliation put forward in *Van der Peet* cannot determine the specific content of Aboriginal rights (this is the role of the courts), but it does play a role in determining the form of the judicial process.

13 *Van der Peet* at para. 50.

This provides us with what could be termed the minimal requirement of the concept of reconciliation (viz. equal weight on Crown and Aboriginal perspectives). It is presented to us via the long-standing juridical metaphor of the scales of justice. But it fails to reflect on the vulnerability of this metaphor. Weights and measures are not objectively determined; they are standards. In order for the scales to be seen as a metaphor for justice or "true reconciliation," the parties to the dispute must agree on the standards used to determine weight. But it is precisely here that the conflict between the concept of reconciliation and the process adopted by the Court is clearest.[14] The Court simply assumes the validity of the Crown's claim. This has led to a procedure in which the only check on

14 A clear example of this conflict can be seen in McLachlin CJ's discussion of "due weight" in *Mitchell v. MNR* at paras. 37–9. The stated aim of this discussion is to "clarify the general principles" that the Court provided in *Van der Peet* and *Delgamuukw* regarding the assessment of evidence in Aboriginal right claims (at para. 37). She informs us, "There is a boundary that must not be crossed between a sensitive application and a complete abandonment of the rules of evidence" (at para. 39). Exactly where this boundary lies is far from clear. She cites *Van der Peet* to remind us that the "accommodation" of the "perspective" of Aboriginal peoples "must be done in a manner that does not strain the Canadian legal and constitutional structure'" (at para. 38, citing *Van der Peet* at para. 49). She also makes use of Binnie J's caution that "generous rules of interpretation should not be confused with a vague sense of after-the-fact largesse" in *Marshall* at para. 14. This leads her to an articulation of "due weight": "Placing 'due weight' on the aboriginal perspective, or ensuring its supporting evidence an 'equal footing' with more familiar forms of evidence, means precisely what these phrases suggest: equal and due treatment" (para. 39). I have trouble seeing how this discussion clarifies anything, let alone provides the courts with "general principles." We are effectively presented with what amounts to something like a reminder that the phrase "due weight" requires that the courts refrain from placing either too much or too little weight on the evidence before them. It is true that this is indeed "an obvious proposition," but it is unclear why it needs to be stated (at para. 39). That is, unless we read past this arbitrary equivocation and see that what we are presented with are not two equal terms (i.e., the Aboriginal perspective and the common law rules of evidence) but that one term must be held to the standards of the other. It seems to me that the real emphasis of these "general principles" is on the requirement that, whatever accommodations are made, they *must not strain the Canadian legal and constitutional structure*. On this point it appears that the "clarification" being offered in *Mitchell* prefigures the chief justice's conception of translation in *Marshall; R v. Bernard* at paras. 48, 51, 58, 69–70. The problem here is that this seems to assume that the Canadian legal and constitutional structure is somehow fixed, objective, or value-free, and thus not subject to the shifting tides and cross-pressures of history, perspective, and interpretation. Brian Slattery has argued that translation "artificially constrains and distorts the true character of Aboriginal title" and that this distortion "risks compounding the historical injustices visited on Indigenous peoples" in such a way that it will likely "exacerbate existing conflicts and grievances." See Slattery, "Metamorphosis of Aboriginal Title." I would adapt this argument somewhat (I hope in a manner that its author with concur with) and say that this ridged or fixed picture of the Canadian legal and political structure that the Court presents us with "artificially constraints and distorts the true character" of the Canadian constitutional structure, and it does so by covering over its history.

the Crown's ability to unilaterally infringe on Aboriginal rights is a proportionality test, which occurs after the infringement.[15] This minimal protection can be accessed only by groups that have the time, energy, and resources to engage in lengthy and complicated litigation. And even if a claim does finally make it through, it is going to be put on the scales against the undetermined value, or to borrow Selden's phrasing, the "uncertain measure" of the judicial interpretation of Crown sovereignty.[16]

As the Court so aptly put it in *Sparrow*, "There was from the outset never any doubt that sovereignty and legislative power, and indeed the underlying title, to such lands vested in the Crown."[17] This same absence of doubt is repeated in *Tsilhqot'in Nation* when the Court states that "at the time of the assertion of European sovereignty, the Crown acquired radical or underlying title to all the land in the province."[18] This same absence of doubt serves as the basis for the "broad view" of s. 91(24). It is the background of the Court's picture of the Canadian legal and constitutional structure. The consequences for Aboriginal

---

15 I am not suggesting that this combination of judicially mediated standards of justification and procedural restraints are somehow inconsequential. The last few decades of s. 35 litigation have shown that it can indeed be a source or real, meaningful protection for the rights it recognizes and affirms. My aim is not to argue that s. 35 (as it is understood) is trivial and should be disregarded. Rather its tests to determine the existence of those rights and the interpretation of treaties are built upon the presumption of *thick* Crown sovereignty, so the rights they do find are made-to-measure a colonial picture of the constitutional order. Furthermore, the protections that it offers for these proven rights occur within a larger picture or framework of the Canadian legal and political structure. This framework determines the constitutional character of these protections and so sets their limits. This framework is based on the unquestioned presumption that the Crown has sovereignty, legislative power, and underlying title, and that this bundled conception of sovereignty is non-justiciable. Once this is accepted as the background of the Canadian constitutional order, it artificially constrains and distorts (to borrow Slattery's phrase) our view of the Canadian legal and political structure and its history. It makes it seem as if reconciliation is a game whose rules are set by Crown sovereignty. This leaves the Canadian constitutional order without a legitimate constitutional foundation. The courts are left scrambling to borrow the force of the legal fictions of discovery and *terra nullius* while conscientiously avoiding any explicit reference to them. It is, in my view, little more than legerdemain, and, as such, it is vulnerable to simple re-description (i.e., sleight-of-hand appears to be magic by limiting the field of view, so that the decisive move occurs out of sight; when this move is exposed, the mysterious aura of magic is stripped away). My aim in this book is to bring these background presuppositions into the foreground so that the actual legal and political tools and resources that have been constructed can be put to another use. That is, I want to alter the view of the framework and in order to up our perspective on what is possible within the criss-crossing and overlapping legal and political structures that make up what we commonly refer to as Canada.

16 Selden, *Table Talk* at 223–4.

17 *Sparrow*, *supra* note 4 at 1109.

18 *Tsilhqot'in Nation v. British Columbia*, [2014] SCC 44 at para. 69.

peoples are difficult to overstate. As Lamer CJC explained in *Van der Peet*, when the courts are "assessing a claim for the existence of an aboriginal right," they "must take into account the perspective of the aboriginal people claiming the right."[19] But, he continues, the court must also recognize that the Aboriginal perspective "must be framed in terms cognizable to the Canadian legal and constitutional structure."[20] This can be read over as a rather common-sense requirement. After all, what judicial process can operate without mutually understandable terms? But if the limits of cognizability are in fact set by the Crown's unquestioned claim to a version of sovereignty that is bundled with legislative power and underlying title, then we are dealing with a very different requirement. In this case, cognizability (as well as the related concepts of "due weight" in *Mitchell* and "translation" in *Marshall; Bernard*) functions as a Procrustean bed. Aboriginal peoples bring their claims to the courts, who then determine their measure by placing them in an iron bed version of the Canadian legal and constitutional structure. If we return to the metaphor of the scales, we see that the process of determining weight is simply a show. Once the court has come to a determination of the weight, then it is placed on the scales with the undetermined power of s. 91(24), and anything that does not fit into that picture of the constitutional order is deemed non-cognizable. The Aboriginal claim is subjected to the strict judicial scrutiny via a set of unilaterally determined standards. This effectively sets the limits of what is possible in the game.

This exercise is, to my mind, simply another version of the "public interest" justification that Dickson CJC and La Forest J reject because they find it to be "so vague as to provide no meaningful guidance and so broad as to be unworkable as a test for the justification of a limitation on constitutional rights."[21] The common ground between the "broad view" of s. 91(24) and the "public interest" justification is *vagueness*. Any game based on this version of reconciling will result in little more than a kind of sleight of hand and showmanship that accompanies magic shows.

In *Tsilhqot'in Nation* the Court does seem to signal a concern with the unbalanced nature of this game. As they put it, "To justify an infringement, the Crown must demonstrate that: (1) it complied with its procedural duty to consult with the right holders and accommodate the right to an appropriate extent at the stage when infringement was contemplated; (2) the infringement is backed by a compelling and substantial legislative objective in the public interest; and (3) the benefit to the public is proportionate to any adverse effect on the Aboriginal interest."[22]

---

19 *Van der Peet* at para. 49.

20 Ibid.

21 *Sparrow* at 1113.

22 *Tsilhqot'in Nation* at para. 125 (emphasis added).

But without some definite limitations on the scope of "public interest" (and with it, the Crown's legislative power over Aboriginal peoples), this does not overcome the problem; it simply repeats it. The sword of legislative power can (we are told) be used liberally by either Parliament or the legislatures (such is the substance of the Crown's claim to bundled sovereignty, the "broad view" of s. 91(24), and the modern theory of federalism). Meanwhile s. 35 does not provide a usable shield for Aboriginal peoples; at its best it provides a (uncertain) measure of constitutional shelter from unilateral Crown infringement, and at its worst it leaves them with a limited right for after-the-fact compensation. In other words, what we are left with is a procedural game that is designed to *finesse* rather than *face* the actual challenge of reconciliation.

This is, in my view, why reconciliation so quickly moved from being the rather solitary process of constitutional jurisprudence we find in *Sparrow* to being referred to by the Supreme Court as the "governing ethos" and "grand purpose" of s. 35.[23] This inflated language (generally more common in the rhetoric of political speeches than the more controlled and dispassionate climes of common law decisions) with all of its grand proclamations is, I argue, little more than the product of the Court's self-imposed blindness. By assuming the legitimacy of Crown sovereignty and its claims to legislative power and underlying title, it has placed itself in a fixed position that can only attempt to manufacture the appearance of change by what Dickens aptly termed the "superlative degree of comparison," which is to say, it finesses comparison altogether.[24] There is no recollection in this reconciliation, no memory, no context. By this I do not mean that *nothing* is remembered and the court meets each case as if it was the first of its kind. Rather, what is repeated (ad infinitum, ad nauseam) is a claim that is never put into question: the Crown has sovereignty, legislative power, and underlying title. There is no historical moment that can be referred to that could possibly explain how the Crown acquired these powers; therefore, there can be no recollection, no memory, and no context for them. No matter what arcane judicial semantics are marshalled to its cause, the basis of these powers is simply a form of proof by assertion. This is a reconciliation without recollection precisely because the very terms that are being used to determine the game are, like the view from nowhere, metahistorical. What is left is a judicial process by which the Crown's unquestioned *power-over* Indians and their lands allows them to unilaterally reconcile the duties that are "recognized and affirmed" in s. 35 to this power (viz. the Crown's claim to the bundled

23 Ibid. at para. 17; *Beckman v. Little Salmon/Carmacks First Nation*, 2010 SCC 53, [2010] 3 SCR 103 at para. 10.

24 Legitimacy is not merely a political question: it is a foundational concept in our constitutional order. As the Court rightly states in the *Reference re Secession of Quebec* at para. 33, "In our constitutional tradition, legality and legitimacy are linked."

conception of sovereignty sets the terms of cognizability for s. 35). If this is what we are calling reconciliation, then it is a game whose outcome is fixed in advance. Aboriginal peoples live under the vast administrative despotism of the *Indian Act*, they are counted by a federal register that determines who is and is not an "Indian," their governmental systems are cast (by analogy or the dubious fiction of the "as if" we find used in *Chief Mountain*[25]) as municipal creatures of statute with devolved powers, poverty, illness, and over-incarceration are endemic, but the Court keeps weaving on its empty loom. "Come with us into the future" it urges, "the future is more important than the past. A canoeist who hopes to make progress faces forwards, not backwards."[26] It continues forward as if it could overcome an antinomy (viz. the inherent rights of Aboriginal peoples and Crown sovereignty) by simply getting into its canoe and paddling off in hunt of snarks.[27] In other words, it seems to me that reconciliation has *gone on holiday*.[28]

Given the happy connotations of the term *reconciliation*, it is unsurprising that it has come to be the "grand purpose" of s. 35. It is, to borrow Wittgenstein's phrasing, as if the word has led us on a road that we were inclined to go on, but it has led us away from where we were, and didn't show us clearly the place

25 I provide an analysis of this case in part 4.

26 *Beckman v. Little Salmon/Carmacks First Nation.*

27 See Carroll, *Annotated Hunting of the Snark*. In its commitment to the presumption of the bundled version, Crown sovereignty, and the "broad view" of s. 91(24) the Court has locked itself into a rather Kantian trap. The Crown is positioned as a "necessary being" and so they are confronted with the fourth antinomy. According to Kant, in order to posit the existence of a "necessary being," reason must contradict itself and place it outside the sensible realm. In other words, to defend the claim that God necessarily exists, we must place God safely outside the sensible realm. If we fail to do this, the claim for God's necessary existence is immediately confronted by the demand for proof, and (barring the second advent) there is nothing convincing to offer. The analogy I see here is that court has posited the bundled version of Crown sovereignty as unquestionable or necessary, and yet it cannot offer any proof or evidence to support this beyond the bare assertion of it. This leaves it in the same unenviable position as theologians attempting to prove the existence of God; they both have to hide God in a mysterious magical cupboard. See Immanuel Kant, *The Cambridge Edition of the Works of Immanuel Kant: The Critique of Pure Reason*, trans. and ed. Paul Guyer and Allen Wood (Cambridge: Cambridge University Press, 1998) at 548–9. It is left split between the metaphysical dream of necessity and the nightmare of unlimited contingency. I would say that on a rough-and-ready analysis the court has adopted the Kantian solution of continually moving forward "as if" the necessary being was there buried under appearances. If this fits, it can hardly be surprising that they would also adopt his Bluebeard logic to the question of the sovereign's historical warrant. See Kant, *Metaphysics of Morals* at 111–12, 136.

28 To paraphrase Wittgenstein, we pack our bags for such a holiday as soon as the Court tries to "bring out the relation between *the* name and the thing by staring at an object in front of [it] and repeating a name or even the word 'this' innumerable times." See Wittgenstein, *Philosophical Investigations* at §38.

we had been all along.[29] When we fail to examine the differences between the Court's version of reconciliation and our everyday sense of the term, we allow the former to clothe itself in the legitimacy we commonly assign to the latter. Put somewhat differently, by accepting the Court's use of *reconciliation* as equivalent to the everyday sense of the term, we play a role in legitimating the conduct of the courts and the settler state.

My suggestion is that the term that fits the everyday reality of Aboriginal peoples in Canada (at least since the failure of the White Paper) is "indirect rule." But what does this term mean? I do not intend it as merely an accusation or empty indictment. I am arguing that the term *reconciliation does not fit* as a description of the framework that the Court is using to mediate the relationship between the Crown machine and Aboriginal peoples. It only obscures the practices that give it meaning. I am arguing that this framework can be better understood as part of a system of indirect rule. In my view, indirect rule is a helpful substitute for the Court's current version of reconciliation because it highlights the very aspects that the latter term obscures. I am not advocating for the complete removal of the term *reconciliation* from our shared legal and political registers. Rather, I want to use *indirect rule* as a temporary heuristic to help us think differently about the Court's use of *reconciliation*. If we follow Skinner's argument that "any principle that helps to legitimize a course of action will … be among the enabling conditions of its occurrence," then by redescribing the framework we gain a more perspicuous perspective, and this can change the available range of actions by showing us the other possibilities.[30] These possibilities are not new; rather, they have been there all along, in each act of resistance. They simply need to be remembered, rearranged, so that we can begin to see reconciliation again, from a different angle, under a different light: so that we can bring it back to its everyday use.

The explosive potential of this redescription is that it can change the way that we see a given set of actions. Allow me to use an object of comparison to illustrate this point. In *Theses on the Philosophy of History* Walter Benjamin presents us with the story of a chess-playing automaton. As he puts it, "The story is told of an automaton constructed in such a way that it could play a winning game of chess, answering each move of an opponent with a countermove. A puppet in Turkish attire and with a hookah in its mouth sat before a chessboard placed on a large table. A system of mirrors created the illusion that this table was transparent from all sides. Actually, a little hunchback who was an expert

29 I am paraphrasing Wittgenstein's phrase from the *Blue Book*. See Wittgenstein, *Blue and Brown Books* at 41.

30 Skinner, *Visions of Politics* at 1:156.

chess player sat inside and guided the puppet's hands by means of strings."[31] The basic structure of this stage exposes the potential of aspect perception: if it is seen as it is intended to be, then it appears magical, but if the stage is seen from a different angle, then all that remains is a clever piece of deception. If we use this to think through the problem of reconciliation, we can see it like this: there are two chess players on a stage. The game seems fair, as the rules of chess are known to both and the moves occur in the open for all to see. But one player seems to consistently win.[32] Hidden under the table is another player who moves the pieces to ensure the result. This combination of a visible and hidden player is the system of indirect rule; it employs misdirection and sleight of hand to conceal the decisive moves. The hidden player is, for us, the presumption of Crown sovereignty, legislative power, and underlying title. When this is seen, the seemingly equal playing field is exposed as rigged. This brings the possibility of changing the way in which the game is played in the future. If it is to continue under the name *reconciliation*, then the hidden player must be removed. If not, then at the very least the nature of the game that is being played will be available for all to see.

Returning to the task at hand, in order to show how indirect rule can change our perspective and expose the still unexplored possibilities of reconciliation, I will need to do more than simply substitute the descriptive term. If it is, as I believe it to be, a description of a certain displacement or configuration of what I have termed the "Crown machinery," then we will have to offer a survey of it from another, broader angle. This means that we will need to move from the fine grain details and criss-crossing conversations of the common law that formed the focus of the previous chapter and try to find our bearings from a different vantage point. The line of inquiry that leads us to this vantage point begins when we ask the following question: how do s. 91(24), the *Indian Act*, and the practices of governance that they set in place fit into the current legal-political architecture of Canada and the ongoing struggles that continue to shape it?

This is, naturally, far too broad. The territory that it opens up is vast and undetermined. It is as if it is being constructed ad hoc as it is being mapped, or

31 Walter Benjamin, *Illuminations: Essays and Reflections*, ed. Hannah Arendt (New York: Schocken Books, 1968) at 253.

32 One could argue that this comparison does not fit, as in litigation the Crown often loses (e.g., *Badger, Gladstone, Marshall, Haida, Morris, Tsilhqot'in Nation, Clyde River*, etc.), but I would argue that these "wins" occur within a picture of the constitutional order premised on unquestionable Crown sovereignty, legislative power, and underlying title. Within the chess-playing automaton comparison I am making here, these "wins" are more like "moves" on the board. Whatever moves are made the hidden player (i.e., presumption of bundled Crown sovereignty) ensures that the results of the game are the same.

as if the territory is moving and rearranging itself behind our backs. As soon as we feel that we know our way about, we turn around and realize that we have lost sight of the landmarks we had relied on. This is not surprising; contested territories are often covered in fog. So we will need to make do with sketches of landscape. This is not to say that these sketches are *merely sketches* so we should feel free to ignore them, or that they are parts that could, at some point, be assembled into *the* map. The use of these provisional maps is that they can draw our attention to the distinction between *the map* and *the territory*. This kind of reminder is needed when we become so convinced of the truth of our map that we insist on following it, even when it bears no resemblance to the territory.

This is, to my mind, where we are with reconciliation. The framework that is being used as the map of reconciliation starts from the premise that the Crown has sovereignty, legislative power, and underlying title, and so the map cannot distinguish between the unilateral sense of *reconciliation-to* and the mutual requirements of *reconciliation-with-recollection*.[33] This framework cannot function without the hidden player; it needs the presumption of this bundled form of sovereignty to ground the unilateral right of infringement. It is this presumption that (over)inflates the Court's interpretation of s. 91(24) and leads us to what I have been referring to as the "broad view" of this particular provision. This is the alchemy that sets the framework in motion. With it in place, the rules of the game appear fixed; reconciliation becomes little more than a set of substantive limits and procedural checks on unquestioned Crown sovereignty. But the game is not entirely bounded by rules. By redescribing this framework as part of a system of indirect rule I am not simply accusing or condemning; rather, my intent is to shift the perspective. By moving the background assumptions into view, we can begin to see both the visible and hidden player; this changes the game. My aim is to rearrange the perspective so that we can see that the rules are open to contestation. There are and have always been different moves in the game of reconciliation; it is true that we are all here to stay, but this does not mean that we should turn our back on the past. Nor does it mean that we can settle grievances by placing them in the past and looking only towards the future. The Court's forward-facing canoe may bear the name

33 By "framework" I am referring to how the Court in *Tsilhqot'in Nation* makes use of the term. For example, consider para. 118: "Section 35 of the Constitution Act, 1982 represents 'the culmination of a long and difficult struggle in both the political forum and the courts for the constitutional recognition of [A]boriginal rights' (*Sparrow* 1105). It protects Aboriginal rights against provincial and federal legislative power and provides a *framework* to facilitate negotiations and reconciliation of Aboriginal interests with those of the broader public." Here's an example of an account of reconciliation that foregrounds not Crown sovereignty, but the interests of Indigenous and non-Indigenous peoples. We are told later on that "this *framework* permits a principled reconciliation of Aboriginal rights with the interests of all Canadians." See *Tsilhqot'in Nation* at paras. 118, 125 (emphasis added).

"reconciliation" but it can carry only those who are hunting snarks.[34] There is no reconciliation without recollection; this is, to my mind, the meaning of *The Spirit of Haida Gwaii.*

As Tully rightly states, "The answer given by the black canoe is that, although the passengers vie and negotiate for recognition and power, they always do so in accord with the three conventions [viz. mutual recognition, consent, and continuity].... [W]e must listen to the description of each member of the crew, and indeed enter into conversation ourselves, in order to find the redescriptions acceptable to all which mediate the differences we wish each other to recognize."[35] It is time that we stop playing the rigged game of reconciliation and explore other avenues and possibilities that this word holds.

In order to follow this line of inquiry I have divided this chapter into two sections:

1 *The change in policy from* Calder *to the* Indian Act, 1985: In this section, my focus will be on covering the overall shift in Indian policy that follows the failure of the White Paper. Part of this territory was covered in the previous chapter (e.g., the case law that defines – or, more accurately, leaves undefined – the scope of s. 91(24), *Bill C-31*, the jurisdiction of bands, etc.), so I will focus my attention on the *Penner Report* and *Bill C-52*. Although the former was largely disregarded and the latter was never enacted, they offer us an invaluable snapshot of policy formulation in the wake of the *Constitution Act, 1982*. This transition from parliamentary to constitutional supremacy is key. This significance of this shift is that, as Noel Lyon phrased it, "It renounces the old rules of the game under which the Crown established courts of law and denied those courts the authority to question the sovereign claims made by the Crown."[36]

   The *Penner Report* was commissioned in order to try to make sense of this transition in the rules of the game.[37] It provides us with a vision of a new sort of game. We will follow the various threads that lead to it (e.g., the White Paper, the beginning of the modern land claim process with the *James Bay and Northern Quebec Agreement* in 1975, and the constitutional consultations leading up to 1982) and explore how it can help us

34 This canoe is just another version of the ship of state, and, as Cavell maintains, this myth is "not merely false, but mythically false. Not just untrue but destructive of truth." See Cavell, *Claim of Reason* at 365. For the snark, see Carroll, *Annotated Hunting of the Snark.*

35 Tully, *Strange Multiplicity*, at 212 and 111.

36 Lyon, "Essay on Constitutional Interpretation" at 1106.

37 Parliament of Canada, Special Committee on Indian Self-Government, *Indian Self-Government in Canada* (Ottawa: Ministry of Supply and Services, 1983) [hereinafter the *Penner Report*].

to reimagine the game we now find ourselves playing. The *Penner Report* remains relevant; it is, from the perspective of the current framework, radical. Its contours include recommendations for redrawing the meaning of s. 91(24) in light of the inherent rights that were "recognized and affirmed" in s. 35. This would take place by the federal government enacting legislation to occupy the field of s. 91(24) and then vacate it in favour of Aboriginal nations who could then have the jurisdictional space to formally govern their lands.[38] The parallels with Laskin CJ's "enclave theory" from *Cardinal, Natural Parents*, and *Four B* are clear. This map of the possibilities of the inherent right of self-government was clearly rejected by the government of the day in *Bill C-52*, and it remains unexplored, as today the framework of s. 35 is constructed on the "broad view" of s. 91(24). As I have shown, this allows the Court in *Tsilhqot'in Nation* to claim that *terra nullius* has never applied in Canada, but it also leaves it incapable of accounting for the legitimacy of Crown sovereignty, legislative power, and underlying title. Everything is anchored in the silent (or, rather, unspeakable) foundations of Crown sovereignty, which is, in turn, concealed by the Court's "broad view" of s. 91(24). This (over)inflated interpretation of s. 91(24) provides a stalking horse for the colonial constitutional order: viz. it offers the *appearance* of a constitutional source for the Crown's mysterious power-over "Indians" and their "lands." But it is only an *appearance*; s. 91(24) can constitutionally ground the Crown machinery only if it is interpreted as conferring *power-over*. The *Penner Report* draws our attention to the fact this is by no means the only possible interpretation. By returning to this particular moment we are able to explore the possibilities of a turning point that was not adopted (at least not formally). Both the *Penner Report* and *Bill C-52* set out to tackle the problem of self-government on a constitutional level and, by my reading, the positions taken continue to shape law and policy (e.g., the *Charlottetown Accord*). As such, a comparative analysis of them offers us an invaluable snapshot of policy formulation in the wake of the *Constitution Act, 1982*.

2 *Reconciliation and the implementation of the* United Nations Declaration of the Rights of Indigenous People (UNDRIP): On 10 May 2016 Canadian Indigenous Affairs Minister Carolyn Bennett addressed the

38 We can get a better sense of the significance of this "occupy and vacate" strategy by referring to chapter 4 of the *Penner Report* (which is entitled "Self-Government for Indian First Nations"). This chapter outlines seven points that make it clear that this strategy is an initial step within a larger project that sets out to recognize the inherent right of self-government by substantially reordering the constitutional structure. In the words of the committee, "Indian First Nation governments would form a distinct order of government in Canada, with their jurisdiction defined" (44).

Permanent Forum on Indigenous Issues at the United Nations and officially endorsed *UNDRIP*, without the qualifications attached by the previous government. She further stated that Canada intends "nothing less than to adopt and implement the declaration in accordance with the Canadian Constitution."[39] This signals a shift from the previous government's approach to *UNDRIP*, which held it to be "aspirational" and therefore not legally binding. The actual meaning of this apparent change in policy hinges on the question of what implementation in accordance with the Canadian Constitution looks like. Minister Bennett also stated that s. 35 of the *Constitution Act, 1982* provides a "robust framework" and a "full box of rights." This could be read as a signal that the current legal framework (with all of its unilateral principles and doctrines) of s. 35 and s. 91(24) of the *Constitution Act, 1867* will be used to restrict the content of *UNDRIP*.[40] If this is the case, then it seems that, from the perspective of the federal Crown, the "box of rights" is already full and the change of policy is little more than a slight shift of emphasis. But this is simply one of many possibilities. The one thing that this announcement makes clear is that the conversation about the future of reconciliation in Canada is not confined strictly to the domestic legal sphere. While this may seem to be a sudden and abrupt change, it is by no means a new development. From the Pre-Confederation Treaties, the Delegation of British Columbia Chiefs meeting with King Edward to discuss the Indian Land Question in the early 1900s, and the Six Nations bringing their concerns to the *League of Nations* in the 1920s, to the *Lovelace* case in the 1970s, international law has always been part of the conversation in Canada. This fact has been obscured by a 150-year-old legal narrative that has characterized Aboriginal peoples as wards of the Crown and, since 1982, by the predominance of constitutional law. My aim in this section will be to explore what implementation could mean if the government and the courts were to reject the "broad view" of s. 91(24) and the colonial version of federalism that it entails. This will be a mapping out of an imaginary space, but it is not utopian. That is, it does not come from nowhere (despite its name, utopia really does reflect a context). Rather, it draws on the resources of the 250-year-old tradition of constitutional law that is reflected in the treaties, the *Royal Proclamation, 1763*, s. 25 of the *Constitution Act, 1982*, and the everyday practices of resistance of Aboriginal peoples. It will offer a rough-and-ready account of both what I have termed *reconciliation-with-recollection*, and what that could

39 Carolyn Bennett speech, 10 May 2016.

40 One possible version of this kind of "restriction" of *UNDRIP* by s. 35 would be to argue that the "rights" outlined in the former do not qualify as Aboriginal rights under the latter because they have not been proven via the *Van der Peet* test.

mean in practice. This will offer a way to reimagine both the possibilities of reconciliation in Canada and the so-called Fourth World.

5.1 The Hidden Player: Policy from *Calder* to the *Indian Act, 1985*

Prior to *Calder* the legitimacy of Crown sovereignty, legislative power, and underlying title was not in question. Since 1888, the decision of the Privy Council in *St Catherine's Milling* had clarified precisely this point. As Lord Watson put it, "The Crown has *all along* had a present proprietary estate in the land, upon which the Indian title was a mere burden."[41] Now, there is something undoubtedly strange about this assertion. It presents us with an ordered field of view, which effectively settles the conflict before it. That is, the conflict between Parliament and the legislatures (we should always remember that there were no Aboriginal representatives party to this case) over which of them had administration and control of the Crown's underlying title is decided from this perspective. Indian title is a "mere burden." It seems to produce a clear and unambiguous picture of the place of Indians and their lands in Canadian federalism: namely, Indians and their claims to lands are a "mere burden" that is to be administered by the executive, regulated, if at all, by Parliament; and underlying title remains vested in the Crown in right of the provinces (this is a picture we have yet to escape).

But there is, even here, something that cannot be accounted for. It is like the case of the eye and the field of sight; as Wittgenstein puts it, "You really do not see the eye."[42] This unseen seer is implicated by two related features of this picture: (1) the Crown is positioned outside the confines of history (i.e. it has *all along* had ...); and (2) Indian title is a "mere burden" that entitles them to nothing more than is "a personal and usufructuary right, dependent upon the good will of the Sovereign."[43] Within the picture it is the Crown's ever-present

---

41 *St Catherine's Milling and Lumber Company v. R* (1888), 14 App. Cas. 46 at 58. Strictly speaking, all this assertion does is secure the Crown's underlying title. Lord Watson seems to base his theory of Crown sovereignty in the *Royal Proclamation, 1763* and the treaties (viz. by interpreting the former as an assertion of sovereignty and the latter as surrenders). But this is buffered by his view that Indian title has no pre-existence (i.e., it is created by the imperial Crown). In this he adopts a diminished view of the legal rights and capacities of Indigenous peoples that resembles the doctrine of discovery. He does not rely or even refer to this legal fiction; rather, he manages to achieve its effect by adopting a strictly positivist account of the law. The legislative supremacy of the dominion is anchored in s. 91(24), which is read as an indication that it was "the plain policy of the Act that, in order to ensure uniformity of administration, all such lands, and Indian affairs generally, shall be under the legislative control of one central authority" (ibid. at 59).

42 Wittgenstein, *Tractatus Logico-Philosophicus* at §5.633.

43 *St Catherine's Milling* at 54 (emphasis added).

claim to sovereignty, legislative power, and underlying title that transforms Aboriginal peoples into "mere burdens" (viz. Indians), but how this occurs is left unexplained.[44] It takes place off-stage. Despite the simple matter-of-fact manner in which this picture is conveyed, in true Hegelian fashion, it contains its own contradiction. It is this contradiction that formally enters Canadian legal discourse in *Calder*. The majority of the Supreme Court (six of the seven justices involved in the decision) found that Aboriginal title was grounded in prior Aboriginal occupation of the land. As Hall J puts it, "The right to possession claimed is not prescriptive in origin because a prescriptive right presupposes a prior right in some other person or authority."[45] In other words, the Crown's claim that its title was effectively outside history was refused. This effectively undoes any claim to internal continuity for the picture of federalism found in *St Catherine's Milling*.

In *Calder*, "Aboriginal perspective" (and by this I mean the *inherent* basis of Aboriginal rights) enters Canadian legal discourse. Its arrival is, to put it mildly, belated. After all, Lord Watson's view that Indian title had no pre-existence had been undone by the Judicial Committee of the Privy Council by 1921. The 1918 decision in *Re Southern Rhodesia Land* and the 1921 decision in *Amodu Tijani v. Secretary, Southern Nigeria* had held that Aboriginal title *pre-existed* British authority and remained in place unless explicitly extinguished.[46] Canada managed to avoid the implications of this decision by using the unchecked power of s. 91(24) to enact s. 141 of the *Indian Act*, which barred Indians from accessing legal representation from 1927 to 1951. By the time it was repealed, the Supreme Court of Canada had become the final court of appeal, and so decisions of the Judicial Committee were no longer simply imposed as law. This decision could be cited by Canadian judges, but until they did so it was safely outside

44 Strictly speaking, it's not the Aboriginal peoples that are said to be the "mere burdens"; it's their pre-existing interests in certain lands. But when we consider how the Crown exercised its legislative powers under s. 91(24), it seems to me that this burden is understood somewhat differently. The Crown machinery was certainly geared to resolve the legal problems associated with the pre-existing legal interests, but its manner of operation was to assimilate Indians and in doing so cancel out their legal interests. In other words, it was geared to *unburden* the Crown's claim to underlying title by decoupling the rightful claimants from their legal interests (viz. if there are no Indians left, then there are no remaining legal interests burdening Crown title).

45 *Calder* at 353.

46 *Re Southern Rhodesia Land* (1918), 88 LJPC 1; *Amodu Tijani v. Secretary, Southern Nigeria* (1921) 2 AC 399. These decisions retained the notion that Aboriginal title is susceptible to unilateral extinguishment, and in that sense they agree with Lord Watson's assertion that the interests are "dependent on the goodwill of the Sovereign." But the notion that Aboriginal title pre-existed British authority was a significant change in the law at the time. For an insightful analysis of these cases and their reception in the Canadian context, see Tennant, *Aboriginal Peoples and Politics* at 214–15.

of Canadian law.[47] It takes nineteen years to finally enter Canadian law. Once it actually arrives it is a sea change in Canadian legal and political history, one whose full implications, to my mind, remain unexplored. Its appearance is not the action of some mysterious deus ex machina; it has a history. This perspective had been there, to repurpose Lord Watson's phrasing, *all along*. Aboriginal peoples have never accepted that their interests were a "mere burden." In each and every act of resistance they have put the legitimacy of Crown sovereignty, legislative power, and underlying title into question. The question of why this finally moves from the everyday reality of Aboriginal life in Canada to the more rarefied confines of the common law is a complicated one.

The answer, in my view, is entangled with the history of the terms that have been marshalled to legitimate the European colonial empires over the last 500 years. By the early twentieth century the legal fictions that had grounded these claims to legitimacy had worn thin. This is clearly seen in the conflict between the Six Nations and Canada at the League of Nations. The dominion's arguments for the legitimacy of its sovereignty, legislative power, and underlying title *all hinge* on a *unilateral* power of recognition. It is this miraculous and unaccounted for power that transforms the Six Nations into subjects of the British Crown and their treaties into little more than surrender documents. These arguments did not hold water with their intended audience in 1924. Several members of the league pushed to formally hear the case, but they dropped the issue when the British Foreign Office intervened. The fact that the British needed to resort to such an explicit use of realpolitik indicates that the range of terms that could be used to legitimize their behaviour had changed. As Skinner rightly maintains, "The range of terms that innovating ideologists can hope to apply to legitimize their behavior can never be set by themselves. The availability of such terms is a question about the prevailing morality of their society; their applicability is a question about the meaning and use of the terms involved, and about how far these can plausibly be stretched."[48]

Simply put, the vocabulary of legitimation had shifted; the legal fictions that had once supported the European colonial empires and their claims of universal history were now seen as shabby and embarrassing relics. Their magical power (viz. to set a universal standard to determine the limits of human rationality and with it the capacity for self-government) had vanished. The consequences of this change flow through the mandate system, the United Nations Trusteeship Council, to the process of decolonization in the 1960s, and bring us to the White Paper and *Calder*.

47 The argument for the convenient timing of the repeal is made by Tennant, ibid. at 215.
48 Skinner, *Regarding Method*, *supra* note 2 at 156.

There is, in my view, a very real sense in which we have never left the shores of *Calder*. We remain struck on its bizarre non sequitur. As Judson J states,

> Although I think that *it is clear that Indian title in British Columbia cannot owe its origin to the Proclamation of 1763, the fact is that when the settlers came, the Indians were there, organized in societies and occupying the land as their forefathers had done for centuries.* This is what Indian title means and it does not help one in the solution of this problem to call it a "personal or usufructuary right." What they are asserting in this action is that they had a right to continue to live on their lands as their forefathers had lived and that this right has never been lawfully extinguished. *There can be no question that this right was "dependent on the goodwill of the Sovereign."*[49]

Aboriginal title inheres in the fact that "when the settlers came, the Indians were there, organized in societies and occupying the land as their forefathers had done for centuries." But, at the very same time we find that, this right was dependent on the goodwill of the sovereign. How so? How can an inherent right become dependent on the goodwill of the sovereign?[50] Courts in other jurisdictions have responded to this contradiction by simply excluding this question from their jurisdictional purview altogether.

In *Johnson v. M'Intosh*, Marshall CJ of the United States Supreme Court drew this line: "We will not enter into the controversy whether agriculturists, merchants, and manufacturers have a right on abstract principles to expel hunters from the territory they possess or to contract their limits. *Conquest gives a title which the courts of the conqueror cannot deny*, whatever the private and speculative opinions of individuals may be, respecting the original justice of the claim which has been successfully asserted.... *It is not for the courts of this country to question the validity of this title or to sustain one which is incompatible with it.*"[51]

There is another version of this approach in the Australian case law. In 1979 Jacobs J of the High Court of Australia states in *Coe v. Commonwealth of Australia* that a challenge to a nation's sovereignty is "not cognizable in a court exercising jurisdiction under that sovereignty which is sought to be challenged."[52] The Canadian Supreme Court has, much to their credit, not adopted this

49 *Calder, supra* note 5 at 328 (emphasis added).

50 One could argue that the answer is the doctrine of continuity coupled with parliamentary supremacy and the unilateral power to extinguish. But this presumes that the imperial Crown was in possession of a kind of sovereign authority that allowed them to pass on (seemingly unlimited) legislative power and underlying title to the dominion. In other words it simply begs the question of the ultimate source of the bundled version of Crown sovereignty.

51 *Johnson v. M'Intosh* at 588–9 (emphasis added).

52 *Coe v. Commonwealth of Australia*, [1979] HCA 68 at 3.

all-encompassing view of Crown sovereignty (i.e., they have veered away from the doctrine of sovereign incompatibility).[53] Instead they have attempted to maintain an impossible, or even schizophrenic, position: Aboriginal rights and title are, at one and the same time, *inherent and dependent*. This is the beginning of what I have termed "indirect rule." The picture had changed; Aboriginal peoples had *inherent rights*. But the legitimacy of Crown sovereignty, legislative power, and underlying title was, according to the courts, *still not in question*.

The result of this judicial compromise is nothing more than a house built on sand. The question of how exactly the Crown obtained this unquestioned power gained emphasis from the court's refusal to question it. In the terms of rhetoric, the court's actions effectively constitute an unconscious paralipsis.[54] Quite simply, the more the courts stated that the Crown's sovereignty was unquestionable, the more questionable it became. As I have argued, this Bluebeard logic, which attempts to set limits on further inquiry by deflection (e.g., "There is nothing to see here") or threat (e.g., "Do not go in, or else") does not dissuade further inquiry; it attracts it. The development of the "broad view" of s. 91(24) is, to my mind, a response to this very problem. The legitimacy of the

53 There are a number of lower court decisions where the doctrine of sovereign incompatibility has been adopted. See *RO: RI: WI: IO v. Canada (AG)*, 2007 ONCA 100; *R v. Pena*, 103 BCAC 273 (BCCA); *R v. David*, 2000 CarswellOnt 540 (SCJ); *R v. Cook et al.*, 2010 ONSC 675; *R v. Francis*, 2007 CarswellOnt 1548 (SC). In *Beaver v. Hill*, Chappel J provides a helpful overview of how this doctrine has been received in Canada: "The notion of one, all-encompassing sovereignty that is vested in the Crown has been revisited in the aboriginal rights jurisprudence in the past two decades" (at para. 111). She continues to note that while *Sparrow* has been used to lend support to arguments of sovereign incompatibility, "a careful review of that decision indicates that the court questioned the notion that aboriginal rights claims could be summarily dismissed on the basis of arguments based on an exclusive sovereignty vesting in the Crown" (ibid.). After a detailed review of the last twenty years of SCC jurisprudence, she concludes that the Court has acknowledged that

> aboriginal self-governance claims can fall within the purview of aboriginal rights protected by s. 35(1). Furthermore, the court appears to have accepted a vision of "Canadian" sovereignty that includes elements of aboriginal sovereignty that may be officially defined and recognized through either the voluntary treaty process or alternatively, recognized by the courts as aboriginal rights pursuant to s. 35(1). The doctrine of sovereign incompatibility is in my view antithetical to this vision. It derived from the common law of succession and was based on the historical all-encompassing concept of sovereignty that did not allow room for any form of aboriginal sovereignty. (at para. 121)

54 Paralipsis is a technique of giving emphasis to something by claiming to say little or nothing about it. A frequently cited example of an unconscious paralipsis occurs in Hamlet during the famous play-within-the-play scene. Hamlet asks his mother how she likes the play, and she replies, "The lady doth protest too much, methinks." This has become a figure of speech that is used to describe how repeated denials can indicate that the opposite may in fact be the case.

Crown's sovereignty had become inexpressible. Its only remaining defence was to focus on the unimaginable nature of the consequences that would flow from its unilateral powers being removed. This is the only remaining substance of the dominion's response to the Six Nations' case in 1924. As D.C. Scott put it, "Naturally and obviously it was not the intention in this or preceding 'treaties' to recognize or infer the existence of any independent or sovereign status of the Indians concerned. Such a principle, if admitted, would apply as much, if not more, to these other groups of Indians as to the Six Nations, and the entire Dominion would be dotted with independent, or quasi-independent Indian States 'allied with but not subject to the British Crown.' It is submitted that such a condition would be untenable and inconceivable."[55]

After *Calder*, the magic that had made Aboriginal peoples appear to be "mere burdens" could no longer be openly used. Something else was needed to keep the game moving. My position is that the "broad view" of s. 91(24) has served just this purpose. It contains all of the magic of the bundled version of Crown sovereignty and the forbidden legal fictions (i.e., *terra nullius*, discovery, etc.) without having to go to the trouble of actually expressing them. They could therefore be put into play without responsibility; the courts simply need to point to the clear, black letters of s. 91(24) of the *Constitution Act, 1867*, and the Crown's unquestionable aura appears. But this works only if the source of the magic goes unseen. It is a trick of perspective; it works so long as we do not ask where this interpretation came from.[56] This is why I have argued that it acts

55 Canada, "Appeal" at 836.

56 Let us imagine it this way: There are three people in a room playing a game – a judge and two players. At first it appears to be a close game, as each player makes moves that seem to be successful (Aboriginal peoples do win cases). But as we continue to watch the game, it becomes clear that one player is able to win each game because the judge allows it to make a decisive move that the other cannot (i.e., we can think of this as a trump card that it can play at any point in any game). When we ask why this player gets to make this move and the other cannot; in response, the judge points to a door that is labelled "s. 91(24)" and acts as if that was a complete answer. The door itself is locked. One of Wittgenstein's remarks in *Culture and Value* provides us with a way of seeing this again: "If you do not want certain people to get into a room, put a lock on it for which they do not have the key. But it is senseless to talk with them about it, unless you want them all the same to admire the room from the outside!" He continues on the same remark: "The decent thing to do is: put a lock on the doors that attracts only those who are able to open it & is not noticed by the rest." Ludwig Wittgenstein, *Culture and Value: A Selection from the Posthumous Remains*, ed. G.H. von Wright, rev. ed. (Oxford: Blackwell, 1998) at 10e. The "decent thing" cannot be done because of the role that the door has been assigned in the game. In order to allow the one player to always win, the judge has to point to it and the other player must admire it (i.e., accept its legitimacy and inquire no further). This is precisely how I read Binnie J's claim that "the future is more important than the past" and Kant's warnings to not inquire into the "historical warrant" of sovereigns. *Beckman v. Little Salmon/Carmacks First Nation* at para. 10; Kant, *Metaphysics of Morals* at 111–12, 136. It is what I have been referring to as Bluebeard logic (see note 79 of part 1). It is

as the "hidden player" – or, to borrow Gilbert Ryle's evocative phrase, the *ghost in the machine* – that allows the game to continue on, despite the fact that the contradiction expressed so clearly in *Calder* remains open and unresolved. It is this combination of the open contradiction and the hidden player that characterizes the gradual re-articulation of the Crown machinery from *Calder* to the *Constitution Act, 1982*.

Three Lines of Re-articulation

In the last chapter I detailed how the Supreme Court struggled to generate a workable solution to the contradiction it exposed in *Calder*. The immediate questions concerning the meaning of s. 91(24) for federalism and the implications of the *Bill of Rights* have already been surveyed. The lines of constitutional interpretation that emerge from this period contain the Aboriginal perspective by shoring up the Crown's claim to sovereignty, legislative power, and underlying title. Through *Cardinal*, *Natural Parents*, and *Four B*, the Supreme Court provides us with an interpretation of s. 91(24) and s. 88 of the *Indian Act* that places Aboriginal peoples under concurrent and overlapping spheres of jurisdiction. Through *Canard* and *Lavell* the Court uses s. 91(24) to read down the equality provisions of the *Bill of Rights* on the *Indian Act*. These cases work to together to present a picture of federalism that grants the Crown all-encompassing *power over* Aboriginal peoples. They contain the potential implications of *Calder* by preserving and extending the reasoning of *St Catherine's Milling*. Simply put, in these cases we see the Court hard at work trying to put the fly of inherent Aboriginal rights back into the fly bottle of parliamentary supremacy.

---

undone when the door is open. This resolution is not magical, though; it does not determine the result in advance or end all games. It simply exposes the nature of the game that is being played. The player that once had the trump card now must either find a new way to legitimate its powers (e.g., find a vocabulary that can accommodate these powers) or forgo legitimation altogether and use force to win. This is the message I take from Kafka's parable in "Before the Law," in *The Complete Stories*, ed. Nahum N. Glatzer (New York: Schocken Books, 1983) at 3–4. If we choose to the follow the doorkeeper's warning and wait, the door never opens. On the other hand, if we refuse the warning, then it may well be that behind this door there is another and another with more and more powerful guards (after all, a quest for *the* Law has no possible end point because there is no such destination), but this does not mean that the game does not change with each door that is opened. The key, in my mind, is that the very attempt to open the door *changes the game* (i.e., at the very least it moves from waiting to confronting the doorman). As Wittgenstein puts it, "If we think of the world's future, we always mean the place it will get to if it keeps going as we see it going now and it doesn't occur to us that it is not going in a straight line but in a curve & that its direction is constantly changing" (*Culture and Value* at 5e). Opening the door exposes this curve and the possibility of things being otherwise than they are.

The period from the failure of the White Paper to the *Constitution Act, 1982* is a kind of interregnum. The Crown machinery is being re-articulated to address the challenge that *Calder* poses to its legitimacy. Before we follow the various lines this re-articulation gives rise to, we must we must remember two points:

1 The picture that *St Catherine's Milling* gives us is that Indians are a federal burden and the provinces hold underlying title.
2 The process of assimilation was designed to use the unlimited administrative powers of the federal government to finalize this picture. The jurisdictional questions raised by s. 91(24) would be resolved by removing Indians from the picture (viz. it would be, in effect, a self-cancelling head of power or, to borrow Mill's apt phrasing, a "temporary despotism").

This reminder is important, because the processes of re-articulation that follow from *Calder* all stem from it. The Court's recognition of the *inherent* basis of Aboriginal rights and title exposes the problem that was already contained within this picture from the very beginning. Simply put, as soon as Aboriginal peoples are recognized as being more than "mere burdens" whose rights were given to them by the Crown, the question of Crown legitimacy is opened within the law. This, in effect, recognizes that the picture offered in *St Catherine's Milling* was always just that, a picture, a field of view, and, as such, not complete unto itself. Like all pictures, it reflects a particular perspective, which can be put into question. *Calder* introduces the Aboriginal perspective into Canadian law and with it the question of the legitimacy of the Crown's claim to sovereignty, legislative power, and underlying title.

The processes of re-articulation that have stemmed from this can be grouped into two general perspectives.

1 The first attempts to capture and contain Aboriginal peoples within the confines of *St Catherine's Milling* by moving towards a model of indirect rule. It positions the right of self-government as being strictly historical and focuses instead on delegating powers of self-management similar to that of a municipality, while retaining the Crown's claim to ultimate sovereignty and underlying title. Seen from this perspective, s. 35 is little more than a self-imposed limitation on the otherwise unlimited power of s. 91(24) (viz. the tail on the dog of the presumption of the all-encompassing version of Crown sovereignty). The presumption of an all-encompassing concept of Crown sovereignty occupies the picture of the constitutional order. This unquestioned presumption of Crown sovereignty determines the dimensions of the constitutional protections and procedural limitations put in place via s. 35. By maintaining this version of Crown sovereignty, the courts foreclose on the hard-constitutional

question of Aboriginal sovereignty and thereby treat s. 35 as a subspecies of administrative law.[57] This is what I have referred to as *reconciliation to* or *reconciliation-without-recollection.*

2 The second focuses on the *inherent* nature of Aboriginal rights and refuses the picture of *St Catherine's Milling* altogether. It references the *Royal Proclamation, 1763* and the treaties as the sources of a 250-year-old constitutional principle that is grounded in the recognition of the inherent and continuous nature of their right to govern both themselves and their lands. This necessarily requires a rejection of the bundled version of Crown sovereignty, the "broad view" of s. 91(24), the *Indian Act*, and its "vast administrative despotism." It also rejects the view of federalism that is based on it, which excludes the possibility of Aboriginal jurisdiction by placing them and their lands under the concurrent and overlapping jurisdictions of Parliament and the provincial legislatures. It holds the line so clearly articulated by the *Two Row Wampum Treaty Belt* in 1613, repeated in the *Royal Commission* of 1664 (viz. that Aboriginal nations are equal "partners in confederation") and can even be seen in the late nineteenth century (e.g., Lord Dufferin's speech at Government House, Victoria, British Columbia in 1876).[58] This perspective can be thought of as the Aboriginal or Indigenous Constitution (following Borrows and Slattery), treaty-federalism (following Barsh and Henderson), common or diverse constitutionalism (following Tully), or, in my own terms, as *reconciliation with*.[59]

57 By this I mean that it simply takes Crown sovereignty for granted and focuses its attention on reviewing the use of this all-encompassing power. It thereby converts a substantive constitutional issue into a procedural administrative one.

58 Lord Dufferin stated, "In Canada, no Government, whether provincial or central, has failed to acknowledge that the original title to the land existed in Indian Tribes and the communities that hunted or wandered over them, [therefore] … not until [we negotiate treaties] do we consider that we are entitled to deal with a single acre." This is cited in Asch, *On Being Here to Stay* at paras. 158–9. I would like to thank him for pointing it out to me, as it highlights the point that even during this phase of Indian policy the treaty approach was alive and actively contesting the extinguishment strategy that was being pursued in British Columbia. For the references to the Two-Row Wampum and the *Royal Commission of 1664*, see Tully, *Strange Multiplicity* at 127–37, and the Royal Commission on Aboriginal Peoples, *Partners in Confederation, Aboriginal Peoples, Self-Government, and the Constitution* (Ottawa: Minister of Supply and Services, 1993) at 14–15.

59 For the concept of the Aboriginal or Indigenous constitution, see John Borrows, *Canada's Indigenous Constitution* (Toronto: University of Toronto Press, 2010); Borrows, *Freedom and Indigenous Constitutionalism*; and Borrows, "Canada's Colonial Constitution" (paper delivered at the Faculty of Law, University of British Columbia, 19 January 2016) (unpublished); and Slattery, "Aboriginal Constitution." For more on the concept of treaty-federalism, refer to Barsh and Henderson, *The Road: Indian Tribes and Political Liberty*; and, more recently, Asch, *On Being Here to Stay*. For Tully's account of common constitutionalism, see his *Strange Multiplicity* at 184.

These two perspectives have shaped law and policy on the Aboriginal question since the nineteenth century. There is a kind of dialogical relationship between them. They continually relate and respond to one another. This continual contestation has resulted in policy formation characterized by a kind of haphazard movement between confrontation and concession. At one time, a given policy will be clearly grounded in one perspective, but, at the very same time, it will attempt to co-opt the other by adopting its techniques (e.g., the use of consent in the making of the numbered treaties). There are, for lack of a better word, phases in the dispute between these perspectives. At one time the lines between them may be relatively bright (e.g., the high points of assimilation policy in the late nineteenth and early twentieth centuries); at another, blurred. The crisis of legitimacy that occurs with the White Paper and *Calder* marks a phase in which the lines begin to blur. This is because the language that was used to legitimate the Crown machinery from the mid-nineteenth century on had lost its ability to do so. From this point it becomes increasingly difficult to find a clear and plain expression of either perspective in law and policy. This is not to say that there are not lines, or limits that demarcate between them, but rather that the lines become harder to read.

With this in mind, let us turn our attention to three of the lines of re-articulation that follow from *Calder*. For the sake of simplicity, I will refer to them as legislative renovation, land claim agreements, and constitutional change. I am not suggesting that these "lines" constitute entirely separate parallel processes. Nor do I mean to suggest that they have a single author or source. Rather, they are actively contested processes that criss-cross and overlap one another. Their commonality is that they stem from the ultimate failure of the project of assimilation. The White Paper attempted to complete the substantive aims of that project (the disappearance of Indians and their claims to their lands) under the aegis of the principle of equality. Its failure brought with it a crisis of legitimacy that formally enters Canadian law with *Calder*. These lines originate in this crisis and aim, in one way or another, to resolve it. They cover a vast and complicated territory that extends from *Calder* through to today. My aim is not to provide a complete map of this territory, but rather three brief surveys to help us find our way around. Following the surveys, I will shift to a more detailed analysis of the *Penner Report* and *Bill C-52*.

A. Line One: Legislative Renovation

In the wake of the failure of the White Paper, the Department of Indian Affairs (DIA) began to search for a self-government policy that could replace its previous goal of assimilation.[60] The results of this research are expressed in a

60 Giokas, "Indian Act" at 90.

discussion document released in 1982 entitled *Strengthening Indian Band Government*. This document identified five areas of the existing *Indian Act* that reduced the effectiveness of band councils. These five problem areas can be summarized as follows:

1 All of the powers granted to band councils are subject to control by the minister and/or the Governor-in-Council.
2 The land tenure system within the Act restricts the abilities of bands and individuals to actually make use of their lands.
3 The minister's trust responsibilities for band monies prevent band governments from controlling their own assets.
4 Band governments do not have defined legislative powers to address social and economic development. This results in a situation where the DIA devolves administrative responsibilities to bands for programs they are unable to define and reshape.
5 The band council's legal capacities in terms of contract law were unclear, restricting their ability to relate to third parties.[61]

In order to address these problems, the DIA presented a number of possible legislative avenues for Parliament: (1) revising the *Indian Act* in whole or in part; (2) developing a series of Acts to deal with each aspect of band self-government; (3) regional or individual band Acts; or (4) providing companion legislation to the *Indian Act* that bands could opt to enter.[62] It is surprising that the fourth approach was favoured, because the optional structure avoids the appearance of a unilateral exercise of power. The general contours of approach were outlined by the DIA in another discussion document from 1982, *The Alternative of Optional Indian Band Government Legislation*. Its recommendations (which I summarize below) correspond to the problems identified by its companion document above.

1 The ministerial authority over bands should be removed or delegated to bands, but the powers of supervision over bands and disallowance of their by-laws should be retained.
2 Bands should develop constitutions to establish their political structure and accountability to their membership.
3 Bands should have the authority to determine their own membership, but this ability should be restricted by a federally determined standard of "minimal connection."

61 Cited in ibid. at 90–1.
62 Ibid.

4 Federal authority over Indian land, social services, and monies should be delegated to bands. This should include the power to tax their own population, but federal protection of Indian lands under the *Indian Act* should be retained.
5 Bands should have a more clearly defined legal status that would enable them to enter into the existing legal framework of contract law.[63]

There is, as Giokas rightly notes, a strong resemblance between this approach and the one adopted by the United States in the *Indian Reorganization Act* of 1934.[64] This can be seen in the recommendation for band constitutions and a clearly defined legal identity that would enable bands to conduct business within existing frameworks. The difference between these approaches – and this difference makes the comparison with the US legislation so very relevant for our purposes – is in how they account for the source of the band's authority to govern itself. The United States based its approach on the inherent nature of tribal sovereign powers. By contrast, the Canadian approach is based on the delegation of federal power to the band councils, which exist as little more than creatures of statute.[65]

This proposed approach is a re-articulation of the picture from *St Catherine's Milling*. It follows the logic of indirect rule. This logic is clearly spelled out in a comment made by M. Yanaghita (the Japanese member of the Permanent Mandates Commission of the League of Nations) in 1923: "We find that under this system many chiefs, both great and small, are given charge of matters of minor importance connected with village administration. They are permitted to carry out these duties in a most imposing manner, taking advantage of the great traditional respect which they still receive from those under them. Scarcely aware of the fact that their little sovereignty has been transferred to a higher group, they will assist in the work of the mandatory government and will be content with the empty title and modest stipend."[66]

This provides us with a useful representation of the basic structure of indirect rule. At its basis it is simply delegated authority. There is a source of authority (in this case the "mandatory government") and a local administrator (the "chiefs"). There is, in this respect, no difference between this model and the more familiar form of municipal governance. Municipalities are, after all, creatures of statute. Their powers are devolved by the legislative body that created

63 Ibid.
64 Ch. 574, 48 Stat. 984, codified at 25 USC, ss. 461–79.
65 *Giokas*, "Indian Act" at para. 92.
66 League of Nations, *Permanent Mandates Commission, Minutes of the Third Session* (Geneva: League of Nations Publications, 1923) at 283.

them. Generally speaking, this arrangement is not problematic. Within the familiar setting of a constitutional democracy, the residents of the municipality are also citizens of the state; their interests are represented in the state's legislative body. This means that the entire relationship is conducted openly, and its legitimacy is maintained by the principles of representative democracy.

This is where the difference between the familiar model of municipal governance and indirect rule comes into play. In a system of indirect rule the basic municipal structure of power is hidden from all, aside from those in the "higher group" who actually hold sovereign power (e.g., the imperial Parliament). This concealment is the magic that defines indirect rule. It is what this remark from 1923 so clearly illustrates: from the perspective of the villagers, the chief is sovereign. This appearance is advantageous to the mandatory government, because it is able to cloak itself in borrowed legitimacy. This was the substance of Henry Maine's insight in the nineteenth century: culture was, contrary to J.S. Mill's civilizing thesis, *thick*, so colonial governance required the maintenance of traditional forms and structures of law and self-government.[67] By maintaining the *appearance* of traditional forms of self-government, the mandatory government was able to avoid the resistance that accompanied direct rule. This, in turn, enabled it to minimize administrative costs and maximize the extraction of resources. The advantages of indirect rule are contingent on the *magic of appearances* being maintained (viz. the "empty title" must appear to be real). If the actual structure of the relationship becomes clear to all parties involved, the advantages vanish. This is, to my mind, what Hannah Arendt so effectively captures with her phrase "the rule of nobody."[68] Once the "empty title" is visible, all that remains is, as Mahmoud Mamdani aptly put it, a system of "decentralized despotism."[69]

The challenge in the Canadian context is that the Crown machinery was geared explicitly to assimilate the traditional leadership structures. This was the very purpose of band councils, stretching back into their origins in the *Gradual Enfranchisement Act* in 1868. This meant that, following the collapse of the project of assimilation, the DIA was faced with the task of converting these fabricated political structures (the band councils) into legitimate ones, while ensuring that these structures remain fixed within the municipal level of the division of powers.

67 See part 2 for a detailed account.

68 Here Arendt is pointing out the rise of bureaucracy and its contrast with the earlier system of personal rulership. It works in this context because in a system of indirect rule the local sovereign is a stalking horse for a larger administrative system. I do not mean to suggest that once the true structure is exposed there is actually no one in charge; rather, there is a vast and complicated administrative system. There will likely be some final source of authority but it is by no means a system of "personal rulership." Arendt, *Human Condition* at 45.

69 Mahmoud Mamdani, *Citizen and Subject: Contemporary Africa and the Legacy of Colonialism* (Princeton: Princeton University Press, 1996) at 25.

This was the only way to ensure that the *St Catherine's Milling* model of federalism could continue to exist (i.e., the model that places the burden of Indian administration on Parliament and the underlying title to their lands in the hands of the Crown in right of the provinces). This is, in my view, what accounts for the disconnect between the problems that the DIA identifies in *Strengthening Indian Band Government* and the piecemeal nature of the responses it recommends. The responses are constrained by the need to maintain a model of federalism that fundamentally excludes Aboriginal peoples as anything other than the subject of a head of constitutional power. This is why the recommendations so clearly maintain *unilateral* Crown power over band councils and membership (through the use of the "minimal standards" of blood quantum).

It is unclear exactly what would constitute success under this approach. The best case scenario is that band councils and the bands they serve would need to accept this legislative change as the legitimate reflection of their rights. This requires that they either knowingly accept the very *power-over* relationship that they have actively resisted for the last 150 years or simply fail to see its true nature. This is highly unlikely. What seems more likely is that this kind of incremental adjustment would provide the federal government with the appearance of action (at least to some members of the non-Aboriginal electorate). It would doubtlessly be presented as a necessary exercise in capacity building, a step on the way to the full acceptance of inherent self-government. But without a clear picture of either the current or the proposed constitutional order, it would be little more than another quest guided by a blank map. Putting the political pageantry and Panglossian spin to the side for a moment, this approach amounts to little more than a dressed-up version of the common practice of deferred maintenance. Its sole virtue is deferral. It enables political actors to push costly maintenance and repair into the future, which leads to further deterioration and ultimately collapse. For Aboriginal peoples this approach is a familiar one; the best outcome amounts to little more than a lengthening of the leash. In other words, even in the best-case scenario the crisis of legitimacy remains. The project of legislative renovation is little more than an attempt to substitute an "empty title and modest stipend" for the inherent right of self-government.

B. Line Two: Land Claim Agreements

This process begins with the *James Bay and Northern Québec Agreement* of 1975 and the *Northeastern Québec Agreement* of 1978.[70] Through these agreements the

70 *James Bay and Northern Québec Native Claims Settlement Act*, SC 1976–7, c. 32. This agreement and its associated documents are collected in the *James Bay and Northern Québec Agreement and Complimentary Agreements* (Quebec: Les Publications du Québec, 1991) [hereinafter *JBNQA*].

vast traditional territories of the Cree and the Naskapi were ceded to the Crown. In exchange, three categories of lands were created over which the Cree and Naskapi have descending degrees of proprietary interest and control. The agreements also establish a system of self-government via provisions that are tellingly referred to as "special legislation concerning local government."[71] The overall purpose of the agreement itself is clearly set out in the opening section of the agreement:

> These people are inhabitants of the territory of Québec. It is normal and natural for Québec to assume its responsibilities for them, as it does for the rest of the population. And that is what the Québec Government will be in a position to do as a result of this Agreement. It will be the guarantor of the rights, the legal status and the well-being of the native peoples of its northern territory. Until now, the native peoples have lived, legally speaking, in a kind of limbo. The limits of federal responsibility were never quite clear, nor was it quite clear that Québec had any effective jurisdiction. The land these people inhabited was in Québec, after 1912, and yet Québec's title was not properly defined. This Agreement will remove any grounds for further doubt or misunderstanding. Jurisdiction will be established in a precise and definitive manner. Until now, Québec's presence in the North has not been complete. Today we are completing and reaffirming this presence.[72]

This account of the historical relationship between the parties is strange, but it is by no means unfamiliar. This area of Quebec (comprising one million square kilometres) was transferred from the Northwest Territories to the province via the *Quebec Boundaries Extension Act* of 1912.[73] In this transfer Quebec assumed obligations to, as Ciaccia puts it, "settle such land questions and other claims as the native peoples might raise."[74]

Let us consider this a bit more closely. According to the logic that is set out in the selection above, the relationship between the parties from 1912 on was unclear. Now, this lack of clarity is by no means complete. That is, it does not assume that each party had an equal claim to sovereignty, legislative power, and underlying title to the territory. The legal interests of the Cree and the Naskapi (who had never ceded title to their lands) are limited to that of a "mere burden." There is no explanation offered for why this is so. It is simply an unstated assumption that is borrowed from the case law. The Cree and the Naskapi are simply "two minorities" who have special "needs and interests" and are "closely

71 Ibid. at §5.1.2.

72 Ibid. at 6. This opening section is entitled "Philosophy of the Agreement" and was written by John Ciaccia (who was then a member of the National Assembly for Mount Royal and the special representative of Premier Robert Bourassa).

73 *Quebec Boundaries Extension Act*, 1912, Can. 2 Geo. V, c. 45.

74 *JBQNA* at 5.

tied to their lands."[75] What the agreement actually clarifies is who is legally responsible for administering this burden. The answer is found in the agreement, which supersedes the *Indian Act*.[76] It replaces the "historic approach of Indian affairs," which it deems to be "no longer valid."[77] As Ciaccia states, "We did not want to create 'reserves' in the conventional meaning of that word and, in fact, we are not creating them."[78] Instead, it creates a new land regime of "self-administration" which provides that "local matters will be regulated by the people who live there, as they are in any other municipality anywhere else in Québec."[79] And as in "any other municipality," the underlying title to the lands and the ultimate legislative powers remain with the Crown.

As Ciaccia reassuringly maintains,

> There will be public roads in and near these communities, for example. It's not going to take any red tape to get to them, either. *The Government will have the normal right to expropriate land for public purposes.* There will be servitudes for utilities. And the general public will have the same rights on land in the public domain, such as the roads, as it has anywhere else – and the same limited rights on land not in the public domain as it has on private property anywhere else. That is to say, there is a normal right of access for lawful and legitimate purposes. The Category 1 lands are not to be walled off or cloistered. Nobody will automatically be guilty of trespass simply for entering Category 1 lands. We are not creating shelters or confinements for wards of the State, for the simple reason that the concept expressed in the Agreement aims at wiping out the stigma attached to being a ward of the State. In reality, we are giving *cultural minorities* the chance of collective survival, and we are doing this *without in any way diminishing the Province's power to use the resources of Quebec for the good and the benefit of all the people of Quebec.*[80]

The rights of the Cree and the Naskapi are reduced in advance to those of "cultural minorities." There is no mention of the inherent nature of their rights, nor is there an explanation for how their rights were diminished prior to even sitting down at the negotiating table. The reasoning of *St Catherine's Milling*

---

75 Ibid. at 7 and 10.

76 As Ciaccia states, "This Agreement will, in fact, take precedence over the federal Indian Act. It is our aim that a new concept will exist, to be implemented by Quebec law. This concept is that of a community with the Crees or the Inuit, as the case may be, will inhabit as their own, and which will be built around their traditional activities, but which will be accessible to the rest of society" (ibid. at 6). For more details on how the *JBQNA* takes "precedence" over the *Indian Act*, see ss. 3.1.1; 3.1.3; 3.2; 3.5.4; 5.1.2; 5.1.6; 9.0.1; 9.0.3; 18.0.8; 18.0.9.

77 Ibid. at 9–10.

78 Ibid.

79 Ibid. at 8.

80 Ibid. at 10 (emphasis added).

determines the result of the agreement in advance. They are subjects simply by virtue of being Indians under the unquestioned and undefined limits of s. 91(24), and, as such, their consent is unnecessary. Parliament could simply extinguish their rights, but, in its mercy, it grants them "the chance of collective survival." It does so because direct extinguishment would require legitimation, and, as we have already seen, by the 1970s there was no legitimating vocabulary available to cover such an act. The modern land claim agreements do not set out to face the challenge of reconciling the Crown's claim to sovereignty and underlying title with the inherent rights of Aboriginal peoples; they finesse it. What is left is, as Ciaccia twice assures us, not "reserves in the classical sense."[81] But it just so happens that these new communities fit precisely into the space available in the picture of federalism we find in *St Catherine's Milling*. The Cree and the Naskapi remain under the status provisions of the *Indian Act*, and their ability to govern their lands is devolved to them from the Crown. This may be a change from the "historic approach of Indian affairs," but it follows the same old rules of the game. It may seem that there is a return to the 250-year-old tradition of treaty making, but it is a return whose limits are set in advance by the presence of the Crown machinery and the "broad view" of s. 91(24). They are negotiated in a context where the Crown explicitly controls the membership, funding, and everyday legal reality of the party with which it is negotiating. The only possible product is municipal.[82] There is no acknowledgment of the inherent nature of Aboriginal rights in these agreements. They are, much like the White Paper that preceded them, designed to resolve the anxiety of legitimation once and for all. Simply put, the "old rules" remain in place, but they are not mentioned. They operate as a hidden premise (or, to adopt the terms of our chess analogy, a hidden player), which sets the relationship between the parties

---

81 Ibid.

82 While the *Nisga'a Final Agreement* does have provisions that make it so that it prevails over conflicting federal or provincial legislation, the courts have not provided a clear picture of where it actually fits within the division of powers. See *Nisga'a Final Agreement* (Canada, British Columbia, Nisga'a Nation) 4 August 1998. Instead we have a decision in *Campbell* that offers a possibly useful (but limited) reading of residual spaces within the *Constitution Act, 1867*, and in *Chief Mountain* the court simply uses the theoretical possibility of devolution to sidestep the issue. I analyse both decisions in part 4. In my view, the potential exemplary value of the *NFA* is limited by the current picture of federalism, which has captured the courts (not to mention the federal and provincial governments) since 1888. If the Crown holds sovereignty, legislative power, and underlying title by virtue of an unquestioned presumption that the courts hold to be non-justiciable, then federalism remains a straitjacket for Aboriginal peoples. Within this picture the *NFA* just has looser straps. But if we place the *NFA* in a different picture of federalism, one where the Crown's sovereignty is not bundled with non-justiciable claims to legislative power and underlying title, then its significance changes.

that, in turn, ensures the result. These "old rules" ground the agreement that finally completes and affirms "Quebec's presence in the North."[83]

C. Line Three: Constitutional Change

The third line of re-articulation is, for many, the most familiar, as it is the dominant feature of our current landscape. The repatriation of the constitution meant fundamentally changing the legal and political architecture of Canada. It seemed that the move from a system organized on the principle of parliamentary sovereignty to one of constitutional supremacy would necessarily change the rules of the game. After all, such a change would enable the Supreme Court to bind all governmental authority to the terms of the constitution. But this characterization of the shift is, obviously, abstract and oversimplified.

The actual Canadian legal structure was never organized on the principle of parliamentary sovereignty. At least not the sovereignty of the Canadian Parliament. Until 1931 it was a Commonwealth dominion and so operated under the sovereign legislative power of the British Crown in Parliament and the judicial decisions of the Privy Council.[84] The nature of the problem in *St Catherine's Milling* clearly illustrates this complicated relationship. Nevertheless, constitutional change offered the possibility of a way out of the antinomy brought about by the Court's simultaneous acknowledgment of the inherent basis of Aboriginal rights and the supremacy of Crown sovereignty in *Calder*. This fact was by no means lost on the national Aboriginal organizations of the day, who were intent on changing the "old rules" of the game. The National Indian Brotherhood (NIB), Native Council of Canada, and Inuit Committee on National Issues were all active on this front.[85] They were invited to attend the first ministers' meetings on constitutional change in 1978 and 1979, but as observers. They successfully pressed for more direct involvement in the negotiations. This success was due, in large part, to the political pressure they were able to exert through the highly publicized lobbying efforts of the NIB and close to three hundred chiefs in England in 1979.[86] But the success was partial. They were

83 *JBQNA* at 6.

84 In 1931 the Statute of Westminster established the legislative independence of Canada and the other self-governing dominions of the British Empire. It was a step towards the transformation of the dominions into separate states. This was a gradual process, as the Judicial Committee of the Privy Council remained the highest court of appeal (for most areas of law) in Canada until its abolishment in 1949. See *Statute of Westminster, 1931* (UK), 22–3 Geo. V, c. 4 and *An Act to Amend the Supreme Court Act*, SC 1949 (2nd Sess.), c. 37, s. 3.

85 The NIB represented the interests of status Indian, the NCC non-status and Métis, and the ICNI Inuit. See Giokas, "Indian Act" at 89.

86 Ibid.

consulted during the process, but not present for the actual negotiations at the bargaining table.

The result of this process was the inclusion of three provisions (ss. 25, 35, and 37) relating to Aboriginal peoples within the *Constitution Act, 1982.* The actual effect of these provisions was – and in many respects still is – unclear. As Peter Hogg points out, s. 35 was a late addition to the *Constitution Act, 1982.* It was not included in the October 1980 version and then it appears in the April 1981 version, without the word *existing*, only to vanish entirely in the 5 November 1981 version. The omission drew intense criticism; as a result, it was added in November with the addition of the word *existing.* The history of the provision alone demonstrates that it was the product of contention and compromise. This is evident in both the vague drafting and placement of s. 35 (viz. s. 35 is not a part of the *Charter* and so not subject to either s. 1 or s. 33). What does "recognized and affirmed" mean? Does "existing" open the door for extinguishment?[87] These issues could have been settled by the future constitutional conferences promised by s. 37, but this problem was not resolved in those conferences. All that remained of this possibility of substantial constitutional change was seemingly spent in the failures of the Meech Lake and Charlottetown accords.[88]

This brings us back to more familiar territory. From this point the landmarks carry names such as *Sparrow*, *Delgamuukw*, and, most recently, *Tsilhqot'in Nation.* But self-government has remained unexplored. Its possibilities remain concealed by the Court's unquestioning acceptance of the "broad view" of s. 91(24). This has transformed s. 35 into a *Charter*-like judicial check on the exercise of Crown sovereignty. That is, it takes Crown sovereignty, legislative power, and underlying title for granted and confines itself to reviewing the use of this undetermined power. It thereby (magically) converts a substantive constitutional issue pertaining to the division of powers into a *Charter*-like test for justified infringement and a set of administrative procedures. The forms of Aboriginal governance are, to borrow the words of Ciaccia in the *James Bay and Northern Québec Agreement,* "in a kind of limbo" between the devolved powers of a municipality and the possibility of something else.[89] But this was by

87 Hogg, "Constitutional Basis of Aboriginal Rights" at 5–7.

88 The Meech Lake Accord was negotiated without any input from Aboriginal peoples. In 1990 Elijah Harper (a former chief of the Red Sucker Lake First Nation who was then the MLA for Rupertsland in Manitoba) protested this fact by filibustering the motion in the legislature and preventing ratification. The Charlottetown Accord sought to avoid this by including a constitutional amendment that would explicitly recognize Aboriginal peoples' "inherent right of self-government within Canada." But the 1992 referendum to implement it failed. While the amending formula does not technically require a referendum, the lack of a democratic mandate (or its appearance) led to a failure of political will.

89 *JBQNA* at 6.

no means the only possible course of events. In the immediate aftermath of the *Constitution Act, 1982* the *Penner Report* offered another way forward on self-government. It still holds the potential to change our perspective.

D. The Penner Report

In order to get a sense of the significance of the report's recommendations, we need to begin by briefly explaining the composition, process, and mandate of the committee that drafted it. The report itself is the product of the Special Committee on Indian Self-Government. This committee originated from a request issued on 1 June 1982 by the Standing Committee on Indian Affairs and Northern Development to the House of Commons for authority "to examine the government of Canada's total financial and other relationships … with Indian people."[90] The House of Commons responded to this request on 4 August 1982 by issuing a two-part order of reference. Initially this took the form of two subcommittees.

1 The first was the Subcommittee on Indian Women and the Indian Act. It was directed to "to study the provisions of the Indian Act dealing with band membership and Indian status, with a view to recommending how the Act might be amended to remove those provisions that discriminate against women on the basis of sex."[91]
2 The second was called the Subcommittee on Indian Self-Government. It was directed to make recommendations to Parliament "in regard particularly to possible provisions of new legislation and improved administrative arrangements to apply to some or all Band Governments on reserves taking into account the various social, economic, administrative, political and demographic situations of Indian bands, and the views of Indian bands in regard to administrative or legal change."[92]

In December of that same year the House of Commons changed its rules on committees and decided to merge the two subcommittees into a single special committee known as the Parliamentary Task Force on Indian Self-Government.

---

90 *Penner Report* at 3. I wish to, once again, acknowledge my deep and abiding debt to John Giokas for his incisive analysis. His interpretation of the *Penner Report* provided the basis for my own reading and can be found at Giokas, "Indian Act" at 93–103.

91 This was undoubtedly triggered by the fact that the United Nations Human Rights Committee had released its decision in *Lovelace* just the year before which, inter alia, found Canada to be in breach of Article 27 of the *International Covenant on Civil and Political Rights*.

92 *Penner Report* at 3.

The special committee was composed of ten members; seven members of Parliament and three representatives from national Aboriginal organizations. The Aboriginal members were limited to having non-voting ex officio and liaison status.[93] The committee received information in three ways: oral testimony taken at public meetings between members and witnesses; written submissions; and research projects that it commissioned. Its investigations were expansive, including some 567 witnesses and involving trips to the United States for comparative purposes.[94]

It is crucial to note that the *Constitution Act, 1982* was proclaimed as law by Queen Elizabeth II in Ottawa on 17 April 1982. This is less than two months prior to the initial request from the standing committee and less than four before the mandate was given to the two subcommittees. There is clear evidence that the report was meant to assist Parliament in determining the practical meaning of the new relationship promised by the suggestive (but vague) language of s. 35. For example, the special committee temporarily suspended its hearings in response to the confusion from overlap between its inquiry and the Federal-Provincial Conference of First Ministers on Aboriginal Constitutional Matters on 15 March 1983. During this constitutional conference an accord was signed to place the issue of self-government on the agenda for the next conference, which was to be held on 8 March 1984. The special committee was thus well aware of the potential impact of its report; they were providing what could well be the road map for achieving "permanent and fundamental change in the relationship between Indian peoples and the federal government."[95] The committee's mandate was thus undeniably broad, but it was by no means *complete*.

As the introduction of the report itself states, "It should be pointed out that the Special Committee was directed to examine *Indian self-government, not aboriginal self-government*. The Committee therefore devoted its efforts exclusively to discussing changes in the relationship between Canada and Indian peoples, even though the Constitution identifies three aboriginal peoples – Indians, Inuit and Métis. Inuit were not among the witnesses. Although some

93 The seven voting members were Keith Penner (Lib.) MP for Cochrane – Superior (Ontario) (chairman); Stan Schellenberger (PC) MP for Wetaskiwin (Alberta) (vice-chairman); Warren Allmand (Lib.) MP for Notre-Dame-de-Gráce – Lachine East (Quebec); Jim Manly (NDP) MP for Cowichan – Malahat – The Islands (BC); Frank Oberly (PC) MP for Prince George – Peace River (BC); Raymond Chénier (Lib.) MP for Timmins – Chapleau (Ontario); and Henri Tousignant (Lib.) Témiscamingue (Quebec). The three non-voting Aboriginal representatives were Roberta Jamieson (*ex officio* member) for the Assembly of First Nations; Sandra Isaac (liaison member) for the Native Women's Association of Canada; and Bill Wilson (liaison member) for the Native Council of Canada. See *Penner Report* at 4–5.

94 Ibid. at 5; Giokas, "Indian Act" at 93.

95 *Penner Report* at 44.

Métis people were included as witnesses as part of delegations from the Native Council of Canada and its affiliates, the Committee did not have a mandate to report on issues of concern to the Métis."[96] This distinction between Indian and Aboriginal self-government makes it clear that the report was focused on *Indian Act* bands and status Indians. The full implications of this narrowing of the issue of self-government will become clear as we outline the substance of its recommendations.

The overall approach that the special committee took to its (almost impossibly) wide-ranging mandate is, to my mind, captured in the epigraph they selected: "I sit on a man's back choking him and making him carry me and yet assure myself and others that I am sorry for him and wish to lighten his load by all possible means – except by getting off his back."[97]

This evocative image (reminiscent of a scene from the works of Kafka or Beckett) offers a different perspective – or to borrow Wittgenstein's terms, it serves as an "object of comparison" – on the relationship between the Crown and Aboriginal peoples. Seen in this light, the nature of the problem seems clear: it is the fundamental asymmetry between the parties (viz. the fact that one sits on the other's back). But this is only one aspect of this picture and one that almost every approach to the problem would likely concede. Where the approaches tend to diverge is on the question of the cause, which then shapes the prescribed resolution (e.g., the civilizing narrative grounds the cause of the asymmetry in the "backwardness" of Aboriginal peoples; this naturally leads to both the ward–guardian relationship and, if that fails, the extinction thesis). This is precisely what the picture offered in the epigraph fails to show: there is no historical context to explain the relationship it depicts. The most significant aspect of the relationship between the Crown and Aboriginal peoples – and the one on which, in my view, the committee bases its approach – concerns the way this relationship began. It is this inquiry that is required if we are to begin to understand why the dominant party is seemingly unable to see the solution that is so manifestly clear to everyone else.

The committee is able to show us this aspect by providing a historical account of the "old relationship" that the epigraph so effectively captures. They begin their version with a basic restatement of *Calder*. "For thousands of years prior to European immigration, North America was inhabited by many different self-governing aboriginal peoples, speaking many languages and having widely differing cultures and economies. The Royal Proclamation

96 Ibid. at 5 (emphasis added).

97 Ibid. at 2. The words are taken from Leo Tolstoy's *What Then Must We Do?* (a non-fiction work on the social conditions of Russia published in 1886). The report credits the citation itself to a submission to the Special Committee by the Mayo Indian Band.

of 1763, which formalized British colonial policy for North America, recognized this situation."[98]

This initial relationship is characterized by two familiar features. First, Aboriginal peoples pre-existed the arrival of Europeans and were *self-governing*. There are no diminishing narratives in play here. By this I mean any legal fictions that could reduce or eliminate the legal rights and capacities of Aboriginal peoples (i.e., they are not described as merely "occupying" the land). The specific term *self-governing* does not actually appear in *Calder*, but it is implied in Judson J's use of the phrase "organized in societies."[99] Second, it interprets the *Royal Proclamation of 1763* as recognizing the fact that Aboriginal peoples were self-governing and establishing relationships with them on a nation-to-nation basis. This rejects the reading found in *St Catherine's Milling*, which interprets it as a document establishing sovereignty over them. It also entails that the treaties are not, as D.C. Scott maintained, merely part of "the plan of negotiation adopted by the Government in dealing with ... usufructuary rights."[100] Rather, they are further recognition of the nation-to-nation relationship established in the *Royal Proclamation of 1763*. This also means that they are not sui generis in international law (the implications of which will become clearer later on).

With this set of initial conditions in place, the committee move on to their account of how this initial relationship of mutual consent changes.

> Over the years, however, the initial relationship between Indian people and the British Crown changed. In the evolution of Canada from colonial status to independence, the Indian peoples were largely ignored, except when agreements had to be made with them to obtain more land for settlement. The Indian peoples played no part in negotiating Confederation, or in drafting the *British North America Act of 1867* which, under section 91 (24), assigned legislative authority with respect to "Indians, and Lands reserved for the Indians" to the federal government.

---

98 Ibid. at 39. It is curious that the committee adopts the terms of *Calder* here (i.e., "self-governing aboriginal peoples"), but then reverts to its narrower concept of "Indian self-government." It seems to be aware, to at least some degree, of the historical problems that their approach creates as the flawed colonial process of band creation and Indian registration are effectively repeated, but they nonetheless remain committed to it. The likely cause is not a gap in its imagination but rather the limits that were imposed on its mandate.

99 *Calder* at 328. Anyone who would object to this line of reasoning would be faced with the impossible task of providing an example of an isolated group of human beings who are organized into a society, but not self-governing. I specify "isolated," as referring to examples of colonized societies that simply repeat the problem. For a helpful analysis that highlights this, see Catherine Bell and Michael Asch, "Challenging Assumptions: The Impact of Precedent in Aboriginal Rights Litigation," in *Aboriginal and Treaty Rights in Canada*, ed. Michael Asch, 38–74 (Vancouver: UBC Press, 2000).

100 Canada, "Appeal" at 835–6.

> The government assumed increasing legislative control over Indian communities, leading to The Indian Act, 1876, which, with minor modifications, remains in effect today. The result, over the years, has been the steady erosion of Indian governmental powers. Under the Indian Act, traditional Indian governments were replaced by band councils that functioned as agents of the federal government, exercising a limited range of delegated powers under federal supervision.[101]

Two related features characterize this change in the relationship: first, there is a change from the consent-based model to a unilateral one. Second, the federal government grounds this unilateral approach by interpreting s. 91(24) as granting them *power over* Indians and their lands (i.e., it adopts what I have been referring to as the "broad view"), but the meaning of the provision is not self-evident. The fact that the *British North American Act, 1867* confers legislative authority *in relation to* "Indians and lands reserved for Indians" to Parliament cannot serve as a final or unquestionable ground for the "broad view." That is, it does not interpret itself. This, combined with the fact that Aboriginal peoples "played no part" in negotiating this provision, highlights the unilateral, arbitrary, and self-serving nature of this interpretation. This perspective is contrary to Lord Watson's in *St Catherine's Milling*; he views the only limitation on the power of s. 91(24) as stemming from the provinces' interests in land in s. 109 (viz. he treats it as a *complete code*). Adoption of this positivist approach suddenly and completely obscured the more lateral structure of the pre-existing relationship. Simply put, Lord Watson uses a judgment as if it were a principle of judgment.[102] As a result, the only possible explanation that this approach leaves open to the courts who are asked to explain or account for the legitimacy of this unilateral relationship is the magical power of the Crown to provide proof by assertion, which, as we well know, is a proof that can only ever be accepted if you never doubt or question it.

If we recast this into the image from the epigraph, we find that the dominant party simply cannot account for how it got onto the other's back. It has come to accept this condition as a given (or even as a condition of its possibility), so it remains fixed in place. The "Emperor's New Clothes" helps us to understand this curious form of blindness that afflicts the dominant party in this picture. The emperor falls for the weavers' trick because he believes that this invisible suit will show the people the truth of his power (viz. the weavers claimed that the fabric was invisible only to the unworthy). His gullibility is a product of his condition: he needs to find an answer to the question that the people pose to kings (viz. "who are you to rule?"). It is not simply pride that leads him to the parade; rather, it is his need for some external, objective, and final ground

101 *Penner Report* at 39–40.

102 The phrase is Wittgenstein's. See *On Certainty* at §124.

for his unilateral power over them. If the weavers had been able to deliver the new clothes, they would have made the emperor immune to further contestation; the visibility/invisibility of the clothes would have become the criteria for determining the rational capacity of the viewer only. This same blindness afflicts the dominant party in the epigraph; he cannot see the problem with his position because of his desire to remain in power. If he was willing, even for a moment, to entertain the possibility that the problem was his position on the other's back, then he would have to answer for his position and possibly end up walking on his own two feet; it seems to me that this is precisely what he wishes to avoid. The point of both stories is that the contestability of the asymmetrical relationship between the parties is open for all to see. It is *hiding in plain sight*. All that is needed is a change in perspective.

This is what the approach taken by the committee offers us.[103] It changes our perspective by placing the relationship in its historical context and so is able to account for how this relationship began. Simply put, it makes the illegitimacy of it open for all to see.

In my view, it is this more perspicacious perspective (one that they gained by actually listening to Aboriginal peoples and not taking the confines of *St Catherine's Milling* as the limits of all possible relationships) that convinces the committee that it was not enough to simply renovate the existing Crown machinery, which was, as we have seen, the approach advocated for by the DIA in its *Strengthening Indian Band Government*. Rather, they recommended that the very basis of the relationship had to be changed. This is reflected in the starting point that the committee adopted for its model of self-government: it rejected the delegated authority model entirely – which had served as the basis for the Crown's Indian policy for well over 100 years by this point – in favour of one predicated on the inherent nature of what it refers to as "Indian self-government."[104]

The committee's rejection of the DIA's approach was direct and to the point:

> The Committee's assessment is that the DIAND approach would be unacceptable as the basis of a new relationship for a variety of reasons. First, it was described by the Minister, and perceived by the witnesses, as a revision within existing arrangements which have been found to be unsuccessful and limiting; *it is a further extension of "devolution," which has been rejected. The proposal envisages Indian governments as municipal governments and fails to take account of the origins and*

103 Their approach is, in my view, a version of the 250-year-old constitutional principle that Borrows and Slattery refer to as the Aboriginal Constitution. See Borrows, *Canada's Colonial Constitution*; and Slattery, "Aboriginal Constitution" 319.

104 I am using the term of the report itself, which, as I have already noted, confined itself explicitly to the narrower issue of Indian self-government, as opposed to the wider field of Aboriginal self-government.

> *rights of Indian First Nations in Canada.* A major objection is that permission to opt in would be a favour granted to bands that the Minister of Indian Affairs, in his discretion, deemed to be sufficiently "advanced." The paternalistic role of the Department would be maintained.[105]

The upshot of this position can be found in the following recommendation: "The Committee does not support amending the Indian Act as a route to self-government. The antiquated policy basis and structure of the Indian Act make it completely unacceptable as a blueprint for the future."[106]

Given the foundational nature of this shift, the next question that we need to address, naturally, concerns the practical steps that the committee proposes for implementing this within the new constitutional framework.

E. The Problem of Implementing the New Relationship

The committee was well aware of the challenges involved in amending the constitution. The Indian self-government amendment that they were recommending would require the approval of the federal government and seven provinces constituting at least half of the population of Canada. Given that this process would likely be protracted, they considered three other courses of action for achieving self-government. They referred to them as the courts, the bilateral process, and legislative action. Their position on the first option was clear: "Obtaining a judgement in the Supreme Court of Canada is a very lengthy process. The fundamental issue may not be directly addressed. In any event, a single court ruling could not define the full scope of Indian government or even design a new structure accommodating Indian government, although it might provide some impetus to political action. Clearly, it is an option that Indian First Nation governments might pursue, and they are free to do so. But *the Committee regards this procedure as difficult to execute and uncertain in its outcome.*"[107]

Their insight here is prescient. The process has proven to be difficult and uncertain (not to mention costly). It has given rise to a kind of labyrinthine jurisprudence. In each case a certain corner is moved, a wall shifted, but the position of *Calder* remains fixed (viz. the Crown possesses unquestioned sovereignty, legislative power, and underlying title, and Aboriginal peoples have both inherent and treaty rights). No matter how Crown sovereignty is qualified or limited (by suggestive qualifying terms such as *de facto* or *assertion*), the Court has designed its tests for determining the limits of Aboriginal rights with the presumption of bundled Crown sovereignty in mind (e.g., the *Van*

105 *Penner Report* at 47.
106 Ibid.
107 Ibid. at 45 (emphasis added).

der Peet test, the *Sparrow*/*Badger* framework, etc.). In fact, even these made-to-measure rights are subject to a judicially mediated version of the Crown's unilateral power; the Court determines if infringement is justifiable. It has contained the possibility of s. 35 by turning it into a proportionality test via the "broad view" of s. 91(24) (i.e., the stalking horse of the thick version of Crown sovereignty). This opens up a kind of creeping procedural legitimation of Crown sovereignty; the sheer fact that the Crown's claim to sovereignty, legislative power, and underlying title is never in doubt allows a hidden player to ensure the outcome of the game. This provides the appearance of movement towards a new relationship while maintaining the same old municipal limits of self-government. In other words, the combination of the thick version of Crown sovereignty and the "broad view" of s. 91(24) act as the hinge proposition upon which the entire system of indirect rule moves. While the outcomes of this line can be seen only from our current position, the limitations of using the courts to settle this constitutional problem were clearly evident to the committee in 1983. These limitations led them to focus on the combination of the bilateral process and legislative action.

Their suggestion on these fronts was – and, to my view, still is – largely consistent with the 250-year-old tradition of Aboriginal constitutionalism. As the Aboriginal witnesses pointed out to the committee, the starting point is found in the proposition that "an Indian order of government already exists in Canada."[108] It is manifest in the bilateral nature of the treaty-making process and the *Royal Proclamation of 1763*. As they put it, "The treaty-making process also provided a direct government-to-government link between the Crown and Indian peoples. This, in the Indian view, was confirmed by the setting aside of 'Indians, and Lands reserved for the Indians' in a unique manner when the *British North America Act* was passed in 1867. They therefore viewed the passage of successive *Indian Acts* as a misinterpretation of federal authority. Instead of continuing to enter into agreements with Indian nations, the federal government legislated over them and imposed restrictions on them."[109]

This misinterpretation highlights the role that s. 91(24) has played from Confederation on. As they state further down the same page, "Parliament has not attempted to exercise the full range of its powers under section 91(24), which sets apart 'Indians, and Lands reserved for the Indians.' Consequently, the limits of these powers have not been established. In the past, Parliament has, through the *Indian Act*, legislated in a manner that has regarded Indian communities as less than municipalities. On the few occasions where it has legislated in a more wide-ranging manner – for example, with respect to liquor, which is a provincial

108 Ibid.
109 Ibid. at 46.

responsibility when not related to Indians, the courts have upheld the exercise of its powers."[110] This is a clear and plain articulation of what I have referred to as the "broad view." The key here is that because of the starting point that the committee members take, they are able to see that this is not the only possible interpretation of this provision. In fact, it is an interpretation that requires the historical blinders of legal formalism (which were provided by Lord Watson in *St Catherine's Milling*) in order to maintain itself. Once this is put in question from a historically informed perspective (as Aboriginal peoples have continually presented and represented to the Crown), its status as *an interpretation* is exposed. This opens up the possibility of reading, and indeed, using s. 91(24) otherwise. The committee correctly saw that this reading is bolstered by the addition of ss. 25 and 35 to the *Constitution Act, 1982*. This is what they refer to as the "new context" for legislation.[111] It leads them to recommend "that Parliament should move to occupy the field of legislation in relation to 'Indians, and Lands reserved for the Indians' and then vacate these areas of jurisdiction to recognized Indian governments."[112] The fact that this suggestion still strikes us as radical is, to my mind, a testament to just how fixed the picture of *St Catherine's Milling* remains. The recommendation itself is by no means without precedent; it is a recognition of the fact that s. 91(24) can be interpreted in light of the 250-year-old tradition of Aboriginal constitutionalism. The courts are not entirely unaware of this (as Laskin's "enclave theory" clearly shows), but they have continued to uphold the "broad view" and its regime of administrative despotism. What the committee is recommending here would unhinge the Crown machinery. After all, it cannot function without unquestionable and unilateral sovereignty, legislative power, and underlying title. Now that we can see how the committee would ground the "new relationship" within the existing constitutional architecture, we can move on to the more specific details of implementation.

The basic architecture of implementation consisted of three legislative measures. The last of these measures was for Parliament to "occupy and vacate" s. 91(24). The first was to be the creation of an "Indian First Nations Recognition Act." The purpose of this Act was to transition away from the devolved model of *Indian Act* bands and a federally administered registration system to the inherent model of Indian First Nation governments. This task in and of itself was, as the committee recognized, deeply complicated. The administrative policy of assimilation, with its basic transitional units of Indian and band, had been designed to dissolve or de-constitute all of the pre-existing models of governance and leadership. But this process of conversion had stalled. What had

110 Ibid.

111 Ibid. at 49.

112 Ibid. at 59.

been designed to be transitional administrative units had remained in place, so the Indian and the band were the only political units recognized by the settler state. This meant that the relationship between membership and political structure was fractured along innumerable lines. The divisions between status/non-status and traditional/band criss-crossed and overlapped in such a way that the process of reconstituting legitimate political entities would be, in many respects, the primary challenge. As the committee put it,

> Band membership has for many years been determined not by Indian people but by federal standards, which have excluded some people who properly belong. In the process of constituting a First Nation, the true community identified with the band must be consulted. Although the primary unit would therefore be based on current band groupings, restrictive *Indian Act* definitions of membership would be inappropriate in the context of self-government. The number of people involved in the process would be greater than the present membership through the inclusion of some people now excluded from membership by the operation of the Act.[113]

The process that they envisioned to resolve this problem was both flexible and narrow. The narrowness of the process was a product of its starting position. The fact that they adopted the *Indian Act* band as the only eligible political unit left a number of issues unresolved (in particular the question of the Métis, non-status Indians, and Inuit). They recommended membership processes that would attempt to address this by virtue of their flexibility. A five-step procedure was put forward as a possible model:

1. The people in each community would begin with the *Indian Act* list, in addition to those who might be reinstated by any changes in legislation.
2. These people would get together to ask who might be missing and to include those they wished to include.
3. These people would agree on membership criteria and thus decide who else might be included or excluded. The criteria would be balanced with the standards in international covenants concerned with human rights.
4. These same people would agree on appeal procedures and mechanisms.

---

113 Ibid. at 54. The 2017 amendments to the *Indian Act* that amend the rules for Indian status and band membership to take account of *Descheneaux* also mandate a consultation with First Nations to discuss what role Canada should continue to play in dealing with these identity questions. The implications of this legislation are (much like the language used in its drafting) unclear. What seems clear to me is that the notion that the *Indian Act* can be modified ad hoc and thereby converted into a vehicle for achieving meaningful self-government for Aboriginal peoples is nonsensical. The *Indian Act* fits within a picture of Crown sovereignty and the constitutional order that fundamentally positions Aboriginal peoples as subjects. The committee was clearly aware of this and advised the federal government accordingly.

5 The whole group would then determine their form of government and apply for recognition.[114]

This approach could address at least some of the problems by opening up the lines of membership and political form. This would address, at least in part, the non-status question and open up the possibility of larger political units (i.e., several bands could potentially combine themselves into a unitary or federal structure). In order to attempt to cover those not included in this process, the committee recommended that special federal support programs be generated to address their needs. The result would be a "two-tier" system of First Nations citizens and "free-floating Indians" who remain under a new federal administrative system.[115] The committee had little to say about what the latter would look like or how it would do justice to the inherent rights of the "free-floating" Indians. They focused their attention on the procedures required for recognizing the new First Nation governments.

The "Indian First Nations Recognition Act" was to be a product of bilateral cooperation. It had two primary roles:

1 Specify minimum criteria, such as popular support, accountability, and a membership code, and establish a process for verifying that Indian bands wishing to be recognized as self-governing had met these criteria.
2 Elaborate a procedure under which recognition would be accorded.[116]

This required a second legislative stage to authorize the federal government to enter into these agreements. This involved the creation of a new Ministry of State for Indian First Nations Relations, which would be linked directly to the Privy Council Office.[117] This new ministry would then help to form a bilateral panel that would receive and adjudicate the recognition applications. The committee provided three criteria as examples that the panel could use:

1 Demonstrated support for the new governmental structure by a significant majority of all the people involved in a way that left no doubt as to their desires;
2 Some system of accountability by the government to the people concerned;

---

114 Ibid. at 55.
115 Giokas, "Indian Act" at 93.
116 *Penner Report* at 58.
117 The continuing relevance of the *Penner Report* can be seen in recent policy decisions of the current Trudeau government. A prime example is the August 2017 announcement that Indigenous and Northern Affairs Canada would be dissolved and replaced with the Department of Indigenous Services and the Department of Crown-Indigenous Relations and Northern Affairs.

3 A membership code, and procedures for decision-making and appeals, in accordance with international covenants.[118]

Once the criteria were met, the First Nation would determine the scope of jurisdiction that it wanted to exercise. This was highly flexible and could be changed through future applications to the panel. The limits of this possible scope were similar to those of a province. As the committee stated, "A First Nation government should have authority to legislate in such areas as social and cultural development, including education and family relations, land and resource use, revenue-raising, economic and commercial development, and justice and law enforcement, among others."[119]

Once the desired scope of initial jurisdiction was settled, the panel would submit their recommendations to the governor in council, which would pass an order to the governor general to affirm the recognition of the individual First Nation.[120] The committee viewed the inclusion of the governor general as necessary to "symbolize the unbroken link with the Crown and confirm that recognition would continue from government to government."[121]

The result of this process could be seen as the realization of the kind of fragmentation that D.C. Scott used to fortify his rejection of the Six Nations' argument that the treaties were government-to-government agreements. His words are worth reconsidering at length. "Naturally and obviously it was not the intention in this or preceding 'treaties' to recognize or infer the existence of any independent or sovereign status of the Indians concerned. Such a principle, if admitted, would apply as much, if not more, to these other groups of Indians as to the Six Nations, and the entire Dominion would be dotted with independent, or quasi-independent Indian States 'allied with but not subject to the British Crown.' It is submitted that such a condition would be untenable and inconceivable."[122]

The committee did not follow this line of reasoning. They attended to the witnesses who offered them another perspective on this possibility. "Many witnesses emphasized that, in seeking to establish Indian First Nation governments, they did not wish to create divisions that would weaken Canada. Their object is to change the relationship of Indian First Nations to other governments, not to fragment the country. In their opinion, the exercise of political self-determination is a necessary step toward national unity. Canada would be strengthened, not weakened as a result."[123]

118 Ibid. at 57.
119 Ibid. at 64.
120 Ibid. at 61.
121 Ibid.
122 Canada, "Appeal" at 836.
123 *Penner Report* at 41–2.

This led them to reject Scott's all-or-nothing conception of the state as being little more than the "barricades of the past."[124] Their starting point was not the abstract categories of international law with its bird's-eye view of uniform sovereign states, but the history of a particular case. This enabled them to move past the self-imposed limits that inform the "broad view" of s. 91(24) and animate the Crown machinery. In place of the *St Catherine's Milling* picture of federalism and its paper-thin foundations (viz. the combination of the Crown's proof by assertion and the judiciary's interpretation without question, which can be held in place only by what I have referred to as Bluebeard logic) they offered a vision of a diversity of governmental styles. As they stated, "These styles will reflect historical and traditional values, location, size, culture, economy, and a host of other factors. This diversity is to be respected. It can further be expected that these developments will proceed at different paces, and no time limits or pressures should be imposed. Indian governments will benefit from each other's experience. Needs will also change as conditions evolve and as structures appropriate for one stage cease to be appropriate for another."[125]

This flexible model would not be without difficulty or conflict. The committee was well aware of the potential for intergovernmental conflicts and, in fact, recommended that a specialized tribunal be constituted to arbitrate such disputes. While the picture they offered was by no means complete, it did offer a path towards a reconciliation based on the principles of mutual recognition, consent, and continuity. It demonstrated that recognizing Aboriginal peoples as "equal partners in confederation" was (contra Scott) neither "untenable" nor "inconceivable."[126] The government's response to their report demonstrated the persistence of the "broad view."

THE GOVERNMENT'S RESPONSE IN BILL C-52

The first part of the federal government's response came in March 1984. It consisted of a seven-page document presented by the minister of Indian affairs and northern development, John C. Munro. While it avoided directly rejecting the substance of the *Penner Report,* it shifted emphasis away from the inherent right of self-government. It maintained that the Aboriginal question "can only be resolved through agreement with Provincial Governments in the context of ongoing constitutional discussions involving First Ministers' conferences."[127]

The implications of this statement require some unpacking. First, by maintaining that the provinces must be involved, the minister was holding to the

124 Ibid. at 60.

125 Ibid. at 56.

126 These are the words of Royal Commission of 1664.

127 *Response of the Government to the Report of the Special Committee on Indian Self-Government* (Ottawa: Indian and Northern Affairs Canada, 1984) at 2.

St Catherine's Milling picture of federalism. The heart of the conflict was set as being between s. 91(24) and s. 109. These provisions were presented as the two halves of the problem: they gave the federal and the provincial governments their respective positions and voices, and in contrast, Indians and their claims to their lands were residual, a "mere burden" that could be worked out without their actual input.

All of this rested on the unstated presumption that grounded this picture of federalism: that the Crown was able to acquire sovereignty, legislative power, and underlying title simply by asserting that it had it. This presumption was the basis of the "broad view" of s. 91(24) and it allowed Lord Watson to use it as the hinge proposition that repositioned the *Royal Proclamation of 1763* and the treaties as being nothing more than confirmations of sovereign power. As a result, Aboriginal peoples did not have a seat at the table of constitutional powers. Rather, the federal government occupied their seat. It was their guardian, their trustee, but unlike any other kind of trustee it was also vested with the unilateral authority to extinguish the trust. In this picture the only barrier to the federal Crown's all-encompassing power over Indians and their lands was the province's interests in land under s. 109. Lord Watson resolved this in favour of the provinces.[128] If the government had adopted the view of s. 91(24) that the Special Committee had offered them, the provinces would not need to be involved. Their reading of the provision started with the *Royal Proclamation of 1763* and the treaties. It read them as constitutional documents that created a lateral government-to-government relationship. This was then read as the context that gave the vague phrase "Indians and lands reserved for Indians" its meaning.

Their lands were not simply vested in the provinces by virtue of s. 109. This position was further bolstered by the (then) new provisions of ss. 35 and 25. The Special Committee characterized this as a "new relationship," but it was actually a renewal. It based itself on the 250-year-old tradition of Aboriginal constitutionalism.

The minister simply rejected this view. There was no explanation for why the provinces needed to be involved. It was simply taken as the reality of the situation (i.e., the picture of *St Catherine's Milling* was not seen as a picture; it was like a pair of spectacles that cannot be taken off).

The Special Committee's bilateral legislative approach was thus rejected. The constitutional conferences promised by s. 37 offered the possibility of revisiting their suggestions. But the language of the minister's response suggested that

---

128 It is safe to assume that this constituted an attempt to maintain a balance of powers that weakens the federal government so as to maintain the position of the dominion in relation to the British Crown.

the horizon of this future was closed in. The new relationship that the Special Committee called for was re-characterized as one that would allow "Indian First Nations and their governments ... to set their own course within Canada to the maximum extent possible."[129] The emphasis here was on "within" and "maximum extent possible." This picture of the constitutional framework suggested the existence of limits that were in some way known in advance. It shifted the focus from reinterpreting the balance of powers to simply pointing to jurisdictional limits. It did so, to my view, because it took those limits as fixed. It continued along this line by focusing on the material needs of Indians (it referred to the need to break the "dependency cycle") and the importance of preserving their culture.[130] The right of self-government was drawn into the historical background, which suggested that this right was no longer "existing" for the purposes of s. 35. Naturally, this picture offered no explanation for how this right could be confined to the bounds of the past. All of this translated into a response that sought to finesse the question of self-government. The hard constitutional question was deferred to the ongoing constitutional conferences. In the meantime, the minister suggested that the government would focus its attention on making improvements to existing legislation. In other words, it would focus on simply adjusting the status quo of the Crown machinery.

This is clearly evidenced in the legislation the government tabled following their response. In Bill C-52 the government set out a detailed legislative program of sixty-five sections to address the issue of self-government.[131] Giokas provides us with a clear and insightful analysis of its substance: "It appears on a close reading to delegate powers instead of recognizing them and continued to permit a considerable degree of oversight including disallowance powers as under the current Indian Act. In addition, the source of Indian Nation power was never stated. In retrospect, it seems clear that despite its recognition language and format, Bill C-52 attempted to skirt the line between true recognition and delegated authority in a way that left many unconvinced that it was true recognition legislation."[132]

The exact status of the Indian Nation governments (the language in the bill avoids the use of the term *First Nation*) that this bill would have created is unclear. The composition of the "recognition panel" weighted towards federal control in its composition and the criteria it would employ. The governor in council could set the "criteria relating to the possession of a land base

129 *Response* at 1.

130 Ibid.; Giokas, "Indian Act" at 103–4.

131 Bill C-52 was entitled *An Act relating to self-government for Indian Nations* and was introduced in the House of Commons on 27 June 1984 by the minister of Indian affairs. See Giokas, "Indian Act" at 103.

132 Giokas, "Indian Act" at 105.

and evidence of viability in terms of population and economic potential."[133] This evaluative power was reminiscent of the one first introduced in the *Indian Advancement Act* of 1884.[134] It allowed the federal government to hold back the delegation of additional powers of local governance until a band could demonstrate that it was at an "advanced stage of development." The real spirit of this power is captured in the title of the 1884 legislation: "*training them for the exercise of municipal powers.*" Once a band was deemed eligible and passed through the Bill C-52 process, its position within the division of powers was unclear. It was still confined to local matters, and these limited powers could be removed via the federal power of disallowance. The *Indian Act* would still apply (the Indian Nations would be exempted only from ss. 32, 33 – which covered the sale and barter of produce in the prairie provinces – and 88) to them. It would still determine their membership, their reserve lands would still be held in trust by the federal government, and the non-reserve lands would still be subject to provincial title under s. 109.

Simply put, everything would seem to change but would really remain the same. It was, by my view, the program for a magic show of sorts. The legislation would set up a stage and a panel of magicians. A band would appear, they would drape a cloth over it, pronounce the appointed words, and then suddenly withdraw the cloth to reveal an Indian nation. The idea was that this would satisfy the desire for self-government. But, like any trick of indirect rule, its success hinged on maintaining the appearance of difference. The "empty title and modest stipend" must be taken as self-government. This is why this legislation failed; the trick was far too obvious. There was no *real* difference between a band and an Indian nation. Sensing this, the government allowed the legislation to die on the order paper.

The moves that follow from this decision are familiar. The *Indian Act* was revised in 1985 and *Bill C-31* replaced the previous system of registration. It allowed for bands to create their own membership lists by separating status from band membership.[135] This could be read as a partial realization of the *Penner Report* recommendation to separate the registrar's general list from the membership of each First Nation government. But this appearance was just that, an appearance. A custom band might well control its membership, but the number of status Indians in its membership was a factor in determining

133 Cited in ibid. at 106.

134 *An Act for conferring certain privileges on the more advanced Bands of the Indians of Canada, with the view of training them for the exercise of municipal powers*, SC 1884, s. 28.

135 This separation is partial, as s. 4(1) of the *Indian Act* deems band members to be Indians for certain specified purposes under the Act.

its funding.[136] The registration system imposed was designed to reduce the number of status Indians over time. As long as individuals continue to marry out, the number of individuals eligible for Indian status declines. It is a waiting game based on probabilities. Current legislative machinery is, as Giokas rightly notes, the same as "the *Indian Act* of 1876 and its precursors in most important respects."[137] It paradoxically continues both the guardianship and assimilative policies of the colonial period. It thus constitutes a system of "protective assimilation."[138]

The sheer obviousness of this brings us to ask how this could be taken as a system of indirect rule. After all, indirect rule hinges on the magic trick of making an "empty title and modest stipend" appear to be a legitimate system of self-government. My response is that it is in the continual strategy of deferral. The current administrative system is always presented as temporary. This is by no means a new strategy. It is a foundational one. But its initial temporary status was different. It began by openly promising assimilation. Now it promises self-government. The machinery remains the same, but how it is used is different. There is a kind of de facto delegation as the minister allows band councils greater control, but the levers and buttons of unilateral oversight remain.[139] The possibility of the future of self-government is always under construction. At first it was pushed to the constitutional conferences, but that path ended with the failure of the Charlottetown Accord in 1992. This left two avenues open: for the Aboriginal peoples who were not covered by treaties, there remained the modern land claim process that began with *James Bay and Northern Québec Agreement* of 1975. As we have already seen, this process has not resulted in anything other than a new form of special municipality. This leaves the final avenue. The question of self-government has been left to the procedure that the *Penner Report* aptly characterized as being "difficult to execute and uncertain in its outcome" (viz. the courts).[140]

136 For more detail on membership controls see Sébastien Grammond, *Identity Captured by Law: Membership in Canada's Indigenous Peoples and Linguistic Minorities* (Montreal and Kingston: McGill-Queen's University Press, 2009).

137 Giokas, "Indian Act" at 2.

138 Ibid.

139 There have been some modest reductions. For example, the minister's power to disallow s. 81 by-laws was repealed in 2014, and First Nations operating under the *First Nations Land Management Act*, SC 1999, c. 24 have considerably greater autonomy in reserve land matters than those still operating under the *Indian Act*. I would like to thank Kerry Wilkins for directing my attention to these changes. While these do not alter the colonial picture of the Canadian constitutional order, they do provide some points of flexibility that could be used to change and/or resist this picture.

140 *Penner Report* at 45.

F. The Era of Indirect Rule and the Mechanism of Deferral

At this point I am in a position to answer the question I posed above. What hides the truth of the municipal nature of the relationship between the Crown and Aboriginal peoples? It seems clear that all of the courses on the table are captured by this framework of "devolved powers." So how can the Crown machinery maintain the illusion of legitimacy? The answer, to my mind, is in the actions of the Supreme Court of Canada. The Court has led us into a system of indirect rule. It provides the illusion of a resolution on the horizon. It is always the next case that promises reconciliation. This promise hides what is otherwise so plainly obvious; the *Indian Act* is not the waiting room for reconciliation, it is simply the same old administrative despotism. The unjustifiable warrant of the Crown machinery is concealed by the Court's elaborate stagecraft. The everyday reality of Aboriginal peoples remains the same. The framework of its justification has changed. It is always a *reconciliation to come*, but for now this leaves us only with *reconciliation to* the unilateral power of the Crown.[141]

This framework of reconciliation is built on the unquestioned presumption of the bundled version of Crown sovereignty. It sets this presumption as the background of the constitutional picture and occupies itself with fitting Aboriginal peoples into (or *reconciling them to*) the remaining space. This framework of reconciliation is Procrustean. Its purpose is to maintain the colonial picture of the Canadian constitutional order by ensuring that Aboriginal peoples fit within it. Rejecting this mode of reconciliation does not necessarily entail that the solution is a complete or final reconciliation (the voyage of the black canoe has no end). But the strategy of justifying the *Indian Act* and its "vast administrative despotism" as temporary necessities cannot be continued. If the Court wishes to continue to speak of the Aboriginal perceptive and reconciliation, it must renounce the "broad view" of s. 91(24). This hidden player has determined the outcome of the game for far too long. If it refuses and continues blindly forward, peddling its *reconciliation without recollection*, then these words should be seen to be hollow. The possibility to change the rules of the game is still there as it has always been, hiding in plain sight.

It is, to my mind, hidden in the way the Court has thus far reconciled s. 91(24) and s. 35 (i.e., in the existing framework of reconciliation). It could have used different spells. It could have simply blinded itself to the historical warrant of the Crown (as did Australia and the United States). But it has kept the question of legitimacy open. This presents us with two challenges. First, if it

141 My intent is not to trivialize the protections that the existing interpretation of s. 35 offers; rather, I am trying to draw attention to the background presumptions that determine the constitutional structure and status of these protections; see note 15.

continues on its current course, then this open door offers only the illusion of a *reconciliation to come*, which conceals the unjustifiable nature of the Crown's legitimacy. But this is not the only course of action available. The Court has signalled its willingness to question the legitimacy of the Crown's claim to sovereignty (by qualifying it as being de facto or an *assertion*). This, in combination with the federal government's recent announcement concerning *UNDRIP*, opens up the possibility of another course of action.

5.2 Reconciliation and Implementation

This brings us to the second question with which we began the chapter: how are we to approach the implementation of the *United Nations Declaration of the Rights of Indigenous Peoples*? It is unprecedented and seems to extend before us as a vast and unexplored territory. It is tempting to cast our gaze to the horizon and try to anticipate the path ahead, but attempting to survey the future is a risky venture. It is, more often than not, the province of prophets and fortune tellers. Their maps of the future are about as useful as the Bellman's map in the *Hunting of the Snark*, which is to say, as helpful as a blank sheet of paper can be.[142] This is what I take to be Hegel's point from the preface to the *Philosophy of Right* when he states (with his characteristic – if not arcane – flair), "The owl of Minerva begins its flight only on the onset of dusk."[143] If we are actually trying to understand where we are, then we cannot begin by consulting blank maps that can only ever hope to "*issue instructions* on how the world ought to be."[144] It is not that such maps have no claim to existence, but rather their claims are nothing more than *opinions*. And as Hegel reminds us, opinion is well suited to this task, as it is "a pliant medium in which the imagination can construct anything it pleases."[145] So if the way forward has so little to offer us, how are we going to get our bearings? Here, yet again, Binnie J's words from *Beckman v. Little Salmon/Carmacks First Nation* can provide some guidance: "The future is more important than the past. A canoeist who hopes to make progress faces forwards, not backwards."[146]

This approach captures what has become of reconciliation in the courts; they have crafted it into a blank map. The government has taken it as their framework and now seems posed to continue the 150-year-old hunt for the snark. How can we bring reconciliation back from this peculiar holiday? My response is that we begin by refusing the temptation to look at blank maps

142 Carroll, *Annotated Hunting of the Snark*.

143 Hegel, *Elements of the Philosophy of Right*.

144 Ibid. at 22.

145 Ibid.

146 *Beckman v. Little Salmon/Carmacks First Nation* at para. 10.

of the future with their endless promises of a *reconciliation to come* (whose reality in the present is always confined to being simply a *reconciliation to* the status quo). In order to bring reconciliation back to its everyday use, we need to start looking behind us; we need a *reconciliation with recollection*. This means that implementation cannot be limited to the abstract and formal application of a domestic constitutional "framework" to an international declaration. This exercise simply uses one "framework" to determine the measure of the other; it is as pointless as putting a square peg into a square hole and seeing that it fits.[147] If reconciliation is to come back from holiday, the question of implementation must begin from the context of the particular case. This means that it must begin by acknowledging that the relationship between the struggle for Aboriginal self-government and international law is by no means new. Nor is implementation merely a domestic issue. It is, as Henderson rightly states, "part of the unfinished business of decolonization."[148]

In order to address the question of implementation I will divide my inquiry into three subsections. First, I will show how the paradoxical position of Aboriginal rights (i.e., that they are not reducible to minority rights or claims for international statehood) is the product of a model of the state that is inseparable from its nineteenth-century context.[149] This helps us to see that the line

---

147 Wittgenstein, *Philosophical Investigations* at §216.

148 James Sa'ke'j Youngblood Henderson, *Indigenous Diplomacy and the Rights of Peoples: Achieving UN Recognition* (Saskatoon, SK: Purich Publishing, 2008) at 34.

149 A brief point of clarification is required here. What I mean by stating that Aboriginal rights are "not reducible to minority rights or claims for international statehood" is that they do not fit within these conceptual confines directly or neatly. Naturally, Aboriginal peoples have taken a diversity of positions on how they see their rights. Some do argue for international statehood and lay claim to a right of succession. This has demonstrably not been the predominant approach overall. My own concerns with adopting this particular sovereigntist tactic are drawn out clearly by Tully:

> Some Quebec and Aboriginal sovereigntists ignore the members within their borders who disagree with their projects and reduce the other members of society to a homogenous "other." By this tactic, they undermine the legitimacy of their own claim to recognition, for they misrecognize, or fail to recognize at all, the claim of others affected by their claim, precisely the injustice they are protesting in their own case. Such performative contradictions violate the first principle of recognition politics, the principle of reciprocity, mutual recognition, mutual acknowledgment or *audi alteram partem* (always listen to the other side). That is, every member affected by the proposed change should be acknowledged and have a say in the discussions and negotiations. (*Public Philosophy in a New Key* at 1:201)

I feel that J.G.A. Pocock offers a similar (if somewhat less clearly expressed) version of this concern when he states, "History, the breakdown of dreamtime, may be the precondition of judgment, and a dreamtime which comes to court for judgment may destroy itself,

that seems to strictly determine the possible outcomes of Aboriginal self-determination cannot sustain its claim to abstract generality; it is the product of a particular perspective and so can be changed. In other words, the presumptions that underlie Binnie J's forward-facing canoe and his reinterpretation of the Two Row Wampum in *Mitchell* are not some neutral set of laws, but a particular (and therefore contestable) narrative (i.e., the ship of state).[150] This allows us to reframe the problem and see that the question of Aboriginal self-determination can be used to rethink the limitations of this model of the state and the international order. Simply put, the current constitutional framework should not be seen as the shape that *UNDRIP* must fit into. Rather, *UNDRIP* should be used to put the hidden presumptions that ground the current

---

win or lose." By "dreamtime" he is, by my reading, referring to Aboriginal claims that are being grounded in mythic terms and are used as irrefutable grounds for a kind of absolute sovereignty. Once entered and expressed in the courts, these positions must become historical (i.e., open to interpretation and contestation). See J.G.A. Pocock, *The Discovery of Island: Essays in British History* (Cambridge: Cambridge University Press, 2005) at 249. This does not mean that Aboriginal peoples do not have the right to refuse to engage in the processes of reconciliation being offered in the settler states. If reconciliation is to have any meaning, there must be an ability to refuse it. The concern here is what this refusal means. There is a strong presumption that the only possible options for political and legal association are for Aboriginal peoples to be either a minority within the settler state or a secessionist movement that aims to establish a separate Westphalian state. This covers over the diverse legal and political traditions of Aboriginal peoples; there are a diversity of other options that could be explored under the broad contours of federalism. My concern (and the concern that I see in both Tully and Pocock) is that some may choose to adopt the Westphalian model of the state as their own and take up the very unilateral model of sovereignty (with its basis in the same mixture of mythology, legal fiction, and Bluebeard logic). If this path is taken, then they have adopted a model of sovereignty that violates, as Tully puts it, "the first principle of recognition politics, the principle of reciprocity, mutual recognition, mutual acknowledgment or *audi alteram partem* (always listen to the other side)." Tully, *Public Philosophy* at 1:201). My hope is to simply highlight two points: (1) those who refuse to engage and seek some alternative course need not be constrained by the false either/or of being a minority within a settler state or a separate state; and (2) whatever course of action is taken, it must face the question of legitimacy (outlined by Tully above). In regard to the minority approach, this has been the dominant approach of the Crown (i.e., that Aboriginal peoples are a sui generis category of British subjects akin to wards, or later, a sui generis category of Canadian citizens by virtue of the mere assertion of sovereignty), and so it has the same legitimacy deficit of the Crown's claims to sovereignty, legislative power, and underlying title. Will Kymlicka has provided a much different sense of the term *minority* in this context. It challenges the simplistic all-or-nothing version of the concept that conflicts with the equality principle of democratic citizenship. My claim that Aboriginal rights cannot be reduced to minority rights refers to the former narrow concept of a minority and not Kymlicka's broadened version. He develops this through a number of works, but the primary point of reference is his *Multicultural Citizenship: A Liberal Theory of Minority Rights* (Oxford: Oxford University Press, 1995).

150 *Mitchell v. MNR* at para. 130.

constitutional framework into question so that we can actually get to the *unfinished business of decolonization*.

Second, I will sketch the points of convergence and overlap that connect the struggle for Aboriginal self-government in Canada and the international project of decolonization beginning in the 1920s. This is a rough and very limited sketch of a vast territory.[151] Its purpose is to show that the struggle for Aboriginal self-government has never been simply a domestic matter. This shows that the stakes of the Indigenous question are not limited to Canadian reconciliation; rather, it extends to the very future of popular sovereignty as the legitimating principle for political organization. In order to see these stakes, I argue that we must reject the simplistic vision of historicism that grounds the myth of the unitary state and its unified and singular people. This means coming to grips with the fact that the struggle for Aboriginal rights and title *was never merely a domestic matter*. The prospect of the implementation of *UNDRIP* is thus not akin to the sudden arrival of a stranger; rather, it is part of the 250-year-old tradition of Aboriginal constitutionalism and diplomacy.

Third, and finally, I will outline how an approach informed by what I have termed *reconciliation with recollection* would work.

A. Unsettling the Ship of State

There is a tendency to see the question of Aboriginal self-government in Canada as a strictly domestic issue. This is by no means strange. After all, Aboriginal law is a part of the common law. It consists of bits and pieces of legislative machinery and constitutional sources. At times the courts will incorporate legal decisions from other jurisdictions, or at least cite them as persuasive, but this is part of the ordinary practice of the common law. But it is an *unsettled* one. It does not easily fit into the lines that determine this difference between international and domestic law. This is clearly exemplified in the contested status of treaties in Canada. From the perspective of the Crown they are little more than part of "the plan of negotiation adopted by the Government in dealing with … usufructuary rights,"[152] whereas Aboriginal peoples have continually

151 A more adequate approach to it would adopt a comparative and international focus. This would begin by exploring the question of Indigenous self-determination in multiple settler-colonial contexts and how these sets of laws, policies, practices, and institutions (this family of Crown machines), related both to one another and the development of international legal intuitions in the twentieth century. It is, in my opinion, not simply chance that the mandate system of the *League of Nations* so strongly resembles the Crown machinery that we find preceding it in dominions such as Canada. Given the focus of my current investigation, this broader project can be seen only as a possible line of future inquiry.

152 Canada, "Appeal" at 835–6.

maintained that they are lateral *nation-to-nation* agreements. This distinction between these accounts cuts to the very foundation of the relationship.

The typical Crown view begins from the assumption of the thick concept of sovereignty and holds that these treaties and s. 91(24) legitimate a *power-over* relationship in which Aboriginal rights are merely contractual terms that are subject to unilateral extinguishment (prior to 1982) or justified infringement (after 1982). The typical Indigenous view holds that they create a lateral *power-with* relationship that has been unilaterally breached for the last 150 years (viz. legislative power and underlying title are *not* bundled with Crown sovereignty; rather, they are subject to constitutional negotiations based on mutual recognition, consent, and continuity).

In terms of international law, the precise nature of the problem is difficult to categorize. This is, as Tully rightly notes, a product of the form of colonization that was employed: "In external colonization, colonies and the imperial society coexist in different territories. The colonies can free themselves and form geographically independent societies with exclusive jurisdiction over their respective territories (as Canada, United States, Australia and New Zealand have done in relation to the former British Empire). With internal colonization, this is not possible. The problematic, unresolved contradiction and constant provocation at the foundation of internal colonization, therefore, is that the dominant society coexists on and exercises exclusive jurisdiction over the territories and jurisdictions that the Indigenous peoples refuse to surrender."[153]

As a result, the conflict between settler states and Indigenous peoples is caught between the conceptual lines that define the Westphalian system of states. It seems that it must be either a domestic conflict between a state and a minority, or an international conflict between a colonial power and a separate nation (or group of nations). Both perspectives distort the reality of the conflict: the first because of its complete inability to provide a legitimate account for how Aboriginal peoples became a cultural minority within the settler body-politic (i.e., there is no evidence of the kind of mutual consent to this sovereign-to-subjects form of relationship or military conquest that could legitimate the unilateral *power-over* relationship); the second, because Aboriginal peoples cannot be simply and uniformly defined as secessionist movements. This has left Aboriginal peoples caught in what Roger Merino helpfully terms the "paradox of inclusion-exclusion."[154] As he puts it, "After colonization the political and economic elites constructed states under European models according to which the state was the legal and political expression of a homogeneous social

153 Tully, *Public Philosophy* at 1:262.

154 Roger Merino, "Law and Politics of Indigenous Self-Determination: The Meaning of the Right of Prior Consultation" (unpublished) at 2.

collective (a 'nation'). Therefore, Indigenous Peoples have to be either included within these new nation-states (denying their different social, political and economic arrangements) or excluded from them (which meant in some contexts the legal and material elimination of these peoples). Thus, in the new state model 'Indigenous Nations' were not accepted."[155]

The persistence of Indigenous resistance to both the logic of assimilation and the path of secession leaves the basic conceptual machinery of international law stuck. It seems that Indigenous peoples must choose one of two paths; first, they can concede that they are cultural minorities and thereby avail themselves of the human rights regime. This requires that they accept the thick or bundled version of Crown sovereignty and thereby accept the diminished forms of title and self-government that fit in this picture of the constitutional order. Second, they can maintain that they are a separate nation and struggle for international recognition. This is a *false dilemma* akin to the robber's choice: "Your money or your life." The real issue is not which option is selected but the illegitimacy of the use of force to impose it.

This false dilemma is a product of the nineteenth century. Its foundations can be seen in the Crown's claim that Aboriginal peoples are strictly a domestic concern. In order for this line (or any of the many versions of it) to hold true, there needs to be some account of why self-governing Aboriginal peoples are treated as if they were a cultural minority with a historical claim to some *lesser-than* set of property rights and not equal partners in confederation. In the nineteenth century the explanation was provided by civilizing discourses and the legal fictions associated with them (viz. *terra nullius* and discovery). This legitimating framework was useful, because it could be unilaterally imposed. There was no need to explain it. As J.S. Mill so clearly put it, "Despotism is a legitimate mode of government in dealing with barbarians, provided the end be their improvement, and the means justified by actually effecting that end. Liberty, as a principle, has no application to any state of things anterior to the time when mankind have become capable of being improved by free and equal discussion."[156]

The notion of historical stages provided the ground for determining the boundaries of applicability for the concept of *liberty*. Simply put, the accepted model of legitimation did not require mutual consent in all cases. This produced a model of the nation state whose boundaries were taken as the line that separated liberty from despotism (viz. only the civilized were capable of free political association, only they could form states).[157] This model of the state fit

155 Ibid.

156 Mill, *On Liberty* at 9.

157 This kind of exclusive coupling of the concept of civilization with the state led to the development of colonies *within the state*, as those individuals and groups who were deemed

within a larger international community of nations, which used the concept of civilization as the criterion for membership. Thus, the line between this free community of nations and the barbarians (who had no claim to liberty) was maintained by a unilateral use of the concept of recognition.

This led to a rather simplistic model of the state, which was conceived of as the legal and political expression of a singular people or nation. The unity of the people was their access to the concept of liberty, but this was defined in opposition to the barbarians who lacked such access.[158] The problem was that this boundary was the product of a *unilateral assertion*. All that distinguished it from a simple assertion of the right of the strongest (whose rather obvious flaws are drawn out by Hobbes) was the civilized/uncivilized distinction. This distinction provided legitimation to the colonial empires, but it came at a high cost. It was predicated on a claim concerning the nature and structure of historical progress. Those at the highest stage had access to liberty and a duty to educate those at the lower stages (i.e., to civilize them).

The form of this education was peculiar, to say the least; it maintained that the ends and the means could be categorically distinct. Much like alchemy's claim to convert lead into gold, the civilizing thesis held that violent and coercive means could lead to peaceful ends (this line of reasoning connects Hobbes, Kant, Hegel, Mill, and Marx, among others). There was effectively no real limit on the means used to educate barbarians; as Mill so clearly maintains, even despotism is legitimate. This was practically very useful, as it covered any and all forms of domination and coercion, but it was not unconditional. As Skinner rightly notes, "Any principle that helps to legitimize a course of action will therefore be among the enabling conditions of its occurrence."[159]

The legitimating power of the civilizing thesis was connected to the improvement of barbarians. But this raised two related problems. There was no standard or criterion that could measure their progress. There was no possible *objective*

---

to be deviant or abnormal were (to use Foucault's term) disciplined. For more on this process, refer to central texts within Foucault's extensive oeuvre such as *History of Madness*, ed. Jean Khalfa, trans. Jonathan Murphy and Jean Khalfa (London: Routledge, 2006); and *Discipline and Punish*. For more on the history of internal (or domestic) colonies, see Barbara Arneil, *Domestic Colonies: The Turn Inward to Colony* (Oxford: Oxford University Press, 2017).

158 I would like to note that the concepts of liberty, freedom, and self-determination are related to one another and essentially contested. This means that while a certain interpretation of these concepts may well claim general acceptance at a given time, it does not *capture the field* of these concepts (so to speak). They remain open to (and are enriched by) other contesting approaches and perspectives. It is a mistake to allow these invaluable concepts to remain the exclusive province of any particular tradition of political thought. For more on this line of reasoning, see Skinner, *Liberty before Liberalism*.

159 Skinner, *Regarding Method* at 156.

standard that could legitimate the line between liberty and despotism. In other words, legitimacy was connected directly to the nowhere of *utopia* and the impossible historical logic of *theodicy*. In order to escape the fray of subjective judgments, the standard of civilization required an absolute judgment. In the end, only *a view from nowhere* could possibly deliver the legitimacy it had promised. This meant that both the colonizer's claim to legitimacy and the barbarian's ability to lay claim to liberty and justice were infinitely deferred. Reaching it was as impossible as obtaining a view from nowhere or reaching the "end of history." Without the promise of legitimacy, all that remained was a despotism that was *continually resisted*. This resistance began to shift the onus from the barbarians (who had been assigned the impossible task of proving that they were *civilized*) to the colonial administrators in charge of the "temporary despotisms" of empire.

Those who were deemed to be barbarians (and so not entitled to liberty or "free and equal discussion") did not accept this designation. Nor did they fail to keep records (as Kant had imagined they would).[160] Rather, they continually pressed for an explanation that could justify the unilateral power of the colonial governments (e.g., see the Six Nations' status case in part 3). This resistance and contestation takes a wide number of forms, but it collectively shifted the available terms of legitimation. The only terms of legitimation left standing were those that applied to free and equal subjects (i.e., mutual recognition and constitutional democracy). This left the European colonial empires with little room to respond, other than a kind of rearguard position that claimed that their models of political association were all that was possible – that it was either their version of the nation state or Hobbes's *bellum omnium contra omnes*.[161] This position is clearly expressed in D.C. Scott's claim that the treaties between the Crown and Aboriginal peoples cannot be regarded as treaties in the normal sense, because the result would be "untenable and inconceivable."[162]

160 Kant, *Metaphysics of Morals* at 111–12.

161 In effect, the European colonial powers used the conditions of conflict and deprivation that they created under their temporary despotisms as evidence of a threat that could ground their legitimacy on the promise of security (viz. the colonial empire exists as both the problem and its solution; it is a racketeering scheme). But security alone is insufficient. It always needs recourse to the horizon of a future reconciliation. Without it there is no means of deferral aside from the use of violence, which, as non-violent praxis clearly shows, simply adds emphasis to the question of legitimacy.

162 Canada, "Appeal" at 836. In my mind there is a family resemblance between this position and the one expressed in the claim that "if God is dead then everything is permitted" (i.e., the fear of moral relativism). Both are predicated on a hidden premise that maintains that the only possible criteria or standards for law, justice, and truth are *absolute*. They thus concede that the "view from nowhere" is impossible, but continue to prop it up by maintaining its impossible criteria. The everyday practices of dialogue, consent, and mutual recognition are

Wittgenstein captures the basis of this problem perfectly: "The idea, as we think of it, is unshakable. You can never get outside it; you must always turn back. There is no outside; outside you cannot breathe. – Where does this idea come from? It is like a pair of glasses on our nose through which we see whatever we look at. It never occurs to us to take them off."[163]

What D.C. Scott's glasses obscure is what Tully helpfully refers to as the "plurality" of contests over recognition. As he explains, "This concept refers to two features of recognition politics. (1) that struggles over the mutual recognition of identities are too complex, unpredictable and mutable to admit of definitive solutions, and (2) that the intersubjective activity of striving for and responding to forms of mutual recognition is an intrinsic public good of modern politics that contributes to legitimacy and stability whether or not the form of recognition demanded is achieved."[164]

This further entails that "*the primary question is thus not recognition, identity or difference, but freedom*; the freedom of the members of an open society to change the constitutional rules of mutual recognition and association from time to time as their identities change. This is an aspect of the freedom of self-determination of peoples, one of the most important principles of modern politics from the American and French revolutions to the Universal Declaration of Human Rights."[165]

The only way to continue to avoid the implications of this plurality was to avoid the question of legitimation altogether by borrowing the magicians' techniques of sleight of hand to conceal it (and then protecting the secrets of the trade with the "Do not enter" warnings of Bluebeard logic). The colonial governments found that the unilateral power that the civilization distinction offered could still be used, as long as its basis was hidden from sight. This was (and is) the secret of indirect rule. If it is successful, it allows an "empty title and modest stipend" to be passed off as real self-determination, but when its mechanisms are exposed it suddenly collapses like a house of cards. The only justification available after this is that "might makes right," which is no justification at all.[166] This sets the stage for the process of decolonization, which begins in the early twentieth century, and the conflict between the right of self-determination and territorial integrity.

---

simply ignored. This is, to my mind, akin to using darkened glasses to stare at the horizon and then shifting your gaze back to the immediate surroundings and believing that there is either nothing to see or that you are blind – the point being that the source of the problem is not everyday reality, but the criteria that you are using to judge it.

163 Wittgenstein, *Philosophical Investigations* at §103.

164 Tully, *Public Philosophy* at 1:189.

165 Ibid., emphasis added.

166 Ibid. at 234.

B. Recollection without Historicism

There is a pattern of criss-crossing and overlapping lines that connects the struggle for Aboriginal self-government in Canada with the international process of decolonization. This is evident in the course of events that we have already covered. The Six Nations presenting their case at the League of Nations in the 1920s (a tactic that was also used by the Maori during the same period) and the *Lovelace* case in the 1970s clearly show that international law has always been part of the conversation in Canada.[167] It has been a part of each major shift in Canadian Indian policy. This should be of no surprise. After all, the international legal institutions of the twentieth century were designed to restructure the colonial system of the preceding century.[168] From their inception these institutions became avenues for *all colonized peoples* (by this I mean both those subjected to the external and the internal forms of colonization) to contest the legitimacy of the system created by the colonizing powers. This meant that the language and practices of colonial legitimation were being simultaneously contested and reasserted at both the *intra*national and *inter*national stages. The arguments that Indigenous peoples in Canada have been continually reasserting over the last 250 years (i.e., what Tully refers to as the "prior and coexisting sovereignty argument" and what many others – following Barsh and Henderson – have called "treaty federalism") were applied to the emerging field of international legal discourse.[169] They applied and adapted the historical and contextual resources of the "prior and coexisting sovereignty argument" to the concept of self-determination on the international stage. This means that the self-determination argument was never a separate and discrete line, but rather a related and parallel path.

This relationship between self-determination and prior and coexisting sovereignty can be easily seen as soon as we begin to consider the course of the *intra*national struggle in Canada over the development of international law. The second wave of international indigenous diplomacy (following the failure of the League of Nations) begins with the rise of international human rights in the 1960s.[170] In the mid-1960s the *Declaration on the Elimination of All Forms of Racial Discrimination* and (a few years later) the *International Convention on*

---

167 Henderson, *Indigenous Diplomacy* at 24. For more detail on the Maori at the League of Nations, see Tracey Banivanua Mar, *Decolonization and the Pacific: Indigenous Globalization and the Ends of Empire* (Cambridge: Cambridge University Press, 2016) at 86–95.

168 See Anghie, *Imperialism, Sovereignty and the Making of International Law*; and Koskenniemi, *Gentle Civilizer of Nations*).

169 Tully, *Public Philosophy* at 1:278; Barsh and Henderson, *The Road: Indian Tribes and Political Liberty*; and Asch, *On Being Here to Stay* draws out this point in relationship to the treaties.

170 Henderson, *Indigenous Diplomacy* at 24.

the Elimination of All Forms of Racial Discrimination provided a definition of "racial discrimination" that delegitimized the maintenance of separate rights for different racial groups.[171] While it did not mention Indigenous peoples, it was clear that it could be used to terminate their treaty rights, and this is precisely what the White Paper set out to do in 1969.[172]

This (unintentional) shift against the rights of Indigenous peoples was counterbalanced by the human rights covenants in 1966 (the *International Covenant on Economic, Social, and Cultural Rights* and the *International Covenant on Civil and Political Rights*); the first article of both asserts, "All peoples have the right of self-determination."[173] Adoption of these covenants brought a new wave of international diplomatic efforts by Indigenous peoples. It was through their concerted efforts that in 1972 (a year before the Court released the decision in *Calder*) the Sub-Commission on the Prevention of Discrimination and Protection of Minorities of the UN Commission on Human Rights appointed a special rapporteur to study "the problem of discrimination against Indigenous populations."[174]

In 1975 the International Court of Justice (ICJ) released its advisory opinion in the *Western Sahara* case.[175] Tully provides a useful summary of their opinion: "The ICJ rejected the doctrine of discovery and asserted that the only way a foreign sovereign could acquire a right to enter into territory that is not terra nullius is with the consent of the inhabitants by means of a public agreement. The Court further advised that the structure and form of government and whether a people are said to be at a lower level of civilization are not valid criteria for determining if the inhabitants have rights, such as the right of self-determination. The relevant consideration is if they have social and political organization."[176]

---

171 *Declaration on the Elimination of All Forms of Racial Discrimination*, GA Res 1904 (XVIII), UNGAOR, 18th Sess, UN Doc A/RES/18/1904 (20 November 1963); *International Convention on the Elimination of All Forms of Racial Discrimination*, 21 December 1965, 660 UNTS 195 (entered into force 4 January 1969), www.ohchr.org/EN/ProfessionalInterest/Pages/CERD.aspx.

172 Canada, "Statement of the Government of Canada on Indian Policy."

173 *International Covenant on Economic, Social and Cultural Rights*, 16 December 1966, 993 UNTS 3, 6 ILM 360 (entered into force 3 January 1976), www.ohchr.org/EN/ProfessionalInterest/Pages/CESCR.aspx; *International Covenant on Civil and Political Rights*, 16 December 1966, 999 UNTS 171 (entered into force 23 March 1976), www.ohchr.org/en/professionalinterest/pages/ccpr.aspx.

174 Sub-commission on Prevention of Discrimination and Protection of Minorities, José R. Martinez Cobo, *Study of the Problem of Discrimination against Indigenous Populations*, E/CN.4/Sub.2/1986/7/Add.4 (1987).

175 *Western Sahara: Advisory Opinion of 16 October 1975* (The Hague: ICJ Reports, 1975).

176 Tully, *Public Philosophy* at 1:281.

This decision was yet another blow to the nineteenth-century doctrines that had legitimated the European colonial projects. Its ramifications were not (and could not be) limited to those who experienced the external form of colonization. It added to the building international momentum on Indigenous self-determination.

In 1977, at the International NGO Conference on Discrimination against Indigenous Populations in the Americas in Geneva, Indigenous leaders moved towards developing human rights standards appropriate to this concern. The result of this diplomatic effort was the *Declaration of Principles for the Defense of Indigenous Nations and Peoples of the Western Hemisphere.*[177] This was followed in 1982 by the formation of a Working Group on Indigenous Populations. The group was established within the Sub-Commission on the Prevention of Discrimination and Protection of Minorities of the Commission of Human Rights. This was the beginning of the long and arduous process that resulted in the 2007 *United Nations Declaration on the Rights of Indigenous Peoples.*[178] While the 2007 declaration constitutes a major advance in the Indigenous struggle for self-determination, it is not without its limitations. As Tully notes, "Under the 2007 Declaration, the transcendent priority of existing exclusive state jurisdiction and territorial integrity is reproduced rather than questioned by the way the distinction between internal and external self-determination can be interpreted."[179] The main issue to be decided concerns the conflict between territorial integrity (Article 46) and self-determination (Articles 3 and 4).[180] This conflict is not a new one. It has shaped the course from the intra-national to the international legal stage.

The rejection of the Indigenous question at the League of Nations by the settler states and their colonial powers (via the concept of territorial integrity) was extended into the United Nations. This extension can be seen in the General

177 *Declaration of Principles for the Defense of Indigenous Nations and Peoples of the Western Hemisphere*, UN Doc E/CN.4/Sub.2/476/Add.5, Annex 4 (1981).

178 *United Nations Declaration on the Rights of Indigenous Peoples [UNDRIP]*, 2007, Doc. A/61/L.67.

179 Tully, *Public Philosophy* at 1:285.

180 *UNDRIP*. This conflict also necessarily concerns the phrase "free, prior and informed consent" (Articles 10, 11, 19, 28, and 29). In order for the concept of "consent" to have meaning, Indigenous peoples must have the ability to say no. This "veto" over proposed developments is not the pernicious bugbear that settler states present it is. It appears to be so only when one presumes that Indigenous peoples are a cultural minority within the body politic. With that background presumption in place, it makes it seem as if they are able to step outside of democratic decision-making processes to enforce their will on the state in ways that other citizens are not. Once this background is investigated and removed, it becomes clear that Indigenous peoples are "partners in Confederation" (i.e., an order of government within the division of powers). The concept of consent is thus simply a feature of their self-governance and jurisdiction over their territory.

Assembly's *Declaration on the Granting of Independence to Colonial Countries and Peoples*, which legitimated the dismantling of the external colonial projects while excluding the internal ones.[181] The "saltwater thesis" denied Indigenous peoples living in predominantly settler states the right to self-determination. The basis of its denial was, once again, territorial integrity. It was attractive to the newly independent states that had inherited the deep social and cultural fractures left by the colonial powers and were concerned by the prospect of intra-national division.

The basic structure of the territorial integrity argument was by no means new to Aboriginal peoples. It exists within *St Catherine's Milling*, which positions them (without their consent) as already a part of a state. It magically converts their interests in their lands and the pre-existing nation-to-nation treaties as being little more than gifts from the imperial Crown that, following its gradual retreat, become the burdens of the dominion – burdens that, as we well know, could be extinguished at will. This magical argument hides its presumptions by presenting itself as a simple application of the rules of formal legal interpretation. This enables Lord Watson to read s. 91(24) as a complete and final grant of unilateral power over Indians and their lands. What it ignores (and must always refuse) is any and all references to the context for this constitutional provision. In order to continue to serve as a foundation, it requires that either the British Crown was able to give what it did not have or that it could unilaterally interpret all pre-existing agreements in its favour. As Pocock rightly points out, this bizarre logic reinterprets treaties as constituting "a kind of legal self-annihilation or suicide on the part of the indigenous contractor, so that to enter into a treaty was to lose the right to enforce it and consequently all rights under it."[182] At its basis, once its foundations are laid bare, all that remains of it is that "might makes right." This absence of a foundation is propped up by Bluebeard logic and theatrical displays of violence (e.g., the use of police force to suppress the Six Nations in the 1920s and Canada's use of the police and military power to respond to the resistance of the Mohawk of Kanesatake in the Oka Crisis in 1990).[183]

The fixed nature of this response can be seen in the similarity between the arguments used by Canada against the Six Nations in the 1920s and those used against the Mi'kmaw Nation in the 1980s. In 1980 the United Nations Human Rights Committee accepted a complaint from the Mi'kmaw Nation that alleged violations to their right of self-determination. Just one month after Canada received notice of the complaint from the secretary general, the Sûreté du Québec (provincial police) conducted a raid on the Mi'kmaq Reserve at Listuguj.

181 Tully, *Public Philosophy* at 1:283.

182 Pocock, *Discovery of Island* at 230.

183 For more on the Oka crisis and its context, see Gerald R. Alfred, *Heeding the Voices of Our Ancestors: Kahnawake Mohawk Politics and the Rise of Native Nationalism* (Oxford: Oxford University Press, 1995) at 93–114.

Canada followed this action with a formal response to the Mi'kmaw. Their position was simple: (1) self-determination "cannot affect the national unity and territorial integrity of Canada," and (2) the treaties "are merely considered to be nothing more than contracts between a sovereign and a group of its subjects."[184] Both the pattern of response and its conceptual basis are the same. The conceptual basis of this position appeared again in 1993 at the World Conference on Human Rights in Vienna during the drafting of the *Vienna Declaration and Program of Action.*[185] Canada (along with Indonesia and India) took the position that Indigenous peoples should be described as a "people" and not "peoples" – the basis of this absurd position being that the use of the singular term *people* would provide a kind of formalistic bar to the application of human rights doctrines so that these states could continue treating Indigenous peoples as a minority.[186] Quite simply, Canada has continually maintained that Aboriginal peoples can only ever be a minority or a secessionist movement. The process of reconciliation has been constructed on this very basis; it is a *reconciliation to* the Crown's unilateral *power over* Aboriginal peoples and their lands via the "broad view" of s. 91(24).[187] Aboriginal peoples have continually

---

184 "Response of the Government of Canada respecting Communication submitted by Mr. Alexander Denny on behalf of the people of the Mi'kmak tribal society on September 30, 1980 (date of initial letter)," 21 July 1981 at 2 and 4, www.usask.ca/nativelaw/unhrfn/mikmaqfiles/No4.pdf. See also Henderson, *Indigenous Diplomacy* at 38–9.

185 UN General Assembly, *Vienna Declaration and Programme of Action*, 12 July 1993, A/CONF.157/23.

186 Henderson, *Indigenous Diplomacy* at 53 and 122.

187 By "reconciliation to" the Crown's unilateral power I am not suggesting that the current s. 35 framework offers no meaningful limits to unilateral Crown power of Indigenous peoples. The phrase is not to be understood as a simple substitute for coercion. As I state in note 15 of this part, s. 35 litigation has indeed shown that it can be a source of real, meaningful protection for the rights it recognizes and affirms. My concern is that s. 35 (as it is currently understood) is built upon the presumption of *thick* Crown sovereignty. Thus, all of the tests that the courts have designed to determine the limits of these rights are built on this background presumption (viz. the court is unwittingly designing Procrustean beds). This means that in the process of litigation Aboriginal and treaty rights are a made-to-measure colonial picture of the constitutional order. These made-to-measure rights are provided with constitutional protections, but these are *Charter*-like protections. They presume a sovereign–subject relationship wherein the court places reasonable limits on the Crown's exercise of sovereign authority. The problem here is not simply that this version of s. 35 lacks meaningful protections, but that it is categorically the wrong type of protections altogether. Aboriginal peoples are *peoples*, and the courts should not be reconciling them to the position of a cultural minority within the state. Put differently, by accepting this thick or bundled version of Crown sovereignty, they have imposed a colonial picture of the constitutional order on Aboriginal peoples. This is not the only possible approach. The transition from parliamentary to constitutional supremacy has placed the courts in the difficult position of having to legally mediate the relationship between the Crown and Aboriginal peoples. While the Canadian courts cannot question Crown sovereignty full stop, they can determine what legal consequences flow from this sovereignty. They can

responded to this argument by reminding the Crown of their treaties and the nation-to-nation relationship that the *Royal Proclamation of 1763* recognized.

This context helps to frame exactly what is at stake in the possible implementation of the *UNDRIP*. The stakes are, quite simply, the future of popular sovereignty as the legitimating principle for political organization. This could well strike some readers as little more than hyperbole, but I would ask those readers to pause and consider the situation carefully. The conflict between the concepts of territorial integrity and self-determination is foundational. The question of Indigenous self-determination exposes this clearly. If the Westphalian model of the state is to be retained, then we must refuse to recognize Indigenous peoples as *peoples*. They must be nothing more than a cultural minority (or minorities) within currently existing states. The cost of this position is high; it must withstand the historical reality that Aboriginal peoples *did not consent to this relationship*.[188] This means it must either simply draw a line that forbids inquiry

---

decouple (or unbundle) Crown sovereignty from legislative power and underlying title. This opens up the possibility of a federal solution (one that has roots that stretch back over 250 years) to the problems that the colonial constitutional order has generated. This solution involves remapping the jurisdictional lines within Canada; it retains the "territorial integrity" of the state. By doing so they can begin to treat Aboriginal peoples as *equal partners in Canadian confederation*. While this is not a problem that the courts can hope to resolve on their own, they can initiate the process by holding Crown sovereignty to constitutional limitations. They can help guide the process of constitutional decolonisation by adhering to the model of constitutional negotiations that they so clearly mapped out in the *Secession Reference*. This significance of this shift is that, as Noel Lyon phrased it, "it renounces the old rules of the game under which the Crown established courts of law and denied those courts the authority to question the sovereign claims made by the Crown." See Noel Lyon, "Essay on Constitutional Interpretation" at 100.

188 Referring to the treaties as sources of this consent requires the use of a set of special constructive techniques. I say "special" because those who employ them expend considerable effort in distinguishing these treaties from international treaties. The legal principles used to interpret international treaties are founded on the presumption of free consent, good faith, and the *pacta sunt servanda* rule (see the preamble of the *Vienna Convention on the Law of Treaties*, 1155 UNTS 331, 8 ILM 679 (entered into force 27 January 1980)). The treaties in Canada are interpreted from within a constitutional framework where the Crown is presumed to have a thick or bundled form of sovereignty. The Crown's position within this frame is so all-encompassing that it leaves little to no space for Aboriginal sovereignty. This leads to the construction of a (pseudo-)categorical distinction of the treaties from international treaties. For example, Duncan Campbell Scott (who was the head of the Department of Indian Affairs from 1913 to 1932 and drafted the response) argued that the treaties are not treaties "in the meaning comprehended by international law" but simply part of "the plan of negotiation adopted by the Government in dealing with the usufructuary rights which the aboriginal peoples have been recognized as possessing in the land from the inception of British rule." See Canada, "Appeal" at 835–6. Canada's response to the Mi'kmaw Nation's complaint in the 1980s reiterated this position by stating that (1) self-determination "cannot affect the national unity and territorial integrity of Canada," and (2) the treaties "are merely considered to be nothing more than contracts between a sovereign and a group of its

into the historical warrant of sovereignty or judicially reinterpret each and every piece of historical evidence. Both options rely on *unilateral* power over Aboriginal peoples; neither is convincing. They are attempts to finesse rather

---

subjects." See *The Mikmaq Tribal Society v. Canada*, Communication No. 78/1980 at 2–6; and Henderson, *Indigenous Diplomacy* at 38–9. We can see a prime example of this argument in Norris JA's decision in *White and Bob R. v. White and Bob* (1964) 50 DLR (2d) 613 at 649 (aff'd [1965] SCR vi, 52 DLR (2d) 481).

> In the section "Treaty" is not a word of art and in my respectful opinion, it embraces all such engagements made by persons in authority as may be brought within the term "the word of the white man" the sanctity of which was, at the time of British exploration and settlement, the most important means of obtaining the goodwill and co-operation of the native tribes and ensuring that the colonists would be protected from death and destruction. On such assurance the Indians relied. In view of the argument before us, it is necessary to point out that on numerous occasions in modern days, rights under what were entered into with Indians as solemn engagements, although completed with what would now be considered informality, have been whittled away on the excuse that they do not comply with present day formal requirements and with rules of interpretation applicable to transactions between people who must be taken in the light of advanced civilization to be of equal status. Reliance on instances where this has been done is merely to compound injustice without real justification at law. The transaction in question here was a transaction between, on the one hand, the strong representative of a proprietary company under the Crown and representing the Crown, who had gained the respect of the Indians by his integrity and the strength of his personality and was thus able to bring about the completion of the agreement, and, on the other hand, uneducated savages. The nature of the transaction itself was consistent with the informality of frontier days in this Province and such as the necessities of the occasion and the customs and illiteracy of the Indians demanded. The transaction in itself was a primitive one – a surrender of land in exchange for blankets to be divided between the Indian signatories according to arrangements between them – with a reservation of aboriginal rights, the document being executed by the Indians by the affixing of their marks. The unusual (by the standards of legal draftsmen) nature and form of the document considered in the light of the circumstances on Vancouver Island in 1854 does not detract from it as being a "Treaty."

Roger B. Taney CJ took much the same position in the mid-nineteenth century in *United States v. Rogers* 45 US 567 (1846) at 572:

> The native tribes who were found on this continent at the time of its discovery have never been acknowledged or treated as independent nations by the European governments, nor regarded as the owners of the territories they respectively occupied. On the contrary, the whole continent was divided and parceled out, and granted by the governments of Europe as if it had been vacant and unoccupied land, and the Indians continually held to be, and treated as, subject to their dominion and control. It would be useless at this day to inquire whether the principle thus adopted is just or not, or to speak of the manner in which the power claimed was in many instances exercised. It is due to the United States, however, to say, that while

than face the challenge of reconciliation. Tully draws out the consequences of this strategy: "*Unilateral* defence of the status quo, unilateral constitutional change and unilateral succession are all unjust in the sense that they violate with respect to other members the very principle that is invoked to justify the act. Moreover, such unilateral acts are unstable, for the disregarded members are seldom silenced for long. All the force of existing society or of the secessionist state cannot stabilize effectively the unjust situation or gain the recognition they need from others, as we have seen in many tragic cases."[189]

The implications are unavoidable; either find a way to finesse legitimation (and paint continued resistance as secessionist) or forgo legitimation altogether. In any case, what is clear at this point is that the Westphalian model of the state is caught in this dilemma. Simply put, the picture of the ship of state is no longer a sustainable one. Clifford Geertz captures the situation: "The diffusionist notion that the modern world was made in northern and western Europe and then seeped out like an oil slick to cover the rest of the world has obscured the fact … that rather than converging toward a single pattern those entities called countries were ordering themselves in novel ways, ways that put European conceptions, not all that secure in any case, of what a country is, and what its basis is, under increasing pressure. The genuinely radical implications of the decolonization process are

---

> they have maintained the doctrines upon this subject which had been previously established by other nations, and insisted upon the same powers and dominion within their territory, yet, from the very moment the general government came into existence to this time, it has exercised its power over this unfortunate race in the spirit of humanity and justice, and has endeavored by every means in its power to enlighten their minds and increase their comforts, and to save them if possible from the consequences of their own vices.

Lamar J (as he was then) uses a less explicit version of this argument in *R v. Sioui*:

> Without deciding what the international law on this point was, I note that the writers to whom the appellant referred the Court studied the rules governing international relations and did not comment on the rules which at that time governed the conclusion of treaties between European nations and native peoples. In any case, the rules of international law do not preclude the document being characterized as a treaty within the meaning of s. 88 of the *Indian Act*. At the time with which we are concerned relations with Indian tribes fell somewhere between the kind of relations conducted between sovereign states and the relations that such states had with their own citizens.

This (deeply unpersuasive) distinction is then coupled with the construction of a narrow and technical set of judicial interpretative tools that, in my view, retain their persuasive force only for those who benefit directly from them. Once the sui generis distinction is removed, even this highly selective persuasive power evaporates.

189 Tully, *Public Philosophy* at 1:201 (emphasis in original).

only just now coming to be recognized. For better or for worse, the dynamics of Western nation building are not being replicated. Something else is going on."[190]

It is precisely the "implications of the decolonization" that are at stake in the question of implementation. If the Canadian government continues forward with the status quo and uses its framework to read down the right of self-determination to fit the municipal model of *St Catherine's Milling*, then reconciliation will continue its current holiday. As Tully reminds us, "If the Constitution does not rest on the consent of the people or their representatives, or if there is not a procedure by which it can be so amended, then they are neither self-governing nor self-determining but are governed and determined by a structure of laws that is imposed on them. They are unfree. This is the principle of popular sovereignty by which modern peoples and governments are said to be free and legitimate."[191] The consequence is that Aboriginal peoples will effectively be left in a constitutional prison fashioned by the Court, and when they inquire why, the response will be that it is *how power is reconciled with duty*.

This is not the only available course of action. It is also possible to use implementation to work through and remove the barricades of the past from the current framework. It is possible for Canada to lead the way towards a post-Westphalian model of the state that takes the open-ended *plurality* of contests over recognition as its starting point. This would replace the unitary model of the ship of state and its endless historical progress towards reconciliation – which has never been anything more than a theological mechanism of deferral – with the diverse and unmoving black canoe. In other words, it is possible to use this moment as an opportunity to find a reconciliation *with* Aboriginal peoples and thereby shape future processes of internal self-determination.

C. Implementing Reconciliation-with-Recollection

It may well seem that the challenge of articulating what I have termed *reconciliation-with-recollection* (or simply *reconciliation-with*) will require another long and difficult journey; that we should busy ourselves by stocking up discursive provisions to rig ourselves "out for the fight" (to borrow Carroll's phrasing). But this is not the nature of the task at hand. There is no need to attempt to leap over our own time or craft (yet another) blank map. Our itinerary is not set by a horizon that is yet to come; it is not speculative. Rather, as Wittgenstein maintained, "What *we* do is to bring back words from their metaphysical to their everyday use."[192] There is, as such, no need to set out towards

190 Clifford Geertz, *Available Light: Anthropological Reflections on Philosophical Topics* (Princeton: Princeton University Press, 2000) at 230–1.

191 Tully, *Public Philosophy I* at 1:286.

192 Wittgenstein, *Philosophical Investigations* at §116.

the horizon. The resources that are required were already there – hidden in plain sight, so to speak. I could say that (following Hegel – or one of his many versions) the task is to recognize the "rose in the cross of the present."[193] The difficulty is in finding a way to help us see what is already there. Not that "what is there" is somehow simple: a final truth that is simply buried and that, once uncovered, will provide reconciliation in the blink of an eye. Rather, the challenge lies in seeing the diverse possibilities that are already there. As Wittgenstein reminds us, no game, no matter how detailed, is bounded on all sides by rules. The task "consists in assembling reminders for a particular purpose."[194] This means that the resources that we require are already there; *they never left.*

Reconciliation *with* Aboriginal peoples is just that; it is carried out with them. It requires that the *bundled* conception of Crown sovereignty and the "broad view" of s. 91(24) be abandoned by the Court. This is no small task. It has served as the "hinge proposition" around which the entire body of the current framework moves. It is the magical or alchemical (to follow Borrows's helpful metaphor) provision that acts as the ground for all unilateral barricades that have constrained the Aboriginal perspective. It grants the Court the magical power that is needed to determine that it is contact with Europeans that determines the line for Aboriginal rights (as it did in *Van der Peet*), whereas it is the assertion of sovereignty for title,[195] not to mention the very idea that Aboriginal rights can be articulated on a spectrum that runs from rights to title.[196] This kind of patent absurdity is captured by the joke about three blind men and an elephant.[197] All of this complicated and convoluted jurisprudence is carried out on the basis of the idea that "there was from the outset never any doubt that sovereignty and legislative power, and indeed the underlying

---

193 Hegel, *Philosophy of Right* at 22.

194 Wittgenstein, *Philosophical Investigations* at §127.

195 *Van der Peet*; *Delgamuukw v. British Columbia.*

196 *Haida Nation v. British Columbia.* It is interesting to note that the concept of the "spectrum" is said to be helpful "not to suggest watertight legal compartments but rather to indicate what the honour of the Crown may require in particular circumstances." This is interesting because while the concept of a spectrum provides gradation (whereas the watertight compartments are clearly divisible units with strict limits), it remains *contained* within the ship of state. The constitutional metaphor of the living tree is not put to use. As Roger Merino helpfully points out, "Self-determination must be understood as the main right for Indigenous Peoples, a *foundational right* in the sense that it is the basis of a whole legal, political and economic system rooted in non-Western ontologies and epistemologies." See Merino, "Law and Politics of Indigenous Self-Determination" at 22.

197 The story is a familiar one: each believes that he discovers a separate and divisible object, but this is simply a problem of perspective. If each begins to listen to one another and collaborate it is possible to see that all are really just describing one thing. In this case what is being described is Aboriginal self-government.

title, to such lands vested in the Crown."[198] As we have already seen (and as the Court's recent qualifications of Crown sovereignty suggest), as soon as we begin to question the basis of this undoubted claim, we find nothing but the barricades of the past (i.e., *terra nullius*, discovery, the civilization thesis, etc.). There is, simply put, no legitimate basis for either the *bundled* conception of Crown sovereignty or the "broad view" of s. 91(24) that it gives rise to. And as the Court rightly maintained in the *Reference re Secession of Quebec*, "In our constitutional tradition, legality and legitimacy are linked."[199]

The way to begin *reconciliation with* is thus to remove the hinge of the current framework and all of the unilateral rights that it carries. This may well seem (to use D.C. Scott's terms) "untenable" and "inconceivable," but it is actually consistent with another aspect of Canada's constitutional tradition. As the Lord Chancellor, Viscount Sankey stated in *Edwards v. Canada (AG)*,

> The British North America Act planted in Canada a living tree capable of growth and expansion within its natural limits. The object of the Act was to grant a Constitution to Canada. Like all written constitutions it has been subject to development through usage and convention.... Their Lordships do not conceive it to be the duty of this Board – it is certainly not their desire – to cut down the provisions of the Act by a narrow and technical construction, but rather to give it a large and liberal interpretation so that the Dominion to a great extent, but within certain fixed limits, may be mistress in her own house, as the provinces to a great extent, but within certain fixed limits, are mistresses in theirs.[200]

The ship of state (whether it is outfitted with watertight compartments or spectrums) has never been the appropriate metaphor for the constitutional relationship between Aboriginal peoples and Canada. But it has persisted. This is, to my mind, because of the exceptional treatment that the *thick* conception of Crown sovereignty required. It simply could not grow and develop with the rest of the tree. It has been confined by a set of constitutional interpretive practices that Borrows has termed "(Ab)originalism."[201] He provides us with a reminder of what is at stake in this: "While Aboriginal and treaty rights are exercisable only by Aboriginal peoples, and thus do not flow from the liberal enlightenment in this respect, this should not cause us to overlook the truth that they likewise exist to restrain government action. They are living constitutional traditions.... Thus, we must take care to ensure that while we appropriately define Aboriginal rights as having different contours, we do not place them entirely outside of the constitution's broader framework."[202]

198 *Sparrow* at 1103.

199 *Reference re Secession of Quebec* at para. 33.

200 *Edwards v. AG for Canada* at 136.

201 Borrows, *Freedom and Indigenous Constitutionalism* at 128.

202 Ibid. at 144.

But the current framework for reconciliation does precisely this. By beginning with the presumption of Crown sovereignty, legislative power, and underlying title (which I have termed the *bundled* or *thick* conception of sovereignty) the courts have constructed a picture of the constitutional order that has no place for the "living constitutional traditions" of Aboriginal peoples. The Aboriginal rights that are "recognized and affirmed" in the current framework are made-to-measure for this picture. Their "different contours" have been cut away to make room for the all-encompassing dimensions of *thick* Crown sovereignty. But this can be changed. There is also no need for the Court to point to the need for a negotiated political process or constitutional amendment to do so.

The Court may feel that the problem of Crown sovereignty is beyond the scope of its jurisdiction. After all, Crown sovereignty is non-justiciable in Canadian courts. But this status does not necessarily extend to legislative power and underlying title. The way out of this problem is to adopt an *unbundled, thin, deflated,* or *limited* concept of Crown sovereignty.

This *thinning* of the concept of sovereignty via judicial interpretation is not an entirely novel solution.[203] In the *Marshall Trilogy* the chief justice moves from a *thick* version of state sovereignty in *Johnson v. M'Intosh* to a *thinner* one in *Worcester v. Georgia*. Similarly, the Judicial Committee of the Privy Council altered the thickness of its notion of sovereignty from *St Catherine's Milling* to *Re Southern Rhodesia Land* and *Amodu Tijani v. Secretary, Southern Nigeria*. The jurisdictional space that these courts created for Indigenous peoples was still a diminished one. These decisions retain a view of state sovereignty that has the power to unilaterally extinguish the rights of Aboriginal peoples. This power is built on a narrow view of the legal personality of Indigenous peoples (e.g., they "occupy" but cannot "own" their lands, and their right of self-determination is limited). Simply put, these decisions are still reliant on the legerdemain of racist nineteenth-century legal fictions. But they do have value. They remind us that state sovereignty is by no means a *fixed* legal concept. And so the non-justiciability of sovereignty cannot be used as full answer to questions concerning either the sources or the legitimacy of its legal qualities. Put otherwise, the Crown's claim to legislative power and underlying title should be justiciable questions.

By continuing to uphold the Crown's claim to sovereignty, legislative power, and underlying title, the Court is confining Aboriginal peoples to the very "straitjacket" they cautioned against in the *Reference re Secession of Quebec*. "The Constitution is not a straitjacket. Even a brief review of our constitutional history demonstrates periods of momentous and dramatic change. Our democratic

203 See Chappel J at n 53. While she retains the current s. 35 framework, her analysis of the changes in the courts' understanding of Crown sovereignty from *Sparrow* to today is useful.

institutions necessarily accommodate a continuous process of discussion and evolution, which is reflected in the constitutional right of each participant in the federation to initiate constitutional change. This right implies a reciprocal duty on the other participants to engage in discussions to address any legitimate initiative to change the constitutional order."[204] It is time to acknowledge that Aboriginal peoples are not "mere burdens" to be divided between s. 91(24) and s. 109, but full participants in the federation.

In order to do so, they must decouple (or unbundle) Crown sovereignty from legislative power and underlying title. This would unhinge ss. 91(24) and s. 35 so that the Aboriginal rights that the latter "recognizes and affirms" can no longer be subject to reasonable infringement. Instead these rights would take on a jurisdictional status that is analogous to ss. 91 and 92 of the *Constitution Act, 1867*. This solution involves remapping the jurisdictional lines within Canada, but it does so in a manner that retains the "territorial integrity" of the state. While this is not a problem that the courts can hope to resolve on their own, they, as the "guardians of the constitution" can initiate the process by interpreting Crown sovereignty in a manner that allows for a legitimate and lawful constitutional order with Aboriginal peoples. They can help guide constitutional decolonization by adhering to the model of constitutional negotiations that they so clearly mapped out in the *Secession Reference*.

The *thinned* version of sovereignty that I would recommend would restrict the non-justiciable shield to minimal settings (e.g., external legal personality, territorial integrity, etc.) and thus place legislative power and underlying title within the arena of constitutional law and negotiation.[205] This would also *unhinge* the Court's current framework of reconciliation. Let me unpack what I mean by "unhinge." In *Sparrow* the Court made use of a *thick* concept of Crown sovereignty to ground their interpretation of federal "power" under s. 91(24) and thereby justify treating s. 35 as if it was subject to the reasonable limitations of s. 1. Put differently, the *thick* concept of Crown sovereignty provides them with the means to reconcile the division between the *Constitution Acts* of 1867 and 1982. Once this hinge is removed, s. 35 can no longer be treated "as if" it was a part of the *Charter*. The existing framework of reconciliation collapses. But I do not feel that we should see this as a loss. Rather, it provides us a clearer

---

204 *Reference re Secession of Quebec* at para. 150.

205 I would also note that this strategy works around the limitations of "territorial integrity" in Article 46(1) of the *UNDRIP*, as remapping the jurisdictional lines within a state does nothing to "dismember or impair, totally or in part" either the "territorial integrity" or the "political unity of sovereign and independent States." Rather, were such a solution to the conflict between Aboriginal peoples and Canada to be successful, it would doubtlessly enhance their "political unity."

view of the colonial structure of our shared constitutional order, which, in turn, offers us new opportunities to continue the work of decolonizing it.

An intermediate step that the Court could take is to shift the hinge of the framework from the presumption of *thick* Crown sovereignty and the "broad view" of s. 91(24) to *thin* Crown sovereignty and a *broader view* of s. 25. As Tully points out, "Section 91(24) of the Constitution can be read as recognizing the existence of the first confederation. Section 25 specifies the treaty character of the relations of the first confederation, and Section 35 can be interpreted to recognize and affirm an inherent right to self-government."[206]

This realignment may seem radical, and it doubtlessly will require a process that will be complex and unpredictable, but this is no reason to maintain the status quo.[207] Legitimacy and legality cannot be held apart by simply begging the question and pointing to a *reconciliation to come*. Rather, as the Court correctly reminds us in the *Reference re Secession of Quebec*, "In our constitutional tradition, legality and legitimacy are linked."[208] Tully draws our attention to what is at stake in this link between legality and legitimacy: "Indigenous peoples will be free and self-determining only when they govern themselves by their own constitutions, and these are equal in international status to Western constitutions. That is, they will have an effective say in having their constitutions recognized and accommodated in a negotiated treaty relationship *with* the present constitutions of existing states, not *within* them."[209] This difference between what I have referred to as *reconciliation with* and *reconciliation to* is clearly exposed here.

The stakes of these two approaches are drawn out by the prospect of implementing *UNDRIP*. On the one hand, Canada could continue following its blank map. This would make implementation into little more than a coronation of the status

206 Tully, *Public Philosophy* at 1:238.

207 One issue that needs to be addressed regarding this re-hinging is that s. 25 is within the *Charter* and limits the *Charter*'s impact on Aboriginal, treaty, and certain "other" rights of Indigenous peoples. Given its place in the structure, can it bear the constitutional weight needed? My response is that a *broader view* of s. 25 could be constructed on the basis of its connection to what Tully terms "the treaty character of the relations of the first confederation." See Tully, *Public Philosophy* at 1:238. This allows the court to use s. 25 to draw on the 250-year history of treaty federalism to read s. 91(24) and s. 35 in a way that engages with Aboriginal peoples as *equal partners in Confederation*. In terms of the more technical questions of constitutional interpretation, I would argue that this re-positioning of the hinge from federal "power over" in s. 91(24) to "power-with" under s. 25 is more persuasive and, I would argue, has a more secure claim to the kind of legitimacy that accords with the Canadian legal order.

208 *Reference re Secession of Quebec* at para. 33.

209 Ibid. at 286.

quo. This would effectively defer the meaning of internal self-determination. On the other hand, Canada could listen to the Aboriginal perspective and begin working through the current impasse together. This entails, as Asch maintains, returning to the treaties and reading them *with* Aboriginal peoples and thus treating them as constitutional documents that continue to live and grow over time.[210] The work of reconciliation does not begin from nothing; its foundations are there already, hiding in plain sight. We need to see that the view of the treaties that is put forward by Lord Watson in *St Catherine's Milling*, articulated by D.C. Scott, and perpetuated by the Court's use of (Ab)originalism is only *one perspective*. It has been this perspective that has dominated the last 150 years under the "broad view" of s. 91(24) and the "vast administrative despotism" that it empowers. The history of the numbered treaties shows that there were many others within the Crown who did not take this view, even after Confederation.[211] It is still possible to listen to Aboriginal peoples as equal partners in confederation and thereby return to the relationship of mutual recognition. By my view, it was this possibility that Lord Denning had in mind when he stated,

> There is nothing, so far as I can see, to warrant any distrust by the Indians of the Government of Canada. But, in case there should be, the discussion in this case will strengthen their hand so as to enable them to withstand any onslaught. They will be able to say that their rights and freedoms have been guaranteed to them by the Crown – originally by the Crown in respect of the United Kingdom – now by the Crown in respect of Canada – but, in any case, by the Crown. No Parliament should do anything to lessen the worth of these guarantees. They should be honoured by the Crown in respect of Canada "so long as the sun rises and the river flows." That promise must never be broken.[212]

If Canada were to listen to Aboriginal peoples as equal partners in confederation, this could serve as a model for other states who are experiencing conflicts over recognition within multinational societies. It is not only part of the unfinished business of decolonization, but also, to my mind, that of the Enlightenment. By this I mean that it is part of living up to the requirements of the principles of freedom and equality without the barricades and "temporary despotisms" of the past.

This latter option would minimally require that *the hinge of the current framework must be shifted from thick Crown sovereignty and the "broad view" of s.* 91(24) *to shared sovereignty and a broader view of s. 25.* This realignment entails a fundamental rethinking of the jurisprudence on Aboriginal rights and title.

---

210 Asch, *On Being Here to Stay*, at 162–65.

211 Ibid. at 157.

212 This is from the decision of the British Court of Appeal on an appeal brought by the Indians of Alberta in 1982. It is cited in the *Penner Report* at 49.

The unilateral right of infringement would need to be removed. Consent would become the standard, and it would need to be acquired before any projects or activities take place.[213] In order to be workable, this requires that Aboriginal peoples have self-government with jurisdiction over clearly defined territorial boundaries. This, in turn, means that the related questions of political form, membership, and territory must be dealt with. As I have already detailed, none of the current forms of self-governance satisfy this. The model in all cases is some variant of a municipality with devolved powers. The minimal requirement of meaningful self-government is the recognition of its inherent claim to internal sovereignty, legislative power, and underlying title. The *Penner Report* and the *Report of the Royal Commission on Aboriginal Peoples* both provide guidance on how this could be carried out. Doubtlessly a diversity of forms of governance will grow and develop as this process takes shape. This is neither "untenable" nor "inconceivable"; it is simply what is already there, hidden in plain sight. It offers us a way to move towards a post-Westphalian model of political association that is based on a concept of sovereignty that is no longer taken to be absolute, but rather is suited to the overlapping and interdependent terrain of everyday reality. It is time to stop following blank maps and hunting snarks. Mutual reconciliation (or *reconciliation with*) cannot be achieved through unilateral assertions. It requires that the means and ends be the same; it begins with free and equal discussion. This is the answer given by the black canoe, it is the *Spirit of Haida Gwaii*.[214]

---

213 The standard of consent is often dismissed as being a "right to veto" that cuts against the principle of equality. This mischaracterizes the nature of the conflict altogether; it presents a view in which Indigenous peoples are already a part of *the people* within the settler state and are demanding the kind of "power over" relationship that grants undoubted sovereignty, legislative power, and underlying title. At its heart, this is a false dilemma that is based on two hidden premises: (1) it presumes that Indigenous peoples are part of *the people* without their consent and so their claims cut against the other citizens, and (2) it is based on an all-or-nothing (or absolutist) understanding of sovereignty that obscures the possibilities of democratic constitutionalism and federalism. The consistent position of Indigenous diplomacy over the last 250 years (indeed stretching back to the Two Row Wampum in 1613) has been premised on something other than this absolutist "power over" view. After all, "treaty federalism" is a way of dividing sovereignty and holding *power-with*. Roger Merino ("Law and Politics of Indigenous Self-Determination" at 22) provides a clear and direct response to the "right to veto" argument: "Self-determination and territoriality support the right of consent, wrongly called 'right to veto,' because it does not derive from a special power conferred to Indigenous Peoples due to their hegemonic position in the democratic system (as is the case with the presidential veto power), but it is an expression of their self-determination as peoples." It does not offend the principle of equality to recognize this; rather, it offends the principle of equality to simply presume that Indigenous peoples are a part of *the people* within a settler state without their free, prior, and informed consent.

214 Tully, *Strange Multiplicity* at 212.

Select Bibliography

Alfred, Taiaiake. *Peace, Power, Righteousness: An Indigenous Manifesto.* 2nd ed. Oxford: Oxford University Press, 2009.

Anghie, Antony. *Imperialism, Sovereignty and the Making of International Law.* Cambridge: Cambridge University Press, 2005.

Arendt, Hannah. *The Human Condition.* 2nd ed. Chicago: University of Chicago Press, 1958.

Asch, Michael. "From 'Calder' to 'Van der Peet': Aboriginal Rights in Canadian Law, 1973–1996." In *Indigenous Peoples' Rights in Australia, Canada and New Zealand,* edited by Paul Havemann, 428–45. Oxford: Oxford University Press, 1999.

– *On Being Here to Stay: Treaties and Aboriginal Rights in Canada.* Toronto: University of Toronto Press, 2014.

Baker, Gordon P. *Wittgenstein's Method: Neglected Aspects.* Edited by Katherine Morris. Oxford: Blackwell, 2004.

Baker, Gordon P., and P.M.S. Hacker. "Surveyability and Surveyable Representations." In *Wittgenstein: Understanding and Meaning.* Vol. 1 of *An Analytical Commentary on the Philosophical Investigations. Part I: Essays,* 307–34. 2nd ed. Oxford: Blackwell, 2009.

Barron, F. Laurie. "The Indian Pass System in the Canadian West, 1882–1935." *Prairie Forum* 13 (1988): 323–52.

Barsh, Russel Lawrence, and James Youngblood Henderson. *The Road: Indian Tribes and Political Liberty.* Berkeley: University of California Press, 1980.

– "The Supreme Court's *Van der Peet* Trilogy: Naive Imperialism and Ropes of Sand." *McGill Law Journal* 42 (1997): 993–1010.

Beaton, Ryan. "Aboriginal Title in Recent Supreme Court of Canada Jurisprudence: What Remains of Radical Crown Title?" *National Journal of Constitutional Law* 33 (2014): 61–81.

Bell, Duncan. *Reordering the World: Essays on Liberalism and Empire.* Princeton, NJ: Princeton University Press, 2016.

Benjamin, Walter. "Critique of Violence." In *Reflections: Essays, Aphorisms, Autobiographical Writings*, 277–300. Edited by Peter Demetz. Translated by Edmund Jephcott. New York: Schocken Books, 1986.

– *Illuminations: Essays and Reflections*. Edited by Hannah Arendt. New York: Schoken, 1968.

Bennington, Geoffrey. *Legislations*. New York: Verso, 1994.

Bentham, Jeremy. *The Works of Jeremy Bentham*, vol. 2. Edited by John Bowring. Edinburgh: William Tait, 1838–43.

Berger, Carl. *The Sense of Power: Studies in the Ideas of Canadian Imperialism 1867–1914*. Toronto: University of Toronto Press, 1970.

Berlin, Isaiah. *The Crooked Timber of Humanity: Chapters in the History of Ideas*. Princeton, NJ: Princeton University Press, 2013.

Borges, J.L. *Collected Fictions*. Translated by Andrew Hurley. New York: Penguin, 1998.

Borrows, John. "(Ab)Originalism and Canada's Constitution." *Supreme Court Law Review* 58 (2012).

– "Canada's Colonial Constitution." Paper delivered at the Faculty of Law, University of British Columbia, 19 January 2016. Unpublished.

– "The Durability of Terra Nullius: Tsilhqot'in Nation v British Columbia." *UBC Law Review* 48, no. 3 (2015): 701–42.

– *Freedom and Indigenous Constitutionalism*. Toronto: University of Toronto Press, 2016.

– "A Genealogy of Law: Inherent Sovereignty and First Nations Self Government." *Osgoode Hall Law Journal* 30, no. 2 (1992): 291–353.

– "Seven Generations, Seven Teachings." Research paper for the National Centre for First Nations Governance, 2008.

– "Sovereignty's Alchemy: An Analysis of Delgamuukw v. British Columbia." *Osgoode Hall Law Journal* 37 (1999): 537–96.

– "The Trickster. Integral to a Distinctive Culture." *Constitutional Forum constitutionnel* 8, no. 2 (1997): 27–32.

– "Unextinguished: Rights and the Indian Act." Unpublished.

Boyd, Robert. *The Coming of the Spirit of Pestilence: Introduced Infectious Diseases and Population Decline among the North-West Coast Indians*. Vancouver: UBC Press, 1999.

Brantlinger, Patrick. *Dark Vanishings: Discourse on the Extinction of Primitive Races, 1800–1930*. Ithaca, NY: Cornell University Press, 2003.

British Parliamentary Papers. Vol. 12, *Correspondence, Returns and Other Papers Relating to Canada and to the Indian Problem Therein, 1839*. Shannon: Irish University Press, 1969.

Canadian Federal Court Case Law. *Anisman v. Canada (Border Services Agency)*, [2010] FCA 52.

– *Canada (Indian Affairs) v. Daniels*, [2014] FCA 101.

- *Daniels v. Canada,* [2013] FC 6.
- *Devil's Gap Cottagers (1982) Ltd. v. Rat Portage Band No. 38B,* [2009] 2 FCR 276.
- *Elders of Mitchikinabikok Inik v. Algonquins of Barriere Lake Customary Council,* [2010] FC 160.
- *Gabriel v. Canatonquin,* [1978] 1 FC 124.
- *Gamblin v. Norway House Cree Nation Band Council,* [2012] FC 1536.
- *Wood Mountain First Nation No. 160 Council v. Canada (AG)* (2006), 55 Admin LR (4th) 293 (FC).

Capaldi, Nicholas. *John Stuart Mill: A Biography.* Cambridge: Cambridge University Press, 2004.

Carroll, Lewis. *The Hunting of the Snark.* Edited by Martin Gardner. New York: Norton, 2006.

- *Sylvie and Bruno Concluded.* London: Macmillan, 1893.

Cavell, Stanley. *The Claim of Reason: Wittgenstein, Skepticism, Morality and Tragedy.* New York: Oxford University Press, 1999.

Chartrand, Larry. "The Failure of the Daniels Case: Blindly Entrenching a Colonial Legacy." *Alberta Law Review* 50, no. 1 (2013): 181–90.

Chomsky, Noam, and Edward S. Herman, *The Washington Connection and Third World Fascism.* Montreal: Black Rose Books, 1979.

Christie, Gordon. "The Court's Exercise of Plenary Power: Rewriting the Two-Row Wampum." (2002) SCLR 16:285–301.

- "Justifying Principles of Treaty Interpretation." *Queen's Law Journal* 26 (2000): 143–224.
- "Who Makes Decisions over Aboriginal Lands?" *UBC Law Review* 48, no. 3 (2015): 743–92.

Chute, Janet E. "Singwaukonse: A Nineteenth-Century Innovative Ojibwa Leader." *Ethnohistory* 45 (1998): 65–101.

Cohen, Felix. *Handbook of Federal Indian Law.* New York: LexisNexis, 2012.

Conway, Kyle S. "Inherently or Exclusively Federal: Constitutional Preemption and the Relationship between Public Law 280 and Federalism." *University of Pennsylvania Journal of Constitutional Law* 15, no. 5 (May 2013): 1323–72.

Cooper, John Milton. *Breaking the Heart of the World: Woodrow Wilson and the Fight for the League of Nations.* Cambridge: Cambridge University Press, 2001.

Cover, Robert. *Justice Accused: Antislavery and the Judicial Process.* New Haven, CT: Yale University Press, 1975.

Daschuk, James. *Clearing the Plains: Disease, Politics of Starvation, and the Loss of Aboriginal Life.* Regina: University of Regina Press, 2014.

Derrida, Jacques. *Politics of Friendship.* Translated by George Collins. New York: Verso, 2000.

Deskaheh. "The Redman's Appeal for Justice." In *Strange Visitors: Documents in Indigenous-Settler Relations in Canada from 1876,* edited by Keith D. Smith, 143–7. Toronto: University of Toronto Press, 2014.

Diamond, Jared. *Guns, Germs and Steel: The Fates of Human Societies*. New York: Norton, 1999.

Eco, Umberto. *Semiotics and the Philosophy of Language*. London: MacMillan, 1984.

Eden, Lorraine, and Maureen Appel Molot. "Canada's National Policies: Reflections on 125 Years." *Canadian Public Policy* 19, no. 3 (1993): 232–51.

Elliot, Robin. "Interjurisdictional Immunity after Canadian Western Bank and Lafarge Canada Inc.: The Supreme Court Muddies the Doctrinal Waters – Again." *Supreme Court Law Review* 43 (2008): 433–98.

Fenn, Elizabeth. *Pox Americana: The Great Smallpox Epidemic 1775–1782*. New York: Hill and Wang, 2001.

Fichte, J.G. *Foundations of Natural Right*. Edited by Frederick Neuhouser. Translated by Michael Baur. New York: Cambridge University Press, 2000.

Fitzmaurice, Andrew. "The Genealogy of Terra Nullius." *Australian Historical Studies* 38, no. 129 (2007): 1–15.

Foucault, Michele. *Discipline and Punish: The Birth of the Prison*. Translated by Alan Sheridan. New York: Vintage Books, 1995.

– "Nietzsche, Genealogy, History." In *The Foucault Reader*, edited by Paul Rabinow, 76–100. New York: Pantheon, 1991.

– *On the Government of the Living (Lectures at the Collège de France 1979–1980)*. Translated by Graham Burchell. New York: Palgrave Macmillan, 2014.

– *Power/Knowledge: Selected Interviews and Other Writings, 1972–1977*. Edited by Colin Gordon. New York: Pantheon, 1980.

Freud, Sigmund. *The Interpretation of Dreams*. Translated and edited by James Strachey. New York: Basic Books, 2010.

– *Jokes and Their Relation to the Unconscious*. Translated and edited by James Strachey. New York: W.W. Norton, 1989.

Furet, Francois, and Mona Ozouf, eds. *A Critical Dictionary of the French Revolution*. Translated by Arthur Goldhammer. Cambridge: Belknap, 1989.

Gallie, W.B. *Philosophy and the Historical Understanding*. London: Chatto & Windus, 1964.

Gavigan, Shelley A.M. *Hunger, Horses, and Government Men: Criminal Law on the Aboriginal Plains, 1870–1905*. Vancouver: UBC Press, 2013.

Geertz, Clifford. *Available Light: Anthropological Reflections on Philosophical Topics*. Princeton, NJ: Princeton University Press, 2000.

Gell, Alfred. *Art and Agency: An Anthropological Theory*. Oxford: Oxford University Press, 1998.

Giokas, John. "The Indian Act: Evolution, Overview and Options for Amendment and Transition." Research paper prepared for the Royal Commission on Aboriginal Peoples, 1995.

Government of Canada. "Appeal of the 'Six Nations' to the League." *League of Nations Official Journal* 5, no. 6 (1924): 829–42.

Hamilton, Robert. "After Tsilhqot'in Nation: The Aboriginal Title Question in Canada's Maritime Provinces." *University of New Brunswick Law Journal* 67 (2016): 58–108.

– "'They Promised to Leave Us Some of Our Land': Aboriginal Title in Canada's Maritime Provinces." LLM thesis, York University Osgoode Hall Law School, 2015.

Hart, H.L.A. *The Concept of Law.* 2nd ed. Oxford: Oxford University Press, 1994.

Hegel, G.W.F. *Elements of the Philosophy of Right.* Edited by Allen W. Wood. Translated by H.B. Nisbet. Cambridge: Cambridge University Press, 2004.

– *Lectures on the Philosophy of World History.* Translated by H.B. Nisbet. Cambridge: Cambridge University Press, 1980.

– *Phenomenology of Spirit.* Translated by A.V. Miller. Oxford: Oxford University Press, 1997.

– *Philosophy of History.* Translated by J. Sibree. New York: Prometheus Books, 1991.

Henderson, J.Y. *Indigenous Diplomacy and the Rights of Peoples: Achieving UN Recognition.* Saskatoon: Purich Publishing, 2008.

– "Interpreting *Sui generis* Treaties." *Alberta Law Review* 36 (1997): 46–96.

Herder, J.G. *Herder on Social and Political Culture.* Edited and translated by F.M. Barnard. Cambridge: Cambridge University Press, 1969.

Hobsbawm, Eric. *The Age of Capital, 1848–1875.* New York: Vintage Books, 1996.

Hoehn, Felix. *Reconciling Sovereignties: Aboriginal Nations and Canada.* Saskatoon: Native Law Centre, 2012.

Hogg, Peter W. "The Constitutional Basis of Aboriginal Rights." In *Aboriginal Law since Delgamuukw*, edited by Maria Morellato, 176–96. Aurora, ON: Canada Law Book, 2009.

– *Constitutional Law of Canada.* 5th ed. Toronto: Carswell, 2007.

Hollis, Duncan B., ed. *The Oxford Guide to Treaties.* Oxford: Oxford University Press, 2012.

Honig, Bonnie. *Emergency Politics: Paradox, Law, Democracy.* Princeton, NJ: Princeton University Press, 2009.

Hopkins, Donald R. *The Greatest Killer: Smallpox in History.* Chicago: University of Chicago Press, 2002.

Indian Association of Alberta. "Citizens Plus." Edmonton: Indian Association of Alberta, 1970.

Jeffries, Samantha, and Philip Stenning. "Sentencing Aboriginal Offenders: Law, Policy, and Practice in Three Countries." *Canadian Journal of Criminology and Criminal Justice* 56, no. 4 (2014): 447–94.

Jenkins, Christopher D. "Marshall's Aboriginal Rights Theory and Its Treatment in Canadian Jurisprudence." *University of British Columbia Law Review* (2001): 1–42.

Johnson, Darlene. "The Quest of the Six Nations Confederacy for Self-Determination." *University of Toronto Faculty of Law Review* 44, no. 1 (1986): 1–32.

Judicial Committee of the Privy Council. *AG for Canada v. AG for Ontario*, [1937] AC 326 (PC).

– *The Collector of Voter for the Electoral District of Vancouver City and the Attorney General for the Province of British Columbia v. Tomey Homma and the Attorney General for the Dominions of Canada (British Columbia)* [1902] UKPC 60.

– *St Catherine's Milling & Lumber Company v. R* (1888), 14 App Cas 46 (PC).

Kafka, Franz. *The Complete Short Stories*. Edited by Nahum N. Glatzer. Translated by Willa and Edwin Muir. New York: Schocken Books, 1971.

Kant, Immanuel. *The Cambridge Edition of the Works of Immanuel Kant: The Critique of Pure Reason*. Translated and edited Paul Guyer and Allen Wood. Cambridge: Cambridge University Press, 1998.

– *The Metaphysics of Morals*. Edited and translated by Mary Gregor. Cambridge: Cambridge University Press, 2006.

– *Political Writings*. Edited by Hans Reiss. Translated by H.B. Nisbet. New York: Cambridge University Press, 1991.

Kennedy, Dawnis Minawaanigogizhigok. "Reconciliation without Respect? Section 35 and Indigenous Legal Orders." In Law Commission of Canada, *Indigenous Legal Traditions*, 77–113. Vancouver: University of British Columbia Press, 2008.

Koskenniemi, Marti. *The Gentle Civilizer of Nations: The Rise and Fall of International Law 1870–1960*. Cambridge: Cambridge University Press, 2001.

Kymlicka, Will. *Multicultural Citizenship: A Liberal Theory of Minority Rights*. Oxford: Oxford University Press, 1995.

Lambert, Douglas. "Where to from Here: Reconciling Aboriginal Title with Crown Sovereignty." In *Aboriginal Law since Delgamuukw*, edited by Maria Morellato, 31–54. Aurora: Canada Law Book, 2009.

League of Nations. *Permanent Mandates Commission, Minutes of the Third Session*. Geneva: League of Nations Publications, 1923.

Leslie, John F., ed. *Commissions of Inquiry into Indian Affairs in the Canadas, 1828–1858: Evolving a Corporate Memory for the Indian Department*. Ottawa: Treaties and Historical Research Centre, DIAND, 1985.

Levin, Michael. *Mill on Civilization and Barbarism*. New York: Routledge, 2004.

Lindberg, Tracey. "The Doctrine of Discovery in Canada" and "Contemporary Canadian Resonance of an Imperial Doctrine." In *Discovering Indigenous Lands: The Doctrine of Discovery in the English Colonies*, edited by Robert J. Miller, Larissa Behrendt, and Tracey Lindberg, 89–125. Oxford: Oxford University Press, 2010.

Lyon, Noel. "Constitutional Issues in Native Law." In *Aboriginal Peoples and the Law: Indian, Metis and Inuit Rights in Canada*, edited by B.W. Morse, 408–51. Ottawa: Carleton University Press, 1984.

– "An Essay on Constitutional Interpretation." *Osgoode Hall Law Journal* 26 (1988): 95–126.

Macklem, Patrick. "First Nations Self-Government and the Borders of the Canadian Legal Imagination." *McGill Law Journal* 36 (1991): 382–456.

– *Indigenous Difference and the Constitution of Canada*. Toronto: University of Toronto Press, 2001.
– "What Is International Human Rights Law? Three Applications of a Distributive Account." *McGill Law Journal* 52 (2007): 575–604.
Mamdani, Mahmoud. *Citizen and Subject: Contemporary Africa and the Legacy of Colonialism*. Princeton, NJ: Princeton University Press, 1996.
Manela, Erez. *The Wilsonian Moment: Self-Determination and the International Origins of Anticolonial Nationalism*. Oxford: Oxford University Press, 2007.
Marx, Karl. "The British Rule in India." *New York Daily Tribune*, 25 June 1853.
Marx, Karl, and Frederick Engels. *Collected Works*. New York: International Publishers, 1983.
Matena, Karuna. *Alibis of Empire: Henry Maine and the End of Liberal Imperialism*. Princeton, NJ: Princeton University Press, 2010.
McHugh, P.G. *Aboriginal Societies and the Common Law: A History of Sovereignty, Status and Self-Determination*. Oxford: Oxford University Press, 2004.
McNeil, Kent. "Aboriginal Title and Section 88 of the Indian Act." *University of British Columbia Law Review* 34 (2000): 159–94.
– "Challenging Legislative Infringements of the Inherent Aboriginal Right of Self-Government." *Windsor Yearbook of Access to Justice* 22 (2003): 329–62.
– "Fiduciary Obligations and Federal Responsibility for the Aboriginal Peoples." In *Emerging Justice? Essays on Indigenous Rights in Canada and Australia*, 309–55. Saskatoon: University of Saskatchewan Native Law Centre, 2001.
– "How Can Infringements of the Constitutional Rights of Aboriginal Peoples Be Justified?" *Constitutional Forum* 8, no. 2 (1997): 33–9.
Merino, Roger. "Law and Politics of Indigenous Self-Determination: The Meaning of the Right of Prior Consultation." Unpublished.
Mill, J.S. "Civilization." In *Collected Works of John Stuart Mill*, edited by J.M. Robson, 18:117–48. Toronto: University of Toronto Press, 1977.
– *The Collected Works of John Stuart Mill*. Vol. 7, *A System of Logic Ratiocinative and Inductive, Being a Connected View of the Principles of Evidence and the Methods of Scientific Investigation (Books I–III)*. Edited by John M. Robson and introduction by R.F. McRae. Toronto: University of Toronto Press, 1974.
– *The Collected Works of John Stuart Mill*. Vol. 8, *A System of Logic Ratiocinative and Inductive, Being a Connected View of the Principles of Evidence and the Methods of Scientific Investigation (Books IV–VI and Appendices)*. Edited by John M. Robson and introduction by R.F. McRae. Toronto: University of Toronto Press, 1974.
– *The Collected Works of John Stuart Mill*. Vol. 9, *An Examination of William Hamilton's Philosophy and of the Principal Philosophical Questions Discussed in His Writings*. Edited by John M. Robson and introduction by Alan Ryan. Toronto: University of Toronto Press, 1979.
– *The Collected Works of John Stuart Mill*. Vol. 10, *Essays on Ethics, Religion, and Society*. Edited by John M. Robson and Introduction by F.E.L. Priestley. Toronto: University of Toronto Press, 1985.

– *The Collected Works of John Stuart Mill*. Vol. 16, *The Later Letters of John Stuart Mill 1849–1873 Part III*. Edited by Francis E. Mineka and Dwight N. Lindley. Toronto: University of Toronto Press, 1972.
– *The Collected Works of John Stuart Mill*. Vol. 17, *The Later Letters of John Stuart Mill 1849–1873 Part IV*. Edited by Francis E. Mineka and Dwight N. Lindley. Toronto: University of Toronto Press, 1972.
– *The Collected Works of John Stuart Mill*. Vol. 23, *Public and Parliamentary Speeches Part I November 1850–November 1868*. Edited by John M. Robson and Bruce L. Kinzer. Toronto: University of Toronto Press, 1988.
– *On Liberty and Considerations on Representative Government*. Edited by R.B. McCallum. Oxford: Basil Blackwell, 1948.
Miller, Bruce. *Invisible Indigenes: The Politics of Nonrecognition*. Lincoln: University of Nebraska Press, 2008.
Miller, Cary. "Gifts as Treaties: The Political Use of Received Gifts in Anishinaabeg Communities, 1820–1832." *American Indian Quarterly* 26, no. 2 (2002): 221–45.
Milloy, John S. "The Early Indian Acts: Developmental Strategy and Constitutional Change." In *Sweet Promises: A Reader on Indian-White Relations in Canada*, edited by J.R. Miller, 145–56. Toronto: University of Toronto Press, 1991.
– *A Historical Overview of Indian-Government Relations 1755–1940*. Ottawa: Department of Indian Affairs and Northern Development, 1992.
Moore, G.E. *Principia Ethica*. Amherst: Prometheus Books, 1988.
Moore, Robert G. *Historical Development of the Indian Act*. Edited by J. Leslie and R. Maguire, 2nd ed. Ottawa: Treaties and Historical Research Centre, Indian and Northern Affairs, 1978.
Morse, Brad. "Permafrost Rights: Aboriginal Self-Government and the Supreme Court in *R. v. Pamajewon*." *McGill Law Journal* 42, no. 4 (1997): 1011–44.
Nichols, Joshua. *The End(s) of Community: History, Sovereignty and the Question of Law*. Waterloo, ON: Wilfrid Laurier University Press, 2013.
– "A Reconciliation without Recollection? *Chief Mountain* and the Sources of Sovereignty." *University of British Columbia Law Review* 48, no. 2 (2015): 515–40.
Nietzsche, Friedrich. *Thus Spoke Zarathustra*. Translated by Graham Parkes. Oxford: Oxford University Press, 2005.
Orwell, George. *Animal Farm and 1984*. New York: Houghton Mifflin Harcourt, 2003.
Pagden, Anthony. *The Burdens of Empire 1539 to the Present*. Cambridge: Cambridge University Press, 2015.
– *The Fall of Natural Man: The American Indian and the Origins of Comparative Ethnology*. Cambridge: Cambridge University Press, 1986.
– *Lords of All the World: Ideologies of Empire in Spain, Britain and France c. 1500–c. 1800*. New Haven, CT: Yale University Press, 1995.
Parliament of Canada, Special Committee on Indian Self-Government. *Indian Self-Government in Canada*. Ottawa: Ministry of Supply and Services, 1983.

- *Response of the Government to the Report of the Special Committee on Indian Self-Government*. Ottawa: Indian and Northern Affairs Canada, 1984.

Pascal, Blaise. *Pensées and Other Writings*. Edited by Anthony Levi. Translated by Honor Levi. New York: Oxford University Press, 1995.

Pitts, Jennifer. *A Turn to Empire: The Rise of Imperial Liberalism in Britain and France*. Princeton, NJ: Princeton University Press, 2005.

Pocock, J.G.A. *The Discovery of Island: Essays in British History*. Cambridge: Cambridge University Press, 2005.

Posel, Deborah. *The Making of Apartheid 1948–1961: Conflict and Compromise*. Oxford: Oxford University Press, 1991.

Provincial Case Law. *Ahousaht Indian Band and Nation v. Canada (AG)*, [2009] BCSC 1494.

- *Ahousaht Indian Band and Nation v. Canada (AG)*, [2011] BCCA 237.
- *Davey v. Isaac* [1977] 77 DLR (3d) 481.
- *Delgammuukw v. British Columbia* (8 March 1991), Smithers No 0843 (BCSC).
- *Isaac v. Davey* [1973] 3 OR 677, 38 DLR (3d) 23 (Ont HC).
- *Leighton v. British Columbia* (1989) 57 DLR (4th) 657 (BCCA).
- *Logan v. Styres* [1959] OWN 361, 20 DLR (2d) 416 (Ont HC).
- *McIvor v. Canada (Registrar of Indian and Northern Affairs)*, [2009] BCCA 153.
- *McIvor v. the Registrar, Indian and Northern Affairs Canada*, [2007] BCSC 827.
- *R v. Hill* (1907) 15 OLR 406 (CA).
- *R v. Martin* (1917), 41 OLR 79.
- *R v. Rogers* (1923), 33 Man R 139, [1923] 3 DLR 414 (CA).
- *R v. Syliboy* (1929), 1 DLR 307 (NS Co Ct).
- *Re Whitebear Indian Council and Carpenters Provincial Council of Saskatchewan* (1982), 135 DLR (3d) 128, 3 WWR 554, 15 Sask R 37 (Sask CA).
- *Sga'nism Sim'augit (Chief Mountain) v. Canada (AG)*, 2013 BCCA 49, 359 DLR (4th) 231.

Roach, Kent. "Blaming the Victim: Canadian Law, Causation, and Residential Schools." *University of Toronto Law Journal* 64, no. 4 (2014): 566–95.

Roach, Kent, and Jonathan Rudin. "Gladue: The Judicial and Political Reception of a Promising Decision." *Canadian Journal of Criminology* 42, no. 3 (2000): 355–88.

Rotman, Leonard I. "Defining Parameters: Aboriginal Rights, Treaty Rights, and the Sparrow Justificatory Test." *Alberta Law Review* 36 (1997): 149–79.

- "Hunting for Answers in a Strange Kettle of Fish: Unilateralism, Paternalism and Fiduciary Rhetoric in *Badger and Van der Peet*." *Constitutional Forum constitionnel* 8, no. 2 (1997): 40–6.

Rousseau, Jean-Jacques. *The Basic Political Writings*. Translated by Donald A. Cress. Indianapolis: Hackett Publishing, 1987.

Royal Commission on Aboriginal Peoples. *Partners in Confederation, Aboriginal Peoples, Self-Government and the Constitution*. Ottawa: Minister of Supply and Services, 1993.

– *Report of the Royal Commission on Aboriginal Peoples.* Vol. 1, *Looking Forward Looking Back.* Part 2, *False Assumptions and a Failed Relationship.* Ottawa: Canada Communication Group, 1996.
– *Report of the Royal Commission on Aboriginal Peoples.* Vol. 2, *Restructuring the Relationship.* Ottawa, Minister of Supply and Services, 1996.
Ryder, Bruce. "The Demise and Rise of the Classical Paradigm in Canadian Federalism: Promoting Autonomy for the Provinces and First Nations." *McGill Law Journal* 36 (1991): 308–81.
Said, Edward. *Culture and Imperialism.* New York: Vintage Books, 1993.
Sanders, Douglas. "The Application of Provincial Laws." In *Aboriginal Peoples and the Law: Indian, Metis and Inuit Rights in Canada*, edited by B.W. Morse, 452–66. Ottawa: Carleton University Press, 1984.
Santayana, George. *The Life of Reason: Reason in Common Sense.* Critical edition. Co-edited by Marianne S. Wokeck and Martin A. Coleman. Vol. 7, bk 1 of *The Works of George Santayana.* Cambridge, MA: MIT Press, 2011.
Sartre, Jean-Paul. *Colonialism and Neocolonialism.* Translated by Azzedine Haddour, Steve Brewer, and Terry McWilliams. New York: Routledge, 2006.
Selden, John. *Table Talk*, quoted in *Sources of English Legal and Constitutional History*, edited by M.B. Evans and R.I. Jack. Sydney: Butterworths, 1984.
Skinner, Quintin. *Hobbes and Republican Liberty.* Cambridge; Cambridge University Press, 2008.
– *Liberty before Liberalism.* Cambridge: Cambridge University Press, 1998.
– *Visions of Politics.* Vol. 1, *Regarding Method.* Cambridge: Cambridge University Press, 2002.
Slattery, Brian. "The Aboriginal Constitution" (2014) 67 SCLR (2d) 319–36.
– "The Constitutional Guarantee of Aboriginal Treaty Rights." *Queen's Law Journal* 8 (1982): 232–73.
– "Making Sense of Aboriginal Treaty Rights." *Canadian Bar Review* 79 (2000): 196–224.
– "The Metamorphosis of Aboriginal Title." *Canadian Bar Review* 85 (2006): 255–86.
Smith, Adam. *The Wealth of Nations.* Vol. 1. Edited by Edwin Cannan. Chicago: University of Chicago Press, 1976.
Stannard, David E. *American Holocaust: The Conquest of the New World.* New York: Oxford University Press, 1994.
Supreme Court of Canada. *AG of Canada v. Canard*, [1976] 1 SCR 170, 52 DLR (3d).
– *AG of Canada v. Lavell*, [1974] SCR 1349.
– *Beckman v. Little Salmon/Carmacks First Nation*, [2010] 3 SCR 103.
– *Behn v. Moulton Contracting Ltd*, [2013] 2 SCR 227.
– *Bell Canada v. Quebec (Commission de la Santé et de la Sécurité du Travail)*, [1988] 1 SCR 749.
– *Calder et al. v. AG of British Columbia*, [1973] SCR 313.

- *Cardinal v. Alberta (AG)*, [1974] SCR 695.
- *Cherokee Nation v. Georgia*, 30 US 1, 8 L Ed 25 (1831).
- *Daniels v. Canada (Indian Affairs and Northern Development)*, 2016 SCC 12.
- *Delgamuuku v. British Columbia*, [1997] 3 SCR 1010.
- *Dick v. R* [1985] 2 SCR 309.
- *Four B Manufacturing v. United Garment Workers* [1980] 1 SCR 1031.
- *Guerin v. R*, [1984] 2 SCR 335, 1984 CanLII 25 (SCC).
- *Haida Nation v. British Columbia (Minister of Forests)*, [2004] 3 SCR 511.
- *Hunter v. Southam Inc.*, [1984] 2 SCR 145.
- *In the matter of a reference as to the validity of the Industrial Relations and Disputes Investigation Act*, [1955] SCR 529.
- *Johnson v. M'Intosh*, 21 US 543, 5 L, Ed 681 (1823).
- *Kitkatla Band v. British Columbia* [2002] 2 SCR 146.
- *Kruger et al. v. R*, [1978] 1 SCR 104.
- *Manitoba Metis Federation Inc v. Canada (AG)*, [2013] 1 SCR 623.
- *McEvoy v. New Brunswick (AG)*, [1983] 1 SCR 704.
- *Mitchell v. MNR*, [2001] 1 SCR 911.
- *Multiple Access Ltd. v. McCutcheon*, [1982] 2 SCR 161.
- *Natural Parents v. Superintendent of Child Welfare et al.*, [1976] 2 SCR 751.
- *NIL/TU,O Child and Family Services Society v. BC Government and Service Employees' Union* [2010] 2 SCR 696.
- *Nova Scotia (AG) v. Canada (AG)*, [1951] SCR 31.
- *OPSEU v. Ontario (AG)*, [1987] 2 SCR 2.
- *Paul v. British Columbia* [2003] 2 SCR 585.
- *Reference whether "Indians" includes "Eskimo,"* [1939] SCR 104.
- *R v. Badger*, [1996] 1 SCR 771.
- *R v. Crown Zellerbach Canada Ltd.*, [1988] 1 SCR 401.
- *R v. Drybones*, [1970] SCR 282.
- *R v. Francis* [1988] 1 SCR 1025.
- *R v. Gladstone*, [1996] 2 SCR 723.
- *R v. Marshall*, [1999] 3 SCR 456.
- *R v. Marshall; R v Bernard*, [2005] 2 SCR 220.
- *R v. Morris*, [2006] 2 SCR 915.
- *R v. Pamajewon*, [1996] 2 SCR 82.
- *R v. Sioui*, [1990] 1 SCR 1025.
- *R v. Sparrow*, [1990] 1 SCR 1075.
- *R v. Sutherland*, [1980] 2 SCR 451.
- *R v. Van der Peet*, [1996] 2 SCR 507.
- *Rizzo & Rizzo Shoes Ltd (Re)*, [1998] 1 SCR 27.
- *Simon v. R.*, [1985] 2 SCR 387.
- *State of Washington v. Washington State Commercial, Passenger, Fishing Vessel Association*, 443 US 658 (1979).

Supreme Court of the United States of America. *Taku River Tlingit First Nation v. British Columbia (Project Assessment Director)*, [2004] 3 SCR 550.
- *Tsilhqot'in Nation v. British Columbia*, [2014] SCC 44.
- *Worcester v. Georgia*, 31 US 515, 8 L Ed 483 (1832).

Temelini, Michael. *Wittgenstein and the Study of Politics*. Toronto: University of Toronto Press, 2015.

Tennant, Paul. *Aboriginal Peoples and Politics: The Indian Land Question in British Columbia, 1849–1989*. Vancouver: University of British Columbia Press, 1992.

Titley, E. Brian. *A Narrow Vision: Duncan Campbell Scott and the Administration of Indian Affairs in Canada*. Vancouver: University of British Columbia Press, 1986.

Tobias, John L. "Protections, Civilization, Assimilation: An Outline History of Canada's Indian Policy." In *As Long as the Sun Shines and Water Flows*. Edited by I.A.L. Getty and A.S. Lussier, 39–55. Vancouver: University of British Columbia Press, 1983.

Tocqueville, Alexis de. *Democracy in America*. Edited by J.P. Mayer. Translated by George Lawrence. New York: Harper and Row, 1988.

Toulmin, Stephen. *Return to Reason*. Cambridge, MA: Harvard University Press, 2001.

Thompson, Leonard Monteath. *A History of South Africa*. 3rd ed. New Haven, CT: Yale University Press, 2001.

Tucker, Jonathan B. *Scourge: The Once and Future Threat of Smallpox*. New York: Grove, 2001.

Tully, James. "Deparochializing Political Theory and Beyond: A Dialogue Approach to Comparative Political Thought." *Journal of World Philosophies* 1, no. 1 (2016).
- *Public Philosophy in a New Key*. Vol. 1, *Democracy and Civic Freedom*. Cambridge: Cambridge University Press, 2008.
- *Public Philosophy in a New Key*. Vol. 2, *Imperialism and Civic Freedom*. Cambridge: Cambridge University Press, 2008.
- "Richard Gregg and the Power of Nonviolence: The Power of Nonviolence as the Unifying Animacy of Life." J. Glenn and Ursula Gray Memorial Lecture, delivered at Colorado College, 1 March 2016. Unpublished.
- *Strange Multiplicity: Constitutionalism in an Age of Diversity*. Cambridge: Cambridge University Press, 1995.
- "Violent Power-Over and Nonviolent Power-With: Hannah Arendt on Violence and Nonviolence." Paper delivered at Goethe University, 7 June 2011. Unpublished.

United Kingdom. *Report of the Parliamentary Select Committee on Aboriginal Tribes (British Settlements)*. London: William Ball, Aldine Chambers, Paternoster Row, 1837.

Upton, Leslie F.S. *Micmacs and Colonists: Indian-White Relations in the Maritimes, 1713–1867*. Vancouver: University of British Columbia Press, 1979.

Walters, Mark D. "The Jurisprudence of Reconciliation: Aboriginal Rights in Canada." In *The Politics of Reconciliation in Multicultural Societies*, edited by Will Kymlicka and Bashir Bashir, 165–91. Oxford: Oxford University Press, 2008.

– "The Morality of Aboriginal Law." *Queen's Law Journal* 31 (2006): 470–520.

Weaver, Sally M. *Making Canadian Indian Policy: The Hidden Agenda 1968–1970*. Toronto: University of Toronto Press, 1981.

Webber, Jeremy. *The Constitution of Canada: A Contextual Analysis*. Portland, OR: Hart Publishing, 2015.

Wilkins, Kerry. "'Still Crazy after All These Years': Section 88 of the Indian Act at Fifty." *Alberta Law Review* 38, no. 2 (2000): 458–503.

Williams, Gareth. *Angel of Death: The Story of Smallpox*. London: Palgrave Macmillan, 2010.

Williams, Robert A. Jr. *The American Indian in Western Legal Thought: The Discourses of Conquest*. New York: Oxford University Press, 1990.

Wittgenstein, Ludwig. *The Blue and Brown Books*. 2nd ed. New York: Harper & Row, 1964.

– *Culture and Value: A Selection from the Posthumous Remains*. Rev. ed. Edited by G.H. von Wright. Oxford: Blackwell, 1998.

– *On Certainty*. Edited by G.E.M. Anscombe and G.H. von Wright. Oxford: Blackwell, 1974.

– *Philosophical Investigations*. Translated by G.E.M. Anscombe. 3rd ed. Oxford: Blackwell, 2001.

– *Tractatus Logico-Philosophicus*. Translated by C.K. Ogden. London: Routledge, 1981.

– *Tractatus Logico-Philosophicus*. Translated by D.F. Pears and B.F. McGuinness. London: Routledge, 2001.

Index